Contents

KT-482-909

About the Author   4

Timeline to a University Place   5

How This Book Can Help You   7

Introduction   9

  1 The University League Table   17

  2 Choosing What and Where to Study   28

  3 Assessing Graduate Job Prospects   49

  4 The Bottom Line: Tuition Fees and Finance   60

  5 Making Your Application   67

  6 Where Students Come From   80

  7 Finding Somewhere to Live   100

  8 Enjoying University Sport   112

  9 Staying Safe and Seeking Help on Campus   117

10 Going Abroad to Study   124

11 Coming to the UK to Study   134

12 Subject by Subject Guide   143

13 Applying to Oxbridge   281

14 University Profiles   314

Specialist Institutions of Higher Education   586

Index   590

About the Author

Zoe Thomas is a journalist and education writer. She has worked on *The Times and Sunday Times Good University Guide* since 2005 and is a former staff journalist for the Sunday newspaper. For the past 13 years, she has written extensively for the *Guide*, both its UK and Irish editions, and its sister publication *The Sunday Times Schools Guide*, *Parent Power*, the annual review of Britain's leading primary and secondary schools. She has a degree in media studies from the University of Sussex.

Acknowledgements

We would like to thank the many individuals who have helped with this edition of *The Times and Sunday Times Good University Guide*, particularly Alastair McCall, Editor of *The Sunday Times Good University Guide*, and John O'Leary, journalist, education consultant and the former author of this *Guide*. Thanks also go to Jethro Lennox at HarperCollins Publishers and to Lucy Reichwald, Sophie Bradford, Andrew Farquhar and Fiona Kugele at UoE Consulting Limited, which has compiled the main university league table and the individual subject tables for this *Guide* on behalf of *The Times*, *The Sunday Times* and HarperCollins Publishers.

To the members of *The Times and Sunday Times Good University Guide* Advisory Group for their time and expertise: Patrick Kennedy, Consultant, Collective Intelligence Limited; Christine Couper, former Head of Planning and Statistics, University of Greenwich; James Galbraith, Senior Strategic Planner, University of Edinburgh; Josh Gulrajani, Bath Spa University; Daniel Monnery, Head of Corporate Strategy, Northumbria University; Bojan Cvijan at Imperial College London; Jackie Njoroge, Head of Strategic Planning, University of Salford; Steve Walsh, Head of Planning, Aberystwyth University; David Totten, Head of Planning, Queen's University, Belfast; Jenny Walker, Planning Officer, Loughborough University; to Denise Jones, Emily Raven, Kathryn Heywood and Jonathan Waller of HESA for their technical advice; also to Richard Puttock, Director of Data, Foresight and Analysis, Office for Students. To Nick Rodrigues, Senay Boztas, Charlie Burt, Georgie Campbell, Catherine Lally and Katie Meynell for their contributions to the book.

We also wish to thank all the university staff who assisted in providing information for this edition.

Timeline to a University Place

This book will help you find a university place in September 2023. Meeting the deadlines that punctuate the journey from sixth form to Freshers' Week in good time, allows for greater flexibility and options – and brings on the feelgood factor from beating procrastination.

Those applying for degrees in medicine, veterinary medicine and dentistry have an earlier application deadline than the majority of applicants, which is 15 October 2022, the same date that Cambridge and Oxford universities also require applications to have been submitted. Relevant work experience is required for some degrees including medicine, as are aptitude and pre-assessment tests (detailed further on page 34).

Use the dates below to find the key stages to a university place.

Key dates
February to July 2022
Use this time to mull over the subject you would like to study and where you would like to study it. The chapters of this book will help distil your thinking on how to choose a subject and a university.

March 2022 onwards
Go to university Open Days. By attending Open Days, you can develop a personal impression of what a university feels like, its location, and what studying in a particular department or faculty would be like. This year's applicants have the advantage of the return of on-campus Open Days. Go to as many as you can within reason. Plan carefully and make each one count. Online Open Days are also being offered by many universities; they require less legwork and are more accessible, so make the most of this upside of the pandemic's impact on university life. For Open Day dates, consult each university's website – as detailed in Chapter 14.

July 2022
Registration starts for UCAS Apply, the online application system through which you will apply to universities. You will have a maximum of five choices when you complete your form.

September 2022
UCAS will begin to accept completed applications.

15 October 2022
Deadline for applications to Oxford or Cambridge (you can only apply to one of them), and for applications to any university to study medicine, dentistry or veterinary science. Some courses require you to have completed a pre-application assessment test by this date.

15 January 2023
Deadline for applications for all other universities and subjects (excluding a few art and design courses with a March 2023 deadline). This is the last date you can apply by, but it is better to get your application in beforehand; aim for the end of November 2022.

End of March 2023

Universities should have given you decisions on your applications by now if you submitted them by 15 January 2023.

April onwards

Apply for student loans to cover tuition fees and living costs.

Early May 2023

By this time, you should have responded to all university decisions. You must select a first choice, and if your first offer is conditional, a second choice, and reject all other offers.

Once you have accepted an offer, apply for university accommodation if you are going to need it. Universities have their own housing application deadlines – getting in early will often guarantee a space and may allow you first dibs on your choice of room.

First week of August 2023

Scottish examination results. If your results meet the offer from your first choice (or, failing that, your second choice), your place at university will be confirmed. If not, you can enter Clearing for Scottish universities to find a place on another course.

Second week of August 2023

A-level results announced. If your results meet the offer from your first choice (or, failing that, your second choice), your place at university will be confirmed. If not, you can enter Clearing to find a place on another course offered by any university. If you did better than expected and exceeded the conditions of your firm choice you can enter Adjustment, which gives you the chance to "trade up" and apply for a different course or university.

Mid to late September 2023

Arrive at university for Freshers' Week.

How This Book Can Help You

What and where to study are the fundamental decisions in making a successful university application.

How do I choose a course?
Most degrees last three or sometimes four years, some even longer, so you will need enthusiasm for, and some aptitude in, the subject. Also consider whether studying full-time or part-time will be best for you.
» The first half of chapter 2 provides advice on choosing a subject area and selecting relevant courses within that subject.
» Chapter 12 provides details for 70 different subject areas (as listed on page 147). For each subject there is specific advice and a league table that provides our ranking of universities offering courses

How will my choice of subject affect my employment prospects?
The course you choose will influence your job prospects after you graduate, so your initial subject decision will have an impact on your life long after you have finished your degree.
» The employment prospects and average starting salaries for the main subject groups are given in chapter 3.
» The subject tables in chapter 12 give the employment prospects for each university offering a course.
» Universities are now doing more to increase the employability of their graduates. Examples are given in chapter 3 and in the profiles in chapter 14.

How do I choose a university?
While choosing your subject comes first, the place where you study also plays a major role. You will need to decide what type of university you wish to go to: campus, city or smaller town? How well does the university perform? How far is the university from home? Is it large or small? Is it specialist or general? Do you want to study abroad?
» Central to our *Guide* is the main *Times and Sunday Times* league table in chapter 1. This ranks the universities by assessing their performance not just according to teaching quality and the student experience but also through seven other factors, including research quality, the spending on services and facilities, and graduate employment prospects.
» The second half of chapter 2 provides advice on the factors to consider when choosing a university.
» Chapter 14, the largest chapter in the book, contains two pages on each university, giving a general overview of the institution as well as data on student numbers, contact details, accommodation provision, and the latest fees available. Note that fees and student support for 2023–24 will not be confirmed until August 2022, and you must check these before applying.
» For those considering Oxford or Cambridge, details of admission processes and of all the undergraduate colleges can be found in chapter 13.
» Chapter 9 gives advice about student life; focusing on alcohol, drugs, mental health and staying safe on campus.

» If you are considering studying abroad, chapter 10 provides guidance and practical information.
» Specific advice for international students coming to study in the UK is given in chapter 11.

How do I apply?

» Chapter 5 outlines the application procedure for university entry. It starts by advising you on how to complete the UCAS application, and then takes you through the process that we hope will lead to your university place for autumn 2023.

Can I afford it?

Note that most figures in chapter 4 refer to 2022 and there will be changes for 2023, which you will need to check.

» Chapter 4 describes how the system of tuition fees works and what you are likely to be charged, depending upon where in the UK you plan to study. It also provides advice on the tuition fee loans and maintenance loans that are available, depending upon where you live in the UK, other forms of financial support (including university scholarships and bursaries), and how to plan your budget.
» Chapter 7 provides advice on where to live while you are at university. Sample accommodation charges for each university are given in chapter 14.

How do I find out more?

The Times and Sunday Times Good University Guide website at **https://www.thetimes.co.uk/gooduniversityguide** will keep you up to date with developments throughout the year and contains further information and online tables (subscription required).

You can also find much practical advice on the UCAS website (**www.ucas.com**), and on individual university websites. There is a wealth of official statistical information on the Discover Uni website (which has replaced Unistats) **https://discoveruni.gov.uk**

Introduction

Extraordinary times have called for extraordinary measures in higher education since the outbreak of the Covid-19 pandemic. Universities showed remarkable resilience in moving to an online model, as did students in adapting their learning styles. The closure of campuses taught universities lessons in how to harness digital technologies alongside in-person teaching, bringing advances that will be here to stay across the sector. At the same time, closed campuses taught us just how highly students value in-person teaching and face-to-face contact time with academic staff and with each other.

Results of the National Student Survey (NSS) published in 2021 found that a year of pandemic disruption on campuses caused dramatic falls in student satisfaction. Students returned often damning judgements on how the year of blended online learning had impacted their university experience. A *Good University Guide* analysis of 2020 and 2021 NSS results revealed that out of the 132 universities in our league table just two – Imperial College London and Surrey – improved their NSS scores year-on-year. Its results shed light on the institutions that adapted better than others to the new ways of operating – proficiency that remains relevant for the applicants of 2023–24, given the ongoing uncertainty around evolving Covid-19 variants. The university profiles in Chapter 14 go into more details on how individual institutions got on.

The University of St Andrews managed to flip its small-class teaching model to online delivery during the pandemic and registered only a tiny decline in student satisfaction rates in the NSS. The university already had a strong record in student satisfaction and the results from 2021, while almost all others nosedived, helped boost St Andrews' overall ranking in our league table from third to first place. In topping our institutional table this year, St Andrews has displaced Cambridge and Oxford from the top of the academic tree – a feat no other university has achieved in the near 30-year history of our (or any other domestic UK) university ranking.

That some remote learning continued once campuses re-opened for the 2021–22 academic year was met with discontent. Students felt short-changed by any ongoing reduction in face-to-face teaching once the lockdowns had been lifted. Through the course of the pandemic an in-person university experience has in some ways become a signifier of value for money.

Even so, lectures had been recorded for playback by lots of universities well before Covid-19. Among the positives that have emerged from the acceleration in online provision is universities' ability to offer students extended access to support services via digital platforms.

Many undergraduates have also expressed a preference for online assessment. And for students juggling work, family and caring responsibilities the flexibility offered by online and hybrid teaching has been beneficial, as it has for those with disabilities and for international students coping with travel disruption.

Covid-19 did not stall the upward trend for young people to go to university. The proportion of all young people across the UK getting an undergraduate place reached record levels in 2021's admissions round, at 38.3%, representing 275,235 new students. Eighty-one per cent of them got a place at their first-choice university. The rise in the 18-year-old population is not expected to be back to its 2010 peak until 2024 and with offer rates continuing to rise in most subjects, next year's applicants should still benefit from relatively favourable odds.

Chris Whitty was credited with prompting a surge in school-leavers applying to medicine and nursing courses in autumn 2021, according to a report by UCAS. The Chief Medical Officer for England is among the inspirational figures to have emerged from the pandemic. The focus on frontline health workers and the stability of job prospects in medicine and nursing are also factors behind the phenomenon, which saw applications to medical degrees rise by a fifth for places in 2021, for nursing courses they rose by a quarter. With the number of places to study medicine capped centrally, the surge in interest made for an even more competitive environment for applicants than usual.

Universities experienced a downward trend in the numbers of students from European countries, however, as the withdrawal of home fee status for EU students following Brexit prompted those from the Continent to vote with their feet. EU student acceptances to undergraduate degree courses were 50% lower in the 2021 admissions round than the year before. But in the same cycle the number of international students from further afield increased for the fifth consecutive year – despite the health pandemic – and more than 54,000 students from non-EU countries won places to study at British universities in 2021. Britain's universities are a magnet for students worldwide, and for those who have them on their doorstep they offer a valuable resource. Even so, the opportunity to study abroad – especially in America – is increasingly attractive to UK students – which we look into in more detail in Chapter 10 Going Abroad to Study.

Among the points raised by the 2019 Philip Augar review of post-18 education and funding was that some university courses offer students little or no financial or professional benefits after graduation, in spite of the big investment. This is an issue our *Guide* has long sought to help students avoid. In an interim report in early 2021, the government stated its aim "to create a system whereby the quality of our technical and academic education is on a par, and the two are equally accessible." A skilled workforce – not only of graduates – is central to Britain's goal of building back better from the pandemic. "We want every student with the aptitude and desire to go to university to be able to do so and we want technical, employer-centric training to be a viable option for many more people," the report continued.

Interest in degree apprenticeships, which dovetail degrees with on-the-job experience, pay a salary and do not cost a penny in tuition fees, is already growing. Clare Marchant, chief executive of UCAS noted that "interest in apprenticeships has never been higher, with now over two million searches annually on UCAS Career Finder." Michelle Donelan, the universities minister, wants every university to offer degree apprenticeships. Their number has increased by 8% since the start of the pandemic and they are now offered by 94 universities.

Efforts to diversify the social profiles of entrants to UK universities are ongoing and their success patchy. As discussed in Chapter 6 Where Students Come From, children from whole sections of society and from disadvantaged backgrounds continue to be shut out of parts of our higher education system in anything other than insignificant numbers. But more encouragingly our fourth annual social inclusion table shows universities of all kinds are more socially diverse now than they were when we first analysed inequalities in 2018.

Some of the most academically-selective universities – Oxford and Cambridge to the fore – have accelerated their progress in admitting more of the brightest students from non-selective state secondary schools. The black achievement gap appears to be narrowing, but at the same time the dropout gap between those recruited from the fifth of postcodes with the lowest higher education participation and the other four-fifths is as wide as ever.

The return of intramural sport, following its Covid-induced off season, has also precipitated the return of our chapter on Enjoying University Sport. The Tokyo 2020 Olympics proved the extraordinary strength of elite sport at UK universities, as exemplified by Loughborough University, which if it were a country would have outperformed Sweden, Switzerland and Belgium in the medals table. Current and past Loughborough students, as well as those who trained at the university's world-class sports facilities, won 14 medals, including three golds. UK campuses boast some of the country's best facilities for sport and participation, just for fun or to keep fit, is encouraged as much as elite-level performance.

Chapter 9 of our *Guide* looks at how students can find help and support when needed and what families can do to assist. Drinking, drug-taking and personal safety on campuses are front and centre, and the chapter aims to set a realistic tone. It offers helpful advice on how it is possible to give your child their autonomy whilst also checking in with them around the matters of drink, drugs and staying safe. With sexual assault claims levelled at two thirds of British universities we look into the tragic case of one student, Emily Drouet, who took her own life following a campaign of abuse by a fellow student, her boyfriend. Scarcely any universities have introduced compulsory consent training for students yet, but with growing momentum they may start to do more.

The price of tuition fees has not gone up for students from the UK and Ireland for now, but it has not gone down either – as had been proposed by the Augar review in 2019. But in February 2020, research by the Institute of Fiscal Studies (IF) reconfirmed the salary premium, finding that a degree from a UK university increases a person's net earnings by at least £100,000 over their lifetime, after student loan repayments and taxes are factored in.

Some degrees do not offer good value for money though, and applicants need to find a sensible balance between following their dreams and getting into debt unwisely when choosing what and where to study. Investigate the findings of the new Graduate Outcomes survey, which shows what graduates are doing 15 months after finishing their degrees. Ideally, in the subjects you want to apply to study, you will see high proportions in high-skilled jobs and/or postgraduate study, and far fewer in jobs deemed low-skilled, or unemployed.

Most graduates do not regret going to university and carry fond memories of their undergraduate years with them through life – along with career advantages and intellectual enrichment. The right university cannot be pinpointed simply by a league table, but this *Guide* should provide all the information needed to draw up a shortlist for further investigation, which will help you make the right choice in the end.

Evolving higher education

In the 28 years that this book has been published, higher education has experienced numerous changes. Recommendations made in 2019 by the Augar review into post-18 education and funding have been slow to bear fruit as the government's attention has been focused elsewhere, but tuition fees – which it recommended reducing – remain in the news. As recently as October 2021, officials from No 10, the Treasury and the Department for Education (DfE) were engaged in talks about a possible cut to fees but failed to reach an agreement in time for the chancellor's spending review that month. Loan repayment thresholds have also been the subject of debate, with minsters said to be considering cutting the repayment threshold from over £27,000 to £23,000 – in an effort to save the Treasury billions. At the time of going to press no changes had been made.

Britain's withdrawal from the European Union has brought significant change for students coming to the UK. As part of the Brexit divorce deal, students from EU countries, Iceland, Liechtenstein, Norway (EEA) and Switzerland are no longer eligible for "home" tuition fees of up to £9,250 in Britain. Nor can they continue to access tuition fee loans here. Instead, from the 2021–22 academic year they have qualified for the higher rate of "international" tuition rates payable by those from the rest of the world. The UK has also left the Erasmus foreign exchange programme, an EU operation, and replaced it with the Turing scheme – a national version that has funding confirmed until 2024–25.

The pattern of applications and enrolments has changed since the introduction of higher fees in 2012. Students are opting in larger numbers for subjects that they think will lead to well-paid jobs. While there has been a recovery in some arts and social science subjects, the trend towards the sciences and some vocational degrees is unmistakeable. Engineering and computer science degrees experienced significant upturns in the 2021 cycle, along with medicine and nursing. The decline in languages at degree level, meanwhile, is ongoing.

Most students take a degree at least partly to improve their career prospects, so some second-guessing of the employment market is inevitable. But most graduate jobs are not subject-specific and even the keenest future forecasters are hard-pressed to predict employment hotspots four or five years ahead – which is when today's applicants will be looking for jobs.

Just as it may be unwise to second-guess employment prospects, the same goes for the competition for places in different subjects. Universities may close or reduce the intake to courses that have low numbers of applicants while some of the more selective institutions may make more places available, especially to candidates who achieve good grades at A-level.

Using this Guide

The merger of *The Times and Sunday Times* university guides eight years ago began a new chapter in the ranking of higher education institutions in the UK. The two guides had 35 editions between them and, in their new form, provide the most comprehensive and authoritative assessments of undergraduate education at UK universities. Hartpury University enters our main ranking in =112th place this year and ministers are keen for new institutions to shake up the higher education system. Even those with university titles – the first criterion for inclusion in our table – take time to build up the body of data required to make meaningful comparisons.

Some famous names in UK higher education have never been ranked because they do not fit the parameters of a system that is intended mainly to guide full-time undergraduates. The Open University, for example, operates entirely through distance learning, while the London and Manchester Business Schools have no undergraduates. Birkbeck University of London, which operates a broadly part-time course model, has dropped out of the table, though we still publish a profile of it in chapter 14.

There are now 70 subject tables, and others will be added in due course because there is growing demand for information at this level. Successive surveys have found that students are more influenced by subject rankings than those for whole institutions.

Since the separation of National Student Survey (NSS) scores, outlined below, there has been no change in the basic methodology behind the tables, however. The nine elements of the main table are the same, with the approach to scores in the 2014 Research Excellence Framework mirroring as closely as possible those for previous assessments. In order to reflect the likelihood of undergraduates coming into contact with outstanding researchers, the proportion of eligible academics entered for assessment is part of the calculation, as well as the average grades achieved.

The graduate prospects measure, derived from the new Graduate Outcomes survey, has made allowance for 15 months' worth of feet-finding among graduates before taking a census of their job status, which makes it a better reflection of their prospects than the six-months-on survey that went before it.

Guide Award Winners

University of the Year	**Imperial College London**
Runner-up	**Warwick**
Shortlisted	**Edge Hill**
	Ulster
	York
Scottish University of the Year	**Glasgow**
Welsh University of the Year	**Cardiff**
Modern University of the Year	**Edge Hill**
Sports University of the Year	**Loughborough**
University of the Year for	
Teaching Quality	**Warwick**
Student Experience	**Imperial College London**
Graduate Employment	**Surrey**
Student Retention	**Sussex**
Social Inclusion	**Teesside**

The methodology for the new edition remains stable. The *Guide* has always put a premium on consistency in the way that it uses the statistics published by universities and presents the results. The overriding aim is to inform potential students and their parents and advisors, not to make judgments on the performance of universities. As such, it differs from the Government's Teaching Excellence Framework (TEF), which uses some of the same statistics but makes allowance for the prior qualifications of students and uses an expert panel to place the results in context. Our tables use the raw data produced by universities to reflect the undergraduate experience, whatever advantages or disadvantages those institutions might face. We also rank all 132 universities, while the TEF uses only three bands, leaving almost half of the institutions in our table on the same middle tier.

The TEF represents the first official intervention in this area since the Quality Assurance Agency's assessments of teaching quality were abolished more than a decade ago. Scores in those reports correlated closely with research grades, and the first discussions on the framework in the Coalition Government envisaged one comparison taking account of both teaching and research. This remains our approach, to look at a broad range of factors (including the presence of excellent researchers on the academic staff) that will impact on undergraduates.

This year's tables

St Andrews has shaken Cambridge and Oxford from the top of the academic table. For several years, St Andrews has been closing in on the top spot with levels of student satisfaction that most other academically elite universities can only marvel at. Oxford has swapped places with Cambridge this year, to sit second. The global significance of Oxford's vaccine work was key in it winning our University of the Year award in 2021–22. That title is taken by Imperial College London this year. Ranking fourth in our academic league table, this specialist in science, engineering, medicine and business has gained 80 points in our measures in the past year – closing on Cambridge in third place. Imperial made sure its international community of 10,500 undergraduates and 9,000 postgraduates did not feel displaced from its academic heart in central London in a year when the pandemic left most students feeling stranded. In recognition of its achievements Imperial also wins our University of the Year for Student Experience award.

Cambridge is again the most successful university among our subject rankings. It tops 23 of the 70 tables; St Andrews leads in seven; Oxford in six; Strathclyde, Imperial College London and Glasgow top three each while Queens, Belfast, Bath, UCL, Warwick, LSE and Edinburgh come first in two tables each. Thirteen other universities top one table each.

St Andrews is no longer only Scotland's top university, it leads the whole of the UK. But it is Glasgow that takes our Scottish University of the Year award, having risen for the fifth consecutive year to its highest ever ranking of 12th. Queen's Belfast is Northern Ireland's top university by a clear margin. In Wales, Cardiff, which has held on to its lead over Swansea, wins our Welsh University of the Year award.

Impressive rises in our table include Goldsmiths, which has gained 36 places to 61st, Arts London (up 31 places to =52nd) and Bolton in =89th place – a 29-place rise. Going in the opposite direction, Royal Agricultural has fallen 43 places to 116th and Leeds Arts has declined by an even bigger margin of 48 places, to =103rd.

In the top ten, Warwick, in 8th place, wins our University of the Year for Teaching Quality award. It has risen two places and maintained its record of never dropping outside the top ten. Aberdeen has risen seven places to join the top 20 in 20th place and King's College London has shot up from 30th to 18th place this year.

Queen Mary, University of London, continues to prove that academic success and social inclusion are not mutually exclusive. It ranks 40th in our academic table and 47th for social inclusion.

Edge Hill, ranked at 68th, its highest position yet in our academic league table, wins our Modern University of the Year award. One of the shining stars of the modern sector, Edge Hill has established a profile nationally as a go-ahead institution with ambition for its students. A new medical school is the latest addition to its estate and its course offering is expanding all the time.

Making the right choices

This *Guide* is intended as a starting point to finding the right course, a tool to help navigate the statistical minefield that applicants face, as universities present their performance in the best possible light. There is advice on fees and financial questions, as well as all-important employment issues, along with the usual ranking of universities and 70 subject tables.

While some of the leading universities have expanded considerably in recent years, most will remain selective, particularly in popular subjects. Although the offer rate is promising, that does not mean that all students secure the university or course of their dreams. The demand for places is far from uniform, and even within the same university the level of competition will vary between subjects. The entry scores quoted in the subject tables in Chapter 12 offer a reliable guide to the relative levels of selectivity, but the figures are for entrants' actual qualifications.

The standard offers made by departments will invariably be lower, and the grades those departments were prepared to accept were often lower still.

Making the right choice requires a mixture of realism and ambition. Most sixth-formers and college students have a fair idea of the grades they are capable of attaining, within a certain margin for error. Even with five course choices, there is no point in applying for a degree where the standard offer is so far from your predicted grades that rejection is virtually certain. If your results do turn out to be much better than predicted, there will be an opportunity through the Adjustment system, or simply through Clearing, to trade up to an alternative university.

Since the relaxation of recruitment restrictions, universities that once took pride in their absence from Clearing have continued to recruit after A-level results day. As a result, the use of insurance choices – the inclusion of at least one university with lower entrance standards than your main targets – has been declining. It is still a dangerous strategy, but there is now more chance of picking up a place at a leading university if you aimed too high with all your first-round choices. Some may even come to you if you sign up to the system that allows universities to approach unplaced candidates on Results Day if their grades are similar to those of other entrants.

The long view

School-leavers who will enter higher education in 2023 were not born when our first league table was published and most will never have heard of polytechnics, even if they attend a university that once carried that title. But it was the award of university status to the 34 polytechnics, over a quarter of a century ago, that was the inspiration for the first edition of *The Times Good University Guide*. The original poly, the Polytechnic of Central London, had become the University of Westminster, Bristol Polytechnic was the University of the West of England and – most mysteriously of all – Leicester Polytechnic had morphed into De Montfort University. The new *Guide* charted the lineage of the new universities and offered the first-ever comparison of institutional performance in UK higher education.

The university establishment did not welcome the initiative. The vice-chancellors described the table as "wrong in principle, flawed in execution and constructed upon data which are not uniform, are ill-defined and in places demonstrably false." The league table has changed considerably since then, and its results are taken rather more seriously. While consistency has been a priority for the *Guide* throughout its 28 years, only six of the original 14 measures have survived. Some of the current components – notably the National Student Survey – did not exist in 1992, while others have been modified or dropped at the behest of the expert group of planning officers from different types of universities that meets annually to review the methodology and make recommendations for the future.

While ranking is hardly popular with academics, the relationship with universities has changed radically, and this *Guide* is quoted on numerous university websites. As Sir David Eastwood, now vice-chancellor of the University of Birmingham, said in launching an official report on university league tables that he commissioned as Chief Executive of the Higher Education Funding Council for England: "We deplore league tables one day and deploy them the next."

Most universities have had their ups and downs over the years, with the notable exceptions of Oxford and Cambridge. Both benefit from top research grades – a measure that carries an extra weighting in our table. They also have famously high entry standards, much the largest proportions of first and upper-second class degrees and consistently good scores on every other measure. St Andrews, which also performs superbly across the board, has the edge over Oxbridge on student satisfaction – while Oxbridge has boycotted the NSS since 2016. Imperial College London and University College London have seldom been out of the top five, with St Andrews joining them in recent years, while the London School of Economics, Durham and Warwick have all been fixtures in the top ten.

There have been spectacular rises. As Thames Valley University in 2001, West London was bottom of our rankings, it is 74th this year and won our award for Student Experience last year. Lincoln is another former incumbent of the bottom spot (in 1999) when it was the University of Lincolnshire and Humberside. It is 49th this year.

Since this book was first published, the number of universities has increased by a third and the full-time student population has rocketed. Individual institutions are almost unrecognisable from their 1993 forms. Nottingham, for example, had fewer than 10,000 students then, compared with more than 30,000 now. Manchester Metropolitan, the largest of the former polys, has experienced similar growth. Yet there are universities now which would have been too small and too specialist to qualify for the title in 1992. The diversity of UK higher education is celebrated as one of its greatest strengths, and the modern universities are neither encouraged nor anxious to compete with the older foundations on some of the measures in our table.

The coming years may bring more transformation in the higher education landscape, not just from increased blended online learning, but from private sector universities competing strongly with established institutions in some fields. The rising 18-year-old population will increase the demand for higher education places over the next few years, but it remains to be seen whether the finances of universities and the regulatory restrictions they might face will enable them to satisfy that demand. Recent experience has reminded us what enduring institutions universities are.

1 The University League Table

What Makes a Top University?

With the introduction of tuition fees in 1998 came the opening of the floodgates of information and statistics about universities and students. Higher education became accountable for the investment it represented to students, their families and to taxpayers more widely. The transparent approach adopted by universities and the government to sharing information is to be commended and is surely an improvement on the somewhat nebulous notion of "reputation" that largely counted as the means of judging a university's quality before. But for those embarking on their application for a university place, navigating the plethora of publicly available information is a complicated and at times confusing process.

The Times and Sunday Times University Guide weighs up university performance measures and combines them in a straightforward way that has armed generations of students with the knowledge and insights to make informed choices. The table in this chapter focuses on the fundamentals of undergraduate education and makes meaningful comparisons. Every element of the table has been chosen for the light it shines on the experience undergraduates encounter during their degrees, and their future prospects.

The information contained within our league table gives readers the chance to look under the bonnet of universities' performance. To get the most out of its content, take some time to read through this introduction to our league table and gain an understanding of the measures used. There is no panel of "experts" involved in creating our league table, the statistics do the talking. Critics may have reasons to discount any of the measures we use, but the package has struck a chord with readers. Our ranking has built a reputation as the most authoritative arbiter of changing fortunes in higher education.

Over 28 years of publication, our *Guide* has maintained consistency in its evaluations, confident that the measures used are the best currently available for the task. Some changes have been forced upon us though, naturally enough during the course of nearly three decades. When universities stopped assessing teaching quality by subject, our table lost its most heavily weighted measure. However, we now have the benefit of the National Student Survey (NSS), which allows us to reflect the student experience. More than two-thirds of final year undergraduates give their views on the quality of their courses, a remarkable response rate that makes the results impossible to dismiss.

The student satisfaction measure is split in two. The "teaching quality" indicator reflects the average scores of the survey's sections on teaching, assessment and feedback, learning opportunities and academic support. The "student experience" indicator is drawn from the average of the sections on organisation and management, learning resources, the student voice and the learning community, as well as the final question on overall satisfaction. Teaching quality is favoured over student experience in our table and accounts for 67% of the overall student satisfaction score, with student experience making up the remaining 33%.

The basic information that applicants need in order to judge universities and their courses does not change, however. A university's entry standards, staffing levels, completion rates, degree classifications and graduate employment rates are all vital pieces of intelligence for anyone deciding where to study.

Research grades, while not directly involving undergraduates, bring with them considerable funds and enable a university to attract top academics.

The measures used are kept under review by a group of university administrators and statisticians, which meets annually. The raw data that go into the table in this chapter and the 70 subject tables in chapter 12 are all in the public domain and are sent to universities for checking before any scores are calculated.

The various official bodies concerned with higher education do not publish league tables, and the Higher Education Statistics Agency (HESA), which supplies most of the figures used in our tables, does not endorse the way in which they are aggregated. But there are now numerous exercises, from the Teaching Excellence Framework to the annual "performance indicators" published by HESA on everything from completion rates to research output at each university, that invite comparisons.

Scrutiny of institutional league table positions is best carried out in conjunction with an examination of the relevant subject table – it is the course, after all, that will dominate your undergraduate years and influence your subsequent career.

How *The Times and Sunday Times* league table works

The table is presented in a format that displays the raw data, wherever possible. In building the table, scores for student satisfaction (combining the teaching quality and student experience scores) and research quality were weighted by 1.5; all other measures were weighted by 1.

For entry standards, student/staff ratio, good honours and graduate prospects, the score was adjusted for subject mix. For example, it is accepted that engineering, law and medicine graduates will tend to have better graduate prospects than their peers from English, psychology and sociology courses. Comparing results in the main subject groupings helps to iron out differences attributable simply to the range of degrees on offer. This subject-mix adjustment means that it is not possible to replicate the scores in the table from the published indicators because the calculation requires access to the entire dataset.

The indicators were combined using a common statistical technique known as z-scores, to ensure that no indicator has a disproportionate effect on the overall total for each university, and the totals were transformed to a scale with 1,000 for the top score. The z-score technique makes it impossible to compare universities' total scores from one year to the next, although their relative positions in the table are comparable. Individual scores are dependent on the top performer: a university might drop from 60% of the top score to 58% but still have improved, depending on the relative performance of other universities.

Only where data are not available from HESA are figures sourced directly from universities. Where this is not possible scores are generated according to a university's average performance on other indicators, apart from the measures for research quality, student/staff ratio and services and facilities spend, where no score is created.

The organisations providing the raw data for the tables are not involved in the process of aggregation, so are not responsible for any inferences or conclusions we have made. Every care has been taken to ensure the accuracy of the tables and accompanying information, but no responsibility can be taken for errors or omissions.

The Times and The Sunday Times league table uses nine important indicators of university activity, based on the most recent data available at the time of compilation:

» Teaching quality
» Student experience
» Research quality
» Entry standards
» Student/staff ratio

» Services and facilities spend
» Completion
» Good honours
» Graduate prospects

Teaching quality and student experience

The student satisfaction measure has been divided into two components which give final-year undergraduates' views of the quality of their courses. The National Student Survey (NSS) published in 2021 was the source of the data.

Where no data were available in the 2021 survey, the score from the 2020 survey was used. Where no data from the 2020 survey were available, the 2019 score was used.

» The National Student Survey covers eight aspects of a course, with an additional question gauging overall satisfaction. Students answer on a scale from 1 (bottom) to 5 (top) and the score in the table is the percentage of positive responses (4 and 5) in each section
» The teaching quality indicator reflects the average scores of the first four sections, which contain 14 questions
» The student experience indicator is drawn from the average scores of the remaining four sections, containing 12 questions, and the additional question on overall satisfaction.
» Teaching quality accounts for 67% of the overall score covering student satisfaction, with student experience making up the remaining 33%.
» The survey is based on the opinion of final-year undergraduates rather than directly assessing teaching quality. Most undergraduates have no experience of other universities, or different courses, to inform their judgements. Although all the questions relate to courses, rather than other aspects of the student experience, some types of university – notably medium-sized campus universities – tend to do better than others, while those in London in particular tend to do worse.

Research quality

This is a measure of the quality of the research undertaken in each university. The information was sourced from the 2014 Research Excellence Framework (REF), a peer-review exercise used to evaluate the quality of research in UK higher education institutions undertaken by the UK Higher Education funding bodies. Additionally, academic staffing data for 2013–14 from the

Higher Education Statistics Agency have been used. (The next REF is due to be published in 2022.)

» A research quality profile was given to every university department that took part. This profile used the following categories: 4* world-leading; 3* internationally excellent; 2* internationally recognised; 1* nationally recognised; and unclassified. The Funding Bodies have directed more funds to the best research by applying weightings, and for the 2015 *Guide* we used the weightings adopted by HEFCE (the funding council for England) for funding in 2013–14: 4* was weighted by a factor of 3 and 3* was weighted by a factor of 1. Outputs of 2* and 1* carried zero weight. This meant a maximum score of 3. In the interests of consistency, the above weightings continue to be applied.

» The scores in the table are presented as a percentage of the maximum score. To achieve the maximum score all staff would need to be at 4* world-leading level.

» Universities could choose which staff to include in the REF, so, to factor in the depth of the research quality, each quality profile score has been multiplied by the number of staff returned in the REF as a proportion of all eligible staff.

Entry standards

This is the average score, using the UCAS tariff (see page 32), of new students under the age of 21 who took A and AS-Levels, Scottish Highers and Advanced Highers and other equivalent qualifications (eg, International Baccalaureate). It measures what new students achieved rather than the entry requirements suggested by the universities. The data comes from HESA for 2019–20. The original sources of data for this measure are data returns made by the universities to HESA.

» Using the UCAS tariff, each student's examination results were converted to a numerical score. HESA then calculated an average for all students at the university. The results have then been adjusted to take account of the subject mix at the university.

» A score of 144 represents three As at A-level. Although all but five of the top 40 universities in the table have average entry standards of at least 144, it does not mean that everyone achieved such results – let alone that this was the standard offer. Courses will not demand more than three subjects at A-level and offers are pitched accordingly. You will need to reach the entry requirements set by the university, rather than these scores.

Graduate prospects

This measure is the percentage of full-time, UK-resident graduates undertaking further study or in a high-skilled job 15 months after graduation. The high-skilled employment data came from the new Graduate Outcomes survey published by HESA in July 2021. It is based on 2018 and 2019 graduates interviewed up to September 2019 and September 2020 respectively. The results have been adjusted for subject mix.

Good honours

This measure is the percentage of graduates achieving a first or upper-second class degree. The results have been adjusted to take account of the subject mix at the university. The data comes from HESA for 2018–19 and 2019–20 averaged to offset any classification inflation due to the pandemic. The original sources of data for this measure are data returns made by the universities to HESA.

» Four-year first degrees, such as an MChem, are treated as equivalent to a first or upper-second.

» Scottish Ordinary degrees (awarded after three years of study) are excluded.

» Universities control degree classification, with some oversight from external examiners. There have been suggestions that, since universities have increased the numbers of good honours degrees they award, this measure may not be as objective as it should be. However, it remains the key measure of a student's success and employability.

Completion

This measure gives the percentage of students expected to complete their studies (or transfer to another institution) for each university. The data comes from the HESA performance indicators published in March 2021 and based on students entering in 2016–17 through to 2018–19.

» This measure is a projection, liable to statistical fluctuations.

Student/staff ratio

This is a measure of the average number of full-time equivalent students to each member of the academic staff, apart from those purely engaged in research. In this measure a low value is better than a high value. The data comes from HESA for 2019–20. The original sources of data for this measure are data returns made by the universities themselves to HESA.

» The figures, as calculated by HESA, allow for variation in employment patterns at different universities. A low value means that there are a small number of students for each academic member of staff, but this does not, of course, ensure good teaching quality or contact time with academics.

» Student/staff ratios vary by subject; for example, the ratio is usually low for medicine. In building the table, the score is adjusted for the subject mix taught by each university.

» Adjustments are also made for students who are on industrial placements, either for a full year or for part of a year.

Services and facilities spend

The expenditure per student on staff and student facilities, including library and computing facilities. The data comes from HESA for 2018–19 and 2019–20. The original data sources for this measure are data returns made by the universities to HESA.

» This is a measure calculated by taking the expenditure on student facilities (including sports, grants to student societies, careers services, health services, counselling, etc.) and library and computing facilities (books, journals, staff, central computers and computer networks, but not buildings) and dividing this by the number of full-time-equivalent students. Expenditure is averaged over two years to even out the figures (for example, a computer upgrade undertaken in a single year).

Rank	Last year's rank		Teaching quality (%)	Student experience (%)	Research quality (%)	Entry standards (UCAS points)	Graduate prospects (%)	Good honours (%)	Completion rate (%)	Student-staff ratio	Services & facilities spend per student (£)	Total
1	3	St Andrews	86.5	84.2	40.4	207	80.4	91.8	95.7	11.1	3,943	1,000
2	2	Oxford	n/a	n/a	53.1	198	89.2	95.1	99.1	10.1	3,610	978
3	1	Cambridge	n/a	n/a	57.3	206	88.5	95.1	99.0	11.4	3,972	977
4	5	Imperial College London	77.7	79.3	56.2	197	92.0	92.4	97.5	11.1	4,047	939
5	4	London School of Economics	75.3	69.8	52.8	175	92.0	94.1	96.5	12.4	2,983	928
6	6	Durham	76.4	70.2	39.0	182	84.5	93.2	96.8	13.5	3,846	883
7	8	University College London	72.8	69.9	51.0	177	85.3	92.6	94.3	10.1	2,961	851
8	10=	Warwick	78.5	74.5	44.6	169	85.4	87.8	95.1	12.8	2,649	842
9	9	Bath	76.8	79.0	37.3	167	85.7	90.6	96.0	15.1	2,965	822
10	7	Loughborough	78.3	80.6	36.3	150	80.6	86.0	93.4	13.5	3,425	818
11	10=	Lancaster	77.3	74.3	39.1	144	79.9	83.1	93.3	13	3,509	796
12	14	Glasgow	76.3	74.2	39.9	202	75.7	86.9	88.2	13.1	2,843	774
13	17	Edinburgh	69.6	64.6	43.8	187	79.0	90.9	93.3	11.7	2,466	755
14	13	Bristol	72.9	67.4	47.3	164	79.7	91.3	95.3	13.4	2,704	752
15	15=	Leeds	73.6	69.6	36.8	159	79.7	88.5	93.4	13.7	3,211	749
16	15=	Southampton	75.8	71.8	44.9	151	76.0	87.3	93.2	13.2	2,772	744
17	23=	Strathclyde	77.5	77.3	37.7	199	80.3	85.5	89.5	18.9	2,278	742
18	30	King's College London	71.5	65.6	44.0	164	82.8	88.1	91.3	11.7	3,242	732
19	20	York	76.7	72.1	38.3	149	78.1	82.9	93.3	13.6	2,273	725
20	27	Aberdeen	77.5	76.0	29.9	184	77.3	88.2	88.5	15.7	2,624	723
21	12	Exeter	72.6	70.1	38.0	156	77.4	88.9	94.5	15.1	2,688	721
22	23=	Sheffield	76.1	73.7	37.6	150	77.4	85.3	92.8	14	2,497	708
23	18	Manchester	69.8	65.1	39.8	161	79.4	84.8	93.0	13.1	3,332	707
24	31=	Queen's Belfast	74.5	72.8	39.7	148	83.1	86.1	91.0	14.6	2,410	703
25	19	Birmingham	68.8	64.7	37.1	152	78.0	89.2	94.6	14.7	3,854	701

Rank	Last year's rank		Teaching quality (%)	Student experience (%)	Research quality (%)	Entry standards (UCAS points)	Graduate prospects (%)	Good honours (%)	Completion rate (%)	Student-staff ratio	Services & facilities spend per student (£)	Total
26	22	Royal Holloway, London	74.5	70.5	36.3	130	72.5	86.5	91.2	15.1	2,820	696
27	21	East Anglia	74.6	71.3	35.8	133	75.3	85.5	88.6	13.2	3,087	695
28	26	Nottingham	73.5	68.4	37.8	146	81.0	84.7	93.0	14.8	3,009	691
29	28	Harper Adams	79.3	76.1	5.7	121	75.7	76.5	91.8	14.2	4,101	689
30=	35	Heriot-Watt	73.0	73.1	36.7	170	74.3	82.6	84.6	17.3	3,723	688
30=	29	Liverpool	75.9	72.4	31.5	140	75.6	81.3	91.3	13.9	3,387	688
32	39	Surrey	77.1	76.3	29.7	136	81.5	81.0	89.3	16.7	2,809	675
33	50	SOAS, London	72.1	66.4	27.9	148	67.8	85.2	83.5	12.8	3,304	673
34	31=	Reading	72.0	68.3	36.5	122	76.5	85.6	91.4	16.4	2,859	662
35=	34	Cardiff	71.0	66.2	35.0	145	80.4	84.1	91.8	13.7	2,686	660
35=	23=	Dundee	75.1	71.0	31.2	177	76.3	78.8	89.0	14.5	2,718	660
37	37	Leicester	74.5	71.3	31.8	129	73.5	82.9	90.5	13.8	2,871	656
38	42	Aberystwyth	81.8	77.9	28.1	118	65.0	72.8	85.0	16	3,277	651
39	36	Swansea	77.7	73.5	33.7	131	75.0	80.4	89.4	14.8	2,143	650
40	41	Queen Mary, London	72.1	69.3	37.9	146	74.6	87.5	91.6	13	2,146	649
41	38	Stirling	77.9	73.3	30.5	167	71.5	75.1	83.9	15.8	2,191	648
42	31=	Newcastle	69.4	63.5	37.7	144	76.4	85.2	94.0	14.9	2,675	635
43	40	Essex	70.7	67.6	37.2	115	67.6	77.6	86.8	15.5	4,027	626
44	51=	Ulster	77.7	74.6	31.8	126	72.1	80.9	87.1	18.9	2,792	625
45	43	Aston	72.3	69.9	25.8	126	77.4	83.3	90.1	15.8	2,234	615
46	48	Kent	74.5	70.4	35.2	125	68.2	81.4	88.2	16.7	1,985	599
47	44	Sussex	71.6	67.7	31.8	136	68.2	78.4	92.2	17.4	2,450	594
48	51=	Keele	75.9	73.4	22.1	121	77.5	77.7	88.0	14.8	2,225	580
49	45	Lincoln	76.5	72.2	10.3	118	68.4	78.0	88.1	15.7	2,409	571
50	46=	Chichester	80.5	76.3	6.4	122	62.9	78.4	86.4	14.9	1,783	566

Rank	Last year's rank		Teaching quality (%)	Student experience (%)	Research quality (%)	Entry standards (UCAS points)	Graduate prospects (%)	Good honours (%)	Completion rate (%)	Student-staff ratio	Services & facilities spend per student (£)	Total
51	46=	Coventry	78.0	74.4	3.8	113	70.8	77.0	80.0	14.2	2,805	565
52=	83=	Arts London	70.9	56.7	8.0	140	58.2	76.8	85.5	12.8	3,566	561
52=	60=	Hull	76.6	71.9	16.7	124	73.9	77.2	80.9	15.5	2,561	561
54	56	Oxford Brookes	70.9	67.0	11.4	114	74.7	81.3	90.7	14.2	2,246	560
55	82	City, London	68.5	67.5	22.6	131	79.0	77.8	88.1	17.6	2,793	557
56	77	Norwich Arts	79.8	69.7	5.6	129	58.0	71.1	83.7	15.6	2,931	552
57	63	Edinburgh Napier	78.4	75.0	4.6	149	71.6	80.5	80.3	19.9	2,585	549
58=	70	Edge Hill	74.9	70.5	4.9	129	67.4	73.5	86.2	14.3	2,781	546
58=	59	Plymouth	76.5	70.7	15.9	125	73.1	81.0	84.0	17.1	2,378	546
60	75	Glasgow Caledonian	74.8	72.5	7.0	165	75.3	84.0	85.1	22.3	2,006	544
61	97	Goldsmiths, London	67.4	57.7	33.4	127	61.3	82.7	79.1	14.3	3,120	542
62=	57	Northumbria	71.8	64.2	9.0	139	73.8	80.8	82.5	15.5	2,482	540
62=	66	Robert Gordon	79.7	75.4	4.0	154	71.9	73.0	84.3	18.7	2,001	540
64	62	Bangor	74.8	69.3	27.2	123	66.3	76.1	81.4	15.9	2,141	538
65	78	Roehampton	73.1	68.3	24.5	100	60.2	71.4	77.5	15.2	3,596	537
66	89	Queen Margaret, Edinburgh	78.2	74.0	6.6	160	66.8	80.4	81.5	20.8	1,541	535
67	86	St Mary's, Twickenham	80.4	78.1	4.0	105	66.6	78.6	81.1	18	1,879	534
68	69	Chester	75.4	67.0	4.1	117	71.0	74.8	81.1	14.7	2,953	531
69	71	Creative Arts	76.6	65.1	3.4	134	51.0	78.7	84.5	14.1	2,749	529
70	53	Nottingham Trent	74.0	67.1	6.5	120	65.8	73.4	88.4	15.3	2,430	525
71	65	Manchester Metropolitan	72.3	64.1	7.5	127	63.6	77.9	85.5	16	3,152	524
72	67	Sheffield Hallam	73.1	66.0	5.4	115	73.5	78.6	84.2	17.2	2,893	520
73	58	West of England	76.4	70.9	8.8	123	74.2	75.6	82.0	15.8	1,888	519
74	60=	West London	80.3	75.5	1.6	117	62.4	78.8	77.5	15.9	2,526	518
75	73=	Huddersfield	72.0	64.7	9.4	121	65.3	78.9	83.5	13.7	2,567	516

Rank	Last year's rank		Teaching quality (%)	Student experience (%)	Research quality (%)	Entry standards (UCAS points)	Graduate prospects (%)	Good honours (%)	Completion rate (%)	Student-staff ratio	Services & facilities spend per student (£)	Total
76	76	Staffordshire	78.1	70.5	16.5	117	68.0	74.4	77.8	17.7	2,063	509
77	103	Sunderland	79.6	74.9	5.8	116	61.8	66.1	77.4	15.5	3,010	505
78	49	St George's, London	64.5	59.2	22.2	144	94.4	80.5	93.0	13.3	2,637	501
79=	54	Arts Bournemouth	75.4	68.8	2.4	145	53.5	69.0	88.4	14.3	1,806	500
79=	79	Cardiff Metropolitan	74.9	70.2	3.9	123	68.4	75.4	78.9	18.5	2,629	500
81	80=	Liverpool Hope	75.4	67.3	9.2	113	61.3	74.4	82.6	14.8	2,170	499
82	64	Bishop Grosseteste	75.5	67.3	2.1	107	75.0	72.1	88.1	19.1	2,200	497
83=	90=	Birmingham City	76.4	69.3	4.3	118	69.4	76.7	82.7	16.5	2,039	495
83=	101=	Wales Trinity St David	79.5	70.0	2.6	136	60.7	74.4	78.8	18.8	2,153	495
83=	83=	York St John	77.5	71.3	4.1	108	64.7	76.1	84.5	18.1	2,203	495
86	101=	Worcester	78.1	74.5	4.3	114	73.1	66.6	85.3	16.9	1,885	494
87	94=	Falmouth	76.6	69.0	4.6	123	54.5	76.5	84.6	15.3	2,042	493
88	72	Portsmouth	72.8	66.5	8.6	111	68.2	76.3	83.5	16.3	2,405	488
89=	118	Bolton	81.3	75.9	2.9	116	60.2	63.7	75.8	14.5	2,779	485
89=	106	Bradford	74.8	71.4	9.2	123	71.7	82.9	83.7	18.7	2,005	485
89=	108	Buckingham	79.0	73.4	n/a	118	87.1	67.7	85.0	18.8	1,644	485
89=	98	Greenwich	74.9	70.0	4.9	114	71.0	79.5	81.7	18.5	2,116	485
93	85	Liverpool John Moores	72.4	67.8	8.9	143	67.0	76.6	82.7	17.3	1,826	484
94=	80=	Abertay	78.3	71.7	5.1	144	68.5	78.5	73.6	22.4	1,780	481
94=	94=	Derby	78.2	72.1	2.5	116	67.0	69.3	78.5	14.7	1,884	481
96=	109	Gloucestershire	75.8	69.9	3.8	117	63.3	75.8	80.8	17.3	1,930	478
96=	99	Hertfordshire	74.6	70.2	5.6	103	69.4	70.3	82.0	15.6	2,793	478
98	100	Salford	72.0	65.6	8.3	126	70.1	75.5	80.1	16.8	2,416	477
99	90=	South Wales	75.5	68.4	4.0	116	63.7	73.1	81.8	15.5	2,281	476
100	125	London Metropolitan	81.0	74.9	3.5	100	57.1	66.7	68.0	18.5	3,817	469

Rank	Last year's rank	Teaching quality (%)	Student experience (%)	Research quality (%)	Entry standards (UCAS points)	Graduate prospects (%)	Good honours (%)	Completion rate (%)	Student-staff ratio	Services & facilities spend per student (£)	Total
101=	104= Kingston	75.1	69.2	5.1	116	62.2	73.7	82.4	17.6	2,589	463
101=	115 Plymouth Marjon	81.6	77.2	0.0	117	61.8	77.4	78.3	16.4	983	463
103=	104= Bath Spa	74.4	67.0	7.9	106	54.4	81.9	84.5	18	2,135	462
103=	55 Leeds Arts	72.3	64.9	n/a	149	51.7	76.7	93.5	15.1	1,287	462
105	122 Suffolk	76.1	67.8	n/a	112	75.2	70.8	65.0	16.5	2,788	459
106=	68 Bournemouth	67.0	60.2	9.0	110	72.4	80.0	80.9	18.6	2,511	456
106=	96 Winchester	72.5	65.3	5.8	108	63.7	76.5	84.4	17.4	1,754	456
108=	87 Central Lancashire	72.8	66.4	5.6	124	67.7	72.8	72.4	14.3	2,428	455
108=	111 Northampton	72.2	64.4	3.2	104	69.3	68.1	79.2	16.8	3,363	455
110=	116 West of Scotland	72.8	65.5	4.3	136	69.3	77.0	78.1	20.9	2,559	451
110=	124 Wrexham Glynd r	82.0	73.8	2.3	113	64.0	76.2	73.2	21.9	1,773	451
112=	Hartpury	78.3	73.4	n/a	117	61.6	62.9	n/a	22.2	3,012	449
112=	107 Leeds Beckett	74.9	69.4	4.1	104	66.2	75.7	77.6	20	2,384	449
112=	93 Solent, Southampton	76.0	68.8	0.5	110	59.1	75.5	76.2	16.1	2,146	449
115	117 Anglia Ruskin	76.3	71.3	5.4	109	71.3	76.2	79.9	20	1,596	447
116	73= Royal Agricultural	72.4	68.5	1.1	111	63.2	67.9	89.5	21.7	3,214	443
117	120 Brighton	69.1	59.3	7.9	109	71.6	72.6	82.8	16.7	2,462	437
118	92 Teesside	72.1	63.9	3.6	115	74.1	74.2	75.6	17.9	2,781	434
119=	112= Buckinghamshire New	75.8	68.2	1.5	108	64.6	60.3	73.1	17.4	3,660	425
119=	127 Canterbury Christ Church	73.3	62.9	4.5	98	70.4	68.9	77.3	16.4	2,223	425
121	88 Brunel London	63.4	59.2	25.4	118	67.1	77.0	87.4	17	1,591	423
122	112= Newman, Birmingham	78.0	73.1	2.8	103	63.8	68.4	75.3	17.7	1,899	422
123	121 Middlesex	71.6	66.8	9.7	105	59.3	72.2	76.2	17.5	2,645	415
124	110 Leeds Trinity	71.1	63.9	2.0	103	61.8	81.8	81.3	22.9	2,031	406
125	114 Cumbria	73.3	66.5	1.2	120	68.5	66.5	81.7	16.6	1,748	401

Rank	Last year's rank		Teaching quality (%)	Student experience (%)	Research quality (%)	Entry standards (UCAS points)	Graduate prospects (%)	Good honours (%)	Completion rate (%)	Student-staff ratio	Services & facilities spend per student (£)	Total
126	119	De Montfort	67.7	61.6	8.9	105	65.0	76.1	80.2	20.2	2,353	392
127	123	London South Bank	71.8	63.1	9.0	106	65.4	71.2	75.2	16.8	2,391	389
128	128	Wolverhampton	74.4	67.1	5.9	107	64.6	70.2	71.4	17	2,161	383
129	126	Westminster	70.7	66.5	9.8	118	57.3	70.2	80.2	20.9	1,992	381
130	129	East London	74.8	69.4	7.2	97	57.7	73.1	76.5	21.9	1,556	354
131	130	Ravensbourne, London	65.8	54.7	n/a	113	61.4	80.9	79.7	22.6	1,561	341
132	131	Bedfordshire	74.0	67.6	7.0	106	66.2	63.8	53.1	26.3	1,693	261

last year's data
2017–18 data only

2 Choosing What and Where to Study

Decisions, decisions. Picking what and where to study is up there with some of the biggest. The degree and university you choose will impact the rest of your life, to one extent or another, on so many levels – from professional and intellectual to personal and emotional. This is not the time to be guided by where most of your mates are going, the miles of motorway that keep your mum and dad at bay or what drinks deals are offered at the local night spots. Careers, scholarship and lifelong friendships are shaped during the undergraduate years. Many people meet their wives and husbands at university, too. Things that seem light years away to most school leavers filling out their UCAS forms can turn out to be driven by where they end up at university; it may become the area where you buy your first home, the place you put down roots.

Naturally, all considerations about what and where to study are under the microscope in light of the student debt that is racking up to cover tuition fees and living costs. Those who graduated in 2020 took out an average of £45,060 in loans, according to a report from the Higher Education Policy Institute. Making informed but also aspirational decisions about a degree course is key to ensuring a wise choice that is likely to stand the test of time.

Choice runs through education, from selecting from over 50 GCSE and A-level subjects in England, Northern Ireland and Wales, and 70 Higher and Advanced Higher subjects in Scotland, to figuring out the right university. There are more than 35,000 undergraduate courses on offer in Britain, as totted up by UCAS in its *Where Next?* analysis of school leavers' choices in the 2020 admissions cycle. This *Guide* features 132 universities, plus there are lots of specialist colleges to consider. Such breadth of choice may seem overwhelming, but there are plenty of tangible ways to begin whittling down your options.

The UCAS report polled 27,000 individuals and found that their decision-making motivations ranged from the rational and logical to the inexplicable and emotive. A common thread, though, and one that chimes with widespread research, was that subject choice came first: 83% of students said they decided on their degree subject before thinking about the institution at which they would study it.

Enjoying a subject was the guiding principle for a resounding 99% of the students surveyed, but employability prospects are also increasingly taken into consideration – as they should be –

with more than half of respondents reporting that high graduate employment rates have become more important to them since the start of the pandemic. The following chapter *Assessing Graduate Job Prospects* looks into this in greater detail.

The demand for places at university is continuing to climb. Not even a global health pandemic has stalled the upward trajectory of applications and enrolments to UK higher education institutions. The charms of university have perhaps seemed more appealing while the alternatives have been so limited by Covid-19, with opportunities to travel limited and job prospects confusing or sparse. In 2020, just 18% of graduates found a job, compared with 60% in a normal year.

The new Graduate Outcomes survey shows what graduates of the subjects you are interested in are doing 15 months after finishing their degrees. Ideally, you will see high proportions in high-skilled jobs and/or postgraduate study, and far fewer in jobs deemed low-skilled, or unemployed. It is a useful tool for new applicants.

Some subjects and some universities carry more prestige than others. Such judgements are worth bearing in mind, as your future CV will be assessed according to them. This kind of thinking may not sit easily with everyone, but employers treat universities and subjects as yardsticks, not just the results gained on courses. Certain universities, however, may not occupy our upper rankings, but they might have particularly strong departments for individual subjects. Make the most out of this *Guide*, and cross reference the subject-by-subject information in chapter 12 with the university profiles and rankings in chapter 14. The options are not endless, but they are many.

Be realistic in your choices, the course you apply to should be within your capabilities, though it will also need to keep you interested for three or four years. A degree should broaden your options later in life, so be sensible about choosing one that can do that for you and keep an eye on the jobs horizon. The technological advancements of the fourth industrial revolution are continually reshaping the world of work, and you want to be abreast of developments. Narrowing your focus at degree stage could limit what is open to you in five to ten years' time. This *Guide* can inform you of what is possible, and what will make a wise choice.

Is higher education for you?
Being carried along with the flow is all too easy. Maybe all your friends are going to university, or your parents expect it. If you apply for a course in your strongest A-level subject, things should work out ok and your career will look after itself, right? Or perhaps your driving motivation is to leave home and go a bit wild. Such considerations are natural and will not necessarily lead to disaster. But now is the time to question whether university is the best way of fulfilling your ambitions. There are degree apprenticeships, or training schemes at big firms which could equally help you achieve what you want, minus the need to take out a Student Loan.

If studying for A-levels or equivalent qualifications has felt like torture, now may not be the time for you to go to university. Perhaps a job would be better, and possibly a return to education later in life would suit you more. Love of a subject is an excellent reason for taking a degree; it will help you focus your course search on those that reflect your passion. But if a degree is a means to a career for you, look carefully at employment rates for any courses you consider.

Setting your priorities
The majority of graduate jobs are not subject-specific; employers value the transferable skills that higher education confers. Rightly or wrongly, however, most employers are influenced by which university you went to, as mentioned above, so the choice of institution remains important.

Consider boosting your CV while studying by choosing a university that offers some sort of employment-related scheme. It could be work experience built into your degree, or a particularly active careers service.

Narrowing down the field

There is only a scramble for places on a relatively small proportion of courses that attract intense competition. Otherwise, there are plenty of places at good universities for candidates with sufficient qualifications, you just need to find the one that suits you best. For older applicants returning to education, relevant work experience and demonstrable interest in a subject may be enough to win a place.

Too much choice is more of an issue. Narrow down your options by choosing a subject – or subject area – first, rather than a university. This can reduce the field considerably as not all universities offer all subjects. Having made this first edit by subject, then factor in personal preferences such as location and type of university – campus or city? – and by this point you may already have the beginnings of a manageable list.

Next up is course content and what life is really like for students. Today's budding undergraduates are at an advantage in this regard. As well as having access to the informative and accurate contents of university prospectuses and websites, they can connect with current students online and do some digging. Most universities have an "Ask a Student" function, or similar, on their website, which will link you with a student ambassador for a live chat or call back. Another helpful source of information is **www.thestudentroom.com** the country's largest online student community. You may already have used it while studying for your A-levels. The peer-to-peer platform offers forums for students to discuss their options, ask for advice and build relationships. Current students on the courses and at the universities you are interested in may be happy to share their appraisals – though bear in mind that what they tell you may be biased in some direction or another, and cross-reference anything you have been told with factual sources of information such as ours, or the UCAS website.

The National Student Survey is an objective source of information which is available online, with a range of additional data about the main courses at each institution, at **www.officeforstudents.org.uk/advice-and-guidance/student-information-and-data**.

Visiting the university will give a truer picture yet; better still go to the department where you would be studying.

What to study?

As well as an interest that is sustainable for three-plus years in the subject you pick, you need to ensure you have the right qualifications to meet its entry requirements. Many economics degrees require maths A-level, for example, while most medical schools demand chemistry or biology. The UCAS website **www.ucas.com** is a good starting point; it contains course profiles and entrance requirements, while universities' own sites offer more detailed information. The Russell Group of 24 leading universities' Informed Choices website is another go-to source of information regarding required subjects.

Your school subjects and the UCAS tariff

The official measure by which your results will be judged is the UCAS tariff, which gives a score for each grade of most UK qualifications considered relevant to university entrance, as well as for the International Baccalaureate (IB). The points system is shown on Page 32. Two-thirds of offers are made in grades, rather than tariff points. This means universities may stipulate the grades they require in specific subjects, and determine which vocational qualifications are relevant to different degrees. In certain universities, some departments, but not others, will use the tariff to set offers. Course profiles on the UCAS website and/or universities' own sites should show whether offers are framed in terms of grades or tariff points. It is important to find out which, especially if you are relying on points from qualifications other than A-level or Scottish Highers.

Entry qualifications listed in the *Guide* relate not to the offers made by universities, but to the actual grades achieved by successful candidates who are under 21 on entry. For ease of comparison, a tariff score is included even where universities make their offers in grades.

"Soft" subjects

These are another big factor in what and where you study. The Russell Group of 24 research-led universities scrapped its controversial list of preferred A-levels in 2019, after criticism that it contributed to a devaluation of creative and arts subjects. Previously however, the group's Informed Choices website had a list of "facilitating subjects" comprising: maths and further maths, English, physics, biology, chemistry, geography, languages (classical and modern) and history, which are required by many degrees and welcomed by Russell Group universities generally. The website advised sixth formers to pick the majority of their A-levels from this list and to include at most one "soft" subject. Although these "soft subjects" were not listed specifically, a previous Informed Choices report named media studies, art and design, photography and business studies among the subjects that would normally be given this label. The current Informed Choices website offers more personalised guidance on A-level choices.

The facilitating subjects list may be gone, but its legacy is entrenched, and applicants to these universities should be very aware of that when selecting A-levels. It is better to keep more doors open than close any off at sixth form.

For most courses at most universities, there are no such restrictions, as long as your main subjects or qualifications are relevant to the degree you hope to take. Even so, the Russell Group lists are an indication of the subjects that admissions tutors may take more or less seriously, especially if you plan to apply to at least one leading university. Although only the London School of Economics has published a list of "non-preferred" subjects (see page 33), others may take a less formal approach but still apply similar weightings.

General studies is a separate matter, and some universities still do not regard it as a full A-level for entry purposes, while others – including some leading institutions – do.

Vocational qualifications

The Education Department downgraded many vocational qualifications in school league tables from 2014. This has added to the confusion surrounding the value placed on diplomas and other qualifications by universities. The engineering diploma has won near-universal approval from universities (for admission to engineering courses and possibly some science degrees), but some of the other diplomas are in fields that are not on the curriculum of the most selective universities. Regardless of the points awarded under the tariff, it is essential to contact universities direct to ensure that a diploma or another vocational qualification will be an acceptable qualification for your chosen degree.

UCAS tariff scores for main qualifications:

A-levels		AS levels	
Grade	**Points**	**Grade**	**Points**
A*	56	A	20
A	48	B	16
B	40	C	12
C	32	D	10
D	24	E	6
E	16		

Scottish Advanced higher		Scottish higher	
Grade	**Points**	**Grade**	**Points**
A	56	A	33
B	48	B	27
C	40	C	21
D	32	D	15

BTec Level 3			
National Diploma (post-2016)		**Extended Certificate**	
Grade	**Points**	**Grade**	**Points**
D*	28	D*	56
D	24	D	48
M	16	M	32
P	8	P	16

International Baccalaureate*			
Higher level		**Standard level**	
H7	56	S7	28
H6	48	S6	24
H5	32	S5	16
H4	24	S4	12
H3	12	S3	6

*The Extended Essay and Theory of Knowledge course are awarded A 12, B 10, C 8, D 6, E 4
For Foundation Diploma, Extended Diploma and other BTec levels see UCAS website
For other qualifications see: **ucas.com/ucas/ucas-tariff-points**

Admission tests

The growing numbers of applicants with high grades at A-level have encouraged the introduction of separate admission tests for some of the most oversubscribed courses. There are national tests in medicine and law that are used by some of the leading universities, while Oxford and Cambridge have their own tests in a growing number of subjects. The details are listed on page 34. In all cases, the tests are used as an extra selection tool, not as a replacement for A-level or other general qualifications.

Making a choice

Your A-levels or Scottish Highers may have been straightforward to choose, but the range of subjects at university is vast. Even subjects you have studied at school may be quite different at degree level – some academic economists prefer their undergraduates not to have taken A-level economics because they approach the subject so differently. Other students are disappointed because they appear to be going over old ground when they continue with a subject that they enjoyed at school. Universities now publish quite detailed syllabuses, and applicants are advised to go through the fine print.

The greater difficulty comes in judging your suitability for the many subjects that are not on the school or college curriculum. Philosophy and psychology sound fascinating (and are), but you may have no idea what degrees in either subject entail – for example, the level of statistics that may be required. Forensic science may look exciting on television – more glamorous than plain chemistry – but it opens fewer doors, as the type of work portrayed in *Silent Witness* is very hard to find.

Academic or vocational?

There is frequent and often misleading debate about the differences between academic and vocational higher education. It is usually about the relative value of taking a degree, as opposed to a directly work-related qualification. But it also extends to higher education itself, with jibes about so-called "Mickey Mouse" degrees in areas that were not part of the higher education curriculum when most of the critics were students.

Such attitudes ignore the fact that medicine and law are both vocational subjects, as are architecture, engineering and education. They are not seen as any less academic than geography or sociology, but for some reason, social work or nursing, let alone media studies and sports science, are often looked down upon. The test of a degree should be whether it is challenging and a good preparation for working life. Both general academic and vocational degrees can do this.

Nevertheless, it is clear that the prospect of much higher graduate debt is encouraging more students into job-related subjects. This is understandable and, if you are sure of your future career path, possibly also sensible. But much depends on what that career is – and whether you are ready to make such a long-term commitment. Some of the programmes that have attracted

---

"Traditional academic" and "non-preferred" subjects

The London School of Economics expects applicants to offer at least two of the traditional subjects listed below, while any of the non-preferred subjects listed should only be offered with two traditional subjects.

Traditional subjects

- Ancient history
- Biology
- Classical civilisation
- Chemistry
- Computing
- Economics
- Electronics
- English
- Further mathematics
- Geography
- Government and politics
- History
- Law
- Mathematics
- Modern or classical languages
- Music
- Philosophy
- Physics
- Psychology
- Religious studies
- Sociology

Non-preferred subjects

- Any Applied A-level
- Accounting
- Art and design
- Business studies
- Citizenship studies
- Communication and culture
- Creative writing
- Design and technology
- Drama/theatre studies
- Film studies
- Health and social care
- Home economics
- Information and communication technology
- Leisure studies
- Media studies
- Music technology
- Physical education/ Sports studies
- Travel and tourism

General studies, critical thinking, thinking skills, knowledge and enquiry, global perspectives and research and project work A-levels will only be considered as fourth A-level subjects and will not therefore be accepted as part of a conditional offer.
Accounting and Drama/theatre studies may be considered by certain departments.

Admissions tests

Some of the most competitive courses now have additional entrance tests. The most significant tests are listed below. Note that registration for many of the tests is before 15 October and you will need to register for them as early as possible. All the tests have their own websites. Institutions requiring specific tests vary from year to year and you must check course website details carefully for test requirements. In addition over 50 universities also administer their own tests for certain courses. Details are given at: **www.ucas.com/undergraduate/applying-university/admissions-tests**

Law
Cambridge Law Test: for entry to law at Cambridge; candidates called for interview sit the test in late November.
Law National Admissions Test (LNAT): for entry to law courses at Bristol, Durham, Glasgow, King's College London, London School of Economics, Nottingham, Oxford, SOAS, University College London. Register from August; tests held from September to July.

Mathematics
Mathematics Admissions Test (MAT): for entry to mathematics at Imperial College London and mathematics and computer science at Oxford. Advised but not compulsory for applicants to mathematics at Warwick. Test held in early November.
Sixth Term Examination Papers (STEP): for entry to mathematics at Cambridge, Warwick and Imperial College London (also occasionally requested by other universities). Check for registration and test dates at **www.admissionstesting.org/for-test-takers/step/about-step**
Test of Mathematics for University Admission: results accepted by Bath, Cardiff, Durham, Nottingham, Lancaster, London School of Economics, Sheffield, Southampton, Warwick, registration opens early September, test held early November.

Medical subjects
BioMedical Admissions Test (BMAT): for entry to medicine at Brighton and Sussex Medical School, Cambridge, Imperial College London, Keele (international applicants only), Lancaster, Leeds (also for dentistry), Manchester (for some groups of international students only, check university website), Oxford (also for biomedical sciences) and University College London. Check: Check **www.admissionstesting.org/for-test-takers/bmat** for registration and test dates.
Graduate Medical School Admissions Test (GAMSAT): for graduate entry to medicine at Cardiff, Exeter, Liverpool, Nottingham, Plymouth (and dentistry), St. George's, London, Swansea, Keele and St Andrews, Dundee, Sunderland, Ulster and Worcester. Register by July 20, test held September 3–16.
Health Professions Admissions Test (HPAT-Ulster): for certain health profession courses at Ulster. Register by January 11, test held 22–23 January.
University Clinical Aptitude Test (UCAT): for entry to medical and dental schools at Aberdeen, Anglia Ruskin, Aston, Birmingham, Bristol, Brunel, Cardiff, Chester, Dundee, East Anglia, Edge Hill, Edinburgh, Exeter, Glasgow, Hull York Medical School, Keele, Kent and Medway, King's College London, Leicester, Liverpool, Manchester, Newcastle, Nottingham, Plymouth, Queen Mary, University of London, Queen's University Belfast, Sheffield, Southampton, St Andrews, St George's, London, Sunderland, Warwick and Worcester. Register between early May and mid-September; tests held between late July and late September.

Cambridge University
Pre-interview or at-interview assessments take place for most subjects. Full details given on the Cambridge admissions website. See also STEP and BMAT above.

Oxford University
Pre-interview tests take place in many subjects that candidates are required to register for specifically by early October. Full details given on the Oxford admissions website. Tests held in early November, usually at candidate's educational institution. See also LNAT, MAT and BMAT above.

public ridicule, such as surf science or golf course management, may narrow graduates' options to a worrying extent, but often boast strong employment records.

As you would expect, many vocational courses are tailored to particular professions. If you choose one of these, make sure that the degree is recognised by the relevant professional body (such as the Engineering Council or one of the institutes) or you may not be able to use the skills that you acquire. Most universities are only too keen to make such recognition clear in their prospectus; if no such guarantee is published, contact the university department running the course and seek assurances. In education, for example, by no means all degrees qualify you to teach.

Even where a course has professional recognition, a further qualification may be required to practise. Both law and medicine, for example, demand additional training to become a fully qualified solicitor, barrister or doctor. Neither degree is an automatic passport to a job: only about half of all law graduates go into the profession. Both law and medicine also offer a postgraduate route into the profession for those who have taken other subjects as a first degree. Law conversion courses, though not cheap, are increasingly popular, and there are a growing number of graduate-entry medical degrees.

One way to ensure that a degree is job-related is to take a "sandwich" course, which involves up to a year in business or industry. Students often end up working for the organisation which provided the placement, while others gain valuable insights into a field of employment – even if only to discount it. The drawback with such courses is that, like the year abroad that is part of most language degrees, the period away from university inevitably disrupts living arrangements and friendship groups. But most of those who take this route find that the career benefits make this a worthwhile sacrifice. Growing numbers of traditional degrees now offer shorter periods of work experience.

Employers' organisations calculate that more than half of all graduate jobs are open to applicants from any subject, and recruiters for the most competitive graduate training schemes often prefer traditional academic subjects to apparently relevant vocational degrees. Newspapers, for example, may prefer a history graduate to one with a media studies degree; computing firms are said to take a disproportionate number of classicists. A good degree classification and the right work experience are more important than the subject for most non-technical jobs. But it is hard to achieve a good result on a course that you do not enjoy, so scour prospectuses, and email or phone university departments to ensure that you know what you are letting yourself in for. Their reaction to your approach will also give you an idea of how responsive they are to their students.

Most popular subject areas by applications 2021

1	Nursing	229,555
2	Psychology	134,905
3	Law	129,480
4	Computer science	103,345
5	Medicine	102,240
6	Management studies	92,590
7	Design studies	89,715
8	Education	87,750
9	Subjects allied to medicine	83,955
10	Combinations with business and admin studies	80,815

Source: UCAS End of Cycle report 2021

Most popular subjects by acceptances 2021

1	Nursing	37,805
2	Psychology	25,455
3	Law	23,965
4	Business studies	21,820
5	Computer science	18,885
6	Education	18,620
7	Combinations within business and admin studies	17,725
8	Design studies	17,535
9	Management studies	16,975
10	Sport and exercise science	15,660

Source: UCAS End of Cycle report 2021

Subject areas covered in this *Guide*

The list below gives each of the 70 subject areas that are covered in detail later in the book (in chapter 12). For each subject area in that chapter, there is specific advice, a summary of employment prospects and a league table of universities that offered courses in 2019–20, ranked on the basis of an overall score calculated from research quality, entry standards, teaching quality, student experience and graduate employment prospects.

Accounting and Finance
Aeronautical and Manufacturing
  Engineering
Agriculture and Forestry
American Studies
Anatomy and Physiology
Animal Science
Anthropology
Archaeology and Forensic Science
Architecture
Art and Design
Bioengineering and Biomedical
  Engineering
Biological Sciences
Building
Business Studies
Celtic Studies
Chemical Engineering
Chemistry
Civil Engineering
Classics and Ancient History
Communication and Media Studies
Computer Science
Creative Writing
Criminology
Dentistry
Drama, Dance and Cinematics
East and South Asian Studies
Economics
Education
Electrical and Electronic Engineering
English
Food Science
French
General Engineering
Geography and Environmental Sciences
Geology

German
History
History of Art, Architecture and Design
Hospitality, Leisure, Recreation and
  Tourism
Iberian Languages
Information Systems and Management
Italian
Land and Property Management
Law
Liberal Arts and Humanities
Linguistics
Materials Technology
Mathematics
Mechanical Engineering
Medicine
Middle Eastern and African Studies
Music
Natural Sciences
Nursing
Other Subjects Allied to Medicine
Pharmacology and Pharmacy
Philosophy
Physics and Astronomy
Physiotherapy
Politics
Psychology
Radiography
Russian
Social Policy
Social Work
Sociology
Sports Science
Theology and Religious Studies
Town and Country Planning and
  Landscape
Veterinary Medicine

Studying more than one subject

If more than one subject appeals, you could consider Joint Honours – degrees that combine two subjects – or even Combined Honours, which will cover several related subjects. Such courses obviously allow you to extend the scope of your studies, but they should be approached with caution. Even if the number of credits suggests a similar workload to Single Honours, covering more than one subject inevitably involves extra reading and often more essays or project work. Applicants should also be sure to discuss their even-handed interest in both subjects in the personal statement of their UCAS form.

Many students choose a "dual" to add a vocational element to make themselves more employable – business studies with languages or engineering, for example, or media studies with English. Others want to take their studies in a particular direction, perhaps by combining history with politics, or statistics with maths. Some simply want to add a completely unrelated interest to their main subject, such as environmental science and music, or archaeology and event management – both combinations that are available at UK universities.

At most universities, however, it is not necessary to take a degree in more than one subject in order to broaden your studies. The spread of modular programmes ensures that you can take courses in related subjects without changing the basic structure of your degree. You may not be able to take an event management module in a single-honours archaeology degree, but it should be possible to study some history or a language. The number and scope of the combinations offered at many of the larger universities is extraordinary. Indeed, it has been criticised by academics who believe that "mix-and-match" degrees can leave a graduate without a rounded view of a subject. But if you are looking for breadth and variety, scrutinise university prospectuses closely as part of the selection process.

What type of course?

Once you have a subject, you must decide on the level and type of course. Most readers of this *Guide* will be looking for full-time degree courses, but higher education is much broader than that. You may not be able to afford the time or the money needed for a full-time commitment of three or four years at this point in life.

Part-time courses

Tens of thousands of people each year opt for a part-time course – usually while holding down a job – to continue learning and to improve their career prospects. The numbers studying this way have dropped considerably, but loans are available for students whose courses occupy between a quarter and three-quarters of the time expected on a full-time course. Repayments are on the same conditions as those for full-time courses, except that you will begin repaying after three years of study even if the course has not been completed by then. The downside is that universities have increased their fees in the knowledge that part-time students will be able to take out student loans to cover fees, and employers are now less inclined to fund their employees on such courses. At Birkbeck, University of London, a compromise has been found with full-time courses taught in the evening. For courses classified as part-time, students pay fees in proportion to the number of credits they take.

Part-time study can be exhausting unless your employer gives you time off, but if you have the stamina for a course that will usually take twice as long as the full-time equivalent, this route should still make a degree more affordable. Part-time students tend to be highly committed to their subject, and many claim that the quality of the social life associated with their course makes up for the quantity of leisure time enjoyed by full-timers.

Distance learning

The pandemic has shown that undergraduate teaching and learning is perhaps far more possible to achieve remotely than many thought pre-Covid. If you are confident that you can manage without regular face-to-face contact with teachers and fellow students, distance learning is an option. Courses are delivered mainly or entirely online or through correspondence, although some programmes offer a certain amount of local tuition. The process might sound daunting and impersonal, but students of the Open University (OU), all of whom are educated in this way, are frequently among the most satisfied in the country, according to the results of the annual National Student Survey. Attending lectures or oversized seminars at a conventional university can be less personal than regular contact with your tutor at a distance – factors that mainstream universities have cottoned on to since being forced to pivot to remote teaching and learning in the pandemic.

Results of 2021's National Student Survey – in which all but two universities (Imperial College London and Surrey) saw their student satisfaction scores decline – evidenced that not all universities are as good, or practised, at communicating with their distance-learning students as the OU. Neither do they all offer such high-quality course materials remotely, but this mode of study does give students ultimate flexibility to determine when and where they study. Distance learning is becoming increasingly popular for the delivery of professional courses, which are often needed to supplement degrees. The OU takes students of all ages, including school-leavers, not just mature students.

In addition, Massive Open Online Courses (MOOCs) are provided by many of the leading UK and American universities, usually free of charge. As yet, most such courses are the equivalent of a module in a degree course, rather than the entire qualification. Some are assessed formally but none is likely to be seen by employers as the equal of a conventional degree, no matter how prestigious the university offering the course. For those who are uncertain about committing to a degree, or who simply want to learn more about a subject without needing a high-status qualification, they are ideal.

A number of UK universities offer MOOCs through the Futurelearn platform, run by the Open University (**www.futurelearn.com**). But the beauty of MOOCs is that they can come from all over the world. Perhaps the best-known providers are Coursera (**www.coursera.org**), which originated at Stanford University, in California, and now involves a large number of American and international universities including Edinburgh, and edX (**www.edx.org**), which numbers Harvard among its members. MOOCs are also being used increasingly by sixth-formers to extend their subject knowledge and demonstrate their enthusiasm and capability to admissions tutors. They are certainly worth considering for inclusion in a personal statement and/or to spark discussion at an interview.

Foundation degrees

Even if you are set on a full-time course, you might not want to commit yourself for three or more years. Two-year vocational Foundation degrees have become a popular route into higher education in recent years. Many other students take longer-established two-year courses, such as Higher National Diplomas or other diplomas tailored to the needs of industry or parts of the health service. Those who do well on such courses usually have the option of converting their qualification into a full degree with further study, although many are satisfied without immediately staying on for the further two or more years that will be required to complete a BA or BSc.

Foundation courses

A growing number of short courses, usually lasting a year, are designed for students who do not have the necessary qualifications to start a degree in their chosen subject. Foundation courses in art and design have been common for many years and are the chosen preparation for a degree at leading departments, even for many students whose A-levels would win them a degree place elsewhere. Access courses perform the same function in a wider range of subjects for students without A-levels, or for those whose grades are either too low or in the wrong subjects to gain admission to a particular course. Entry requirements are modest, but students have to reach the same standard as regular entrants to progress to a degree.

Other short courses

A number of universities are experimenting with two-year degrees, encouraged by the Government, squeezing more work into an extended academic year. The so-called "third semester" makes use of the summer vacation for extra teaching, so that mature students, in particular, can reduce the length of their career break. But only at the University of Buckingham, the UK's longest-established private university, is this the dominant pattern for degree courses. Other private institutions – notably BPP University – are following suit.

Higher and Degree Apprenticeships

Apprenticeships have been a serious alternative to university for more than a decade. They give students the best of both worlds at a growing number of universities by combining study at degree level with extended work experience at a named industrial or business partner. The range of programmes is growing and includes accountancy, computing, nursing, healthcare sciences, data science, management and some branches of engineering.

The government wants more degree apprenticeships and universities are expanding their offerings. Clare Marchant, the chief executive of UCAS, told the *Sunday Times* in our *Guide's* newspaper edition in September 2021 that she believes the days of the three-year degree as the only qualification for 18-year-olds are numbered. UCAS's website has a Career Finder service, which helps students find jobs and apprenticeships. Applications for an apprenticeship are made directly to employers and, if successful, a student is then linked to a university to study part-time for the associated degree. In August 2020 alone, Career Finder registered more than 11,000 applications to start an apprenticeship. There are about 9,000 apprenticeship openings on **ucas.com**.

Applicants can also make a direct application to the company. Weigh up the options on the gov.uk website's "Find an Apprenticeship" section. Once you register, you can set up email and text alerts to inform you about new apprenticeship roles. You can also find a range of vacancies at **www.ratemyapprenticeship.co.uk**, which carries thousands of reviews.

Such apprenticeships take up to five years to complete and leave the graduate with a Bachelor's or even a Master's degree. Employers including Deloitte, PwC, BMW, Microsoft and the BBC are offering higher-level apprenticeships, although naturally not all are with household names such as these.

Students are paid employees of the sponsoring company, with a contract of employment and holiday entitlement, as well as annual salaries which averaged £17,875 back in 2019.

Yet more choice

No single guide can allow for personal preferences in choosing a course. You may want one of the many degrees that incorporate a year at a partner university abroad, or to try an exchange via the government's new Turing scheme, which has replaced Erasmus post-Brexit. Either might prove a valuable experience and add to your employability. Or you might prefer a January or February start to the traditional autumn start – there are plenty of opportunities for this, and not only at post-1992 universities.

In some subjects – particularly engineering and the sciences – the leading degrees may be Masters courses, taking four years rather than three (in England). In Scotland, most degree courses take four years and some at the older universities will confer a Masters qualification. Those who come with A-levels may apply to go straight into the second year. Relatively few students take this option, but it is easy to imagine more doing so in future at universities that charge students from other parts of the UK the full £9,250 for all years of the course.

Where to study

Several factors might influence your choice of university or college. Obviously, you need to have a reasonable chance of getting in, you may want reassurance about the university's reputation, and its location will probably be important to you as well. On top of that, most applicants have views about the type of institution they are looking for – big or small, old or new, urban or rural, specialist or comprehensive. Campus universities tend to produce the highest levels of student satisfaction, but big city universities continue to attract sixth-formers in the largest numbers. You may surprise yourself by choosing somewhere that does not conform to your initial criteria but working through your preferences is another way of narrowing down your options.

Entry standards

Unless you are a mature student or have taken a gap year, your passport to your chosen university will probably be a conditional offer based on your predicted grades, previous exam performance, personal statement, and school or college reference. The practice of making unconditional offers to candidates in selected subjects who have a strong academic record and are predicted high grades was suspended during the pandemic until September 2021. It remains to be seen whether many universities will return to such offers once the restrictions are lifted.

Supply and demand dictate whether you will receive an offer, conditional or otherwise. Beyond the national picture, your chances will be affected both by the university and the subject

Universities with highest and lowest offer rates

Highest		Lowest	
1 Aberystwyth	96.6%	1 Oxford	21.5%
2 Bishop Grosseteste	94.5%	2 Cambridge	26.5%
3 Ravensbourne	92.9%	3 LSE	36.5%
4 Creative Arts	92.5%	4 St George's London	38.7%
=5 Roehampton	89.3%	5 St Andrews	41.0%
=5 Sussex	89.3%	6 Imperial College London	42.9%
7 Northumbria	88.7%	7 Leeds Arts	43.5%
=8 Kent	88.6%	8 Arts, London	45.5%
=8 Nottingham Trent	88.6%	9 Strathclye	48.0%
10 York St John	88.5%	10 Bolton	50.6%

UCAS: Applications 2020

you choose. A few universities (but not many) at the top of the league tables are heavily oversubscribed in every subject; others will have areas in which they excel but may make relatively modest demands for entry to other courses. Even in many of the leading universities, the number of applicants for each place in languages or engineering is still not high. Conversely, three As at A-level will not guarantee a place on one of the top English or law degrees, but there are enough universities running courses to ensure that three Cs will give you a chance somewhere.

University prospectuses and the UCAS website will give you the "standard offer" for each course, but in some cases, this is pitched deliberately low in order to leave admissions staff extra flexibility. The standard A-level offer for medicine, for example, may not demand A*s, but nearly all successful applicants will have one or more. In Scotland, universities have started to publish two sets of standard offers: their normal range and another with lower grades for applicants from disadvantaged backgrounds. A similar practice elsewhere in the UK uses contextualised information about applicants' backgrounds to reduce the entry grades.

As already noted, the average entry scores in our tables give the actual points obtained by successful applicants – many of which are far above the offer made by the university, but which give an indication of the pecking order at entry. The subject tables (in chapter 12) are, naturally, a better guide than the main table (in chapter 1), where average entry scores are influenced by the range of subjects available at each university.

Best paid graduates

(Median salary 15 months after graduating)

1	Imperial College London	£33,500
2	London School of Economics	£32,000
3	Cambridge	£30,100
=4	Oxford	£30,000
=4	University College London	£30,000
=6	King's College London	£29,000
=6	St George's, London	£29,000
=6	Warwick	£29,000
9	Bath	£28,500
=10	Bristol	£28,000
=10	Queen Mary, London	£28,000

HESA 2019–20 graduates

Location

The most obvious starting point is the country you study in. Most degrees in Scotland take four years, rather than the UK norm of three, which makes them more expensive, especially given the loss of the year's salary you might have been earning after graduation. A later chapter will go into the details of the system but suffice to say that students from Scotland pay no fees, while those from the rest of the UK do. Nevertheless, Edinburgh and St Andrews remain particularly popular with English students, despite charging them £9,250 a year for the full four years of a degree starting in 2021. The number of English students going to Scottish universities has increased almost every year since the fees went up, even though there would be no savings, perhaps because the institutions have tried harder to attract them.

Most popular universities by applications 2020

1	University of Manchester	79,925
2	University of Edinburgh	64,225
3	University of Leeds	62,250
4	UCL (University College London)	58,690
5	King's College, London	57,470
6	University of Birmingham	55,935
7	University of Nottingham	54,170
8	University of Bristol	52,385
9	Manchester Metropolitan University	48,270
10	Nottingham Trent University	46,670

Source: UCAS End of Cycle report 2020

Fees – or the lack of them – are by no means the only influence on cross-border mobility: the number of Scots going to English universities rose sharply, despite the cost, probably because the number of places is capped in Scotland, but not any longer in England.

Close to home

Far from crossing national boundaries, however, growing numbers of students choose to study near home, whether or not they continue to live with their family. This is understandable for Scots, who will save themselves tens of thousands of pounds by studying at their own fees-free universities. But there is also a gradual increase in the numbers choosing to study close to home either to cut living costs or for personal reasons, such as family circumstances, a girlfriend or boyfriend, continuing employment or religion. Some simply want to stick with what they know.

The trend for full-time students who do go away to study, is to choose a university within about two hours' travelling time. The assumption is that this is far enough to discourage parents from springing unannounced visits, but close enough to make the occasional trip home to get the washing done, have a decent meal and see friends. The leading universities recruit from all over the world, but most still have a regional core.

City universities

The most popular universities, in terms of total applications, are nearly all in big cities with other major centres of population within the two-hour travelling window. Students are drawn by the best nightclubs, top sporting events, high-quality shopping, cultural diversity and access to leading galleries, museums and theatres. Especially for those who live in cities already, city universities are a magnet. The big universities also, by definition, offer the widest range of subjects, although that does not mean that they necessarily have the specific course that is right for you. You might not actually go clubbing a lot or hit the shops that much, in spite of the inspiring marketing material that suggests you will, either because you cannot afford to, or because student life is more focused on the university than the city, or even because you are too busy studying.

Campus universities

City universities are the right choice for many young people, but it is worth bearing in mind that the National Student Survey shows that the highest satisfaction levels tend to be at smaller universities, often those with their own self-contained campuses. It seems that students identify more closely with institutions where there is a close-knit community and the social life is based around the students' union rather than the local nightclubs – at least in the first-year when more students tend to live in campus accommodation. There may also be a better prospect of regular contact with tutors and lecturers, who are likely to live on or near the campus. Few UK universities are in genuinely rural locations, but some – particularly among the more recently promoted – are in relatively small towns. Several longer-established institutions in Scotland and Wales also share this type of setting, where the university dominates the town.

Importance of Open Days

By far the best way to be confident that any university is for you is to visit. Physical events have returned, Covid restrictions permitting, in tandem with virtual tours. Our profiles give each university's website for the latest information. Schools often restrict the number of open days that sixth-formers can attend in term-time, but some universities offer a weekend alternative.

A full calendar of events is available at **www.opendays.com**. Bear in mind, if you only attend one or two, that the event has to be badly mismanaged for a university not to seem an exciting place to someone who spends their days at school, or even college. Try to get a flavour of several institutions before you make your choice.

How many universities to pick?
When that time comes, of course, you will not be making one choice but five; four if you are applying for medicine, dentistry or veterinary science. (Full details of the application process are given in chapter 5.) Tens of thousands of students each year eventually go to a university that did not start out as their first choice, either because they did not get the right offer or because they changed their mind along the way. UCAS rules are such that applicants do not list universities in order of preference anyway – indeed, universities are not allowed to know where else you have applied. So do not pin all your hopes on one course; take just as much care choosing the other universities on your list.

The value of an "insurance" choice
Until recently, nearly all applicants included at least one "insurance" choice on that list – a university or college where entry grades were significantly lower than at their preferred institutions. This practice has been in decline, presumably because candidates expecting high grades think they can pick up a lower offer either in Clearing or through UCAS Extra, the service that allows applicants rejected by their original choices to apply to courses that still have vacancies after the first round of offers. However, it is easy to miscalculate and leave yourself without a place that you want. You may not like the look of the options in Clearing, leaving yourself with an unwelcome and potentially expensive year off at a time when jobs are thin on the ground.

The lifting of recruitment restrictions in 2015 has increased competition between universities and seen more of the leading institutions taking part in Clearing. For those with good grades, this makes it less of a risk to apply only to highly selective universities. However, if you are at all uncertain about your grades, including an insurance choice remains a sensible course of action. Even if you are sure that you will match the standard offers of your chosen universities, there is no guarantee that they will make you an offer. Particularly for degrees demanding three As or more at A-level, there may simply be too many highly qualified applicants to offer places to all of them. The main proviso for insurance choices, as with all others, is that you must be prepared to take up that place. If not, you might as well go for broke with courses with higher standard offers and take your chances in Clearing, or even retake exams if you drop grades. Thousands of applicants each year end up rejecting their only offer when they could have had a second, insurance, choice.

Reputation
The reputation of a university is something intangible, usually built up over a long period and sometimes outlasting reality. Before universities were subject to external assessment and the publication of copious statistics, reputation was rooted in the past. League tables are partly responsible for changing that, although employers are often still influenced by what they remember as the university pecking order when they were students.

The fragmentation of the British university system into groups of institutions is another factor: the Russell Group (**www.russellgroup.ac.uk**) represents 24 research-intensive universities, nearly all with medical schools; the million+ group (**www.millionplus.ac.uk**) contains many of the former polytechnics and newer universities; the University Alliance (**www.unialliance.ac.uk**) provides a home for 18 universities, both old and new, that did not fit into the other categories; while GuildHE (**www.guildhe.ac.uk**) represents specialist colleges and the newest universities. The Cathedrals Group (**www.cathedralsgroup.ac.uk**) is an affiliation of 16 church-based universities and colleges, some of which are also members of other groups.

Many of today's applicants will barely have heard of a polytechnic, let alone be able to identify which of today's universities had that heritage, but most will know which of two universities in the same city has the higher status. While that should matter far less than the quality of a course, it would be naïve to ignore institutional reputation entirely if that is going to carry weight with a future employer. Some big firms restrict their recruitment efforts to a small group of universities (see chapter 3), and, however short sighted that might be, it is something to bear in mind if a career in the City or a big law firm is your ambition.

Facilities

The quality of campus facilities is an important factor in choosing a university for most students. Only the course and the university's location tend to have a higher priority. Accommodation is the main selling point for those living away from home, but sports facilities, libraries (24-hour, ideally) and computing equipment also play an important part. Even upgraded campus nightclubs have become part of the facilities race that has followed the introduction of higher fees.

Many universities guarantee first-year students accommodation in halls of residence or university-owned flats. It is a good idea to know what happens after that. Are there enough places for second or third-year students who want them, and if not, what is the private market like? Rents for student houses vary quite widely across the country and there have been tensions with local residents in some cities. All universities offer specialist accommodation for disabled students – and are better at providing other facilities than most public institutions.

Special-interest clubs and recreational facilities, as well as political activity, tend to be based in the students' union – sometimes known as the guild of students. In some universities,

---

Top 10 Universities for Quality of Teaching, feedback and support 2020
% satisfied with teaching quality

1	St Andrews	86.5%
2	Wrexham Glyndwr	82.0%
3	Aberystwyth	81.8%
4	Plymouth Marjon	81.6%
5	Bolton	81.3%
6	London Metropolitan	81.0%
7	Chichester	80.5%
8	St Mary's Twickenham	80.4%
9	West London	80.3%
10	Norwich Arts	79.8%

Source: National Student Survey 2021

Top 10 Universities for Overall Student Experience 2020

1	St Andrews	84.2%
2	Loughborough	80.6%
3	Imperial College London	79.3%
4	Bath	79.0%
5	St Mary's Twickenham	78.1%
6	Aberystwyth	77.9%
7	Strathclyde	77.3%
8	Plymouth Marjon	77.2%
=9	Surrey	76.3%
=9	Chichester	76.3%

Source: National Student Survey 2021

the union is the focal point of social activity, while in others the attractions of the city seem to overshadow the union to the point where facilities are underused. Students' union websites are included with the information found in the university profiles (chapter 14).

University or college?

This *Guide* is primarily concerned with universities, the destination of choice for the vast majority of higher education students. But there are other options – and not just for those searching for lower fees. A number of specialist higher education colleges offer a similar, or sometimes superior, quality of course in their particular fields. The subject tables in chapter 12 chart the successes of various colleges in art, agriculture, music and teacher training in particular. Some colleges of higher education are not so different from the newer universities and may acquire that status themselves in future years.

Further education colleges

The second group of colleges offering degrees are further education (FE) colleges. These are often large institutions with a wide range of courses, from A-levels to vocational subjects at different levels, up to degrees in some cases. Although their numbers of higher education students have been falling in recent years, the current fee structure presents them with an opportunity because they tend not to bear all the costs of a university campus. For that reason, too, they may not offer a broad student experience of the type that universities pride themselves on, but the best colleges respond well to the local labour market and offer small teaching groups and effective personal support.

FE colleges are a local resource and tend to attract mature students who cannot or do not want to travel to university. Many of their higher education students apply nowhere else. But, as competition for university places has increased, they also have become more of an option for school-leavers to continue their studies, as they always have been in Scotland.

Their predominantly local, mature student populations do FE colleges no favours in statistical comparisons with universities. But it should be noted that the proportion of college graduates unemployed six months after graduation tends to be higher than at universities, and average graduate salaries lower. However, 14 further education colleges secured "gold" ratings in the first year of the Government's Teaching Excellence Framework (TEF) – although more than twice as many found themselves in the lowest "bronze" category.

Both further and higher education colleges are audited by the Quality Assurance Agency and appear in the National Student Survey, as well as the TEF. In all three, their results usually show wide variation. Some demonstrate higher levels of satisfaction among their students than most universities, for example, while others are at the bottom of the scale

Private universities and colleges

These were relatively insignificant in terms of size until recently, but the current fee regime may cause numbers at private universities and colleges to grow. Courses are mainly in business and law, and also in some other specialist fields.

By far the longest established – and the only one to meet the criteria for inclusion in our main table – is the University of Buckingham, which is profiled on pages 358–9. The best-known "newcomer" currently is BPP University, which became a full university in 2013 and offers degrees, as well as shorter courses, in both law and business subjects. Like Buckingham, BPP offers two-year degrees with short vacations to maximise teaching time – a model that other private providers are likely to follow. Fees were £9,000 a year for UK students taking BPP's three-year degrees in 2020 and £13,500 a year for the accelerated version.

The New College of the Humanities, which graduated its first students in 2015, started out with fees of nearly £18,000 a year for all undergraduates, guaranteeing small-group teaching and some big-name visiting lecturers in economics, English, history, law and philosophy. The college is now matching the "public sector" at £9,250 a year and has been bought by the Boston-based Northeastern University.

Two other private institutions have been awarded full university status. Regent's University, attractively positioned in London's Regent's Park, caters particularly for the international market with courses in business, arts and social science subjects priced at £18,500 – £21,500 a year for 2021–22. However, about half of the students at the not-for-profit university, which offers British and American degrees, are from the UK or other parts of Europe. The University of Law, as its name suggests, is more specialised. It has been operating as a college in London for more than 100 years and claims to be the world's leading professional law school. It offers law degrees, as well as professional courses, with fees for three-year degrees set at £9,250 in 2021–22 for UK students and £11,100 for the two-year version. The university has 15 UK campuses, in locations including London (where it has two), Nottingham, Birmingham, Bristol, Chester, Guildford, Manchester and Leeds, as well as at Exeter, East Anglia, Reading, and Liverpool universities.

There are also growing numbers of specialist colleges offering degrees, especially in the business sector. The ifs School of Finance, for example, also dates back more than 100 years and now has university college status (as ifs University College) for its courses in finance and banking.

Some others that rely on international students have been hit by tougher visa regulations, but the Government is keen to encourage the development of a private sector to compete with the established universities. Two newcomers will focus on engineering, for example. The Dyson Institute of Engineering and Technology, based at Malmesbury, in Wiltshire, welcomed its first 33 undergraduates in 2017. Funded entirely by Sir James Dyson, there are no fees, and students work at the nearby Dyson headquarters for 47 weeks a year. The New Model in Technology and Engineering, in Hereford, has received more than £20million in Government funding and promises to give students a "head start on becoming a work-ready, world-conscious engineer."

So far, there are few multi-faculty private institutions, but the range of specialisms is certainly growing. There are two high-profile colleges specialising in football, for example, and the London Interdisciplinary School was founded in 2017. Inevitably, they will take time to build up a track record, but there should be a market in the areas they offer. A listing of some of the more popular private institutions begins on Page 587.

Sources of information

With more than 130 universities to choose from, the Discover Uni and UCAS websites, as well as guides such as this one, are the obvious places to start your search for the right course. Discover Uni includes figures for average salaries at course level, as well as student satisfaction ratings and some information on contact hours, although this does not distinguish between lectures and seminars. The site does not make multiple comparisons easy to carry out, but it does contain a wealth of information for those who persevere. Once you have narrowed down the list of candidates, you will want to go through undergraduate prospectuses. All are available online and many universities still print hard copies, should you want a hefty book that includes

Checklist

Choosing a subject and a place to study is a major decision. Make sure you can answer these questions:

Choosing a course

» What do I want out of higher education?
» Which subjects do I enjoy studying at school?
» Which subject or subjects do I want to study?
» Do I have the right qualifications?
» What are my career plans and does the subject and course fit these?
» Do I want to study full-time or part-time?
» Do I want to study at a university or a college?

Choosing a university

» What type of university do I wish to go to: campus, city or smaller town?
» How far is the university from home?
» Is it large or small?
» Is it specialist or general?
» Does it offer the right course?
» How much will it cost?
» Have I arranged to visit the university?

---

details of every course to arrive in the post. Beware of generalised claims about the standing of the university, the quality of courses, friendly atmosphere and legendary social life. Stick to the factual information.

While the material that the universities publish about their own qualities is less than objective, much of what you will find on the internet may be completely unreliable, for different reasons. A simple search on the name of a university will turn up spurious comparisons of everything from the standard of lecturing to the attractiveness of the students. These can be seriously misleading and are usually based on anecdotal evidence, at best. Make sure that any information you consider comes from a reputable source and, if it conflicts with your impression, try to cross-check it with this *Guide* and the institution's own material.

Useful websites

The best starting point is the UCAS website (**www.ucas.com**), there is extensive information on courses, universities and the whole process of applying to university. UCAS has an official presence on Facebook (**www.facebook.com/ucasonline**) and Twitter (@UCAS_online) and now also has a series of video guides (**www.ucas.tv**) on the process of applying, UCAS resources and comments from other students.

For statistical information which allows limited comparison between universities (and for full details of the National Student Survey), visit: **www.discoveruni.gov.uk**

On appropriate A-level subject choice, visit **www.informedchoices.ac.uk**

Narrowing down course choices: **www.ukcoursefinder.com**

For a full calendar of university and college open days: **www.opendays.com**

Students with disabilities: Disability Rights UK: **www.disabilityrightsuk.org/how-we-can-help**

3 Assessing Graduate Job Prospects

"The only way to do great work is to love what you do," Steve Jobs, the founder of Apple, once said. Such wisdom affirms the approach of many students in selecting degrees that light their intellectual fire – especially as that fire needs to keep burning across three-plus years of focused study. While university is not the only – or even a guaranteed – route into a fulfilling and rewarding career, many students who opt for higher education do so with thoughts of securing themselves professional work afterwards. Rather than a future that involves merely making ends meet, the hope is that a degree will help to secure a career that offers fulfilment, social standing and at least above average pay.

Degrees also need to represent a fair return on students' investment – a consideration that has been under scrutiny in the UK ever since the introduction of £9,000 tuition fees in 2012.

From the government's perspective, a degree should provide value for money to the taxpayer as well as to the student, partly because so many student loans will not be fully paid back: if graduates either never earn above or slip below earning £27,295 they do not need to make Student Loan repayments.

Graduate salaries are one way of evaluating whether a degree represents a good bet, although they are a blunt tool and liable to vary depending on whether a university is located in an area of high or low employment, with high or low wages. *The Times and the Sunday Times Good University Guide* league table rankings have never used salary data as a performance measure. Few would attempt to argue that trainee nurses and teachers, for example, should be put off going to university because the professions they are studying towards do not promise megabucks. We do, though, list median salaries for each subject group in this chapter's second table, and with the subject guides in Chapter 12, for reference.

That said, going to university is a very good investment for most students. According to the Institute of Fiscal Studies, male graduates can expect to earn about £240,000 more and females about £140,000 more across a working lifetime than if they had not gone to university – which translates to benefits of about £130,000 for men and £100,000 for women after Student Loan repayments and extra taxes. The higher earnings of – and therefore taxes paid by – graduates also mean that sending about half of young people to university is a good deal overall for the taxpayer.

There are enormous variations in the difference a degree makes, however, the IFS found in its 2020 research for the Department for Education. Only a tiny proportion, around 10%, are likely to rake in an extra £500,000 or more during their lifetime, with students of medicine and law among those in line for very high returns, while few creative arts students are likely to gain financially from their degree at all. Using the Longitudinal Education Outcomes (LEO) dataset it found that a typical student can expect to gain about £70,000 from their degree, but that one in five students (or about 70,000 each year) is likely to end up financially worse off as a result of going to university.

Such a mismatch between students' investment and effort and their outcomes is naturally a cause for concern – and a driving force behind the relevance of university guides such as ours in helping applicants make well-informed choices. The 2019 Philip Augar review of post-18 education and funding called for varying rates of funding support for different subjects to reflect the economic and social "value" of degrees, and how much they cost to teach.

Early in 2021 the government finally responded to the review's recommendations: "We need a better balance between academic and technical education – we are currently too skewed towards degrees above all else," said its interim review. "In line with this…we aim to create a system whereby the quality of our technical and academic education is on a par, and the two are equally accessible. We want every student with the aptitude and desire to go to university to be able to do so, and we want technical, employer-centric training to be a viable option for many more people."

While no one can see into the future, applicants must attempt to evaluate the kind of career trajectory their potential degree could lead to. To spend money and time on university and then work in a job that could have been accessed without a degree adds up to a bad deal, however much you enjoyed the teaching, learning and broader all-round experience.

Median earnings by degree subject five years after graduation (2012–13 graduates)

Subject	Earnings	Subject	Earnings
Medicine and dentistry	£49,300	Philosophy and religious studies	£27,700
Economics	£42,700	Materials and technology	£27,000
Engineering	£36,500	Biosciences	£26,300
Architecture, building and planning	£35,000	Allied health subjects	£26,300
Mathematical sciences	£34,700	English studies	£25,200
Physics and astronomy	£34,700	Sport and exercise science	£25,200
Pharmacology, toxicology and pharmacy	£32,500	General, applied and forensic sciences	£24,800
Medical sciences	£32,100	Health and social care	£24,500
Veterinary science	£31,800	Sociology, social policy and anthropology	£24,500
Politics	£31,000	Psychology	£24,500
Computing	£30,700	Celtic studies	£24,500
Chemistry	£30,300	Education and teaching	£24,100
Geography, earth and environmental studies	£29,600	Media, journalism and communications	£24,100
Languages and area studies	£29,200	Combined and general studies	£24,100
Nursing and midwifery	£28,800	Agriculture, food and related subjects	£23,400
Business and management	£28,800	Creative arts and design	£22,300
Law	£27,700	Performing arts	£21,200
History and archaeology	£27,700		

Source: Department for Education, Graduate Outcomes March 2021

The Covid-19 effect

UCAS's *Where Next?* analysis in 2021 revealed that more than 50% of university applicants reported that high graduate employment rates had become more important to them since the start of the pandemic. Meanwhile, the latest figures from the UK Labour Force Survey, run by the Office for National Statistics (ONS) showed that graduates remained at a career advantage over those without degrees during a global pandemic. Coronavirus had a marked impact on the UK labour market in 2020, with unemployment increasing across the board, but graduates suffered less acutely than those without degrees. The unemployment rate for graduates was 4.6% in July to Sept 2020, compared with 5.1% overall, rising to 5.2% for October to December 2020. The average unemployment rate for graduates between 2017 and the latter part of 2020 was 3%, compared with the total average unemployment rate of 4.2%.

Graduates are among the highest-skilled workers and play an important role in the economy, the ONS pointed out, they promote innovation and growth – crucial contributions in dealing with the challenges imposed by the pandemic. Graduates are also more occupationally and geographically mobile, which helps explain their employment in times of crisis. As well as specific skills related to their subject, graduates also have more general transferrable skills – such as writing, communication and critical thinking – that contribute to greater resilience in times of economic crisis.

Graduate prospects in *Good University Guide* rankings

The measure we use to assess graduate prospects takes account of the rates of employment for graduates in the 70 subject areas in our *Guide* and distinguishes between types of work.

After several years in development a new way of making these assessments is now in its second year. The Graduate Outcomes (GO) survey replaced the Destination of Leavers from Higher Education (DLHE) survey. Both measure the same thing: what graduates do next, but the previous system gathered information six months after graduation, whereas GO conducts its survey 15 months after graduates have finished their degrees. The longer timeframe better reflects changes in work patterns, with many graduates doing internships, travelling or sampling the jobs market before plumping for a career path.

The new GO survey has caused our graduate prospects measure to evolve. So, we now look at the proportion of graduates in high-skilled (instead of graduate-level) jobs or postgraduate study. This *Guide* uses a definition of a high-skilled job from the Higher Education Statistics Agency (HESA), which conducts the GO survey. Universities that got the best graduate prospects scores in the previous measure have been largely unaffected by the new measure and continued to perform strongly, while for some universities very different results emerged.

In 2020, the employment rate for working-age graduates aged 16 to 64 – was 86.4% (down 1.1 percentage points from 2019) and for working-age postgraduates it was 88.2%, compared with 71.3% for non-graduates. Of these, 66% of graduates were in high-skilled employment (up 0.4%), compared with 78.4% of postgraduates (a 0.5% decrease on 2019) and 24.5% of non-graduates (down 0.6%). The median salary for working-age graduates was £35,000 in 2020, which was £9,500 more than the median salary earned by non-graduates (£25,500) and £7,000 less than postgraduates (£42,000).

Future-proof degrees?

Automation is reshaping some jobs and the traditional nine-to-five is giving way to more independent ways of working. Economists have said young people should plan for five careers

What graduates are doing 15 months after leaving university by subject studied

	Subject	High-skilled job %	High-skilled job and studying %	Studying %	Lower-skilled job and studying %	Lower-skilled job %	Unemployed %	Total with positive outcome %
1	Medicine	89	7	3	—	0	0	99.2
2=	Nursing	94	3	1	0	2	1	97.4
2=	Physiotherapy	95	2	1	—	2	1	97.4
4	Veterinary Medicine	95	1	1	0	1	1	97.2
5	Radiography	91	3	1	—	1	3	95.6
6	Dentistry	85	6	0	—	1	8	91.2
7	Civil Engineering	75	4	7	0	6	8	86.0
8	Pharmacology and Pharmacy	68	7	10	0	6	9	85.7
9	General Engineering	70	3	11	0	9	8	83.3
10=	Subjects Allied to Medicine	65	4	13	1	13	5	81.9
10=	Chemistry	53	3	25	1	10	8	81.9
12	Building	74	6	2	0	10	8	81.8
13	Physics and Astronomy	50	3	28	0	9	9	81.3
14	Chemical Engineering	66	4	11	1	10	8	81.1
15	Town and Country Planning and Landscape	64	6	9	1	11	8	80.4
16	Computer Science	71	3	5	0	10	11	79.4
17=	Mathematics	57	7	14	1	13	8	78.9
17=	Celtic Studies	52	1	23	4	15	6	78.9
19	Materials Technology	53	3	22	0	12	9	78.6
20	Electrical and Electronic Engineering	66	3	8	0	12	10	78.1
21	Economics	59	8	10	1	14	8	77.8
22	Architecture	66	4	6	0	13	11	76.1
23	Mechanical Engineering	64	3	8	0	14	10	75.8
24	Food Science	65	2	8	1	17	7	75.7
25	Bioengineering and biomedical engineering	52	3	18	1	16	9	75.1
26	Anatomy and Physiology	40	4	30	1	19	7	74.7
27	Aeronautical and Manufacturing Engineering	61	4	10	1	15	10	74.5
28=	Middle Eastern and African Studies	54	5	14	1	13	13	74.0
28=	Social Work	63	5	5	1	20	6	74.0
30	Land and Property Management	64	5	4	—	22	5	73.2
31	Education	63	3	7	1	21	6	72.8
32	Biological Sciences	42	3	25	1	20	9	71.2
33	Information Systems and Management	63	3	5	0	18	11	71.1
34	French	51	4	14	1	22	8	70.1
35	Geology	39	3	27	1	19	12	69.8
36	Russian	45	8	15	1	19	12	69.1
37	Law	44	7	15	2	23	9	67.8
38	German	52	5	10	1	22	10	67.6
39	Theology and Religious Studies	47	5	14	1	26	6	67.5
40	Italian	52	1	13	1	23	10	66.8

	Subject	High-skilled job %	High-skilled job and studying %	Studying %	Lower-skilled job and studying %	Lower-skilled job %	Unemployed %	Total with positive outcome %
41	Geography and Environmental Sciences	46	4	15	1	25	8	**66.6**
42	Politics	45	5	15	1	24	10	**65.9**
43=	Iberian Languages	50	3	12	1	23	11	**65.7**
43=	Philosophy	44	4	16	1	23	11	**65.7**
45	Anthropology	42	5	17	1	25	11	**64.6**
46	Business, Management and Marketing	54	4	5	1	26	10	**63.6**
47	Classics and Ancient History	41	3	18	2	27	9	**63.5**
48	English	43	4	15	1	27	10	**63.0**
49	History	38	4	19	2	29	9	**62.3**
50	Sport Science	43	5	12	1	32	6	**62.0**
51	Accounting and Finance	43	10	6	3	29	9	**61.7**
52	Music	49	4	8	1	29	10	**61.5**
53=	Archaeology and Forensic Science	40	2	15	2	31	10	**59.5**
53=	Linguistics	37	3	17	2	30	11	**59.5**
55	History of Art, Architecture and Design	41	2	15	1	28	12	**59.4**
56	Agriculture and Forestry	50	4	3	1	38	3	**59.2**
57	East and South Asian Studies	43	1	13	1	28	13	**59.1**
58	Art and Design	51	2	4	1	31	12	**56.7**
59	Communication and Media Studies	49	2	4	1	31	13	**56.3**
60	American Studies	39	2	12	1	34	12	**54.7**
61	Social Policy	37	4	11	2	37	10	**53.8**
62	Psychology	32	4	14	3	38	8	**53.3**
63	Creative Writing	36	5	8	2	34	15	**51.5**
64	Animal Science	31	2	16	2	39	9	**51.4**
65	Sociology	35	3	11	2	40	9	**51.0**
66	Drama, Dance and Cinematics	42	2	4	1	38	13	**49.0**
67	Hospitality, Leisure, Recreation and Tourism	40	2	5	1	41	12	**47.3**

Note: Note: This table is ranked on the proportion of graduates in high-skilled jobs and/or further study, and those combining lower-skilled jobs with further study. This total is shown in the final column in bold. Source: Hesa, 2018–19

in a lifetime. Yes, lots is changing, but the oft-quoted estimate that 65% of primary school age children will end up working in jobs that don't yet exist, was debunked by a BBC investigation and found to be a statistical urban myth. A figure of around a third was more likely, it suggested.

Everyone knows that there have been changes to the world of work in the last few decades but repeating to young people that the jobs they will do have not been invented yet, can be unhelpful, dispiriting and confusing. As we saw during the pandemic, the so-called "Chris Whitty effect" has boosted applications to study nursing and medicine to new heights. Applicants were driven not only by the desire to help others in front line roles, but also attracted by the security of such jobs – especially as furlough and job losses created disruption in many other fields.

What graduates are earning 15 months after graduation by subject studied

Subject	High skilled work (median) £	Low and medium skilled £
1 Dentistry	38,694	
2 Medicine	35,000	
3 Pharmacology and Pharmacy	31,040	20,000
4 Veterinary Medicine	31,000	
5 Chemical Engineering	30,000	22,000
6 General Engineering	29,000	22,500
7 Economics	29,000	22,000
8 Social Work	29,000	19,000
9 Middle Eastern and African Studies	29,000	
10 Aeronautical and Manufacturing Engineering	28,000	25,000
11 Electrical and Electronic Engineering	28,000	24,000
12 Mechanical Engineering	28,000	23,000
13 Mathematics	28,000	20,500
14 Physics and Astronomy	28,000	20,000
15 Computer Science	27,500	20,000
16 Materials Technology	27,500	
17 Civil Engineering	27,000	23,000
18 Building	27,000	21,000
19 Bioengineering and biomedical engineering	26,000	19,110
20 Politics	25,800	21,000
21= Accounting and Finance	25,000	21,000
21= Italian	25,000	21,000
23 East and South Asian Studies	25,000	20,500
24 German	25,000	20,400
25= Chemistry	25,000	20,000
25= Town and Country Planning and Landscape	25,000	20,000
25= Information Systems and Management	25,000	20,000
25= Business, Management and Marketing	25,000	20,000
25= Iberian Languages	25,000	20,000
30 Philosophy	25,000	19,000
31 Russian	25,000	
32 Radiography	24,995	
33 Anatomy and Physiology	24,907	19,000
34 Physiotherapy	24,907	
35 Celtic Studies	24,906	
36 Food Science	24,900	19,000
37 Subjects Allied to Medicine	24,900	18,200
38 History	24,800	19,500
39 Agriculture and Forestry	24,699	21,000
40 French	24,662	20,101
41 Nursing	24,500	20,400

Subject	High skilled work (median) £	Low and medium skilled £
42 Geography and Environmental Sciences	24,500	20,000
43 Education	24,500	17,633
44 Theology and Religious Studies	24,400	17,775
45= Anthropology	24,000	20,000
45= Land and Property Management	24,000	20,000
45= Classics and Ancient History	24,000	20,000
48 Social Policy	24,000	19,595
49= Biological Sciences	24,000	19,000
49= American Studies	24,000	19,000
49= Linguistics	24,000	19,000
52 Geology	23,500	19,000
53 History of Art, Architecture and Design	23,000	20,000
54 Sociology	23,000	19,000
55 English	23,000	18,933
56 Sport Science	23,000	18,005
57 Psychology	22,500	18,258
58 Architecture	22,000	20,000
59 Hospitality, Leisure, Recreation and Tourism	22,000	19,968
60 Law	22,000	19,800
61 Drama, Dance and Cinematics	22,000	18,000
62 Art and Design	21,500	18,720
63 Music	21,493	18,000
64 Communication and Media Studies	21,234	19,500
65 Archaeology and Forensic Science	21,100	19,000
66 Animal Science	21,000	18,000
67 Creative Writing	20,000	18,000

Note: The salaries table is ranked by the median salary of those in highly skilled employment in each subject area. Where high-skilled salaries are equal, medium-skilled salaries are used as a separator.

Source: Higher Edeucation Statistics Agency, Graduate Outcomes Survey 2018–19, published July 2021
Covers graduates in employment and self-employment/freelance work, first degree UK-domiciled students only

Advances in robotics and artificial intelligence will mean some jobs are on the way out, but roles needed to develop new technologies and new solutions are expanding. The stuff that makes us different from machines, such as emotional intelligence, analytical skills and caring, will also be vital in the future jobs market, as will creativity and resilience. A rounded university education with experience in and out of the classroom or laboratory will help to hone such "soft" skills. As for resilience, current and incoming students have been building their bounce-back-ability through the many adaptations they have had to make to what used to be normal life, such as adjusting to blended online learning, examination changes, vaccines and social distancing.

Parents' well-meant career advice is often 20 or 30 years out of date. Careers experts recommend finding something you care about, and something you are good at, and linking the two together to find a job that will be rewarding. Some suggest looking at the United Nations' Sustainable Development Goals (SDGs) and aligning careers to them: improving health and education, reducing inequality, spurring economic growth and conserving the environment – these are problems whose solutions are long-term, and their higher purpose chimes with the interests of the current generation of students. You could work as an expert in these fields or use other professional skills within the context of these SDGs.

By keeping your eye on the horizon to see what trends and changes are coming, you stand a chance of picking a future-proof field of work. Automation is changing professions, but not wiping them out entirely.

Graduate employment and underemployment

Competition for graduate jobs, with their salary premium over a working lifetime, remains stiff. There are more than 14 million graduates in the UK, and in Inner London they make up 56% of the adult population. The northeast is the region with Britain's lowest proportion of graduates, yet 34% of those aged 20-plus there have a degree. The high proportion of graduates in the overall population means that they may now take longer than their predecessors to find the right career opening and might experiment with internships before committing themselves. Employers' ideas of which jobs require a degree, and of the roles for which they prefer graduates change over time. Nurses have not always been required to take a degree, but the job now needs skills that were not part of the profession 20 years ago. The same is true of many occupations. Even in jobs where it may be possible to do the work involved without a degree, having taken one makes it easier to get hired in the first place.

Surveys have found that a sizeable proportion of graduates consider themselves working in a job that does not require a degree – an experience known as being underemployed. Scoping out a job via internships rather than going for whatever is immediately available for the highest salary can be a wise move. Almost 60% of graduates said they would take a lower salary for a more fulfilling job, in a survey by the consultancy Accenture, and only 55% were working in their chosen field.

The graduate labour market

The contents of this *Guide* – particularly in the subject tables – should help to create a nuanced picture. A close examination of individual universities' employment rates in your subject – possibly supplemented by the salary figures on the Discover Uni website **https://discoveruni.gov.uk** – will tell you whether national trends apply to your chosen course.

The health pandemic continues to to impact businesses and the economy. Brexit has wrought its own, separate havoc in areas such as supply chains. Even without such circumstances, for the boom years of graduate employment to return, there will have to be stronger recruitment by small and medium-sized companies, as well as the big battalions. The number of self-employed graduates will increase, in line with universities reporting growing demand for their business start-up and incubator services. If you are considering the graduate entrepreneur route, explore what your chosen university offers, because business hub services vary considerably in scale and sophistication.

Subject choice and career opportunities

For those thinking of embarking on higher education in 2023, the signs are still positive. But in any year, some universities and some subjects produce better returns than others. The tables in this chapter give a more detailed picture of the differences between subjects at a national level, while the rankings in chapters 1 and 12 include figures for each university and subject area. There are a few striking changes, but mainly among subjects with relatively small and fluctuating numbers of graduates.

In the employment table, subjects are ranked according to the proportion employed in jobs categorized by HESA as high-skilled, and include those undertaking further study, whether or not combined with a high-skilled job. The level of detail we provide about types of job is illuminating; some similar tables do not make a distinction between different sorts of work, which can mislead applicants into thinking all universities and subjects offer uniformly rosy employment prospects.

The definitions of both a high-skilled and a graduate job are controversial. But HESA relies on the Standard Occupational Classification, a complex series of definitions drawn up by the Office for National Statistics (ONS). New universities, in particular, often claim that the whole concept of a graduate job immediately after graduation fails to reflect reality for their alumni. In any case, a degree is about enhancing your whole career, your way of working and your view of the world, not just your first job out of college.

That said, the tables in this chapter will help you assess whether your course is likely to pay off in career terms, at least to start with. They show both the amount you might expect to earn with a degree in a specific subject, and the odds of being in work. They reflect the experience 15 months after graduation of those who completed their degrees in 2018, so the picture may have improved by the time you leave university. The pattern of success rates for specific subjects and institutions are unlikely to have changed radically, though.

It is worth considering that at age 25 the average male graduate earns 5% more per year than the average female graduate, even though women are more likely to get first class or upper second degrees, and by age 30 – before most graduates start having children – the gender pay gap in annual earnings has extended to 25%. Without maternity leave to explain such a pay gulf, analysts have suggested it may be down to women choosing degrees that are less likely to translate into as high-paying careers as their male counterparts.

The table of employment statistics from the new Graduate Outcomes survey reveals some unexpected results. For example, only 63.6% of business, management and marketing graduates are working in high-skilled jobs or doing further study, though this is slightly more than the 61.7% of of accounting and finance graduates who achieved similar positive outcomes. The town and country planners, economists and food scientists fare a lot better. All seven branches of engineering are in the top 20 subjects for both graduate outcomes and starting salaries.

The employment table also shows that graduates in some subjects, especially sciences such as physics and astronomy, biological sciences, chemistry and geology, are more likely to undertake further study than in others, such as those in art and design or hospitality. A range of professions now regard a Masters degree as a basic entry-level qualification.

Those going into subjects such as art and design appreciate that it too has its own career peculiarities. Periods of freelance or casual work are common at the start of a career and may become an enduring choice. Less surprisingly, doctors and dentists are virtually guaranteed a job if they complete a degree, as are nurses.

The second table, on pages 53–54, gives average earnings of those who graduated in 2019, recorded 15 months after leaving university. It contains interesting, and in some cases surprising, information about early career pay levels. Few would have placed social work in the top ten for graduate pay. However, nursing is now in 41st place, having been in the top 20 a few years ago.

It is important, of course, to consider the differences between starting salaries and the long-term prospects of different jobs. Over time, the accountants may well end up with bigger rewards, despite being only £500 a year better off than the nurses in our early-career snapshot. In any case, it is important to realise that once you ignore the higher incomes available to medics and other elite professionals, early graduate incomes vary less than you might think from subject to subject.

Five subjects from chemistry to Iberian languages tie at 25th in our salary ranking. A further three tie for 45th. But the difference between these two groups is only £1,000 a year, with the first set on £25,000 and the second on £24,000. There is so little between them in fact, that where high-skilled salaries are equal, medium-skilled salaries are used as a separator. That's why you should consider the lifetime earnings you might derive from these subjects, and your own interests and inclinations, at least as much as this snapshot.

Enhancing your employability

Graduate employability has become the holy grail of degree education since higher fees were introduced in most of the UK. Virtually every university has an initiative to enhance their graduates' prospects. Many have incorporated specially designed employability modules into degree courses; some are certificating extra-curricular activities to improve their graduates' CVs; and many more are stepping up their efforts to provide work experience to complement degrees. Opinion is divided on the value of such schemes.

Some of the biggest employers restrict their recruitment activities to a small number of universities, believing that these institutions attract the brightest minds and that trawling more widely is not cost-effective. In 2020–21, High Fliers reported that the ten universities most targeted by the largest number of top graduate employers were Birmingham, Manchester, University College London, Nottingham, Leeds, Warwick, Bristol, Cambridge, Oxford and Imperial College London.

Some top law firms and others in the City of London have introduced institution-blind applications, but big employers' links with their favourite recruiting grounds are likely to continue. Widening the pool of universities from which they set out to recruit is costly, and can seem unnecessary if employers are getting the people they think they need. They will expect outstanding candidates who went to other universities to come to them, either on graduation or later in their careers. But most graduates do not work in the City and most students do not go to universities at the top of the league tables.

University schemes

If a university offers extra help towards employment, consider whether its scheme is likely to work for you. Some are too new to have shown results in the labour market yet, but they may have been endorsed by big employers or introduced at an institution whose graduates already have a record of success in the jobs market. They might involve classes in CV writing, interview skills, personal finance, entrepreneurship and negotiation skills, among many other topics. There can be guest lectures and demonstrations, or mock interviews, by real employers, to assess students' strengths and weaknesses. In time, these extras may turn into mandatory parts of a degree, complete with course credits.

The value of work experience

The majority of graduate jobs are open to applicants from any discipline. For these general positions, employers tend to be more impressed by a good degree from what they consider a prestigious university than by an apparently relevant qualification. Here numeracy, literacy and communications – the skills needed to function effectively in any organisation – are vitally important.

Specialist jobs, for example in engineering or design, are a different matter. Employers may be much more knowledgeable about the quality of individual courses, and less influenced by a university's overall position in league tables, when the job relies directly on knowledge and skills acquired as a student. That goes for medicine and architecture as well as computer games design or environmental management.

In almost all fields of employment, however, work experience has become increasingly valuable. Results of the High Fliers survey show that work experience schemes have become an integral part of recruiting new graduates. Students who apply for work experience in their first or second year at university go through similar selection processes to graduates, which works as a kind of pre-vetting for a job after graduation. The number of paid placements has risen sharply, reflecting the increased role of work experience in graduate recruitment.

Even during the pandemic, employers continued to engage young people for internships by transitioning from in-person placements to virtual activities – although how effective these were for either party is debatable. Companies large and small commonly hire graduates who have already worked for them, whether in holiday jobs, internships or placements.

Sandwich degrees, which include extended programmes of up to a year at work, have always boosted employment prospects. Graduates – often engineers – frequently end up working where they undertook their placement. And while a sandwich year will make your course take longer, it will not cost a full year's-worth of tuition fees.

Many conventional degrees now include shorter work placements that should offer some advantages in the labour market. Not all are arranged by the university – most big graduate employers offer some provision of this nature, although access to it can be competitive.

Although there is no guarantee of employment at the end of the course, employment rates from sandwich degrees suggest that companies are likely to want to retain those in whom they have invested considerable time and money.

A growing number of employers are also offering degree apprenticeships, in partnership with a wide range of universities. Even Cambridge has some at postgraduate level and is developing more. They generally take longer than a traditional degree, but there are no tuition fees, apprentices are paid a salary and there is usually a guaranteed job at the end. Michelle Donelan, the Minister of State for Universities, (at the time of writing) said in October 2021 that the number of degree apprentices had increased 8% since the pandemic began – and they were now available at 94 universities – but the figures were "not good enough", because, she stated, "I want every university to be holding degree apprenticeships".

If you opt for a traditional degree without a work placement, consider arranging your own part-time or temporary employment. The majority of full-time students now take jobs during term time, as well as in vacations, to make ends meet. But such jobs can boost your CV as well as your bank balance. Even working in a bar or a shop shows some experience of dealing with the public and coping with the discipline of the workplace. Inevitably, the more prosperous cities are likely to offer more employment opportunities than rural areas or conurbations that have been hard hit by recession.

Consider part-time degrees

Another option is part-time study. Although enrolments have fallen sharply both before and since the big 2012 increases in fees, there are now loans available for most part-time courses. Employers may be willing to share the cost of taking a degree or another relevant qualification, and the chance to earn a wage while studying has obvious attractions. Bear in mind that most part-time courses take twice as long to complete as the full-time equivalent. If your earning power is linked to the qualification, it will take that much longer for you to enjoy the benefits.

Plan early for your career

Whatever type of course you choose, it is sensible to start thinking about your future career early in your time at university. There has been a growing tendency in recent years for students to convince themselves that there would be plenty of time to apply for jobs after graduation, and that they were better off focusing entirely on their degree while at university. In the current employment market, all but the most obviously brilliant graduates need to offer more than just a degree, whether it be work experience, leadership qualities demonstrated through clubs and societies, or commitment to voluntary activities. Many students finish a degree without knowing what they want to do, but a blank CV will not impress a prospective employer.

Sometimes a side hustle can work out well for your CV as well as your bank balance; big brands use student ambassadors to help spread the word about their latest projects, providing the opportunity to develop your skills in marketing, social media strategy and content creation, while also earning money.

Useful websites

Prospects, the UK's official graduate careers website: **www.prospects.ac.uk**
For career advice, internships and student and graduate jobs: **www.milkround.com**
For graduate employment (and other) statistics: **www.discoveruni.gov.uk**
High Fliers research: **www.highfliers.co.uk**

4 The Bottom Line: Tuition Fees and Finance

Ever a thorny issue whether in Whitehall, over the dinner table or at student demonstrations, tuition fees continue to make the news. An announcement on potential changes to them is long overdue following the 2019 Augar review of post-18 education, which recommended tuition fees were cut from £9,250 a year to £7,500 as part of a radical overhaul of university funding. As recently as October 2021, officials from No 10, the Treasury and the Department for Education (DfE) were engaged in impassioned talks about a possible cut to fees but failed to reach an agreement in time for the chancellor's spending review that month. The proposed new rate was £8,500, reportedly, £1,000 adrift of Augur's pre-pandemic figure.

While such a reduction is an attractive prospect – as it reduces the perceived student debt – commentators have noted that in practical terms it means taking money away from universities and benefitting high-earning graduates.

Loan repayment thresholds have also been the subject of debate. As it stands, graduates only start repaying their tuition fee and maintenance loans once they earn more than £27,295, but in autumn 2021 minsters were said to be considering cutting that threshold to £23,000 – in an effort to save the Treasury billions. However, students, unions and the Institute of Fiscal Studies (IFS) warned against mandating earlier repayment of student loans, saying it would hit lower earners hardest and pile pressure on the Covid generation.

The IFS even created an online calculator showing the options and costs available to the Treasury. The tool illustrated that any substantial changes to the loan system means the richest graduates pay proportionately less, while those on average earnings have to pay more. The IFS suggested the income tax system would be a better way of raising revenue from the highest-paid graduates.

Tony Blair, the former Prime Minster and the architect of the drive to get half of all young people into higher education, has also been shining the spotlight on university funding. Writing in our *Guide's* newspaper edition in the *Sunday Times*, Blair called for the return of maintenance grants and a new generation of universities to help cater for disadvantaged students.

"High levels of university participation is one of the defining characteristics of advanced economies," maintains Blair, whose suggestions include, "no cap on student numbers, no upfront payment, better per student resources and higher earners paying their fair share."

Meanwhile, there was renewed pressure to cut university tuition fees upon the publication of international research showing England to have the most expensive undergraduate courses in the world. A study from the Organisation for Economic Co-operation and Development (OECD) said that English universities charged more than publicly funded institutions in any other country even though students often reaped lower economic benefits.

Blair, now executive chairman of the Institute for Global Change concedes that, "while young people see enough value in higher education to pursue it despite the very high fees, they still graduate, on average, with £47,000 of debt. Repayment may be income-contingent, but this headline figure ranks with some of the highest in the world. There is a strong case for reforms that would significantly reduce it, especially for those from disadvantaged backgrounds."

The debate is ongoing. But what of the candidates of 2022–23? The simple answer is: Nothing has changed. Tuition fees for UK students in England, Northern Ireland, Scotland and Wales will remain at a maximum of £9,250 for most courses. Scots studying in Scotland pay nothing, Northern Ireland students at Queen's, Belfast or Ulster pay much less and Wales caps fees at its own universities at £9,000 and gives grants to its own students.

Tuition fees history

Up until 1998, tuition at UK universities was free. The £1,000 annual fees introduced that year represented a seismic shift in higher education at the time, and in British society more widely. These fees were paid upfront by students at the start of the academic year. In 2006 fees were raised to £3,000 and a new system of variable deferred fees and tuition fees loans was introduced. From 2006, fees rose gradually by inflation until 2012 when tuition fees were raised to £9,000 per year – a move met by protest marches, campus occupations and students voting with their feet as evidenced by a downturn in applications to university. Student finance reformed at the same time, to include raising the repayment threshold to £21,000 and introducing a variable tiered rate of interest on student loans. Fees up to £9,250 were first introduced in 2017–18 and have not gone up since. Application and enrolment numbers have regained the ground they lost in the immediate years after 2012, students appearing to have become resigned to the regime.

There are some exceptions to these upper limits; private providers are not subject to fee caps, and the maximum fee for accelerated degree courses in England is £11,100. However, a fee loan will only be made available up to £9,250 and any shortfall must be met by the student.

Most students pay the maximum fees, but tuition costs vary more widely than the upper limits suggest, with bursaries and fee waivers bringing down the price for students from low-income households, while merit-based scholarships – which are sometimes, but not always linked to household incomes – are similarly valuable to those in receipt of them.

Some universities have substantial endowments to fund their bursaries and scholarships programmes, such as the prestigious London School of Economics and Political Science, which each year awards around £4million in scholarships and financial support to its undergraduates.

The University of West London uses the surplus money it generates to effectively reduce the cost of going to university from the tuition fees rack rate of £9,250 to about £8,550 for some students. Everyone gets an annual £200 Aspire card for study essentials and fulltime undergraduate scholarships, worth £500 a year, are awarded to 400 entrants from households with incomes under £25,000.

This *Guide* quotes the higher headline fees, but even these will vary according to whether you are from the UK or overseas, studying full-time or part-time, and whether you are taking a Foundation degree or an Honours programme. For 2022 entry, international medical students at Imperial College London are paying £46,650 per year in tuition fees (a figure that will rise with inflation). Not far away at Kingston University, UK students on the second year of their early-years foundation courses are being charged £6,000. Pre-Brexit, EU students qualified for "home" fees of £9,250, which those already on courses before the transition period ended on 31 December 2020 still pay, but any who have joined since are classed as international students – with higher fees to match.

Here we focus on full-time Honours degrees for British undergraduates, and the EU students who escaped the higher international fees: these students make up the biggest group on any UK campus.

An important fact easy to overlook is that some universities guarantee fees will be fixed at the first-year rate for the whole of your course, while others make no such promise. Applicants are advised to check the fees pages of individual universities closely.

It is also worth noting that during work placements or years abroad fees cannot exceed £1,850 (20% of the full-year fee) for work placements and £1,385 for a year abroad and are often less. So, the costs incurred by extending an undergraduate degree to four years by adding a year abroad or in industry are mainly living related only.

Fees and loans

Marginal fluctuations in fee levels and bursary provision between universities tend not to be the basis upon which applicants make their degree choices. Numbers from the poorest socio-economic groups are at record levels, although they remain severely underrepresented compared with more affluent groups.

Most readers of *The Times and Sunday Times Good University Guide* will be choosing full-time undergraduate or Foundation degree courses. The fees for 2022 entry are listed alongside each university's profile in chapter 14 wherever available. Details of English universities' bursaries and scholarships are on the website of the Office for Students (OfS) in the pages on access and participation plans. Universities have their own fees and funding web pages as well, which are good places to source up-to-date information regarding financial help.

Institutions in Scotland, Wales and Northern Ireland continue to have lower charges for their own residents but charge varying amounts to students from other parts of the UK. Only those living in Scotland and studying at Scottish universities will escape all fees, although there are reduced fees for those normally living in Wales and Northern Ireland.

The number of bursaries and scholarships offered to reduce the burden on new students has been falling since OFFA, the former Office for Fair Access, suggested that such initiatives do little to attract students from low-income households. Following this logic, the Government turned the grants paid to the poorest students into loans, although it is restoring some maintenance grants, for example for nurses.

Alternative options

Some further education colleges offer substantial savings on the cost of a degree, or of a Foundation degree, but they tend to have very local appeal, and their subject range tends to be largely vocational. The private sector may grow in popularity, following the success of two-year degrees at the University of Buckingham and BPP University in particular. Regent's University, one of the latest to be awarded that title, is charging £18,500 in 2022–23 for all students, irrespective of their place of origin, although less for some foundation years. The New College of the Humanities, also in London, now charges the standard £9,250, having originally come in at twice the price charged by mainstream institutions. The international fee is £14,000.

Impact on subject and university choice

Fee levels have had little impact on students' choices of university, but that is not the case for choices of subject. Predictions that old universities and/or vocational subjects would prosper at the expense of the rest have been shown to be too simplistic. Some, but not all, arts subjects have suffered, while in general science courses have prospered. For many young people, the options have not changed. If you want to be a doctor, a teacher or a social worker, there is no alternative to higher education. And, while there are now more options for studying post A-level, it remains to be seen whether they offer the same promotion prospects as a degree.

Even among full-time degrees, the pattern of applications and enrolments has varied considerably since the introduction of higher fees. In 2018, the big losers among disciplines included technology subjects and languages and literature, European and global. Winners included medicine and, perhaps unexpectedly, the social sciences. Nursing and medicine experienced application booms in 2020 as a result of the health pandemic's spotlight on frontline health workers. The career security offered by these subjects is also of value to students. Medicine, dentistry and veterinary science have been growing in popularity even pre-Covid, and new medical schools are opening to meet the demand for more doctors.

In general terms, over the eight years since higher fees were introduced, science and business subjects have done better than the arts, as students have made their own assumptions about future career prospects. IT, engineering, physical sciences and law are ahead of 2010 application numbers and languages and linguistics are down. In the 2020 admissions cycle business and management courses had the most enrolments.

Universities vary the courses they offer, in response to the perceived demand from students, much more frequently than they used to. A drop in applications may mean less competition for places, or it may lead universities to close courses, possibly intensifying the race for entry. The only reliable forecast is that competition for places on the most popular courses will remain stiff, just as it has been since before students paid any fees.

Two-year degrees are so far mainly the domain of the private universities. The University of Law, for example, already does degrees in this way. It charges £11,100 per year, a saving of £5,550 on a three-year course, which the same institution also offers at the standard £9,250, alongside less expensive online options. A two-year course also gets you into the workforce faster and reduces spending on living costs. However, this approach also cuts out much chance of holiday earnings and of sandwich courses or placements, where students can often get paid and gain work experience. It remains to be seen whether the idea will catch on with traditional universities and if so, whether it will be applicable to the full range of academic subjects.

Degree Apprenticeships

There is the option of studying for a degree with no fees at all, by taking a degree apprenticeship sponsored by an employer. So far, the range of subjects in which these are available is relatively narrow – they have to go through a cumbersome accreditation procedure – but the number of universities offering them had grown to 94, at the last count.

Many degree apprenticeships are in professional areas, such as childcare, accounting, policing and social work, but there are others in the sciences, business subjects, some social sciences and IT. On the whole students spend the majority of their time at work with their sponsoring employer – and receiving a wage, rather than having to access loans – with varying periods at university. Those on PwC's "Flying Start" computer science or software engineering degree apprenticeships have a different experience, however. Their fees at Birmingham, Leeds,

Queen Mary, London or Queen's, Belfast universities are paid by their employer for a full BSc, and they earn a salary throughout their course. Instead of being based mostly at work, the student-trainees experience university life more traditionally and both live and study largely alongside fellow undergraduates in term time, with work placements taken in chunks throughout their degrees. A graduate scheme place awaits at the end, with a head start straight into the second year.

The degree versus degree apprenticeship debate is fairly even-handed. Financially, degree apprenticeships – which are known as graduate apprenticeships in Scotland – are a no-brainer; you do not pay tuition fees, plus you will get a salary for a job that is building experience for your future career, rather than a typical part-time role just to boost your current account. Those who last the course of up to five years will be met with immediate employment levels that are guaranteed to be excellent, and many employers pay those who complete the qualification more than traditional graduates because they will have been with them for longer and be more valuable in the short term. However, the degree apprenticeship route is too new for the long-term prospects to be certain, and it is impossible to say whether the qualification will have the same currency and be as portable as a traditional degree in mid-career.

Getting the best deal

There will still be a certain amount of variation in student support packages in 2023 and it will be possible to shop around, particularly if your family income is low. But remember that the best deal, even in purely financial terms, is one that leads to a rewarding career. By all means compare the full packages offered by individual universities but consider too whether marginal differences of a few hundred pounds in headline fees, repaid over 30 years, matter as much as the quality of the course and the likely advantages it will confer in the employment market. Scottish students can save themselves £27,750 by opting to study north of the border. That is a very different matter to the much smaller saving that is available to students in England, particularly if the Scottish university is of comparable quality to the alternatives elsewhere. So, it is all a matter of judgement.

The financial relief offered by means-tested bursaries may be impossible to ignore for those who qualify for them. No one has to pay tuition fees while they are a student, but you still have to find thousands of pounds in living costs to take a full-time degree. In some cases, bursaries may make the difference between being able to afford higher education and having to pass up a potentially life-changing opportunity. Some are worth up to £3,000 a year, although most are less generous than this, often because large numbers of students qualify for an award.

Some scholarships are even more valuable, and are awarded for sporting and musical prowess, as well as academic achievement. Most scholarships are not means-tested, but a few are open only to students who are both high performers academically and from low-income families.

International students

The higher fees now charged to EU students, post-Brexit, have naturally impacted recruitment from EU countries. UCAS figures show that across UK universities, applications from EU students were 28,400 in 2021 compared with 49,650 in 2020 – a 43% drop. On the other hand, non-EU student applications increased by 14% – from 89,130 in 2020 to 102,000 in 2021. For more information on international tuition fees, please refer to Chapter 11: Coming to the UK to Study.

Financing Your Studies

The need for enough money to live on at university and the likelihood that for the majority of students, some debt will be involved, remain constants in higher education – whatever changes in fees may be dictated by government policies.

Most students take out both tuition fee and maintenance loans to cover the cost of studying and living. These are technically two types of funding, but the total amount borrowed is known as their Student Loan. Try not to focus on the scaremongering headlines you may have noticed, flagging eyewatering sums of money students owe upon graduation. Yes, there is going to be a debt and it is likely to be considerable, but (and this is a big "but") – student loan debts are not quite like other sorts of commercial borrowing – such as on credit cards or via a mortgage. Some commentators argue they work out more like a graduate tax.

Each UK country has its own student finance system. The following sections of this chapter relate to the loans and costs incurred by students from England, while the broader content relates to students across the UK. The facts and figures for those from Northern Ireland, Wales and Scotland are detailed separately later in the chapter.

Tuition fee loans

Full-time students can borrow up to the full amount of £9,250 needed to cover tuition fees wherever they study in the UK. Those studying an accelerated degree course could get up to £11,100. This loan is not dependent upon household income. New part-time students can apply for loans of up to £6,935 for tuition fees in an academic year.

Students never get their hands on the tuition fee loans cash, the money is paid straight to the university. This way there is no risk of blowing the lot on something other than funding studies or running late with payments and being chased by the university.

Maintenance Loan entitlement, England 2021–22

Household income	Living at home	Living away from home but not in London	Living away from home and studying in London
£25,000	£7,987	£9,488	£12,382
£30,000	£7,315	£8,809	£11,692
£35,000	£6,642	£8,130	£11,001
£40,000	£5,969	£7,450	£10,311
£45,000	£5,296	£6,771	£9,620
£50,000	£4,623	£6,092	£8,929
£55,000	£3,950	£5,412	£8,239
£58,220	£3,516	£4,974	£7,794
£60,000	£3,516	£4,733	£7,548
£62,286	£3,516	£4,422	£7,232
£65,000	£3,516	£4,422	£6,858
£70,000	£3,516	£4,422	£6,167
£70,004+	£3,516	£4,422	£6,166

Source: Student Finance England

Maintenance Loans

These are designed to help full-time home students pay for their living expenses – rent, food, travel, bills, going out, clothes, gym fees and so on. Maintenance loans are partly means-tested and the amount that can be borrowed depends on family income, whether the university is in London or elsewhere in the UK, and whether students live at home with their family or independently.

Maximum loan amounts in 2021/22:

» £7,987 for students living at their family home during term time.
» £9,488 for students living away from home outside London.
» £12,382 for students living away from home in London.
» £10,866 for students living and studying abroad for at least one term as part of their UK course.

In general, students must be under 60 on the first day of the first academic year of their course. However, in England over-60s can access a lower means-tested loan for living costs, of up to £4,014.

Maintenance loans are paid straight into students' bank accounts in three instalments throughout the year. Budgeting to make each loan last until the next instalment is down to students. The final Maintenance loan payment is a bit smaller than in the years before, because student life ends in June/July of that year, and with it the entitlement to a Student loan.

The first loan instalment creates a bit of a heaven-and-hell moment. For most 18-year-old freshers there is the thrill of their current account probably experiencing its biggest single cash injection ever, combined with the more sobering surprise that the interest clock starts ticking on the loan from the day of the initial payment, usually the first day of the first term. It keeps ticking until the April after students finish their course, which is when repayment may or may not begin. For part-time students earning over £27,295 (this threshold increases every year for all students) repayment starts four years after starting to receive the loan, even if they are furthering their studies rather than working at that time.

The most recent significant change to the student finance system, in 2016–2017, was the abolition of grants – which do not require repayment – in England for students from low-income families, and their replacement by increased maintenance loans. As with the introduction of tuition fees, there has been no immediate impact on students. Repayments are in line with those for tuition fee loans. But critics have said many low and middle-income students could be put off university by having to accrue more debt, and in 2020 the Government reintroduced maintenance grants for nurses, as detailed below.

NHS Bursaries

Eligible full-time NHS students can apply for a bursary from the NHS, plus a £1,000 grant from the NHS and a reduced Maintenance loan from Student Finance England. For those eligible for an NHS bursary, the NHS pays their standard tuition fees directly to their university.

The student nursing bursary returned in September 2020, having been scrapped in 2015. Under the funding arrangements, all nursing students qualify for at least £5,000 a year maintenance grant – which is commonly known as the bursary. Those who plan on working in a branch of nursing suffering from severe shortages can also access a further £1,000.

Beyond this, another £2,000 is accessible in childcare allowances. Only part of the bursary is means-tested, and some student nurses may be eligible for more bursary funding subject to the means-testing.

Student nurses do not have to repay the maintenance grants, as they are not loans. And having the bursary doesn't impact a student nurse's access to a full Student loan through the Student Loans Company.

Interest rates

Student loan interest rates are based on the Retail Prices Index (RPI), the rate at which prices rise. While studying, until the April following graduation, students are charged RPI + 3%. From that point, interest accrues on a sliding scale of RPI plus up to 3% until they reach a salary of £47,835, after which it remains at RPI plus 3% however much they earn. As an idea of what to expect on the sliding scale, those earning a midway salary of £37,205 will accrue interest of RPI + 1.5%.

The interest rate is reduced to RPI alone if a student leaves college and gets a job paying less than £27,295 (from1 April 2021). In other words, as the personal finance whiz, Martin Lewis, points out on his **www.moneysavingexpert.com** website, "Unlike other debt, the interest added ISN'T the interest paid. That depends on future earnings. Some won't repay any interest and most won't earn enough to repay close to all of it."

The interest rate changes every September, based on the RPI rate of inflation in the year to the previous March. The RPI rate was 2.6% in March 2020, so in 2021 Student loan interest was currently charged at 2.6% to 5.6%, depending on whether the student was still studying and how much they were earning. If students lose touch with the Student Loans Company, RPI plus 3% is automatically applied to their debt.

The disappearing debt

After 30 years in England (this varies a little elsewhere in the UK – please see further down this chapter), the debt is written off. Because the repayments seem modest for anyone with a qualifying income, and because of the 30-year rule, student debt is a lot more forgiving than a mortgage or a credit card, where the bills keep on coming even if you are out of work. The Student Loans Company is probably the only lender in Britain that hands out tens of thousands of pounds without a credit check.

Repaying the Student Loan

Some students may never earn the £27,295-plus per year which triggers repayments, although few go to university with that expectation. In practice, only a handful will be in that position, and they will mostly be there because of their own life decisions. At the other extreme, graduates may land such well-paid jobs that university was cheap at the price. Most will be somewhere in the middle. Contrary to the majority of debts, which are better to clear as early as possible, students should not start repaying Student Loans before the April after leaving university, as this can result in overpaying – which tens of thousands of students have done in the past and can now reclaim. From this point students repay their loans at a rate of 9% of their earnings above £27,295 from April 1 2021. In this way, the amount owed (the borrowed money plus interest) does not affect what is repaid each year.

On his website, Martin Lewis, the Money Saving Expert, provides helpful advice to demystify Student loan repayments. His example uses the 2021 threshold of £27,295, as follows:

Student loan & interest: £20,000. *Your earnings: £37,295.*
As you repay 9% of everything above £27,295 your annual repayment is £900.
Student loan & interest: £50,000. *Your earnings: £37,295.*
As you repay 9% of everything above £27,295 your annual repayment is £900.
To get silly to prove a point: student loan & interest:
£1 billion. *Your earnings: £37,295.*
As you repay 9% of everything above £27,295 your annual repayment is **£900**.

The Student Loans Company website **www.studentloanrepayment.co.uk** has information to guide prospective students through these arrangements and also gives examples of levels of repayment.

Affording to live

Analysis by the National Union of Students confirmed what students already knew, that the maintenance loan does not provide enough money to cover the real cost of living. Making ends meet is a constant university challenge, and students have always proved resourceful. Typically, the number one source of help is parents, whose financial assistance is implied, if not explicit, in the government's approach to student funding. Part-time jobs, savings and bursaries and scholarships also contribute to the student purse.

The Student Money Survey 2020 from **www.savethestudent.org** found that average undergraduate spending was £795 per month, with rent the biggest outlay at an average of £418 per month, equivalent to 73% of a maintenance loan. The survey revealed that 71% of students worried about not being able to make ends meet and that 36% had considered dropping out for that reason. Which is why savings, earnings from part-time work and help from family and friends have to be added to the pot.

The annual Natwest Student Living Index for 2021 reported that student loans continue to make up the majority of students' income, with 54% relying on student finance to cover their rent – a decrease on the year before as reliance on parental support and personal revenue has increased – likely due to many students choosing to live at home during remote learning. The 2021 index shows 37% rely on the Bank of Mum and Dad to pay rent, while 13% use their own income and 13% use their personal savings.

The index confirmed that for students across the UK, rent remains the biggest monthly spend, followed by supermarket shopping, clothes, and eating out. Students in Manchester spend the most money per month on clothes, shoes and accessories, while those in Oxford spend the most on going out or socialising with friends. The remainder of students' money is spent on alcohol, takeaways, bills, travel and activities with a small amount going to charity and investing in cryptocurrency.

Value for money

Most surveys suggest that on average, a degree still offers a worthwhile return on the financial investment involved in going to university. Future salary expectations are better for graduates than those without degrees, even taking into consideration the wages that might otherwise have been earned while studying instead. Our Subject-by-Subject Guide in Chapter 12 delves deeper into graduate outcomes and salaries.

Budgeting

One in four freshers spend their first student loan instalment within a month, according to Endsleigh Insurance. Help is at hand to avoid such financial abandon. University websites, UCAS at **www.ucas.com/finance/managing-money/student-budgeting-tips** and many others offer guidance on preparing a budget. List all likely income (loans, bursaries, part-time work, savings, parental support) and compare this with expected outgoings. It pays to be realistic, rather than too optimistic, about both sides of the equation. With care, it should be possible to end up either only slightly in the red, or preferably far enough in the black to be able to afford some of the things you like.

Aldi, Lidl and other budget supermarkets are godsends when it comes to stretching the budget, even if shopping at one means needing to get a taxi home – share with a housemate and split the cost, there will still be significant savings on the prices at the nearby Tesco Metro or Sainsbury's Local. No one is condoning binge drinking, but with "pre-drinks" before a night out popular, great savings can be made by stocking up on the budget supermarket versions of well-known drinks and snacks. Shopping online, while not offered by the budget supermarkets, can also be cost effective if you stick to own-brand products, as the temptation of popping extra items into the trolley at will is removed and any delivery fee can be shared with housemates. Learn to cook at least a few basics and make use of leftovers in packed lunches the next day – a Tupperware pot is an invaluable weapon in the fight against splurging more than is affordable on daily café lunches. The same goes for a carry-cup for coffee.

Funding timetable

It is vital that you sort out your funding arrangements before you start university. Each funding agency has its own arrangements, and it is very important that you find out the exact details from them. The timings below give general indications of key dates.

March/April
» Online and paper application forms become available from funding agencies.
» You must contact the appropriate funding agency to make an application. This will be the funding agency for the region of the UK that you live in, even if you are planning to study elsewhere in the UK.
» Complete application form as soon as possible. At this stage select the university offer that will be your first choice.
» Check details of bursaries and scholarships available from your selected universities.

May/June
» Funding agencies will give you details of the financial support they can offer.
» Last date for making an application to ensure funding is ready for you at the start of term (exact date varies significantly between agencies).

August
» Tell your funding agency if the university or course you have been accepted for is different from that originally given them.

September
» Take letter confirming funding to your university for registration.
» After registration, the first part of funds will be released to you.

More than two-thirds of 18–24-year-olds reported they received no financial education at school, according to a report by the National Association of Student Money Advisors (NASMA). Keeping track of finances is not every student's idea of a good time but it is certain to provide greater freedom for enjoying university life. Most graduates will have to grapple with spreadsheets during their working life, and they make balancing the student budget simpler. Nobody wants any cash-machine-ate-my-card situations.

Make full use of student travel cards and shopping discounts, and shop around for the best calls and data deals on mobile phones. The 2020 Natwest Student Living Index put average monthly mobile phone spending at £12.40, while groceries and household items came in at £81.60 a month, £29.30 went on alcohol and £15.10 on books and other course-related material.

Study costs

The average student spent about £1,000 a year on costs associated with course work and studying, a survey by the NUS estimated – mainly on books and equipment. Some courses require much higher spends than others, and extra financial support may be available for certain – but not all – things. Take out library text books or buy them second-hand from students who don't need them anymore, to avoid racking up huge bookshop bills incurred by a long reading list.

Overdrafts and credit cards

These are the more expensive forms of debt, and best avoided if at all possible. Many banks offer free overdraft facilities for students but going over the limit without prior arrangement can result in high charges. Credit cards can be useful if managed properly, ideally by setting up a direct debit to pay off the full balance every month, thus avoiding paying any interest. To pay only the minimum charge each month can end up costing a small fortune over a long period. Those inclined to spend impulsively without keeping track of spending are probably better off without a credit card and should stick with a debit card.

Insurance

Most students arrive at university with laptops and other goodies such as games consoles, sports equipment, musical instruments, mobile phones and bikes that are tempting to thieves. It is estimated that around a third of students fall victim to crime at some point during university. A reasonable amount of cover for these items should be found by shopping around, without it costing you an arm and a leg. It may also be possible to add this cover cheaply to parents' domestic contents policy (probably at their expense).

Living in one country, studying in another

As each of the countries of the UK develops its own distinctive system of student finance, the effects on students leaving home in one UK nation to go and study in another have become knottier. UK students who cross borders to study, pay the tuition fees of their chosen university and are eligible for a fee loan, and maybe a partial grant, to cover them. They are also entitled to apply for the scholarships or bursaries on offer from that institution. Any maintenance loan or grant will still come from the awarding body of their home country. If you are in this position, you must check with the authorities in your home country about the funding you are eligible for. You should also contact your own government about support on offer if you are from the Channel Islands or the Isle of Man.

Following Britain's departure from the European Union, EU students from outside the UK will be charged the same tuition fees as those paid by international students, which are often much higher. They may be considered for some of the scholarships and bursaries offered by individual institutions.

Applying for support

English students should apply for grants and loans through Student Finance England, Welsh students through Student Finance Wales, Scottish students through the Student Awards Agency for Scotland, and those in Northern Ireland through Student Finance NI or their Education and Library Board.

Applications should be made as soon as the offer of a place at university has been received. Don't expect things to happen automatically. For instance, students have to tell the Student Loans Company to pay the tuition fees they owe to the university.

University scholarships and bursaries

Shop around for university bursaries, scholarships and other sponsorship packages, and seek other forms of supplementary support. There may be fee reductions for groups, including local students, which are usually detailed on university websites. There is funding for students with disabilities or family responsibilities; or for those taking subjects with wide public benefit, such as social work or medicine. Funding is also available from a range of charities with their own criteria.

The Scholarship Hub, a database of scholarships, suspects UK students could be missing out on funding worth up to £150million a year as organisations offering scholarships often struggle to get enough applications. The database is free, but it requires a subscription to access advice about how to apply and to use enhanced search tools.

Most bursaries are means-tested, while scholarships are awarded via open competition. Some universities offer eligible students the choice of accommodation discounts, fee waivers or cash. Most also have hardship funds for those who find themselves in financial difficulties. Many charities for specific industries or professions have a remit to support education, and many have bursaries for anyone studying a related subject. The Directory of Grant-Making Trusts lists bodies that make one-off or regular awards to all kinds of causes, often including deserving students. Only available in hard copy, a library visit may be required to see it for free.

Take note of the application procedures for scholarships and bursaries. They vary between institutions, and even from course to course within institutions. Specific awards may have specific application deadlines. In some cases, the university will work out for you whether you are entitled to an award by referring to your funding agency's financial assessment. If your personal circumstances change part-way through a course, entitlement to a scholarship or bursary may be reviewed.

Advice on scholarships and bursaries is usually included in a university's website or prospectus and many institutions also maintain a helpline. Is the bursary or scholarship automatic or conditional? When will you find out whether your application has been successful? For some awards, this won't be until after exam results.

Students with disabilities

Extra financial help is available to disabled students, whether studying full-time or part-time, through Disabled Students' Allowances, which are paid in addition to the standard student finance package. They are available for help with education-related conditions such as dyslexia, and for other physical and mental disabilities. They do not depend on income and do not have to be repaid. The cash is available for extra travel costs, equipment and to pay helpers. For 2020–21 the maximum for students in England for a non-medical helper was £23,258 a year, or £17,443 a year for a part-time student. In addition, there was a maximum equipment allowance of £5,849 for the duration of the course and £1,954 (£1,465 part-time) for general expenses a year, although the government warns that most students get less than these amounts. There is also needs-based funding for travel costs.

The National Health Service has its own Disabled Students Allowance system. The NHS Business Services Authority has a Student Services Arm which runs the NHS Learning Support Grants and the NHS Education Support Grant, again worth investigating by those planning to study health or social work.

Further sources of income

There are various types of support available for students in particular circumstances, other than the main loans, grants and bursaries.

» Undergraduates in financial difficulties can apply for help from their university's student hardship fund. These provide support for anything from day-to-day study and living costs to unexpected or exceptional expenses. The university decides which students need help and how much to award them. These funds often target older or disadvantaged students, and finalists in danger of dropping out. The sums range up to a few thousand pounds, are not repayable and do not count against other income.

» Students with children can apply for a Childcare Grant. For 2020–21 this was up to £174.22 a week for a first child and up to £298.69 for two or more children under 15, or under 17 with special educational needs, calculated on the basis of 85% of childcare costs. There was also a Parents' Learning Allowance of up to £1,766, for help with course-related costs.

» Students with a partner, or another adult family member who is financially dependent on them, can apply for an Adult Dependants' Grant, worth up to £3,094 a year for 2020–21.

Part-time work

A part-time term-time job is a fact of life for almost half of students. The challenge is to not let the part-time job get in the way of studying. A survey by the NUS found that 59% of students who worked felt it had an impact on their studies, with 38% missing lectures and over a fifth failing to submit coursework because of their part-time jobs.

Student employment agencies, found on many university campuses, match employers with students seeking work, sometimes offering jobs within the university itself. They also ensure both minimum wages and the maximum number of hours worked in term time, typically 15 hours a week. Students sometimes make money from freelance work and student businesses, but most take casual work in shops, restaurants, bars and call centres. Most students get a job during the holidays, including those who don't have one in the term.

How the £9,250 fee system works

What follows is a summary of the position for British students in late 2021. While there are substantial differences between the four countries of the UK, there is one important piece of common ground. Up-front payment of fees is not compulsory, and students can take out a fee loan from the Student Loans Company to cover them. This is repayable in instalments after graduation when earnings reach £27,295 for English students, a threshold set by the Government.

The most you can borrow to pay fees is £9,250, with lower sums for private colleges (up to £6,165) and part-time study, where the cap is £6,935 at public institutions and £4,625 at private ones. There are different levels of fees and support for UK students who are not from England. New students enrolling at UK universities from all other countries, including those in the EU, will pay the same international rate, which is usually much higher than the home rate. EU students already registered on courses before 31 December 2020 will qualify for the home rate of fees for the remainder of their course. The latest information on individual universities' fees at the time of going to press is listed alongside their profiles in chapter 14.

With changes, large or small, becoming almost an annual occurrence, it is essential to consult the websites of the relevant Government agencies.

Tuition fees by region for courses starting in 2022

Student's home region	Studying in England	Studying in Scotland	Studying in Wales	Studying in Northern Ireland
England	£9,250	Up to £9,250*	£9,000	£9,250
Scotland	£9,250	No fee	£9,000	£9,250
Wales**	£9,250	Up to £9,250	£9,000	£9,250
Northern Ireland	£9,250	Up to £9,250	£9,000	£4,530
EU and Other international	Variable	Variable	Variable	Variable

*Note that Honours Degrees in Scotland take four years and some universities charge £9,250 for each year.
**Students who live in Wales will be entitled to tuition fee loans and means-tested maintenance grants.
NB: Correct at time of going to press.
Source: UCAS

Fees in England

In England, the maximum tuition fee for full-time undergraduates from the UK will be £9,250 a year in 2022–23. As we have seen, most courses will demand fees of £9,250 or close to it.

In many public universities, the lowest fees will be for Foundation degrees and Higher National Diplomas. Although some universities have chosen to charge the full £9,250 a year for all courses, these two-year courses will remain a cost-effective steppingstone to a full degree, or a qualification in their own right, at many universities and further education colleges. Those universities that offer extended work placements or a year abroad as part of a degree course, will charge much less than the normal fee for this "year out". The maximum cost for a placement year is 20% of the tuition fee (£1,850), and for a full year abroad, 15%. If you spend only part of the year abroad, you will probably have to pay the whole £9,250.

Fees in Scotland

At Scottish universities and colleges, students from Scotland pay no fees directly. The universities' vice-chancellors and principals have appealed for charges to be introduced at some level to save their institutions from falling behind their English rivals in financial terms, but Alex Salmond, when he was Scotland's First Minister, famously declared that the "rocks will melt with the sun" before this happens.

Students whose home is in Scotland and who are studying at a Scottish university apply to the Student Awards Agency for Scotland (SAAS) to have their fees paid for them. Note, too, that three-year degrees are rare in Scotland, so most students can expect to pay four years of living costs.

Students from England, Wales and Northern Ireland studying in Scotland will pay fees at something like the scale that applies in England and will have access to finance at similar levels to those available for study in England. It is worth noting, however, that some courses offer considerable savings, Robert Gordon University in Aberdeen, for example, has a fee of £6,000 per year for some four-year courses, including a BA in Accounting and Finance.

The majority of Scottish universities offer a "free" fourth year to bring their total fees into line with English universities, but Edinburgh and St Andrews are charging £9,250 in all four years of their degree courses.

Scottish maintenance bursaries and loans 2021–22

Young student (under 25 at start of course)				Independent student (25+)			
Income	Loan	Bursary	Total	Income	Loan	Bursary	Total
Up to £20,999	£5,750	£2,000	£7,750	Up to £20,999	£6,750	£1,000	£7,750
£21,000–£23,999	£5,750	£1,125	£6,875	£21,000–£23,999	£6,750	–	£6,750
£24,000–£33,999	£5,750	£500	£6,250	£24,000–£33,999	£6,250	–	£6,250
Over £34,000	£4,750	–	£4,750	Over £34,000	£4,750	–	£4,750

UK Nursing and Midwifery students studying in Scotland are eligible for bursaries of £10,000 for the first three years and £7,500 for the fourth year of a course. There is a separate dental bursary scheme.

Source: Students Awards Agency Scotland

Student loans and grants for Scottish students

Scottish students pay no tuition fees at their own universities and can apply for up to £9,250 per year as a loan for fees elsewhere in the UK. They must reapply for this loan each year.

The Scottish Government has a commitment to a minimum income, currently £7,750 per year for students from poorer backgrounds. So, in 2021–22, students from a family with an income below £20,999 could get a £2,000 Young Students' Bursary (YSB) as well as a loan of £5,750. Unlike the other UK countries, Scotland uses a band system to calculate the combination of bursary and loan, rather than precise household income. So, for incomes from £21,000 to £23,999, the bursary is £1,125 and the loan remains the same, making a total of £6,875 and for those earning £24,000 to £33,999, the bursary is only £500, making a total of £6,250. Above £34,000, no bursary is available and the maximum loan falls to £4,750. These figures remain the same regardless of whether students live at home or where they are studying in the UK. Higher loans but more limited bursaries are available for "independent" students – those who are married, mature (25 or over) or without family support. Maintenance support loans in Scotland are not available to students aged over 55, and students must be under 60 to enrol on the first day of their course.

The Scottish government's Student Awards Agency Scotland has raised the repayment threshold to £25,000. Interest is linked to the RPI, as in Northern Ireland. Repayments will continue until the loan is paid off, with any outstanding amount being cancelled after 35 years, five years later than for the English, and ten years later than in Wales.

As elsewhere in the UK, there are special funds for people with disabilities and other special needs, and for those with children or adult dependants. No tuition fee loans are required by Scottish students studying in Scotland, but such loans are available for Scottish students studying elsewhere in the UK.

Fees in Wales

All Welsh universities apply £9,000 tuition fees. Students who live in Wales will be able to apply for a Tuition Fee Loan as well as a Tuition Fee Grant, wherever they study. You can get a combined loan and grant for up to £9,000 if you study in Wales, or £9,250 for Scotland, England or Northern Ireland, but only a loan, of up to £6,165, for study in a private institution.

Student loans and grants for Welsh students

For 2021–22 the maximum maintenance award is £8,790 for students living at home, £10,350 for those living away from home and outside London, and £12,930 for those living in London. These sums are mainly an outright grant to those from low-income households. So, if total household income is £18,370 or less, £8,100 of the £10,350 is a grant (and therefore does not need to be repaid) and only £2,250 a loan, but if income is over £59,200, then £9,350 is repayable and only £1,000 is a grant. The same logic applies to other levels of support, while part-time students can get a variable loan or grant that depends upon income and the intensity of their course.

Tuition fee loans are available to cover the whole £9,000 of tuition fees in Wales, or £9,250 for Welsh students in Scotland, England or Northern Ireland (£6,165 for a private provider). Those studying part-time in Wales (or at the Open University) can apply for a loan of up to £2,625. Elsewhere in the UK they can apply for up to £6,935, or for courses at private institutions, £4,625.

Repayment of loans starts once a graduate's income reaches £27,295. Interest repayments and the length of loan are as for England (see above). In addition, students in Wales are also able to apply for Welsh Government support for parents of young children, for adult learners, for those with adult dependants and for those with disabilities. This support can cover carer costs as well as equipment and general expenditure.

Fees in Northern Ireland

The two universities of Northern Ireland are charging local students £4,530 a year for 2021–22. For students from elsewhere in the UK, the fee is £9,250 for Queen's, Belfast and for the University of Ulster.

Student loans and grants for Northern Ireland students

Maintenance grants range from £3,475 for students with household incomes of £19,203 or below, to zero if the figure is £41,540 or above. The maximum loan is reduced by the size of any grant received. Loan repayments of 9% of salary start once income reaches £19,390, a lower threshold than in England, and interest is calculated on the RPI or 1% above base rate, whichever is lower, again less than for England. The loan will be cancelled after 25 years, also quicker than in England.

There are also special funds for people with disabilities and other special needs, and for those with children or adult dependants. Students studying in the Republic of Ireland can also borrow up to €3,000 a year to pay their Irish tuition contribution and may be able to get a bursary to study there. Tuition fee loans are available for the full amount of tuition fees, regardless of where you study in the UK.

Useful websites

The "fees and funding" pages on university websites provide the most up-to-date information on costs of individual courses – especially for rates paid by international students, which vary. Universities also publish details of the financial help available, and how to apply.

It is essential to consult the latest information provided by Government agencies. The following websites will outline any major developments.

England: **www.gov.uk/student-finance**
Wales: **www.studentfinancewales.co.uk**
Scotland: **www.saas.gov.uk**
Northern Ireland: **www.studentfinanceni.co.uk**

Office for Students: **www.officeforstudents.org.uk**

For the basics of fees, loans, grants and other allowances: **www.gov.uk/student-finance**

UCAS provides helpful advice: **www.ucas.com/money**

Office for Students: **www.officeforstudents.org.uk**

All UK student loans are administered by the Student Loans Company: **www.gov.uk/government/organisations/student-loans-company**

HMRC information on the tax position of students: **www.gov.uk/student-jobs-paying-tax**

For finding out about availability of scholarships: **www.thescholarshiphub.org.uk** (requires subscription fee). Or go direct to university websites, where their scholarship and bursary provision will be detailed.

5 Making Your Application

A rarity in the education sector globally, the UK's predicted grades admissions system is unique among developed countries. We have been on the cusp of reforms to the application and admissions process for several years, and the move to a post-qualifications admissions model has been described by government advisors as "readyish" to go. The shift – which would mean applicants could receive university offers only once they have obtained their final grades – would bring Britain in line with most other countries and had the backing of former Education Secretary Gavin Williamson. His successor Nadhim Zahawi has yet to confirm any changes. Therefore, the advice in this chapter is correct at the time of writing, but applicants for 2022 or 2023 entry should stay abreast of any developments.

The crucial elements of making your application will remain constant, however. The University and Colleges Admissions System, more commonly known by its acronym UCAS, was formed in 1992 through the merger of the former university admissions system UCCA and the former polytechnics admissions system PCAS. UCAS makes the process of applying to university as straightforward as possible. Everything happens online and UCAS provides clear instructions, tips and suggestions of how best to navigate each section along the way.

Be prepared for the UCAS website to oust Instagram from your browser's top spot, at least in the run up to submitting your application, and for its various stages to be part of your life until a university place has been secured. The UCAS hub is your one-stop-shop for everything from details of more than 35,000 courses, open days and key dates to top tips based on where you are in the application process, handy to-do lists and reminders to keep you on track.

Your grades will be the most important factor in winning a place at university, but what goes on the application form is more important than many students realise. There is a knack to making the kind of application that will stand out to admissions tutors, and which will convey your knowledge of and enthusiasm for your chosen subject, preferably with supporting evidence from your school or college.

It pays to keep your eye on the ball at this stage on the journey to university. Under the current system, applicants must decide on up to five choices months before they take their final exams, you do not have to use all five of them but doing so gives you the best chance of success.

The application process

Almost all applications for full-time higher education courses go through UCAS, including those to the conservatoires which come with separate guidance and processes on the UCAS website.

Applications for degree apprenticeships are exceptions to the rule, however, and should be made to employers rather than universities. Deadlines differ between employers. You can apply for as many apprenticeships as you want, on top of your university applications. Many recruit through the **www.gov.uk/apply-apprenticeship** website, which also has links to vacancy information, as does UCAS at **https://careerfinder.ucas.com/**

Some universities that have not filled all their places on conventional degrees, even during Clearing, will accept direct applications up to and sometimes after the start of the academic year, but UCAS is both the official route and the only way into the most popular courses. The "Apply" system is available 24 hours a day, and, when the time comes, information on the progress of your application may arrive at any time.

Registering with Apply

Applications kick off by registering with Apply. School and college students will be given a "buzzword" by their tutor or careers adviser – you need this in order to login to register. It links your application to the school or college so that the application can be sent electronically to your referee (usually one of your teachers) for your reference to be attached. If you are no longer at a school or college, you do not need a "buzzword", but you will need details of your referee. More information is given on the UCAS website.

Clicking on "Apply" begins the process for providing your personal details and generating a username and password, as well as reminding you of basic points, such as amending your details in case of a change of address. You can register separate term-time and holiday addresses – a useful option for boarders, who could find offers and, particularly, the confirmation of a place, going to their school when they are miles away at home. Remember to keep a note of your username and password in a safe place.

Throughout the process, you will be in sole control of communications with UCAS and your chosen universities. Only if you nominate a representative and give them your unique nine-digit application number (sent automatically by UCAS when your application is submitted), can a parent or anyone else give or receive information on your behalf, perhaps because you are ill or out of the country.

Video guides on the application process are available on the UCAS website. Once you are registered, you can start to complete the Apply screens. The sections that follow cover the main screens.

The main screens to be completed in UCAS Apply

» Personal and contact details and some additional non-educational details for UK applicants.
» Your course choices.
» Details of your education so far, including examination results and examinations still to be taken.
» Details of any jobs you have done.
» Your personal statement.
» A reference from one of your teachers.
» View all details to make sure they are correct and reflect your preferences.
» Pay for the application (applications for 2022 cost £26.50, or £22 to apply to just one course).

Personal details

This information is taken from your initial registration, and you will be asked for additional information, for example, on ethnic origin and national identity, to monitor equal opportunities in the application process. UK students will also be asked to complete a student finance section designed to speed up any loan application you might make.

Choices

In most subjects, you will be able to apply to a maximum of five universities and/or colleges. The exceptions are medicine, dentistry and veterinary science, where the maximum is four, but you can use your fifth choice as a back-up to apply for a different subject.

The other important restriction concerns Oxford or Cambridge, because you can only apply to one or the other; you cannot apply to both universities in the same year, nor can you apply for more than one course there. For both universities you may need to take a written test (see page 34) and submit examples of your work, depending on the course selected. In addition, for Cambridge, many subjects will demand a pre-interview assessment once the university has received your application from UCAS, while the rest will set written tests to be taken at interview.

The deadline for Oxbridge applications – and for all medicine, dentistry and veterinary science courses – is 15 October. For all other applications the deadline is 15 January (or 24 March for some specified art and design courses). The other exceptions to this rule are the relatively small but growing number of courses that start in January or February. If you are considering one of these, contact the university concerned for application deadlines.

Most applicants use all five choices. But if you do choose fewer than five courses, you can still add another to your form up to 30 June, as long as you have not accepted or declined any offers. Nor do you have to choose five different universities if more than one course at the same institution attracts you – if you are keen on one institution in particular, applying for one course with lower entrance requirements than the other is a good way of hedging your bets. Universities are not allowed to see where else you have applied, or whether you have chosen the same subject elsewhere. But they will be aware of multiple applications within their own institution. Remember that it is more difficult to write a convincing personal statement if it has to cover two subjects.

For each course you select, you will need to put the UCAS code on the form – and you should check carefully that you have the correct code and understand any special requirements that may be detailed on the UCAS description of the course. It does not matter in what order you enter your choices as all are treated equally. You will also need to indicate whether you are applying for a deferred entry (for example, if you are taking a gap year – see page 88).

Education

This is where you provide details of the schools and colleges you have attended, and the qualifications you have obtained or are preparing for. The UCAS website gives plenty of advice on the ways in which you should enter this information, to ensure that all your relevant qualifications are included with their grades. While UCAS does not need to see qualification certificates, it can double-check results with the examination boards to ensure that no one has exaggerated their results.

In the Employment section that follows, add details of any paid jobs you have had (unpaid or voluntary work should be mentioned in your personal statement).

Personal statement

It is never too early to get cracking on your personal statement, as you will need it finished and in pristine form before making applications. Plan, write and check this statement with consideration and care – but do not agonise over the first line, this is best left to the end once the rest of the content has been included and distilled. Before sending, check again, and then once more for luck. A sloppily written personal statement is a wasted opportunity; like all elements of your UCAS form the level of attention to detail conveys a message to its readers about the author. One statement goes to all the universities you are applying to, so do not mention any universities by name. You have between 1,000 and 4,000 characters (including spaces) over a maximum of 47 lines to make a winning case for the strength of your application, and if it comes to a tie-break in admissions departments, the strongest personal statement gives that applicant the competitive edge. Even if yours does not reach such a deal-breaking stage, it is not worth taking the chance.

While stopping short of exaggerating or out-and-out lying, this is an opportunity to promote yourself; if that makes you cringe and clam up, ask for help from your parents, friends and teachers who will be able to list your talents.

The personal statement is not the place to discuss exam grades – qualifications are covered elsewhere on your UCAS form. Academic staff in charge of admissions look for potential beyond the high grades that increasing numbers of candidates bring. To stand out, do your homework on your chosen degree, show an interest in the subject by listening to podcasts, following lecturers on Twitter, reading articles. Highlight the experiences you've gained that are related to the syllabus you are applying to – clubs, lectures, visits, vlogs you have created, blogs you have written, work experience and wider reading around the subject.

Admissions tutors also value success in extracurricular activities such as drama, sport and the Duke of Edinburgh Award along with more individual or unusual interests. Standing out from the crowd is a good thing; if you enjoy reading, which many people do, say which authors or books inspire you, and why. Again, ensure your account is based on lived experiences, not what you think the UCAS admissions tutor would want you to say. Your UCAS form also has your teacher's reference and your statement should be in line with their summary of your abilities and interests.

Practical work experience or volunteering in medical or caring settings should be included by those applying to study medicine – but don't just list what you've done, reflect on what these experiences taught you about working as a doctor and how you are suited to the training and profession. The same approach goes for other vocational degrees; explain how you see yourself using the qualification. Work experience in any setting requires a similar approach; merely namechecking a prestigious company you have been lucky enough to get a placement with will not impress admissions tutors – tell them what you learnt from the organisation and how it relates to the degree you are applying to study.

Take advice from teachers and, if there is still time before you make your application, look for some subject-related activities that will help round out your statement. The admissions departments will understand the difficulties that the last two years' candidates will have had in getting real-life work experience during the pandemic and will take it into consideration.

Mention the accomplishments which suggest you will turn out to be a productive member of the university and, eventually, a successful graduate. Leading activities outside your school or college are ideal, or other responsibilities you have taken on. Show the admissions tutors that you can take initiative and be self-disciplined, since higher education involves much more independent study than sixth-formers are used to.

Think hard about why you want to study your chosen subject – especially if it is one you have not taken at school or college – and align your interests and skills with the course. Showing commitment to the full course is important, so admissions officers are convinced you will get good results for its duration. Some applicants' five choices will cover more than one subject, and in this situation try to make more general comments about your academic strengths and enthusiasms and avoid focusing on just one of the courses.

If you are an international (EU and non-EU) student you should also include why you want to study in the UK, detail your English language skills, and any English courses or tests you've taken and why you want to be an international student, rather than study in your own country. Mature students can talk about any alternative entry requirements you've used – such as an Access course – that show skills and knowledge you've gained through your previous experiences.

Take advantage of the help offered by your school or college. Your teachers see personal statements every year and will have a feel for ones that have gone down well for former students. UCAS provides a checklist of themes to cover and websites such as **www.studential.com** and **www.thestudentroom.co.uk** provide tips as well. By this point in your academic career the perils of plagiarism are probably clear to you, but do not be fooled into thinking you can cut and paste from one of the personal statement help websites. UCAS and universities have software that spots plagiarism and have caught out plenty of applicants over the years.

It may be tempting to shoehorn in as much information as the space will allow but err on the side of reserve. Admissions officers will have piles of these to read and giving them a thoughtfully edited statement is likely to be looked upon kindly. Compose your statement on Word or similar and avoid kicking off with a dreary cliché. Equally, though, do not start with an overly florid introduction – the best personal statements get to the point quickly. Let someone you trust proofread your statement before you paste a copy into Apply and press send; a second pair of eyes is hugely beneficial to a piece of work like the personal statement.

References

Hand-in-hand with your personal statement goes the reference from your school, college or, in the case of mature students, someone who knows you well, but is not a friend or family member.

UCAS tips on how to write your personal statement

Your personal statement should be unique, so there's no definite format for you to follow here – just take your time. Here are some guidelines for you to follow, but remember your personal statement needs to be 'personal'.

» Write in an enthusiastic, concise, and natural style – nothing too complex.

» Try to stand out, but be careful with humour, quotes, or anything unusual – just in case the admissions tutor doesn't have the same sense of humour as you.

» Structure your info to reflect the skills and qualities the unis and colleges value most – use the course descriptions to help you.

» Check the character and line limit – you have 4,000 characters and 47 lines. Some word processors get different values if they don't count tabs and paragraph spacing as individual characters.

» Proofread aloud, and get your teachers, advisers, and family to check. Then redraft it until you're happy with it, and the spelling, punctuation, and grammar are correct.

We recommend you write your personal statement first, then copy and paste it into your online application once you're happy with it. Make sure you save it regularly, as the site times out after 35 minutes of inactivity.

Timetable for applications for university admission in 2023

At the time of writing UCAS had not confirmed the exact dates for the application schedule. Please check the UCAS website for the most recent information.

2022

January onwards	Find out about courses and universities. Check schedule of open days.
February onwards	Attend open days.
early July	Registration starts for UCAS Apply.
mid September	UCAS starts receiving applications.
15 October	Final day for applications to Oxford and Cambridge, and for most courses in medicine, dentistry and veterinary science.

2023

15 January	Final day for all other applications from UK and EU students.
16 January–end June	New applications continue to be accepted by UCAS, but only considered by universities if the relevant courses have vacancies.
late February	Start of applications through UCAS Extra.
24 March	Final day for applications to art and design courses that specify this date.
end March	Universities should have sent decisions on all applications received by 15 January.
early May	Final time by which applicants have to decide on their choices if all decisions received by end March (exact date for each applicant will be confirmed by UCAS). **If you do not reply to UCAS, they will decline your offers.** UCAS must have received all decisions from universities if you applied by 15 January.
early June	Final time by which applicants have to decide on their choices if all decisions received by early May.
start of July	Any new application received from this time held until Clearing starts. End of applications through UCAS Extra.
early July	International Baccalaureate results published.
early August	SQA results published. Scottish Clearing starts. (to be confirmed)
mid August	A-level results published. Full Clearing and Adjustment starts. (to be confirmed)
end August	Adjustment closes. Last time for you to meet any offer conditions, after which university might not accept you.
late October	End of period for adding Clearing choices and last point at which a university can accept you through Clearing.

Since 2014, even referees who are not your teachers have been encouraged to predict your grades, although they are allowed to opt out of this process. Whatever the source, the reference has to be independent – you are specifically forbidden to change any part of it if you send off your own application – but that does not mean you should not try to influence what it contains.

Most schools and colleges conduct informal interviews before compiling a reference, but it does no harm to draw up a list of the achievements that you would like to see included, and ensure your referee knows what subject you are applying for. Referees cannot know every detail of a candidate's interests and most welcome an aide-memoire.

The UCAS guidelines skirt around the candidate's right to see their reference, but it does exist. Schools' practices vary, but most now show the applicant the completed reference. Where this is not the case, the candidate can pay UCAS a small fee for a copy, although at this stage it is obviously too late to influence the contents. Better, if you can, to see it before it goes off, in case there are factual inaccuracies that can be corrected.

Timing

The general deadline for applications through UCAS is 15 January, but even those received up to 30 June will be considered if the relevant courses still have vacancies. After that, you will be limited to Clearing, or an application for the following year. If your form arrives with the deadline looming, you may appear less organised than those who submitted in good time; and your application may be one of a large batch that receives a more cursory first reading than the early arrivals. Under UCAS rules, last-minute applicants should not be at a disadvantage, but why take the risk?

The best advice is to get your application in early: before Christmas, or earlier if possible. Applications are accepted from mid-September onwards, so the autumn half-term is a sensible target date for completing the process. Universities tend to start considering applications as soon as they arrive, so some early applicants will already be holding offers from universities. Other universities will not start making offers until after all applications are in, so offers will be sent out after 15 January.

Next steps

Once your application has been processed by UCAS, you will receive an email confirming that your application has been sent to your chosen universities and summarising what will happen next. The email will also confirm your Personal ID, which you can use to access "Track", the online system that allows you to follow the progress of your application. Check all the details carefully: you have 14 days to contact UCAS to correct any errors. Universities can make direct contact with you through Track, including arranging interviews.

After that, it is just a matter of waiting for universities to make their decisions, which can take days, weeks or even months, depending on the university and the course. Some obviously see an advantage in being the first to make an offer – it is a memorable moment to be reassured that at least one of your chosen institutions wants you – and may send their response almost immediately. Others take much longer, perhaps because they have so many good applications to consider, or maybe because they are waiting to see which of their applicants withdraw when Oxford and Cambridge make their offers. Universities are asked to make all their decisions by the end of March, and most have done so long before that.

Interviews

Unless you are applying for a course in health or education that brings you into direct contact with the public, the chances are you will not have a selection interview. For prospective medics, vets, dentists or teachers, a face-to-face assessment of your suitability (social distancing measures allowing) will be crucial to your chances of success. Likewise in the performing arts, the interview may be as important as your exam grades. Cambridge still interviews most applicants in all subjects and Oxford interviews about 40 to 45% of applicants, while a few of the other top universities also see a significant proportion. But the expansion of higher education has made it impractical to interview everyone, and many admissions experts are sceptical about interviews.

What has become more common, however, is the "sales" interview, where the university is really selling itself to the candidate. There may still be testing questions, but the admissions staff have already made their minds up and are actually trying to persuade you to accept an offer. Indeed, you will probably be given a clear indication at the end of the interview that an offer is on its way. The technique seems to work, perhaps because you have invested time and nervous energy in a sometimes lengthy trip, as well as acquiring a more detailed impression of both the department and the university.

The difficulty can come in spotting which type of interview is which. The "genuine" ones require lengthy preparation, revisiting your personal statement and reading beyond the exam syllabus. Impressions count for a lot, so dress smartly – even if your interview is being held via video call – and make sure that you are on time. Have a question of your own ready, as well as being prepared to give answers.

While you would not want to appear ignorant at a "sales" interview, lengthy preparation might be a waste of valuable time during a period of revision. Naturally, you should err on the side of caution, but if your predicted grades are well above the standard offer and the subject is not one that normally requires an interview, it is likely that the invitation is a sales pitch. It is still worth going, unless you have changed your mind about the application.

Offers

When your chosen universities respond to your application, there will be one of three answers:

» Unconditional Offer (U): This used to be a possibility only if you applied after satisfying the entrance requirements – usually if you were applying as a mature student, while on a gap year, after resitting exams or, in Scotland, after completing Highers. However, a number of universities competing for bright students now make unconditional offers to those who are predicted high grades – just how high will depend on the university. If you are fortunate (and able) enough to receive one, do not assume that grades are no longer important because they may be taken into consideration when you apply for jobs as a graduate.

» Conditional Offer (C): The vast majority of students will still receive conditional offers, where each university offers a place subject to you achieving set grades or points on the UCAS tariff.

» Rejection (R): You do not have the right qualifications or have lost out to stronger competition.

English universities were banned from making "conditional unconditional" offers during the pandemic until September 2021. This controversial type of offer – which only becomes unconditional once an applicant accepts it as their firm choice – was the focus of controversy pre-Covid, with more than 20 universities that were making the highest proportions of "conditional unconditional" offers named and shamed by the Education Secretary of the time, who argued that it was unethical to restrict such offers to those who made the university their first choice. Many of those on the list – and others – have now abandoned the practice.

One danger, from the student's point of view, is that an unconditional offer might tempt a candidate to lower their sights and accept a place that would not have been their first choice otherwise. As long as this is not the case, however, there is no reason to spurn such an offer if it comes, as long as you do not take your foot off the pedal in the run-up to exams.

If you have chosen wisely, you should have more than one offer to choose from, so you will be required to pick your favourite as your firm acceptance – known as UF if it was an unconditional offer and CF if it was conditional. Candidates with conditional offers can also accept a second offer, with lower grades, as an insurance choice (CI). You must then decline any other offers that you have.

You do not have to make an insurance choice – indeed, you may decline all your offers if you have changed your mind about your career path or regret your course decisions. But most people prefer the security of a back-up route into higher education if their grades fall short. Some 27,825 took up their insurance choice in 2020 – around 6% of the total number of the admission cycle's acceptances and a decline of 11% compared with 2019's insurance choice acceptances. You must be sure that your firm acceptance is definitely your first choice because you will be allocated a place automatically if you meet the university's conditions. You cannot change your mind at this stage if you decide you prefer your insurance choice because UCAS rules will not allow a switch.

The only way round those rules, unless your results are better than your highest offer (see Adjustment, below), is through direct contact with the universities concerned. Your firm acceptance institution has to be prepared to release you so that your new choice can award you a place in Clearing. Neither is under any obligation to do so but, in practice, it is rare for a university to insist that a student joins against their wishes. Admissions staff will do all they can to persuade you that your original choice was the right one – as it may well have been, if your research was thorough – but it will almost certainly be your decision in the end.

UCAS Extra

If things do go wrong and you receive five rejections, that need not be the end of your higher education ambitions. From late February until early July, you have another chance through UCAS Extra, a listing of courses that still have vacancies after the initial round of offers. Extra is sometimes dismissed (wrongly) as a repository of second-rate courses. In fact, even in the boom years for applications, most Russell Group universities still have courses listed in a wide variety of subjects.

You will be notified if you are eligible for Extra and can then select courses marked as available on the UCAS website. In order to assist students who choose different subjects after a full set of rejections in their original application, you will be able to submit a new personal statement for Extra. Applications are made, one at a time, through UCAS Track. If you do not receive an offer, or you choose to decline one, you can continue applying for other courses until you are successful. About half of those applying through Extra normally find a place. The numbers using Extra in 2020 declined for the fourth consecutive year to 4,450, but it remains a valuable route for those who need it. Why wait for the uncertainty of Clearing if there are places available on a course that you want?

Results Day

Rule Number One on results day is to be at home, or at least within easy communication – this is not the day to rely on intermittent Wi-Fi reception in a far-flung location, especially if there are complications. Not that you need to be at home to wait for the post or look for your name on a sixth-form noticeboard; Track has removed the agony of opening the envelope or scanning a results list. On the morning of A-level results day, the system informs those who have already won a place on their chosen course. You will not learn your grades until later, but at least your immediate future is clear.

The day might be stressful, unless you are absolutely confident that you achieved the required grades – more of a possibility in an era of modular courses with marks along the way.

If you get the grades stipulated in your conditional offer, the process should work smoothly, and you can begin celebrating. Track will let you know as soon as your place is confirmed, and the paperwork will arrive in a day or two. You can phone the university to double check, but it should not be necessary, and you will be joining a long queue of people doing the same thing.

If the results are not what you hoped – and particularly if you just miss your grades – you need to be on the phone and taking advice from your school or college. In a year when results are better than expected, some universities will stick to the letter of their offers, perhaps refusing to accept your AAC grades when they had demanded ABB. Growing numbers will forgive a dropped grade to take a candidate who is regarded as promising, rather than go into Clearing to recruit an unknown quantity. Admissions staff may be persuadable – particularly if there are extenuating personal circumstances, or the dropped grade is in a subject that is not relevant to your chosen course. Try to get a teacher to support your case and be persistent if there is any prospect of flexibility. Showing commitment is a good thing.

If your results are lower than predicted, one option is to ask for papers to be re-marked, as growing numbers do each year. The school may ask for a whole batch to be re-marked, and you should ensure that your chosen universities know this if it may make the difference to whether or not you satisfy your offer. If your grades improve as a result, the university will review its decision, but if by then it has filled all its places, you may have to wait until next year to start.

If you took Scottish Highers, you will have had your results for more than a week by the time the A-level grades are published. If you missed your grades, there is no need to wait for A-levels before you begin approaching universities. Admissions staff at English universities may not wish to commit themselves before they see results from south of the border, but Scottish universities will be filling places immediately and all should be prepared to give you an idea of your prospects.

Adjustment

If your grades are better than those demanded by your first-choice university, there is an opportunity to "trade up". The Adjustment Period runs from when you receive your results until 31 August, and you can only use it for five 24-hour periods during that period, so there is no time to waste. First, go into the Track system and click on "Register for Adjustment" and then contact your preferred institutions to find another place. If none is available, or you decide not to move, your initial offer will remain open. The number of students switching universities in this way has not increased as much as many observers expected, perhaps because Clearing has become much more flexible. Indeed, following several big drops numbers declined by 56% in 2020, but there were still 260 successful candidates. The process has become an established part of the system and, without the previous restrictions on the number of students they could recruit, many leading universities see it as a good source of talented undergraduates. UCAS does not publish a breakdown of which universities take part, but it is known that many students successfully go back to institutions that had rejected them at the initial application stage. Even if you are eligible for Adjustment, you may decide to stick with the offer you have, but it is worth at least exploring your options.

Clearing

If results morning did not elicit a "yay, I got in!" moment, put plan B into action and find a university place through Clearing. There will be plenty of options at a good range of universities. In 2020 nearly 70,500 students (nearly 14% of placed applicants) found a place via this route. The process is also increasingly popular as a sole route, and 17,800 entered Clearing direct in 2020 without submitting an initial application. Contrary to popular belief Clearing does not open for the first time on A-level results day, it begins on 5 July, IB results day, and runs until 19 October in 2022. The busiest day however, will be 18 August (in 2022), when A-level students find out their grades. As long as you are not holding any offers and you have not withdrawn your application, you are eligible automatically. You will be sent a Clearing number via Track to quote to universities.

With recruitment restrictions lifted, universities that used to regard their absence from Clearing as a point of pride are appearing in the Clearing vacancy lists, and candidates will see options at the coveted research-led institutions included. Certain courses have more availability than others though, and more universities are seeking to expand particularly in arts, social sciences and business subjects. Some subjects, such as medicine and dentistry, do not show up in Clearing as they are so oversubscribed. Only a handful of universities do not take part these days, including Oxford, Cambridge, Imperial, the LSE and St Andrews.

The most popular courses may fill up quickly, but many remain open up to and beyond the start of the academic year. And, at least at the start of the process, the range of courses with vacancies is much wider than in Extra. Most universities will list some courses, and most subjects will be available somewhere.

There are now two ways of entering Clearing: the traditional method of ringing universities that still have vacancies, or by signing up for the service in which up to five universities approach candidates with suitable grades for one of their courses. The latter, newer way of entering begins with an email from UCAS issuing a code word that universities will use when they make contact with applicants on Results Day or later. UCAS advises students to approach universities themselves in any case, but the new system may take some of the anxiety out of Clearing.

On the basis of making your own approaches, the first step is to trawl through the lists on the UCAS website, and elsewhere, before ringing the university offering the course that appeals most, and where you have a realistic chance of a place – do not waste time on courses where the standard offer is far above your grades. Universities have all hands on deck running Clearing hotlines and are adept at dealing with lots of calls in a short period, but even so you can spend a long time trying the phone while the most desirable places are beginning to disappear. If you can't get through, send an email setting out your grades and the course that interests you, but keep trying by phone too. Schools and colleges open on Results Day, and teachers should be willing to help with these calls, especially if you are in a panic. A good way of managing the calls is to let the teacher ring, get through to the university and then pass the phone to the applicant. At the end of calls do a round-up of next steps, as in the melee it is possible to misunderstand or forget things, such as requests for more information or follow-up forms to be filled out.

Wise students will not have waited for Results Day to draw up a list of possible Clearing targets. They will have had their list researched and ready to deploy if the time comes in advance. This way students can target the courses they know they want, without having to do so much last-minute research. Many universities publish lists of courses that are likely to be in Clearing on their websites from the start of August. Reconsider some of the courses you mulled over when making your original application, or others at your chosen universities that had lower entrance requirements. But beware of switching to another subject simply because you have the right grades – you still have to sustain your interest and be capable of succeeding over three or more years. Many of the students who drop out of degrees are those who chose the wrong course in a rush during Clearing.

In short, start your search immediately if you find yourself in Clearing, and act decisively, but do not panic. You can make as many approaches as you like, until you are accepted on the course of your choice. Remember that if you changed your personal statement for applications in Extra, this will be the one that goes to any universities that you approach in Clearing, so it may be difficult to return to the subjects in your original application.

Most of the available vacancies will appear in Clearing lists, but some of the universities towards the top of the league tables may have a limited number of openings that they choose not to advertise – either for reasons of status or because they do not want the administrative burden of fielding large numbers of calls to fill a handful of places. If there is a course that you find particularly attractive – especially if you have good grades and are applying late – it may be worth making a speculative call. Sometimes candidates holding offers drop grades and you may be on the spot at the right moment.

What are the alternatives?

If your results are lower than expected and there is nothing you want in Clearing, there are several things you can do. The first is to resit one or more subjects. The modular nature of most courses means that you will have a clear idea of what you need to do to get better grades. You can go back to school or college or try a "crammer". Although some colleges have a good success rate with re-takes, you have to be highly focused and realistic about the likely improvements. Some of the most competitive courses, such as medicine, may demand higher grades for a second application, so be sure you know the details before you commit yourself.

Other options are to get a job and study part-time, or to take a break from studying and return later in your career. You may have considered an apprenticeship before applying to university; the number and variety are growing all the time, so it may be worth another look. The UCAS Progress service provides information on apprenticeship opportunities post-16 and has a search tool for higher and degree apprenticeship vacancies.

The part-time route can be arduous – many young people find a job enough to handle without the extra burden of academic work. But others find it just the combination they need for a fulfilling life. It all depends on your job, your social life and your commitment to the subject you will study. It may be that a relatively short break is all that you need to rekindle your enthusiasm for studying. Many universities now have a majority of mature students, so you need not be out of place if this is your chosen route.

Taking a gap year

The other popular option is to take a gap year. In most years, about 7% of applicants defer their entry until the following year (though this declined in 2020's unusual recruitment round) while they travel or do voluntary or paid work. A whole industry has grown up around tailor-made activities, many of them in Asia, Africa or Latin America. Some have been criticised for doing more for the organisers than the underprivileged communities that they purport to assist, but there are programmes that are useful and character-building, as well as safe. Most of the overseas programmes are not cheap but raising the money can be part of the experience.

Various organisations can help you find voluntary work. Some examples include vInspired (**www.vinspired.com**) and Plan my Gap Year (**www.planmygapyear.co.uk**). Voluntary Service Overseas (**www.vsointernational.org**) works mainly with older volunteers but has an offshoot, run with five other volunteering organisations, International Citizen Service (**www.volunteerics.org**), that places 18–25-year-olds around the world.

The alternative is to stay closer to home and make your contribution through organisations like Volunteering Matters (**http://volunteeringmatters.org.uk**) or to take a job that will make higher education more affordable when the time comes. Work placements can be casual or structured, such as the Year in Industry Scheme (**www.etrust.org.uk**). Sponsorship is also available, mainly to those wishing to study science, engineering or business. Buyer beware: we cannot vouch for any of these and you need to be clear whether the aim is to make money or to plump up your CV. If it is the second, you may end up spending money, not saving it.

Many admissions staff are happy to facilitate gap years because they think it makes for more mature, rounded students than those who come straight from school. The longer-term benefits may also be an advantage in the graduate employment market. Both university admissions officers and employers look for evidence that candidates have more about them than academic ability. The experience you gain on a gap year can help you develop many of the attributes they are looking for, such as interpersonal, organisational and teamwork skills, leadership, creativity, experience of new cultures or work environments, and enterprise.

There are subjects – maths in particular – that discourage a break because it takes too long to pick up study skills where you left off. From the student's point of view, you should also bear in mind that a gap year postpones the moment at which you embark on a career. This may be important if your course is a long one, such as medicine or architecture.

If you are considering a gap year, it makes sense to apply for a deferred place, rather than waiting for your results before applying. The application form has a section for deferments. That allows you to sort out your immediate future before you start travelling or working and leaves you the option of changing your mind if circumstances change.

Useful websites

The essential website for making an application is, of course, that of UCAS:
www.ucas.com/undergraduate/applying-to-university
For applications to music conservatoires: **www.ucas.com/conservatoires**
For advice on your personal statement:
www.ucas.com/ucas/16-18-choices/search-and-apply/writing-ucas-progress-personal-statement

Gap years

For links to volunteering opportunities in the UK: **www.do-it.org**
For links to many gap year organisations: **www.yearoutgroup.org**

6 Where Students Come From

A long journey

The social profile of entrants to universities is as varied as the universities themselves. While there continues to be a focus on equal opportunities, whether expressed through the government's somewhat fuzzy "levelling up" agenda, or through pronouncements from the Office for Students on the need for fair admissions decisions that recognise the context in which qualifications at school have been gained – particularly now in light of the pandemic – the effectiveness of university actions in this area remains patchy.

Looking at current admissions figures only tells part of the story, however, as each university has begun its journey towards fairer admissions from a different place. It is unreasonable, therefore, to expect them all to reach the same destination simultaneously. Context is critical.

So, it is still true to say that children from whole sections of society and from disadvantaged backgrounds continue to be shut out of parts of our higher education system in anything other than insignificant numbers, while also acknowledging that our fourth social inclusion table shows universities of all kinds are more socially diverse now than they were in 2018.

There is accelerating progress at some of the most academically-selective universities – Oxford and Cambridge to the fore – in admitting more of the brightest students educated in non-selective state secondary schools. The black achievement gap appears to be narrowing, but at the same time the dropout gap between those recruited from the fifth of postcodes with lowest higher education participation and the other four-fifths is as wide as ever.

Chris Millward, the former director of fair access and participation at the Office for Students, warned shortly before his term of office ended in December: "Progress on the attainment gap between the most and least advantaged students moved into reverse towards the end of the last decade. These results precede the pandemic, which is considered to have harmed the learning of disadvantaged pupils more than others. If…universities are to improve equality of opportunity – and indeed avoid it worsening due to lost learning – they will need to take positive action during the coming years."

Some positive action appears to have been taken. Oxford soared to a record 68% admissions from the state sector (selective schools and comprehensives) in 2020, and maintained that in 2021, as public examinations endured a second year of disruption with grades awarded by teachers. Cambridge hit a record also with 70.6% state school admissions in 2020 and beat that again in 2021, getting above 71%. Full data from the pandemic years will start to filter through in next year's ranking, which will reveal whether Covid stalled or boosted progress towards greater equality.

The table

So why produce social inclusion tables? As well as providing a benchmark to measure change going forward, the key reason is that today's applicants want to know about the composition of the student body they will be joining. In the same way, today's students are interested in where their university ranks on green issues, through assessments such as that provided by People and Planet. Our fourth table shows why so much attention is being focused on the fairness or otherwise of the admissions process. Broadly speaking, the universities at the top of our academic ranking – those with the highest entry standards, the best job prospects and most competition for places – find themselves at the bottom of our social inclusion ranking. They recruit the bulk of their students from a much narrower cross-section of British society than those lower down our academic ranking.

The purpose of the table is not to point the finger. It is unfair to expect universities to magically overcome through admissions choices the inequalities built into the education system from nursery provision upwards and present in society more widely. However, the table does accurately reflect the reality on campus, identifying those institutions with fewer students educated in comprehensives or those where BAME students will find themselves among a very small minority.

We have two rankings; one for England and Wales, with Scotland standing alone on account of its different measure of social deprivation – the Scottish Index of Multiple Deprivation (SIMD) – which captures better the position in the 15 Scottish universities than the POLAR4 (Participation of Local Areas) measure used for England and Wales, but is not directly comparable. The two universities in Northern Ireland, Queen's Belfast and Ulster, are excluded from the ranking because differences in their school system, with a high proportion of selective grammar schools, make comparisons with the rest of the UK on social mix invalid via our methodology.

We do not include measures contained within the social inclusion tables as part of our wider academic ranking. There is good reason for this: a university with a poor record for social inclusion may still have an excellent record for teaching and research. It might be a very good university with an outstanding global and national reputation, but with a socially-narrow recruitment profile. By using the two multi-indicator, multi-institution tables that we publish together (alongside the relevant subject table) prospective students can identify the universities which are the best fit for them academically and where they might feel most at home socially or in tune politically.

We have added a new measure this year – bringing the social indicators in the ranking to nine for England and Wales and eight for Scotland – covering recruitment of white working class males. Although a lot of focus is rightly put on the representation and progression of ethnic minority students, one of our most intractable social problems is the academic under-achievement at all ages of boys from white, working class backgrounds, who are the least likely of any group to go to university. A report from the Education Select Committee in June 2021 highlighted the huge under-achievement of white pupils receiving free school meals compared to those of other ethnicities.

Looking at university entry specifically for children in receipt of free school meals, the committee's report showed that 16% of white British pupils won places, compared to 59% of black African pupils, 59% of Bangladeshi pupils and 32% of black Caribbean pupils. The chairman, Robert Halfon, MP, described it as a "major social injustice" that so little had been done over the years to address this gap in attainment.

The full list of equally-weighted indicators used in *The Times and The Sunday Times* social inclusion ranking for England and Wales is:

» recruitment from non-selective state schools

» recruitment from all ethnic minorities

» a measurement of the black attainment gap

» recruitment from deprived areas (using POLAR4)

» a measurement of the deprived areas dropout gap

» recruitment of white, working class males

» recruitment of first generation students

» recruitment of mature students (those 21 or older on admission)

» recruitment of disabled students

For Scottish institutions, there is no measure of the deprived areas dropout gap and the deprived areas measure is based on SIMD, rather than POLAR4, as outlined above.

With the exception of the admissions data for non-selective state schools, all the other indicators are in the public domain. This ranking is unique in combining these strands of data to build an overall picture of the social mix at each institution, and to measure university performance in the two key areas of black achievement and whether more students from the most deprived areas fail to complete their courses than those recruited from more advantaged districts.

The table is presented in a format that displays the raw data in all instances. No adjustment is made for university location, so a university with a strong, local recruitment pattern in an area of low ethnic minority population is unlikely do well on the two measures covering the ethnicity of the intake. This was most notably the case with Glyndŵr, which is for the fourth successive year the most socially inclusive university in the UK according to our ranking, but had just 5% of its 2020 entrants drawn from ethnic minorities.

However, by combining the indicators using a common statistical technique known as z-scoring, we have ensured no single indicator has a disproportionate effect on the overall score. The totals for each university were transformed to a scale with 1,000 for the top score and the performance of all universities measured relative to that of the university ranked No 1.

Just as with our academic ranking, the organisations providing the raw data for the table are not involved in the process of aggregation, and are not responsible for any conclusion or inferences we have made. Every care has been taken to ensure the accuracy of the table and accompanying analysis, but no responsibility can be taken for errors or omissions. The indicators used and what can be learned from them are outlined in turn below.

Non-selective state school admissions

For many years, the Higher Education Statistics Agency (HESA) has published as part of its Performance Indicators, the proportion of students admitted to universities from all state schools. Among the entrants included in this proportion are those attending the 163 state grammars in England and the voluntary grammars in Northern Ireland. However, state school admissions to all universities stripped of the academically-selective grammar school sector are not published elsewhere. Removing the grammars from the equation reveals the proportion of students admitted to each university in 2019–20 from the largely non-selective state secondary schools (comprehensives and most academies) attended by around 80% of university applicants.

This is the indicator that has seen greatest change over the four editions of our ranking. At five universities – one fewer than last year – less than half the students admitted came from comprehensives and academies: Imperial College London (42.4%, down 1 percentage point on last year's data), Oxford (45.6%, up 3.1 percentage points), the London School of Economics (47%, down 2 percentage points), Cambridge (47.8%, up 4.8 percentage points), and Durham (49%, up 0.3 percentage points). While the number of universities where the figure is less than 50% has only shifted down by one over our four years, it is particularly noticeable that Oxbridge has made significant efforts to recruit more equitably. The rate of change in the school backgrounds of entrants at Oxbridge is outstripping that at the other 22 Russell Group universities.

In our 2018 table, at Oxford, recruits from independent schools held a 2.9 percentage point lead over those from comprehensives and other non-selective state schools, 42.3% against 39.4%. This year, the figures are 37.8% and 45.6% respectively, a lead for the non-selective state sector of 7.8 percentage points, a swing of 5.35%. At Cambridge, even in 2018, the non-selective schools held a lead of 2.7 percentage points – 40.1% against 37.4% – over the private sector. This has widened to 16.9 percentage points – 47.8% against 30.9%, a swing of 7.1%. This trend is expected to continue.

Where are the independently educated school leavers going instead? More are going abroad, some to the United States, certainly, but other UK universities are seeing a significant upturn in recruitment of privately-educated students. Exeter has seen the proportion rise from 30.6% in our 2018 tables to 35.5% now, while St Andrews, the London School of Economics and Nottingham are among those to record smaller swings towards the independent sector.

The majority of universities (95, up one on last year) admit more than 80% of their students from non-selective state schools, and just 22 (two more than last year) take less than 70% of their intake from this demographic, 14 of these are members of the Russell Group of highly-selective, research-led universities.

Ethnic minority admissions

Data gathered from the 2020 admissions cycle by UCAS shows the proportion of entrants to each university drawn from black, Asian, mixed and other ethnic (BAME) minorities.

Eight London universities feature in the top ten, all with at least 70% of BAME students – ranking behind Aston which recruited 84.7% of its students from ethnic minorities in 2020. Bradford (77.3%), our University of the Year for Social Inclusion in 2019, is the only other non-London university in the top ten. The most ethnically diverse London universities are City (79.3%), SOAS (77.3%), Queen Mary (76.5%), Middlesex (76.4%), and Brunel (75.5%). Queen Mary, London is by some distance the most ethnically diverse of the Russell Group student communities.

The least ethnically diverse university is Harper Adams, in rural Shropshire, where 2.8% of the intake was drawn from ethnic minorities in 2020, closely followed by the Royal Agricultural University (4.4%). Both are institutions offering largely land-based courses, traditionally attracting low ethnic minority participation. The top two in our ranking, Bishop Grosseteste, in Lincoln, with 4.7% and Wrexham Glyndŵr (5%) have the third and fourth smallest proportions of BAME students

Black attainment gap

One of the two university output measures in the social inclusion ranking, the data here is among the most shocking in the survey. We were unable to create a reliable measure of the black achievement gap in ten universities – St Andrews (top of our academic ranking), Abertay,

Aberystwyth, Bishop Grosseteste, Harper Adams, Hartpury, Highlands and Islands, Leeds Arts, Queen Margaret, and Royal Agricultural University – because there were simply too few black graduates (91 in total between the ten universities) for effective analysis in the period 2017–19.

Where we could compare the proportion of white and black students gaining first-class or 2:1 degrees, the negative gap in achievement between the groups was at least 20 percentage points in 60 institutions. It was commendably narrow (less than ten percentage points) in 13. In none of them did black students achieve as well – or better even – than their white counterparts.

The universities with the widest negative percentage point gap for black achievement (showing low attainment by black students) were Buckingham (-41.2%), York St John (-40.1%), Arts University Bournemouth and Canterbury Christ Church (both -38.5%) and South Wales (-33.1%). On an encouraging note, the achievement gaps at these five poorest performing universities were all narrower than last year's bottom five. Those where black students performed the best in relation to their white counterparts were St George's, London (-1.1%) Edinburgh Napier (-2.8%), Imperial College London (-3.8%), Oxford (-4.1%) and the LSE (-5.4%), three of the top five places taken by Russell Group institutions, so often lagging in other areas of the social inclusion ranking.

White working class males

This measure of social inclusion is included for the first time and has triggered a few significant moves in the wider ranking. Its significance is discussed above, and it is one of the key metrics that universities are focusing on as they seek to diversify their intakes and make them as inclusive as possible. The highest achievers are Plymouth Marjon (13.4% of entrants in 2020), Staffordshire (12.4%), Sheffield Hallam (11.7%), Solent (11.4%) and Liverpool John Moores (11.1%). In each instance, the universities make gains in our overall ranking.

At the opposite end of the spectrum, at these five institutions white male students with a working class background make up between 1 in 90 and 1 in 55 of students: Buckingham (1.1%), University College London (1.7%), and St George's London, Cambridge and SOAS (all 1.8%). While more common than unicorns, white working class men are a rare sighting here and at the 40 universities where they make up fewer than one in 25 of the student population.

Deprived areas

This data is drawn from the 2020 UCAS admissions cycle and looks at the home postcode of all recruits, putting them into one of five pots, according to the level of participation in higher education. For England and Wales, this indicator records the proportion of students recruited from Quintile 1 (of POLAR4 data) – the 20% of areas that have the lowest participation rates. In Scotland, it records the proportion of students recruited from postcodes which fall into the 20% with the highest levels of deprivation measured by the Scottish Index of Multiple Deprivation (SIMD20).

Like all indicators, this one has limitations, chief among which is that London overall has high participation rates in higher education relative to the rest of the UK, so very few London-based entrants fall into Quintile 1. This means that London universities score relatively poorly across the board on this measure, even if they have a socially diverse intake.

Teesside (31%), our University of the Year for Social Inclusion and Sunderland (28.6%), which held the title in our previous edition, record the highest proportions of students recruited from Quintile 1. Both institutions recruit heavily within their immediate region, the northeast being the English region with the lowest participation rate in higher education. Staffordshire (28.4%)

is ranked third on this measure. City University London (2.1%), followed by the Royal Agricultural University (2.3%) and SOAS (2.8%) have the lowest rates of recruitment from Quintile 1.

In Scotland, the highest rates of recruitment of students falling into SIMD20 are to be found at West of Scotland (29.6%) and Glasgow Caledonian (22.5%), while the two Aberdeen universities, Robert Gordon (5.2%) and Aberdeen (8.6%) have the lowest rates.

Deprived areas dropout gap

This indicator is used in the England and Wales social inclusion ranking only. Drawing upon the same POLAR4 data as above, it measures student outcomes from each of the five social quintiles. The proportion of students dropping out who were recruited from Quintile 1 is compared to the same proportion from Quintiles 2, 3, 4 and 5. A negative score indicates a higher proportion of students is dropping out from Quintile 1 than those recruited from more advantaged areas. It identifies those universities where Quintile 1 students who do get in are more likely to fail to see their courses through.

The universities with the biggest negative percentage point gap for deprived area dropouts are Liverpool Hope (-9%), Chichester (-7%), Cumbria and Falmouth (both -6%), and York St John (-5.7%). This is especially concerning for Liverpool Hope, York St John and Chichester, which are among the 20 universities to admit most students from Quintile 1.

As Chris Millward observed in a blog for the Higher Education Policy Institute in November 2021: "The promotion of equality of opportunity is only meaningful if it improves outcomes: there is no point to it otherwise, let alone spending more than half a billion pounds on it each year as we do in English higher education today."

The universities performing most strongly, where a smaller proportion of students from the most deprived areas dropout compared to the rest, are Suffolk (+7%), Ravensbourne and Bedfordshire (both +6%), Goldsmiths, London (+5.9%) and West London (+4%).

First generation students

This measure records the proportion of students recruited from homes where neither parent attended university. It is considered one of the most informative in assessing the overall inclusiveness of recruitment strategies. Once again, performance varies considerably from those recruiting 60% or more first generation students – Newman (75.2%), Bradford (66.5%), Bedfordshire and Wolverhampton (both 65.8%), Bishop Grosseteste (63.9%), and Wrexham Glyndŵr (60.6%) – to those where fewer than 25% of students come from such homes – Oxford (14.8%), Cambridge (15.4%), St Andrews (18%), Edinburgh (20.3%), Bristol (22.9%), Durham (23%), and Bath and Imperial College London (24.3%). Among those admitting fewest first generation students, only Edinburgh and Durham were admitting fewer than in last year's ranking. So, again slow progress is being made.

Mature students

Mature students are returners to education and often win places with "life" qualifications, rather than A-levels. This immediately makes the group more diverse than younger entrants. The number of young entrants (those aged 20 or under) was subtracted from the overall number of entrants recorded by HESA in 2019–20 to calculate the proportion of mature students (those aged 21 or over).

The age of the student population can have a major impact on the social scene on campus. Older students, particularly those with partners (and even children) are less likely to be found clubbing or propping up the bar late into the evening. Universities with a very small proportion of mature undergraduates – the LSE (1.8%), Loughborough (1.9%), Oxford (2.2%), Bath

(2.9%) and Durham (4%) – are likely to have a livelier campus social life than Buckinghamshire New (78% mature admissions) Suffolk (77.1%), Wrexham Glyndŵr (76.2%), Bedfordshire (74.4%), and London Metropolitan (69%).

Disabled students

This indicator measures the proportion of all students in receipt of Disability Support Allowance (DSA). It is part of the bigger HESA dataset on widening participation, published in February 2021, and is based on data from the 2019–20 academic year.

As with other indicators, there is a significant difference between the universities at the top – Wrexham Glyndŵr where HESA records 20% of students in receipt of DSA, Harper Adams (18%) and Arts London (17%) – and those at the bottom – West of Scotland (1.5%), Highlands and Islands (1.7%) and Imperial College London (2.3%).

The overall picture

It is not possible to appear near the top of the social inclusion rankings if an institution is only achieving well on one or two of the nine measures that *The Times and The Sunday Times* have chosen. Success in the table comes from broadly-based achievement in recruiting from areas of society least represented in higher education, and then seeing those students complete their degrees and achieve well. Equally, a university that appears near the bottom is not falling short in one or two regards; it reflects a pattern of recruitment – or poor performance – affecting swathes of society.

A different set of metrics looking at the same subject might produce a very different looking table, which is why it is necessary to understand what is being measured here. Based on the measures we have chosen the top three in the academic rankings – St Andrews, Oxford and Cambridge – appear at the bottom (or second bottom in Scotland in St Andrews' case) of our social inclusion rankings. Wrexham Glyndŵr, placed =110th in our academic ranking of 132 institutions, is top for social inclusion. Sixteen of the bottom 20 universities for social inclusion in England and Wales (and two of the bottom three in Scotland) are highly selective Russell Group universities.

Used in conjunction, our academic and social inclusion rankings provide an intriguing insight into likely academic and professional success, the quality of the student experience, and the mix of students to be found in lecture theatres and after-hours clubs and bars. But whatever the student recruitment profile of the university you are considering, don't rule it out on that basis. If applicants from non-traditional backgrounds don't apply to universities – all of which are now pledging to broaden their intakes – it will only make it easier for the status quo to prevail.

Alastair McCall

Social Inclusion Ranking for England and Wales

Rank	Last year's rank	Institution	State educated (non-grammar) (%)	Ethnic minorities (%)	Black achievement gap (%)	White working class males (%)	Low participation areas (%)	Low participation areas dropout gap (%)	First generation students (%)	Disabled (%)	Mature (%)	Total
1	1	Wrexham Glyndŵr	97.9	5.0	-23.3	6.2	27.1	n/a	60.6	20.0	76.2	1,000
2	21	Bishop Grosseteste	95.4	4.7	n/a	6.0	27.9	1	63.9	15.8	28.9	899
3	6	Plymouth Marjon	97.2	6.4	-29.6	13.4	19.3	1	58.2	15.6	37.8	888
4	8	Teesside	98.6	12.5	-20.3	10.5	31.0	-2.6	57.2	10.2	44.8	867
5	2	Bolton	97.7	32.7	-21.4	5.4	21.3	1	54.7	10.3	66.8	848

Rank	#	Institution										
6	13	Staffordshire	97.2	19.1	-32.2	12.4	28.4	-1.9	59.7	11.2	35.1	843
7	25	Suffolk	97.3	32.8	-30.0	2.6	23.7	7	59.2	5.3	77.1	831
8	17=	Wales Trinity St David	98.0	6.5	-12.2	5.9	13.6	n/a	45.9	14.2	66.6	823
9	11	Sunderland	95.8	27.5	-27.1	7.9	28.6	-2.2	59.5	6.3	65.3	808
10=	4	Bedfordshire	98.1	58.3	-31.9	2.4	9.0	6	65.8	4.5	74.4	781
10=	22	West London	94.9	66.7	-21.5	3.1	7.2	4	53.2	8.5	57.6	781
12=	3	Newman	98.3	44.1	-30.9	4.6	18.4	-3	75.2	11.4	43.0	780
12=	5	Bradford	93.8	77.3	-10.1	2.2	10.4	-1.7	66.5	10.2	25.1	780
14	12	East London	96.3	70.1	-21.5	3.3	8.5	2.7	56.6	7.2	55.2	775
15	7	Wolverhampton	97.0	51.2	-22.8	4.6	21.7	-4.3	66.4	8.6	46.5	771
16	17=	Derby	96.2	30.2	-26.5	6.9	23.8	-1.6	53.3	11.2	36.0	764
17	9	Anglia Ruskin	92.3	36.6	-15.0	4.5	16.1	-0.3	53.9	5.4	67.8	753
18	10	London South Bank	95.7	70.4	-22.5	3.1	6.0	3.5	52.2	8.8	47.0	752
19	30	Hull	91.9	11.5	-10.8	8.4	27.6	-3.4	50.3	7.4	31.9	751
20	24	Huddersfield	95.4	44.2	-14.2	6.0	15.3	-0.2	56.7	8.3	21.2	750
21	64	Ravensbourne, London	92.9	48.3	-13.9	6.1	5.9	6	46.6	8.6	17.4	745
22=	14	Greenwich	92.9	56.2	-18.3	6.1	6.9	3	56.0	5.8	34.0	735
22=	15	Leeds Trinity	96.1	45.8	-17.6	4.1	19.8	-4	59.8	4.9	62.1	735
24	44	Sheffield Hallam	94.5	22.4	-25.9	11.7	23.6	-3.1	51.7	8.5	20.1	733
25	86	Cardiff Metropolitan	94.0	14.3	-16.4	8.2	16.1	n/a	48.9	10.1	23.9	722
26	34	Buckinghamshire New	94.7	30.4	-12.4	5.4	10.7	0.5	47.2	2.7	78.0	721
27	20	Middlesex	98.2	76.4	-15.5	2.8	4.0	1.9	57.5	5.7	34.3	720
28	27	Goldsmiths, London	89.6	48.8	-19.7	4.4	5.3	5.9	45.5	9.8	22.0	701
29	28=	London Metropolitan	96.9	62.4	-24.9	2.3	6.9	1	54.2	5.3	69.0	700
30	31	Roehampton	96.3	63.9	-24.3	5.3	4.2	2.9	49.2	5.9	43.6	699
31	48=	Chester	93.2	9.6	-18.3	7.8	21.3	-2.9	54.3	6.9	33.4	692
32	54	Solent	96.2	18.4	-30.6	11.4	18.3	-0.8	48.5	5.5	35.0	689
33=	19	Birmingham City	97.3	59.1	-17.1	3.7	15.2	-1.2	56.2	5.5	22.7	687
33=	36	Gloucestershire	92.4	9.7	-19.2	7.4	13.4	-0.1	47.1	11.0	28.9	687
35	35	Northampton	97.2	42.3	-23.6	4.5	16.8	0.3	52.2	5.7	34.2	680
36	83	Aberystwyth	90.4	7.2	n/a	9.9	14.1	n/a	39.1	12.1	16.2	678
37	40=	De Montfort	95.0	54.2	-24.2	4.9	14.7	-0.9	47.9	10.4	15.4	675
38	62=	Portsmouth	91.5	30.3	-20.2	7.7	15.6	-1	48.1	8.5	13.3	664
39	43	Norwich Arts	93.8	11.5	-20.5	8.8	18.2	-5	45.8	13.1	13.4	662
40	56	Keele	84.4	34.1	-15.2	5.9	19.8	-0.3	43.7	7.8	15.0	661
41	38=	Creative Arts	93.6	24.3	-23.1	5.4	15.1	0	47.5	10.6	17.2	652
42	33	South Wales	95.5	10.9	-33.1	7.0	23.8	n/a	44.5	8.4	36.9	650
43	42	Edge Hill	96.8	8.6	-21.5	7.6	18.8	-3.4	55.3	6.8	25.0	647
44=	32	Central Lancashire	96.2	30.9	-26.8	7.0	14.3	-3.6	51.1	7.5	39.2	645
44=	51	Cumbria	95.7	13.4	-24.3	5.2	18.2	-6	45.8	8.8	52.6	645
46	59=	Winchester	93.8	11.5	-26.8	6.3	14.9	-0.8	49.6	12.1	18.4	644
47	46	Queen Mary, London	81.0	76.5	-5.7	2.5	3.6	1.9	46.0	6.5	9.0	638
48	37	Brunel London	89.6	75.5	-18.7	3.6	3.9	1.9	51.2	6.3	11.2	635
49	79	Worcester	95.2	12.6	-24.1	6.0	14.7	-5	51.2	11.6	35.6	634
50	26	Arts London	90.0	31.7	-23.4	4.0	7.2	-0.3	38.2	17.0	18.0	632
51=	57=	Bangor	92.0	7.9	-24.7	7.1	13.1	n/a	43.1	10.8	30.0	625
51=	57=	Canterbury Christ Church	94.3	27.5	-38.5	6.7	18.0	-3.3	59.2	7.8	37.0	625
53	62=	Hertfordshire	95.3	57.1	-23.7	3.6	7.0	1.7	50.9	5.4	23.9	624

Social Inclusion Ranking for England and Wales cont

Rank	Last year's rank	Institution	State educated (non-grammar) (%)	Ethnic minorities (%)	Black achievement gap (%)	White working class males (%)	Low participation areas (%)	Low participation areas dropout gap (%)	First generation students (%)	Disabled (%)	Mature (%)	Total
54=	66=	Salford	96.7	34.8	-26.2	6.4	15.6	-2	46.1	6.3	26.9	619
54=	72=	Essex	91.2	43.8	-15.6	5.6	13.9	-1.6	46.9	4.7	17.5	619
56	52	Coventry	92.6	60.8	-22.5	4.1	12.2	-0.8	45.7	4.2	32.8	618
57=	38=	Aston	99.5	84.7	-16.2	2.1	10.8	-1.6	53.1	3.2	5.4	616
57=	70=	Liverpool John Moores	88.8	13.1	-22.1	11.1	17.3	-4.2	52.2	4.7	17.3	616
59	16	Kingston	95.2	62.6	-19.3	3.3	6.1	-2.4	52.7	6.9	24.4	614
60	69	Plymouth	87.4	13.0	-24.1	7.4	15.1	-3.1	45.0	10.0	29.3	611
61	59=	Northumbria	89.7	11.2	-25.2	8.4	17.5	-2.2	51.3	6.3	19.7	608
62	28=	Liverpool Hope	89.7	12.8	-27.2	8.9	24.9	-9	50.2	10.5	19.2	605
63	23	Westminster	94.7	70.2	-23.2	3.3	4.3	0.2	55.3	5.2	15.7	604
64	50	Leeds Arts	93.1	9.8	n/a	4.1	13.1	0	42.4	12.5	9.6	603
65	61	Lincoln	93.2	10.1	-29.5	9.0	19.4	-3.2	52.1	6.7	10.5	591
66	68	West of England	91.3	19.4	-31.1	6.9	15.6	-1.5	42.5	9.3	24.9	590
67	72=	Bournemouth	90.8	14.9	-26.0	7.7	11.4	-1.1	46.8	8.3	17.7	588
68	45	St Mary's, Twickenham	91.8	31.9	-14.2	6.5	6.8	-4	44.7	7.0	23.3	582
69	55	St George's, London	67.9	63.4	-1.1	1.8	5.1	n/a	35.3	7.4	31.8	576
70=	70=	Manchester Metropolitan	93.5	38.6	-20.5	5.4	14.0	-3.9	50.6	5.0	14.0	572
70=	84	Leeds Beckett	91.9	21.7	-19.4	7.8	17.2	-4.1	39.1	6.5	13.5	572
72	47	City, London	87.8	79.3	-16.9	2.1	2.1	n/a	58.1	3.8	13.0	565
73	77	Leicester	81.1	57.3	-15.3	3.4	10.1	0.6	39.4	5.8	9.4	564
74=	65	Bath Spa	91.1	8.7	-21.9	5.1	14.6	-5.6	42.6	11.4	29.6	563
74=	66=	Brighton	89.4	20.8	-27.3	7.1	12.9	-5.3	45.7	10.1	24.3	563
76=	48=	SOAS, London	79.9	77.3	-13.6	1.8	2.8	n/a	43.4	8.1	15.2	562
76=	88=	Swansea	90.7	18.0	-13.5	6.9	11.6	n/a	36.9	4.8	19.7	562
78	81	Harper Adams	76.1	2.8	n/a	5.6	7.1	n/a	36.2	18.0	11.3	556
79	85	Sheffield	76.3	22.1	-8.7	4.9	10.4	-1.4	32.7	9.9	12.0	553
80	82	Kent	90.3	42.7	-21.3	5.4	10.2	-2.2	46.4	5.6	8.5	550
81	40=	Chichester	94.4	6.8	-30.7	6.7	19.5	-7	47.6	10.7	18.7	548
82	74	Hartpury	90.1	5.6	n/a	5.9	11.5	-4	48.1	9.2	16.7	542
83	80	Royal Holloway, London	76.1	52.1	-16.8	3.3	5.5	1.2	39.0	7.6	5.7	530
84	76	East Anglia	78.7	21.4	-11.5	6.3	11.7	-3.4	39.5	6.5	11.3	529
85	75	King's College London	64.4	63.0	-9.7	2.0	3.7	-0.5	37.2	6.4	21.3	511
86	87	Sussex	80.0	26.5	-18.7	4.7	7.9	-2.9	39.8	10.0	10.7	510
87	91	Nottingham Trent	87.2	28.0	-27.4	5.5	13.4	-2.8	42.8	7.0	9.7	507
88	53	York St John	94.8	6.6	-40.1	6.3	19.8	-5.7	47.5	8.1	19.3	488
89	93	Lancaster	78.6	18.9	-17.2	5.3	8.2	-0.4	35.2	7.2	4.4	483
90	94	Manchester	71.9	32.8	-13.7	3.2	8.9	-0.2	33.0	7.1	8.2	481
91	88=	Surrey	77.5	34.6	-17.5	4.3	6.8	-1.3	41.5	4.9	11.4	479
92	92	Reading	73.6	33.2	-16.3	3.4	7.0	-1.3	35.1	7.4	8.3	463
93	97	Falmouth	91.3	6.4	-25.8	5.7	9.5	-6	33.3	10.9	18.1	461
94	78	Arts Bournemouh	92.9	13.2	-38.5	4.5	11.1	-1	39.3	9.0	12.3	458

Rank	Last year's rank	Institution									
95=	90	Loughborough	68.5	24.9	-12.0	5.3	7.9	-3.6	32.9	8.4	1.9	450
95=	109	York	70.9	14.3	-12.9	5.1	9.5	-2	31.9	6.9	6.1	450
97	99	Southampton	72.3	23.2	-18.8	4.8	7.4	-0.6	34.4	6.1	8.9	447
98	95	Oxford Brookes	64.8	19.6	-22.3	3.5	6.9	-2.5	37.5	9.3	15.9	420
99	102	Warwick	62.4	42.5	-11.2	3.2	6.6	-3.3	31.2	5.7	9.0	411
100	110	University College London	50.6	55.5	-5.9	1.7	3.8	0.6	26.7	4.5	8.0	409
101	105	Cardiff	77.1	18.5	-18.7	4.1	9.8	n/a	31.4	5.3	10.9	407
102	103=	Leeds	70.0	22.1	-18.8	3.8	8.1	-3.1	32.9	6.9	7.5	397
103	100=	Birmingham	68.4	34.1	-15.0	2.4	7.6	-1.6	30.7	5.2	4.4	394
104	98	Liverpool	74.5	16.8	-24.2	4.8	8.6	-4.5	40.6	6.3	7.4	393
105	103=	London School of Economics	47.0	61.4	-5.4	2.4	4.8	n/a	31.3	4.2	1.8	376
106	107	Newcastle	64.8	14.0	-12.3	4.8	8.3	-4.1	33.0	4.0	5.5	367
107	106	Bath	54.1	18.3	-7.0	3.6	5.5	-0.8	24.3	5.7	2.9	366
108	108	Nottingham	63.4	29.6	-18.7	3.2	7.1	-2.5	30.1	5.5	7.4	361
109	111	Exeter	52.8	10.7	-13.4	3.6	6.3	-1.5	26.3	7.8	7.1	355
110	115	Durham	49.0	13.5	-8.7	3.0	6.9	0.4	23.0	5.8	4.0	351
111	96	Buckingham	68.5	38.7	-41.2	1.1	7.8	n/a	35.0	5.9	42.1	331
112	112	Imperial College London	42.4	60.6	-3.8	2.2	4.1	n/a	24.3	2.3	9.7	329
113	100=	Royal Agricultural	54.7	4.4	n/a	3.0	2.3	n/a	38.4	9.5	22.1	316
114	113	Bristol	59.0	20.3	-11.7	2.6	6.1	-3.9	22.9	5.5	5.8	308
115	114	Oxford	45.6	23.8	-4.1	2.1	4.2	n/a	14.8	7.9	2.2	289
116	116	Cambridge	47.8	29.3	-6.6	1.8	4.8	n/a	15.4	3.9	4.6	246

Social Inclusion Ranking for Scotland

Rank	Last year's rank	Institution	State educated (non-grammar) (%)	Ethnic minorities (%)	Black achievement gap (%)	White working class males (%)	Deprived areas (%)	First generation students (%)	Disabled (%)	Mature (%)	Total
1	1	Abertay	96.4	9.5	n/a	11.3	16.3	47.5	6.2	35.6	1,000
2	2	West of Scotland	98.4	9.3	-22.4	7.5	29.6	47.0	1.5	54.2	960
3	7	Edinburgh Napier	94.5	10.5	-2.9	7.5	15.1	39.7	5.3	39.2	918
4	3	Queen Margaret, Edinburgh	97.6	7.6	n/a	6.3	13.8	38.2	12.0	38.0	892
5	4	Glasgow Caledonian	96.0	13.5	-32.0	8.7	22.5	43.9	2.4	38.8	876
6	11	Stirling	89.1	6.7	-5.7	6.3	13.1	38.1	10.4	24.3	812
7	9	Highlands and Islands	97.4	3.9	n/a	11.1	10.5	43.9	1.7	51.1	796
8	5	Heriot-Watt	83.9	15.0	-16.0	7.7	11.0	32.7	5.2	23.0	756
9	6	Dundee	83.5	11.5	-14.4	5.5	16.2	40.8	4.5	26.6	752
10	10	Strathclyde	88.9	12.5	-23.5	6.7	19.6	36.5	3.1	17.0	711
11	12	Aberdeen	79.2	14.5	-12.3	7.6	8.6	30.0	5.1	15.6	687
12	8	Robert Gordon	94.3	10.0	-32.5	6.9	5.2	34.4	6.1	34.6	633
13	14	Glasgow	80.1	11.9	-13.0	4.5	13.5	25.9	3.1	15.6	566
14	15	St Andrews	57.5	15.3	n/a	3.4	11.0	18.0	5.7	8.9	404
15	13	Edinburgh	56.6	13.1	-20.0	2.8	10.8	20.3	5.5	7.1	386

7 Finding Somewhere to Live

A bottle of Fairy Liquid and a packet of sponge scourers – plus some aptitude for putting them to use – should be among the must-haves for any student if smooth relations with housemates are to be achieved. Leaving the dirty dishes out is the biggest bugbear among student house-sharers, the National Student Survey 2021 revealed. Failing to help with cleaning comes second and making too much noise ranks as the third most annoying habit.

For most freshers, starting university will be the first taste of independent living, and learning the ropes of looking after themselves and rubbing along with others takes a little practice. But there are bigger issues regarding student housing than whether one flatmate has finished another's milk without asking. Safe, comfortable and affordable accommodation is key to ensuring students can settle happily into all that university life has to offer. And aside from tuition fees, it represents the biggest financial outlay.

According to the latest figures published by student housing charity Unipol and the National Union for Students (NUS) in their 2021 Accommodation Costs Survey, the average annual cost for a room in purpose-built accommodation in the UK now stands at £7,374 outside London, and £9,488 in the capital. This works out at an average weekly rent of £166 in the 2021–22 letting year. It is worth noting that these rents almost always include all utilities and the internet. University-owned halls are only marginally cheaper, at £13 less per week on average than those in the private sector. Rents have risen by 16% since the last Unipol/NUS survey in 2018/19 and 61% since its 2011–12 edition. Save the Student put average rents across all types of housing slightly lower in their 2021 report, at £421 per month.

At either rate, even if students receive the full maintenance loan, rent consumes almost all of it. Going by the Unipol/NUS figures, 88% of a maintenance fund gets eaten by rent in London, leaving students just £38 per week to spend on anything else. Outside of London, accommodation costs account for 72% of the maximum loan, leaving students with £69.52 to spend on other living costs.

The most common source of rent help comes from parents, who on average stump up £44 per week for their student's accommodation, or £2,288 over a 12-month period, according to Save the Student.

So, what are students getting in return for such investment? The chances are it will bear little resemblance to the standard of accommodation their parents put up with when at university. Student accommodation has evolved enormously over the years. As universities move away from their own accommodation provision, private providers now dominate the market, and represented 70% of the bed spaces surveyed in the new Unipol/NUS report. En-suite and studio rooms are replacing cheaper, older stock in university-owned halls, as ambitious refurbishments modernise campuses up and down the country.

With demand for halls greater than supply, rents rising, and billions of pounds committed to residences each year, private student housing has become one of the property market's biggest growth areas. But not all developments are completed on time. A recent example of students being let down by unfinished housing was in Glasgow at Bridle Works, which was advertised as luxury new accommodation featuring top-class amenities including a gym, home cinema and roof terrace. But when students arrived at the complex in autumn 2021 it was still under construction and they were met with holes in floors, exposed wiring and leaking plumbing.

Some 38 international students wrote to the accommodation provider, Novel Student, detailing issues such as a lack of hot water for long periods, dust and dirt in bedrooms from ongoing building work, and radiators falling off walls. The complainants said they were "misled" because the company never revealed that the 20-storey, 422-room block was still being built. Novel Student blamed Covid-19 for being behind schedule. It offered to reimburse students for days missed at the property and accommodated them in hotels, but reportedly did not address student requests for reduced rent for disruption and discomfort faced while living there.

Lockdown life

The unique and unsettling experience of living in student digs through a global health pandemic, of course, created its own challenges. Lockdowns forced students to spend endless hours confined to their bedrooms. As venues and high streets shuttered, students' social lives were disrupted beyond all recognition. Online learning meant that in practice students could study from anywhere that had decent Wi-Fi, and many looked to decamp home and save on rent. However, they were often still locked into their residential contracts and many students felt that they were paying out large sums of money in rent for accommodation they had no use for.

The National Student Accommodation Survey 2021 found that although around 42% of students in the survey had been able to spend the entire 2020–21 year in their properties,

Term-time accommodation of full-time and sandwich students 2019–20		
University provided accommodation	360,745	18.1%
Private sector halls	175,255	8.8%
Parental home	368,475	18.5%
Own residence	379,205	19.0%
Other rented accommodation	569,130	28.6%
Other	67,425	3.4%
Not in attendance/unknown	72.565	3.6%

Source HESA 2020 (adapted)

Top Tenancy Problems for Students		
1	Lack of water/heating	32%
2	Damp	29%
3	Disruptive building work	21%
=4	Rodents and pests	16%
=4	Inappropriate landlord visits	16%
=6	Dangerous living conditions	5%
=6	Break-in or burglary	5%
8	Other	8%

Source: National Student Accommodation Survey 2021
Based on 1,300 responses **www.savethestudent.org**

another 43% spent three months or less there. In hindsight, more than two in five would have chosen their accommodation differently. Meanwhile the numbers who moved in with their parents after Christmas 2020 went up by a third, following the government's "travel window" for them to return home in December.

Variant coronavirus strains permitting, students of 2022 onwards will not have to cope with lockdown living. The Unipol/NUS 2021 Accommodation Costs Survey revealed that when students applied for price reductions in the pandemic, private providers were more responsive in adjusting pricing to fill rooms: 29% reported having significantly discounted rents and 41% were offered greater incentives such as cashback and vouchers. By contrast, the university sector was far less agile in dealing with altered conditions: 84% said they had not been offered any changes to pricing. The National Student Accommodation Survey calculated that the average partial rent discount was £75 per week. It also estimated that across the whole UK student population nearly £1billion (£933,270,890) of rent was spent on rooms that sat empty during 2020–21.

With the pandemic shift to online learning, student accommodation became a place of work as well as a place to live. Virtual learning to one extent or another is here to stay in undergraduate teaching, and so students should look for good working and learning conditions in accommodation.

Halls of residence
First-years are guaranteed a space in halls by many universities, but spaces are usually limited so it pays to meet application deadlines. Applying early might help you get first pick of the different types of room available, too. Any rooms left over are allocated to postgraduates, international students in any year of study and some returning, non-first-year students. Institutions that recruit significant numbers in Clearing have rooms available late in the admissions cycle. Some universities reserve a small proportion of accommodation for students with families.

While halls are generally the preferred option for freshers, they are also the priciest – not only in private developments but in many cases in university-owned accommodation too, making affordability a sticking point – as discussed earlier. Some private blocks come with high-spec interiors and swanky extras including gyms. Most developments are in big complexes, but there are also niche providers such as Student Cribs, which converts properties to a more luxurious standard than usual digs and rents them to students. It now operates in 25 cities.

Unite Students is one of the country's biggest providers and has 73,000 beds across 173 properties in 25 university towns and cities in the UK, some provided in partnership with universities and others in developments that serve more than one institution. UPP has over 36,000 residential places in operation or under construction in complexes built for 15 universities, usually on campus, and where rents are negotiated with the university, often in consultation with the students' union.

The 2021 National Student Accommodation Survey found that 15% of students were living in private halls, up from 8% four years ago, but university accommodation still accounts for a much higher 34% of students, while 39% have a private landlord, 10% live with their parents, and 1% own their home.

The Student Housing Awards are a recently launched roll of honour for halls of residence, both university-owned and private. The top private provider in 2021 was Fresh, which has accommodation in 29 UK locations. Liverpool won the award for best university accommodation. DIGS Student Accommodation was named the best value for money provider, and students at its Huddersfield, Wolverhampton and Sheffield developments get 100mb broadband and gym membership included in one weekly price.

Price and location are likely to be more important to students than who owns the property, but when it comes to student accommodation: caveat emptor! Standards can be variable, prices may leave little to live on, and horror stories recounted in surveys by the NUS and Save the Student mention heating and hot water issues, rodents and pests, inappropriate visits from landlords and damp.

Living at home

If students live within commuting distance of a good university, the option of dodging hefty rent and household bills is tempting. This may be a permanent shift, given the rising costs of student housing and the willingness of many young people, student or not, to live with their parents well into their twenties. What effect the health pandemic has on the popularity of studying from home remains to be seen, but it would seem natural for risk-averse types to see this as a more reliable option within an ongoing health pandemic.

Stay-at-home students tend to have longer commutes to campus than those in their own digs, the extra journey time a worthwhile compromise. Not only school-leavers live at home, the proportion includes mature students, many of whom live in their own homes rather than with their parents. The trend is four times more common at post-1992 universities than at older universities, reflecting the larger numbers of mature students with family responsibilities at the newer universities and a generally younger and more affluent student population at the older ones.

Before opting to stay at home solely on the basis that it makes financial sense, it is important to consider the relationship with your parents and the availability of quiet space in which to study. You will still be entitled to a maintenance loan, although for 2021–22 it is a maximum of £7,987 in England, rather than £9,488 if you were living away from home outside London, or £12,382 in London. There is no higher rate for anyone living at home in London, which seems unreasonable given the high cost of transport and other essentials there. There may be advantages in terms of academic work if the alternative involves shopping, cooking and cleaning as well as the other distractions of a student flat. The downside is that you may miss out on a lot of the student experience, especially the social scene and the opportunity to make new friends.

Research has found that students who live at home are less likely than others to say they are learning a lot at university, and a survey by the Student Engagement Partnership suggests that they find life unexpectedly "tiring, expensive and stressful". Issues affecting their quality of life include travel, security and the lack of their own space. But remember that you can always move on later if you think you are missing out. Many initially home-based students do so in their second year.

Living away from home

Most of those who can afford it, still see moving away to study as an integral rite of passage. There is no other option for those whose chosen course is at a university further than commuting distance. Others look forward to broadening their experiences in a new, unexplored location.

For the fortunate majority, the search for accommodation will be over quickly because the university can offer a place in one of its halls of residence or self-catering flats. The choice may come down to the type of accommodation and whether or not to do your own cooking. But for others, there will be an anxious search for a room in a strange city. Most universities will help with this if they cannot offer accommodation of their own.

The practicalities of living independently loom large for students who go away to university. The location and the type of accommodation may even influence your choice of university, since there are big differences across the sector and the country in the cost and standard of accommodation, and in its availability.

How much will it cost?

Rents vary so much across the UK that national averages can bear little resemblance to what you end up paying. The 2021 NatWest Student Living Index found a range from £447.40 a month in Glasgow and £465.30 in Newcastle to £619.90 in London and £578.70 in Cambridge, the next dearest.

Such figures conceal a wide range of actual rents, particularly in London. This was always the case but has become even more obvious with the rapid growth of a luxury market at the same time as many students have become willing to accept sub-standard accommodation to keep costs down.

A series of recent reports suggest that the need for good Wi-Fi has overtaken reasonable rents as students' top priority in choosing accommodation. A survey by mystudenthalls.com found that a big, bright room, good Wi-Fi, friendly people, a clean kitchen and a good gym are the top things students say they value in a place to live. The same website lists a top ten of the most Instagrammable student accommodation (won by Ernest Place, Durham with its rooftop communal areas).

Fabulous though such digs sound, being able to afford them must be a priority. Many students will not receive the full maintenance loan, due its means-testing against household income. Cash is needed up front for deposits, and/or a guarantee, probably from your parents, that the rent will be paid. Most universities with a range of accommodation find that their most expensive rooms fill up first, and that students appear to have higher expectations than they used to.

Another consideration is that both living costs and potential earnings should be factored into calculations when deciding where to live. While living costs in London are by far the highest, potential part-time earnings are, too. Taking account of both income and outgoings, the 2021 NatWest index made Sheffield the most affordable student city, followed by Cambridge and Glasgow.

The choices you have

» University hall of residence, with individual study bedrooms and a full catering service. Many will have en-suite accommodation.
» University halls, flats or houses where you provide your own food.
» Private, purpose-built student accommodation.
» Rented houses or flats, shared with fellow students.
» Living at home.
» Living as a lodger in a private house.

Making your choice

Choosing somewhere cheap is a false economy if it ends up making you feel depressed and isolated. Financial considerations should be weighed up in terms of the value that your living environment will contribute to your enjoyment of student life. Most students who drop out of university do so in the first few months, when homesickness and loneliness can be felt most acutely.

Being warm and well-fed is likely to have a positive effect on your studies. University halls offer a convenient, safe and reliable standard of accommodation, along with a supportive community environment. The sheer number of students – especially first-years – in halls makes this form of accommodation an easy way of meeting people from a wide range of courses and making friends.

If meals are included, this extra adds further peace of mind both for students and their parents. But only a tiny proportion of places are catered, compared with the standard format of en-suite rooms and a shared kitchen. So, some basic cooking skills might help build your popularity and self-confidence when you first reach university.

Wherever you choose to live, there are some general points you will need to consider, such as how safe the neighbourhood seems to be, and how long it might take you to travel to and from classes, especially during rush hour. A survey of travel time between term-time accommodation and university found that most students in London can expect a commute of at least 30 minutes and often over an hour, while students living in Wales are usually much less than 30 minutes away from their university.

In chapter 14, we provide details of what accommodation each university offers, covering the number of places, the costs, and their policy towards first-year students.

New student accommodation

At the top end of the market, private firms usually lead the way, at least in the bigger student cities. Companies such as UPP and Unite Students offer some of the most luxurious student accommodation the UK has seen, either in partnership with universities or in their own right. Rooms in these complexes are nearly always en-suite and with internet access and may include other facilities such as your own phone line and satellite TV. Shared kitchens are top-quality and fitted out with the latest equipment.

This kind of accommodation naturally comes at a higher price but offers the advantages of flexibility both in living arrangements and through a range of payment options.

University halls of residence

Many new or recently refurbished university-owned halls offer a standard of accommodation that is not far short of the privately-built residences. This is partly because rooms in these halls can be offered to conference delegates during vacations. Even though these halls are also at the pricier end of the spectrum, you will probably find that they are in great demand, and you may have to get your name down quickly to secure one of the fancier rooms. That said, you can often get a guarantee of accommodation if you give a firm acceptance of an offered place by a certain date in the summer.

If you have gained your place through Clearing, this option may not exist, although rooms in private halls might still be on offer at this stage. The delays experienced in development completions in recent years underline the importance of ensuring, as far as possible, that any new builds are on time and have the seal of approval (even in the absence of a formal arrangement) of the university. Cladding is a particular concern and not one that is easily assuaged. An incident in Bolton raised safety concerns as fire ripped through a relatively new hall of residence with cladding, though it appeared to have met building regulations and not be the type used on Grenfell Tower. Students were evacuated and two were treated by paramedics but fortunately none came to serious harm.

While a few halls are single-sex most are mixed, and often house over 500 students. In student villages, the numbers are now counted in thousands and these are great environments for making friends and becoming part of the social scene.

One possible downside is that big student housing developments can also be noisy places where it can be difficult at times to get down to some work. Surveys of students have revealed that for those who found noise a problem, peace and quiet was a higher priority than access to public transport or good nightlife. The more successful students learn, before too many essay deadlines and exams start to loom, to get the balance right between all-night partying and escaping to the library for some undisturbed study time. Many libraries, especially new ones, are now open 24 hours a day.

Self-catering

Very few universities offer catered halls of residence and self-catering is the norm. Invest in sturdy crockery and basic utensils – the sort of kit that will survive novice cookery skills and shared kitchens. To avoid reliance on instant noodles and takeaways it is wise to master at least a few culinary basics – pasta bakes are hard to get wrong and affordable to whip up. Sharing meals with housemates can be a sociable way of settling in at university.

Catering in university accommodation

Many universities have responded to a general increase in demand from students for a more independent lifestyle by providing more flexible catering facilities. A range of eateries, from fast food outlets to more traditional refectories, can usually be found on campus or in student villages. Students in university accommodation may be offered pay-as-you-eat deals as an alternative to full-board packages.

What to do after the first year?

After your first year of living in university residences you may well wish, and will probably be expected, to move out to other accommodation. The main exceptions are the collegiate universities, particularly Oxford and Cambridge but also others, which may allow you to stay on in college for another year or two, and particularly for your final year. Students from outside the EU are also often guaranteed accommodation. At a growing number of universities, where there is a sufficiently large stock of residential accommodation, it is not uncommon for students to move back into halls for their final year.

Practical details

Whether or not you have decided to start out in university accommodation, you will probably be expected to sign an agreement to cover your rent. Contract lengths vary. They can be for around 40 weeks, which includes the Christmas and Easter holiday periods, or for just the length of the three university terms. These term-time contracts are common when a university uses its rooms for conferences during vacations, and you will be required to leave your room empty during these weeks. Check whether the university has secure storage space for you to leave your belongings. Otherwise, you will have to make arrangements to take all your belongings home or store them privately between terms. International students may be offered special arrangements by which they can stay in halls during the short vacation periods. Organisations like **www.hostuk.org** can arrange for international students to stay in a UK family home at holiday times such as Christmas.

Parental purchases

One option for affluent families is to buy a house or flat and take in student lodgers. This might not be the safe financial bet it once appeared, but it is still tempting for many parents. Agents Knight Frank have had a student division since 2007, mostly working with new developers to sell specially adapted homes. Those who are considering this route tend to do so from their first year of study to maximise the return on their investment.

Being a lodger or staying in a hostel

A small number of students live as a lodger in a family home, an option most frequently taken up by international students. The usual arrangement is for a study bedroom and some meals to be provided, while other facilities such as the washing machine are shared. Students with certain religious affiliations or from a particular country may wish to consider living in a hostel run by a charity catering for a specific group. Most of these are in London. There are also specialist commercial providers such as Mansion Student India, which runs housing for Indian students in the UK.

Renting from the private sector

Around a third of students live in privately rented flats or houses. Every university city or town is awash with such accommodation, available via agencies or direct from landlords. Indeed, this type of accommodation has grown to the point where so-called "student ghettoes," in which local residents feel outnumbered, have become a hot political issue in some cities. Into this traditional market for rented flats and houses have come the new private-sector complexes and residences, adding to the options. Some are on university campuses, but others are in city centres and usually open to students of more than one university. Examples can be seen online; some sites are listed at the end of this chapter.

While there are always exceptions, a much more professional attitude and approach to managing rented accommodation has emerged among smaller providers, thanks to a combination of greater regulation and increasing competition. Nevertheless, it is wise to take certain precautions when seeking out private residences.

How to start looking for rented property

Start this process as soon as you have accepted a place. Contact your university's accommodation service and ask for its list of approved rented properties. Some have a Student Accommodation Accreditation Scheme, run in collaboration with the local council. To get onto an approved list under such schemes, landlords must show they are adhering to basic standards of safety and security, such as having an up-to-date gas and electric safety certificate. University accommodation officers should also be able to advise you on any hidden charges. For instance, you may be asked to pay a booking or reservation fee to secure a place in a particular property, and there are sometimes fees for references or for drawing up a tenancy agreement. The practice of charging a "joining fee", however, has been outlawed.

Speak to older students with first-hand experience. Most universities have a clickable "Chat to a Student" icon on their website, and **www.thestudentroom.com** the online community of students nationwide is another helpful source for getting your ear to the ground. Certain areas of town may be notorious among second and third-years and you can try to avoid them.

Making a choice

Once you have made an initial choice of the area you would like to live in and the size of property you are looking for, the next stage is to look at possible places. If you plan to share, it is important that you all have a look at the property. If you will be living by yourself, take a friend with you when you go to view a property, since he or she can help you assess what you see objectively, and avoid any irrational or rushed on-the-spot decisions. Don't let yourself be pushed into signing on the dotted line there and then. Take time to visit and consider options, as well as checking out the local facilities, transport and the general environment at various times of the day and on different days of the week.

If you are living in private rented accommodation, it is likely that at least some of your neighbours will not be students. Local people often welcome students, but resentment can build up, particularly in areas of towns and cities that are dominated by student housing. It is important to respect your neighbours' rights, and not to behave in an anti-social manner.

Preparing for sharing

Because you enjoy spending time with someone socially does not mean they will be free of annoying habits if you choose to share a house. How well you cope with some of the downsides of sharing will be partly down to the kind of person you are and where you are on the spectrum between laid back and highly strung. But it will help a lot if you are co-habiting with people whose outlook on day-to-day living is not too far out of line with your own. According to Unite Students, 31% of female students find sharing more difficult than they had expected, compared with 22% of men.

Some students sign for their second-year houses as early as November. While it is good to be ahead of the rush, you may not yet have met your best friends at this stage. If you have not selected your own group of friends, universities and landlords can help by taking personal preferences and lifestyle into account when grouping tenants together.

How students annoy their housemates

1	Leaving dirty dishes out	55%
2	Not helping with cleaning	47%
3	Making too much noise	39%
4	Leaving lights/appliances on	34%
5	Leaving food to rot	32%
6	Not removing hair from plugholes	22%
=7	Stealing food	18%
=7	Not changing the toilet roll	18%

Source: National Student Accommodation Survey 2021

Security in Student Housing

» Before you rent, check that front and back doors have five-lever mortise locks as well as standard catch locks and use them when you go out

» Invest in a light-timer, so the house looks occupied even when you're out and don't advertise your departure on social media

» If you put your desk in a window, make sure you move your laptop, phone and any other valuable equipment away when you're not using them

» Get insurance for your valuables and take them home if you're leaving the house for any length of time. You may be able to add your valuables to your parents' home insurance

» Ask the landlord or letting agency to make sure previous tenants have returned any keys and discuss any security concerns with them

» Register your valuables (see www.immobilise.com) makes it more likely you'll be re-united if things do get stolen and invest in a good bike lock

Source: www.savethestudent.org and NUS (adapted)

Potential issues to consider when deciding whether to move into a shared house include whether any of the housemates smoke or own a loud musical instrument or DJ decks. It will also be important to sort out broadband arrangements that will work for everyone, and that will enable you to access the university system. It is a good idea to agree a rota for everyone to share in the household cleaning chores from the start. Otherwise, it is almost certain that you will live in a state of unhygienic squalor, or that one or two individuals will be left to clear up everyone else's mess.

The practical details about renting

It is a good idea to ask whether your house is covered by an accreditation scheme or code of standards. Such codes provide a clear outline of what constitutes good practice as well as the responsibilities of both landlords and tenants. Adhering to schemes like the National Code of Standards for Larger Student Developments compiled by Accreditation Network UK (**www.anuk.org.uk**) may well become a requirement for larger properties, including those managed by universities, now that the Housing Act is in force.

At the very least, make sure that if you are renting from a private landlord, you have their telephone number and home address. Some can be remarkably difficult to contact when repairs are needed or when deposits are due to be returned.

Multiple occupation

If you are renting a private house, it may be subject to the 2004 Housing Act in England and Wales (similar legislation applies in Scotland and Northern Ireland). Licenses are compulsory for all private Houses in Multiple Occupation (HMOs) with three or more storeys and that house five or more unrelated residents. The provisions of the Act also allow local authorities to designate whole areas in which HMOs of all sizes must be licensed. The regulations may be applied in sections of university towns and cities where most students live. This means that a house must be licensed, well-managed and must meet various health and safety standards, and its owner subject to various financial regulations. There is more on this at **www.gov.uk** under Private Renting.

Tenancy agreements

Whatever kind of accommodation you go for, you must be sure to have all the paperwork in order and be clear about what you are signing up to before you move in. If you are taking up residence in a shared house, flat or bedsit, the first document you will have to grapple with is a tenancy agreement or lease offering you an "assured shorthold tenancy". Since this is a binding legal document, you should be prepared to go through every clause with a fine-tooth comb. Remember that it is much more difficult to make changes or overcome problems arising from unfair agreements once you are a tenant than before you become one.

You would be well advised to seek help in the likely event of your not fully understanding some of the clauses. Your university accommodation office or students' union is a good place to start. They should know all the ins and outs and have model tenancy agreements to refer to. A Citizens Advice Bureau or Law Advice Centre should also be able to offer you free advice. In particular, watch out for clauses that may make you jointly responsible for the actions of others with whom you are sharing. If you name a parent as a guarantor to cover any costs not paid by you, they may also be liable for charges levied on all tenants for damage that was not your fault. A rent review clause could allow your landlord to increase the rent at will, whereas without such a clause, they are restricted to one rent rise a year. Make sure you keep a copy of all documents and get a receipt (and keep it somewhere safe) for anything you have had to pay for that is the landlord's responsibility.

Contracts with private landlords tend to be longer than for university accommodation. They will frequently commit you to paying rent for 52 weeks of the year. Leaving aside the cost, there are probably more advantages than disadvantages to this kind of arrangement. It means you don't have to move out during vacations, which you will have to in most university halls. You can store your belongings in your room when you go away (but don't leave anything valuable behind if you can help it). You may be able to negotiate a rent discount for periods when you are not staying in the property. The other advantage, particularly important for cash-strapped students, is that you have a base from which to find work and hold down a job during the vacations. Term dates are also not as dictatorial as they might be in halls. If you rent your own house, then you can come back when you wish.

Deposits

On top of the agreed rent, you will need to provide a deposit or bond to cover any breakages or damage. This will probably set you back the equivalent of another month's rent. The deposit should be returned, less any deductions, at the end of the contract. However, be warned that disputes over the return of deposits are common, with the question of what constitutes reasonable wear and tear often the subject of disagreements between landlord and tenant. To protect students from unscrupulous landlords who withheld deposits without good reason, the 2004 Housing Act introduced a National Tenancy Deposit Scheme under which deposits are held by an independent body. This is designed to ensure that deposits are fairly returned, and that any disputes are resolved swiftly and cheaply. There are details at citizensadvice.org.uk. You may also be asked to find guarantors for your rent payments – in practice, usually your parents.

Inventories and other paperwork

You should get an inventory and schedule of condition of everything in the property. This is another document that you should check carefully and make sure that everything listed is as described. Write on the document anything that is different. The NUS suggests taking photographs of rooms and equipment when you first move in (setting the correct date on your camera), to provide you with additional proof should any dispute arise when your contract ends, and you want to get your deposit back. If you are not offered an inventory, then make one of your own. You should have someone else witness and sign this, send it to your landlord, and keep your own copy. Keeping in contact with your landlord throughout the year and developing a good relationship with him or her will also do you no harm and may be to your advantage in the long run.

You should ask your landlord for a recent gas safety certificate issued by a qualified CORGI engineer, a fire safety certificate covering the furnishings, and a record of current gas and electricity meter readings. Take your own readings of meters when you move in to make sure these match up with what you have been given or make your own records if the landlord doesn't supply them. This also applies to water meters if you are expected to pay water rates (although this isn't usually the case). The NUS issues its own advice on how to keep down energy bills, at **http://studentswitchoff.org/save-energy-rented-accommodation**. The NUS says that the average student in private rented accommodation spends £500 a year on energy, so you can save money and cut down carbon emissions.

Finally, students are not liable for Council Tax. If you are sharing a house only with other full-time students, then you will not have to pay it. However, you may be liable to pay a proportion of the Council Tax bill if you are sharing with anyone who is not a full-time student. You may need to get a Council Tax exemption certificate from your university as evidence that you do not need to pay Council Tax.

Safety and security

Once you have arrived and settled in, remember to take care of your own safety and the security of your possessions. You are particularly vulnerable as a fresher, when you are still getting used to your new-found independence. This may help explain why so many students are burgled or robbed in the first six weeks of the academic year. Take care with valuable portable items such as mobile phones, tablets and laptops, all of which are desirably saleable items for thieves. Ensure you don't leave them obviously on display when you are out and about and that you have insurance cover. If your mobile phone is stolen, call your network or 08701 123123 to immobilise it. Students' unions, universities and the police will provide plenty of practical guidance when you arrive. Following their advice will reduce the chance of you becoming a victim of crime and help you to enjoy living in the new surroundings of your chosen university town.

Useful websites

For advice on a range of housing issues, visit: **www.nus.org.uk/more/faqs/housing-and-rent**

The Shelter website has separate sections covering different housing regulations in England, Wales, Scotland and Northern Ireland: **www.shelter.org.uk**

As examples of providers of private hall accommodation, visit:
www.upp-ltd.com
http://www.unitestudents.com/
http://thestudenthousingcompany.com
www.student-cribs.com

A number of sites will help you find accommodation and/or potential housemates, including:
www.accommodationforstudents.com
www.uniplaces.com
www.sturents.com,
www.studentpad.co.uk
www.studentcrowd.com
http://student.spareroom.co.uk
http://uk.easyroommate.com

Accreditation Network UK is at: **https://www.anuk.org.uk**

www.hostuk.org helps international students meet British people and families in their homes

8 Enjoying University Sport

If Loughborough University were a country, it would have outperformed Sweden, Switzerland and Belgium at the Tokyo 2020 Olympics. A stellar team of current and past students, together with others who trained at the university's world-class sports facilities, won 14 medals – including three golds. Among those to podium was the swimmer Adam Peaty, who won two gold medals in the men's 100m breaststroke and the mixed 4 x 100m medley relay, and the triathlete Alex Yee, who won gold and silver in the individual and mixed relay. There were further medals for Loughborough in the Paralympics, with six golds, six silvers and nine bronzes brought home by students, alumni and others who trained there.

Loughborough is also the *Sunday Times* Sports University of the Year – a trophy it has earned three times (more often than any other university) in recognition of its unparalleled elite success, the best sports facilities in the country and an atmosphere that encourages widespread participation among students whose sporting ambitions stop short of the Olympics and who just want to keep fit and enjoy being active.

For most applicants, the sports facilities are not what is going to seal the deal on their university choice, but nearly a third say they played some part in their decision-making. Clued-up universities are aware they have to work harder to meet the expectations of fee-paying students who want to play sport, workout and try new activities. They have boosted provision to meet this demand on such a scale in recent years that nationally, UK university sports facilities are said to be worth an astonishing £20billion.

In the past 15 years Loughborough alone has invested £60million in sporting facilities on its 440-acre campus on the edge of the Leicestershire market town. An exhaustive – and, presumably, exhausting – list of new resources includes two world-class gyms, a High Performance Athletics Centre, the Paula Radcliffe Athletics Track, the National Cricket Performance Centre, its Netball Centre hosting England Netball, and a huge range of pitches – plus the £6million pool where Peaty has been training since 2017. It is also a British Swimming National Centre and British Triathlon Performance Centre. All this is backed up by technical facilities such as a human performance laboratory, technical analysis suite, nutritional analysis room and sports medicine service.

Naturally the extraordinary sporting successes of Loughborough – as with all the leading sporting universities – are the result of considerable investment in sports scholarships and training programmes, as well as campus facilities.

Ever competitive, Loughborough claims its campus represents the best square mile of sports facilities in the world, let alone the British higher education sector. Its student athletes across sporting disciplines have topped the British Universities and Colleges Sport (BUCS) points table for inter-university competition almost throughout the league's 40-year history.

But when the table was suspended in 2020 because of the Pandemic, Nottingham, just a half-hour's drive from Loughborough, was at the top and it continued to outperform its neighbour in the partial results posted in 2021, although because of the disruption no official table was drawn up. Nottingham students have access to £40million sports facilities used by elite athletes, and under a "sport for all" banner the university's ambition is to engage, inspire and excel. Two-times winner of our Sports University of the Year award, Nottingham has never finished outside the BUCS league's top ten.

Building on its strong sporting tradition, in 2016 Nottingham raised the money to build a sports village with the help of alumnus and Carphone Warehouse founder, David Ross. The wide range of facilities at the David Ross Sports Village includes a high-performance athletics zone, dedicated martial arts studio and all-glass squash court. There is a sports injury clinic in the complex – as well as a Finnish sauna, steam room, arctic ice fountain and ice-cold bucket shower. About 25,000 of the university's 36,000 students engage with sporting programmes at some level – from using one of the 200 stations at the gym now and again to winning one of 200 sports scholarships and competing at the Olympics.

At the University of Birmingham, a £55million sports centre includes the only 50m pool in the region, to add to its already impressive facilities, while Solent has a recently-opened £28million sports development. Bath was the first UK university to offer sporting scholarships to student athletes in 1976 and now provides more than 50 each year. Its £30million Sports Training Village hosts 1.6 million visits each year, by everyone from high-performance athletes and the public to students and staff, including 43 community sports clubs. Bath has a £1.6million London 2012 legacy swimming pool, which is used by 310,000 people a year, and a £3.5million extension to the Team Bath gym is due to open in 2022.

Such facilities attract elite performers and are often used for high-level teaching, but they are also available for day-to-day use by undergraduates. Comparing such facilities is not easy, but most universities display them prominently on their websites and offer taster sessions on open days. There are brief descriptions of the bigger developments in the university profiles in Chapter 14.

Research for BUCS suggests that at least 1.7 million students take part in regular physical activity, from gym sessions to competitive individual or team sports. There are good reasons, beyond fitness, for doing so, according to BUCS reports. Those who are physically active expect higher grades and are more confident of securing a graduate job than less active students. There are 53 sports listed on the BUCS website, from American Football to Windsurfing.

During the pandemic, universities dug deep to provide sports activities to boost students' mental health. The University of Worcester's dance society implemented virtual events during lockdown, including daily physical and creative challenges, virtual quizzes and fundraising for the NHS. Worcester's "Cheers" mental health marathon, launched in November 2020, involved sports clubs and societies members walking, jogging or running 26.2 miles over the month to raise money for Mind UK. The initiatives were nominated for the BUCS Diversity and Inclusion Award 2021.

Another nominee for the BUCS award was Liverpool John Moores University's (LJMU) "InclusActivity Week", which included sessions focusing on barriers to students who identify as disabled, LGBTQA+, BAME, mature, postgraduate and women – with the intention of encouraging these students to engage in university sports teams. LJMU opened its new Sports Centre last year – featuring an eight-court sports hall, two multifunctional studio rooms and a two-floor gym.

Sporting opportunities

Some specialist facilities may be reserved at times for elite performers, but all universities are conscious of the need for wider access. Many institutions still encourage departments not to schedule lectures and seminars on Wednesday afternoons, to give students free time for sport. There are student-run clubs for all the major sports and – particularly at the larger universities – a host of minor ones. In addition, there are high-quality gyms, with staff on hand to devise personalised training regimes and to run popular activities such as Zumba and Pilates. The cost varies widely between universities, and membership fees can represent a large amount to lay out at the start of the year, but most provide good value if you are going to be a regular user.

Sport for all

At most universities, attention is mainly focused on "sport for all". Beginners are welcomed and coaching provided in a range of sports, from Ultimate Frisbee to tai-chi, that would be difficult to match outside the higher education system. Check on university websites to see whether your usual sport is available, but do not be surprised if you come across a new favourite when you have the opportunity to try out something different as a student. Many universities have programmes designed to encourage students to take up a new sport, with expert coaching provided.

All universities are conscious of the need to provide for a spread of ability – and disability. University teams demand a hefty commitment in terms of training and practice sessions – often several times a week – and in many sports standards are high. University teams often compete in local and national leagues.

For those who are looking for competition at a lower level, or whose interests are primarily social, there are thriving internal, or intramural, leagues. These provide opportunities for groups from halls of residence or faculties, or even a group of friends, to form a team and participate on a regular basis.

Some universities have cut back sports budgets, but representative sport continues to grow. There are home nations competitions at international level in some sports and in London over 30 institutions take part in the London Universities Sport League. This now involves almost 450 teams – male, female and mixed – competing at a variety of levels in 15 different sports.

First-year sport

Halls of residence sport is a great way of meeting like-minded people from your accommodation and over the course of the years, friendly rivalries often develop with other halls or flats. Generally, there will be teams for football (five-a-side and 11-a-side), hockey, netball, cricket, tennis, squash, badminton and even golf.

Other opportunities

You may even end up wanting to coach, umpire or referee – another area in which higher education has much to offer. Many university clubs and sports unions provide subsidised courses for students to gain qualifications. Or you might want to try your hand at some sports administration, with an eye to your career. In most universities there is a sports (or athletic) union, with autonomy from the main students' union, which organises matches and looks after the wider interests of those who play.

Universities that excel

Winners of the *Sunday Times* Sports University of the Year award, launched in 2014, represent some – but not all – of the UK's leading sporting universities.

2022 Loughborough
2021 Nottingham
2020 Stirling
2019 Nottingham
2018 Bath
2017 Loughborough
2016 Exeter
2015 Durham
2014 Loughborough

Leeds Beckett, Brunel, Cardiff Metropolitan and St Mary's Twickenham are some of the other institutions with excellent sports pedigrees.

The Boat Race between Oxford and Cambridge universities and the Varsity Match (in rugby union) are the only UK university sporting events with a big popular following – although there are varsity matches in many university cities that have become big occasions for students. Be aware, though, that success in school sport is not a passport to an Oxbridge place; such special consideration for sporty undergraduates is long gone.

Representative sport

There were over 120 BUCS athletes representing Team GB and other countries in the Tokyo Olympics. If BUCS was a country, based on the number of its athletes who won medals, it would have placed seventh in the Olympic medal table and ninth in the Paralympic table, with 88 medals in total.

BUCS is the national organisation for higher education sport in the UK, providing a comprehensive, multi-sport competition structure and managing the development of services and facilities for participatory, grass-roots sport and healthy campuses, through to high-performance elite athletes.

BUCS (**www.bucs.org.uk**) lists 53 sports and runs championships, leagues and/or individual competitions in almost all of them. It ranks participating institutions based on the points earned in the competitive programme, although the pandemic has disrupted this for the past two years. Between September and December 2021, 5,092 teams from 130-plus universities had competed in over 15,000 BUCS matches. There is also international competition in a number of sports, and the World Student Games have become one of the biggest occasions in the international sporting calendar.

How much?

Students who are used to free (if inferior) facilities at school often get a nasty surprise when they find that they are expected to pay to join the Athletic Union and then pay again to use the gym or play football. Because most university sport is subsidised, the charges are reasonable compared to commercial facilities, but the best deal may require a considerable outlay at the start. Some universities include sports facility membership as part of the £9,250 fee, but most offer a variety of peak and off-peak membership packages.

Outdoor sports are usually charged by the hour, although clubs will also charge a membership fee. You may be required to pay up to £90 for membership of the Athletic Union, although most universities also offer pay-as-you-play options. Fees for intramural sport are seldom substantial; teams will usually pay a fee for the season, while courts for racket sports tend to be marginally cheaper per session than in other clubs.

How far away?

The other common complaint by students is that the playing fields are too far from the campus – understandable in the case of city-centre universities, but still aggravating if you have to arrange your own transport. This is where campus universities have a clear advantage. For the rest, there has to be some trade-off between the quality of outdoor facilities and the distance you have to travel to use them.

Sport as a degree subject

Over 15,000 students started sports science courses in 2020, making it one of the most popular degree choices. A separate ranking for the subject is on page 272.

Many degrees in the sports area focus on management, with careers in the leisure industry in mind.

Sports scholarships

Sports scholarships are for elite performers, regardless of what they are studying – indeed, they exist at universities with barely any degrees in the area. Imported from the USA, scholarships now exist in an array of sports. Their value varies considerably – sometimes according to individual prowess. Many offer benefits in the form of coaching, equipment or access to facilities. The Government-funded Talented Athlete Scholarship Scheme (TASS) is worth up to £3,500 per year for students at English universities who have achieved national recognition at under-18 level and are eligible to represent England in one of 32 different sports. Sixty-six medals were won by TASS athletes at the Tokyo Olympic and Paralympic Games. The Scottish equivalent, Winning Students Scotland, awards scholarships worth up to £6,000 a year.

Part-time work

University sports centres are an excellent source of term-time (and out-of-term) employment. You may also be trained in first aid, fire safety, customer care and risk assessment – all useful skills for future employment. The experience could help secure a job in commercial or local authority facilities – and even for roles such as stewarding at football grounds and music venues. Most universities also have a sabbatical post in the Athletic Union or similar body, a paid position with responsibility for organising university sport and representing the sporting community within the university.

British Universities Tokyo Medal Table

Students and alumni at the Olympic Games

University	Gold	Silver	Bronze	Total
1 Bath	5	–	–	5
2 Leeds Beckett	2	4	–	6
3 Stirling	2	3	–	5
4 Cambridge	1	–	–	1
=4 Leeds	1	–	–	1
6 Loughborough	–	2	10	12
7 Glasgow	–	2	–	2
8 Durham	–	1	1	2
=8 Cardiff	–	1	1	2

Students and alumni at the Paralympic Games

University	Gold	Silver	Bronze	Total
1 Loughborough	3	1	1	5
2 Manchester Metropolitan	3	1	–	4
3 East Anglia	2	–	1	2
4 Leeds Beckett	2	–	–	2
=4 Coventry	2	–	–	2
6 Northumbria	1	2	2	5
7 St Mary's Twickenham	1	1	–	2
=7 Birmingham	1	1	–	2
9 Salford	1	–	1	2
=9 Leeds	1	–	1	2

*University facilities are used for training by many elite athletes who are not students or alumni
Source: BUCS

9 Staying Safe and Seeking Help on Campus

Driving down the motorway, the boot fit to burst with your child's worldly possessions – plus the new toastie maker and saucepan set – dropping off at university is a school run on another level. Saying goodbye as you leave them at halls for the first time is a moment for tears, jubilation or probably a combination of both. Parents, step-parents and carers know that university is most likely to be a brilliant experience that will help their charge grow into a well-rounded, self-sufficient adult. But it may also be their first experience of unfettered access to alcohol, drugs and relationships. Or maybe they feel daunted at the prospect of degree-level academia.

With such a lot of change – and an unprecedented loosening of the apron strings – even the most chilled out parents fret when their new undergraduate flies the nest. Worrying is natural, but it shouldn't absorb every waking thought. It is possible to give your child autonomy whilst also checking in with them around the major issues: drinking, taking drugs and staying safe – both physically and mentally – on campus.

To find out how far universities are going to support students, we used our annual survey to ask them what compulsory modules they ran covering alcohol use, drug-taking, social tolerance and sexual consent. Their responses revealed that support was patchy, at best. Only two universities, Abertay and Swansea, required students to attend sessions in all four categories, while two more, Cardiff and Chester offered obligatory courses, covering drugs and alcohol, and another 11 had compulsory classes on sexual consent: Durham, Kent, SOAS, Southampton, Plymouth Marjon, St Andrews, Cardiff, University of Wales Trinity St David, Warwick, Newcastle and Nottingham Trent. Although some student unions offered advice on the four topics, 119 institutions said they did not run any obligatory courses.

There is a fine line between supporting and meddling, but by researching what to expect, how best to react if things go awry, and support available, a balance should be within reach.

The first round

Much of the university social scene inevitably revolves around campus or college bars, and Freshers Week traditionally has a packed itinerary of club nights and boozy social mixer events. This extends to accommodation, with pre-drinks ever popular as a cheap alternative to paying bar prices. Students gather in their kitchens for drinking games, often aiming to get sozzled enough before they go out, to ensure an inexpensive night once they do. In an Alcohol Impact survey carried out by the NUS in 2018–2019, over half of the 793 respondents said they regularly drank at home or a friend's house before a night out, and 29% stated they deliberately got drunk at pre-drinks.

Sobering thoughts

The long-term health conditions caused by regular over-consumption of alcohol are unlikely to be at the forefront of the minds of freshly independent 18-year-olds as they knock back another Jagerbomb, but the impact that the culture of student drinking can have on their social circle and academic progress may hit home. Teetotal students can feel isolated, whilst those hellbent on drinking to excess can find themselves missing deadlines, involved in anti-social behaviour or letting their guard down around personal safety. Universities and student organisations have woken up to these issues and campaigns to promote responsible drinking have sprung up nationwide.

Last orders

The National Union of Students (NUS) runs the Alcohol Impact programme, which partners with universities to reduce harm. Originally set up to tackle drunk, antisocial behaviour, the programme had the knock-on effect of increasing student wellbeing, whilst making campus a more inclusive place for non-drinkers. It recommends 50 different actions to reduce harm around drinking, from training bar staff to help intoxicated students, to working with the local community to ensure students get home safely from a night out. So far, 30 universities have participated, and you can see if the institution you are considering is part of the programme at **https://alcoholimpact.unioncloud.org/**.

For non-drinkers, there may well be an active sober social scene on campus. In the 2018–19 NUS Alcohol Impact Report, 40% of respondents said they got drunk less than once a week. There are an increasing number of dry societies and booze-free social events at universities.

Offering sober-minded advice

Michelle Hemmingfield, co-ordinator of NUS Alcohol Impact, recommends a harm reduction approach. Rather than preaching sobriety to your children, foster open conversation in which you can inform them about alcohol overconsumption. A good way to get the conversation going is by explaining how to take care of someone else who has drunk to excess.

A harm reduction approach is even more important when bars and pubs close and hall parties take over. Hemmingfield recommends buying students an alcohol measure, to help them more accurately keep track of the units they consume. Cringe though some might when unpacking their drinks measure in a halls kitchen, you never know, it might just work. And if having a measure does not result in your child fastidiously updating a drinks diary, it could at least make them think twice before sloshing in another huge home measure or help them create concoctions that might even be savoured rather than inhaled.

Finally, trust them. The Alcohol Impact survey revealed 80% of respondents agreed that drinking too much can spoil a good night. Parents who are worried about their child's drinking can find useful resources at DrinkAware online, including tips on how to facilitate conversations around alcohol.

Chasing the High

Parents cannot pull the wool over their own eyes any longer; it is easier than ever to score drugs on campus. Dealers are on the way out though, and buying through the dark web or peer hook-ups is more common and more difficult to trace. Furthermore, with Covid restrictions on bars and clubs stretching into the future, drugs are more likely to be taken at a flat or house party. This removes the limiting influence of bouncers and bar staff, along with increasing peer pressure as students try to fit in with their restricted social bubbles. It's never been more important to ensure students are equipped with harm prevention methods around drugs.

Despite being illegal, drugs are ever-present on campuses. Taking the Hit, a 2018 NUS study into drugs at university, surveyed 2,081 students at 151 institutions. It found that 39% said they currently used drugs, and 19% had used them in the past. Cannabis was the most popular, having been used at some point by 94% of respondents. It was closely followed by "club drug" Ecstasy/MDMA, with cocaine and nitrous oxide also making the list.

"Study drugs" are also favourites on campuses across the UK, purportedly taken by students to improve concentration and keep them writing essays into the early hours. Substances such as Ritalin and Modafinil were taken by one in ten of the 2,081 respondents, utilising prescription-only medicines usually procured via other methods to keep them focused during deadlines.

Historically, universities have responded punitively to students caught with drugs. A solely disciplinary approach has limited success however, isolating students rather than aiding them. Four in ten of the respondents to Taking the Hit said they wouldn't feel comfortable disclosing their drug use to their university for fear of punishment, and as such, do not seek out help when they need it.

Changing the game

The "abstinence only" approach to drug taking at universities is slowly changing. Students for Sensible Drug Policy, (SSDP) is an international grassroots organisation, advocating a change in drug policy on campuses.

Iulia Vatau, founder of SSDP at University College, London, believes in a harm reduction approach. She argues that the many reasons behind drug use, including mental health management and peer pressure, should be acknowledged. The organisation provides online Harm Prevention packs for incoming students, containing information and advice on drugs and seeking help. The goal is to empower students to make informed decisions, stating that pastoral and medical needs will always be prioritised over disciplinary proceedings.

This is not to say that drugs will soon be permissible on campuses. Of the 151 institutions surveyed in the Taking the Hit report, over half took a firmer line than the law, penalising students for technically legal drug use. Accommodation contracts often have an outright ban on drugs, threatening eviction.

A spoonful of sugar

Foster an open dialogue to equip your child with harm reduction knowledge. By discussing the effects of certain drugs, and what to do if someone has a bad reaction or overdoses, they'll garner information that could end up saving a life. To facilitate such a potentially thorny chat, Hemmingfield, who also co-ordinates the NUS Alcohol and Drugs impact scheme, recommends taking a bystander approach. She advises:

"A way to frame it is saying, 'your friends may take drugs, these are the risks they are undertaking.' By doing that, you make sure that they get the information for themselves whilst still not directly tackling them on it. This can make for a less awkward conversation, and it helps young people to understand the risks in a non-judgemental, safe space."

University drug policies vary, so read the fine print. Websites such as Talk to Frank and Volteface provide information on the effects that different substances can have and advice on how to talk to young people about drugs.

Facts of life

Sexual assault and violence on UK campuses is a serious problem and some institutions are rife with misconduct and ill-equipped to deal with the problem. In the past year, the website everyonesinvited.uk reported survivors' testimonies of sexual abuse in 93 institutions profiled in the *Good University Guide*. Through freedom of information requests, Eva Tutchell and John Edmonds, authors of *Unsafe Spaces: Ending Sexual Abuse in Universities,* estimate there are between 50,000 and 100,000 sexual assaults at British universities every year.

"The first thing that amazed us was that universities, research-based organisations, have made no real attempt to collect authoritative information about sexual assaults on campuses," Edmonds said. "If you haven't got the evidence, the specialist knowledge, how do you put together a programme that is likely to work? They rely on reports made by students and by junior staff, but everybody knows that these sexual assaults are massively underreported."

How widespread is the problem?

In a nationwide study, Revolt Sexual Assault polled 4,500 students from 135 universities in 2018. About 70% of women respondents said they experienced sexual violence at university; among males the figure was 26%; for non-binary 61% and for disabled respondents 73%. Just 6% reported it to the university.

Sara Khan, vice-president (liberation and equality) at the National Union of Students, says there are several reasons for this, including students not feeling they'll be heard or protected, and many learning, perhaps for the first time, what sexual assault and consent really mean.

"Before I joined the NUS, I was a sabbatical officer at the University of Manchester Student Union and I was on the receiving end of disclosures," she explained. "The experience of students is essentially that they're being put on trial, they have to prove that they've been sexually assaulted, but providing hard evidence in many cases is near impossible."

Most processes for reporting incidents are decades old, out of touch and not fit for purpose, says Edmonds. Some universities even suggest that victims should talk to their attacker and see if they can reach an accommodation.

"One university, which we haven't named, although honestly, the temptation is enormous, suggested that if you find it difficult to confront the person you're complaining about, you might want to consider assertiveness training," he said.

Khan says the NUS thinks that universities need to take a hard look at their reporting systems, how they are structured and whether they centre on the needs of survivors, their safety and their mental health. Edmonds and Tutchell believe that universities hope to avoid legal cases, protect their reputation and "keep everybody quiet". A report by the BBC in 2019 showed that universities had spent £87million in 2017–18 on non-disclosure agreements to stop bullying, discrimination and sexual misconduct allegations being made public.

"I think that this fear, that if people know that sexual violence happens at a university, no one will want to go to that university, is a very unproductive mindset because, realistically, we know that it happens in every university," Khan said.

An affair of the heart

Are any universities getting it right? Edmonds and Tutchell, conclude that there are a few who "haven't always got it right, but are taking it seriously". They include: Aberdeen; Cambridge; Goldsmiths; Imperial College London; Lancaster; London School of Economics; Oxford, and Sussex.

Unfortunately, scandal and media pressure have been the main influences in instigating change.

St Andrews found itself in the firing line in 2020 after dozens of allegations of sexual assault were made, several against an American-style fraternity at the university. A freedom of information request found that 42 reports of sexual assault and harassment had been made in the five years to 2020. Last August the university announced that it would be hiring a sexual violence worker to support survivors.

Fiona Drouet's daughter, Emily, was subjected by her boyfriend, Angus Milligan, to a brutal campaign of physical and emotional abuse, at Aberdeen University, which ended in her taking her own life. Today, Drouet is the chief executive of the charity Emily Test, which campaigns for better protection for students.

The organisation is asking universities to commit to a Gender-Based Violence (GBV) charter, where they must examine their current systems and policies to see if they pass the "Emily test" – whether they could have saved Emily's life. The charity has drafted a list of minimum standards such as GBV data collection, educating and empowering staff and students, risk assessment processes, departments working together to spot warning signs, and easily accessible and compassionate help for victims and survivors.

"It won't stop assaults and rape on campus, but it will tackle the issue of a generation that do not understand consent, sexual assault or rape," Drouet says.

Reframing the birds and the bees

Mandy Saligari, a therapist who specialises in treating teenagers and young adults, says that understanding the intricacies of consent is the key to helping your child protect themselves and others. So, start off by saying, "I know you are going to roll your eyes, but I need you to listen because this is important". Do not get put off by your child saying, "Oh, no!" – you have the right to fulfil your parental duty.

"Teenagers need to understand that there is no 'point of no-return'. At any stage, either party can stop and say, 'I do not want to do this'. You are not a prick-tease if you go three quarters of the way and then say you don't want to continue. And if you are a boy and you hear 'No', stop straight away. Tell your teenager they should not be afraid to assert their sexual boundaries."

Khan says that the uncomfortable truth is that a rapist or someone who commits sexual violence is not usually a "monster". "Most people who experience sexual violence, experience it from a close loved one, or someone who is known to them, someone who often doesn't actually understand what consent is or that they're violating consent," she said.

In retrospect, following Emily's suicide, Drouet thinks that she was a naive parent. She'd tell her daughter to mind her drink wasn't spiked and not be out alone, but never discussed coercion or abuse.

"I never said: this is what you should do if you find yourself in a relationship where you feel you're not free to do the things that you want to do, you're being put down all the time, you're being blackmailed or asked to do things sexually that you're not comfortable with," she said.

Another thing to do as a parent, is to make sure your child feels able to talk to you without judgement or blame. According to Edmonds, until you start talking to victims, you don't realise "how little you know – the hurt, the secrecy, the guilt, the whole gamut is just awful."

"So, if the worst should happen, think before you react," Drouet says. "Remember that no one asks to be abused. We need to educate ourselves as parents. It's never the victim's fault and if your child comes to you, make sure you know where you can get professional help and reassure them that there is never a problem that can't be fixed together."

Sex education in schools rarely covers issues of consent, so equip your child with practical information about support services on offer. Finally, if your child is sexually active, make sure they know how to access contraceptive services and sign up to a GP as soon as possible.

Troubled Times

The kids are not always alright, so friends and family are correct to be vigilant. Jenny Smith, Policy Manager at Student Minds, is particularly concerned for new students. "The start of a new academic year is a key pressure point. Students may be worried about their academic capability, establishing new friendships, or making ends meet financially."

The onset of mental health conditions often overlaps with the age when most students go to university. Research shows that both the number of suicides and of those dropping out were increasing before the pandemic, and in 2019 mental health conditions were the second most declared disability following a 20% increase.

Depression rates across the general public have doubled, according to the Office for National Statistics. John de Pury, mental health policy lead for Universities UK, believes that financially disadvantaged, BAME, disabled and LGBTQ students are most acutely at risk.

Trying to find your feet without sufficient funds makes things more difficult. Part-time jobs were squeezed as Covid shut down the economy, and ongoing Covid restrictions have made shifts in pubs and restaurants much rarer. As a result, students have struggled to make ends meet and universities have faced unprecedented pressures on hardship funds

Tackling the load

Universities are also struggling to meet the increased demand for mental health services. Long waiting times are, sadly, par for the course. Geraldine Dufour, Head of Counselling Services at Cambridge, said: "Cambridge, the education sector and society more widely were already facing challenges in relation to mental health services every year."

There is some light on the horizon and most universities are expanding their mental health service provision. Bristol offers a ten-week Science of Happiness course, which teaches exercises to improve mental wellbeing. Ten other universities will benefit from a £1.5million partnership between the charity Mind and Goldman Sachs investment bank to deliver wellbeing, resilience and mindfulness training.

Many support services have moved online since Covid-19, hastening a trend that was already emerging. Although this reduces face-to-face support it makes accessing services easier, both practically and psychologically, by avoiding the daunting walk to an in-person appointment.

How can parents help?

The role of a parent or guardian has never been more important. Family and friends are often the first to know when students are unwell, so breaking down the stigma by talking freely about mental health will help them reach out for support when they need it.

Graham Virgo, Senior Pro-Vice Chancellor at Cambridge, urges parents to get involved: "If your prospective student is worried about the future, tell them that they are not alone. Suggest that, while there are many things that are out of our control, they can always reach out to you with their concerns and other people at university." Research what support is available to your child and spend time brainstorming helpful strategies together.

Student Minds has launched Student Space, offering free wellbeing resources and support via phone, text, webchat or email to all university students in England and Wales. For parents and carers worried about their child's mental health, the Parents Helpline at Young Minds offers free, confidential advice. For other resources and information visit the Student Minds parent's FAQ page at **https://www.studentminds.org.uk/supportforparents.html**.

Digital universities

Even with the re-opening of campuses, this generation of students is facing the most online-based experience to date. In the last decade higher education has increasingly seen coursework set, essays handed in and gradings taking place digitally. Lectures are recorded and uploaded onto student interfaces.

Along with online learning, students should be aware of the impact their online persona has. Posting on social media and messaging online are not private affairs, and many students have been exposed in supposedly confidential group chats, or by statuses on a private profile. Once posted online – be it a compromising photo, crass opinion or cruel "banter" – then it is there to stay. Digital footprints follow you, whether you like it or not.

Students at Durham rightly fell foul of this in September 2020, when a group chat containing multiple misogynistic, racist and discriminatory views was leaked. One student had his offer withdrawn. In a similar online exposure, 11 students at Warwick were suspended for making rape jokes, racist statements and anti-Semitic slurs in an online conversation.

With the popularity of social media sites, where opinions can be fired off in a matter of seconds, and TikToks or Instagram Reels serving as currency, remind your child that things they post today may be seen not only by their university but by future employers. Caution them not to post anything they wouldn't be comfortable having read back to them in an interview, or in front of a lecture hall of peers.

Universities have social media guidelines for students and your child will be seen as a representative of the university, whether posting on a private page or not. Bullying, harassment and discrimination, no matter how jokily intended, won't be tolerated. Clue them up on this before they go and remind them that nothing is truly private.

Keeping an eye online

Try not to fall into "helicopter" parenting. Your child is unlikely to accept you as a friend on social media sites or share everything with you. They are entitled to their own privacy, and if you give them space, they are more likely to willingly share when they want to.

Encourage privacy settings so their posts can't be shared beyond the intended audience. This won't give them free rein to post whatever they like, but hopefully serve as damage limitation if something does go awry.

If you're concerned that they might be feeling isolated, stay in touch. As with all the issues outlined above, the key is open dialogue and reserving your own judgement. Developing this relationship before your child goes to university will reap dividends as they navigate their time away.

Nick Rodrigues, Charlie Burt and Georgie Campbell

Useful websites

For alcohol information: **https://alcoholimpact.nus.org.uk   www.drinkaware.co.uk**
For information about drugs: **www.talktofrank.com   www.ssdp.org**
For information around consent: **www.nusconnect.org.uk**
www.revoltsexualassault.com
www.consentcollective.com
For information about mental health services the first point of reference should be a university's student support services.
For more general information: **www.studentminds.org.uk   www.youngminds.org.uk**

10 Going Abroad to University

For British students considering studying abroad, American universities are in a league of their own. More than twice the number of UK students went to the US in 2020 than went to Germany, the country that hosted the second-largest cohort. Sharing a common language is a big plus for Brits in the US, as is the liberal arts curriculum Stateside: there is no picking of chemistry, history, political science or whatever, you apply to university undecided and spend the first two years of a four-year Bachelors degree studying a wide range of classes before majoring in a specific field.

The Fulbright Commission, which promotes US-UK educational exchanges, estimates that most years there are between 11,000 and 11,500 British students studying at US universities at all levels, undergraduate, postgraduate and study abroad programmes. Although the pandemic reduced the numbers in 2020–21, numbers are on the rise again.

Applications from UK students to American universities were up 23% part way through the 2021 cycle, according to Common App, the closest equivalent to UCAS in the USA and an application system used by about 900 of the 4,000-plus US universities.

Unesco, which monitors the global flow of students in Higher Education, registers a slightly lower figure and also reported a slight decline in UK students going to the US in 2020 to 9,934. But this followed several years when the number was well over 10,000.

The popularity of American higher education among UK students is on the rise especially in private schools – many of which have dedicated staff to assist in US university applications, and where sixth formers' US destination successes are flagged on a par with their Oxbridge numbers. Some experts fear a "brain drain" of talented British students to American universities, as Oxford and Cambridge make efforts to reduce the number of offers they make to private school pupils. At Eton College, 36 sixth-formers were holding offers at US universities for the current academic year including Yale, Princeton, Harvard and Stanford – a third more than did so in 2016. At King's College School in Wimbledon, southwest London, about one in eight of the year group applied to American universities for this academic year. Westminster School in central London has seen offers from US universities almost double since 2015, from 23 to 41.

The Sutton Trust educational charity and champion of social mobility delivers a US programme in conjunction with the Fulbright Commission. The scheme is directed at low-income, first generation students in year 12 at British state schools. It sent 44 state-educated teenagers to America last autumn – including to highly selective institutions Harvard, in Cambridge Massachusetts, Stanford in California and Duke in North Carolina.

The big-name universities – and global ranking big hitters – attract a lot of interest from UK students. But Rowena Boddington, advising and marketing director at the Fulbright Commission, encourages applicants "to recognise that there's more than six or seven universities in the US. I see students who are willing to be open minded and explore what's out there be particularly successful in winning places."

Getting to grips with a whole continent of higher education institutions takes some doing. "It's worth considering what the Ivy League is and what it isn't," advises Boddington. "Some people think it's the equivalent of the Russell Group – it's not. The Ivy League is only universities in the northeast corner of the US, and it is a sports league. They are within driving distance of each other, they play football against each other. But there are lots of other selective schools that are not in the Ivy League – Stanford, MIT etc."

"Ivy Plus" is the term that encompasses both the Ivy League and a handful of similarly prestigious universities with lively traditions, large endowments and renowned alumni – such as Stanford, MIT (the Massachusetts Institute of Technology also in Cambridge), the University of Chicago and Duke. Some lists also count Northwestern, in Illinois, Johns Hopkins, in Baltimore, and Caltech, in Pasadena, California, as Ivy Plus.

Half the global top ten universities in the QS ranking are in America, but David Hawkins, founder of The University Guys – which helps students make successful applications to international universities – points out a fact that UK families often overlook. "America also has colleges," he notes, "that only do undergraduate degrees, like Amherst (in Massachusetts), and Pomona (in California), – some of them are more selective than the Ivy League but they aren't in the rankings because they don't have academic research and postgraduate degrees."

In light of the global pandemic, many US universities have made their SAT or ACT entry tests optional, thus extending the application window for UK students. This contributed to quite a significant rise in University Guys clients, "of 20–25% in students from the UK applying to US universities last year," says Hawkins. However, he did not see many more actually going. "It was 'I'll have a crack at Harvard, Princeton, Stanford' without really knowing what it means to do that. Applying to Columbia and applying to Brown is like trying to do a UCAS application for physics and fine art – they are two completely different experiences, and people here tend not to know that."

Fears of a brain drain of elite British students to American universities are out of proportion, believes Hawkins. "Oxford last year took 2,500 students from the UK, Harvard only has 1,600 spots and it only took 34 from the UK. But the perception out there is that 'all our good kids will get into the Ivies'. There were 65 US universities last year more selective than Oxford. Harvard isn't your cosy backup. Our students who get into the Ivies are your cast-iron certainties for Oxbridge, and then they might get into an Ivy League or an Ivy Plus, it's not the other way round – which unfortunately is what a lot of families think."

Character

Applicants to US universities should ask questions they might not ask about a UK university – such as: what is the culture of this institution? America's polarised states offer varying experiences, explains Hawkins:

"Going to university in Georgia is going to feel different to going to a university in Massachusetts. Going to a university with a catholic tradition, like Boston College or Notre Dame, is going to feel very different to going to a very urban, secular university like Northeastern (in Boston) or NYU (New York). The Canadian universities McGill, British Columbia and Toronto are great but they're huge – they educate about as many undergraduates as the top 20 in America put together."

Universities have their quirks, too – did you know that you have to pass a swimming test to get a degree from Columbia in New York? "Columbia also has a very defined curriculum – even the physicists and the mathematicians are going to be reading the Bible, Aristotle, Shakespeare," says Hawkins.

How much will it cost?

Fees vary; there are so many universities in the US, some with much lower fees and some with mind-bogglingly high prices. At Harvard, for example, in 2021/22, the total cost per year for a UK student – including tuition, fees, room and board, books, travel, and personal expenses is between \$78,000 and \$82,000 (approx. £59,000 – £62,000).

According to College Board, for tuition alone the average published annual fees are \$26,820 per year (£20,000) at public universities for out-of-state students and \$36,880 (£28,000) at private universities. However, not everyone pays these sticker prices – scholarships and grants can significantly reduce fees – but only for those who qualify. Unfortunately, you cannot take a student loan to the US. So, it's down to families to find the fees.

American universities extend the same financial aid to international students as they do to home undergraduates, which comes either as a sport scholarship, merit scholarship or as needs-based help. The most common awards are in sport scholarships, Hawkins explains: "US college sport is big business. The scholarship is a coach of a team using some of his or her budget to recruit students. So, if you are a very talented hockey player and the coach at Duke wants you, the coach at Duke is using his or her budget to fund you through university. The whole thing is about getting a coach to want you."

Merit scholarships can be in a wide range of talents such as volunteering or music, and different universities offer different awards. Needs-based aid is a means-tested form of funding, "So you could have two students going to Harvard, one of them could be paying \$80,000 or so a year, the other one could be paying nothing. And that determination is entirely based on the family's financial circumstances," explains Hawkins. Middle class dreams of packing your teen off to a prestigious US university on a massive scholarship should be reined in, however. "Harvard can be \$80,000 for a lot of families," he advises.

American dream job?

Student visas end when students have finished studying, and if they don't have a US visa or citizenship then they need to return to their home country. But an Optional Practical Training visa is offered to graduates. They can apply as they finish their studies. "It means that they don't have to have an employer who is willing to sponsor a work visa for them," explains Boddington. In practical terms it extends the student visa into this OPT period. "The idea is that a graduate can get a job in a field related to their major and get practical experience before returning home. For students in STEM fields an OPT visa can be for up to three years and for students in non-STEM fields it lasts for up to one year." Meanwhile students who return to Britain to apply for jobs have gained international experience and cross-cultural competency that makes them stand out.

Where do I start?

The University Guys has two big messages to everyone considering applying to the US: "Start early and work harder," says Hawkins. Year 12 is when students should really ramp up their application efforts. Organisations such as The University Guys (**https://www.theuniversityguys. com**) help families navigate the process and make sense of the stuff that gets lost in translation as it crosses the pond. The Fulbright Commission offers free online guides on applying to US universities, an advice phone line and organises USA College Day each September, Europe's largest US university college fair. The last time it happened in person was 2019 and 179 universities flew in just to meet British students. (**www.fulbright.org.uk/going-to-the-usa/ undergraduate/educationusa-advice**)

Europe

British students already living in an EU country before the clock struck midnight on 31 December 2020 have continued to have the same educational rights as that country's nationals. UK citizens studying – or planning to study – in Ireland continue to be covered by the Common Travel Area arrangements, which guarantees "home" fees, lower than those charged to international students, for the future. Applications to Trinity College Dublin surged by 11% in 2020 – dubbed the "Normal People bounce" due to the cult hit television series. Trinity's rise in applications included a small increase from UK applicants, halting a slide blamed on Brexit over recent years

It is up to individual EU member states to determine their approach to tuition fees for UK nationals, post-Brexit. Some countries, such as Germany – the second most popular destination for UK students studying abroad – have always charged the same fees to students from anywhere else in the world, not just the EU, and will continue to do so post-Brexit. In other countries, such as Denmark, British citizens without permanent residency are now liable to pay university tuition fees.

The Netherlands, which regularly promotes its universities to UK students and offers more undergraduate degrees taught in English than many other countries withdrew funding and fee benefits post-Brexit for UK students, who now pay international fees which range from around £5,500 a year to £13,500 for most courses, and over £30,000 a year for medicine. Dutch tuition fee loans, available for the full amount to EU students who are resident in the Netherlands throughout their studies, have stopped for UK students.

Top ten destinations for UK students studying abroad		Best Student Cities in the World	
1 United States	9,934	1 London	United Kingdom
2 Germany	4,746	2 Munich	Germany
3 Netherlands	3,163	=3 Seoul	South Korea
4 Australia	2,568	=3 Tokyo	Japan
5 Bulgaria	2,441	5 Berlin	Germany
6 Ireland	1,960	6 Melbourne	Australia
7 Canada	1,431	7 Zurich	Switzerland
8 Spain	1,117	8 Sydney	Australia
9 France	1,042	=9 Montreal	Canada
10 Denmark	979	=9 Paris	France
Source: 2020 Unesco figures		=9 Boston	United Stated
		QS ranking 2021	

Since Brexit, UK students have had to wrangle with immigration regulations in the EU. UK nationals are only able to stay in an EU country for 90 out of every 180 days without a visa.

There are more than 10,000 UK students at Continental European universities and colleges, according to Unesco. But a minority are undergraduates. More courses are taught in English at postgraduate level.

Nearly all first degrees in France are taught in the mother tongue, though there are 100 programmes taught in English listed on the Campus France website (**www.campusfrance.org/en**) at the Licence (Bachelors equivalent) level.

Germany attracts large numbers of international students and the DAAD website (**www.daad.de/en**) lists 249 undergraduate programmes taught wholly or mainly in English. Many are at the 20 private German universities, however, like Jacobs University in Bremen, which charges €20,000 (approx. £17,000) tuition fees a year. The public sector has abolished tuition fees, but you need to hunt down the courses as they are relatively scarce.

Most Continental courses are longer than their UK equivalents, adding to the cost and to lost earnings from extra time at university. Travel costs will of course be higher. The cost of living varies, from lower than the UK in southern Europe, to higher in Scandinavia.

The shorter-term schemes offered by the new national exchange scheme detailed below or arranged by UK universities with partners across the world, represent much less of a commitment academically, emotionally and financially than taking your whole degree abroad.

Exchange students

Named after the mathematician Alan Turing, the UK's new Turing scheme replaces Erasmus, the EU student exchange programme which UK students can no longer take part in. The UK was offered the opportunity to continue participating in Erasmus after Brexit but turned it down. The £110million Turing scheme provides funding for students in study and work placements across the world. More than 41,000 were able to benefit from it during the 2021–22 academic year. The government has confirmed funding for the scheme to 2024–25.

Under the Turing scheme, schools, colleges and higher education providers apply for funding for exchange projects on behalf of their students. If successful, they are then able to provide their students with funding to support study and work placements abroad. Funding amounts vary, depending on where students are going and for how long. For example, a student going to France for six months would get €390 (£335) per month under the Turing scheme, while the Erasmus scheme paid €370 (£317) per month in 2020–21. There is a more generous rate for disadvantaged students, plus help with travel costs.

The new programme has a global reach and provides placements across the world, whereas Erasmus is limited to EU and some non-EU countries that pay to be part of it. UK students did not have to pay tuition fees when studying abroad under Erasmus because the reciprocal scheme allowed EU students to come and study in the UK as well. The Turing scheme will not pay tuition fees for UK students studying abroad or for students from other countries studying in the UK. Instead, it expects the fees to be waived by the universities that take part.

As part of an arrangement with the Irish government, students at universities in Northern Ireland, however, will be able to participate in either Erasmus or the Turing scheme.

Exiting Erasmus has not been met with widespread enthusiasm. "Despite the claims of this government, they have not backed up the new Turing scheme with the funding required to support disadvantaged students to study abroad," Hillary Gyebi-Ababio, NUS vice-president for higher education, said. "This will harm the futures of thousands of students for years to come." However, 48% of the Turing scheme's first 41,024 participants were from disadvantaged backgrounds.

The path less trodden

As a nation, the British are historically not prolific student-travellers. There are more than 5.3 million students worldwide pursuing their higher education abroad – which represents two out of every 100 students, according to Unesco, but the British contingent contributes little to the global campus stampede. This is due in part to the good quality higher education at home – with UK universities second only to those in the US in all international rankings, and which at present offer enough places to meet demand. Our collectively dreadful ability to speak any language other than English also crucially limits the British taste for foreign study, unlike in most other countries where young people tend to be proficient in at least one second language by their late teens.

Cost is another factor that deters Brits from going abroad to study. Predictions that price would become less of a barrier once UK degrees charged £9,000-a-year from 2012 have been slow to translate into a long-term overseas applications boom. Even taking into account grants, loans and scholarships, access to studying at university abroad is limited to those with the finances to make it happen. Universities in some Continental cities, such as those in Scandinavian countries, may come with accommodation costs that are hard to swallow. Another major money concern is that, although support from the Student Loans Company continues for a year abroad during a UK degree course, those studying for their whole degrees from non-UK institutions do not qualify for a loan at all.

Advantages of studying abroad

Schools, universities and students themselves are enthusiastic about studying abroad. It is exciting, it broadens horizons, offers new challenges and introduces young people to a global working environment sure to prove helpful in future careers. A study stint abroad on a CV shows employers that the applicant is flexible and culturally mobile, with a maturity and breadth of experience that stands out from other candidates.

The numbers going abroad as part of a UK degree have grown by more than 50% in recent years, topping 39,000. But France has over 100,000 studying abroad and Germany more than three times as many, according to Unesco. Nepal has half the UK's population but many more students overseas.

It is possible to have your academic cake and eat it, by attending a British university in another country. Nottingham University has campuses in China and Malaysia; Middlesex can offer Dubai or Mauritius, where students registered in the UK can take part or all of their degrees. Other universities, such as Liverpool, also have joint ventures with overseas institutions which offer an international experience (in China, in Liverpool's case) and degrees from both universities.

In most cases, however, an overseas study experience means a foreign university. Postgraduate degrees used to be the preferred qualification to pursue abroad, and it is worth considering spending your undergraduate years in the UK before going abroad for more advanced study. Older students focused on more specialised programmes may get more out of living and studying abroad than 18-year-olds, and since first degrees in the UK are shorter than elsewhere, it could also work out cheaper.

Top Universities in the World

Rank	(Last year)	Institution	Country
2021	**(2020)**		
1	**(2)**	Harvard University	USA
2	**(1)**	Stanford University	USA
=3	**(3)**	Massachusetts Institute of Technology (MIT)	USA
=3	**(4)**	University of Oxford	UK
5	**(=5)**	University of Cambridge	UK
6	**(=5)**	California Institute of Technology (Caltech)	USA
7	**(8)**	University of Chicago	USA
8	**(7)**	Princeton University	USA
9	**(9)**	Yale University	USA
10	**(13)**	Columbia University	USA
11	**(=15)**	University of Pennsylvania	USA
12	**(=11)**	UCL (University College London)	UK
=13	**(14)**	Imperial College London	UK
=13	**(10)**	ETH Zurich (Swiss Federal Institute of Technology)	Switzerland
15	**(=11)**	University of California, Berkeley (UCB)	USA
16	**(17)**	Johns Hopkins University	USA
17	**(=15)**	Cornell University	USA
18	**(=18)**	Tsinghua University	China
19	**(21)**	University of Toronto	Canada
20	**(20)**	University of Michigan Ann Arbor	USA
21	**(=18)**	University of California, Los Angeles (UCLA)	USA
22	**(27)**	Peking University	China
23	**(23)**	University of Tokyo	Japan
24	**(26)**	University of Edinburgh	UK
25	**(22)**	Northwestern University	USA
26	**(24)**	New York University (NYU)	USA
27	**(28)**	University of California, San Diego (UCSD)	USA
28	**(29)**	The University of Melbourne	Australia
=29	**(32)**	National University of Singapore (NUS)	Singapore
=29	**(25)**	Duke University	USA
31	**(31)**	University of Manchester	UK
32	**(30)**	King's College London (KCL)	UK
33	**(36)**	Université PSL (Paris Sciences & Lettres)	France
34	**(=33)**	University of British Columbia	Canada
35	**(35)**	Kyoto University	Japan
36	**(=33)**	University of Washington	USA
37	**(41)**	McGill University	Canada
38	**(42)**	Nanyang Technological University (NTU)	Singapore
39	**(38)**	Technische Universität München	Germany
40	**(=39)**	Ludwig-Maximilians-Universität München	Germany
41	**(37)**	Ecole Polytechnique Fédérale de Lausanne (EPFL)	Switzerland

42	**(=45)** The University of Queensland (UQ)	Australia
43	**(=45)** University of Hong Kong (HKU)	Hong Kong
44	**(43)** University of Texas at Austin	USA
45	**(44)** Australian National University (ANU)	Australia
46	**(47)** Ruprecht-Karls-Universität Heidelberg	Germany
47	**(=39)** University of Wisconsin-Madison	USA
48	**(48)** The University of Sydney	Australia
49	**(=61)** Fudan University	China
50	**(63)** Zhejiang University	China
51	**(=49)** Washington University in St Louis	USA
52	**(52)** London School of Economics and Political Science (LSE)	UK
=53	**(56)** The University of New South Wales (UNSW)	Australia
=53	**(=49)** Carnegie Mellon University	USA
55	**(53)** University of North Carolina, Chapel Hill	USA
56	**(54)** Karolinska Institute, Stockholm	Sweden
57	**(51)** University of Illinois at Urbana-Champaign	USA
58	**(69)** The Chinese University of Hong Kong (CUHK)	Hong Kong
59	**(=58)** Seoul National University (SNU)	South Korea
60	**(65)** Shanghai Jiao Tong University	China
=61	**(=61)** Monash University	Australia
=61	**(64)** Sorbonne University	France
=63	**(=73)** Katholieke Universiteit Leuven	Belgium
=63	**(=58)** University of Zurich	Switzerland
65	**(55)** The Hong Kong University of Science and Technology (HKUST)	Hong Kong
66	**(57)** University of Copenhagen	Denmark
67	**(68)** Paris-Saclay University	France
68	**(=75)** Utrecht University	Netherlands
69	**(=75)** University of Amsterdam	Netherlands
70	**(72)** University of California, San Francisco	USA
=71	**(71)** Brown University	USA
=71	**(67)** University of Southern California	USA
73	**(69)** University of California Santa Barbara	USA
74	**(=73)** University of Minnesota, Twin Cities	USA
=75	**(78)** Delft University of Technology	Netherlands
=75	**(66)** University of Bristol	UK
77	**(70)** Georgia Institute of Technology (Georgia Tech)	USA
78	**(79)** The University of Warwick	UK
80	**(77)** KAIST – Korea Advanced Institute of Science and Technology	South Korea
81	**(=81)** Rockefeller University	USA
82	**(=84)** University of Groningen	Netherlands
83	**(83)** University of Colorado at Boulder	USA
84	**(=88)** University of Science and Technology of China	China
85	**(=84)** The University of Texas Southwestern Medical Center at Dallas	USA
=86	**(90)** Institut Polytechnique de Paris	France
=86	**(80)** University of Maryland, College Park	USA

Top Universities in the World cont.

=88	(=84)	City University of Hong Kong	Hong Kong
=88	(98)	Wageningen University	Netherlands
=88	(87)	Leiden University	Netherlands
=91	(92)	Tokyo Institute of Technology	Japan
=91	(=81)	Boston University	USA
93	(-)	University of Glasgow	UK
94	(=93)	University of Geneva	Switzerland
95	(95)	University of Oslo	Norway
=96	(=93)	Universiti Malaya (UM)	Malaysia
=96	(=96)	Vanderbilt University	USA
=98	(-)	The Hong Kong Polytechnic University	Hong Kong
=98	(=90)	University of California Davis	USA
100	(-)	The University of Texas M. D. Anderson Cancer Center	USA

Averaged from positions in the QS World University Ranking (QS); the Academic Ranking of World Universities (ARWU – Shanghai ranking) and *Times Higher Education* (THE) for 2021

Where do students go to?

There is remarkably little official monitoring of how many students leave the UK, let alone where they go. But the USA remains by far the most popular student destination. The latest figures from Unesco put Germany, the Netherlands, Australia, Bulgaria and Ireland after it. A few British students find their way to unexpected locations, like the Republic of Moldova or Indonesia, but usually for family reasons or to study the language.

Bear in mind that studying abroad can be the start of a much lengthier relocation, visa regulations allowing. University is where lots of people meet their spouses and set sail in their careers. Is the other side of the Atlantic, or the world, where you see yourself potentially settling down?

Which countries are best?

A memorable and valuable all-round experience is up there with the need for a good course when searching for a university overseas. Location is a big deal for most students – the country and the city – as is the reputation of the institution. QS publishes an annual ranking of student cities, based on quality-of-life indicators as well as the number of places at world-ranked universities. London topped the ranking in 2021, followed by Munich, Seoul and Tokyo.

Many Asian countries, such as Japan, are looking to recruit more foreign students. The high cost of living and unfamiliar language in Japan may seem hard to crack, but support for international students and courses taught in English are on the rise. As with any non-English speaking country though, even if you are taught in English, you still need enough of the local language to get by in shops, on transport and to make friends – to sign up for an exciting study experience abroad but only mix with expats would be a wasted opportunity.

China is worth considering, if you can get used to the dormitory accommodation that is the norm at most universities. The country's leading institutions are climbing the world rankings and improving their facilities, and the potential headstart in business offered by studying in China is hard to ignore. Hong Kong, which has several world-ranked universities and feels familiar for Britons, is a popular alternative to mainland Chinese universities, although the security situation has to be kept under review.

Will my degree be recognised?

Even in the era of globalisation, you need to bear in mind that not all degrees are equal. Unlike the MBA, which has an international system for accrediting courses and a global admissions standard, many professional courses need a qualification recognised by the relevant professional body. It is understandable that to practise law in England, you need to have studied the English legal system. For other subjects, the issues are more about the quality and content of courses outside UK control.

Contact the National Recognition Centre for the UK (**www.enic.org.uk**), which examines the compatibility and acceptability of qualifications from around the world, or ask the UK professional body in question – an engineering institution, law society or dental council, for instance – about the qualification you are interested in.

Global rankings: which university is best?

Going abroad to study is a big and expensive decision, and you want to get it right. A university that is taken seriously around the world should be your ambition, whatever you hope to do after graduation.

At the moment, there are three main systems for ranking universities internationally. One is run by QS (Quacquarelli Symonds), an educational research company in London (**www.topuniversities.com**). Another is by Shanghai Ranking Consultancy, a company set up by Shanghai Jiao Tong University, in China, and is called the Academic Ranking of World Universities (ARWU) (**www.shanghairanking.com**). The third is produced by *Times Higher Education* (**www.timeshighereducation.com/world-university-rankings**), a weekly magazine with no connection to *The Times,* which published the QS version until 2010.

The QS system uses measures including academic opinion, employer opinion, international orientation, research impact and staff/student ratio to create its listing, while the ARWU takes account of Nobel Prizes and highly-cited papers, which are more related to excellence in scientific research. *Times Higher Education* added a number of measures to the QS model, including research income and a controversial global survey of teaching quality.

Naturally, the different methodologies produce some contrasting results – as evidenced by the three main rankings each having a different university at the top. The table on these pages is a composite of the three main rankings, which places Harvard at the top and includes four UK universities in the top 15.

In practice, if you go to a university that features strongly in any of the tables, you will be at a place that is well-regarded around the world. Even the 200th university on any of these rankings is an elite institution in a world with way more than 5,000 universities.

The main international rankings focus largely on research and tend to favour universities which are good at science and medicine. This is why places that centre on the humanities and the social sciences, such as the London School of Economics, can appear in deceptively modest positions. It is also worth bearing in mind that the rankings look at universities as a whole and offer limited information on specific subjects. QS first published global rankings in 26 subjects in 2011 and has increased its output now to 51 subjects.

Other options for overseas studies

A language degree will typically involve a year abroad, and a look at the UCAS website will show many options for studying another subject alongside your language of choice.

Many degrees offer a year abroad, either studying or in a work placement, even to those who are not taking a language. Shorter credit-bearing courses with partner institutions overseas are another option offered by UK universities. The best approach is to decide what you want to study and then see if there is a UK university that offers it as a joint degree or with a placement abroad. Do a background check on all the universities involved to ensure they are well-regarded, which is where the websites of global rankings will come in handy.

Useful websites

Prospects: studying abroad: **www.prospects.ac.uk/postgraduate-study/study-abroad**
Association of Commonwealth Universities: **www.acu.ac.uk**
Campus France: **www.campusfrance.org/en**
College Board (USA): **www.collegeboard.org**
DAAD (for Germany): **www.daad.de/en**
Study in Holland: **www.studyinholland.co.uk**
Education Ireland: **www.educationinireland.com/en**
Erasmus Programme (EU): **www.erasmusplus.org.uk**
Finaid (USA): **www.finaid.org**
Fulbright Commission: **www.fulbright.org.uk**
Study in Australia: **www.studyinaustralia.gov.au**
Study in Canada: **www.studyincanada.com**

11 Coming to the UK to Study

Against a backdrop of uncertainty caused by the Covid pandemic and hefty hikes in tuition fees for EU students following Brexit, EU student acceptances to undergraduate degree courses were 50% lower in the 2021 admissions cycle than in 2020. The withdrawal of home fee status for EU students prompted those from the Continent to vote with their feet. However, the number of overseas students from further afield increased for the fifth consecutive year and over 54,000 international students from non-EU countries won places to begin studying at British universities in 2021.

Evidently, the underlying strength of UK universities has caused demand to hold up among students outside the EU, even in the face of the first global health pandemic since the Spanish Flu a century ago. As for the halving of EU students on British campuses, it is likely this will not be evenly distributed across the country; with the most esteemed UK universities and those which do well in league tables such as ours experiencing less of a hit than more modest institutions.

International undergraduate degree fees vary by course but most fall broadly between £10,000 and £20,000 per year, although subjects such as engineering disciplines can cost £35,100 and medical degrees cost up to £64,652. Classroom-based subjects such as the humanities are less expensive, and cost around £12,000 per year, on average. Compared with the far more affordable £9,250 for all courses charged to EU students pre-Brexit, the new international rates counterbalance the reduced student numbers to some extent.

The UK higher education sector takes great pride in its renown for being welcoming, diverse and offering easy access to international students. Fewer EU students on campuses represents a sore loss of some of that prized cultural diversity, and the change in fee status is a blow to the social and academic mobility offered by the formerly good-value higher education available to students from EU countries.

Paradoxically, the UK's international education strategy includes a target of increasing the number of international students to at least 600,000 by 2030. In 2018–19, there were 485,645 international students studying at UK higher education institutions, accounting for 20.7% of the total student population. Almost 15% of all undergraduates and 37.1% of all postgraduates were international students.

There is much to recommend a degree in Britain. Global surveys have shown that British universities are seen to offer high quality in a relatively safe environment, with the added bonus of students being immersed in the English language. Degree courses here, both undergraduate and postgraduate, are shorter than the average length worldwide, which helps balance our relatively high living costs. The fall in the value of the pound recently has added to the country's appeal and makes a UK higher education cheaper in real terms than it has been before

In terms of academic standing, the QS World University Rankings 2021 include 90 UK universities – six more than last year. Four of them are in the global top ten, with a further four in the global top 50. *Times Higher Education's* World University Rankings 2022 include 101 British institutions, 28 of them in the top 200.

The relationship between the UK and its international students is reciprocal, as highlighted by a report by educational thinktank the Higher Education Policy Institute (HEPI) in 2021. The analysis calculated the valuable contribution of international students to the UK's economic prosperity, finding that first-year international students contribute £28.8billion to the national economy, spread across every part of the UK – significantly less than the costs incurred to the UK by hosting them, which are put at £2.9billion.

The top countries for sending international students to the UK

EU countries	Number	%	Non-EU countries	Number	%
Romania	9,133	9.4	China	51,777	29.9
France	8,887	9.1	India	14,161	8.2
Italy	7,827	8.0	Hong Kong (Special Administrative	12,698	7.3
Spain	7,688	7.9	Region of China)		
Poland	7,557	7.7	Malaysia	10,420	6.0
Cyprus (European Union)	6,610	6.8	United States	7,849	4.5
Germany	5,900	6.1	Singapore	5,269	3.0
Portugal	5,397	5.5	Nigeria	4,328	2.5
Greece	5,273	5.4	Kuwait	4,128	2.4
Bulgaria	5,074	5.2	United Arab Emirates	4,114	2.4
Ireland	4,557	4.7	Korea (South)	3,443	2.0
Lithuania	3,905	4.0	Canada	3,422	2.0
Czech Republic	2,204	2.3	Pakistan	2,939	1.7
Hungary	1,985	2.0	Norway	2,787	1.6
Belgium	1,947	2.0	Saudi Arabia	2,592	1.5
Sweden	1,947	2.0	Switzerland	2,579	1.5
Netherlands	1,656	1.7	Thailand	2,118	1.2
Finland	1,513	1.6	Russia	2,058	1.2
Slovakia	1,506	1.5	Qatar	2,049	1.2
Latvia	1,141	1.2	Egypt	1,640	0.9
			Turkey	1,640	0.9
Total (all non-UK EU)	**97,517**		**Total (all non-EU)**	**156,485**	

Note: First degree non-UK students

Nick Hillman, director of HEPI, said: "This report confirms higher education is one of the UK's greatest export earners. The benefits reach every part of the UK, from Land's End to John O'Groats. But international students do not just bring financial benefits. They also bring educational benefits by making our campuses more diverse and exciting places to be."

Unesco data shows that the UK has been the second most popular destination in the world for international students throughout the years, behind the USA. But research published by Universities UK in 2020 showed that its annual growth is concerningly modest, at 0.9%, especially compared with Australia – which at 13.6% has the fastest-expanding growth rate of international students among English-speaking destinations.

Chinese students make up the UK's largest cohort of international students, representing almost three in every ten overseas students in 2020 – by far the highest proportion from a single country. India, Hong Kong and Malaysia follow in second, third and fourth places, and among EU countries Romania, France and Italy send the most students, in that order.

More than 50 of Britain's universities went all out to ensure their Chinese students were able to travel to the UK for the start of the 2021 academic year, amid the global travel restrictions that risked students being unable to make the trip. Institutions including Russell Group members Imperial College London, Bristol and Exeter, chartered flights to bring students over in time for the start of term. Airport transfers, quarantine hotels and food supplies were also taken care of. Students who could not come to the UK for the start of their course were provided with online learning and multiple start dates.

Evidently, the extent to which UK universities seek out and strive to foster the recruitment of international students will weather the impacts of Covid-19 and Brexit.

Why study in the UK?

As well as the strong reputation of UK degrees and the opportunity to be taught in and soak up the English language, research shows that most international graduates are well-rewarded when they return home. A Government-commissioned report showed that graduates of UK universities earn much higher salaries than those who studied in their own country. The starting salaries of UK graduates in China and India were more than twice as high as those for graduates educated at home, while even those returning to the USA saw a salary premium of more than 10%. Students who take the plunge to travel abroad to study are likely to be bright and highly motivated, so some uplift in such students' outcomes is to be expected. Unless they have government scholarships, most international students have to be from relatively wealthy backgrounds to afford the fees and other expenses involved. The hopes of a higher salary upon graduation are likely to be part of the equation when taking on the cost of the course. But the scale of increase demonstrated in the report suggests that a UK degree remains a good investment. Three years after graduation, 95% of the international graduates surveyed were in work or further study. More than 90% had been satisfied with their learning experience and almost as many would recommend their university to others.

A popular choice

Nearly all UK universities are cosmopolitan places that welcome international students in large numbers. In many UK universities you can expect to have fellow students from more than 100 countries. Almost one student in five is from outside the UK – 6% from the EU and 14% from the rest of the world. More full-time postgraduates – the fastest-growing group – come from outside the UK than within it.

More than 90% of international students declare themselves satisfied with their experience of UK universities in surveys by i-graduate, the student polling organisation, although they are less enthusiastic in the National Student Survey and more likely than UK students to make official complaints. Nevertheless, satisfaction increased by eight percentage points in four years, according to i-graduate, reflecting greater efforts to keep ahead of the global competition. International students are particularly complimentary about student unions, multiculturalism, teaching standards and places of worship. Their main concerns tend to be financial, partly because of a lack of employment opportunities. However, since summer 2021, international students who have successfully completed an undergraduate or Master's degree have been able to benefit from two years' work experience in the UK upon graduation, through the new Graduate Route. Students who complete their PhD will be able to stay for three years.

The number of students taking UK degrees through a local institution, distance learning or a full branch campus of a UK university was already growing even before the pandemic heralded wide-spread blended online learning. The numbers grew by 70% in a decade and are likely to rise further as a result of the post-Brexit fee changes. Over 30 UK universities have a physical presence overseas, hosting a growing number of students and local staff. The success of these international hubs has led to the formation of a new UK University Overseas Campuses Network representing institutions providing a British education to more than 60,000 students and employing upwards of 5,000 staff across their international campuses. Most branch

The universities most favoured by EU and non-EU students

Institution	EU students	Institution	Non-EU students
Coventry University	3,349	University College London	6,675
King's College London	3,046	Coventry University	6,234
University College London	2,973	The University of Manchester	6,152
The University of Aberdeen	2,254	The University of Liverpool	5,315
The University of Manchester	2,209	University of the Arts, London	5,164
The University of Edinburgh	2,139	The University of Edinburgh	5,062
The University of Warwick	2,123	King's College London	4,528
University of the Arts, London	2,069	Imperial College London	3,567
The University of Glasgow	2,068	The University of Birmingham	3,404
University of Bedfordshire	1,960	The University of Sheffield	3,275
The University of Essex	1,823	University of Nottingham	3,232
Anglia Ruskin University	1,773	The University of Leeds	3,133
The University of Westminster	1,674	The University of Warwick	3,040
Imperial College London	1,600	The University of Exeter	2,754
Middlesex University	1,523	University of Durham	2,752
The University of Surrey	1,413	The University of Sussex	2,636
The University of Bath	1,370	The University of Bristol	2,558
Solent University	1,350	The University of St Andrews	2,550
The University of Southampton	1,241	The University of Portsmouth	2,486
De Montfort University	1,233	De Montfort University	2,457

Note: First degree non-UK students

campuses are in Asia or the Middle East, but some universities are now planning campuses in other parts of the EU. Coventry – which was the most popular UK university with EU students in 2020 – has set up in Poland.

Where to study in the UK

The vast majority of the UK's universities and other higher education institutions are in England. Of the 132 universities profiled in this *Guide*, 107 are in England, 15 in Scotland, eight in Wales and two in Northern Ireland. Fee limits in higher education for UK and EU students are determined separately in each administrative area, which historically in some cases brought benefits for EU students, such as those who chose to study in Scotland where they paid no tuition fees. Under the new regulations however, all undergraduates from outside the UK will be charged the international rate of fees.

Within the UK, the cost of living varies by geographical area. London is home to University College London, the most popular university with non-EU students in 2020, and although it is the most expensive city, accommodation costs can also be high in many other major cities. Incoming students should find out as much as they can about what living in Britain is like. Further advice and information is available through the British Council at its offices worldwide, at more than 60 university exhibitions that it holds around the world every year, or at its Education UK website: **https://study-uk.britishcouncil.org**. Also useful for international students is the information provided by the UK Council for International Student Affairs (UKCISA) at **www.ukcisa.org.uk**.

Universities in all parts of the UK have a reputation for high quality teaching and research, as evidenced in global rankings such as those shown on page 131. They maintain this standing by investing heavily in the best academic staff, buildings and equipment, and by taking part in rigorous quality assurance monitoring. The Office for Students is the chief regulatory body for higher education in England, overseeing organisations such as the Quality Assurance Agency for Higher Education (QAA), which remains the arbiter of standards. Professional bodies also play an important role in relevant subjects.

Although many people from outside the UK associate British universities with Oxford and Cambridge, the reality at most higher education institutions is quite different. Some universities do still maintain ancient traditions, but most are modern institutions that place at least as much emphasis on teaching as on research and offer many vocational programmes, often with close links to business, industry and the professions. The table on page 139 shows the universities that are most popular with international students at undergraduate level. Although some of those at the top of the lists are among the most famous names in higher education, others achieved university status only in the last 30 years.

What subjects to study?

Strongly vocational courses are favoured by international students. Many of these in professional areas such as architecture, dentistry or medicine take one or two years longer to complete than most other degree courses. Traditional first degrees are mostly awarded at Bachelor level (BA, BEng, BSc, etc.) and last three to four years. There are also some "enhanced" first degrees (MEng, MChem, etc.) that take four years to complete. The relatively new Foundation degree programmes are almost all vocational and take two years to complete as a full-time course, with an option to study for a further year to gain a full degree. The table on page 141 shows the most popular subjects studied by international students. You need to consider the details of the degree you wish to study and ensure that you have looked at the ranking of that university in our main league table in chapter 1 and in the subject tables in chapter 12.

English language proficiency

The universities maintain high standards partly by setting demanding entry requirements, including proficiency in English. For international students, this usually includes a score of at least 5.5 in the International English Language Testing System (IELTS), which assesses English language ability through listening, speaking, reading and writing tests. Under visa regulations introduced in 2011, universities are able to vouch for a student's ability in English. This proficiency will need to be equivalent to an "upper intermediate" level (level B2) of the CEFR (Common European Framework of Reference for Languages) for studying at an undergraduate level (roughly equivalent to an overall score of 5.5 in IELTS).

There are many private and publicly funded colleges throughout the UK that run courses designed to bring the English language skills of prospective higher education students up to the required standard. However, not all of these are Government approved. Some private organisations such as INTO (**www.intostudy.com**) have joined with universities to create centres

The most popular subjects for international students

Subject Group	EU students	Non-EU students	Total students	% of all international students
Business, Management and Marketing	12,060	22,862	34,922	12.9
Accounting and Finance	2,357	15,277	17,634	6.5
Computer Science	7,899	9,351	17,250	6.4
Law	4,163	10,346	14,508	5.4
Art and Design	5,067	8,687	13,754	5.1
Economics	2,872	8,200	11,072	4.1
Psychology	4,539	4,161	8,700	3.2
Politics	3,786	4,121	7,907	2.9
Mathematics	1,886	5,722	7,607	2.8
Electrical and Electronic Engineering	1,305	5,832	7,138	2.6
Mechanical Engineering	1,705	5,381	7,085	2.6
Drama, Dance and Cinematics	3,989	2,989	6,978	2.6
Biological Sciences	3,397	3,467	6,863	2.5
Communication and Media Studies	2,699	3,776	6,475	2.4
Medicine	1,481	4,259	5,740	2.1
Hospitality, Leisure, Recreation and Tourism	2,613	2,418	5,031	1.9
Architecture	1,601	3,219	4,820	1.8
Aeronautical and Manufacturing Engineering	1,732	2,929	4,661	1.7
Civil Engineering	765	3,702	4,467	1.7
Physics and Astronomy	1,630	1,761	3,392	1.3
Total	**97,517**	**172,899**	**270,416**	

Note: First degree non-UK students
Note: 'Other' excluded from subject rank but numbers are included in total, which are also used to calculate the %s.

running programmes to prepare international students for degree-level study. The British Council also runs English language courses at its centres around the world.

Tougher student visa regulations were introduced in 2012 and have since been refined. Although under the current system, universities' international students should not be denied entry to the UK, as long as they are proficient in English and are found to have followed other immigration rules, some lower-level preparatory courses taken by international students have been affected. It is, therefore, doubly important to consult the official UK government list of approved institutions (web address given at the end of this chapter) before applying.

How to apply

The information below is best read in conjunction with that provided in chapter 5, which deals with the application process in some detail.

Some international students apply directly to a UK university for a place on a course, and others make their applications via an agent in their home country. But most applying for a full-time, first degree course do so through the Universities and Colleges Admissions Service (UCAS). If you take this route, you will need to fill in an online UCAS application form at home, at school or perhaps at your nearest British Council office. There is plenty of advice on the UCAS website about the process of finding a course and the details of the application system.

Whichever way you apply, the deadlines for getting your application in are the same. Under the regulations at the time this *Guide* went to press, for those applying from within an EU country, application forms for most courses starting in 2022 had to be be received at UCAS by 15 January 2022. Note that applications for Oxford and Cambridge and for all courses in medicine, dentistry and veterinary science have to be received at UCAS by 15 October, while some art and design courses have a later deadline of 24 March.

If you are applying from a non-EU country to study in 2023, you can submit your application to UCAS at any time between 1 September 2022 and 30 June 2023. Most people will apply well before the 30 June deadline to make sure that places are still available and to allow plenty of time for immigration regulations, and to make arrangements for travel and accommodation.

Entry and employment regulations

Visa regulations have been the subject of continuing controversy in the UK and many new rules and regulations have been introduced, often hotly contested by universities. Recent governments have been criticised for increasing visa fees, doubling the cost of visa extensions, and ending the right to appeal against refusal of a visa.

The current points system for entry – known as Tier 4 – came into effect in 2009. Under this scheme, prospective students can check whether they are eligible for entry against published criteria, and so assess their points score. Universities are also required to provide a Confirmation of Acceptance for Studies (CAS) to their international student entrants, who must have secured an unconditional offer, and the institution must appear as a "Tier 4 Sponsor" on the Home Office's Register of Sponsors. Prospective students have to demonstrate that, as well as the necessary qualifications, they have English language proficiency and enough money for the first year of their specified course. This includes the full fees for the first year and, currently, living costs of £1,265 a month, up to a maximum of nine months, if studying in London (£1,015 a month in the rest of the UK). Under the current visa requirements, details of financial support are checked in more detail than before.

All students wishing to enter the UK to study are required to obtain entry clearance before arrival. The only exceptions are British nationals living overseas, British overseas territories citizens, British Protected persons, British subjects, and non-visa national short-term students who may enter under a new Student Visitor route. All overseas students must now obtain a Tier 4 student visa, including those from EU countries, Iceland, Liechtenstein, Norway and Switzerland. Fees are £348, plus an annual healthcare surcharge. As part of the application process, biometric data will be requested and this will be used to issue you with a Biometric Residence Permit (BRP) once you have arrived in the UK. You will need a BRP to open a bank account, rent accommodation or establish your eligibility for benefits and services or to work part-time, for example. The details of the regulations are continually reviewed by the Home Office. You can find more about all the latest rules and regulations for entry and visa requirements at **www.gov.uk/tier-4-general-visa**.

Irish nationals have the right to live and work in the UK under the UK-Ireland Common Travel Area arrangements. Irish students will not need to apply for a student visa or the graduate immigration route.

Bringing your family

Since 2010, international students on courses of six months or less have been forbidden to bring a partner or children into the UK, and the latest reforms extend this prohibition to all undergraduates except those who are government sponsored. Postgraduates studying for 12 months or longer will still be able to bring dependants to the UK, and most universities can help to arrange facilities and accommodation for families as well as for single students. The family members you are allowed to bring with you are your husband or wife, civil partner (a same-sex relationship that has been formally registered in the UK or your home country) or long-term partner and dependent children.

You can find out more about getting entry clearance for your family at **www.ukcisa.org.uk**.

Support from British universities

Support for international students is more comprehensive than in many countries and begins long before you arrive in the UK. Many universities have advisers in other countries. Some will arrange to put you in touch with current students or graduates who can give you a first-hand account of what life is like at a particular university. Pre-departure receptions for students and their families, as well as meet-and-greet arrangements for newly-arrived students, are common. You can also expect an orientation and induction programme in your first week, and many universities now have "buddying" systems where current students are assigned to new arrivals to help them find their way around, adjust to their new surroundings and make new friends. Each university also has a students' union that organises social, cultural and sporting events and clubs, including many specifically for international students. Both the university and the students' union are likely to have full-time staff whose job it is to look after the welfare of students from overseas.

International students also benefit from free medical and subsidised dental and optical care and treatment under the UK National Health Service (non-EU students will have had to pay a healthcare surcharge when paying for their visa to benefit from this), plus access to a professional counselling service and a university careers service.

EU students studying full-time may be entitled to a full or partial refund of the immigration health surcharge payment if you have an EHIC issued in an EU country and you do not work in the UK. Further guidance about this is currently limited but the information available is outlined on the Government website **www.gov.uk/guidance/healthcare-for-eu-and-efta-nationals-living-in-the-uk** under the heading "Students" in the section "When your healthcare costs in the UK are covered by an EU country".

At university, you will naturally encounter people from a wide range of cultures and walks of life. Getting involved in student societies, sport, voluntary work, and any of the wide range of social activities on offer will help you gain first-hand experience of British culture, and, if you need it, will help improve your command of the English language.

Useful websites

The British Council, with its dedicated Study UK site designed for those wishing to find out more about studying in the UK:
https://study-uk.britishcouncil.org/

The UK Council for International Student Affairs (UKCISA) provides a wide range of information on all aspects of studying in the UK:
www.ukcisa.org.uk

UCAS, for full details of undergraduate courses available and an explanation of the application process:
www.ucas.com/undergraduate/applying-university/international-and-eu-students

For the latest information on entry and visa requirements:
www.gov.uk/tier-4-general-visa

Register of sponsors for Tier 4 educational establishments:
www.gov.uk/government/publications/register-of-licensed-sponsors-students

For a general guide to Britain, available in many languages:
www.visitbritain.com

12 Subject by Subject Guide

Perhaps surprisingly, the best course in the subject you want to study might not be at the university with the highest league table position or the oldest foundation. Some fairly modest universities are specialists in niche areas – as evidenced by their research outputs, graduate career successes and feedback from current students. Conversely, it could turn out that the best course happens to be offered at a top-end, ancient university that you had not considered before.

Or maybe the subject you loved at A-level is taught quite differently at degree level and would turn out an uninspiring choice for a three-year undergraduate commitment. Employment prospects are another factor; they might be dire for the subject you love – but some digging down can elicit the individual institutions that buck that trend, thus bringing the best of both worlds within sight.

The wealth of publicly available statistics means applicants can be well-equipped to make a thorough assessment of whether a certain subject – or course in that subject at a particular university – is going to give them what they are looking for. Research shows that applicants are wise to how important subject rankings are; the majority take more notice of subject tables than of institutional rankings – though it is the latter that tend to grab the headlines.

This chapter offers pointers to the leading universities in a wide range of subjects. Many, such as psychology and mechanical engineering, have their own table. Others are grouped together in broader categories, such as "subjects allied to medicine". If you see a dash (–) this denotes a score is not available because the number of students is too small for the outcome to be statistically reliable. In 2019/20 HESA, the Higher Education Statistics Agency, introduced a new coding system for subjects. The crossover to the new format has meant a few subjects have missed Graduate Outcomes data this year – which is why you will see more dashes than usual in these columns. Please also be aware that it is possible not all institutions listed in a particular area will be running courses in 2023, as university curriculums vary frequently.

The subject tables include scores from the National Student Survey (NSS). These distil the views of final-year undergraduates on various aspects of their course, with the results presented in two columns. "Teaching quality" reflects the average scores in the sections of the survey focusing on teaching, assessment and feedback, learning opportunities and academic support. "Student experience" is derived from the average of the NSS sections covering organisation and management, learning resources, student voice and learning community, as well as the survey's final question: overall satisfaction.

The three other measures used in our tables are research quality, students' entry qualifications and graduate employment outcomes. The Education table uses a fifth indicator, Ofsted grades, a measure of the quality of teaching based on Ofsted inspections of teacher training courses. None of the measures is weighted. A full explanation of the measures is given on the next page.

Cambridge is again the most successful university among our subject rankings. It tops 23 of the 70 tables; St Andrews leads in seven; Oxford in six; Strathclyde, Imperial College London and Glasgow top three each; while Queens Belfast, Bath, UCL, Warwick, LSE and Edinburgh come first in two tables each. Thirteen other universities top one table.

Our rankings have gained three new tables this year – Bioengineering and Biomedical Engineering, Liberal Arts and Natural Sciences – only the first features in our subject-based employment and earnings tables yet, but graduate prospects statistics for all are included for individual universities.

Research quality

This information is sourced from the 2014 Research Excellence Framework (REF), a peer-review exercise used to evaluate the quality of research of UK higher education institutions, undertaken by the Higher Education Funding Bodies. As in the university league table, REF results are weighted then multiplied by the percentage of eligible staff entered for assessment. At the time of going to press, results from REF 2021 were not yet available.

For each subject, a research quality profile was given to those university departments that took part, showing how much of their research was in the following quality categories: 4* world leading; 3* internationally excellent; 2* internationally recognised; 1* nationally recognised; and unclassified. The funding bodies directed more funding to the very best research by applying weightings. Those used by HEFCE (the funding council for England) are employed in the tables: 4* is weighted by a factor of 3 and 3* is weighted by a factor of 1. Outputs of 2* and 1* carry zero weight. This results in a maximum score of 3. For consistency, the above weightings continue to be applied this year.

The scores in the tables are presented as a percentage of the maximum scores. To achieve the maximum score, all staff would need to be at 4* world-leading level. Universities could choose which staff to include in the REF, so, to factor in the depth of the research excellence, each quality profile score has been multiplied by the number of staff returned in the REF as a proportion of all eligible staff.

Entry standards

This is the average UCAS tariff score for new students under the age of 21, based on A- and AS-levels and Scottish Highers and Advanced Highers and other equivalent qualifications (including the International Baccalaureate), taken from HESA data for 2019–20. Each student's examination grades were converted to a numerical score using the UCAS tariff. The points used in the tariff appear on page 32.

Teaching quality and student experience

The student satisfaction measure is divided into two components, taken from the National Student Survey (NSS) results published in 2020 and 2021. The latest year's figures are used when only one is available, but an average of the two years' results is used in all other cases. Where NSS data was not available, the latest available scores for Teaching Quality and Student Experience were adjusted by the percentage point change in each subject between that year and 2021. This applies mainly to Oxford and Cambridge, which last met the threshold as entire universities in

2016. The adjusted scores were used for z-scoring only, and do not appear in the final tables.

The NSS covers eight aspects of a course, with an additional question gauging overall satisfaction. Students answer on a scale from 1 (bottom) to 5 (top) and the score in the table is calculated from the percentage of positive responses (4 and 5) in each section. The "Teaching Quality" indicator reflects the average scores for the first four sections of the survey. The "Student Experience" indicator is drawn from the average scores of the remaining sections and the overall satisfaction question. Teaching Quality is favoured over Student Experience and accounts for 67% of the overall student satisfaction score, with Student Experience making up the remaining 33%.

Graduate prospects

This is the percentage of graduates in high-skilled jobs or undertaking graduate-level study 15 months after graduation, recorded in the Graduate Outcomes survey published in June 2021 and based on 2019 graduates.

A low score on this measure does not necessarily indicate unemployment – some graduates may have taken jobs that are not categorised as professional work. The averages for each subject are given at the foot of each subject table in this chapter and in two tables in chapter 3 (see pages 51–54).

Note that in the tables that follow, when a figure is followed by a *, it refers to data from a previous year.

The subjects listed below are covered in the tables in this chapter:

Accounting and Finance
Aeronautical and
    Manufacturing Engineering
Agriculture and Forestry
American Studies
Anatomy and Physiology
Animal Science
Anthropology
Archaeology and Forensic
    Science
Architecture
Art and Design
Biological Sciences
Bioengineering and
    Biomedical Engineering
Building
Business, Management and
    Marketing
Celtic Studies
Chemical Engineering
Chemistry
Civil Engineering
Classics and Ancient
    History
Communication and Media
    Studies
Computer Science
Creative Writing
Criminology
Dentistry

Drama, Dance and
    Cinematics
East and South Asian Studies
Economics
Education
Electrical and Electronic
    Engineering
English
Food Science
French
General Engineering
Geography and
    Environmental Sciences
Geology
German
History
History of Art, Architecture
    and Design
Hospitality, Leisure,
    Recreation and Tourism
Iberian Languages
Information Systems and
    Management
Italian
Land and Property
    Management
Law
Liberal Arts
Linguistics
Materials Technology

Mathematics
Mechanical Engineering
Medicine
Middle Eastern and
    African Studies
Music
Natural Sciences
Nursing
Subjects Allied to Medicine
    (see page 275 for subjects
    included in this category)
Pharmacology and Pharmacy
Philosophy
Physics and Astronomy
Physiotherapy
Politics
Psychology
Radiography
Russian and East European
    Languages
Social Policy
Social Work
Sociology
Sports Science
Theology and Religious
    Studies
Town and Country Planning
    and Landscape
Veterinary Medicine

Accounting and Finance

Often taken together, accounting and finance share a focus on matters monetary, business and management. They also have differentiating features, however; accounting is the more defined topic that looks specifically at how money flows in and out of a company, while finance is broader – encompassing long-term management of assets, liabilities and growth.

Maths A-level is useful but not an essential requirement, except by a few leading universities. Business, economics and statistics are among other A-levels that universities look for. Entry standards vary considerably: students arrived at Buckinghamshire New last year with an average of 70 UCAS points, the lowest tariff score of 97 universities listed – although, conversely, it ranks in the top three for student satisfaction with both teaching quality and the wider experience. At the other end of the scale, students at Glasgow achieved entry grades equating to 223 UCAS points. Twenty-four universities averaged over 144 points – equivalent to three As at A level, and 23 averaged under 100 points.

Strathclyde holds on to first place in this table, its entry standards second only to those at Glasgow – which finishes fifth, and its research quality bettered by the LSE alone – which finishes second. Warwick, winner of our University of the Year for Teaching Quality award, has moved up three places to rank third, helped by strong rates of student satisfaction. Bath is fourth and in seventh place is Leeds, which came top of the table two years ago and second in our previous edition.

Perhaps surprisingly, accounting and finance do not set our graduate prospects measure alight. They rank 51st out of 67 subject areas, down from 43rd last year, with 66% of graduates in high-skilled work or further study 15 months on from their degrees. Some institutions do much better than average, however, led by Queen's Belfast with 95.6% of graduates achieving the top outcomes. Bath and Exeter also scored more than 92%.

Accounting and Finance	Teaching quality	Student experience	Research quality	Entry standards (UCAS points)	Graduate prospects	Overall score
1 Strathclyde	77.5%	80.1%	44.3%	210	81.8%	100.0
2 London School of Economics	77.2%	75.0%	52.3%	169	88.2%	98.5
3 Warwick	80.7%	83.8%	40.4%	158	87.5%	97.0
4 Bath	73.0%	81.0%	41.8%	150	92.2%	95.1
5 Glasgow	74.7%	77.4%	22.1%	223	76.7%	94.7
6 Queen's Belfast	74.8%	76.8%	32.7%	152	95.6%	94.1
7 Leeds	73.0%	69.2%	39.3%	168	86.9%	93.8
8 Durham	83.3%	80.4%	23.1%	153	89.5%	93.7
9 Ulster	83.0%	79.4%	40.4%	120	84.3%	93.1
10 Aberdeen	79.6%	81.4%	24.9%	180	75.8%	93.0
11 Lancaster	79.9%	80.7%	42.6%	126	81.2%	92.8
12 Exeter	78.1%	79.2%	24.4%	143	92.1%	92.1
13 Heriot-Watt	79.2%	80.9%	18.8%	175	80.3%	92.0
=14 Manchester	71.2%	71.1%	33.3%	171	80.8%	91.4
=14 Dundee	82.1%	82.9%	12.1%	183	74.7%	91.4
16 Loughborough	72.9%	77.9%	32.6%	148	82.6%	90.9

17	Cardiff	75.2%	70.1%	32.0%	142	85.6%	90.5
18	Edinburgh	68.1%	68.0%	25.8%	180	85.5%	90.4
19	Liverpool	84.8%	83.4%	20.1%	143	71.6%	89.5
20	Stirling	77.8%	77.2%	25.2%	171	64.8%	89.2
21	Birmingham	73.9%	70.1%	29.1%	149	79.1%	88.9
22	City	69.0%	72.4%	28.7%	156	79.1%	88.4
=23	Reading	74.0%	74.4%	29.3%	121	85.3%	88.2
=23	Bristol	65.3%	64.1%	32.1%	159	83.5%	88.2
25	East Anglia	77.7%	78.1%	28.1%	128	75.0%	88.1
26	Queen Mary, London	71.2%	68.4%	31.3%	153	74.2%	87.9
27	Swansea	79.9%	79.1%	22.0%	132	73.6%	87.5
28	Southampton	70.2%	70.6%	24.0%	146	81.4%	87.2
29	York	73.3%	72.1%	24.0%	151*	—	87.1
30	Sussex	76.2%	75.7%	23.7%	136	72.4%	86.7
31	Nottingham	64.1%	64.3%	32.6%	144	82.9%	86.6
32	Glasgow Caledonian	79.4%	79.2%	1.8%	178	66.1%	86.1
33	Bangor	83.0%	83.5%	23.4%	103	68.7%	85.6
34	Newcastle	71.1%	70.3%	20.7%	142	76.8%	85.5
35	Kent	75.6%	75.7%	24.8%	125	69.8%	85.3
=36	Aston	71.3%	70.2%	19.7%	127	81.1%	84.9
=36	Robert Gordon	82.9%	77.2%	2.6%	166	61.2%	84.9
38	Sheffield	71.3%	69.8%	26.8%	126	73.9%	84.7
39	Abertay	84.4%	87.1%	—	138	65.2%	84.3
40	Royal Holloway, London	74.3%	70.5%	27.0%	123	65.5%	83.7
41	Surrey	72.0%	73.7%	15.8%	126	74.4%	83.3
42	Liverpool John Moores	83.3%	81.0%	—	133	66.3%	83.0
43	Hull	78.9%	76.6%	10.2%	117	67.8%	82.2
44	Leicester	68.7%	67.7%	24.3%	123	69.1%	82.1
45	Portsmouth	78.3%	71.5%	9.5%	101	71.1%	80.6
46	West of England	75.9%	73.1%	5.5%	108	70.8%	79.9
47	Essex	67.1%	65.9%	25.1%	107	66.8%	79.7
=48	Oxford Brookes	66.7%	68.3%	5.1%	124	77.1%	79.4
=48	Lincoln	78.5%	72.9%	4.8%	101	68.9%	79.4
50	Edinburgh Napier	70.4%	71.0%	2.3%	162	53.8%	79.1
51	Aberystwyth	81.2%	79.5%	14.5%	96	51.0%	78.9
52	Greenwich	79.5%	76.6%	3.3%	107	60.8%	78.8
53	Keele	69.6%	73.4%	10.2%	111	66.8%	78.7
54	West London	92.7%	91.0%	—	106	36.7%	78.6
55	Northumbria	71.1%	67.8%	4.0%	135	61.6%	78.3
56	Staffordshire	77.0%	71.0%	2.6%	112	63.2%	78.2
57	Nottingham Trent	71.2%	68.2%	4.6%	112	68.8%	77.9
=58	Leeds Beckett	76.6%	76.4%	0.8%	92	67.6%	77.5
=58	Cardiff Metropolitan	79.5%	74.5%	—	98	62.5%	77.5
=60	South Wales	74.9%	74.2%	0.2%	114	60.0%	77.2
=60	Solent, Southampton	81.5%	85.4%	—	83	58.8%	77.2
62	Chester	77.3%	69.0%	0.5%	114	59.3%	77.0

Accounting and Finance cont.

	Teaching quality	Student experience	Research quality	Entry standards (UCAS points)	Graduate prospects	Overall score
=63 London Metropolitan	82.7%	83.0%	0.6%	87	54.7%	76.9
=63 Sunderland	81.2%	79.9%	0.4%	99	53.3%	76.9
65 Worcester	78.4%	69.6%	0.9%	104	—	76.7
=66 Coventry	73.1%	74.0%	1.6%	101	63.0%	76.3
=66 Salford	72.7%	70.5%	5.9%	116	54.0%	76.3
=68 De Montfort	71.9%	68.2%	10.7%	94	61.3%	76.2
=68 Roehampton	75.1%	76.2%	4.5%	92	—	76.2
=70 Sheffield Hallam	70.5%	69.8%	0.6%	109	63.9%	75.9
=70 Wolverhampton	79.4%	75.8%	2.4%	83	58.6%	75.9
=72 Manchester Metropolitan	70.9%	64.8%	4.7%	121	56.3%	75.8
=72 Birmingham City	77.9%	74.3%	1.3%	105	52.3%	75.8
74 Brighton	64.1%	56.0%	6.5%	96	80.1%	75.6
=75 Hertfordshire	76.8%	76.0%	0.9%	97	54.7%	75.5
=75 Derby	81.9%	77.6%	0.9%	98	46.4%	75.5
77 Kingston	70.7%	71.0%	9.2%	99	55.6%	75.3
=78 Plymouth	59.9%	57.5%	13.1%	105	70.1%	75.0
=78 Buckinghamshire New	86.0%	86.5%	1.8%	70	44.7%	75.0
80 Anglia Ruskin	80.9%	80.8%	3.4%	83	46.7%	74.8
81 Brunel	59.4%	58.7%	23.0%	117	52.9%	74.7
82 Bournemouth	63.5%	62.0%	8.8%	93	69.9%	74.5
=83 Teesside	72.1%	68.8%	2.0%	90	62.5%	74.4
=83 Edge Hill	67.8%	70.6%	—	120	55.2%	74.4
85 Huddersfield	71.7%	64.2%	4.1%	113	50.6%	74.0
86 Westminster	66.1%	71.6%	2.4%	122	48.8%	73.6
87 Winchester	71.8%	65.5%	—	100	56.8%	73.4
88 Bedfordshire	72.7%	71.4%	3.1%	89	50.9%	72.9
89 York St John	72.3%	61.4%	0.8%	100	—	72.8
90 Central Lancashire	57.7%	55.7%	4.4%	120	58.8%	71.6
91 Middlesex	66.7%	65.3%	10.5%	95	43.9%	71.3
92 Northampton	71.5%	65.5%	1.0%	88	49.7%	71.1
93 East London	79.9%	79.0%	0.8%	79	32.8%	70.8
94 Canterbury Christ Church	63.0%	63.1%	—	82	61.0%	70.1
95 London South Bank	70.0%	64.4%	2.1%	96	40.4%	69.7
96 West of Scotland	50.6%	50.0%	2.9%	135	52.4%	68.9
97 Bradford	56.7%	59.7%	11.8%	110	29.4%	66.8

Employed in high-skilled job	43%	Employed in lower-skilled job	29%
Employed in high-skilled job and studying	10%	Employed in lower-skilled job and studying	3%
Studying	6%	Unemployed	9%
High skilled work (median) salary	£25,000	Low/medium skilled salary	£21,000

Aeronautical and Manufacturing Engineering

Imperial College London heads our Aeronautical and Manufacturing Engineering table. It has the top research rating in the subjects, the second-highest proportion of graduates in high-skilled work or postgraduate study 15 months on from their degrees and it also achieved a top 10 result for student satisfaction – often a weak point for research-led universities. Bristol places equal second for research and overall.

Surrey, =10th overall, comes top in our measure of graduate prospects, with 92.5% in professional jobs or furthering their studies 15 months after graduating. Imperial, Ulster and Bath also came close to Surrey, with around nine in 10 graduates having secured the most desirable outcomes.

The courses under this category focus predominantly on aeronautical or manufacturing engineering (often called production engineering), but the table also includes some degrees with the mechanical title. Degree apprenticeships may appeal in this area, with earn-while-you-learn routes offered at leading firms such as Rolls-Royce, though they do not feature in this table. Categorised by UCAS as aerospace engineering, both applications and enrolments rose for the eight successive year in 2020, when 3,820 undergraduates started courses. Production and manufacturing engineering disciplines attracted a further 2,065 students. Entry standards can be stiff: 10 of our table's 39 universities averaged over 150 UCAS points in 2020's admissions round and three: Imperial, Glasgow and Strathclyde, averaged over 200 points. The older institutions dominate the upper end of the table, with West of Scotland in 18th place the highest-ranked post-1992 university, followed by Sheffield Hallam in 20th. Most courses require maths and physics, and other desirable subjects include IT or computing, further maths, and design technology.

West of Scotland has the highest rates of student satisfaction by a clear margin for both teaching quality and the wider experience. Wales Trinity St David (21st overall) ranks second for teaching quality, followed by Leeds. Sheffield and Coventry complete the top three for student satisfaction.

Starting salaries of £28,000 rank the subjects 10th and 61% of graduates were in high-skilled jobs. However, with 15% in work deemed low-skilled, and 10% unemployed, the subjects place 27th overall in our graduate prospects measure.

Aeronautical and Manufacturing Engineering	Teaching quality	Student experience	Research quality	Entry standards (UCAS points)	Graduate prospects	Overall score
1 Imperial College London	72.9%	76.1%	59.6%	207	91.1%	100.0
2 Bristol	73.7%	77.9%	52.3%	184	87.7%	96.3
3 Glasgow	75.4%	77.9%	47.2%	201	78.0%	95.1
4 Bath	79.3%	76.4%	37.4%	177	90.3%	95.0
5 Leeds	82.1%	80.7%	40.9%	174	77.9%	93.4
6 Southampton	68.2%	67.8%	52.3%	171	89.7%	93.2
7 Strathclyde	69.1%	64.1%	37.2%	202*	87.5%	92.9
8 Sheffield	79.8%	83.9%	36.0%	154	86.6%	92.6
9 Loughborough	75.1%	78.8%	41.8%	151	85.8%	91.4
=10 Surrey	69.9%	71.5%	30.8%	139	92.5%	88.1
=10 Queen's Belfast	73.4%	72.0%	36.7%	146	82.2%	88.1

Aeronautical and Manufacturing Engineering cont.	Teaching quality	Student experience	Research quality	Entry standards (UCAS points)	Graduate prospects	Overall score
12 Nottingham	65.3%	65.5%	40.8%	147	89.1%	87.9
13 Swansea	70.8%	70.4%	45.5%	129	81.9%	87.0
14 Queen Mary, London	58.6%	61.1%	46.7%	140	81.0%	84.2
15 Liverpool	62.8%	60.9%	32.1%	138	80.0%	82.4
=16 Coventry	80.6%	81.3%	10.3%	125	71.6%	82.0
=16 Manchester	60.9%	61.7%	35.1%	157	70.3%	82.0
18 West of Scotland	88.6%	90.2%	9.0%	130	58.3%	81.9
19 Hull	75.2%	74.7%	16.5%	118	—	81.4
20 Sheffield Hallam	72.1%	63.3%	17.8%	114	84.7%	81.3
21 Wales Trinity St David	85.8%	74.3%	1.0%	115	—	80.9
22 West of England	71.6%	68.9%	10.6%	123	80.2%	80.4
23 Teesside	71.7%	69.0%	5.8%	128	75.0%	78.9
24 Brunel	59.8%	60.2%	23.7%	130	77.5%	78.8
25 Ulster	61.6%	64.5%	—	123	90.0%	78.2
26 Leicester	78.2%	75.9%	—	133	60.9%	77.4
27 Aston	61.2%	59.0%	20.6%	117	75.0%	76.7
28 Staffordshire	74.0%	67.3%	5.7%	110	—	76.5
29 Central Lancashire	67.1%	64.7%	7.1%	125	—	76.2
30 Huddersfield	65.1%	68.0%	10.2%	120	—	76.1
31 Hertfordshire	66.2%	67.5%	16.5%	100	65.6%	74.3
32 City	56.3%	61.0%	23.1%	111	—	74.0
33 Derby	66.8%	62.4%	6.7%	107	—	73.4
34 Wolverhampton	61.1%	53.0%	4.4%	99	80.0%	72.9
35 Salford	56.1%	59.7%	4.4%	128	66.2%	71.9
36 South Wales	72.9%	66.4%	—	123	50.9%	71.7
=37 Brighton	58.9%	58.3%	7.4%	91	73.5%	71.1
=37 Portsmouth	62.0%	58.0%	9.1%	98	66.7%	71.1
39 Kingston	64.4%	61.4%	2.9%	103	46.4%	66.7

Employed in high-skilled job	61%	Employed in lower-skilled job	15%
Employed in high-skilled job and studying	4%	Employed in lower-skilled job and studying	1%
Studying	10%	Unemployed	10%
High skilled work (median) salary	£28,000	Low/medium skilled salary	£25,000

Agriculture and Forestry

The lead that Queen's Belfast gained over Nottingham in the previous edition of our Agriculture and Forestry table has been maintained. It has the highest research rating in the subjects and comes top for graduate prospects – closely followed by Newcastle. Reading is also strong in research (ranking second), as is Aberystwyth (third). Queen's had the highest entry standards in the 2020 admissions round, with an average of 149 UCAS tariff points.

Bangor, fifth overall, comes top for both teaching quality and student satisfaction.

There are two specialist institutions in this table: Harper Adams and Royal Agricultural. The former has outdone the latter in our Agriculture and Forestry rankings once again this year, helped by more buoyant student satisfaction and research ratings.

Bringing together disciplines ranging from animal and land management to food science, horticulture and environmental conservation, agriculture and related sciences saw a small rise in the number of new students in 2020. Forestry and arboriculture is a niche area and 95 undergraduates enrolled on such courses in 2020.

Agriculture and Forestry ranks 39th for starting salaries (below history and above French), with graduates in professional roles earning median salaries of £24,699. The subjects fall further down our graduate prospects ranking, however, where they sit 56th. When surveyed 15 months after finishing their degrees, half of graduates were in high-skilled employment, 4% were balancing a professional job with further study and 3% were studying full time, but 38% were in lower-skilled jobs.

Agriculture and Forestry	Teaching quality	Student experience	Research quality	Entry standards (UCAS points)	Graduate prospects	Overall score
1 Queen's Belfast	74.3%	67.6%	56.3%	149	75.9%	100.0
2 Nottingham	79.7%	80.1%	36.4%	129	67.1%	91.7
3 Aberystwyth	83.5%	78.7%	38.2%	132	60.7%	91.3
4 Newcastle	70.2%	65.4%	28.4%	128	75.4%	90.2
5 Bangor	88.8%	92.3%	29.7%	115	—	90.1
6 Harper Adams	79.6%	78.1%	5.7%	124	71.9%	87.5
7 Reading	60.3%	45.0%	50.7%	128	55.0%	83.8
8 Royal Agricultural	65.9%	63.5%	2.1%	110	58.2%	76.1

Employed in high-skilled job	50%	Employed in lower-skilled job	38%
Employed in high-skilled job and studying	4%	Employed in lower-skilled job and studying	1%
Studying	3%	Unemployed	3%
High skilled work (median) salary	£24,699	Low/medium skilled salary	£21,000

American Studies

Sussex tops our American Studies table, complementing a long history at the upper end of this ranking – except for last year, when it dropped to seventh place. Improved student satisfaction rates with both the wider experience and teaching quality have boosted its position, along with entry standards and graduate prospects that rank second and a top five research rating.

American Studies students at Hull reported the highest levels of satisfaction with teaching quality by a clear margin in the National Student Survey, as with the wider undergraduate experience. Students at Swansea, 9th overall, and at Canterbury Christ Church, at the foot of the table, awarded the second highest scores for teaching quality.

Most degrees concentrate on the culture, literature, history and politics of America and Canada, and students are often offered the opportunity of spending a year at a university in one of the two countries as part of a four-year course. The leading universities look for English language, English literature and history A-levels, while politics is also considered useful. Entry standards in 2020 went no higher than the 139 UCAS tariff points averaged at Manchester, although all were above 100 points.

Placing 60th out of 67 subject areas, American studies has dropped further down our graduate prospects measure. Fifteen months after finishing their degrees, 39% of graduates were in high-skilled work and a further 14% were either engaged in postgraduate study or combining studies with a professional job. By contrast, 34% were in jobs deemed low-skilled and 12% unemployed.

American Studies	Teaching quality	Student experience	Research quality	Entry standards (UCAS points)	Graduate prospects	Overall score
1 Sussex	76.1%	70.7%	45.6%	138	70.6%	100.0
2 Birmingham	55.0%	59.7%	48.8%	136	74.2%	96.9
3 Manchester	82.6%	70.1%	49.1%	139	55.0%	96.7
4 Nottingham	75.5%	64.9%	39.9%	131	68.5%	96.0
5 Hull	95.4%	92.6%	26.1%	133	55.4%	95.1
6 Leicester	80.5%	76.1%	34.3%	125	65.4%	94.6
7 Essex	81.1%	66.4%	46.9%	106	—	92.9
8 East Anglia	70.3%	66.1%	33.1%	125	68.4%	92.7
9 Swansea	85.7%	79.7%	18.5%	116	70.1%	92.2
10 Kent	69.5%	70.3%	47.3%	102	—	89.7
11 Manchester Metropolitan	76.0%	61.8%	29.0%	118	—	88.7
12 Portsmouth	71.4%	63.9%	32.2%	111*	55.7%	85.5
13 Canterbury Christ Church	85.7%	71.8%	16.3%	100	—	84.1

Employed in high-skilled job	39%	Employed in lower-skilled job	34%
Employed in high-skilled job and studying	2%	Employed in lower-skilled job and studying	1%
Studying	12%	Unemployed	12%
High skilled work (median) salary	£24,000	Low/medium skilled salary	£19,000

Anatomy and Physiology

It is an Oxbridge tie at the top our Anatomy and Physiology table. With 221 UCAS tariff points, Cambridge averaged the highest entry standards in 2020's admissions round, while Oxford just has the edge over its old rival on graduate prospects. However, both have been outdone on that measure by modern institutions, with West of England coming top and Huddersfield second, for the proportion of graduates working in professional jobs or postgraduate study 15 months on from their degrees.

Worcester, =16th overall, and Coventry share the best rates of student satisfaction in the two measures derived from the National Student Survey – with the wider experience considered best at Worcester and teaching quality top at Coventry. Top 10 institutions Oxford, Aberdeen, Dundee, Loughborough and Glasgow also fare well in these areas.

Biomedical science degrees are among a wide range of courses included in this subject table, while very few actually have the title of anatomy or physiology. A two-science minimum at A-level usually means biology and chemistry, although physics is also an option. The leading universities look for maths, too.

The subject area is growing in popularity and attracted 9,325 new undergraduates in 2020. Graduate prospects are good: anatomy and physiology rank 26th in our list, with 40% of graduates in high-skilled employment, 4% engaged in further study and 30% combining the two. Median starting salaries of £24,907 place the subjects midway, at 33rd place.

Anatomy and Physiology	Teaching quality	Student experience	Research quality	Entry standards (UCAS points)	Graduate prospects	Overall score
=1 Oxford	80.8%	75.5%	50.9%	207*	91.1%	100.0
=1 Cambridge	—	—	52.5%	221	89.8%	100.0
3 Aberdeen	84.3%	85.3%	34.7%	215	82.2%	97.6
4 Loughborough	79.2%	83.0%	52.1%	157	—	96.0
5 Dundee	81.8%	75.0%	55.4%	176	76.8%	94.3
6 University College London	76.8%	70.6%	55.4%	186*	79.7%	94.2
7 Bristol	74.8%	70.6%	49.7%	155	86.3%	92.8
8 Glasgow	78.5%	79.5%	33.4%	213	71.8%	92.2
9 Edinburgh	69.0%	63.6%	52.8%	172	85.3%	92.0
10 Leeds	77.3%	73.8%	40.9%	150	85.1%	91.9
11 Queen's Belfast	81.5%	75.4%	33.3%	154	83.0%	91.8
12 Swansea	74.9%	72.7%	44.7%	151	—	91.3
13 Leicester	77.6%	79.0%	36.5%	126	84.2%	90.1
14 Manchester	71.7%	67.4%	38.3%	165*	—	89.7
15 Huddersfield	74.2%	74.2%	7.8%	130	93.5%	88.1
=16 King's College London	71.6%	68.3%	38.0%	157	75.7%	87.3
=16 Worcester	87.0%	86.3%	10.9%	108	—	87.3
18 West of England	75.6%	72.0%	—	112	96.3%	86.7
19 Liverpool	78.8%	72.7%	31.7%	145	70.3%	86.2
20 Manchester Metropolitan	80.2%	76.2%	12.0%	137	75.5%	85.3
21 Nottingham	72.3%	69.4%	26.5%	127	79.7%	85.2
22 Coventry	88.0%	85.8%	4.5%	108	74.4%	84.9
23 Plymouth	73.8%	68.2%	—	131*	87.9%	84.7
24 Newcastle	74.0%	56.8%	47.8%	143	67.7%	84.6
25 Keele	75.7%	79.0%	16.5%	120	77.0%	84.4
26 Bangor	75.9%	72.9%	—	119	83.9%	83.7
27 Reading	67.6%	69.3%	26.6%	122*	79.1%	83.5
=28 Anglia Ruskin	70.7%	69.9%	2.2%	104*	88.0%	82.6
=28 Essex	77.0%	72.5%	17.8%	99	—	82.6
30 Derby	77.6%	77.8%	1.6%	119*	72.1%	81.3
31 St George's, London	63.3%	60.1%	20.0%	132	—	79.9
32 Salford	69.2%	64.5%	12.7%	116*	—	79.6
33 Oxford Brookes	62.9%	64.1%	21.3%	117*	—	79.1
34 Portsmouth	75.4%	69.8%	8.1%	—	66.7%	78.4

	Teaching quality	Student experience	Research quality	Entry standards (UCAS points)	Graduate prospects	Overall score
35 Ulster	63.0%	61.9%	—	123	77.8%	77.8
36 Brighton	59.8%	59.0%	4.8%	102	—	73.1

Employed in high-skilled job	40%	Employed in lower-skilled job	19%
Employed in high-skilled job and studying	4%	Employed in lower-skilled job and studying	1%
Studying	30%	Unemployed	7%
High skilled work (median) salary	£24,907	Low/medium skilled salary	£19,000

Animal Science

Our Animal Science table, first launched seven years ago to reflect the growing interest in the subjects, has gained 13 extra universities. Extracted from the agriculture category, degrees range from animal behaviour to equine science and veterinary nursing. Most degrees will ask for biology and probably chemistry.

The expanded table has shaken up the rankings, led by new entry Stirling in the top spot, its position boosted by the highest research rating. Former leader Glasgow – which averaged the highest entry standards with 199 UCAS points – is second. Manchester, Royal Holloway, Sussex and Surrey (in that order) have also entered our top 10.

For both teaching quality and student experience – which are derived from the National Student Survey (NSS) – Royal Holloway takes the lead, followed by Derby (19th overall) and Swansea (=12th).

Animal science has improved its position in our employment ranking to sit 64th, where it has previously occupied the foot of the table due to the relatively high proportion of graduates starting their careers in jobs classified as medium or low-skilled. When surveyed 15 months after completing their degrees, 31% of graduates were in high-skilled employment, 2% were furthering their studies full-time and 16% were doing both. The subject area is second last in our salaries table, with graduates earning £21,000 per year in high-skilled jobs, and £18,000 in medium-skilled roles.

Some universities buck the overall employment trend, most noticeably Middlesex – where 100% of graduates had secured the top outcomes 15 months after finishing, followed by Edinburgh Napier (97.2%) and Surrey (96.6%).

Animal Science	Teaching quality	Student experience	Research quality	Entry standards (UCAS points)	Graduate prospects	Overall score
1 Stirling	75.9%	76.2%	49.0%	183	—	100.0
2 Glasgow	81.7%	75.9%	42.3%	199	55.0%	96.6
3 Manchester	80.7%	70.3%	38.3%	157	76.4%	92.2
4 Royal Holloway, London	89.6%	84.6%	25.7%	133	—	88.0
5 Bristol	76.5%	72.4%	33.2%	141	75.9%	87.8
6 Nottingham	76.2%	74.5%	36.4%	133	63.4%	85.1
7 Sussex	71.3%	68.5%	46.8%	135	57.1%	85.0

8 Liverpool	62.7%	62.8%	32.9%	144	75.6%	84.1
=9 Surrey	63.8%	63.0%	—	160	96.6%	83.5
=9 Newcastle	71.7%	69.5%	47.8%	135	46.5%	83.5
11 Aberystwyth	79.1%	73.1%	38.2%	116	53.9%	81.8
=12 Swansea	84.1%	83.7%	—	129	70.5%	80.6
=12 Cardiff	66.5%	59.3%	33.3%	—	62.5%	80.6
14 Harper Adams	80.3%	72.3%	5.7%	123	74.7%	79.7
15 Bangor	70.9%	67.1%	29.7%	117	51.1%	77.2
16 Middlesex	59.5%	53.1%	—	128	100.0%	77.1
17 Liverpool John Moores	77.3%	74.8%	—	146	46.7%	76.6
18 Lincoln	78.6%	80.0%	—	127	55.9%	76.1
19 Derby	85.3%	83.2%	1.6%	117	50.5%	75.8
20 Greenwich	72.0%	70.8%	19.5%	119	48.8%	75.4
21 Hartpury	81.5%	76.8%	—	116	56.8%	74.9
22 Oxford Brookes	61.6%	60.8%	21.3%	127	51.1%	74.3
23 Royal Veterinary College	65.0%	53.8%	—	129	75.4%	74.2
24 Edinburgh Napier	41.2%	32.9%	—	143	97.2%	72.9
25 Nottingham Trent	74.5%	62.0%	4.1%	131	42.9%	72.7
26 Royal Agricultural	70.4%	66.2%	—	116	52.9%	70.7
27 Chester	68.1%	57.1%	7.9%	126	30.0%	68.6
28 Plymouth	69.8%	64.8%	—	122	36.5%	68.5
29 Roehampton	63.4%	54.6%	20.6%	97	32.1%	66.0

Employed in high-skilled job	31%	Employed in lower-skilled job		39%
Employed in high-skilled job and studying	2%	Employed in lower-skilled job and studying		2%
Studying	16%	Unemployed		9%
High skilled work (median) salary	£21,000	Low/medium skilled salary		£18,000

Anthropology

The study of humans and human society, from the physical evolution of the body and brain, to the political, cultural and linguistic practices of modern societies, anthropology has tended to be the preserve of old universities. Led by Cambridge they dominate our table's top 10, where University College London (UCL) and the LSE have driven Oxford from second into fourth place this year.

Birmingham claims the top research rating, narrowly ahead of UCL and Queen's Belfast, while St Andrews averaged the highest entry standards with 200 UCAS points. Anthropology attracts well-qualified entrants; 13 of the table's 21 universities average 144 UCAS points or more, equivalent to AAA at A-level.

East London is the top-ranked post-1992 institution in 18th place, followed by Oxford Brookes, Liverpool John Moores and Portsmouth. East London is also top for teaching quality in our measure derived from the National Student Survey (NSS), with St Andrews not far behind. Both universities are also in the top three for the wider undergraduate experience, which Brunel leads.

Applications to study anthropology declined by 9% in 2020, although more students started courses than in 2019 reflecting a slightly increased offer rate of 75.7%.

Employment prospects for anthropology graduates remain rooted in the lower reaches of our table, where the subject sits 45th – an improvement on previous years. When surveyed 15 months on from their degrees, 64.6% of graduates were in professional jobs or postgraduate study. A quarter were working in jobs deemed low-skilled while 11% were unemployed. The subject is also 45th for median starting salaries.

Anthropology	Teaching quality	Student experience	Research quality	Entry standards (UCAS points)	Graduate prospects	Overall score
1 Cambridge	—	—	40.4%	192	88.2%	100.0
2 University College London	76.8%	70.9%	49.3%	172	75.3%	97.4
3 London School of Economics	79.2%	74.4%	41.3%	166	78.8%	97.0
4 Oxford	79.8%	65.5%	38.8%	190	—	96.8
5 St Andrews	88.6%	83.0%	25.0%	200	66.7%	95.8
6 Exeter	76.2%	65.6%	41.0%	155	81.3%	95.0
7 Birmingham	81.1%	67.5%	50.9%	130	—	94.3
8 Aberdeen	76.9%	73.7%	31.8%	183	—	94.0
9 Queen's Belfast	78.8%	74.4%	49.0%	133	70.8%	93.6
10 Durham	74.7%	70.1%	29.1%	165	75.9%	91.6
11 Manchester	74.4%	70.7%	36.7%	152	64.7%	89.1
12 Sussex	76.1%	68.1%	34.4%	139	65.8%	87.9
13 East Anglia	69.8%	68.5%	38.6%	129	—	87.0
14 Brunel	86.8%	83.2%	29.3%	111	60.4%	86.9
15 SOAS, London	70.9%	59.9%	31.1%	156	63.2%	85.7
16 Edinburgh	61.4%	54.2%	42.2%	166	59.9%	85.4
17 Kent	77.0%	68.5%	20.5%	120	67.9%	83.8
18 East London	89.4%	78.1%	13.7%	98	—	83.1
19 Oxford Brookes	79.4%	70.9%	17.3%	104	68.8%	82.8
20 Liverpool John Moores	72.0%	68.4%	15.1%	145	64.7%	82.7
=21 Bristol	60.0%	52.6%	11.2%	144	76.6%	80.5
=21 Portsmouth	70.9%	61.3%	32.2%	113*	56.5%	80.5
23 Roehampton	66.0%	66.9%	27.7%	106	—	79.5
24 Goldsmiths, London	67.0%	53.0%	34.5%	120	52.2%	78.6
25 Bournemouth	67.0%	61.6%	19.9%	105	58.0%	76.5

Employed in high-skilled job	42%	Employed in lower-skilled job	25%
Employed in high-skilled job and studying	5%	Employed in lower-skilled job and studying	1%
Studying	17%	Unemployed	11%
High skilled work (median) salary	£24,000	Low/medium skilled salary	£20,000

Archaeology and Forensic Science

Cambridge holds on to its lead in our Archaeology and Forensic Science table once again this year. Its strength in the field is cemented by having the highest entry standards, the best graduate prospects and the third-highest research rating. Oxford holds on to second place. York, in fourth place overall, is top for both teaching quality and the wider undergraduate experience. Worcester, Swansea, Coventry and Reading are among the other institutions whose students reported high levels of satisfaction with their degrees during the difficult, pandemic-affected year.

West of England, in 32nd place overall, achieved the second-best graduate prospects, followed by Cardiff and then Worcester. Starting salaries, though, are among the lowest of the subject areas covered in this *Guide*, with high-skilled jobs attracting median rates of £21,100 per year. The subjects fare better at =53rd in our employment ranking, with just shy of 60% of graduates in professional jobs and/or postgraduate study 15 months on from finishing their degrees.

While most archaeology courses have no subject requirements, the leading universities will usually require a science subject. Geography and history are also relevant A-levels.

As a single honours degree, archaeology attracts small undergraduate numbers – 840 in 2020 – while subjects classified by UCAS as forensic and archaeological science welcomed 2,540 new undergraduates in the same admissions round.

Archaeology and Forensic Science	Teaching quality	Student experience	Research quality	Entry standards (UCAS points)	Graduate prospects	Overall score
1 Cambridge	—	—	47.2	198	87.3	100.0
1 Cambridge	—	—	47.2%	195	87.3%	100.0
2 Oxford	—	—	42.9%	184	—	96.4
3 Durham	88.0%	78.6%	41.2%	154	75.0%	94.9
4 York	95.5%	91.1%	35.1%	133	74.5%	94.5
5 Swansea	92.2%	85.5%	39.4%	131*	—	94.2
6 Dundee	77.5%	71.7%	55.4%	160*	69.4%	93.5
7 Glasgow	80.3%	81.5%	16.4%	194*	—	93.4
8 Kent	85.2%	84.5%	33.1%	133	78.8%	92.3
9 Southampton	82.5%	74.3%	43.5%	132	75.2%	91.4
10 Sheffield	84.1%	72.4%	31.6%	145*	76.5%	91.2
11 Edinburgh	78.4%	67.9%	20.9%	185	—	90.8
12 Queen's Belfast	81.9%	86.3%	36.9%	126	—	89.9
13 University College London	84.3%	74.0%	51.4%	148	56.0%	89.8
14 Aberdeen	84.4%	78.3%	29.4%	139*	—	89.6
=15 Cardiff	80.5%	67.9%	31.1%	122	82.5%	89.0
=15 Reading	91.9%	75.8%	44.7%	115	63.2%	89.0
17 Robert Gordon	83.8%	83.8%	8.8%	149	76.7%	88.7
18 Exeter	73.4%	64.2%	33.6%	147	74.2%	87.8
19 Worcester	92.3%	89.2%	8.1%	94	80.3%	86.3
20 Birmingham	73.1%	57.1%	40.3%	134	—	85.1
=21 Coventry	90.1%	83.6%	—	108	79.6%	85.0
=21 Manchester	72.5%	71.0%	24.7%	147	—	85.0
23 Glasgow Caledonian	84.9%	85.3%	4.7%	155	60.7%	84.8
24 Leicester	72.2%	65.8%	37.2%	118	68.3%	83.8

		Teaching quality	Student experience	Research quality	Entry standards (UCAS points)	Graduate prospects	Overall score
=25	Newcastle	69.6%	61.5%	25.8%	120	77.8%	83.4
=25	Nottingham	77.9%	62.6%	23.7%	127	68.5%	83.4
27	Hull	69.7%	76.0%	31.7%	121	—	83.0
28	Liverpool	79.8%	66.9%	33.5%	132	54.2%	82.7
29	Anglia Ruskin	78.5%	79.0%	24.6%	110	64.2%	82.5
30	Wolverhampton	87.0%	79.7%	—	108	73.2%	82.3
31	Nottingham Trent	71.0%	67.6%	4.1%	132	77.7%	81.8
32	West of England	69.3%	64.6%	—	128	83.8%	81.6
33	Bradford	77.1%	77.1%	23.6%	107	—	81.5
34	Lincoln	86.5%	82.4%	—	113	65.3%	80.9
35	Derby	79.5%	76.7%	3.6%	113	71.2%	80.8
36	Keele	76.9%	74.0%	—	136	66.2%	80.4
37	Wales Trinity St David	77.0%	62.7%	17.3%	111	63.2%	79.0
38	West of Scotland	69.3%	72.3%	—	134	67.7%	78.7
39	Chester	80.4%	67.8%	15.4%	103	58.6%	77.9
40	Liverpool John Moores	70.8%	62.7%	—	152	58.8%	77.5
41	Kingston	83.8%	75.3%	6.9%	93	—	77.4
42	Staffordshire	74.0%	73.1%	—	113	66.3%	77.3
43	West London	73.8%	72.3%	—	120	63.3%	77.1
44	Cumbria	83.2%	71.5%	1.5%	103	—	76.8
45	Bournemouth	67.2%	60.9%	19.9%	110	57.1%	75.3
46	Canterbury Christ Church	80.7%	72.6%	16.3%	85	52.4%	75.1
47	Winchester	81.4%	67.2%	7.5%	99	53.5%	74.9
48	Teesside	65.6%	61.7%	—	125	61.4%	74.2
49	Central Lancashire	67.4%	62.5%	9.8%	122	54.0%	74.1
50	London South Bank	86.7%	80.2%	—	91	46.2%	73.4
51	De Montfort	69.3%	61.3%	—	106	60.3%	72.7
52	South Wales	62.4%	58.7%	—	107	59.5%	70.8

Employed in high-skilled job	40%	Employed in lower-skilled job	31%
Employed in high-skilled job and studying	2%	Employed in lower-skilled job and studying	2%
Studying	15%	Unemployed	10%
High skilled work (median) salary	£21,100	Low/medium skilled salary	£19,000

Architecture

Bath's position at the top of our Architecture table remains stable this year; bolstered by having the second-highest entry standards, third-highest research rating and fourth-best graduate prospects. Loughborough has overtaken Cambridge to rank second, helped by having the top research rating. Meanwhile, architecture students joining Cambridge averaged 209 UCAS points – the highest entry standards.

But for student satisfaction, the post-1992 universities fare better in general. Plymouth, Arts Bournemouth, Creative Arts and Cardiff Metropolitan lead the field for teaching quality (in that order). For the wider undergraduate experience Cardiff Metropolitan had the highest rates of satisfaction in the National Student Survey (NSS), a measure in which Sheffield came second, ahead of Plymouth and Liverpool.

There are usually no essential subjects required to study architecture, although the leading universities will look for a mixture of art and science, and a portfolio is essential. As an alternative to A-levels, it may be possible to take level 3 applied general qualifications in art and design or the level 3 diploma in foundation studies in art and design.

Career trajectories are positive: two-thirds of graduates were in professional jobs 15 months after their degrees and combined with those in postgraduate study, the subject ranks 22nd in our list. Emerging architects are not put off by the modest starting salaries of £22,000 as those in the industry know this soon changes. It takes most architects seven years to fully qualify, of which a degree is the first step. Such a timeframe asks a lot of students' dedication to the profession and of their financial wherewithal to support themselves. Course materials add to costs.

Architecture	Teaching quality	Student experience	Research quality	Entry standards (UCAS points)	Graduate prospects	Overall score
1 Bath	86.0%	84.8%	52.9%	197	93.0%	100.0
2 Loughborough	82.7%	84.4%	58.3%	159	96.0%	97.4
3 Cambridge	73.2%	75.4%	49.0%	209	90.5%	96.4
4 Sheffield	90.3%	88.0%	36.6%	165	91.6%	94.8
=5 Queen's Belfast	88.4%	82.4%	35.2%	141	94.4%	92.2
=5 Liverpool	90.9%	85.9%	43.5%	150	84.0%	92.2
7 Edinburgh	72.2%	66.7%	35.1%	187	90.0%	90.8
8 University College London	71.4%	54.6%	54.1%	171	88.3%	90.7
=9 Cardiff	72.6%	64.9%	40.7%	172	90.0%	90.2
=9 Strathclyde	78.6%	71.6%	23.0%	197	86.0%	90.2
11 Robert Gordon	80.9%	78.8%	8.3%	160	89.8%	86.2
12 Newcastle	70.8%	59.4%	43.7%	167	75.4%	85.1
13 Plymouth	92.9%	87.4%	13.2%	111	87.3%	84.7
14 West of England	85.7%	78.9%	10.6%	148	82.9%	84.3
=15 Nottingham	74.1%	65.6%	14.8%	152	90.3%	84.2
=15 Reading	73.8%	65.5%	40.0%	129	—	84.2
17 Central Lancashire	89.8%	78.4%	3.0%	130	87.5%	83.4
=18 Ulster	75.8%	68.8%	28.6%	123	84.8%	82.8
=18 Creative Arts	91.0%	84.4%	3.4%	129	82.8%	82.8
=20 Arts Bournemouth	92.1%	81.1%	2.4%	115	88.0%	82.7
=20 Dundee	73.0%	58.9%	8.7%	181	—	82.7
22 Manchester School of Architecture	73.9%	59.7%	12.6%	168	82.8%	82.6
23 Oxford Brookes	82.6%	72.5%	17.6%	131	74.2%	80.3
=24 Liverpool John Moores	68.9%	61.2%	4.9%	149	88.7%	80.2
=24 Coventry	86.4%	84.5%	10.3%	110	79.3%	80.2
=24 Kent	64.7%	63.3%	33.3%	134	78.8%	80.2

	Teaching quality	Student experience	Research quality	Entry standards (UCAS points)	Graduate prospects	Overall score
27 Edinburgh Napier	75.2%	72.8%	5.7%	134	84.6%	80.0
28 Leeds Beckett	76.6%	67.3%	5.6%	100	93.5%	79.0
29 Nottingham Trent	79.0%	70.2%	3.4%	113	87.5%	78.9
30 University of the Arts London	80.0%	70.1%	—	146	76.0%	78.5
31 Kingston	78.5%	66.7%	10.1%	125	78.7%	78.3
=32 Northumbria	71.0%	56.8%	5.9%	135	82.8%	77.4
=32 Birmingham City	80.6%	71.5%	9.6%	132	70.7%	77.4
34 Cardiff Metropolitan	91.0%	88.1%	—	94	76.0%	77.1
35 Wolverhampton	86.2%	78.4%	5.6%	96	—	76.8
36 Brighton	71.1%	59.8%	13.1%	109	82.8%	76.3
37 Sheffield Hallam	71.5%	59.5%	13.4%	116	78.1%	75.8
38 Salford	61.8%	57.7%	19.6%	127	77.9%	75.7
39 Lincoln	74.6%	67.4%	3.2%	113	79.5%	75.4
40 De Montfort	56.4%	48.9%	35.9%	103	79.3%	74.8
41 London Metropolitan	81.6%	74.3%	7.2%	114	67.4%	74.7
42 Westminster	76.3%	66.2%	10.7%	128	66.3%	74.5
43 Portsmouth	71.3%	66.4%	—	104	81.4%	73.8
44 Ravensbourne	68.6%	63.3%	—	97	86.2%	73.7
45 London South Bank	73.3%	62.5%	19.6%	112	60.7%	72.0
46 Greenwich	75.5%	66.8%	2.0%	125	61.1%	71.2
47 Derby	67.0%	63.0%	6.7%	102	66.7%	69.3
48 East London	75.6%	61.6%	8.1%	97	56.3%	67.7
49 Anglia Ruskin	60.7%	52.4%	5.2%	100	—	67.3
50 Huddersfield	45.9%	43.2%	—	127	58.1%	62.2

Employed in high-skilled job	66%	Employed in lower-skilled job		13%
Employed in high-skilled job and studying	4%	Employed in lower-skilled job and studying		0%
Studying	6%	Unemployed		11%
High skilled work (median) salary	£22,000	Low/medium skilled salary		£20,000

Art and Design

Our Art and Design ranking is dominated by the post-1992 university sector, and also features several renowned art schools that are now part of Russell Group and other high-tariff universities: such as the Ruskin School of Art (part of the University of Oxford), Slade School of Fine Art (University College London) and Duncan of Jordanstone College of Art and Design (University of Dundee).

It is many of these schools, often specialising in the fine art aspect of this broad subject area, that dominate the top of this year's ranking. Oxford, which dropped to tenth place last year, returns to the top of the table, due in large part to its staggering score of 251 UCAS points in our entry standards measure, almost 40 points clear of its nearest rival (Newcastle). This is achieved in a subject area where the accent in determining entry is on artwork portfolios.

The Ruskin also stipulates the need for an outstanding portfolio and recommends post-A-level (or equivalent) students complete a post-18 Art Foundation course before applying, but evidently students arrive with a clutch of outstanding A-levels alongside their brushes and oils.

Fine Art has long been a jewel in the crown at Newcastle University and remains so this year, even as the wider university has fallen to the foot of the Russell Group rankings in our institutional league table. After two years as No 1 (jointly with Oxford in 2019), the university's BA in Fine Art ranks third in the UK this year, knocked back only by a poor score for graduate prospects. Just 58.6% of graduates from the course are in high-skilled work or postgraduate study 15 months after leaving the university, down from 64.5% last year.

Art and Design is regularly towards the foot of our employment rankings by subject – which will come as no surprise to the many artists and designers squeezing out a living from their creativity. The latest Graduate Outcomes survey revealed fewer than half of graduates were in high-skilled work or further study at nine of the 82 institutions in our ranking. That figure drops as low as 21.2% at Chichester and 35.3% at Liverpool Hope, among the lowest to be found for any degree subject.

Loughborough, in second place, is one of the notable exceptions with almost four in five graduates in high-skilled work or further study, putting it in the UK top four on this measure. Bangor (92.5%), Bournemouth (89.5%) and Brunel London (86.4%) do even better.

Students of Art and Design are clearly not driven solely by jobs and money however, and the subject area remains one of the most popular with just under 240,000 applications in 2020. Nevertheless, the numbers are down 14% from their peak in 2015 when 278,450 applied for art and design courses across the university sector.

Canterbury Christ Church, ranked 17th overall, tops the subject ranking for student satisfaction with teaching quality and the wider student experience with exceptional scores of 94.9% and 89.8% respectively. Sunderland, home to the National Glass Centre, comes second in these ranking components, while finishing =20th overall.

In a volatile period for student satisfaction after the extensive disruption of the pandemic, the success of Canterbury Christ Church and Sunderland in delivering for their Art and Design students is all the more notable. Even among high-ranking institutions, such as University College London (fifth) and Leeds (15th) scores for satisfaction with the wider student experience in this subject area fell below 60%.

Art and Design	Teaching quality	Student experience	Research quality	Entry standards (UCAS points)	Graduate prospects	Overall score
1 Oxford	77.5%	65.7%	39.7%	251	—	100.0
2 Loughborough	81.7%	78.8%	35.3%	175	79.0%	95.0
3 Newcastle	84.0%	75.7%	37.3%	212	58.6%	94.0
4 Glasgow	69.3%	67.6%	37.2%	199	—	90.9
5 University College London	72.3%	59.6%	44.7%	196	65.2%	90.5
6 Ulster	78.3%	69.1%	57.2%	124	70.1%	90.4
7 Lancaster	73.9%	69.5%	48.0%	158	68.6%	90.2
=8 Brunel	71.6%	64.9%	32.8%	131	86.4%	88.4
=8 Edinburgh Napier	87.1%	81.1%	—	174	70.0%	88.4

Art and Design cont.

		Teaching quality	Student experience	Research quality	Entry standards (UCAS points)	Graduate prospects	Overall score
10	Dundee	73.4%	64.1%	39.9%	172	62.4%	87.8
=11	Reading	71.8%	67.3%	38.9%	129	77.6%	87.5
=11	Goldsmiths, London	78.4%	66.2%	25.9%	181	61.5%	87.5
13	Bangor	83.7%	69.3%	—	126	92.5%	87.4
14	West of England	84.5%	72.2%	15.0%	154	61.7%	85.7
15	Leeds	66.0%	57.1%	33.6%	164	72.1%	85.6
16	Glasgow Caledonian	73.7%	69.4%	1.8%	168	78.0%	85.3
17	Canterbury Christ Church	94.9%	89.8%	7.3%	99	64.4%	85.1
18	Heriot-Watt	73.2%	68.3%	31.1%	167	56.7%	84.9
19	Wales Trinity St David	74.9%	61.4%	39.2%	151	57.5%	84.8
=20	Coventry	83.3%	73.9%	18.1%	127	64.4%	84.5
=20	Sunderland	88.4%	82.7%	9.8%	120	63.6%	84.5
=22	Kent	69.7%	66.1%	44.3%	120	66.8%	84.4
=22	Edinburgh	75.5%	58.7%	27.9%	174	56.2%	84.4
24	Southampton	72.3%	59.3%	35.4%	153	61.2%	84.3
25	Northumbria	77.7%	65.8%	13.3%	150	68.8%	84.2
26	Hull	78.1%	73.4%	11.2%	154*	—	83.8
27	Kingston	76.0%	64.3%	10.1%	174	61.8%	83.4
=28	Bournemouth	69.8%	58.8%	15.0%	104	89.5%	82.6
=28	Lincoln	81.6%	76.9%	7.1%	125	65.9%	82.6
30	Staffordshire	84.1%	77.6%	2.3%	130	63.9%	82.5
31	Glyndŵr	84.9%	72.6%	7.8%	130	60.4%	82.3
=32	Nottingham Trent	77.8%	69.9%	4.7%	140	68.3%	82.2
=32	Sheffield Hallam	80.1%	69.7%	15.5%	119	65.7%	82.2
34	Central Lancashire	86.5%	75.8%	3.9%	125	61.0%	82.0
35	Westminster	71.9%	62.9%	22.5%	143	61.0%	81.5
36	Cardiff Metropolitan	81.7%	72.0%	7.9%	131	60.6%	81.4
37	Suffolk	85.4%	78.0%	—	121	61.8%	81.2
=38	Anglia Ruskin	79.7%	71.9%	8.5%	123	64.0%	81.1
=38	Norwich Arts	83.6%	74.2%	5.6%	133	56.7%	81.1
=40	South Wales	86.3%	79.2%	3.3%	120	57.2%	81.0
=40	Robert Gordon	80.1%	67.9%	11.5%	164	47.8%	81.0
42	West London	81.1%	76.5%	4.5%	117	63.2%	80.6
43	Salford	79.6%	68.0%	8.0%	136	58.8%	80.5
=44	Arts Bournemouth	75.6%	69.5%	2.4%	152	60.6%	80.4
=44	Aberystwyth	81.0%	74.6%	21.6%	131	45.6%	80.4
46	Birmingham City	80.8%	74.1%	9.6%	125	56.7%	80.3
47	Manchester Metropolitan	72.5%	59.7%	9.7%	157	60.2%	80.1
48	Plymouth	76.1%	67.1%	14.7%	125	60.1%	80.0
49	London Metropolitan	81.3%	71.2%	4.7%	122	59.6%	79.8
50	Liverpool John Moores	69.6%	61.6%	7.2%	185	52.5%	79.7
51	Wolverhampton	85.1%	79.8%	8.9%	113	49.6%	79.3

=52	Portsmouth	79.9%	70.1%	—	116	65.0%	79.2
=52	University of the Arts London	73.3%	58.8%	8.0%	149	60.0%	79.2
54	Middlesex	76.8%	64.8%	13.3%	110	61.9%	78.8
=55	Greenwich	76.0%	66.6%	3.5%	120	64.9%	78.6
=55	Brighton	69.5%	52.6%	13.1%	143	63.1%	78.6
=57	Worcester	74.5%	69.4%	11.1%	116	60.6%	78.5
=57	Bath Spa	78.8%	67.5%	9.6%	125	54.4%	78.5
=59	Oxford Brookes	71.5%	60.8%	10.4%	126	63.5%	78.3
=59	London South Bank	81.1%	73.6%	12.8%	103	53.8%	78.3
61	Teesside	75.0%	61.3%	2.9%	113	69.3%	78.2
62	Falmouth	74.5%	64.4%	3.0%	139	58.8%	78.1
63	Northampton	80.7%	71.4%	2.9%	117	55.6%	77.9
64	Leeds Arts	72.2%	63.8%	—	153	56.5%	77.6
=65	De Montfort	71.6%	63.1%	10.2%	122	60.5%	77.4
=65	Chester	76.5%	67.9%	6.2%	122	55.6%	77.4
=67	Leeds Beckett	78.4%	67.1%	1.2%	106	62.7%	77.3
=67	Huddersfield	75.1%	64.4%	4.8%	124	58.7%	77.3
69	Bolton	79.0%	72.1%	—	115	56.7%	77.1
70	Gloucestershire	76.8%	63.0%	—	125	59.3%	77.0
71	Buckinghamshire New	81.5%	76.0%	6.1%	117	45.7%	76.8
72	Creative Arts	76.6%	64.6%	3.4%	139	49.2%	76.5
73	Solent, Southampton	77.7%	68.3%	1.6%	106	57.5%	76.0
74	Ravensbourne	74.2%	63.2%	—	116	59.8%	75.7
75	Hertfordshire	75.4%	62.7%	5.8%	109	53.8%	74.9
76	Cumbria	64.3%	62.6%	6.1%	137	49.1%	73.3
77	Derby	70.8%	61.1%	5.1%	116	50.3%	73.2
78	York St John	62.2%	51.7%	—	116	67.1%	72.9
79	Liverpool Hope	70.3%	57.3%	—	131	35.3%	69.5
80	East London	64.4%	56.3%	9.8%	84	52.0%	69.4
81	Bedfordshire	64.9%	49.7%	—	85	48.9%	66.5
82	Chichester	73.2%	59.2%	—	119	21.2%	66.1

Employed in high-skilled job	51%	Employed in lower-skilled job	31%
Employed in high-skilled job and studying	2%	Employed in lower-skilled job and studying	1%
Studying	4%	Unemployed	12%
High skilled work (median) salary	£21,500	Low/medium skilled salary	£18,720

Bioengineering and Biomedical Engineering

Ageing populations, the demand for new treatments for chronic conditions and the need
to respond rapidly to evolving disease challenges have brought about growth in biomedical
engineering and bioengineering among universities worldwide over the past two decades. The
discipline collectively involves a range of engineering and scientific skills, including some of the
newest areas of science in genomics, imaging, and computing to meet those challenges.

Graduate bioengineers may go on to develop prosthetics and biomedical implants, 3D medical imaging or image-guided and robot-assisted surgery – among a range of career pathways. At Imperial, a number of bioengineering graduates win places on the Graduate Entry into Medicine programme each year.

In this, our first dedicated Bioengineering and Biomedical Engineering table, Dundee has emerged the frontrunner in undergraduate provision. The Scottish university has the third-highest research rating, equal with University College London, along with the second-best scores for both teaching quality and the wider experience – measures derived from the National Student Survey (NSS). Imperial, in third place overall, has the top research rating.

The table is dominated by older institutions – especially at the upper end. Seventeenth-place Birmingham City is the highest-ranked post-1992 institution and outdoes all others for student satisfaction, with teaching quality as well as the wider experience. There is insufficient employment data so far for all but eight universities, of which Salford stands out for achieving a perfect 100% of graduates in high-skilled work or further study 15 months on from their degrees.

Bioengineering and Biomedical Engineering	Teaching quality	Student experience	Research quality	Entry standards (UCAS points)	Graduate prospects	Overall score
1 Dundee	89.4%	89.5%	55.4%	192	—	100.0
2 Strathclyde	72.6%	70.5%	52.2%	214	86.8%	98.4
3 Imperial College London	80.4%	77.9%	61.6%	195	—	97.7
4 Sheffield	80.1%	82.2%	57.4%	169	81.9%	96.7
5 Swansea	78.1%	69.7%	45.5%	141	90.9%	93.4
=6 Leeds	81.4%	70.8%	40.9%	200	—	92.8
=6 King's College London	72.0%	72.6%	38.0%	153	92.6%	92.8
8 Glasgow	61.0%	70.8%	33.4%	209	81.1%	90.9
9 Loughborough	78.4%	82.2%	41.8%	156	—	89.0
10 University College London	65.2%	68.9%	55.4%	157	—	86.8
11 Salford	58.8%	57.2%	12.7%	140	100.0%	85.5
12 Ulster	71.5%	75.2%	37.3%	125	—	81.7
13 Reading	82.5%	84.0%	16.3%	121	—	80.7
=14 Queen Mary, London	69.2%	71.8%	26.1%	144	—	80.3
=14 Surrey	68.6%	68.1%	30.8%	142	—	80.3
16 Cardiff	64.3%	64.1%	33.3%	149	—	80.0
17 Birmingham City	93.9%	90.2%	1.5%	109	—	79.9
18 Essex	75.5%	73.9%	17.8%	133	—	79.0
19 Nottingham Trent	74.1%	77.8%	20.1%	112	—	77.5
20 Birmingham	75.6%	63.0%	19.2%	128	—	77.3
21 Bradford	72.1%	73.1%	9.5%	120	65.5%	76.9
22 Kent	62.8%	63.0%	39.1%	114	—	76.8
23 Bolton	79.0%	78.3%	18.1%	106	56.5%	76.3
24 Aston	68.4%	69.6%	20.6%	124	—	76.2
25 City	50.9%	60.9%	23.1%	109	—	69.4
26 Middlesex	59.7%	61.8%	10.0%	95	—	67.3

Employed in high-skilled job	52%	
Employed in high-skilled job and studying	3%	
Studying	18%	
High skilled work (median) salary	£26,000	

Employed in lower-skilled job	16%	
Employed in lower-skilled job and studying	1%	
Unemployed	9%	
Low/medium skilled salary	£19,110	

Biological Sciences

Biology is the most popular of the specialisms within the biological sciences grouping, attracting 4,520 new students in 2020. It is followed by molecular biology, biophysics and biochemistry – with 3,585 enrolments in the same admissions round. Ecology and environmental biology experienced a 10% increase in the numbers starting courses and zoology also saw an uplift in enrolments, albeit smaller. As a grouping, the biological sciences attracted over 91,000 applications in 2020.

Featuring 97 entries, the Biological Sciences table is among the largest of our 70 subject rankings and 155 universities and colleges are planning programmes for 2022–23.

For the 17th year Cambridge tops the table, its position strengthened by eye-watering entry standards in 2020, when new undergraduates averaged 221 UCAS tariff points. Cambridge also comes top for graduate prospects – closely followed by Oxford, which is fourth. Edinburgh, in ninth place overall, has the highest research rating, beating Imperial into second – the same place it occupies in the main table.

For teaching quality and the wider student experience, both measures derived from the National Student Survey, Gloucestershire (which ranks 38th overall) takes the lead. Lincoln places second for both measures, while Lancaster, Loughborough, Edge Hill and St Andrews also fared better than most for student satisfaction in the pandemic-affected years.

With 71.2% of graduates in high-skilled jobs and/or postgraduate study 15 months on from their degrees, the subject occupies a middling position in our employment measure. Starting salaries of £24,000 for professional roles (or £19,000 for medium-skilled jobs, which a fifth of graduates were employed in) rank biological sciences in the lower half of our earnings table.

Biological Sciences	Teaching quality	Student experience	Research quality	Entry standards (UCAS points)	Graduate prospects	Overall score
1 Cambridge	—	—	52.5%	221	89.8%	100.0
2 Imperial College London	74.5%	75.5%	61.6%	191	87.2%	96.6
3 Strathclyde	78.1%	77.8%	52.2%	202	81.7%	95.4
4 Oxford	75.1%	66.9%	50.9%	198	88.0%	95.1
5 University College London	76.2%	75.7%	55.4%	174	83.4%	93.7
6 St Andrews	82.0%	83.4%	37.6%	201	77.4%	93.4
7 Glasgow	80.2%	79.3%	33.4%	200	82.1%	93.3
8 Durham	81.7%	78.0%	32.9%	178	85.7%	92.9
9 Edinburgh	71.2%	69.3%	62.9%	186	78.6%	92.4
10 York	82.3%	77.0%	41.9%	151	85.2%	92.1
11 Sheffield	76.2%	76.6%	57.4%	150	78.6%	90.7
12 Lancaster	86.0%	78.2%	46.5%	144	76.6%	90.5
13 Dundee	68.0%	66.4%	55.4%	179	79.1%	90.0

Biological Sciences cont.	Teaching quality	Student experience	Research quality	Entry standards (UCAS points)	Graduate prospects	Overall score
14 Bath	78.8%	79.9%	31.5%	158	81.8%	89.6
=15 Stirling	74.4%	76.1%	49.0%	169	74.6%	89.3
=15 Loughborough	83.9%	85.4%	52.1%	144	69.5%	89.3
=17 Queen's Belfast	71.7%	73.9%	47.3%	141	84.2%	89.1
=17 Warwick	80.0%	78.3%	37.1%	155	78.2%	89.1
19 King's College London	77.8%	70.9%	38.0%	156	81.1%	89.0
=20 Surrey	78.8%	76.4%	37.5%	131	84.4%	88.8
=20 Bristol	79.3%	74.6%	46.8%	161	73.0%	88.8
22 Aberdeen	79.1%	78.6%	34.7%	175	71.8%	88.1
23 Manchester	72.2%	66.1%	38.3%	164	79.9%	87.6
24 Exeter	75.3%	74.6%	39.7%	156	74.5%	87.0
=25 Birmingham	73.6%	67.2%	38.1%	148	78.5%	86.3
=25 Leeds	70.9%	68.3%	40.9%	152	78.0%	86.3
27 Kent	78.4%	78.2%	39.1%	122	76.2%	85.9
28 Aston	76.8%	73.9%	39.1%	115	79.9%	85.7
29 Aberystwyth	82.3%	77.1%	38.2%	115	74.6%	85.5
30 Southampton	77.0%	77.0%	34.2%	143	73.1%	85.4
31 Nottingham	72.3%	65.8%	26.5%	138	84.3%	85.3
32 Liverpool	72.8%	67.4%	33.9%	145	78.1%	85.2
33 Sussex	79.0%	76.2%	46.8%	145	64.3%	85.0
=34 East Anglia	74.6%	71.2%	38.8%	124	77.0%	84.7
=34 Swansea	77.5%	75.1%	38.6%	127	72.9%	84.7
36 Nottingham Trent	82.9%	75.7%	24.1%	114	78.1%	84.5
37 Royal Holloway, London	73.1%	73.8%	25.7%	120	82.7%	84.3
38 Gloucestershire	88.2%	89.0%	14.5%	99	76.9%	84.2
39 Leicester	72.8%	71.8%	36.5%	128	76.2%	84.1
40 Glasgow Caledonian	81.3%	75.2%	8.1%	126	81.8%	83.9
41 Keele	77.7%	77.5%	16.5%	115	81.8%	83.7
42 Hull	78.7%	74.2%	31.7%	112	75.2%	83.5
=43 Lincoln	86.6%	85.9%	—	115	79.3%	83.4
=43 Oxford Brookes	82.6%	75.8%	21.3%	115	75.5%	83.4
45 Robert Gordon	66.6%	66.0%	4.9%	163	85.4%	83.3
46 Sunderland	80.2%	71.1%	7.5%	109*	86.2%	83.2
=47 Cardiff	66.5%	59.3%	33.3%	143	78.4%	82.9
=47 Liverpool John Moores	81.1%	75.1%	15.1%	123	76.3%	82.9
=47 West of Scotland	85.5%	81.1%	29.0%	133	62.5%	82.9
50 Newcastle	69.9%	64.4%	28.4%	144	75.2%	82.5
=51 Edge Hill	84.0%	84.2%	6.2%	108	77.5%	82.4
=51 Queen Mary, London	68.3%	68.3%	26.1%	136	77.5%	82.4
53 Worcester	82.9%	81.5%	10.9%	95	75.9%	81.2
54 Edinburgh Napier	82.7%	77.9%	8.9%	146	65.6%	81.1
55 Plymouth	81.8%	75.8%	17.4%	124	68.3%	81.0

=56	Essex	74.5%	69.6%	17.8%	102	79.8%	80.8
=56	Portsmouth	74.0%	66.9%	24.3%	103	77.7%	80.8
58	Chester	83.3%	74.8%	12.0%	107	72.2%	80.5
59	York St John	76.1%	73.0%	—	118*	80.0%	80.3
=60	Bangor	65.3%	67.9%	31.5%	112	76.2%	80.2
=60	Heriot-Watt	62.4%	64.0%	26.3%	163	69.3%	80.2
=60	Middlesex	81.0%	76.0%	10.0%	109	—	80.2
63	Reading	73.2%	70.3%	26.6%	117	70.2%	80.0
=64	Cardiff Metropolitan	76.4%	74.0%	—	115	78.9%	79.9
=64	Roehampton	82.2%	77.3%	20.6%	86	71.6%	79.9
=66	Northumbria	67.9%	62.6%	14.0%	129	78.1%	79.6
=66	Derby	79.6%	74.9%	1.6%	108	76.6%	79.6
=68	Greenwich	74.3%	74.3%	7.4%	105	76.9%	79.1
=68	Central Lancashire	71.3%	73.0%	8.3%	120	75.5%	79.1
70	Teesside	78.1%	78.7%	—	99	77.1%	78.9
71	Huddersfield	71.3%	66.7%	7.8%	118	76.2%	78.5
=72	Coventry	76.4%	74.9%	4.5%	109	72.4%	78.1
=72	West of England	80.8%	75.8%	8.2%	112	66.4%	78.1
74	Abertay	74.5%	66.4%	4.3%	136	69.4%	78.0
75	Manchester Metropolitan	79.4%	68.6%	12.0%	121	65.1%	77.9
76	Westminster	69.6%	69.1%	21.2%	111	69.8%	77.7
77	Staffordshire	78.0%	74.4%	—	101	72.9%	77.3
78	Sheffield Hallam	70.8%	65.2%	10.4%	99	75.4%	77.0
79	Brighton	73.0%	70.7%	4.8%	97	74.9%	76.9
80	Bradford	58.8%	62.4%	9.5%	116	80.4%	76.7
81	Royal Veterinary College	65.9%	55.3%	—	114	81.6%	76.5
82	London Metropolitan	68.8%	68.2%	—	104	74.3%	75.4
83	Bedfordshire	62.1%	67.4%	25.1%	97	69.4%	75.3
=84	Bath Spa	75.8%	69.3%	—	89	71.9%	75.2
=84	Hertfordshire	75.1%	74.9%	10.9%	97	64.0%	75.2
=86	Canterbury Christ Church	73.0%	67.5%	11.9%	64	75.2%	75.1
=86	South Wales	74.1%	63.8%	—	101	71.8%	75.1
88	Leeds Beckett	73.7%	71.3%	3.5%	—	67.3%	75.0
89	Kingston	74.0%	66.1%	2.6%	107	66.4%	74.4
90	St George's, London	56.0%	49.3%	20.0%	140	—	74.3
91	Brunel	58.1%	50.2%	18.2%	117	70.5%	73.6
92	Bournemouth	70.2%	61.0%	4.7%	100	66.5%	72.9
93	Salford	72.4%	64.1%	12.7%	121	54.8%	72.8
94	Anglia Ruskin	71.2%	66.8%	2.2%	93	66.0%	72.7
95	Wolverhampton	69.7%	65.6%	—	106	53.3%	68.9
96	Northampton	49.7%	49.1%	—	91	73.0%	67.9
97	London South Bank	55.4%	46.4%	35.0%	88	41.3%	63.8

Employed in high-skilled job	42%	Employed in lower-skilled job	20%
Employed in high-skilled job and studying	3%	Employed in lower-skilled job and studying	1%
Studying	25%	Unemployed	9%
High skilled work (median) salary	£24,000	Low/medium skilled salary	£19,000

Building

Courses in this category include surveying, construction, building services engineering and construction management. Applications and enrolments edged upwards in 2020, although there are still less than four applicants per place. This is despite solid job prospects; with the latest data showing that 81.8% of graduates were working in high-skilled jobs and/or furthering their studies 15 months on from their degrees – ranking building 12th in our employment measure. Starting rates of pay are also encouraging, the £27,000 median earned by graduates in high-skilled jobs gives Building a top 20 place in our ranking.

University College London (UCL) takes the top spot this year, supported by the second-best research rating and top five scores for both measures of student satisfaction. Former winner Loughborough takes second place, though still leads for research and for graduate prospects, while Ulster is in third.

Students on building courses at Wolverhampton rated their teaching the best in the National Student Survey (NSS), followed by those at Coventry and Robert Gordon. For the wider experience, Derby claims the highest rates of student satisfaction, a whisker ahead of Robert Gordon with Wolverhampton close behind. West of England's graduate outcomes are a close second to those at Loughborough.

Entry standards are generally modest; Heriot-Watt averaged the highest UCAS tariff score of 156 points in 2020. Entrants at Wolverhampton and Derby, which have among the most satisfied students, gained places with less than 100 points. Degree apprenticeships, though not included in our table, offer an increasingly popular route into the construction industry.

Building	Teaching quality	Student experience	Research quality	Entry standards (UCAS points)	Graduate prospects	Overall score
1 University College London	77.4%	74.2%	54.1%	146	—	100.0
2 Loughborough	62.8%	64.9%	58.3%	137	96.9%	94.4
3 Ulster	78.2%	77.2%	28.6%	138	89.5%	92.8
4 Heriot-Watt	64.8%	65.5%	38.1%	156	85.7%	91.2
5 Robert Gordon	78.6%	79.4%	8.3%	128	91.4%	89.2
6 Reading	66.1%	59.8%	40.0%	121	88.4%	87.5
=7 Coventry	79.4%	74.0%	10.3%	109	93.9%	87.3
=7 Northumbria	69.5%	62.0%	5.9%	148	91.8%	87.3
9 West of England	72.6%	70.1%	10.6%	115	95.9%	86.6
10 Glasgow Caledonian	69.7%	67.4%	9.1%	147	80.0%	85.4
11 Oxford Brookes	67.7%	69.0%	17.6%	113	91.8%	85.2
12 Liverpool John Moores	67.4%	65.7%	4.9%	137	84.0%	83.8
13 Westminster	67.3%	63.8%	10.7%	121	88.6%	83.7
14 Sheffield Hallam	71.6%	64.3%	13.4%	111	85.3%	83.1
15 Plymouth	67.0%	61.3%	13.2%	122	85.4%	83.0
16 London South Bank	63.2%	56.3%	19.6%	127	83.9%	82.9
=17 Nottingham Trent	69.2%	67.2%	3.4%	105	93.3%	82.6
=17 Nottingham	69.8%	69.3%	14.8%	128	73.9%	82.6
19 Salford	67.0%	62.9%	19.6%	123	77.2%	82.2

20 Anglia Ruskin	71.3%	69.7%	5.2%	108	81.3%	80.8
21 Derby	69.8%	79.8%	5.6%	98	—	80.2
22 Aston	66.9%	69.4%	20.6%	125	64.0%	80.0
23 Edinburgh Napier	62.3%	60.7%	5.7%	134	76.3%	79.9
24 Portsmouth	67.5%	65.1%	—	105	86.1%	79.5
25 Wolverhampton	87.4%	78.9%	5.6%	95	61.5%	78.8
26 Leeds Beckett	65.0%	61.4%	5.6%	97	82.4%	77.5
27 Central Lancashire	47.8%	43.1%	3.0%	124	92.0%	77.0
28 East London	76.0%	65.1%	8.1%	75	—	76.8
29 Brighton	67.3%	63.2%	—	87	84.2%	76.5
30 Birmingham City	65.9%	61.4%	2.7%	115	68.6%	76.0
31 Greenwich	60.8%	62.2%	2.0%	104	—	75.2
32 Kingston	64.9%	64.3%	—	100	73.4%	74.9

Employed in high-skilled job	74%	Employed in lower-skilled job	10%
Employed in high-skilled job and studying	6%	Employed in lower-skilled job and studying	0%
Studying	2%	Unemployed	8%
High skilled work (median) salary	£27,000	Low/medium skilled salary	£21,000

Business, Management and Marketing

More universities offer business-related courses than any other subject area, with 120 featuring in this edition of our *Guide*. The popularity of these courses shows no signs of abating, with applications for business and administration studies rising from 328,000 to 334,020 in the 2020 application cycle. The huge number of places means there are also plenty of opportunities to secure a spot through clearing.

St Andrews remains top for the third successive year with a consistently strong performance across all the components of our ranking: student satisfaction with teaching quality and the wider student experience (ranking fifth for both); research quality (fourth); entry standards (top) and graduate prospects (fifth). Such consistency gives St Andrews a comfortable lead over the rest and contributes to making the university No 1 in our overall table this year.

Nine of last year's top ten feature once again at the top of the business ranking, one of the most stable subject areas. Only Durham, ninth last year, has dropped out of the top ten, to 15th.

Warwick rises from third to second, partly as the result of an increase in student satisfaction with teaching quality. Against a backdrop of tumbling scores for student satisfaction nationally triggered by the disruption caused by the pandemic, Warwick's achievement is remarkable. It was repeated in other subjects, too, helping Warwick win our award for University of the Year for Teaching Quality.

The universities that nailed the highest scores for satisfaction with teaching quality ranked in the middle to lower reaches of the business table overall. The University for the Creative Arts came top on this measure while ranking 49th for business overall, followed by Buckinghamshire New (=85th), and East London (97th).

Satisfaction with the wider student experience showed a much closer correlation to the overall business ranking. The top three for this – Loughborough, Warwick and St Andrews – made the overall top ten.

But graduate prospects are the most closely correlated aspect of the business ranking to the overall result. All the top five on this measure rank in the top ten for business overall. Our analysis of graduate employment in high-skilled jobs or postgraduate study 15 months after leaving university showed that 96.7% of business students from the London School of Economics achieved this, followed by Oxford (95.4%), Bath (93.2%), Warwick (92.6%) and St Andrews (91.8%).

By contrast, Bolton remains bottom of our business table ranking for graduate prospects, although the 37.5% in high-skilled work or further study is at least an improvement on last year's figure of 31.8%.

Although it is not an ingredient of our subject ranking, graduate salaries are naturally of interest to business students. Oxford, ranked third in the business table, takes the honours here with a median salary of £40,000 among its former students within 15 months of graduating. The London School of Economics occupies the same rank – fourth – in our business rankings as it does for salaries at £34,500.

Business, Management and Marketing	Teaching quality	Student experience	Research quality	Entry standards (UCAS points)	Graduate prospects	Overall score
1 St Andrews	83.2%	81.8%	43.8%	218*	91.8%	100.0
2 Warwick	82.2%	82.6%	40.4%	197	92.6%	97.7
3 Oxford	82.1%	74.6%	32.0%	208	95.4%	96.8
4 London School of Economics	76.7%	74.1%	52.3%	172	96.7%	96.1
5 King's College London	—	—	38.2%	193	86.7%	96.0
6 University College London	78.0%	79.7%	43.9%	180	90.6%	95.1
7 Bath	74.5%	77.6%	41.8%	168	93.2%	93.1
8 Strathclyde	75.4%	76.8%	44.3%	200	76.5%	92.9
=9 Loughborough	76.8%	83.3%	32.6%	154	85.7%	90.1
=9 Leeds	76.2%	75.4%	39.3%	154	85.4%	90.1
11 Lancaster	77.2%	76.8%	42.6%	143	81.5%	89.4
12 Glasgow	68.3%	73.7%	22.1%	198	79.6%	87.5
13 Exeter	69.3%	70.5%	24.4%	156	90.3%	86.5
14 Stirling	80.4%	79.0%	25.2%	158	69.3%	86.3
15 Durham	74.7%	73.2%	23.1%	156	82.3%	86.2
16 Aberdeen	63.8%	72.6%	24.9%	178	83.9%	86.0
17 Edinburgh	68.5%	67.4%	25.8%	179	79.6%	85.9
18 Manchester	67.3%	68.9%	33.3%	158	80.3%	85.4
19 East Anglia	75.5%	77.0%	28.1%	133	79.2%	85.2
20 Bristol	70.2%	68.1%	32.1%	157	76.7%	85.0
21 City	66.4%	68.5%	28.7%	176	74.3%	84.7
=22 Reading	70.5%	69.3%	29.3%	127	87.4%	84.4
=22 Nottingham	66.6%	68.4%	32.6%	142	83.7%	84.4
24 Heriot-Watt	73.6%	70.9%	18.8%	169	73.0%	84.2
25 York	73.1%	72.6%	24.0%	141	78.5%	84.0
26 Ulster	75.4%	72.9%	40.4%	127	66.2%	83.7
27 Dundee	68.5%	69.6%	12.1%	178	77.2%	83.3
28 Cardiff	67.0%	64.9%	32.0%	145	76.5%	82.8

29	Queen's Belfast	66.9%	64.4%	32.7%	141	76.7%	82.5
30	Southampton	68.6%	66.8%	24.0%	146	76.7%	82.2
31	Bangor	76.4%	73.3%	23.4%	122	73.0%	82.0
=32	Aberystwyth	80.0%	74.2%	14.5%	127	72.5%	81.9
=32	Swansea	75.1%	70.9%	22.0%	134	71.5%	81.9
34	Birmingham	60.7%	57.1%	29.1%	148	84.6%	81.7
=35	Buckingham	81.8%	78.8%	—	129	77.2%	81.5
=35	Liverpool	69.8%	70.7%	20.1%	140	75.2%	81.5
37	Robert Gordon	81.9%	80.4%	2.6%	155	62.5%	81.4
=38	Surrey	72.3%	74.9%	15.8%	133	73.6%	81.0
=38	Queen Mary, London	67.2%	64.2%	23.5%	156	70.3%	81.0
40	Sussex	68.3%	67.6%	23.7%	134	75.3%	80.9
41	Kent	71.6%	73.2%	24.8%	127	69.3%	80.8
42	Aston	70.1%	68.4%	19.7%	128	76.0%	80.4
43	Sheffield	62.7%	65.9%	26.8%	139	74.0%	80.0
44	Newcastle	61.6%	60.0%	20.7%	144	80.6%	79.7
45	West of England	79.8%	77.8%	5.5%	114	72.0%	79.5
46	Keele	73.8%	73.2%	10.2%	108	79.3%	79.2
47	Chichester	83.0%	78.5%	—	95	78.0%	79.1
48	Central Lancashire	78.9%	76.4%	4.4%	122	69.0%	79.0
49	Creative Arts	86.9%	76.4%	—	121	62.8%	78.9
50	Harper Adams	69.6%	65.5%	—	131*	84.6%	78.6
=51	Edinburgh Napier	76.2%	74.2%	2.3%	144	63.1%	78.4
=51	Glasgow Caledonian	75.2%	72.4%	1.8%	167	56.4%	78.4
=53	Hull	74.0%	68.9%	10.2%	122	71.0%	78.3
=53	SOAS, London	—	—	25.0%	143	52.8%	78.3
=55	Royal Holloway, London	61.8%	61.6%	27.0%	134	70.9%	78.2
=55	South Wales	81.8%	73.5%	0.2%	134	61.7%	78.2
=57	Lincoln	75.2%	73.6%	4.8%	115	73.1%	78.1
=57	Queen Margaret, Edinburgh	75.6%	72.6%	—	143	66.0%	78.1
59	West London	80.4%	76.2%	—	114	66.2%	77.4
=60	Abertay	69.8%	70.1%	—	135	73.6%	77.3
=60	Coventry	79.5%	77.0%	1.6%	109	67.4%	77.3
=62	Leicester	64.4%	60.3%	24.3%	128	68.1%	77.2
=62	Bradford	81.2%	78.6%	11.8%	115	52.9%	77.2
64	Sheffield Hallam	74.6%	68.4%	0.6%	110	77.4%	77.0
=65	Portsmouth	71.4%	67.7%	9.5%	111	72.6%	76.8
=65	Chester	74.9%	70.9%	0.5%	118	70.9%	76.8
=65	Wales Trinity St David	79.2%	75.1%	—	141	54.1%	76.8
68	Plymouth	70.4%	65.8%	13.1%	118	68.9%	76.7
69	Essex	65.4%	65.5%	25.1%	107	69.1%	76.6
70	Nottingham Trent	69.2%	66.2%	4.6%	121	74.6%	76.5
71	Salford	72.6%	69.4%	5.9%	121	66.4%	76.2
72	Falmouth	79.7%	72.5%	—	112	62.1%	75.7
=73	Solent, Southampton	78.0%	70.2%	—	109	64.9%	75.4
=73	Huddersfield	73.6%	65.8%	4.1%	121	64.6%	75.4

Business, Management and Marketing cont.	Teaching quality	Student experience	Research quality	Entry standards (UCAS points)	Graduate prospects	Overall score
=75 Bournemouth	63.4%	58.9%	8.8%	109	80.2%	75.1
=75 Derby	74.5%	69.3%	0.9%	109	67.8%	75.1
=75 Sunderland	83.3%	80.9%	0.4%	104	52.5%	75.1
78 Royal Agricultural	74.4%	71.0%	—	110	66.7%	75.0
=79 Leeds Beckett	73.2%	71.6%	0.8%	100	70.8%	74.9
=79 Kingston	73.3%	69.8%	9.2%	110	60.8%	74.9
=79 West of Scotland	73.6%	70.0%	2.9%	133	55.8%	74.9
=82 Oxford Brookes	65.2%	65.3%	5.1%	115	73.8%	74.8
=82 Liverpool John Moores	69.6%	66.3%	—	137	62.8%	74.8
=82 Anglia Ruskin	79.0%	77.0%	3.4%	98	58.9%	74.8
=85 Manchester Metropolitan	69.9%	63.6%	4.7%	120	65.1%	74.4
=85 Buckinghamshire New	85.0%	77.3%	1.8%	93	52.6%	74.4
87 Worcester	71.5%	69.6%	0.9%	106	68.5%	74.3
88 Birmingham City	73.7%	69.4%	1.3%	112	61.6%	74.1
89 Northumbria	62.8%	56.7%	4.0%	135	70.5%	74.0
90 Liverpool Hope	76.8%	69.5%	—	106	60.9%	73.9
91 Edge Hill	69.7%	70.3%	.	127	58.9%	73.6
=92 Bath Spa	74.2%	69.6%	—	97	65.1%	73.4
=92 London Metropolitan	82.9%	77.7%	0.6%	99	48.3%	73.4
94 Brunel	58.9%	58.8%	23.0%	120	60.5%	73.2
95 St Mary's, Twickenham	80.3%	80.2%	—	91	52.4%	73.1
96 Greenwich	70.1%	67.0%	3.3%	114	58.3%	72.7
97 East London	84.2%	82.5%	0.8%	91	43.1%	72.6
98 De Montfort	68.1%	62.9%	10.7%	95	63.9%	72.5
99 Staffordshire	72.4%	65.8%	2.6%	107	56.9%	72.2
=100 University of the Arts London	65.1%	55.6%	—	136	61.5%	72.0
=100 Bedfordshire	69.9%	66.9%	3.1%	100	61.3%	72.0
102 Brighton	63.2%	53.4%	6.5%	106	70.8%	71.8
103 Teesside	65.5%	57.2%	2.0%	111	66.5%	71.6
104 Westminster	67.3%	68.6%	2.4%	120	53.2%	71.5
105 Bolton	79.1%	83.2%	—	106	37.5%	71.4
=106 Suffolk	64.9%	58.9%	—	97	71.2%	71.1
=106 Gloucestershire	61.7%	59.5%	—	115	67.4%	71.1
108 Hertfordshire	69.9%	69.1%	0.9%	100	56.8%	71.0
109 Winchester	63.6%	62.1%	—	102	68.0%	70.9
110 Middlesex	67.8%	66.8%	10.5%	100	49.1%	70.3
111 Canterbury Christ Church	71.6%	66.0%	—	91	57.0%	70.2
=112 Cumbria	65.5%	64.7%	5.6%	104	54.8%	70.1
=112 Roehampton	67.6%	67.1%	4.5%	97	54.7%	70.1
114 York St John	67.0%	63.5%	0.8%	102	57.9%	70.0
115 Wolverhampton	71.4%	63.7%	2.4%	103	50.0%	69.9
116 Northampton	66.1%	60.9%	1.0%	97	60.5%	69.6

	Teaching quality	Student experience	Research quality	Entry standards (UCAS points)	Graduate prospects	Overall score
117 Cardiff Metropolitan	58.1%	55.4%	—	106	66.2%	68.7
118 Leeds Trinity	66.0%	60.2%	—	93	57.6%	68.4
119 London South Bank	68.9%	62.6%	2.1%	94	47.4%	67.8
120 Glyndŵr	63.6	64.0	—	97*	53.5	69.9

Employed in high-skilled job	54%	Employed in lower-skilled job	26%
Employed in high-skilled job and studying	4%	Employed in lower-skilled job and studying	1%
Studying	5%	Unemployed	10%
High skilled work (median) salary	£25,000	Low/medium skilled salary	£20,000

Celtic Studies

The content of courses in this grouping caters largely to each university's host Celtic nation. The four universities in Wales focus predominantly on degrees in Welsh history, culture and language, and those in Scotland and Ireland cover similar themes but with the focus on Gaelic, Scottish or Irish studies.

Queen's tops our table this year. It has the highest research rating, healthy rates of student satisfaction and entry standards that averaged 143 UCAS points in 2020, just under the 144 equivalent to AAA at A-level. Cambridge still offers its Anglo-Saxon, Norse and Celtic degree, which attracted 26 entrants in 2020, too few to provide sufficient data for our table.

Students who opt for Celtic studies report high levels of student satisfaction at the majority of universities in our table, led by Aberystwyth which does best for both measures derived from the National Student Survey (NSS): teaching quality (94.1%) and the broader experience (90.4%). At the other end of the satisfaction scale is Ulster, where NSS scores reached only 68.2% for the wider experience and 56.7% for teaching quality.

The subject area attracts a select group of students – and just 155 new undergraduates began Celtic Studies degrees in 2020. Median starting salaries of £24,906 for Celtic studies graduates in professional jobs rank the subject 35th in our table.

Celtic Studies	Teaching quality	Student experience	Research quality	Entry standards (UCAS points)	Graduate prospects	Overall score
1 Queen's Belfast	86.4%	83.6%	53.6%	143	—	100.0
2 Cardiff	84.2%	84.3%	32.5%	168	82.6%	98.0
3 Bangor	87.5%	86.1%	39.6%	148	—	97.1
4 Edinburgh	70.9%	63.5%	30.3%	196*	—	95.5
5 Aberystwyth	94.1%	90.4%	23.7%	153*	—	95.1
6 Swansea	83.5%	73.9%	19.4%	146	—	88.9
7 Ulster	68.2%	56.7%	35.7%	125	—	85.5

Employed in high-skilled job	52%	Employed in lower-skilled job	15%
Employed in high-skilled job and studying	1%	Employed in lower-skilled job and studying	4%
Studying	23%	Unemployed	6%
High skilled work (median) salary	£24,906	Low/medium skilled salary	—

Chemical Engineering

Creating useful products from raw materials, chemical engineering combines natural sciences with life sciences, maths and economics. Imperial College London tops our table this year, with last year's winner Cambridge in second place – by the smallest possible margin of 0.01%. Imperial combines the top score for graduate prospects with the second-best rates for research and for student satisfaction with both teaching quality and the wider undergraduate experience – a rare achievement among prominent research-led institutions which often struggle with student satisfaction.

Entrants to Cambridge averaged the highest UCAS tariff score of 220 points in 2020. More than half the table have entry standards that equate to AAA or above at A-level, but less highly qualified applicants should not be put off as there are plenty of institutions with more accessible entry standards. Swansea, for instance, ranks a very respectable 13th overall and averaged 127 UCAS points.

Maths is essential for chemical engineering degrees and while chemistry or physics are required the leading universities will usually expect both. Most courses offer industry placements in the final year and lead to Chartered Engineer status. Graduates are in-demand; two-thirds had secured professional employment when surveyed 15 months after their degrees, and a further 15% were engaged in postgraduate study or combining it with a good job. Lancaster, Heriot-Watt and Aberdeen place after Imperial for job prospects, while London South Bank and Bradford fare much less well in the same measure.

Surprisingly for a subject with such positive career progression, applications dipped in 2020, although competition for places remained stiff at more than five applications per place.

Chemical Engineering	Teaching quality	Student experience	Research quality	Entry standards (UCAS points)	Graduate prospects	Overall score
1 Imperial College London	83.5%	84.9%	59.6%	198	94.4%	100.0
2 Cambridge	—	—	62.0%	220	90.6%	99.9
3 Heriot-Watt	78.6%	83.7%	47.8%	158	91.3%	93.3
4 Strathclyde	76.1%	79.3%	37.2%	207	85.6%	92.4
5 Birmingham	75.6%	78.4%	47.0%	173	87.9%	92.1
6 Nottingham	82.6%	82.9%	40.8%	153	84.1%	90.4
7 University College London	70.2%	72.4%	44.6%	178	86.6%	89.9
8 Bath	78.2%	82.7%	37.4%	164	82.8%	89.4
9 Aberdeen	69.9%	75.1%	28.4%	181	91.0%	89.3
10 Edinburgh	63.7%	67.9%	50.3%	196	82.6%	89.0
11 Lancaster	75.5%	68.3%	41.6%	134	91.7%	88.7
12 Loughborough	72.7%	77.7%	41.8%	143	87.8%	88.5
13 Swansea	75.3%	72.5%	45.5%	127	85.9%	87.4
14 Sheffield	74.0%	77.2%	36.8%	149	83.3%	87.0
15 Manchester	60.0%	61.2%	48.4%	167	87.5%	86.8
16 Leeds	64.1%	64.3%	30.7%	164	88.6%	85.4
17 Queen's Belfast	70.7%	69.6%	36.7%	148	78.6%	84.0
18 Surrey	71.2%	72.2%	30.8%	129	83.5%	83.6

19 Newcastle	66.9%	64.3%	30.2%	128	88.2%	83.3
20 Aston	75.8%	74.6%	20.6%	117	77.0%	80.5
21 Hull	77.7%	80.2%	16.5%	110	77.2%	80.3
22 Wolverhampton	81.3%	81.9%	4.4%	110	—	80.0
23 Greenwich	70.1%	68.7%	29.5%	86	—	78.1
24 Brunel	63.9%	62.3%	23.7%	117	—	77.2
=25 Chester	72.0%	74.1%	7.1%	101	79.3%	77.1
=25 London South Bank	89.2%	89.5%	19.6%	96	57.7%	77.1
27 West of Scotland	62.5%	56.3%	9.0%	150*	—	76.1
28 Teesside	72.4%	73.3%	5.8%	101	75.7%	75.9
29 Huddersfield	70.5%	64.9%	10.2%	103	—	75.4
30 Bradford	79.9%	73.9%	7.7%	100	67.6%	75.1
31 Portsmouth	49.8%	53.8%	9.1%	102	77.4%	70.3

Employed in high-skilled job	66%	Employed in lower-skilled job	10%
Employed in high-skilled job and studying	4%	Employed in lower-skilled job and studying	1%
Studying	11%	Unemployed	8%
High skilled work (median) salary	£30,000	Low/medium skilled salary	£22,000

Chemistry

Led by Cambridge, the top ten of our chemistry table features almost all the same institutions as it did last year, albeit reshuffled, with Edinburgh and St Andrews rising to second and third place respectively and Oxford dropping to fourth. There are two new entries: Imperial has gained 12 places to rank sixth, driven by improved rates of student satisfaction and high entry standards. Aberdeen has gained ten places to rank seventh.

Entry standards are generally high – 23 universities averaged 144 UCAS tariff points or more (equivalent to AAA at A-level). The top-ranked post-1992 university is Liverpool John Moores, which shares 21st place with Surrey

Chemistry A-level, or equivalent, is almost always a prerequisite and the leading universities will also look for maths and/or at least one other science – it is worth checking which second science individual universities ask for, as these may differ. Courses include laboratory and experimental work alongside independent and group research projects and industry experience or placements.

Lincoln (26th overall) did best in the National Student Survey, achieving outstanding scores for both teaching quality (94.3%) and the wider experience (93.2%).

A quarter of chemistry graduates had progressed to postgraduate study when surveyed 15 months after their degrees – which added to the 53% in professional jobs and 3% juggling both – ranks chemistry among the top ten subjects for graduate prospects. Median salaries of £25,000 put it in the top 25 subjects.

Applications and enrolments dipped slightly in 2020 but chemistry experienced a boom in numbers during the last decade and options for aspiring undergraduates are broad, with 123 universities and colleges offering courses in 2022–23.

Chemistry

		Teaching quality	Student experience	Research quality	Entry standards (UCAS points)	Graduate prospects	Overall score
1	Cambridge	—	—	70.3%	221	—	100.0
2	Edinburgh	82.1%	77.0%	48.4%	203	95.7%	96.5
3	St Andrews	84.9%	84.2%	50.3%	217	86.0%	95.3
4	Oxford	—	—	63.1%	195	91.7%	95.1
5	Strathclyde	91.1%	88.6%	40.1%	196	87.2%	94.7
6	Imperial College London	78.9%	80.8%	54.6%	201	88.4%	94.2
7	Aberdeen	80.9%	83.4%	31.6%	181	94.9%	93.0
8	Durham	80.1%	74.4%	49.1%	185	90.4%	92.9
9	Warwick	84.0%	80.4%	50.8%	157	89.6%	92.4
10	Liverpool	79.3%	77.4%	55.6%	144	88.1%	90.5
11	York	78.5%	73.9%	44.6%	172	87.8%	90.2
12	Bristol	78.3%	69.6%	56.6%	148	87.5%	89.8
13	Lancaster	90.4%	85.8%	37.5%	128	87.0%	89.7
14	Glasgow	78.0%	74.2%	41.1%	197	82.7%	89.4
15	Bath	80.8%	85.1%	43.0%	157	83.4%	88.9
16	University College London	70.7%	66.9%	56.0%	171	85.7%	88.7
17	Southampton	82.6%	81.9%	50.7%	148	79.6%	88.1
=18	Nottingham	78.9%	75.4%	48.5%	136	84.3%	87.5
=18	Birmingham	79.3%	81.1%	37.3%	155	83.6%	87.5
20	Heriot-Watt	73.1%	72.7%	34.2%	164	84.7%	86.1
=21	Liverpool John Moores	82.7%	81.0%	6.0%	147	90.3%	86.0
=21	Surrey	82.4%	82.5%	30.8%	138	82.7%	86.0
=23	East Anglia	74.0%	74.1%	39.2%	128	86.9%	85.6
=23	Leicester	83.5%	81.4%	32.8%	117	84.1%	85.6
25	Loughborough	87.6%	91.0%	23.9%	135	78.9%	85.3
26	Lincoln	94.3%	93.2%	—	106	87.8%	85.2
27	Manchester	66.7%	66.1%	46.0%	165	81.1%	84.6
28	Queen Mary, London	75.1%	74.5%	37.0%	130	83.2%	84.4
29	Queen's Belfast	66.1%	65.1%	34.7%	156	85.1%	83.8
30	Leeds	69.8%	69.6%	35.9%	150	81.7%	83.5
31	Hull	82.7%	74.9%	24.2%	108	84.7%	83.4
32	Sheffield	66.6%	66.8%	38.9%	137	84.3%	83.1
33	Plymouth	81.1%	76.6%	25.3%	108	83.0%	82.8
=34	Newcastle	74.1%	70.4%	28.5%	129	82.9%	82.6
=34	Nottingham Trent	80.5%	77.4%	24.1%	108	82.9%	82.6
=34	Aston	82.4%	79.1%	20.6%	114	—	82.6
37	Cardiff	65.3%	67.9%	30.9%	123	88.2%	82.4
38	Keele	81.1%	78.2%	41.1%	109	74.4%	82.0
=39	King's College London	71.3%	67.1%	—	150	89.8%	81.8
=39	Sheffield Hallam	81.0%	74.7%	17.8%	100	84.9%	81.8
41	Greenwich	82.3%	82.7%	7.4%	121	—	81.2
42	Central Lancashire	75.7%	74.5%	11.7%	112	85.9%	81.1

43 Northumbria		84.6%	85.4%	14.0%	131	72.9%	80.6
44 Kent		74.3%	71.8%	27.5%	104	81.0%	80.3
45 West of Scotland		80.1%	67.3%	29.0%	120	75.0%	80.2
46 Manchester Metropolitan		78.6%	76.6%	16.3%	116	77.3%	79.6
47 Reading		67.1%	48.3%	27.3%	118	85.5%	79.3
48 Brighton		81.2%	77.1%	4.8%	90	82.2%	78.8
49 Sussex		82.3%	75.8%	25.8%	142	64.3%	78.5
50 Huddersfield		66.3%	63.0%	11.0%	123	79.0%	76.4
51 Kingston		80.8%	79.6%	2.6%	99	73.1%	76.0
52 De Montfort		66.0%	67.0%	—	99	84.5%	75.6
53 Bradford		73.4%	65.8%	9.5%	100	72.8%	74.2
54 Salford		61.8%	59.5%	—	116	77.4%	72.7

Employed in high-skilled job	53%	Employed in lower-skilled job	10%
Employed in high-skilled job and studying	3%	Employed in lower-skilled job and studying	1%
Studying	25%	Unemployed	8%
High skilled work (median) salary	£25,000	Low/medium skilled salary	£20,000

Civil Engineering

As the future brains behind the design, construction and maintenance of roads, bridges, pipelines, processing plants, buildings and harbours, civil engineering students learn how to apply physics, maths and mechanics to structural design. Some degrees are four-year courses leading to an MEng, others are sandwich courses that include a work placement.

Job prospects are consistently strong – civil engineering ranks in the top ten of our employment table, with three-quarters of graduates working in professional roles 15 months on from their degrees and a further 11% furthering their studies or doing so while also holding down a good job, which attracts median salaries of £27,000.

As well as A-levels and Scottish Highers, BTEC qualifications are a popular means of entry into a civil engineering degree, but applicants should check with individual universities as to their preferred entry requirements.

For the first time in 16 years Cambridge has been toppled from the top of our Civil Engineering table, replaced by Imperial – a hair's breadth in front – boosted by strong results in the National Student Survey (NSS), the second-best employment outcomes and second-highest research rating. Cambridge boycotts the NSS, thus holding back its overall scores in our subject tables, but entrants in 2020 averaged an extraordinary 230 UCAS tariff points – by far the highest entry standards, and the university has the top-rated research in the field.

Northumbria, in 14th place, bucks the trend for older universities to dominate our top 20, while Glasgow Caledonian is the second-ranked post-1992 institution in 21st position, shared with Newcastle. West London has the best rates of student satisfaction but does less well for graduate prospects and lacks a research rating – and is thus confined to 44th overall.

Civil Engineering

		Teaching quality	Student experience	Research quality	Entry standards (UCAS points)	Graduate prospects	Overall score
1	Imperial College London	85.5%	88.4%	61.5%	189	97.1%	100.0
2	Cambridge	–	–	67.0%	230	94.9%	99.1
=3	Glasgow	65.3%	72.5%	47.2%	204	97.3%	94.3
=3	Bath	78.0%	79.1%	52.9%	175	94.0%	94.3
5	Strathclyde	80.0%	79.6%	35.7%	185	96.4%	94.1
6	Southampton	85.0%	82.2%	52.3%	156	92.1%	93.6
7	Bristol	75.9%	75.3%	52.3%	178	91.7%	93.1
8	Sheffield	80.4%	80.5%	43.1%	157	94.6%	92.2
=9	Leeds	82.4%	85.1%	32.0%	184	88.9%	91.9
=9	Dundee	78.9%	76.9%	46.2%	177	88.7%	91.9
11	Heriot-Watt	75.9%	77.0%	47.8%	167	92.3%	91.8
12	Edinburgh	66.1%	65.3%	50.3%	181	94.9%	91.4
13	Nottingham	81.3%	77.2%	40.8%	144	95.1%	90.9
14	Northumbria	85.0%	82.1%	30.7%	146	93.9%	90.4
15	Aberdeen	74.7%	79.0%	28.4%	158	–	88.1
16	Loughborough	76.7%	79.2%	26.9%	135	94.7%	87.4
17	Swansea	72.9%	71.6%	45.5%	140	89.6%	87.3
18	Manchester	70.7%	65.2%	36.4%	154	90.7%	86.6
19	Ulster	75.9%	72.7%	28.6%	129	93.0%	85.8
20	Queen's Belfast	71.1%	72.8%	31.3%	143	90.2%	85.6
=21	Newcastle	66.4%	59.9%	40.9%	130	95.4%	85.5
=21	Glasgow Caledonian	76.2%	74.6%	9.1%	168	–	85.5
23	Liverpool	66.9%	72.5%	32.1%	132	94.0%	85.2
=24	Cardiff	65.1%	70.9%	35.0%	142	91.0%	85.0
=24	Surrey	73.7%	79.7%	30.8%	130	88.7%	85.0
26	Exeter	62.4%	60.7%	36.4%	143	92.0%	84.2
=27	Plymouth	79.3%	77.9%	15.7%	114	92.3%	83.7
=27	University College London	70.8%	67.7%	23.1%	155	86.1%	83.7
29	Birmingham	59.0%	61.6%	21.9%	148	94.1%	82.8
30	Abertay	86.3%	80.4%	16.3%	114	83.9%	82.4
31	Salford	76.3%	70.2%	19.6%	131	85.6%	82.1
32	Teesside	83.2%	81.7%	5.8%	115	84.6%	80.9
33	Brunel	63.6%	66.1%	23.7%	139	85.2%	80.6
34	Nottingham Trent	72.8%	72.9%	3.4%	122	89.3%	80.0
35	Anglia Ruskin	78.6%	75.0%	5.2%	116	–	79.6
36	Edinburgh Napier	70.6%	76.7%	7.7%	130	83.3%	79.2
37	West of England	70.7%	71.2%	10.6%	124	–	79.1
38	Coventry	80.2%	78.2%	10.3%	118	79.0%	79.0
39	Liverpool John Moores	69.6%	68.0%	–	129	88.6%	78.9
40	Portsmouth	71.5%	70.1%	9.1%	109	87.1%	78.5
41	Derby	74.8%	72.3%	6.7%	112	84.6%	78.4
42	Bradford	69.1%	65.7%	17.8%	113	–	78.1

		Teaching quality	Student experience	Research quality	Entry standards (UCAS points)	Graduate prospects	Overall score
43	Brighton	66.3%	61.1%	5.1%	117	90.3%	78.0
44	West London	91.6%	89.8%	—	109	73.0%	77.9
45	Leeds Beckett	68.8%	64.5%	5.6%	95	92.9%	77.8
46	Central Lancashire	66.9%	62.9%	7.1%	125	—	76.6
47	London South Bank	68.1%	63.6%	19.6%	125	73.9%	75.7
48	Greenwich	61.0%	63.2%	5.5%	124	—	74.9
49	West of Scotland	49.1%	46.5%	9.0%	125*	88.0%	73.9
50	City	44.2%	45.1%	23.1%	121	84.6%	73.4
51	Kingston	73.0%	68.9%	2.9%	111	70.2%	72.3
52	East London	77.9%	78.2%	2.3%	102	64.2%	71.2

Employed in high-skilled job	75%	Employed in lower-skilled job	6%
Employed in high-skilled job and studying	4%	Employed in lower-skilled job and studying	0%
Studying	7%	Unemployed	8%
High skilled work (median) salary	£27,000	Low/medium skilled salary	£23,000

Classics and Ancient History

The degree taken by Boris Johnson, the prime minister (at the time of writing), classics takes in the broad literature, history and culture of Ancient Greek and Roman societies, and can include architecture, religion and philosophy. Some courses will want Latin or Greek A-level, while others will allow students to learn the languages from scratch once they have enrolled. Several universities teach the subjects as part of modular courses, but not on their own.

Cambridge cements its position at the top of our table for the 16th time in a row this year, supported by the best results for research and for graduate prospects. The highest entry standards are at St Andrews, the only university to have averaged over 200 UCAS points among its 2020 intake. For student satisfaction with both the wider experience and teaching quality Winchester (in 21st place overall) is unbeaten, with St Andrews, Swansea, Liverpool and Wales Trinity also performing strongly on teaching quality.

Twenty-seven per cent of classics and ancient history graduates were working in jobs deemed low-skilled 15 months after finishing their degrees, the most recent Graduate Outcomes survey found, and 9% were unemployed – ranking the subjects 47th out of the 67 in our employment table. Starting salaries in high-skilled jobs (which more than four in 10 graduates had secured) of £24,000 give the subjects a similar place for earnings.

Applications to classical studies courses declined a little in 2020, as did enrolments, but the number of students starting courses was higher than it was a decade before. The numbers starting the more specialised Classical Greek studies degrees doubled, to ten, while Latin studies attracted an intake of 35 undergraduates.

Classics and Ancient History	Teaching quality	Student experience	Research quality	Entry standards (UCAS points)	Graduate prospects	Overall score
1 Cambridge	—	—	65.0%	181	86.1%	100.0
2 St Andrews	87.5%	80.7%	43.2%	204	85.1%	98.7

	Teaching quality	Student experience	Research quality	Entry standards (UCAS points)	Graduate prospects	Overall score
3 Durham	84.4%	76.3%	54.3%	179	84.8%	97.5
4 Oxford	—	—	58.3%	193	82.6%	97.2
5 University College London	78.4%	62.0%	42.7%	169	86.0%	91.6
6 Exeter	75.4%	71.0%	45.0%	162	74.9%	89.4
7 Southampton	80.0%	70.7%	43.5%	136	—	87.4
8 Liverpool	88.4%	76.4%	28.9%	129	—	86.8
9 Nottingham	74.5%	65.4%	52.0%	134	69.6%	86.7
10 Warwick	78.5%	69.5%	45.0%	138	66.9%	86.6
11 Glasgow	78.1%	67.4%	32.7%	164	—	86.5
12 King's College London	83.7%	76.1%	43.6%	145	53.5%	86.3
13 Bristol	75.0%	68.5%	42.2%	144	70.0%	86.2
14 Reading	79.2%	73.4%	45.2%	117	68.3%	85.9
15 Edinburgh	69.3%	58.6%	34.9%	164	70.8%	83.9
16 Leeds	72.9%	57.2%	29.1%	145	77.8%	83.6
17 Birmingham	75.6%	61.3%	40.3%	133	65.9%	83.5
18 Newcastle	73.3%	67.0%	44.7%	127	61.8%	83.0
=19 Manchester	76.8%	58.3%	31.0%	143	68.0%	82.9
=19 Kent	86.4%	75.7%	33.1%	107	57.8%	82.9
21 Winchester	91.1%	81.0%	19.1%	94	—	82.3
22 Swansea	87.7%	78.3%	25.0%	107	57.2%	81.8
23 Royal Holloway, London	80.1%	76.0%	20.4%	122	55.8%	79.5
24 Cardiff	73.4%	59.8%	31.4%	124	—	79.2
25 Wales Trinity St David	88.1%	67.5%	15.7%	98	—	78.8
26 Roehampton	81.6%	75.2%	—	100	50.8%	73.3

Employed in high-skilled job	41%	Employed in lower-skilled job	27%
Employed in high-skilled job and studying	3%	Employed in lower-skilled job and studying	2%
Studying	18%	Unemployed	9%
High skilled work (median) salary	£24,000	Low/medium skilled salary	£20,000

Communication and Media Studies

This subject table covers a wide range of courses; some focus on the history and theory of media and culture in society, while others range from practical production for TV, film and radio to script writing or journalism. Options are extensive; for 2022–23 entry, 193 universities and colleges were offering 1,628 courses classified by UCAS under the media studies banner – either as standalone degrees or as part of modular courses.

Warwick takes the top spot this year, having fared more strongly on student satisfaction than previous leader, Loughborough, for both teaching quality and the broader experience. For research, Loughborough, Warwick and Goldsmiths lead the field. The Scottish universities of Strathclyde, Stirling and Glasgow Caledonian averaged the highest entry standards in 2020, with Leeds attracting the highest grades south of the border.

Creative Arts (54th overall) received glowing student satisfaction scores for teaching quality in the NSS, a measure in which West London came second – as it did for the wider experience, with Brunel in first place.

With more than nine in ten graduates working in high-skilled jobs and/or engaged in postgraduate study 15 months on from their degrees, City (=7th overall) does well to buck an otherwise lacklustre trend by media studies in our employment table. The subject sits 59th out of the 67 listed, because 31% of graduates were working in low-skilled jobs at the point of survey. Most communication and media studies students will be wise to the dearth of "professional"-level roles upon graduation, but the worryingly high 13% of graduates who were unemployed is more of a concern. Bedfordshire (=88th overall) had just 37.5% of graduates in high-skilled work and/or further study and Aberystwyth (=75th) did almost as poorly. Median starting salaries of £21,234 place the subjects in the bottom four.

Communication and Media Studies	Teaching quality	Student experience	Research quality	Entry standards (UCAS points)	Graduate prospects	Overall score
1 Warwick	88.9%	78.3%	61.7%	157	66.5%	100.0
2 Strathclyde	72.3%	71.8%	39.4%	200	67.9%	97.6
3 Loughborough	65.6%	73.8%	62.3%	142	82.1%	97.0
4 Leeds	73.5%	68.4%	54.5%	161	72.5%	96.6
5 Sheffield	75.8%	73.6%	37.9%	150	80.3%	96.1
6 Stirling	81.1%	73.2%	36.0%	175	66.8%	96.0
=7 City	75.7%	76.1%	30.9%	130	90.4%	95.8
=7 Exeter	82.1%	78.8%	46.2%	143	—	95.8
9 King's College London	—	—	55.8%	154	58.2%	94.7
10 Lancaster	—	—	51.4%	133	64.3%	92.9
11 Cardiff	70.5%	62.8%	55.4%	142	69.2%	92.2
12 Queen Mary, London	76.1%	62.0%	35.1%	151	64.8%	90.0
13 Newcastle	69.2%	62.5%	37.8%	148	69.1%	89.8
14 Southampton	81.7%	69.5%	42.7%	140	56.7%	89.5
15 Kent	86.0%	78.2%	—	118	80.3%	89.3
16 Sussex	70.0%	62.1%	43.6%	137	67.0%	88.9
17 Leicester	76.7%	70.2%	46.1%	134	57.2%	88.4
18 Edinburgh Napier	82.1%	78.2%	9.5%	150	62.3%	88.2
19 York	76.0%	74.9%	26.0%	136	—	88.0
20 Queen Margaret, Edinburgh	73.1%	65.2%	14.0%	157	66.5%	87.6
21 Royal Holloway, London	71.3%	63.4%	38.1%	141	62.1%	87.5
22 Swansea	85.5%	76.4%	18.5%	134	58.6%	87.3
23 Coventry	84.4%	80.0%	18.1%	117	64.9%	87.1
24 Northumbria	76.3%	66.3%	22.2%	132	66.2%	86.7
25 Westminster	83.5%	81.0%	28.3%	109	61.0%	86.5
26 Leeds Beckett	88.3%	82.6%	11.0%	95	71.0%	86.4
27 Ulster	72.3%	68.5%	34.0%	124	64.4%	86.3
28 Queen's Belfast	65.9%	65.0%	38.3%	137	—	86.1

		Teaching quality	Student experience	Research quality	Entry standards (UCAS points)	Graduate prospects	Overall score
29	Goldsmiths, London	60.5%	49.6%	60.0%	125	65.4%	86.0
30	Robert Gordon	85.1%	78.3%	7.5%	151	51.5%	85.6
31	Surrey	72.1%	67.7%	30.2%	128	—	85.4
32	Brunel	87.1%	88.3%	23.0%	104	55.8%	85.2
33	Nottingham	66.1%	59.2%	45.8%	125	—	85.1
34	Liverpool	73.6%	65.3%	27.5%	129	61.1%	84.9
35	East Anglia	68.5%	64.6%	43.8%	124	59.0%	84.8
=36	Glasgow Caledonian	62.5%	58.6%	15.2%	163	64.4%	84.7
=36	Keele	84.7%	79.7%	25.0%	105	57.8%	84.7
38	Canterbury Christ Church	81.8%	68.3%	7.3%	104	72.7%	84.5
39	Birmingham City	81.6%	71.5%	6.0%	116	67.2%	84.3
=40	Liverpool John Moores	77.9%	73.5%	6.2%	141	58.5%	84.1
=40	Salford	74.4%	66.8%	36.9%	121	55.8%	84.1
42	Derby	78.1%	73.1%	13.5%	110	65.9%	83.8
43	Sheffield Hallam	76.1%	69.1%	14.4%	112	66.7%	83.4
=44	West of England	78.8%	70.9%	18.6%	117	59.1%	83.2
=44	Anglia Ruskin	81.3%	73.2%	26.4%	102	58.2%	83.2
46	Sunderland	80.3%	80.0%	13.0%	106	59.6%	82.6
47	Kingston	70.2%	63.9%	15.7%	104	72.4%	82.4
=48	Solent, Southampton	82.3%	75.6%	0.8%	107	64.4%	82.2
=48	Central Lancashire	80.6%	73.5%	7.9%	112	60.8%	82.2
=48	West of Scotland	80.6%	73.1%	11.3%	133	50.9%	82.2
=51	Oxford Brookes	66.8%	64.4%	25.3%	111	64.8%	81.8
=51	Nottingham Trent	75.3%	66.7%	10.0%	113	64.6%	81.8
=51	West London	89.4%	83.3%	4.5%	111	51.1%	81.8
54	Creative Arts	91.9%	79.7%	3.4%	110	51.2%	81.7
55	Wolverhampton	79.2%	71.7%	33.2%	80	57.9%	80.8
=56	Bangor	64.6%	53.9%	24.7%	122	62.1%	80.6
=56	Manchester Metropolitan	69.9%	59.9%	29.0%	115	56.3%	80.6
58	Bournemouth	62.9%	55.3%	15.1%	110	71.0%	80.1
59	Hull	72.6%	60.4%	11.2%	125	57.1%	80.0
=60	Huddersfield	75.5%	69.6%	—	110	63.5%	79.9
=60	Worcester	77.3%	73.2%	8.2%	101	60.2%	79.9
62	Gloucestershire	80.5%	76.1%	9.3%	117	49.4%	79.8
63	Roehampton	73.2%	64.0%	26.4%	95	58.7%	79.7
64	Lincoln	72.7%	65.0%	4.0%	113	62.2%	79.4
65	Middlesex	70.5%	60.4%	11.0%	109	61.8%	78.9
66	De Montfort	60.7%	52.4%	31.2%	105	63.0%	78.8
67	Winchester	71.0%	63.4%	15.8%	102	59.6%	78.6
68	Portsmouth	73.3%	63.9%	12.8%	105	56.0%	78.0
69	York St John	70.7%	70.1%	4.4%	110	57.5%	77.8
=70	London South Bank	74.6%	65.8%	12.8%	90	59.3%	77.7

=70	St Mary's, Twickenham	84.4%	81.9%	9.1%	99	44.7%	77.7
72	Teesside	73.9%	68.0%	2.9%	113	54.2%	77.4
73	Liverpool Hope	73.3%	62.2%	—	114	56.9%	77.2
74	London Metropolitan	70.3%	62.6%	5.9%	107	58.6%	77.1
=75	University of the Arts London	69.6%	55.7%	—	120	58.7%	76.9
=75	Staffordshire	70.4%	57.9%	6.7%	114	56.4%	76.9
=75	Aberystwyth	78.8%	72.7%	9.2%	121	40.3%	76.9
78	Falmouth	67.7%	59.4%	—	122	56.6%	76.4
79	Brighton	64.3%	52.4%	16.2%	101	60.9%	76.2
80	Chester	74.6%	59.8%	4.3%	117	49.2%	76.0
81	Edge Hill	72.9%	63.1%	10.2%	118	44.7%	75.6
82	Bath Spa	71.1%	65.2%	13.9%	104	48.7%	75.5
83	Leeds Trinity	71.4%	59.6%	3.9%	99	57.1%	75.3
84	Greenwich	68.2%	64.7%	3.5%	103	55.8%	75.1
85	East London	69.6%	60.7%	13.9%	94	52.1%	74.4
86	Northampton	69.1%	62.7%	—	95	57.0%	74.0
87	South Wales	69.2%	62.5%	—	103	50.5%	73.1
=88	Chichester	54.5%	49.8%	—	95	59.3%	69.9
=88	Bedfordshire	77.6%	70.6%	8.2%	75	37.5%	69.9

Employed in high-skilled job	49%	Employed in lower-skilled job	31%
Employed in high-skilled job and studying	2%	Employed in lower-skilled job and studying	1%
Studying	4%	Unemployed	13%
High skilled work (median) salary	£21,234	Low/medium skilled salary	£19,500

Computer Science

Listen to your teacher when they tell you to learn to code. It might be the soundest piece of educational advice they give you. Computer science graduates are among the most sought after in the jobs market – and among the best paid. The subject area is broad, taking in everything from artificial intelligence to computer games design.

Twenty-eight universities report more than 90% of their computer science graduates as being in high-skilled jobs or postgraduate study within 15 months. St Andrews, in first place, achieves a perfect 100% – an outcome usually reserved for medicine courses which have guaranteed jobs at the end.

Job prospects for computer science graduates are pretty good regardless of which university you attend, with only 11 registering rates of high-skilled jobs/postgraduate study less than 70%. Compare these outcomes with art and design, where one university has a rate of 90%+ and 70 have less than 70%.

Salaries are equally attractive and at the very top end of the scale. The median salary across all 109 institutions in our subject ranking is a healthy £27,500, but riches await far beyond that in the upper reaches. Oxford leads the way (£65,000), ahead of Cambridge and Imperial College London (both £50,000), followed by University College London (£42,000) and Warwick (£39,000).

St Andrews takes over at the top of the computer science ranking, knocking Cambridge into second place after a five-year run as No 1. As well as leading the way in the jobs market, St Andrews tops our entry standards measure with average UCAS tariff points for new students at 223, just ahead of Cambridge at 220. St Andrews is also second for student satisfaction both with teaching quality and wider experience.

Computer Science	Teaching quality	Student experience	Research quality	Entry standards (UCAS points)	Graduate prospects	Overall score
1 St Andrews	90.2%	87.6%	33.4%	223	100.0%	100.0
2 Cambridge	—	—	57.1%	220	97.4%	98.2
3 Imperial College London	78.7%	82.3%	64.1%	196	97.6%	98.0
4 Oxford	—	—	60.6%	207	97.9%	96.6
5 Glasgow	71.8%	74.6%	50.3%	205	88.6%	92.3
6 Manchester	66.0%	67.4%	50.7%	189	95.7%	90.7
=7 Durham	71.5%	68.4%	38.8%	183	97.9%	90.6
=7 Warwick	66.6%	64.4%	54.8%	183	95.8%	90.6
9 University College London	62.6%	68.5%	62.7%	188	90.9%	90.3
10 Sheffield	72.8%	74.9%	51.1%	150	93.1%	89.3
11 Southampton	71.1%	71.3%	48.2%	168	89.9%	88.9
12 Lancaster	72.1%	71.1%	44.8%	144	97.3%	88.5
13 Strathclyde	72.2%	75.0%	21.1%	193	90.9%	88.3
=14 Leeds	69.5%	66.5%	41.6%	171	93.5%	88.2
=14 Nottingham	—	—	45.4%	154	87.4%	88.2
=14 Aberdeen	72.5%	76.5%	37.4%	166	—	88.2
=17 Bristol	61.4%	61.5%	49.2%	178	96.2%	88.0
=17 Bath	73.2%	79.2%	33.3%	162	90.6%	88.0
19 Edinburgh	59.8%	61.6%	54.3%	202	86.4%	87.9
20 King's College London	66.2%	69.3%	47.6%	168	91.6%	87.8
21 Exeter	70.2%	70.3%	40.7%	146	97.6%	87.7
22 Swansea	78.9%	76.8%	47.5%	132	87.4%	87.6
23 Birmingham	63.4%	63.2%	46.4%	171	94.3%	87.3
24 Loughborough	77.7%	80.7%	18.7%	151	90.4%	86.3
25 Liverpool	76.2%	73.3%	40.5%	137	86.0%	85.7
=26 Leicester	73.1%	74.5%	30.2%	136	92.5%	85.4
=26 Aberystwyth	80.9%	76.3%	38.4%	120	85.3%	85.4
28 Heriot-Watt	62.4%	66.1%	39.5%	164	90.1%	84.9
=29 Royal Holloway, London	71.3%	72.5%	35.1%	131	91.5%	84.7
=29 York	62.6%	66.9%	46.9%	147	90.8%	84.7
31 Surrey	74.1%	75.2%	25.3%	132	92.2%	84.6
=32 East Anglia	69.0%	67.7%	35.9%	142	89.7%	84.2
=32 Queen Mary, London	69.2%	65.8%	37.4%	150	86.9%	84.2
34 Dundee	70.4%	74.7%	29.4%	171	78.6%	84.1
35 Queen's Belfast	65.4%	68.2%	29.5%	143	93.5%	83.6
36 Hull	75.1%	74.6%	22.2%	129	87.1%	82.9
37 Sussex	71.1%	73.2%	21.6%	138	87.7%	82.7

38 Aston	69.7%	66.7%	21.7%	137	90.4%	82.2
39 Stirling	75.4%	69.7%	14.0%	143	85.1%	82.0
40 Newcastle	55.8%	50.5%	49.7%	140	92.8%	81.7
41 Cardiff	62.1%	61.6%	25.0%	146	91.6%	81.4
42 Robert Gordon	79.5%	76.9%	4.3%	142	80.2%	81.1
43 Kent	63.1%	57.8%	37.8%	136	86.8%	80.8
44 Edinburgh Napier	75.7%	69.6%	5.2%	146	83.3%	80.7
45 Bangor	74.9%	66.6%	17.6%	110	87.9%	80.0
46 Ulster	74.3%	68.3%	16.6%	126	81.8%	79.8
47 Plymouth	69.4%	63.0%	21.8%	125	86.2%	79.7
48 Abertay	75.0%	64.4%	3.4%	149	81.1%	79.5
=49 Oxford Brookes	72.6%	70.7%	13.0%	114	85.0%	79.0
=49 Bath Spa	80.4%	74.0%	13.9%	93	83.0%	79.0
51 Chester	77.9%	69.6%	1.3%	120	84.2%	78.9
=52 Liverpool Hope	79.2%	73.4%	8.8%	108	81.1%	78.8
=52 Glyndŵr	78.9%	81.8%	3.9%	109	80.0%	78.8
=52 Staffordshire	81.0%	73.7%	0.4%	121	79.2%	78.8
55 Brunel	69.9%	62.0%	25.2%	132	77.7%	78.7
=56 South Wales	74.5%	69.1%	3.6%	121	84.1%	78.4
=56 City	67.6%	66.7%	21.8%	124	81.3%	78.4
58 West of Scotland	76.9%	68.8%	3.2%	132	77.7%	78.2
59 Sheffield Hallam	69.3%	60.3%	14.4%	117	85.4%	77.6
=60 Essex	55.8%	56.3%	34.3%	123	86.9%	77.5
=60 Keele	67.4%	68.0%	10.8%	122	83.8%	77.5
62 Coventry	75.3%	69.5%	3.3%	114	81.8%	77.4
63 Reading	59.0%	56.3%	16.3%	124	92.4%	77.3
64 Huddersfield	68.6%	58.6%	7.4%	132	83.5%	77.1
=65 Lincoln	62.2%	59.5%	13.6%	126	87.0%	76.9
=65 Northumbria	67.6%	64.0%	4.0%	139	81.0%	76.9
=65 London Metropolitan	94.9%	91.4%	0.7%	89	61.4%	76.9
=68 Manchester Metropolitan	71.7%	64.4%	5.6%	129	78.4%	76.7
=68 Teesside	79.8%	71.1%	3.4%	122	71.1%	76.7
=70 Derby	74.7%	64.6%	5.0%	114	80.3%	76.6
=70 Suffolk	76.0%	68.7%	—	117	78.8%	76.6
=70 Falmouth	81.1%	72.9%	—	116	72.4%	76.6
=73 Edge Hill	71.1%	68.8%	0.3%	134	77.3%	76.5
=73 Leeds Beckett	78.1%	73.9%	0.2%	109	77.1%	76.5
=75 Wales Trinity St David	63.3%	59.0%	1.0%	166	77.5%	76.4
=75 West of England	72.5%	68.3%	5.9%	125	75.5%	76.4
77 Glasgow Caledonian	71.6%	69.3%	4.0%	143	70.1%	76.1
78 Liverpool John Moores	68.6%	61.0%	3.2%	151	73.7%	76.0
79 Bradford	75.2%	70.8%	—	123	72.8%	75.6
80 Sunderland	70.9%	66.7%	1.8%	100	85.0%	75.5
=81 Nottingham Trent	67.0%	56.1%	5.2%	127	80.7%	75.1
=81 Portsmouth	70.9%	64.0%	7.2%	111	77.9%	75.1
=81 Birmingham City	75.7%	69.4%	4.9%	119	69.5%	75.1

Computer Science cont.	Teaching quality	Student experience	Research quality	Entry standards (UCAS points)	Graduate prospects	Overall score
=84 Middlesex	71.4%	71.5%	14.2%	111	69.0%	74.8
=84 Bolton	81.9%	73.6%	—	115	64.7%	74.8
86 York St John	66.9%	56.8%	—	106	88.5%	74.6
87 Goldsmiths, London	54.0%	51.1%	29.2%	134	76.7%	74.3
88 Bournemouth	63.5%	54.4%	8.5%	119	81.4%	74.0
89 Anglia Ruskin	71.7%	65.6%	—	106	77.3%	73.9
90 Westminster	67.9%	64.3%	2.9%	116	75.7%	73.8
=91 Salford	57.3%	54.5%	15.3%	127	79.5%	73.7
=91 Greenwich	67.2%	61.6%	7.3%	118	74.2%	73.7
93 De Montfort	61.5%	59.9%	13.4%	109	79.9%	73.6
94 West London	80.7%	79.3%	1.2%	116	56.5%	73.5
95 Central Lancashire	68.5%	64.7%	—	132	69.6%	73.4
=96 Cardiff Metropolitan	69.1%	67.8%	—	119	71.4%	73.3
=96 Buckinghamshire New	75.8%	68.0%	—	104	70.3%	73.3
98 Bedfordshire	66.7%	57.5%	9.1%	119	73.1%	73.2
=99 Brighton	67.3%	59.3%	6.4%	92	79.7%	72.5
=99 Hertfordshire	67.3%	63.2%	7.8%	112	70.3%	72.5
101 Kingston	68.3%	61.5%	5.3%	106	72.5%	72.2
=102 Worcester	66.2%	62.2%	—	103	77.3%	72.1
=102 East London	78.3%	79.0%	2.3%	84	63.4%	72.1
104 Northampton	70.9%	63.8%	—	104	71.1%	72.0
105 Gloucestershire	66.0%	63.6%	—	117	70.8%	71.8
106 Solent, Southampton	74.3%	63.6%	—	101	65.4%	71.1
107 Canterbury Christ Church	71.8%	66.3%	—	91	68.8%	70.8
108 Wolverhampton	66.8%	61.4%	—	88	64.8%	67.9
109 London South Bank	53.8%	52.4%	19.6%	98	49.0%	63.4

Employed in high-skilled job	71%	Employed in lower-skilled job	10%
Employed in high-skilled job and studying	3%	Employed in lower-skilled job and studying	0%
Studying	5%	Unemployed	11%
High skilled work (median) salary	£27,500	Low/medium skilled salary	£20,000

Creative Writing

At the top of our Creative Writing table, Royal Holloway has achieved consistently strong results across the measures in our dedicated ranking. It has a good record, having placed second in last year's table and fourth the year before that. But it is Bolton, in 20th place overall, that achieved the best results in the National Student Survey (NSS) – where students returned exceptionally positive responses in the sections relating to teaching quality as well as the broad experience. Aberystwyth received the second-highest ratings for both measures, while Kingston was close behind for teaching quality.

Queen Mary, London (in sixth place overall) has the top research rating, a clear margin ahead of Nottingham (third). Dundee averaged the highest entry standards in 2020 of 166 UCAS tariff points. Only nine universities out of 53 averaged over 144 UCAS points, which are equivalent to AAA at A-level.

Graduate prospects are poor for creative writing degrees, and the subject sits four from the bottom of our employment measure. A higher proportion of graduates (51%) are in jobs classified as "low-skilled" or unemployed, rather than "high-skilled" or studying (49%) 15 months on from their degrees.

That said, applicants to creative writing courses may be less motivated by immediate professional full-time employment than many others. This is perhaps why many universities do not post graduate prospects scores. Graduates of ninth-ranked Derby's creative writing courses fared very well, however, with 86% in professional jobs and/or postgraduate study.

Creative Writing	Teaching quality	Student experience	Research quality	Entry standards (UCAS points)	Graduate prospects	Overall score
1 Royal Holloway, London	82.2%	72.3%	49.9%	145	—	100.0
2 Queen's Belfast	73.9%	69.9%	53.1%	154*	—	99.4
3 Nottingham	65.8%	57.7%	56.6%	160*	—	97.0
4 Birmingham	72.2%	63.7%	37.0%	149	77.1%	96.4
5 Aberystwyth	93.7%	91.4%	31.2%	129	58.9%	95.9
6 Queen Mary, London	73.7%	66.8%	64.0%	124*	—	95.8
7 Lancaster	72.4%	68.2%	47.0%	145	—	95.5
8 Leeds	72.6%	65.1%	38.6%	153	—	94.7
9 Derby	87.6%	77.2%	13.5%	110	86.0%	94.3
10 Newcastle	69.8%	51.9%	54.3%	142	—	93.5
11 Dundee	65.1%	62.8%	32.8%	166		92.9
12 East Anglia	71.4%	61.2%	36.2%	147	64.0%	92.1
13 Surrey	79.8%	74.0%	39.1%	119	—	91.9
14 Nottingham Trent	82.4%	71.8%	30.0%	126	—	91.6
15 Brunel	83.2%	74.7%	30.9%	107	70.3%	91.5
16 Essex	79.1%	69.5%	37.7%	122	—	91.3
=17 Kent	76.1%	60.1%	47.3%	121	—	91.2
=17 West of England	85.7%	76.0%	35.4%	108	—	91.2
19 Bangor	77.4%	68.0%	46.3%	128	51.2%	90.0
20 Bolton	97.8%	93.3%	14.4%	94*	—	89.9
=21 Keele	85.6%	75.7%	29.8%	107	—	89.6
=21 Teesside	88.5%	76.8%	15.6%	119	—	89.6
23 Kingston	92.9%	76.5%	15.7%	109	—	89.0
24 Plymouth	80.4%	68.9%	30.5%	109	—	87.6
25 Birmingham City	78.4%	70.1%	30.9%	110	—	87.3
26 Salford	84.9%	74.3%	7.8%	117	60.3%	86.5
27 Manchester Metropolitan	74.0%	56.4%	29.0%	122	57.8%	85.7
28 Chichester	77.5%	72.1%	16.3%	104	64.7%	85.4
29 Central Lancashire	79.8%	65.2%	9.9%	118	61.7%	85.2

Creative Writing cont.

	Teaching quality	Student experience	Research quality	Entry standards (UCAS points)	Graduate prospects	Overall score
30 Lincoln	82.9%	72.9%	16.2%	107	—	85.1
=31 Hull	74.3%	61.9%	22.7%	121	—	85.0
=31 Westminster	77.3%	67.2%	28.9%	104	—	85.0
33 Canterbury Christ Church	77.8%	67.2%	8.0%	106	68.9%	84.8
34 Liverpool Hope	77.8%	67.5%	26.9%	104	—	84.7
35 Anglia Ruskin	83.2%	69.8%	16.3%	106	—	84.6
36 Liverpool John Moores	62.9%	60.0%	17.9%	145	55.8%	84.2
37 Bournemouth	73.4%	67.3%	15.1%	126	54.8%	84.1
38 Chester	86.6%	71.3%	10.7%	102*	—	83.8
=39 De Montfort	64.2%	48.6%	24.1%	114	69.6%	83.7
=39 Roehampton	77.2%	60.6%	20.8%	103	60.9%	83.7
=39 Bath Spa	79.2%	67.0%	23.5%	100	56.4%	83.7
42 Greenwich	73.5%	68.1%	14.4%	121	—	83.6
43 Portsmouth	74.7%	65.3%	17.1%	101	63.9%	83.4
=44 Worcester	77.4%	71.6%	8.2%	103	59.5%	82.3
=44 Gloucestershire	87.0%	67.7%	9.3%	98	54.7%	82.3
46 Edge Hill	80.7%	69.5%	12.1%	121	44.4%	82.1
47 Coventry	75.8%	57.2%	18.1%	110	—	81.5
48 Sheffield Hallam	78.5%	69.0%	14.6%	107	48.7%	81.0
49 Wolverhampton	83.3%	75.4%	7.6%	90*	—	80.3
50 Falmouth	78.2%	69.7%	—	122	47.1%	80.1
51 York St John	75.4%	70.0%	9.7%	100	52.0%	79.5
52 St Mary's, Twickenham	83.0%	81.0%	14.6%	82*	44.4%	78.8
53 Winchester	68.8%	52.9%	—	112	52.0%	76.0

Employed in high-skilled job	36%	Employed in lower-skilled job	34%
Employed in high-skilled job and studying	5%	Employed in lower-skilled job and studying	2%
Studying	8%	Unemployed	15%
High skilled work (median) salary	£20,000	Low/medium skilled salary	£18,000

Criminology

The scientific study of crime and its causes, criminology is a growing undergraduate field. There are 166 universities and colleges offering the subject for 2022–23, either alone, as part of a joint honours degree, or within a broader social science degree.

Now in its sixth year, our Criminology table has expanded to include an extra 18 universities – including Bath, which joins at No 1. Bath's four-year criminology BSc explores 21st-century issues in crime and criminal justice with a global focus and incorporates a placement year. Bath students returned excellent scores in the sections relating to both teaching quality and the wider undergraduate experience in the National Student Survey (NSS). The university is also top for graduate prospects with 85% in high-skilled jobs and/or further study 15 months after finishing their degrees. Wrexham Glyndŵr, in 30th place overall, does best for student satisfaction with teaching quality, and Kent (=18th) leads in research.

The data in this table previously appeared under sociology and law, and while criminology easily merits its own ranking in our *Guide*, the latest Graduate Outcomes survey rolled criminology's results into the sociology category. On its own, criminology finished second from bottom of our employment table in last year's edition and in the bottom six the year before. This year, sociology – including criminology – ranks third from bottom. The nagging issue is a high proportion of graduates starting out in lower-skilled jobs. Career opportunities include in the police force, prison service, Home Office, charities or law practice.

Criminology	Teaching quality	Student experience	Research quality	Entry standards (UCAS points)	Graduate prospects	Overall score
1 Bath	82.3%	81.1%	43.4%	148	85.0%	100.0
2 Durham	79.9%	70.7%	28.7%	151	75.7%	93.6
3 Leeds	71.7%	65.1%	40.1%	162	69.9%	92.5
=4 Bristol	71.6%	64.6%	47.9%	—	73.3%	92.3
=4 Loughborough	83.4%	82.8%	40.6%	144	61.3%	92.3
6 University College London	72.3%	67.6%	48.7%	145	—	90.9
7 Lancaster	74.1%	71.8%	51.4%	144	61.3%	90.7
8 Nottingham	70.8%	64.9%	43.5%	133	74.6%	90.6
9 Stirling	68.9%	62.0%	33.8%	172	61.8%	89.3
10 Southampton	67.0%	60.5%	52.8%	145	64.3%	89.1
11 Queen's Belfast	77.2%	70.0%	39.3%	149	54.2%	87.6
12 Sheffield	73.5%	68.8%	26.8%	146	61.8%	86.8
13 Swansea	77.7%	75.6%	20.4%	128	66.7%	86.7
14 Surrey	75.6%	69.7%	—	142	74.5%	86.5
15 York	62.3%	58.7%	47.5%	140	63.4%	86.1
16 Manchester	68.1%	56.7%	27.2%	148	66.1%	85.9
17 Edinburgh Napier	83.3%	76.3%	—	158	57.9%	85.8
=18 Leicester	75.8%	70.6%	26.3%	125	62.9%	85.1
=18 Kent	68.6%	61.6%	59.0%	109	60.8%	85.1
20 Essex	66.4%	58.6%	44.3%	114	66.7%	84.3
21 Sussex	69.2%	61.0%	27.9%	135	63.3%	84.2
22 Suffolk	82.3%	71.5%	—	108	74.7%	84.1
23 Cardiff	63.2%	54.7%	30.8%	145	63.3%	83.9
24 Salford	77.1%	67.8%	27.7%	114	56.5%	82.0
25 Aberystwyth	79.7%	77.3%	14.3%	114	56.8%	81.6
26 Royal Holloway, London	77.8%	71.5%	—	126	62.4%	81.4
=27 Abertay	81.6%	70.9%	5.0%	141	50.0%	81.2
=27 Ulster	74.6%	65.4%	39.2%	126	45.7%	81.2
29 Northumbria	76.9%	65.0%	12.7%	138	52.4%	81.1
30 Glyndŵr	89.2%	80.5%	—	95	61.5%	81.0
31 Bolton	86.2%	78.8%	1.0%	109	—	80.9
=32 Liverpool	59.2%	52.9%	24.5%	127	67.6%	80.8

Criminology cont.	Teaching quality	Student experience	Research quality	Entry standards (UCAS points)	Graduate prospects	Overall score
=32 City	67.0%	66.5%	20.8%	139	54.3%	80.8
34 Edge Hill	72.8%	70.7%	12.1%	126	56.8%	80.4
35 Worcester	79.6%	74.0%	—	125	56.6%	80.2
36 Birmingham	64.4%	49.2%	40.1%	143	47.2%	79.8
37 Sunderland	85.6%	78.7%	1.9%	102	57.2%	79.7
38 Liverpool John Moores	70.2%	62.0%	5.8%	138	56.1%	79.2
=39 Portsmouth	70.9%	61.3%	12.1%	122	58.4%	79.0
=39 West of England	76.5%	68.5%	10.9%	113	55.9%	79.0
41 Plymouth	68.3%	62.9%	16.0%	116	59.8%	78.9
42 Greenwich	76.8%	70.8%	2.1%	115	57.8%	78.8
43 Derby	77.3%	73.0%	2.4%	106	58.6%	78.3
44 Lincoln	75.3%	71.4%	5.8%	114	55.3%	78.2
45 Sheffield Hallam	73.0%	64.9%	14.4%	107	57.3%	78.0
46 Bedfordshire	73.3%	67.4%	16.3%	107	54.7%	77.9
47 Chester	69.9%	57.4%	0.3%	117	64.5%	77.8
48 Central Lancashire	68.6%	61.7%	11.8%	122	55.3%	77.6
49 Coventry	74.7%	70.3%	—	100	62.3%	77.4
50 Nottingham Trent	75.1%	63.6%	5.1%	109	57.4%	77.3
51 Bournemouth	71.2%	62.2%	—	108	64.0%	77.2
52 Hull	68.5%	66.0%	14.3%	117	53.4%	77.1
53 London South Bank	68.0%	55.0%	20.1%	96	61.7%	76.8
54 Keele	63.2%	59.6%	34.0%	112	49.8%	76.6
55 West London	75.4%	67.1%	—	117	52.5%	76.4
56 London Metropolitan	81.5%	68.2%	8.8%	81	56.9%	76.2
=57 Birmingham City	73.3%	65.0%	3.8%	113	53.2%	76.0
=57 York St John	81.5%	73.5%	—	101	51.2%	76.0
59 Staffordshire	72.0%	62.2%	—	98	61.8%	75.6
60 Goldsmiths, London	65.9%	49.2%	13.5%	122	53.7%	75.4
61 Kingston	75.9%	67.9%	—	96	55.9%	74.9
=62 Bradford	65.8%	59.1%	10.6%	110	54.8%	74.8
=62 Westminster	74.2%	66.6%	—	113	50.0%	74.8
=62 Gloucestershire	79.9%	73.5%	—	111	44.4%	74.8
65 Bangor	66.5%	56.6%	—	135	50.2%	74.7
66 Teesside	62.6%	49.0%	15.0%	105	59.8%	74.6
67 Huddersfield	69.5%	59.7%	9.5%	111	50.7%	74.4
=68 Brunel	60.7%	55.2%	28.5%	—	50.4%	74.2
=68 Manchester Metropolitan	67.6%	57.3%	6.9%	119	50.4%	74.2
70 Canterbury Christ Church	75.0%	67.7%	3.2%	89	54.8%	74.1
=71 Anglia Ruskin	70.4%	59.6%	5.4%	104	52.8%	73.7
=71 South Wales	62.6%	59.2%	15.4%	106	52.6%	73.7
=71 Liverpool Hope	75.2%	65.2%	8.6%	108	43.8%	73.7
74 Solent, Southampton	74.0%	64.0%	—	104	49.7%	73.3

75 West of Scotland	68.9%	60.2%	7.5%	—	50.0%	72.8
76 Winchester	65.5%	61.9%	4.4%	100	54.5%	72.7
77 Oxford Brookes	73.3%	63.8%	—	107	47.2%	72.6
78 East London	67.5%	56.0%	10.6%	92	53.8%	72.3
79 Middlesex	64.8%	60.6%	14.9%	100	48.2%	72.1
80 Leeds Beckett	68.9%	60.2%	6.4%	94	51.4%	72.0
81 Roehampton	67.9%	63.3%	—	92	53.6%	71.4
82 Brighton	56.9%	45.0%	12.4%	101	52.8%	69.8
83 Buckinghamshire New	77.4%	68.0%	—	74	43.9%	69.0
84 Northampton	64.8%	50.6%	—	94	49.1%	68.3
85 St Mary's, Twickenham	63.6%	51.6%	—	97	45.0%	67.2
86 De Montfort	48.5%	44.6%	11.2%	97	51.2%	66.7
87 Bath Spa	62.9%	49.3%	—	92	43.6%	65.8

Dentistry

Glasgow is the best place to study dentistry, topping our subject ranking for the sixth successive year. The university's dentistry school has students with the highest number of UCAS tariff points on average (228 – 40 points more than its nearest rival). Its strength across all five of our ranking measures keeps the university ahead of the field.

With just 15 dental schools across the country, this is one of the smaller and more stable subject rankings, even in a year that has seen more turmoil than most due to the pandemic-influenced downturn in rates of student satisfaction.

Liverpool – seventh overall – comes top in students' eyes for teaching quality, one of five universities to exceed 90%, an outstanding achievement in the circumstances of the pandemic. Scoring 92.4%, Liverpool is narrowly ahead of two of the newer dental schools: Plymouth (91.8%) and Central Lancashire (91.6%). Queen's Belfast and Newcastle also had scores over 90%.

At the opposite end of the scale, King's College London (KCL) commands the worst scores for satisfaction with teaching quality (63.8%). Queen Mary London (68.9%), Cardiff (70.2%) and Manchester (71.1%) cannot claim a ringing endorsement from their students either.

Plymouth is top for satisfaction with the wider student experience, and it and Newcastle are the only two universities to score more than 90% on this measure. Birmingham – bottom of the dentistry ranking for the second successive year – has students whose dissatisfaction with the wider experience is beaten only by those at KCL.

Four of last year's top five for dentistry reappear, although Dundee drops three places to fifth and Queen's Belfast and Newcastle each gain a place to rank second and third respectively. The only new entry to the top five is Manchester, in fourth place this year, up from tenth.

In common with other medical subjects, applications to dentistry are booming, up 7% on 2019 to stand at 12,220, and up 35% since 2016. Career prospects are good. It is one of the more lucrative options for graduates, with a median salary of £38,694 according to the most recent data. There is considerable variation between universities, however, even those at the very top. Newcastle's dentistry graduates earn £50,000 within 15 months of leaving on average, whereas those who studied at Queen's Belfast command a median salary of £32,000 at the same point in their career, as do graduates from top-ranked Glasgow.

Although graduate outcomes are not as consistently high as for medicine, an overwhelming majority of graduates from five-year dentistry courses are in a high-skilled job as a dentist or enrolled in postgraduate study within 15 months. Leeds tops the table with 97.3% of graduates in one of those two destinations, with Manchester not far behind. Birmingham, again, is last, but still has a respectable 86% of graduates hitting the mark.

Dentistry	Teaching quality	Student experience	Research quality	Entry standards (UCAS points)	Graduate prospects	Overall score
1 Glasgow	82.3%	79.9%	29.3%	228	92.6%	100.0
2 Queen's Belfast	91.3%	87.8%	50.7%	180	96.6%	98.4
3 Newcastle	90.6%	90.1%	43.6%	167	95.8%	93.5
4 Manchester	71.1%	69.6%	57.1%	169	97.1%	89.2
5 Dundee	79.9%	79.9%	22.1%	188	88.1%	87.5
6 Bristol	77.3%	69.4%	47.1%	166	94.5%	87.3
7 Liverpool	92.4%	89.1%	31.7%	154	90.7%	87.2
8 Queen Mary, London	68.9%	67.0%	48.3%	174	87.0%	86.8
9 Sheffield	82.6%	78.3%	28.5%	167	95.2%	85.0
10 Plymouth	91.8%	91.7%	9.5%	164	86.4%	83.5
=11 Leeds	81.4%	76.3%	31.7%	159	97.3%	83.3
=11 Cardiff	70.2%	69.3%	36.8%	170	92.9%	83.3
13 King's College London	63.8%	59.2%	40.9%	178	90.3%	82.9
14 Central Lancashire	91.6%	84.7%	8.3%	155	96.9%	79.9
15 Birmingham	73.9%	65.3%	19.2%	163	86.0%	76.9

Employed in high-skilled job	85%	Employed in lower-skilled job		1%
Employed in high-skilled job and studying	6%	Employed in lower-skilled job and studying		0%
Studying	0%	Unemployed		8%
High skilled work (median) salary	£38,694	Low/medium skilled salary		—

Drama, Dance, Cinematics and Photography

Featuring 97 universities, Drama, Dance, Cinematics and Photography is among the largest of our subject areas. Courses are broad-based, covering the four disciplines (although UCAS pairs photography with cinematics under the same grouping) and ranging from acting, theatre studies and performing arts to professional and commercial dance, film studies and photography. Joint honours courses, such as drama studies and English, are also incorporated.

Exeter tops this year's table, buoyed by excellent results in the National Student Survey sections relating to teaching quality and the wider experience – only Buckinghamshire New (in =85th place overall) did better, scoring an almost perfect 99.5% for teaching quality and 86.7% for the broader experience.

Bournemouth outdoes all others for prospects with 72.6% of its graduates being in high-skilled jobs and/or postgraduate study 15 months after their degrees. West London, Leeds and Trinity Laban conservatoire are not far behind. However, the subjects are only one place off the bottom of our employment ranking, with 41% of graduates in "low-skilled" jobs and 13% unemployed, on average.

Of the five specialist institutions in our table, the Royal Conservatoire of Scotland leads in 12th place, followed by Trinity Laban (15th), Central School of Speech and Drama (18th), Guildhall School of Music and Drama (20th) and Rose Bruford College (39th).

Although 18 institutions averaged 144 UCAS tariff points or more in 2020 (equivalent to AAA), performance or portfolio are often more important criteria for entry.

Drama, Dance, Cinematics and Photography	Teaching quality	Student experience	Research quality	Entry standards (UCAS points)	Graduate prospects	Overall score
1 Exeter	87.5%	84.6%	46.3%	150	68.7%	100.0
2 Queen Mary, London	78.0%	72.2%	68.4%	137	71.4%	99.1
3 Manchester	84.2%	73.7%	58.6%	167	56.3%	98.4
4 Lancaster	83.8%	82.3%	48.0%	150	—	98.3
5 Surrey	85.8%	76.3%	27.2%	158	70.6%	97.7
6 Glasgow	75.1%	72.7%	53.9%	191	51.5%	97.6
7 Warwick	78.6%	71.7%	61.7%	139	68.0%	97.4
8 Edinburgh Napier	80.9%	75.4%	37.9%	169	61.7%	96.8
9 Essex	84.0%	76.7%	37.7%	162	61.8%	96.6
10 Leeds	74.6%	69.5%	28.0%	155	72.2%	95.0
11 Royal Holloway, London	75.4%	67.2%	50.6%	148	61.5%	93.7
12 Royal Conservatoire of Scotland	80.2%	77.9%	11.3%	151	70.5%	93.2
13 Birmingham	79.8%	70.0%	36.9%	160	57.3%	93.0
14 Sussex	75.0%	71.1%	45.6%	141	—	92.2
15 Trinity Laban	72.4%	63.6%	28.7%	136	72.0%	91.2
16 York	74.7%	62.1%	26.0%	156	62.6%	90.8
17 Bristol	63.7%	54.5%	48.7%	159	56.4%	89.7
18 Central School of Speech and Drama	67.1%	55.9%	47.7%	138	62.4%	89.2
19 East Anglia	73.0%	67.2%	43.8%	135	58.7%	89.1
20 Guildhall School of Music and Drama	84.8%	81.1%	12.7%	137	59.7%	88.8
21 Queen's Belfast	76.3%	72.7%	38.3%	140	53.4%	88.5
22 Nottingham	76.1%	66.0%	45.8%	124*	—	88.4
23 Kent	78.6%	68.4%	44.3%	121	58.4%	88.3
=24 West London	80.3%	73.1%	2.3%	123	72.4%	87.7
=24 Queen Margaret, Edinburgh	75.8%	67.1%	14.0%	183	45.3%	87.7
26 East London	86.1%	80.2%	11.2%	116	64.3%	87.2
27 Coventry	86.7%	79.6%	18.1%	128	55.6%	87.1
=28 Bournemouth	71.9%	64.1%	15.1%	116	72.6%	86.3
=28 Aberystwyth	80.1%	77.0%	30.3%	128	52.7%	86.3
30 Edinburgh	49.1%	41.0%	48.0%	157	58.3%	85.6
31 Roehampton	68.9%	61.5%	46.6%	111	61.2%	85.5
32 Reading	67.6%	61.0%	34.8%	120	63.4%	85.4
33 Sunderland	85.4%	79.1%	4.2%	123	59.6%	85.3
34 Ulster	85.9%	79.2%	40.0%	119	44.5%	85.1

Dance, Drama and Cinematics cont.

		Teaching quality	Student experience	Research quality	Entry standards (UCAS points)	Graduate prospects	Overall score
35	London Metropolitan	86.0%	77.3%	—	115	62.7%	84.5
36	Nottingham Trent	78.2%	66.9%	10.0%	134	56.5%	84.0
37	Kingston	74.0%	61.9%	15.7%	144	52.2%	83.6
38	Central Lancashire	74.7%	65.4%	3.9%	126	62.5%	83.2
39	Rose Bruford College	80.4%	70.7%	3.1%	125	56.9%	82.6
=40	Canterbury Christ Church	81.2%	72.3%	15.2%	109	55.3%	81.9
=40	Edge Hill	76.8%	69.8%	3.8%	134	53.0%	81.9
42	Birmingham City	72.8%	63.4%	11.6%	127	56.2%	81.7
=43	De Montfort	69.3%	58.7%	14.5%	121	59.6%	81.3
=43	Chichester	74.1%	71.0%	9.7%	125	53.7%	81.3
45	Lincoln	74.5%	66.9%	6.5%	124	56.2%	81.2
=46	West of Scotland	73.8%	63.6%	—	135	55.4%	81.0
=46	Falmouth	78.0%	73.1%	6.2%	122	52.7%	81.0
=46	Arts Bournemouth	73.5%	67.1%	2.4%	143	49.9%	81.0
=46	Manchester Metropolitan	78.2%	67.0%	7.5%	138	47.2%	81.0
50	West of England	70.9%	61.6%	—	142	54.2%	80.9
=51	Wales Trinity St David	72.8%	56.7%	—	147	51.8%	80.8
=51	Goldsmiths, London	67.8%	60.0%	28.3%	129	49.4%	80.8
=53	Hull	71.3%	66.5%	11.2%	117	57.7%	80.7
=53	Bath Spa	83.2%	74.4%	10.7%	115	49.6%	80.7
=53	Huddersfield	73.8%	64.4%	28.0%	127	45.2%	80.7
=56	St Mary's, Twickenham	70.3%	59.1%	9.1%	118	60.3%	80.5
=56	Leeds Arts	70.4%	65.1%	—	139	53.8%	80.5
=58	Northampton	77.6%	68.6%	—	110	59.4%	80.0
=58	Westminster	74.3%	62.0%	—	130	54.7%	80.0
=60	Norwich Arts	70.6%	61.4%	—	126	57.9%	79.8
=60	Middlesex	71.5%	62.4%	16.1%	113	55.9%	79.8
62	Northumbria	64.3%	51.5%	13.3%	143	50.9%	79.7
63	Portsmouth	76.5%	69.7%	—	119	54.8%	79.6
=64	Brunel	55.3%	53.0%	32.6%	121	56.5%	79.5
=64	Bolton	76.3%	67.3%	—	117	56.2%	79.5
=64	Derby	74.1%	62.1%	5.1%	119	55.9%	79.5
67	Gloucestershire	74.6%	69.5%	—	120	53.4%	78.9
68	Sheffield Hallam	68.4%	58.1%	14.4%	117	54.6%	78.6
69	Salford	70.7%	61.9%	7.2%	130	49.1%	78.5
=70	Greenwich	57.0%	50.9%	3.5%	125	63.9%	78.4
=70	Plymouth	72.7%	62.9%	20.2%	122	45.2%	78.4
72	Staffordshire	77.1%	70.2%	—	119	50.3%	78.2
73	Chester	60.9%	53.0%	4.3%	126	59.1%	78.1
74	Creative Arts	66.6%	54.5%	3.4%	135	51.7%	77.9
75	Liverpool Hope	72.6%	58.5%	3.0%	116	55.1%	77.8
76	Anglia Ruskin	61.6%	51.7%	16.9%	129	51.0%	77.7

77 Worcester	73.1%	70.0%	3.5%	114	51.3%	77.6
78 Oxford Brookes	60.8%	52.7%	27.8%	117	—	77.4
=79 Teesside	74.9%	61.0%	2.9%	—	50.0%	77.1
=79 South Wales	74.9%	66.8%	6.4%	118	47.0%	77.1
81 London South Bank	80.3%	67.6%	—	105	51.3%	76.9
82 Newman, Birmingham	72.2%	68.3%	9.6%	106	—	76.6
=83 Ravensbourne	57.0%	45.6%	—	116	64.8%	76.3
=83 Leeds Beckett	68.6%	54.9%	1.7%	114	55.6%	76.3
=85 Hertfordshire	64.1%	54.8%	5.3%	105	59.6%	76.0
=85 Buckinghamshire New	99.5%	86.7%	—	95	36.7%	76.0
87 Wolverhampton	78.3%	71.0%	—	108	47.5%	75.9
88 Bedfordshire	70.4%	58.8%	5.6%	96	57.1%	75.5
89 Liverpool John Moores	59.0%	52.5%	—	144	46.2%	75.1
90 University of the Arts London	64.4%	47.8%	—	130	49.2%	74.7
91 Newcastle	38.0%	37.7%	40.8%	130	—	74.4
92 York St John	81.1%	74.9%	10.5%	113	33.3%	74.3
93 Solent, Southampton	71.9%	63.7%	—	119	42.6%	73.8
94 Brighton	56.9%	45.7%	13.1%	109	52.8%	73.1
=95 Cumbria	69.0%	62.3%	—	111	44.3%	72.5
=95 Suffolk	74.8%	66.8%	—	105	42.3%	72.5
97 Winchester	64.5%	52.8%	11.2%	105	45.6%	71.9

Employed in high-skilled job	42%	Employed in lower-skilled job		38%
Employed in high-skilled job and studying	2%	Employed in lower-skilled job and studying		1%
Studying	4%	Unemployed		13%
High skilled work (median) salary	£22,000	Low/medium skilled salary		£18,000

East and South Asian Studies

Encompassing Chinese studies, Japanese studies and South Asian studies our table is topped by the same three universities this year as last: Cambridge, Oxford and Durham – in that order. The only university to average 200 UCAS tariff points, Cambridge leads on entry standards, as it does for graduate prospects. Manchester, in eighth place overall, holds the highest rating for research. Results of the National Student Survey revealed the best rates of student satisfaction with teaching quality to be found at Warwick – our University of the Year for Teaching Quality – and that for the broader student experience at East Anglia.

The subjects fare well in our ranking of graduate earnings, where median £25,000 starting salaries for those in "professional" jobs, and £20,500 for "medium-skilled" jobs, are 23rd out of 67 subject areas. They did less well in the most recent Graduate Outcomes survey, however, which looks at what graduates are doing 15 months on from their degrees – with only 58% in high-skilled work and/or postgraduate study, a bottom ten result.

Only four universities in the UK offer South Asian Studies: Central Lancashire, Leeds, Manchester and the School of Oriental and Asian Studies (SOAS) in London, which also offers a range of languages including Burmese, Indonesian, Thai, Tibetan and Vietnamese.

These degrees are afforded extra protection by the Government because of their small size and their economic and cultural significance.

Most undergraduates learn their chosen language from scratch, although universities expect to see evidence of potential in other modern language qualifications. Student numbers are modest; in 2020 there were 110 new Chinese studies undergraduates, 260 in Japanese, 40 in South Asian and 165 in other Asian studies.

East and South Asian Studies	Teaching quality	Student experience	Research quality	Entry standards (UCAS points)	Graduate prospects	Overall score
1 Cambridge	—	—	45.0%	200	85.0%	100.0
2 Oxford	77.8%	68.5%	36.2%	188	—	99.1
3 Durham	75.9%	70.9%	34.6%	178	—	97.0
4 Newcastle	77.3%	72.4%	36.3%	145*	—	94.2
5 Leeds	75.5%	68.3%	30.6%	148	74.3%	92.2
6 East Anglia	78.0%	78.2%	33.1%	126	—	92.0
7 Edinburgh	59.4%	59.4%	30.1%	190	77.3%	91.7
8 Manchester	61.1%	56.2%	48.9%	149	72.3%	91.2
9 Liverpool	70.0%	63.4%	33.4%	136	—	88.2
10 Warwick	81.9%	71.2%	—	165	72.6%	87.8
11 Nottingham	67.2%	52.6%	27.3%	147	69.3%	86.1
12 SOAS, London	71.1%	60.8%	26.3%	146	62.5%	85.9
13 Sheffield	71.2%	60.7%	16.7%	153	61.1%	83.9
14 Hull	72.9%	65.5%	22.7%	116	—	83.5
15 Nottingham Trent	64.3%	53.4%	10.0%	123*	—	75.4
16 Central Lancashire	74.0%	64.3%	—	113	53.0%	75.0

Employed in high-skilled job	43%	Employed in lower-skilled job		28%
Employed in high-skilled job and studying	1%	Employed in lower-skilled job and studying		1%
Studying	13%	Unemployed		13%
High skilled work (median) salary	£25,000	Low/medium skilled salary		£20,500

Economics

Economists – more than anyone – should know the value of a degree. They know the difference between boom and bust and learn to recognise the warning signs that presage either. So, what would they make of this year's economics table? Possibly that you should expect the unexpected, as the table has been led by a different university in each of the past four years. The London School of Economics (LSE) is top, rising from joint-second last year. Counterintuitive though it may be, it is the first time in a decade that the LSE has topped the subject ranking from which it takes its name.

That it has done so now stems in part from its research record, where its 70.7% score for quality and quantity of world-leading and internationally excellent research beats all others. The LSE ranks second for graduate prospects (outdone only by Cambridge) with 95.6% of graduates in high-skilled jobs or postgraduate study within 15 months of leaving.

Warwick moves up from fourth to second place, while University College London (UCL) is the only newcomer in the top five. It achieves this by placing fifth for graduate prospects and second for research, just half a percentage point behind the LSE. Cambridge drops to sixth position, despite leading the field for graduate prospects and entry standards, with an average of 223 UCAS tariff points.

Economics graduates are among the more sought-after products of our higher education system, commanding a median salary of £29,000. Cambridge takes the honours here with a median starting salary of £50,000 for its graduates, more than £14,000 clear of UCL in second place. LSE and Warwick economists earn a median £35,000 salary early in their careers, narrowly ahead of Oxford at £34,500.

We don't take account of salaries in our subject ranking, but it should not be underestimated in the minds of applicants. The number of applications was up in 2020 to 64,665 from 60,880 the previous year, a rise of 6.2%. Fortunately, the number of places rose even faster with a 10.2% increase to 10,480.

For all its excellence in research and success in graduate prospects, it is the improvement in LSE's scores in our two ranking measures derived from the National Student Survey (NSS) that has done most to lift the university to the head of the table. Its scores for teaching quality and for the student experience sit 25th and 35th respectively – indicating how much closer the university now comes to meeting the high expectations of its economics students.

Top of our two NSS-derived rankings is Stirling, which stands at eighth place overall. Both scores clear 90%, an exceptional achievement in a year of pandemic disruption.

Economics	Teaching quality	Student experience	Research quality	Entry standards (UCAS points)	Graduate prospects	Overall score
1 London School of Economics	73.8%	69.8%	70.7%	188	95.6%	100.0
2 Warwick	76.9%	76.0%	49.6%	190	95.3%	98.1
3 University College London	67.3%	69.9%	70.2%	189	93.2%	97.9
4 Strathclyde	78.1%	78.4%	44.3%	197	92.9%	97.7
5 Oxford	—	—	58.0%	207	92.2%	97.6
6 Cambridge	—	—	45.0%	223	97.3%	97.3
7 St Andrews	84.7%	84.0%	23.6%	217	82.9%	95.5
8 Stirling	90.8%	92.8%	25.2%	151	—	95.4
9 Bath	67.6%	73.7%	41.8%	169	92.6%	92.0
10 Glasgow	74.3%	77.8%	26.4%	194	84.6%	91.4
11 Durham	70.2%	67.4%	23.1%	182	94.2%	90.1
12 Leeds	69.5%	69.9%	39.3%	168	86.0%	89.9
13 Heriot-Watt	78.6%	83.2%	18.8%	164	83.9%	89.3
14 Loughborough	71.6%	76.2%	32.6%	150	87.7%	89.0
=15 Nottingham	68.2%	69.1%	31.7%	168	87.8%	88.6
=15 Lancaster	69.8%	71.9%	42.6%	140	86.1%	88.6
17 Surrey	75.6%	77.6%	33.0%	131	86.8%	88.5
18 Bristol	63.1%	60.6%	43.6%	166	88.0%	88.3
19 Queen's Belfast	69.4%	74.9%	32.7%	140	87.5%	87.5

Economics cont.

		Teaching quality	Student experience	Research quality	Entry standards (UCAS points)	Graduate prospects	Overall score
20	Exeter	64.5%	67.5%	26.9%	160	90.4%	86.7
21	Ulster	75.2%	70.7%	39.2%	116	82.6%	86.5
22	East Anglia	77.0%	77.5%	25.7%	129	82.2%	86.3
23	York	71.7%	71.5%	22.6%	144	87.0%	86.2
24	Edinburgh	60.8%	61.6%	30.2%	177	86.3%	86.1
25	Aberystwyth	85.3%	80.8%	14.5%	116*	—	85.8
26	Queen Mary, London	66.2%	72.1%	31.3%	154	79.5%	85.3
27	King's College London	68.7%	68.2%	—	182	90.4%	85.1
=28	Sheffield	75.3%	74.6%	16.6%	147	80.6%	85.0
=28	SOAS, London	76.0%	70.8%	22.9%	145	77.8%	85.0
30	Birmingham	65.7%	63.0%	26.6%	149	85.8%	84.5
=31	Southampton	72.1%	70.5%	23.4%	139	80.9%	84.4
=31	Aberdeen	75.2%	77.9%	16.0%	173	69.2%	84.4
33	Liverpool	72.9%	68.2%	20.1%	139	82.4%	84.2
34	Swansea	77.7%	77.3%	22.0%	116	78.4%	84.0
35	Manchester	65.6%	65.0%	26.8%	158	78.6%	83.6
36	Dundee	68.0%	64.4%	12.1%	176	79.7%	83.4
37	Sussex	68.6%	65.7%	25.1%	131	83.1%	83.3
38	Hull	84.6%	77.1%	10.2%	119*	75.6%	83.1
39	Kent	75.6%	72.6%	14.6%	123	79.5%	82.5
=40	Newcastle	60.0%	58.6%	20.7%	149	88.1%	82.2
=40	Aston	70.9%	68.9%	19.7%	117	83.1%	82.2
42	Essex	72.3%	70.3%	43.6%	104	68.4%	82.1
43	Cardiff	58.2%	57.2%	32.0%	140	81.3%	81.2
44	Reading	66.0%	63.9%	29.3%	117	78.0%	80.8
=45	Keele	69.7%	69.8%	10.2%	98	88.3%	80.3
=45	Royal Holloway, London	64.8%	67.6%	31.3%	115	74.9%	80.3
47	East London	84.2%	89.2%	0.8%	77	—	79.7
48	Salford	76.8%	70.2%	5.9%	115	—	79.5
49	Leicester	68.0%	67.9%	21.4%	124	71.5%	79.4
50	Derby	80.8%	75.1%	0.9%	103	—	79.2
51	Sheffield Hallam	74.2%	72.1%	—	104	80.6%	78.4
52	Greenwich	81.0%	77.0%	3.3%	95	71.7%	78.3
53	West of England	72.0%	66.8%	5.5%	105	78.0%	77.7
54	Hertfordshire	89.1%	85.8%	0.9%	84	62.2%	77.6
55	Oxford Brookes	67.5%	65.4%	5.1%	118	78.3%	77.5
56	Portsmouth	73.6%	67.8%	9.5%	106	70.4%	77.0
=57	Nottingham Trent	69.8%	69.2%	4.6%	112	74.1%	76.8
=57	Bradford	66.8%	68.5%	12.7%	107	—	76.8
59	Central Lancashire	73.8%	64.6%	4.4%	107	—	76.5
60	Manchester Metropolitan	68.7%	55.9%	4.7%	114	75.9%	75.7
61	Coventry	67.1%	68.6%	1.6%	96	78.6%	75.5

62 Westminster	69.6%	72.1%	2.4%	103	—	75.4
63 Brighton	78.2%	58.3%	6.5%	84	—	75.1
64 Goldsmiths, London	75.6%	66.4%	16.8%	103	54.2%	74.3
65 Bournemouth	66.0%	58.7%	8.8%	107	—	74.1
66 City	56.8%	60.1%	15.1%	119	65.0%	72.7
67 Leeds Beckett	61.9%	66.2%	0.8%	93	73.3%	72.3
=68 Middlesex	65.4%	56.4%	10.5%	87	67.1%	71.6
=68 Plymouth	67.0%	67.5%	13.1%	106	52.5%	71.6
70 Huddersfield	61.9%	60.7%	4.1%	110	64.5%	71.3
71 Birmingham City	70.1%	64.6%	1.3%	108	53.8%	70.4
=72 De Montfort	63.5%	57.2%	10.7%	89	59.9%	69.7
=72 Kingston	64.4%	72.7%	9.2%	80	55.7%	69.7
74 Brunel	47.1%	47.4%	9.9%	107	65.6%	67.3

Employed in high-skilled job	59%	Employed in lower-skilled job	14%
Employed in high-skilled job and studying	8%	Employed in lower-skilled job and studying	1%
Studying	10%	Unemployed	8%
High skilled work (median) salary	£29,000	Low/medium skilled salary	£22,000

Education

Our Education table is a little different to the others in this *Guide*, as it includes an extra column to accommodate inspection data by Ofsted for the universities in England. The eight universities that tie for the best scores from Ofsted are: Cambridge, University College London, Durham, Birmingham, Brighton, St Mary's Twickenham, Brunel and Winchester – which all feature in the top 22, in that order.

Teacher training BEd degrees – the most common route into primary teaching – had more than 48,600 applications and 10,455 enrolments in the 2020 cycle. Academic Studies in Education degrees are also encompassed in our ranking and garnered 30,215 applications and 8,885 new undergraduates in the same admissions round.

Secondary school teachers are more likely to take the Postgraduate Certificate in Education, or to train through the Teach First or Schools Direct programmes, which are not included in our table's statistics. Our focus exclusively on undergraduate provision explains the absence of some of the best-known education departments, which only offer postgraduate courses. Prime examples are University College London's Institute of Education, ranked top in the world for education by QS, and Oxford – which was the top-scorer in the Research Excellence Framework in this field.

Cambridge combines the academic study of education with other subjects but does not offer Qualified Teacher Status. It takes the number two spot this year, having been replaced at number one by the Royal Conservatoire of Scotland which has risen from 11th place, driven by increased rates of student satisfaction and the highest entry standards in the table. The top ten is dominated by Scottish universities, which benefit from the favourable tariff conversion for Scottish secondary qualifications, while also performing strongly across other measures.

But it is a Welsh institution that comes top for student satisfaction. Aberystwyth, =44th overall, achieved exceptional scores in the sections of the National Student Survey relating to both teaching quality and the wider experience – despite the difficult conditions of the pandemic. Warwick (which is top-rated for research), St Mary's Twickenham and Bolton also did exceptionally well in these student-led measures.

Education sits 31st in our employment ranking. The demands for new primary and secondary teachers vary across the country, creating differences in graduate outcomes. At the Royal Conservatoire of Scotland, 100% of graduates were in professional jobs and/or postgraduate study 15 months after finishing. Edinburgh and Stirling place second and third for graduate prospects, followed by Durham and Northumbria in the northeast of England.

Education	Teaching quality	Student experience	OFSTED rating	Research quality	Entry standards (UCAS points)	Graduate prospects	Overall score
1 Royal Conservatoire of Scotland	82.2%	78.1%	—	—	213	100.0%	100.0
2 Cambridge	—	—	4.0	36.6%	173	—	98.3
3 Strathclyde	84.3%	78.2%	—	19.8%	196	89.7%	98.2
4 Stirling	79.4%	72.3%	—	29.2%	192	91.6%	98.1
5 Glasgow	81.6%	74.1%	—	32.5%	187	88.1%	98.0
6 Warwick	89.8%	85.7%	3.7	43.6%	134	—	97.6
7 Edinburgh	76.6%	73.5%	—	23.1%	192	93.8%	97.1
8 Bath	83.3%	83.4%	3.5	43.4%	143	—	95.3
9 Dundee	85.2%	78.7%	—	11.7%	176	87.3%	94.5
10 University College London	77.4%	74.8%	4.0	40.2%	161	71.0%	94.4
11 Durham	67.2%	58.2%	4.0	38.9%	150	91.4%	94.1
12 West of Scotland	81.7%	74.6%	—	7.5%	187	86.9%	93.4
13 Birmingham	74.7%	67.6%	4.0	40.9%	140	72.2%	92.0
14 Southampton	79.7%	76.8%	3.0	41.1%	174	77.3%	91.8
15 Brighton	85.9%	79.2%	4.0	1.6%	117	87.0%	90.6
16 St Mary's, Twickenham	87.5%	86.5%	4.0	1.8%	107	83.8%	90.1
17 Aberdeen	74.2%	69.6%	—	7.6%	171	88.1%	89.9
18 Sussex	76.0%	67.0%	3.5	28.7%	134	—	88.5
19 Leeds	84.7%	77.9%	3.0	31.6%	149	71.1%	88.4
20 Reading	79.5%	77.9%	3.0	25.8%	131	86.9%	88.2
21 Brunel	73.2%	73.7%	4.0	20.4%	116	75.0%	88.0
22 Winchester	78.8%	74.4%	4.0	2.2%	120	80.4%	87.9
23 Sheffield	80.4%	77.2%	3.0	32.9%	154	68.6%	87.6
24 West London	87.5%	82.3%	—	7.6%	129	—	87.5
25 York	73.7%	71.8%	3.0	43.3%	129	77.2%	87.0
26 Lincoln	85.8%	81.5%	—	12.1%	120	—	86.7
27 Gloucestershire	83.1%	79.4%	3.7	—	121	76.9%	86.5
28 Sheffield Hallam	80.6%	71.1%	3.7	2.0%	125	78.0%	86.2
=29 Bangor	62.8%	53.5%	—	39.6%	145	78.1%	86.1
=29 Newcastle	80.7%	69.6%	3.1	33.1%	118	75.9%	86.1
31 Chester	77.4%	73.9%	3.7	1.4%	121	79.5%	85.7
32 Coventry	81.2%	69.3%	—	18.1%	122	—	85.4
33 Northumbria	75.8%	67.7%	3.0	—	148	90.8%	85.2

=34	Chichester	86.0%	84.1%	3.0	—	116	86.5%	85.1
=34	Keele	70.6%	70.6%	3.5	25.0%	114	76.4%	85.1
36	Liverpool John Moores	74.9%	71.4%	3.5	3.0%	152	69.1%	84.6
37	Plymouth Marjon	86.6%	83.2%	3.3	—	116	74.1%	84.3
38	York St John	79.9%	72.0%	3.3	1.5%	117	83.0%	84.2
39	Derby	81.6%	76.3%	3.4	1.1%	119	75.3%	84.0
=40	Cardiff	62.5%	59.6%	—	35.3%	155	64.8%	83.6
=40	South Wales	79.2%	74.1%	—	—	117	81.2%	83.6
42	Oxford Brookes	78.7%	72.3%	3.0	3.3%	118	86.4%	83.3
43	West of England	81.4%	74.8%	3.0	5.3%	128	77.1%	83.2
=44	Aberystwyth	90.0%	88.8%	—	—	110	65.5%	83.1
=44	Edge Hill	81.5%	79.0%	3.0	1.4%	129	76.9%	83.1
=44	Greenwich	79.1%	75.7%	3.3	0.8%	121	75.5%	83.1
47	Roehampton	75.7%	72.9%	3.0	20.2%	114	76.4%	82.9
48	Staffordshire	85.3%	75.5%	3.0	7.6%	123	69.9%	82.6
49	Worcester	80.0%	78.3%	3.0	2.5%	118	79.1%	82.5
50	Hertfordshire	86.3%	83.6%	3.0	—	110	74.6%	82.3
=51	Liverpool Hope	81.5%	72.5%	3.0	7.3%	123	73.2%	82.2
=51	Plymouth	78.3%	72.0%	3.0	9.4%	120	76.1%	82.2
53	Bedfordshire	82.4%	74.6%	3.1	3.1%	108	73.3%	81.4
=54	Nottingham Trent	73.6%	65.7%	3.3	2.6%	124	72.9%	81.3
=54	Wales Trinity St David	83.6%	73.6%	—	—	135	61.0%	81.3
56	Sunderland	78.6%	71.5%	3.0	3.8%	127	72.1%	81.2
=57	Cumbria	75.4%	67.7%	3.0	0.4%	125	79.7%	81.1
=57	Kingston	77.0%	74.9%	3.0	—	121	76.8%	81.1
=59	Anglia Ruskin	84.2%	77.4%	3.0	0.8%	114	70.4%	81.0
=59	Hull	76.3%	68.5%	3.0	5.0%	129	72.9%	81.0
=59	Middlesex	74.9%	72.7%	3.0	14.9%	111	72.5%	81.0
62	Bishop Grosseteste	76.5%	71.1%	3.0	1.4%	113	79.8%	80.9
63	Bath Spa	64.4%	58.9%	3.7	3.2%	106	75.9%	80.3
64	Wolverhampton	79.5%	71.2%	3.0	1.9%	123	69.0%	80.2
=65	Newman, Birmingham	77.5%	71.3%	3.0	2.2%	113	74.5%	80.1
=65	Cardiff Metropolitan	76.6%	70.9%	—	—	120	70.3%	80.1
67	East Anglia	78.3%	77.4%	3.0	27.2%	126	47.5%	80.0
68	Canterbury Christ Church	76.0%	64.9%	3.0	2.8%	104	81.0%	79.9
69	Northampton	77.7%	69.7%	3.0	1.8%	111	74.4%	79.8
=70	Birmingham City	75.7%	68.6%	3.0	1.8%	119	73.2%	79.7
=70	Manchester Metropolitan	72.1%	64.6%	3.0	5.8%	131	70.5%	79.7
72	Leeds Beckett	75.2%	69.2%	3.0	2.3%	109	75.4%	79.4
73	Huddersfield	80.7%	71.5%	3.1	5.9%	125	56.6%	79.3
74	Bolton	86.0%	88.8%	—	3.1%	105	55.6%	79.2
75	Glyndŵr	81.5%	69.5%	—	—	102	68.5%	78.8
76	De Montfort	70.8%	65.1%	—	11.2%	107	68.0%	77.9
77	Leeds Trinity	69.8%	67.1%	3.0	—	103	77.8%	77.8
78	Teesside	70.1%	58.9%	—	15.0%	108	66.6%	77.5
79	East London	78.2%	72.1%	3.0	2.8%	118	53.4%	76.7

Education cont.

	Teaching quality	Student experience	OFSTED rating	Research quality	Entry standards (UCAS points)	Graduate prospects	Overall score
80 London Metropolitan	80.2%	71.8%	3.1	3.3%	93	51.7%	75.3
81 Goldsmiths, London	68.9%	57.0%	3.0	17.4%	110	54.0%	75.2
82 Portsmouth	65.1%	50.1%	3.3	—	109	56.7%	73.6
83 London South Bank	59.1%	43.3%	3.0	—	104	64.0%	71.3
84 Suffolk	47.5%	43.7%	—	—	99	57.6%	64.2

Employed in high-skilled job	63%	Employed in lower-skilled job	21%
Employed in high-skilled job and studying	3%	Employed in lower-skilled job and studying	1%
Studying	7%	Unemployed	6%
High skilled work (median) salary	£24,500	Low/medium skilled salary	£17,633

Electrical and Electronic Engineering

Maths A-level, or equivalent qualification, is required to study electrical and electronic engineering, along with a second science such as physics, electronics or chemistry. The subject looks at how industry works and teaches the engineering skills and technological knowledge to design and improve electrical and electronic systems. It attracted the second-highest number of applications among the engineering disciplines in 2020, and an increase in both applications and enrolments.

With more than five applications per place, competition is stiff and entry standards at the leading institutions are high. Led by our table's frontrunner, Cambridge, with 230 UCAS tariff points, four universities averaged over 200 points in 2020's intake. Cambridge also has the edge on research ratings, though Imperial comes a close second. The QS world rankings by subject put Cambridge, Oxford and Imperial in the top ten.

Taking sixth place in the main table, Lancaster tops both measures of student satisfaction derived from the National Student Survey – teaching quality and the wider experience – measures in which Derby (36th) is runner-up.

Surrey fares strongly for student satisfaction too, and finishes second for graduate prospects, beaten only by University College London with a remarkable 100% of graduates in high-skilled jobs and/or further study 15 months after finishing their degrees. Electrical and electronic engineering places 20th in our employment ranking, with an impressive two-thirds of graduates already in professional jobs when surveyed and a further 11% either engaged in postgraduate study full-time or combining it with high-skilled work.

Electrical and Electronic Engineering

	Teaching quality	Student experience	Research quality	Entry standards (UCAS points)	Graduate prospects	Overall score
1 Cambridge	—	—	67.0%	230	94.9%	100.0
2 Imperial College London	70.9%	74.3%	65.0%	196	96.1%	96.9
3 Glasgow	80.8%	80.7%	47.2%	207	86.3%	95.9

4	Strathclyde	78.5%	78.9%	41.7%	210	91.3%	95.7
5	Southampton	79.5%	77.9%	53.3%	171	96.7%	95.4
6	Lancaster	85.7%	87.3%	41.6%	160	—	94.9
7	University College London	70.7%	73.2%	59.0%	171	100.0%	94.5
8	Leeds	78.8%	79.3%	41.8%	172	89.9%	92.2
9	Surrey	83.8%	83.4%	36.3%	138	97.0%	91.5
10	Edinburgh	63.2%	68.3%	50.3%	203	89.4%	91.2
11	Queen's Belfast	75.8%	72.5%	47.3%	159	91.9%	90.9
12	Nottingham	77.8%	78.1%	40.8%	152	85.9%	88.9
13	Bath	73.3%	81.1%	28.6%	157	94.8%	88.7
14	Sheffield	75.2%	76.6%	42.6%	147	86.3%	88.1
=15	Exeter	76.3%	77.0%	36.4%	143	89.2%	87.7
=15	Bristol	66.9%	71.0%	52.3%	160	83.8%	87.7
17	Loughborough	79.2%	80.4%	23.8%	145	88.1%	86.7
18	Swansea	75.5%	76.8%	45.5%	130	81.6%	86.1
19	Birmingham	71.6%	65.3%	32.1%	152	91.3%	86.0
20	Queen Mary, London	71.1%	73.9%	41.9%	143	84.5%	85.9
=21	Manchester	66.3%	65.0%	37.0%	163	88.0%	85.7
=21	Liverpool	76.0%	77.6%	30.4%	140	—	85.7
23	Heriot-Watt	52.1%	57.3%	47.8%	178	91.1%	85.3
24	Ulster	79.6%	72.0%	22.8%	128	91.7%	85.0
25	York	78.7%	73.9%	21.4%	127	91.6%	84.8
26	Bangor	77.9%	81.9%	31.9%	128	75.0%	83.4
27	Aberdeen	65.6%	73.9%	28.4%	155	—	83.2
28	Cardiff	73.2%	76.8%	30.2%	129	81.3%	83.0
29	Newcastle	62.9%	59.9%	39.4%	137	88.4%	82.5
30	Manchester Metropolitan	82.5%	82.9%	16.3%	128	73.3%	81.8
31	Sussex	68.1%	74.1%	24.0%	138*	—	81.2
32	Northumbria	72.1%	61.4%	30.7%	131	75.0%	79.9
33	Hertfordshire	79.4%	84.0%	16.5%	94	—	79.4
=34	Aston	62.9%	66.5%	25.8%	123	85.7%	79.3
=34	Huddersfield	76.6%	74.9%	10.2%	117	81.0%	79.3
36	Derby	85.4%	84.4%	6.7%	116	69.0%	79.0
=37	West of England	77.1%	70.7%	10.6%	120	77.1%	78.5
=37	Sheffield Hallam	78.4%	71.6%	17.8%	114	73.3%	78.5
39	Essex	61.5%	65.8%	34.3%	124	—	78.4
=40	Robert Gordon	65.8%	61.6%	8.8%	133	88.1%	78.2
=40	Brunel	63.2%	66.6%	26.4%	134	76.2%	78.2
=42	Liverpool John Moores	65.2%	65.4%	8.7%	136	85.4%	78.1
=42	Plymouth	69.7%	66.6%	13.3%	115	85.1%	78.1
44	City	66.4%	72.9%	23.1%	115	78.6%	78.0
45	Kent	61.6%	59.7%	27.3%	123	82.6%	77.7
46	Greenwich	75.2%	69.3%	7.5%	113	—	76.3
47	Birmingham City	75.8%	68.3%	—	132	72.0%	76.2
48	Coventry	71.9%	68.7%	10.3%	117	73.8%	75.9
49	Glasgow Caledonian	72.3%	64.1%	4.7%	148	63.7%	75.2

Electrical and Electronic Engineering cont.	Teaching quality	Student experience	Research quality	Entry standards (UCAS points)	Graduate prospects	Overall score
50 Middlesex	72.8%	62.7%	14.2%	94	—	73.8
51 Edinburgh Napier	60.6%	61.8%	6.3%	139	—	73.5
52 Hull	57.6%	57.6%	16.5%	133*	—	73.4
53 South Wales	67.1%	61.3%	—	106	81.5%	73.2
54 Brighton	63.9%	55.0%	7.4%	102	79.2%	72.0
55 De Montfort	65.3%	58.0%	12.5%	107	—	71.9
=56 Portsmouth	60.4%	52.9%	7.2%	96	83.5%	71.5
=56 Teesside	70.2%	64.0%	5.8%	114	62.4%	71.5
58 London South Bank	78.8%	75.2%	19.6%	101	40.6%	70.8
59 Westminster	64.9%	65.5%	2.9%	131	57.7%	70.4
60 Salford	65.4%	56.6%	4.4%	114	60.0%	68.9

Employed in high-skilled job	66%	Employed in lower-skilled job	12%
Employed in high-skilled job and studying	3%	Employed in lower-skilled job and studying	0%
Studying	8%	Unemployed	10%
High skilled work (median) salary	£28,000	Low/medium skilled salary	£24,000

English

The lead changes frequently in our English table, and this year's edition is no exception. St Andrews has moved up from second place into first – which it last held jointly with Durham two years ago. St Andrews has the highest entry standards and on research ratings it beats both Oxford and Cambridge, which rank second and ninth respectively overall. Queen Mary, London leads on research but finishes only 25th in the main table, its rank confined by modest entry standards and student satisfaction rates. For these, Bolton (36th) stands out in both measures derived from the National Student Survey – teaching quality and the wider experience. As in many subject rankings, the post-1992 universities dominate on student satisfaction; with Solent (85th) and Suffolk (=90th), holding second and third among these measures.

English literature A-level is usually required for entry. Some English degrees offer an equal balance of literature and language, while others specialise in one or the other – a distinction usually clear in the course title. English is also frequently paired with other subjects in joint honours degrees, and there were 135 universities and colleges offering 1,988 courses in 2022–23. Such breadth is reflected in our table's size.

English sits 48th in our employment table, below classics and ancient history and above history, 43% of graduates were in high-skilled jobs 15 months after their degrees and 19% were engaged in postgraduate study or combining it with a professional job. Median starting salaries rank English degrees 55th, with high-skilled jobs attracting early career earnings of £23,000 per year.

English

	Teaching quality	Student experience	Research quality	Entry standards (UCAS points)	Graduate prospects	Overall score
1 St Andrews	87.6%	79.6%	60.4%	203	69.6%	100.0
2 Oxford	—	—	50.7%	190	85.7%	99.6
3 Durham	81.8%	66.2%	57.9%	185	84.5%	99.4
4 University College London	79.7%	68.3%	61.7%	182	74.1%	96.5
5 York	82.5%	74.7%	61.5%	154	77.4%	96.4
6 Edinburgh Napier	93.6%	87.1%	37.9%	151	76.1%	96.2
7 Strathclyde	79.2%	77.6%	39.4%	198	73.9%	95.3
8 Loughborough	90.7%	87.0%	32.4%	141	80.7%	95.1
9 Cambridge	—	—	50.0%	186	77.6%	94.8
10 Warwick	76.6%	69.0%	59.8%	153	75.5%	93.5
11 Lancaster	79.0%	73.6%	47.0%	147	80.5%	93.4
12 Glasgow	73.3%	67.1%	52.0%	185	72.6%	93.2
13 Exeter	79.4%	71.0%	46.2%	159	75.2%	92.7
14 Stirling	80.5%	73.8%	29.8%	178	75.1%	92.4
15 Nottingham	77.3%	66.6%	56.6%	146	75.7%	92.3
16 Aberdeen	81.7%	78.0%	46.3%	173	62.6%	91.8
17 Surrey	84.5%	79.3%	39.1%	122	77.1%	91.1
18 Sheffield	78.0%	73.1%	42.2%	150	73.4%	90.7
=19 Manchester	73.4%	62.5%	49.1%	163	72.5%	90.5
=19 Royal Holloway, London	81.2%	69.3%	49.9%	137	71.1%	90.5
21 King's College London	74.0%	62.7%	47.6%	154	74.7%	90.1
22 Sussex	75.5%	66.7%	45.6%	132	77.4%	89.6
23 Swansea	81.6%	75.0%	43.6%	130	70.4%	89.5
24 Edinburgh	72.5%	61.6%	43.6%	175	69.0%	89.3
25 Queen Mary, London	73.8%	66.5%	64.0%	120	70.1%	88.9
26 Liverpool	76.1%	63.2%	47.8%	133	74.2%	88.8
=27 Leeds	71.8%	64.0%	38.6%	157	74.7%	88.6
=27 Queen's Belfast	73.6%	69.7%	53.1%	148	65.6%	88.6
29 Kent	79.6%	72.2%	47.3%	119	70.4%	88.3
=30 Aston	77.1%	72.6%	23.4%	120	84.9%	88.2
=30 Southampton	76.6%	65.2%	38.4%	140	73.8%	88.2
32 Reading	80.1%	75.4%	36.3%	120	69.7%	87.0
=33 Edge Hill	88.6%	83.5%	12.1%	124	70.4%	86.8
=33 Ulster	81.3%	77.9%	35.1%	112	70.0%	86.8
=33 Leicester	78.3%	69.6%	45.4%	123	66.7%	86.8
36 Bolton	98.9%	93.6%	14.4%	80*	—	86.5
37 Bedfordshire	79.4%	74.8%	45.8%	105	67.9%	86.4
38 Birmingham	71.0%	64.2%	37.0%	146	71.0%	86.3
39 Bristol	63.7%	55.2%	30.0%	166	78.4%	86.2
40 Birmingham City	82.7%	77.5%	30.9%	108	69.2%	85.9
=41 Cardiff	74.8%	62.1%	35.1%	138	69.7%	85.6
=41 Newcastle	69.0%	53.4%	54.3%	140	66.8%	85.6

English cont.

		Teaching quality	Student experience	Research quality	Entry standards (UCAS points)	Graduate prospects	Overall score
43	Bishop Grosseteste	84.5%	69.8%	6.7%	86	88.3%	85.2
44	Aberystwyth	89.6%	87.7%	31.2%	112	54.5%	85.0
45	Hull	75.5%	68.9%	22.7%	118	76.0%	84.7
46	Huddersfield	83.2%	67.9%	29.9%	108	68.5%	84.6
47	East Anglia	72.2%	65.4%	36.2%	139	65.3%	84.4
48	Greenwich	86.2%	75.7%	14.4%	109	69.2%	84.2
=49	Coventry	80.0%	70.0%	18.1%	103	76.7%	84.1
=49	Dundee	66.3%	66.3%	32.8%	169	61.8%	84.1
=51	Brunel	79.0%	72.8%	30.9%	101	69.6%	84.0
=51	Plymouth	86.2%	71.2%	30.5%	123	57.0%	84.0
=53	Teesside	82.0%	75.4%	15.6%	99	74.4%	83.8
=53	West of England	83.0%	76.1%	35.4%	112	58.2%	83.8
=55	Nottingham Trent	83.7%	72.6%	30.0%	104	63.7%	83.6
=55	Liverpool John Moores	83.1%	76.0%	17.9%	133	60.6%	83.6
57	Keele	83.4%	74.0%	29.8%	114	59.3%	83.3
58	Essex	71.0%	66.9%	37.7%	110	69.1%	83.1
59	Derby	85.3%	73.0%	13.5%	114	—	82.9
60	Bangor	77.7%	67.3%	46.3%	115	55.4%	82.7
61	Bournemouth	80.5%	69.3%	15.1%	103	72.0%	82.5
62	Gloucestershire	88.4%	76.3%	9.3%	106	63.7%	82.2
63	Liverpool Hope	77.2%	72.0%	26.9%	105	65.2%	82.0
64	Northampton	88.7%	67.8%	15.3%	99	—	81.9
=65	Northumbria	75.1%	69.9%	27.2%	125	61.0%	81.8
=65	Bath Spa	85.3%	74.4%	23.5%	106	58.0%	81.8
67	Newman, Birmingham	92.5%	88.2%	9.6%	93	57.4%	81.7
68	Anglia Ruskin	88.8%	84.5%	16.3%	97	56.5%	81.4
69	Central Lancashire	84.7%	75.5%	9.9%	111	62.2%	81.3
=70	Worcester	82.7%	75.1%	8.2%	102	67.0%	81.1
=70	Portsmouth	83.3%	63.3%	17.1%	100	66.6%	81.1
72	Westminster	75.9%	68.7%	28.9%	101	63.6%	80.9
=73	Oxford Brookes	73.4%	66.9%	27.8%	102	66.6%	80.8
=73	Roehampton	80.8%	70.5%	20.8%	102	62.5%	80.8
=73	Chester	85.0%	74.9%	10.7%	108	60.6%	80.8
=76	Wolverhampton	83.2%	73.7%	7.6%	98	67.3%	80.7
=76	Chichester	80.0%	74.4%	16.3%	109	61.8%	80.7
=76	Lincoln	82.9%	73.2%	16.2%	109	59.3%	80.7
79	St Mary's, Twickenham	88.2%	69.4%	14.6%	89	—	80.6
80	York St John	84.0%	77.7%	9.7%	97	63.2%	80.4
81	Manchester Metropolitan	78.0%	60.6%	29.0%	114	58.3%	80.2
82	Leeds Trinity	80.0%	64.7%	6.2%	95	73.0%	80.1
83	Sheffield Hallam	75.1%	66.2%	14.6%	103	69.1%	79.9
84	Middlesex	82.1%	75.3%	11.0%	96	—	79.5

85	Solent, Southampton	96.4%	83.9%	—	107	47.8%	79.3
86	Winchester	80.0%	66.9%	—	112	65.7%	78.8
87	Goldsmiths, London	68.1%	52.9%	34.9%	116	61.0%	78.7
88	De Montfort	71.2%	63.3%	24.1%	96	65.7%	78.6
89	Kingston	71.5%	58.9%	15.7%	94	70.4%	78.1
=90	Canterbury Christ Church	78.9%	65.7%	8.0%	108	60.2%	77.8
=90	Suffolk	94.2%	90.9%	—	97*	44.9%	77.8
92	Salford	76.5%	69.7%	7.8%	111	58.6%	77.4
93	Leeds Beckett	86.6%	73.0%	11.0%	90	51.8%	77.1
94	Falmouth	79.4%	71.7%	—	114*	52.9%	75.8
95	Hertfordshire	83.3%	71.3%	7.8%	93	50.9%	75.6
=96	Sunderland	65.2%	55.6%	15.3%	91	69.3%	75.5
=96	Cardiff Metropolitan	71.6%	62.4%	—	99	66.7%	75.5
98	Brighton	67.9%	51.6%	16.2%	97	63.1%	74.7
99	South Wales	82.7%	69.1%	12.8%	98	36.2%	72.4

Employed in high-skilled job	43%	Employed in lower-skilled job	27%
Employed in high-skilled job and studying	4%	Employed in lower-skilled job and studying	1%
Studying	15%	Unemployed	10%
High skilled work (median) salary	£23,000	Low/medium skilled salary	£18,933

Food Science

Degrees under this grouping encompass a broad range of courses, from nutrition and dietetics – which offer opportunities to study alongside doctors, nurses and other health professionals in hospitals – to food manufacturing and professional cookery. London South Bank offers a BSc in baking science and technology.

Glasgow leads our table for the third year running. Its entry standards of 214 UCAS points are by far the highest, followed by those at Glasgow Caledonian. King's College London averaged the highest UCAS tariff scores in the rest of the UK and ranks third for research – outdone by Queen's Belfast and Reading on this measure.

Bournemouth, in 16th place overall, has the best rates of student satisfaction with both teaching quality and the wider experience – as derived from the National Student Survey (NSS). Tenth-ranked Abertay achieved the second-best rates of student satisfaction, and Queen's Belfast, in second place overall, received the third-best scores for teaching quality in the NSS.

Food science courses consistently feature in the top 30 of our employment ranking and this year sit 24th. Sixty-five per cent of graduates were in professional jobs 15 months after finishing their degrees and a further 10% were in postgraduate study or combining it with a good job. For starting salaries, the subjects rank 36th with graduates earning median rates of £24,900 in high-skilled jobs.

Food Science

		Teaching quality	Student experience	Research quality	Entry standards (UCAS points)	Graduate prospects	Overall score
1	Glasgow	82.4%	77.5%	42.3%	214*	—	100.0
2	Queen's Belfast	84.6%	82.2%	56.3%	153	88.1%	95.0
=3	Surrey	80.8%	84.2%	37.5%	147	94.4%	92.3
=3	King's College London	76.5%	67.4%	46.8%	162	93.9%	92.3
5	Reading	80.5%	85.1%	50.7%	128	91.0%	91.7
6	Nottingham	83.0%	80.1%	36.4%	144	89.0%	90.8
7	Leeds	84.1%	86.1%	36.8%	152	80.2%	90.6
8	Glasgow Caledonian	82.0%	77.4%	8.1%	189	—	89.9
9	Plymouth	82.7%	73.1%	17.4%	148	85.1%	86.7
10	Abertay	90.6%	86.7%	—	156	71.1%	85.2
11	Ulster	74.6%	79.8%	42.5%	127	73.0%	84.6
12	Coventry	81.2%	79.6%	—	129	91.9%	84.0
13	Northumbria	83.4%	73.7%	14.0%	133*	—	83.7
14	Newcastle	67.4%	54.5%	28.4%	145	86.0%	82.8
15	Hertfordshire	79.4%	84.9%	14.8%	112	81.8%	82.5
16	Bournemouth	93.5%	93.7%	4.7%	111	65.7%	81.7
17	Cardiff Metropolitan	75.1%	73.6%	—	126	90.9%	81.5
18	Oxford Brookes	70.9%	74.5%	3.0%	133	87.5%	81.0
19	Sheffield Hallam	77.1%	75.8%	3.7%	128	79.3%	80.5
20	Chester	65.5%	64.7%	12.0%	110	100.0%	80.4
21	Liverpool John Moores	78.8%	71.3%	6.0%	140	71.4%	80.2
22	Queen Margaret, Edinburgh	72.6%	60.9%	—	152	78.6%	79.5
23	Manchester Metropolitan	72.3%	66.2%	12.0%	123	77.6%	78.7
=24	St Mary's, Twickenham	75.8%	81.2%	—	101	81.3%	77.9
=24	Harper Adams	82.8%	75.6%	5.7%	100	72.5%	77.9
26	Leeds Beckett	77.4%	76.7%	—	115	71.2%	77.0
27	Westminster	81.1%	77.0%	—	89*	72.7%	75.7
28	Edge Hill	83.1%	81.6%	—	110	56.9%	75.4
29	Robert Gordon	58.4%	56.6%	4.9%	160	—	75.1
30	Roehampton	71.1%	69.7%	20.6%	117*	48.6%	73.2
31	Bath Spa	70.4%	70.9%	—	98	61.5%	71.0

Employed in high-skilled job	65%	Employed in lower-skilled job	17%
Employed in high-skilled job and studying	2%	Employed in lower-skilled job and studying	1%
Studying	8%	Unemployed	7%
High skilled work (median) salary	£24,900	Low/medium skilled salary	£19,000

French

Led by Cambridge, Oxford and St Andrews, the top three of our French table reads like the top three of our *Guide's* overall academic ranking – but in reverse. The subject table is almost entirely dominated by the UK's older universities, with just Manchester Metropolitan, Nottingham Trent, Chester and Westminster representing the post-1992 institutions, occupying ranks 37 to 40.

French attracts high entry standards; more than half of the universities in our table averaged upwards of 144 UCAS tariff points (equivalent to AAA at A-level) among 2020's intake of students. For research, Cambridge leads the field, but Queen's Belfast is not far behind it. Leicester, =18th overall, leads for student satisfaction – coming top for both teaching quality and the wider experience – measures derived from the National Student Survey (NSS).

Bath, in 11th place overall, tied with Oxford for the best-employed graduates 15 months on from their degrees, the latest data shows, with 87.2% working in high-skilled jobs and/or engaged in postgraduate study. French sits 34th in our employment ranking, with just under seven in ten graduates achieving those top outcomes, on average.

The long decline in the popularity of modern languages is starkly evident in the case of French. The number of new students who enrolled on French degrees in 2020 was around a third of the number in 2011.

French	Teaching quality	Student experience	Research quality	Entry standards (UCAS points)	Graduate prospects	Overall score
1 Cambridge	—	—	54.0%	189	84.1%	100.0
2 Oxford	—	—	41.3%	184	87.2%	96.7
3 St Andrews	84.1%	88.4%	26.4%	207	77.2%	95.8
4 Durham	79.0%	72.7%	34.6%	181	86.6%	95.2
5 Warwick	82.2%	71.9%	45.2%	159	81.3%	94.8
6 Stirling	85.8%	78.6%	29.8%	174	—	94.0
7 Strathclyde	76.1%	74.8%	42.0%	203	70.9%	93.5
8 Queen's Belfast	82.9%	79.0%	53.6%	149	68.8%	93.1
9 Surrey	85.6%	85.8%	39.1%	133	—	92.9
10 Nottingham	81.9%	70.8%	39.4%	139	84.1%	92.7
11 Bath	79.8%	78.2%	27.4%	146	87.2%	91.9
12 University College London	72.3%	58.2%	43.7%	157	85.1%	91.7
=13 King's College London	75.7%	70.2%	42.1%	156	79.2%	91.6
=13 Aberdeen	74.3%	78.3%	29.3%	190	—	91.6
15 Southampton	90.3%	86.0%	42.7%	154	60.0%	91.4
=16 Royal Holloway, London	74.9%	73.3%	48.3%	139	—	90.9
=16 York	81.7%	75.1%	37.3%	143	—	90.9
=18 Manchester	73.0%	60.9%	48.9%	154	74.4%	89.9
=18 Leicester	93.9%	91.0%	16.9%	127	—	89.9
20 Lancaster	70.6%	69.9%	47.0%	150	—	89.7
=21 Exeter	75.3%	73.3%	35.1%	144	78.6%	89.3
=21 Bristol	74.8%	65.0%	36.0%	161	76.3%	89.3
23 Sheffield	76.8%	77.6%	41.2%	151*	68.6%	89.0

		Teaching quality	Student experience	Research quality	Entry standards (UCAS points)	Graduate prospects	Overall score
24	Newcastle	76.0%	71.5%	36.3%	149	75.2%	88.9
25	Glasgow	70.8%	69.0%	26.3%	204	69.5%	88.2
26	Bangor	79.2%	80.9%	39.6%	113*	—	88.1
27	Leeds	79.1%	75.6%	30.6%	153	68.5%	87.5
28	Liverpool	77.7%	77.6%	33.4%	130	—	87.4
29	Edinburgh	72.6%	64.8%	30.3%	183	68.3%	87.1
=30	Queen Mary, London	77.4%	71.3%	35.1%	129	71.8%	86.5
=30	Kent	84.2%	84.5%	41.9%	112	61.3%	86.5
32	Reading	74.2%	67.2%	41.7%	121	—	86.2
33	Birmingham	69.0%	64.0%	33.7%	146	73.2%	85.2
34	Aberystwyth	84.7%	83.8%	16.6%	107	—	83.6
35	Cardiff	75.2%	64.2%	32.5%	128	65.1%	82.9
36	Aston	72.9%	66.1%	23.4%	116*	—	80.2
37	Manchester Metropolitan	70.9%	58.5%	29.0%	109	—	79.4
38	Nottingham Trent	80.3%	71.5%	7.6%	109	—	78.4
39	Chester	68.0%	54.5%	17.3%	110	—	74.9
40	Westminster	69.2%	59.1%	2.0%	113	—	72.2

Employed in high-skilled job	51%	Employed in lower-skilled job	22%
Employed in high-skilled job and studying	4%	Employed in lower-skilled job and studying	1%
Studying	14%	Unemployed	8%
High skilled work (median) salary	£24,662	Low/medium skilled salary	£20,101

General Engineering

Students opting for the general strand of engineering gain the flexibility such breadth of the subject allows in their future careers, while degrees also provide opportunities to specialise in a specific area. As an undergraduate option, general engineering has undergone a popularity boom over the past decade, with applications and enrolments increasing by around two-thirds since 2011.

Bristol retains its lead in our table for the third year. The university is hitting all the right notes with its general engineering students, who for the second year running returned the top score in the sections of the National Student Survey relating to the wider experience. Bristol also tops the sections about teaching quality this year. Oxford, in second place overall, has the strongest research rating, closely followed by Cambridge – which averaged the highest entry standards in 2020 of an eye-watering 230 UCAS tariff points. The subject can also be accessed with more modest entry standards, and 15 institutions averaged fewer than 144 UCAS points (equal to AAA at A-level). Maths and physics A-levels are usually required.

The subject makes a convincing choice in terms of future careers prospects. It is in the top ten of our employment ranking this year and sits sixth for starting salaries, with graduates earning median rates of £29,000 per year in professional roles – the type of job that seven out of ten were working in 15 months after graduating.

General Engineering	Teaching quality	Student experience	Research quality	Entry standards (UCAS points)	Graduate prospects	Overall score
1 Bristol	91.7%	91.1%	52.3%	196	92.6%	100.0
2 Oxford	80.0%	77.0%	68.7%	216	91.4%	99.6
3 Cambridge	—	—	67.0%	230	94.9%	99.5
4 Sheffield	91.6%	89.0%	51.4%	169	—	98.6
5 Durham	77.4%	72.8%	39.4%	200	87.1%	91.9
6 Loughborough	76.5%	74.6%	41.8%	152	91.5%	89.6
7 Warwick	69.5%	67.2%	47.2%	159	90.3%	88.3
8 Lancaster	75.1%	72.8%	41.6%	156*	—	88.1
9 Cardiff	79.0%	82.8%	30.2%	125	92.3%	87.4
10 Queen Mary, London	67.0%	70.7%	46.7%	152	—	86.0
11 Aberdeen	72.4%	76.1%	28.4%	161	—	85.7
12 Exeter	69.5%	69.0%	36.4%	159	—	85.3
13 Leicester	81.6%	83.6%	34.4%	135	76.2%	85.2
14 London South Bank	80.7%	77.5%	19.6%	122	—	82.6
15 Ulster	70.8%	70.4%	22.8%	127	88.4%	82.3
16 Heriot-Watt	52.1%	54.5%	47.8%	174	—	81.9
17 Bournemouth	75.5%	66.3%	8.5%	114	87.0%	79.5
18 Liverpool John Moores	76.2%	67.9%	14.2%	139	74.6%	79.4
19 Nottingham Trent	71.1%	69.6%	20.1%	126	—	79.2
=20 Glasgow Caledonian	68.4%	66.5%	4.7%	143	80.5%	77.9
=20 Aston	65.3%	62.5%	20.6%	139	—	77.9
22 West of England	70.6%	67.6%	10.6%	121*	—	76.3
23 Central Lancashire	66.9%	62.9%	7.1%	131	—	75.0
24 Coventry	68.1%	56.7%	10.3%	121	—	74.0
25 Greenwich	70.1%	68.7%	5.5%	101*	—	73.2
26 West of Scotland	69.9%	69.7%	9.0%	—	65.2%	72.6
27 Wolverhampton	75.0%	70.4%	—	98*	65.0%	71.4
28 Northampton	61.1%	49.0%	—	86	66.7%	65.6

Employed in high-skilled job	70%	Employed in lower-skilled job	9%
Employed in high-skilled job and studying	3%	Employed in lower-skilled job and studying	0%
Studying	11%	Unemployed	8%
High skilled work (median) salary	£29,000	Low/medium skilled salary	£22,500

Geography and Environmental Sciences

With the best-employed graduates and the top research rating, Cambridge leads our Geography and Environmental Sciences table for the second consecutive year. Oxford is runner-up, ahead of Durham and St Andrews – which averaged the highest entry standards in 2020. The London School of Economics, University College London and Glasgow are also regulars in the ranking's top ten.

Stretching to 68 universities, our table incorporates the different strands of geography – physical and human. The former focuses on physical processes and natural environments, the latter concerns human societies and the links between people and the planet. Environmental science studies the earth's physical, chemical and biological processes and looks at what impacts the planet in terms of social, political and cultural developments.

Application and enrolment numbers vary between the disciplines, with physical geography and environmental science experiencing uplifts in 2020, but human geography undergoing a dip.

In 31st place overall, Gloucestershire outdoes all other institutions for student satisfaction with teaching quality and with the broad experience, as expressed in the National Student Survey (NSS). Other post-1992 universities also do well on these measures, notably Derby and West of England, while of the older institutions Royal Holloway and Loughborough received some of the best NSS results.

Graduate outcomes are among the lower half of subjects, as are starting salaries – in 41st and 42nd place respectively out of 67.

Entry standards do not reach the heights, all universities average less than 200 UCAS tariff points, and 15 average less than 100. Geography at A-level or equivalent is a requirement. For environmental science, the leading universities look for two subjects from geology, maths, psychology, physics, geography, biology or chemistry.

Geography and Environmental Sciences	Teaching quality	Student experience	Research quality	Entry standards (UCAS points)	Graduate prospects	Overall score
1 Cambridge	—	—	57.3%	179	93.7%	100.0
2 Oxford	84.9%	72.8%	41.1%	188	85.7%	98.0
3 Durham	78.6%	70.1%	55.0%	174	86.3%	97.3
4 St Andrews	84.7%	83.7%	44.2%	191	73.0%	96.1
5 London School of Economics	70.2%	70.3%	46.9%	161	89.7%	94.1
6 University College London	67.4%	64.0%	52.3%	176	85.1%	93.5
7 Southampton	81.9%	77.3%	45.8%	140	76.6%	91.8
8 Glasgow	77.6%	73.1%	42.4%	183	70.3%	91.7
=9 Aberdeen	64.7%	66.7%	38.2%	190	82.1%	91.4
=9 King's College London	82.6%	75.0%	40.0%	146	76.5%	91.4
=9 Royal Holloway, London	87.6%	85.7%	45.8%	123	72.5%	91.4
12 Dundee	85.3%	83.4%	28.3%	175	68.7%	91.3
=13 Bristol	68.7%	62.5%	61.3%	155	78.2%	91.2
=13 Lancaster	78.4%	75.6%	46.5%	142	77.0%	91.2
15 Loughborough	85.7%	84.9%	24.3%	139	78.7%	90.9
16 Edinburgh	75.1%	69.5%	38.2%	168	76.1%	90.6
17 Leeds	72.2%	69.4%	42.3%	150	81.1%	90.4
18 Sheffield	83.5%	78.5%	31.1%	141	76.7%	90.3
19 Stirling	79.2%	77.6%	30.3%	163	73.9%	90.1
20 Manchester	74.0%	70.4%	36.6%	155	79.6%	90.0
21 Exeter	73.9%	71.7%	43.7%	148	73.4%	88.8
22 Leicester	83.9%	76.2%	29.7%	113	80.2%	88.6
23 Queen's Belfast	79.5%	72.5%	36.9%	129	75.5%	88.3

24	Aberystwyth	84.6%	79.7%	38.6%	117	71.4%	88.2
25	Queen Mary, London	77.3%	74.9%	45.1%	123	73.8%	88.1
26	Swansea	80.4%	79.1%	39.4%	125	71.4%	88.0
27	Birmingham	67.0%	62.5%	42.0%	141	81.3%	87.7
28	Nottingham	75.1%	67.8%	39.6%	131	76.3%	87.5
29	East Anglia	76.3%	70.5%	47.4%	123	69.3%	86.5
30	Newcastle	68.7%	60.4%	43.1%	134	77.7%	86.4
31	Gloucestershire	97.3%	93.4%	14.5%	96	67.0%	86.1
32	Northumbria	80.5%	76.2%	15.4%	125	75.6%	85.4
33	Cardiff	69.9%	66.1%	36.8%	132	73.5%	85.0
34	Reading	73.9%	69.3%	35.0%	118	72.0%	84.4
35	Liverpool	75.0%	69.1%	26.3%	126	73.0%	84.3
36	Plymouth	81.1%	77.7%	25.8%	111	68.1%	83.9
37	Ulster	83.8%	80.2%	17.2%	110	68.0%	83.4
=38	York	75.3%	67.3%	23.9%	133	68.3%	83.1
=38	West of England	90.7%	86.0%	6.4%	104	66.4%	83.1
=40	Coventry	88.9%	80.0%	2.0%	98	73.8%	83.0
=40	SOAS, London	72.3%	68.7%	–	164	73.1%	83.0
=40	Hull	76.2%	76.3%	31.7%	104	68.6%	83.0
43	Sussex	65.6%	59.7%	35.8%	130	71.1%	82.3
44	Keele	80.8%	74.5%	16.4%	111	68.4%	82.1
45	Worcester	79.2%	77.3%	8.1%	97	76.5%	82.0
46	Bangor	77.9%	77.2%	31.5%	112	60.8%	81.9
47	Derby	90.0%	86.7%	3.6%	119	58.3%	81.5
48	Chester	82.9%	79.5%	6.4%	103	69.1%	81.3
49	Manchester Metropolitan	76.0%	70.5%	14.9%	106	71.3%	80.9
=50	Salford	72.4%	66.9%	16.7%	104	71.9%	79.9
=50	Northampton	84.7%	69.3%	7.7%	95	68.1%	79.9
52	York St John	87.9%	81.9%	–	88	66.2%	79.6
53	Liverpool Hope	75.9%	80.2%	1.6%	107	–	78.4
54	Liverpool John Moores	79.0%	74.8%	–	120	60.7%	77.9
=55	Portsmouth	69.9%	65.5%	14.9%	95	69.6%	77.5
=55	Oxford Brookes	71.4%	64.7%	17.3%	98	66.6%	77.5
57	Sheffield Hallam	70.0%	60.7%	13.4%	101	69.7%	77.3
=58	Hertfordshire	76.6%	67.8%	–	88	71.6%	77.1
=58	Kingston	83.1%	75.1%	6.9%	94	58.4%	77.1
60	Edge Hill	74.4%	68.2%	6.2%	113	62.4%	77.0
61	Brighton	73.7%	62.2%	5.1%	88	69.4%	76.0
62	Bournemouth	73.2%	67.4%	19.9%	95	55.3%	75.0
63	Nottingham Trent	69.1%	62.7%	4.1%	98	64.8%	74.3
=64	Leeds Beckett	72.0%	68.9%	5.6%	105	55.9%	73.8
=64	Central Lancashire	73.9%	51.4%	9.8%	92	–	73.8
66	Winchester	76.5%	66.8%	7.5%	91	55.0%	73.5
67	Cumbria	78.8%	68.0%	1.5%	114	48.8%	73.4
68	Bath Spa	60.8%	56.0%	–	90	61.6%	69.4

Employed in high-skilled job	46%	Employed in lower-skilled job	25%
Employed in high-skilled job and studying	4%	Employed in lower-skilled job and studying	1%
Studying	15%	Unemployed	8%
High skilled work (median) salary	£24,500	Low/medium skilled salary	£20,000

Geology

Life after an undergraduate geology degree often involves postgraduate study, which 27% of graduates were engaged in 15 months on from their courses, the latest data shows – among the highest proportions of any subject. Combined with the 39% who were in professional jobs when surveyed, and the 3% who were juggling both, geology places 35th in our employment ranking of 67 subjects.

Average starting salaries of £23,500 for graduates in high-skilled jobs rank geology 52nd – which perhaps goes some way to explaining the high proportion who choose to study for a further qualification before entering the job market. The study of how the earth was formed and shaped, geology has applications in environmental research and oil and gas exploration as well as the water industries, mapping, remote sensing and engineering.

The leading universities require any two subjects from: biology, chemistry, economics, further maths, geography, geology, maths, physics and psychology. Entry standards can be high; Cambridge – which tops our table for the second year running, averaged 221 UCAS tariff points among 2020's intake, and has attracted even higher standards in the past.

Second-ranked Imperial, which last topped the table two years ago, has the edge in research ratings, closely followed by Southampton, in 16th place overall. Imperial also leads on graduate prospects and for student satisfaction with the broad experience, while Coventry (21st) received the best scores for teaching quality in the National Student Survey (NSS) – narrowly ahead of Exeter's similarly positive reviews.

Geology	Teaching quality	Student experience	Research quality	Entry standards (UCAS points)	Graduate prospects	Overall score
1 Cambridge	—	—	58.0%	221	—	100.0
2 Imperial College London	87.1%	89.7%	59.6%	166	92.8%	98.8
3 Oxford	—	—	52.1%	205	84.2%	96.1
4 St Andrews	82.4%	80.9%	44.2%	190	87.3%	94.8
5 Exeter	90.4%	89.1%	45.7%	146	84.5%	94.1
6 Edinburgh	74.3%	68.7%	38.2%	213	90.0%	93.0
7 Glasgow	81.9%	79.0%	38.5%	179	86.2%	92.6
8 Aberdeen	89.8%	88.7%	38.2%	152	81.2%	92.4
9 University College London	77.4%	75.6%	47.9%	157	89.3%	91.8
=10 Leeds	81.3%	78.4%	41.9%	157	85.2%	91.2
=10 Bristol	87.4%	81.3%	55.8%	149	72.1%	91.2
12 Durham	80.6%	74.6%	42.2%	153	88.3%	91.1

13	Birmingham	77.7%	76.0%	38.6%	141	82.4%	87.7
14	Newcastle	81.8%	81.1%	35.4%	114	85.2%	87.6
15	Leicester	86.9%	84.2%	37.2%	121	74.7%	87.4
16	Southampton	78.3%	72.1%	58.3%	144	66.6%	86.8
17	Manchester	72.2%	68.4%	44.5%	147	69.9%	83.9
18	Royal Holloway, London	67.0%	68.7%	43.4%	123	81.0%	83.5
19	Keele	79.3%	74.3%	12.2%	106	88.7%	83.2
20	Liverpool	75.8%	68.3%	30.3%	127	76.8%	82.9
21	Coventry	91.3%	84.9%	2.0%	115	—	82.7
22	Aberystwyth	82.8%	78.8%	34.9%	99	69.2%	82.6
23	East Anglia	77.7%	72.8%	47.4%	145	54.3%	82.2
24	Cardiff	76.6%	70.1%	21.3%	124	76.5%	81.7
25	Bangor	78.9%	76.6%	31.5%	112	64.4%	80.7
26	Portsmouth	78.8%	72.2%	19.8%	102	73.2%	79.9
27	Derby	83.7%	79.5%	3.6%	108	65.9%	78.1
=28	Hull	61.2%	52.8%	31.7%	105	75.0%	76.0
=28	Kingston	82.3%	76.5%	6.9%	—	59.3%	76.0
30	Brighton	71.9%	64.4%	5.1%	88	74.4%	74.6

Employed in high-skilled job	39%	Employed in lower-skilled job	19%
Employed in high-skilled job and studying	3%	Employed in lower-skilled job and studying	1%
Studying	27%	Unemployed	12%
High skilled work (median) salary	£23,500	Low/medium skilled salary	£19,000

German

The small student numbers that German degrees attract create fluctuations within our table, and almost all universities have changed places apart from Cambridge, which retains the No 1 spot. It has the top research rating, the second-best graduate prospects and the third-highest entry standards.

Applicants are well-qualified; of the 24 institutions in our table, 17 averaged 144 points or more among their 2020 intake, equivalent to AAA at A-level, and none averaged lower than the 118 UCAS points at Kent. In =10th place overall, Kent has outdone all others for student satisfaction with teaching quality and ranks second for the wider experience. St Andrews clinched the top score for wider experience.

The subject's 20-year-plus decline continued in the 2020 recruitment cycle, when just 75 students started degrees – only a quarter of the enrolments a decade earlier. But there are still plenty of places to study German, either as a single honours degree or in combination with subjects including law, film, accountancy and other languages. Most universities in the table offer German from scratch as well as catering for those who took it at A-level.

The latest data shows that 52% of German graduates were in professional jobs 15 months on from their degrees, while 10% were furthering their studies and 5% were combining both. The subject places 38th in our employment ranking of 67. It does better in our salary index – the £25,000 earned on average by those in high-skilled jobs places German 24th.

German

		Teaching quality	Student experience	Research quality	Entry standards (UCAS points)	Graduate prospects	Overall score
1	Cambridge	—	—	54.0%	189	84.1%	100.0
2	Durham	79.0%	72.7%	34.6%	181	86.6%	93.4
3	Oxford	—	—	41.3%	179	81.2%	93.1
4	Warwick	83.2%	73.9%	45.2%	163	78.5%	92.9
5	St Andrews	89.1%	89.5%	26.4%	194	—	92.6
6	King's College London	80.2%	77.1%	42.1%	166	—	92.3
7	Sheffield	79.8%	74.8%	41.2%	157*	—	90.4
8	Glasgow	83.1%	76.8%	26.3%	191	—	89.6
9	University College London	72.6%	59.6%	43.7%	160	—	88.8
=10	Kent	90.4%	79.3%	41.9%	118	—	88.7
=10	Newcastle	85.8%	78.4%	36.3%	146	—	88.7
12	Bristol	78.5%	72.7%	36.0%	166	72.3%	87.3
13	Edinburgh	74.5%	69.4%	30.3%	178	—	87.0
14	Exeter	75.3%	73.3%	35.1%	144	78.6%	86.8
15	Queen Mary, London	86.8%	79.1%	35.1%	129	—	86.5
16	Reading	75.3%	79.1%	41.7%	121	—	85.5
17	Leeds	78.9%	76.2%	30.6%	152	72.1%	84.6
18	Nottingham	78.1%	64.2%	39.4%	136	69.0%	83.7
19	Bangor	67.2%	65.1%	39.6%	137*	—	83.5
20	Liverpool	76.5%	78.0%	33.4%	127	—	83.2
21	Manchester	51.4%	45.5%	48.9%	161	69.1%	83.1
22	Birmingham	69.0%	64.0%	33.7%	146	73.5%	83.0
23	Cardiff	72.4%	56.7%	32.5%	127	71.7%	80.2
24	Bath	64.6%	57.9%	27.4%	156	—	79.8

Employed in high-skilled job	52%	Employed in lower-skilled job	22%
Employed in high-skilled job and studying	5%	Employed in lower-skilled job and studying	1%
Studying	10%	Unemployed	10%
High skilled work (median) salary	£25,000	Low/medium skilled salary	£20,400

History

History remains one of the 20 most popular subjects in higher education, despite both applications and enrolments falling for the fifth year in a row in 2020. The decrease in numbers seems to be confined to the lower and medium tariff institutions, however, according to analysis by UCAS.

The top three of our table is unchanged this year, although St Andrews has closed the gap on Cambridge, its score boosted by improved rates of student satisfaction with teaching quality and the highest entry standards. Cambridge has the leading scores in the Research Excellence Framework (a whisker ahead of Oxford) and tops our table for the seventh successive time. The LSE moves up to fourth place this year, pushing Durham into fifth. The LSE has unsurpassed graduate prospects; 92.7% were in professional jobs and/or postgraduate study 15 months on from their degrees.

Of the top 20 universities only St Andrews and Loughborough (=14th) feature in the upper reaches of student satisfaction measures, which are dominated by post-1992 institutions. Newman, Birmingham leads both our measures from the National Student Survey, for teaching quality and the wider experience.

History does not set our employment ranking alight, placing 49th. In the latest Graduate Outcomes survey 38% of history graduates were in jobs deemed "high-skilled" 15 months after graduation, while 29% were in "low-skilled" employment. More positively, nearly one in five had entered postgraduate study and 4% were juggling it with a professional job. Salaries do better; graduates were earning an average of £24,800 in high-skilled jobs, ranking the subject 38th.

History	Teaching quality	Student experience	Research quality	Entry standards (UCAS points)	Graduate prospects	Overall score
1 Cambridge	—	—	56.3%	192	85.7%	100.0
2 St Andrews	88.8%	83.2%	46.7%	195	78.2%	98.3
3 Oxford	—	—	56.1%	190	86.3%	97.2
4 London School of Economics	79.8%	70.8%	46.8%	165	92.7%	95.8
5 Durham	79.6%	68.3%	41.4%	189	84.7%	94.6
6 University College London	76.8%	66.1%	51.9%	177	79.9%	93.3
7 Warwick	78.9%	67.5%	51.7%	152	84.1%	93.1
8 Sheffield	80.6%	72.3%	53.7%	149	73.1%	91.5
9 York	80.7%	71.9%	43.3%	152	75.2%	90.4
10 Glasgow	79.1%	67.8%	47.7%	183	64.2%	90.2
11 Leeds	77.7%	66.4%	43.6%	160	74.8%	89.7
12 Exeter	73.6%	65.6%	45.6%	160	77.1%	89.4
13 Strathclyde	80.1%	75.3%	42.0%	192	57.4%	89.3
=14 Loughborough	89.1%	88.0%	22.5%	136	73.2%	89.0
=14 Southampton	78.7%	69.6%	50.6%	139	71.3%	89.0
16 Lancaster	83.3%	71.6%	37.0%	144	72.7%	88.8
17 Aberdeen	84.4%	78.5%	36.1%	172	57.9%	88.3
18 Sussex	80.9%	71.3%	41.3%	128	73.1%	87.8
19 Edinburgh	65.7%	51.3%	46.9%	174	79.2%	87.7
20 Manchester	75.8%	61.8%	39.8%	160	72.9%	87.6
21 King's College London	73.6%	59.0%	45.3%	164	69.7%	87.2
=22 Birmingham	68.6%	59.2%	48.8%	148	77.1%	87.1
=22 Queen Mary, London	82.2%	71.7%	43.7%	126	67.7%	87.1
24 Kent	85.6%	75.5%	41.3%	127	63.1%	87.0
=25 Bristol	68.6%	62.4%	40.6%	165	74.9%	86.9
=25 Stirling	84.1%	76.2%	28.5%	173	58.6%	86.9
27 East Anglia	77.4%	67.6%	47.4%	123	71.0%	86.7
28 Derby	91.0%	86.9%	13.5%	105	77.9%	86.6
29 Royal Holloway, London	78.4%	65.8%	40.6%	134	69.6%	86.1
30 Newman, Birmingham	96.4%	92.5%	12.0%	90	72.4%	85.8

History cont.

	Teaching quality	Student experience	Research quality	Entry standards (UCAS points)	Graduate prospects	Overall score
=31 Swansea	82.3%	73.4%	25.0%	125	75.0%	85.7
=31 Hertfordshire	87.0%	75.9%	46.7%	98	61.4%	85.7
=33 Reading	77.2%	69.2%	35.4%	117	76.6%	85.6
=33 Dundee	77.5%	71.7%	30.4%	180	58.3%	85.6
35 Aberystwyth	86.7%	79.5%	19.5%	116	72.7%	85.4
36 Keele	82.1%	75.1%	32.8%	110	71.7%	85.3
37 Liverpool	74.6%	64.8%	38.9%	133	71.9%	85.1
38 Nottingham	74.1%	63.0%	36.9%	141	71.1%	85.0
39 Teesside	—	—	27.9%	108	75.7%	84.9
40 SOAS, London	78.0%	73.4%	20.8%	138	71.7%	84.2
41 Lincoln	85.5%	73.1%	25.9%	107	68.7%	83.8
42 Northumbria	82.3%	67.7%	30.7%	125	64.5%	83.7
43 Sheffield Hallam	84.0%	74.1%	38.3%	102	61.2%	83.5
=44 Wales Trinity St David	93.2%	69.6%	17.3%	105	67.1%	83.4
=44 Hull	87.1%	78.5%	26.1%	104	63.5%	83.4
=46 Queen's Belfast	69.7%	63.0%	46.3%	138	60.5%	82.7
=46 Liverpool John Moores	88.3%	77.4%	15.9%	130	58.7%	82.7
48 Leicester	76.0%	67.5%	34.3%	123	64.0%	82.4
=49 Greenwich	86.9%	78.7%	8.6%	105	70.7%	82.1
=49 Edge Hill	87.5%	74.4%	23.6%	102	61.9%	82.1
=51 Cardiff	72.2%	58.4%	31.4%	129	70.9%	82.0
=51 Ulster	85.4%	79.2%	24.0%	109	58.9%	82.0
53 Newcastle	69.3%	56.7%	29.0%	143	70.2%	81.6
54 Bangor	75.0%	66.5%	24.3%	122	68.4%	81.2
=55 Liverpool Hope	81.5%	77.4%	15.7%	106	66.3%	80.9
=55 Huddersfield	83.9%	75.5%	22.3%	111	58.2%	80.9
57 Roehampton	86.0%	74.9%	21.4%	93	62.3%	80.8
58 Essex	77.5%	74.5%	34.8%	105	57.9%	80.7
59 Suffolk	96.0%	89.2%	—	107	55.3%	80.6
=60 Oxford Brookes	74.4%	67.2%	35.0%	102	64.2%	80.5
=60 Portsmouth	81.9%	66.7%	32.2%	89	62.8%	80.5
62 Wolverhampton	86.0%	76.2%	18.8%	95	59.8%	80.1
63 Bishop Grosseteste	91.4%	72.8%	7.0%	91	64.6%	79.8
64 Central Lancashire	86.8%	74.9%	12.0%	100	61.6%	79.7
65 Goldsmiths, London	78.8%	63.4%	34.5%	112	54.5%	79.6
66 Chichester	86.3%	74.0%	15.8%	103	57.6%	79.5
67 Plymouth	85.2%	77.7%	22.6%	104	51.6%	79.4
68 West of England	84.9%	76.8%	28.9%	102	48.2%	79.3
69 Coventry	85.9%	78.5%	5.6%	111	59.7%	79.2
70 Brunel	75.9%	57.9%	32.4%	103	61.0%	78.8
71 Manchester Metropolitan	79.8%	64.2%	18.0%	112	58.8%	78.2
=72 Canterbury Christ Church	85.7%	72.4%	16.3%	84	57.6%	77.8

=72 Leeds Beckett	91.8%	82.8%	11.0%	88	49.2%	77.8
74 Northampton	78.4%	69.9%	21.5%	93	—	77.5
75 Nottingham Trent	78.1%	65.6%	17.5%	102	59.7%	77.2
76 De Montfort	79.6%	66.6%	23.4%	93	55.4%	77.0
=77 Winchester	79.4%	63.8%	19.1%	97	56.5%	76.5
=77 Anglia Ruskin	84.6%	78.5%	15.3%	84	51.3%	76.5
79 St Mary's, Twickenham	79.5%	73.3%	11.0%	93	58.7%	76.3
=80 Salford	78.6%	72.9%	—	106	62.7%	76.1
=80 South Wales	79.5%	67.2%	15.8%	113	50.7%	76.1
82 York St John	85.6%	76.4%	—	95	53.9%	75.4
83 Chester	82.9%	67.5%	9.1%	96	53.0%	75.2
84 Bath Spa	74.4%	65.1%	8.3%	103	57.2%	74.1
85 Westminster	79.0%	72.7%	11.8%	100	45.4%	73.7
86 Gloucestershire	75.7%	67.0%	11.2%	85	56.5%	73.6
87 Worcester	71.1%	60.0%	19.5%	109	48.9%	73.2
88 Brighton	82.8%	63.1%	13.1%	93	44.5%	73.1

Employed in high-skilled job	38%	Employed in lower-skilled job	29%
Employed in high-skilled job and studying	4%	Employed in lower-skilled job and studying	2%
Studying	19%	Unemployed	9%
High skilled work (median) salary	£24,800	Low/medium skilled salary	£19,500

History of Art, Architecture and Design

While there are usually no essential subjects required for entry to a degree in History of Art, essay-based subjects will prove useful, as the course involves analysing and writing about art, architecture and design across styles, themes and techniques.

The best results in the Research Excellence Framework were produced by the Courtauld Institute, which had 95% of its submission classed as world-leading or internationally excellent. A self-governing college of the University of London, the Courtauld specialises in history of art and conservation. Based in Somerset House, it has previously topped our table – the only specialist institution to have done so in any subject ranking in our *Guide* until this year.

But Cambridge, the longstanding leader in the subject, tops the table once more this year. Oxford averaged the highest entry standards in 2020 and was the only university to attract new students with an average of more than 200 UCAS points in a generally high-tariff academic field. Only six universities averaged fewer than 144 UCAS points, equivalent to AAA at A-level. St Andrews, where the Duchess of Cambridge studied History of Art, ranks third in our table.

In 12th place overall, Sussex students returned the highest rates of satisfaction with the wider undergraduate experience in the National Student Survey (NSS), while Plymouth (14th) did best in sections relating to teaching quality.

The numbers taking History of Art degrees have held up better than in most of the humanities, and even increased a little in 2020's admissions round.

History of Art, Architecture and Design	Teaching quality	Student experience	Research quality	Entry standards (UCAS points)	Graduate prospects	Overall score
1 Cambridge	—	—	49.0%	190	—	100.0
2 Warwick	79.5%	74.3%	53.0%	156	77.4%	98.3
3 St Andrews	86.9%	82.7%	42.1%	168	67.9%	97.2
4 Birmingham	76.4%	67.2%	43.7%	161	81.4%	97.1
5 Oxford	—	—	39.7%	203	—	97.0
6 Courtauld	77.9%	61.1%	66.0%	162	65.4%	95.8
7 SOAS, London	82.5%	79.9%	40.9%	155	—	94.3
8 Aberdeen	84.4%	78.3%	36.1%	159	—	94.2
9 University College London	73.0%	63.1%	44.7%	167	67.9%	92.4
10 Manchester	76.9%	70.5%	54.0%	154	62.0%	92.3
11 York	78.7%	73.8%	53.2%	134	64.1%	91.5
12 Sussex	84.2%	87.4%	25.2%	148	—	91.1
13 Leeds	77.8%	64.2%	30.0%	155	67.8%	89.8
14 Plymouth	91.7%	83.4%	14.7%	137*	—	89.2
15 Exeter	73.1%	66.8%	35.1%	157	—	88.7
16 Nottingham	86.6%	74.7%	30.9%	125	—	88.5
17 Glasgow	74.1%	60.1%	37.2%	166	57.8%	87.8
18 Goldsmiths, London	74.3%	55.4%	25.9%	163	63.0%	86.9
19 Oxford Brookes	85.3%	80.1%	35.0%	116	57.9%	86.5
20 East Anglia	66.5%	59.4%	36.9%	133	67.6%	85.4
21 Edinburgh	71.2%	53.6%	27.9%	155	60.0%	84.5
22 Bristol	75.3%	63.6%	28.3%	149	51.9%	83.2
23 Brighton	87.3%	74.6%	13.1%	96	65.2%	83.0
24 Manchester Metropolitan	71.1%	60.4%	9.7%	156	—	81.2

Employed in high-skilled job	41%	Employed in lower-skilled job		28%
Employed in high-skilled job and studying	2%	Employed in lower-skilled job and studying		1%
Studying	15%	Unemployed		12%
High skilled work (median) salary	£23,000	Low/medium skilled salary		£20,000

Hospitality, Leisure, Recreation and Tourism

The top three in Hospitality, Leisure, Recreation and Tourism remain the same, with Birmingham – which has the top-rated research and second-highest entry standards – leading our table for the sixth consecutive year. Liverpool John Moores is second and Edge Hill is in third place.

The top ten features many familiar institutions, albeit in different spots. The exceptions are new entry, Kent, at fifth, while Arts Bournemouth has plummeted from seventh position last year to 45th – due to drastically reduced rates of student satisfaction in the pandemic-hit National Student Survey (NSS), as well as lower entry standards. Taking seventh place this year is Robert Gordon, which has risen from 20th in our previous edition.

But Sunderland – in 26th place – has the top rates of student satisfaction with both teaching quality and the wider experience – which it has achieved, remarkably, for the second year running. Sixth-ranked Lincoln had the second-best rates of student satisfaction.

The table incorporates a wide variety of courses, all of them directed towards management in the leisure and tourism industries. They include degrees in international hospitality management and adventure tourism management. The post-1992 universities feature more than institutions with older foundations.

Oxford Brookes leads for employment prospects, with almost three-quarters of its graduates in high-skilled jobs or postgraduate study 15 months on from their degrees. But as a whole, the subject area places bottom of our jobs ranking. Slightly more graduates were in "low-skilled" jobs (41%) than "high-skilled" (40%) when the Graduate Outcomes survey took its 2018–19 census – before the pandemic's catastrophic impact on the hospitality and tourism industries – and 12% were unemployed. Salaries fare better, placing 59th out of 67 subject areas.

Hospitality, Leisure, Recreation and Tourism	Teaching quality	Student experience	Research quality	Entry standards (UCAS points)	Graduate prospects	Overall score
1 Birmingham	66.3%	62.1%	63.7%	159	—	100.0
2 Liverpool John Moores	67.2%	63.7%	45.3%	140	55.8%	89.4
3 Edge Hill	82.7%	81.3%	7.7%	147*	—	89.0
4 Surrey	75.4%	74.9%	33.6%	133	56.0%	88.8
5 Kent	78.0%	71.9%	21.0%	137	—	88.0
6 Lincoln	86.0%	83.0%	11.4%	128	60.0%	87.6
7 Robert Gordon	78.9%	76.3%	2.6%	148	57.1%	85.7
=8 Coventry	84.9%	81.1%	1.6%	121	64.1%	85.1
=8 Edinburgh	54.9%	58.9%	26.1%	157	—	85.1
10 Glasgow Caledonian	70.4%	67.8%	15.2%	160	48.7%	85.0
11 Oxford Brookes	69.1%	71.3%	5.1%	119	74.4%	84.0
12 Canterbury Christ Church	83.3%	82.9%	19.0%	98	59.0%	83.9
13 Huddersfield	81.5%	80.1%	—	135	54.5%	83.4
14 Edinburgh Napier	75.2%	72.9%	2.3%	148	51.5%	82.9
15 Queen Margaret, Edinburgh	75.3%	73.9%	—	136	58.6%	82.7
16 Ulster	80.4%	82.1%	31.0%	122	34.7%	82.6
17 Portsmouth	78.2%	77.0%	8.1%	114*	57.8%	81.9
=18 Gloucestershire	73.8%	72.1%	6.0%	118	60.8%	81.5
=18 Chester	81.2%	74.7%	6.6%	127	49.4%	81.5
=20 Plymouth	71.9%	65.5%	13.1%	119	58.8%	81.3
=20 Cardiff Metropolitan	74.5%	71.9%	7.7%	118	58.8%	81.3
=20 Sheffield Hallam	79.4%	73.3%	8.5%	112	56.9%	81.3
=23 Leeds Beckett	79.6%	77.4%	12.6%	100	58.2%	81.2
=23 Greenwich	79.9%	74.8%	3.3%	117	57.0%	81.2
25 Bournemouth	67.2%	62.9%	9.0%	118	66.3%	81.1
26 Sunderland	89.4%	87.9%	2.4%	119	43.2%	80.9
=27 Falmouth	83.4%	69.6%	—	101	65.2%	80.7
=27 Manchester Metropolitan	74.0%	69.2%	4.7%	131	53.6%	80.7

		Teaching quality	Student experience	Research quality	Entry standards (UCAS points)	Graduate prospects	Overall score
29	Westminster	69.7%	73.0%	10.7%	134	47.2%	80.3
30	Central Lancashire	81.5%	74.1%	5.1%	120	49.3%	80.1
31	Winchester	64.6%	62.3%	—	122	69.2%	80.0
32	York St John	81.5%	73.0%	5.5%	111	—	79.9
33	Derby	81.6%	76.0%	0.9%	121	50.0%	79.8
34	Wales Trinity St David	78.8%	74.7%	—	129	46.0%	79.0
35	Middlesex	74.8%	71.7%	10.5%	110	—	78.9
36	West of Scotland	78.5%	74.9%	9.1%	124	39.4%	78.4
37	Liverpool Hope	75.2%	67.9%	10.9%	108*	—	78.2
=38	Northumbria	62.8%	62.3%	4.4%	137	—	77.7
=38	Staffordshire	61.8%	62.9%	19.1%	117	—	77.7
40	Buckinghamshire New	—	—	0.9%	100	64.1%	77.5
41	Wolverhampton	70.0%	60.8%	5.6%	111	56.4%	77.0
42	Chichester	77.1%	68.6%	—	94	59.6%	76.6
43	West London	78.4%	74.5%	—	123	37.6%	75.7
44	Solent, Southampton	69.7%	60.7%	0.6%	116	52.2%	75.6
45	Arts Bournemouth	62.8%	55.8%	—	105	63.3%	74.9
46	Salford	52.2%	54.7%	5.9%	124	56.8%	74.7
47	South Wales	70.4%	61.2%	10.8%	102*	—	74.6
48	London South Bank	57.1%	50.8%	35.0%	106	36.7%	73.3
49	Northampton	67.8%	64.8%	—	120	41.9%	73.1
=50	Brighton	61.5%	54.0%	10.9%	107	46.9%	72.5
=50	Cumbria	59.4%	51.5%	3.2%	125	—	72.5
52	Hertfordshire	67.3%	67.1%	0.9%	101	48.2%	72.4
53	East London	72.3%	74.9%	0.8%	74	53.3%	71.7
54	Anglia Ruskin	78.2%	72.7%	3.4%	76	—	71.2
55	London Metropolitan	67.2%	64.6%	—	102*	33.3%	68.0
56	Bedfordshire	58.7%	58.8%	6.7%	89	31.0%	64.5

Employed in high-skilled job	40%	Employed in lower-skilled job	41%
Employed in high-skilled job and studying	2%	Employed in lower-skilled job and studying	1%
Studying	5%	Unemployed	12%
High skilled work (median) salary	£22,000	Low/medium skilled salary	£19,968

Iberian Languages

The declining popularity of modern language degrees has been well documented. But from a post-Brexit perspective, the 36% drop in the number of accepted applicants between 2011 and 2020, from 6,005 to 3,830, prompted fresh fears of a languages skills gap.

The Iberian languages have suffered the decline along with other modern languages, despite Spanish overtaking French at A-level and closing the gap with it at degree level. There was another

10% decrease in the 2020 admissions round, and 59% fewer students started single honours Spanish degrees than did in 2011. However, many more take Spanish as part of a broader modern language degree or paired with diverse subjects as part of a joint honours programme.

Portuguese has had zero single honours students since 2012 – but it can still be studied, and 21 universities offered it as part of joint honours or combined languages courses in 2022.

Fluctuations in our table include third-ranked Stirling moving up from 17th in our previous edition, while St Andrews places fourth, boosted from 12th by the top score for student satisfaction with teaching quality. But the leading two remain unchanged; top-ranked Cambridge is unbeaten on research, although closely followed by Queen's Belfast. Runner-up Oxford has the best-employed students, with 91.5% of graduates in professional jobs or postgraduate study 15 months on from their degrees. Surrey achieved the best rates of student satisfaction with the broad experience in the National Student Survey.

The Iberian languages tie with philosophy for 43rd place in our employment ranking, with 50% of graduates in professional jobs 15 months after their degrees, 12% furthering their studies and 3% combining both.

Iberian Languages	Teaching quality	Student experience	Research quality	Entry standards (UCAS points)	Graduate prospects	Overall score
1 Cambridge	—	—	54.0%	189	84.1%	100.0
2 Oxford	—	—	41.3%	185	91.5%	97.3
3 Stirling	90.0%	87.5%	29.8%	190	—	96.7
4 St Andrews	91.8%	88.6%	26.4%	188	—	96.2
5 Queen's Belfast	81.8%	81.5%	53.6%	144	78.7%	94.7
6 Durham	79.0%	72.7%	34.6%	181	86.6%	94.5
7 Warwick	83.2%	75.9%	45.2%	160	75.4%	93.0
8 Surrey	90.3%	88.8%	39.1%	128	—	92.9
9 Aberdeen	80.4%	80.7%	29.3%	188	—	92.6
10 Nottingham	82.2%	74.7%	39.4%	141	79.4%	91.2
=11 Strathclyde	73.9%	75.3%	42.0%	184	71.7%	91.0
=11 Southampton	88.6%	82.7%	42.7%	150	66.9%	91.0
=13 University College London	70.4%	61.3%	43.7%	164	80.6%	90.3
=13 King's College London	78.2%	74.5%	42.1%	150	75.4%	90.3
=13 York	84.1%	79.7%	37.3%	137	—	90.3
16 Lancaster	73.1%	71.0%	47.0%	142	—	89.2
17 Bristol	79.6%	71.1%	36.0%	155	73.8%	89.0
18 Exeter	75.3%	73.3%	35.1%	144	78.6%	88.5
19 Edinburgh	72.4%	69.8%	30.3%	180	74.8%	88.3
20 Manchester	71.1%	57.4%	48.9%	151	73.8%	88.2
21 Glasgow	76.6%	74.9%	26.3%	198	67.0%	88.0
22 Leeds	73.8%	64.4%	30.6%	154	79.5%	87.5
23 Kent	87.5%	78.1%	41.9%	115	65.0%	86.8
24 Bath	68.8%	68.5%	27.4%	146	82.8%	86.4
25 Newcastle	76.2%	70.8%	36.3%	147	69.9%	86.3
26 Sheffield	77.0%	76.6%	41.2%	144*	63.4%	86.0

		Teaching quality	Student experience	Research quality	Entry standards (UCAS points)	Graduate prospects	Overall score
27	Reading	74.8%	71.9%	41.7%	119	—	85.9
28	Royal Holloway, London	69.3%	57.8%	48.3%	125	—	85.0
29	Cardiff	78.8%	72.4%	32.5%	123	71.4%	84.8
30	Aston	90.4%	83.4%	23.4%	111*	64.2%	83.5
31	Birmingham	69.3%	64.2%	33.7%	146	66.6%	82.6
32	Aberystwyth	85.1%	86.1%	16.6%	107	—	82.4
33	Queen Mary, London	74.7%	66.8%	35.1%	121	65.6%	82.0
34	Chester	77.5%	74.4%	17.3%	91	77.7%	80.8
35	Bangor	68.2%	69.7%	39.6%	96	—	80.6
36	Swansea	78.5%	66.0%	22.8%	112*	—	80.2
37	Nottingham Trent	76.4%	68.2%	7.6%	104	80.7%	79.8
38	Liverpool	71.6%	67.1%	33.4%	130	57.9%	79.4
39	Manchester Metropolitan	63.9%	46.8%	29.0%	105	—	74.4
40	Westminster	71.8%	64.4%	2.0%	108	—	71.7

Employed in high-skilled job	50%	Employed in lower-skilled job	23%
Employed in high-skilled job and studying	3%	Employed in lower-skilled job and studying	1%
Studying	12%	Unemployed	11%
High skilled work (median) salary	£25,000	Low/medium skilled salary	£20,000

Information Systems and Management

Formerly titled "Librarianship and Information Management", we have broadened this subject grouping and renamed it to better reflect its parameters. Our Information Systems and Management table includes courses ranging from information systems, data management and curatorial studies to bioinformatics, museum studies and systems analysis and design. The ranking still takes in librarianship, which requires some postgraduate training after a first degree to enter the profession and has practically disappeared at undergraduate level.

University College London (UCL) tops the newly expanded table by a clear margin, its performance marked by the best rates of student satisfaction with both teaching quality and the wider undergraduate experience – measures derived from the National Student Survey. UCL also averaged the highest entry standards in 2020, of 178 UCAS tariff points. Runner-up, Loughborough, outdoes all others for its research ratings and is followed in this measure by East Anglia.

Elsewhere in the table, post-1992 universities predominate – such as Gloucestershire, in 14th place, which comes top for graduate prospects with 85.7% of graduates in high-skilled jobs or postgraduate study 15 months after finishing their degrees. More than 80% of graduates from Brunel, Portsmouth, Northumbria and Leeds Beckett had also achieved the top employment outcomes when surveyed.

The subject grouping places in the upper half of our employment ranking, with 71.1% of graduates in good jobs or furthering their studies on average. It ties in 25th place for starting salaries, with graduates commanding £25,000 in professional-level jobs and £20,000 in employment deemed "medium-skilled".

	Teaching quality	Student experience	Research quality	Entry standards (UCAS points)	Graduate prospects	Overall score
1 Loughborough	90.5%	92.3%	45.1%	158	78.3%	100.0
2 East Anglia	73.6%	74.1%	43.8%	137	—	92.4
3 Brunel London	79.5%	81.0%	23.0%	128	100.0%	91.9
4 Northumbria	73.5%	70.0%	21.0%	142	82.6%	87.9
5 Edinburgh Napier	87.2%	83.9%	9.5%	128	77.3%	87.4
6 Wolverhampton	73.6%	70.8%	33.2%	—	77.3%	86.9
7 De Montfort	69.9%	72.6%	31.2%	113*	89.7%	86.4
8 Derby	85.0%	79.2%	13.5%	139*	62.5%	86.2
9 Manchester Metropolitan	84.9%	86.2%	4.7%	134	64.3%	84.9
=10 Birmingham City	77.6%	82.6%	6.0%	126	—	83.6
=10 Gloucestershire	73.4%	70.0%	—	117	100.0%	83.6
12 Aberystwyth	82.9%	83.4%	9.2%	—	66.7%	83.3
13 Portsmouth	79.6%	77.4%	12.8%	110	78.4%	83.2
14 Bradford	78.1%	79.2%	—	114	83.8%	82.4
=15 East London	87.3%	87.2%	13.9%	104	57.1%	81.7
=15 Sheffield Hallam	74.5%	73.9%	14.4%	112	74.7%	81.7
17 Leeds Beckett	75.6%	74.4%	11.0%	107	77.8%	81.2
18 Westminster	62.4%	67.6%	28.3%	122	60.9%	80.0
19 London Metropolitan	69.6%	70.4%	5.9%	93	54.5%	72.6

Employed in high-skilled job	63%	Employed in lower-skilled job	18%
Employed in high-skilled job and studying	3%	Employed in lower-skilled job and studying	0%
Studying	5%	Unemployed	11%
High skilled work (median) salary	£25,000	Low/medium skilled salary	£20,000

Italian

The small cohorts of students taking Italian degrees make for plenty of movement in our table, although Cambridge, which was the top scorer in the Research Excellence Framework, continues to lead the table by a clear margin. Durham has moved up from fourth to second place and has the best-employed graduates. For student satisfaction however, Aberystwyth, at the foot of the table is top in the sections relating to both teaching quality and the wider experience in the National Student Survey (NSS).

Glasgow, in eighth place overall, claims the highest entry standards, its incoming Italian undergraduates having averaged 195 UCAS tariff points in 2020. Although no universities reached the heights of 200-plus UCAS points in 2020, the subject is a high-tariff area generally and only four universities in our table averaged below 144 points – equal to AAA at A-level. One modern language at A-level is required by the leading universities – and some of them require Italian specifically, while others allow it to be learned from scratch. Degree courses often include time spent abroad studying or teaching.

For starting salaries Italian ties in 21st place with accounting and finance degrees, with graduates earning £25,000 per year in professional jobs, on average, and those employed in jobs classified as "medium-skilled" commanding £21,000. Results from the Graduate Outcomes survey place Italian 40th out of 67 subject areas, with 66.8% in "high-skilled" jobs and or further study 15 months after finishing their degrees.

Italian	Teaching quality	Student experience	Research quality	Entry standards (UCAS points)	Graduate prospects	Overall score
1 Cambridge	—	—	54.0%	189	84.1%	100.0
2 Durham	79.0%	72.7%	34.6%	181	86.6%	94.3
3 Warwick	84.0%	75.5%	45.2%	161	75.3%	93.5
4 Oxford	—	—	41.3%	177	—	93.2
5 Leeds	84.8%	80.5%	30.6%	147	—	90.3
6 Manchester	69.4%	58.6%	48.9%	158	—	89.5
7 Reading	84.3%	76.6%	41.7%	115*	—	89.3
8 Glasgow	70.4%	74.3%	26.3%	195	—	89.1
9 Exeter	75.3%	73.3%	35.1%	144	78.6%	88.5
10 University College London	68.1%	61.2%	43.7%	162	—	88.3
11 Bristol	81.3%	69.8%	36.0%	155	66.7%	87.5
12 Edinburgh	73.0%	65.5%	30.3%	170	—	87.2
13 Bath	80.0%	81.3%	27.4%	135	—	86.5
14 Cardiff	79.6%	74.0%	32.5%	124	—	85.7
15 Birmingham	69.0%	64.0%	33.7%	146	67.6%	83.1
16 Aberystwyth	86.1%	83.2%	16.6%	107	—	82.3

Employed in high-skilled job	52%	Employed in lower-skilled job	23%
Employed in high-skilled job and studying	1%	Employed in lower-skilled job and studying	1%
Studying	13%	Unemployed	10%
High skilled work (median) salary	£25,000	Low/medium skilled salary	£21,000

Land and Property Management

Real estate degrees are the biggest recruiters among our Land and Property Management table. The subject grouping also encompasses woodland ecology, surveying and conservation – among others. The degree at Cambridge – which tops our table again this year – encompasses law and economics along with aspects of the environment, business finance and resource management. It attracted five applications per place in 2020 and entry standards are by far the highest in the table. Cambridge was also the top scorer in the Research Excellence Framework.

Students at Ulster, which has moved up from third to second place this year, gave the university the best ratings for both teaching quality and the wider undergraduate experience in the National Student Survey – just as the previous year's cohort did.

Reading, in fourth place, operates the "Pathways to Property" widening participation programme at its Henley Business School. Funded by property firms it aims to attract greater numbers of state school-educated applicants into studying real estate via an annual summer school, work experience opportunities and an online course.

Property and Land Management ranks 30th in our employment index this year. The latest data shows 64% of graduates in jobs deemed "high-skilled" 15 months on from their degrees, while a futher 9% were continuing their studies or combining further study with a good job. Average salaries for graduates in high-skilled jobs are £24,000 – ranking the subject area =45th for earnings.

Land and Property Management	Teaching quality	Student experience	Research quality	Entry standards (UCAS points)	Graduate prospects	Overall score
1 Cambridge	77.6%	71.9%	49.0%	192	—	100.0
2 Ulster	83.5%	80.8%	28.6%	120	—	96.4
3 Manchester	68.6%	71.4%	36.5%	158	—	95.6
4 Reading	71.7%	70.9%	40.0%	131	—	95.0
5 Harper Adams	78.4%	75.1%	—	111	85.1%	93.4
6 Nottingham Trent	78.6%	74.3%	3.4%	106	—	92.3
7 Sheffield Hallam	75.7%	70.3%	13.4%	102	—	92.1
8 Royal Agricultural	77.0%	76.5%	—	110	83.1%	91.8
9 Birmingham City	75.0%	70.7%	2.7%	109	—	91.5
10 Leeds Beckett	73.2%	69.9%	5.6%	107	—	91.3
11 Westminster	67.3%	69.4%	10.7%	116	—	91.1
12 Liverpool John Moores	66.6%	56.3%	4.9%	133	—	90.3

Employed in high-skilled job	64%	Employed in lower-skilled job	22%
Employed in high-skilled job and studying	5%	Employed in lower-skilled job and studying	0%
Studying	4%	Unemployed	5%
High skilled work (median) salary	£24,000	Low/medium skilled salary	£20,000

Law

In a highly competitive marketplace, with 99 universities featuring in our subject ranking for law, it is the ability of students to land the best legal jobs on graduation that correlates most closely to universities' overall rankings. Four of the top five universities for law are among the top five for graduate prospects.

Our graduate prospects measure looks at the proportion of students who go on to secure high-skilled jobs – in this case, jobs within the legal profession – or who go into postgraduate study within 15 months of leaving university. Cambridge and the London School of Economics (LSE), the top and second-ranked universities for law overall, are also first and second respectively for the positive outcomes achieved by their law graduates.

University College London (UCL), in third place overall, ranks fifth for legal jobs, while fourth-placed Oxford also ranks fourth for jobs. Royal Holloway, London is the university to prove the exception; while it ranks a more modest 42nd overall in our ranking, it has the third-highest score for graduate prospects with 93.2%. This success is no flash in the pan; it achieved 100% graduate employment under our definition last year.

This intense competition between the top universities for law in the employment market is repeated across our full ranking with the same universities – Cambridge, the LSE, UCL, Oxford and Glasgow – appearing in our top five this year and last with only LSE and UCL swapping places in second and third.

Law is not like medicine, which has close to full employment on graduation. About half of law graduates do not go on to practise. However, there is always a healthy demand for legal trainees, who often become high earners, so the five universities – West London, Bradford, Middlesex, Wolverhampton and West of Scotland – where our high-skilled employment measure falls below 60% stand out for the wrong reasons.

Salaries commanded by recent graduates are also variable. The median salary of £21,000 earned by legal trainees across all universities does not foretell the relative riches to come for even the more modestly-able lawyer, but within this is a wide band of earnings, ranging from £45,000 (Oxford) at the top to £17,000 (Northampton) at the bottom. In this year's data there is also a surprising £13,000 gap between the median earnings of Oxford law graduates and their Cambridge counterparts.

Modern universities have the happiest law undergraduates, according to data from the National Student Survey (NSS). With scores generally depressed due to the pandemic, Sunderland's 84.1% score for satisfaction with teaching quality is exceptional. It narrowly edges West London (83.9%) into second place. The universities rank =65th and =77th respectively overall, hampered in part by poor graduate employment records under our criteria; West London's 55.6% being the lowest of all.

Roehampton ranks third for satisfaction with teaching quality (82.7%) and tops our second NSS-derived ranking for satisfaction with the wider student experience. St Mary's Twickenham ranks fourth and second for the two satisfaction measures respectively. Swansea, ranked 21st overall for law, is one of just two universities towards the top end of the table to perform very strongly for student satisfaction, placing fifth for satisfaction with teaching quality and fourth for student experience. Glasgow Caledonian (25th overall) ranks fifth for satisfaction with student experience.

Applications are buoyant with 147,490 chasing the 29,105 places available last year. Both applications and places were up once again on the previous year.

Law	Teaching quality	Student experience	Research quality	Entry standards (UCAS points)	Graduate prospects	Overall score
1 Cambridge	—	—	58.7%	198	95.5%	100.0
2 London School of Economics	77.9%	68.1%	64.5%	180	94.9%	98.6
3 University College London	73.1%	71.8%	57.7%	201	89.8%	96.8
4 Oxford	—	—	51.8%	197	91.7%	95.8
5 Glasgow	71.6%	71.1%	33.8%	225	87.6%	94.0
6 Durham	—	—	32.8%	192	87.4%	93.7
7 King's College London	73.3%	67.1%	39.2%	207	84.0%	92.5
8 Strathclyde	74.8%	73.0%	29.4%	207	78.1%	90.4
9 Warwick	72.9%	71.9%	41.9%	163	84.1%	90.2
10 Leeds	74.0%	72.4%	40.1%	167	82.4%	90.1
=11 Edinburgh	64.9%	59.2%	40.8%	207	84.7%	89.9

=11	Aberdeen	76.1%	75.6%	20.9%	195	81.6%	89.9
13	York	74.8%	72.5%	30.3%	167	82.8%	89.0
14	Bristol	66.2%	55.1%	50.5%	174	83.9%	88.7
15	Nottingham	71.1%	65.1%	45.2%	157	81.0%	88.2
=16	Queen's Belfast	68.8%	60.7%	40.3%	156	87.4%	88.1
=16	Kent	77.4%	73.7%	43.9%	137	77.0%	88.1
18	Stirling	77.7%	74.4%	19.4%	176	77.9%	87.5
19	Dundee	70.2%	68.0%	16.3%	186	85.9%	87.4
20	Lancaster	73.8%	65.2%	38.9%	138	82.6%	87.0
21	Swansea	80.4%	75.8%	20.4%	133	82.9%	86.8
22	Sheffield	68.3%	66.3%	31.9%	150	84.0%	86.0
23	Queen Mary, London	68.2%	64.2%	23.7%	172	83.1%	85.8
24	Ulster	76.8%	68.9%	48.5%	131	68.5%	85.3
25	Glasgow Caledonian	75.2%	75.7%	1.8%	197	74.7%	85.0
26	Birmingham	64.3%	63.7%	33.6%	155	82.4%	84.9
27	East Anglia	74.4%	70.6%	26.5%	136	78.6%	84.7
28	Leicester	—	—	26.4%	133	81.2%	84.6
29	Southampton	77.3%	68.4%	18.2%	145	78.5%	84.5
30	Exeter	67.3%	63.4%	21.4%	156	84.5%	84.4
31	Manchester	63.9%	55.6%	27.2%	162	83.2%	83.7
32	Newcastle	69.9%	57.4%	25.4%	149	81.1%	83.6
33	Portsmouth	72.9%	67.2%	32.2%	119	78.2%	83.5
34	Buckingham	79.9%	73.5%	—	109	88.3%	83.2
35	Surrey	73.8%	71.2%	8.5%	125	84.8%	82.9
=36	Keele	72.5%	65.7%	30.5%	111	79.0%	82.7
=36	Edinburgh Napier	78.1%	74.1%	—	163	74.2%	82.7
38	Cardiff	63.2%	57.9%	27.2%	150	81.9%	82.5
=39	Aston	73.3%	67.6%	19.7%	128	77.7%	82.3
=39	Reading	71.5%	67.0%	31.2%	123	74.6%	82.3
41	Robert Gordon	75.1%	68.6%	3.9%	164	73.8%	82.0
42	Royal Holloway, London	68.2%	64.6%	—	124	93.2%	81.7
43	Liverpool	66.0%	61.0%	19.6%	140	79.0%	80.9
44	SOAS, London	67.4%	64.6%	26.7%	145	70.7%	80.8
45	South Wales	78.4%	72.6%	—	110	79.5%	80.4
46	Bangor	72.8%	71.6%	12.0%	122	75.2%	80.3
47	Abertay	73.7%	67.6%	1.2%	148	—	80.1
48	Edge Hill	75.8%	73.0%	12.1%	118	70.9%	79.8
=49	Salford	73.6%	69.9%	5.9%	117	77.5%	79.7
=49	Plymouth	79.3%	70.5%	16.0%	111	68.1%	79.7
=51	London Metropolitan	75.9%	72.1%	0.3%	94	82.0%	79.3
=51	Hull	72.0%	70.2%	12.6%	122	72.1%	79.3
53	Sussex	66.3%	60.7%	23.3%	130	73.1%	79.2
54	Lincoln	70.2%	67.8%	5.0%	112	79.2%	78.6
=55	Northumbria	69.0%	63.1%	2.5%	132	76.8%	78.2
=55	Bedfordshire	76.7%	72.1%	3.6%	107	71.9%	78.2
57	Essex	64.2%	63.0%	31.6%	110	70.4%	78.1

Law cont.

		Teaching quality	Student experience	Research quality	Entry standards (UCAS points)	Graduate prospects	Overall score
58	Greenwich	71.0%	62.4%	2.1%	109	80.6%	78.0
59	Sheffield Hallam	72.0%	61.1%	14.4%	105	73.9%	77.8
60	Manchester Metropolitan	69.6%	66.0%	14.9%	115	69.0%	77.2
=61	Chester	69.7%	59.4%	—	110	79.3%	76.7
=61	City	63.3%	60.4%	9.1%	134	73.4%	76.7
63	London South Bank	77.7%	67.2%	20.1%	98	60.1%	76.5
64	St Mary's, Twickenham	82.2%	77.8%	—	86	65.5%	76.4
=65	Oxford Brookes	67.0%	60.7%	5.1%	98	79.6%	76.2
=65	Sunderland	84.1%	70.4%	0.7%	100	62.5%	76.2
=67	Aberystwyth	67.4%	64.4%	14.3%	97	72.7%	76.1
=67	Staffordshire	74.7%	70.9%	—	104	69.5%	76.1
=67	Derby	77.0%	67.0%	2.4%	120	63.6%	76.1
=67	Bradford	78.4%	72.8%	11.8%	111	56.9%	76.1
71	Gloucestershire	75.4%	66.7%	—	103	69.6%	75.8
=72	Nottingham Trent	70.6%	62.6%	2.3%	113	71.5%	75.7
=72	Roehampton	82.7%	78.3%	—	92	60.7%	75.7
74	Anglia Ruskin	69.7%	63.2%	5.2%	90	74.8%	75.3
75	Leeds Beckett	72.7%	69.9%	—	100	69.3%	75.2
76	West of England	67.1%	61.7%	3.5%	109	73.1%	75.1
=77	Westminster	68.3%	62.3%	7.5%	110	69.2%	75.0
=77	West London	83.9%	77.5%	—	99	55.6%	75.0
=79	Teesside	68.8%	60.5%	15.0%	102	66.5%	74.8
=79	Central Lancashire	70.2%	65.5%	5.3%	122	63.6%	74.8
81	Birmingham City	65.2%	63.3%	2.8%	111	72.1%	74.6
82	Hertfordshire	67.7%	63.3%	—	95	75.3%	74.5
83	Liverpool John Moores	60.3%	51.8%	2.7%	129	75.0%	74.1
=84	Huddersfield	64.9%	58.3%	—	120	71.4%	73.9
=84	Kingston	72.5%	67.7%	—	95	66.9%	73.9
86	Winchester	63.1%	53.9%	—	101	78.5%	73.6
87	De Montfort	66.4%	62.0%	5.2%	92	69.9%	73.1
88	Coventry	67.2%	62.6%	5.6%	103	65.0%	72.9
89	West of Scotland	69.3%	67.8%	—	115	59.0%	72.3
90	Middlesex	66.0%	63.2%	21.4%	93	57.3%	72.2
91	Wolverhampton	72.3%	66.8%	2.7%	93	57.4%	71.4
92	Bournemouth	54.7%	48.2%	8.8%	99	75.3%	71.2
93	Brighton	56.8%	46.6%	6.5%	98	75.3%	71.1
94	Northampton	57.9%	52.4%	—	101	74.3%	71.0
95	Brunel	51.5%	46.9%	20.3%	115	67.3%	70.9
=96	Liverpool Hope	62.6%	52.9%	—	106	66.7%	70.5
=96	East London	63.9%	55.1%	8.6%	92	63.3%	70.5
98	Canterbury Christ Church	66.3%	54.7%	3.2%	89	63.9%	70.1
99	Solent, Southampton	49.9%	44.7%	—	97	67.4%	66.0

Employed in high-skilled job	44%	
Employed in high-skilled job and studying	7%	
Studying	15%	
High skilled work (median) salary	£22,000	

Employed in lower-skilled job	23%	
Employed in lower-skilled job and studying	2%	
Unemployed	9%	
Low/medium skilled salary	£19,800	

Liberal Arts and Humanities

Warwick – our University of the Year for Teaching Quality – helps launch our inaugural Liberal Arts and Humanities table in pole position. Formerly the preserve of American universities, liberal arts programmes are a growing area in UK higher education and elsewhere globally. UCAS registered a 14% increase in student numbers on liberal arts courses in 2020 and a 10% rise in applications. Interdisciplinary by design, degrees encompass the arts, humanities and social sciences and provide undergraduates with opportunities to hone their analysis, communication and critical thinking skills. As students progress through the degree they begin to specialise in areas of particular interest.

Warwick has the most satisfied students in the subject by a clear margin, having scored an exceptionally high 96.6% in the sections of the National Student Survey relating to teaching quality, and 91.8% for the wider experience. Fifth-place Leeds finishes second in each of these student-led measures. For research, Warwick is out in front once again, followed by University College London (UCL) – where students averaged the highest entry standards in 2020. In a generally high tariff subject, only Royal Holloway and Essex averaged fewer than 144 UCAS points (equivalent to AAA at A-level).

The best-employed graduates were from UCL at the time of the most recent Graduate Outcomes survey, with 88.4% employed in professional-level jobs or postgraduate study 15 months after their degrees. Career paths include roles in the media, communications, PR, politics and art galleries.

Liberal Arts and Humanities	Teaching quality	Student experience	Research quality	Entry standards (UCAS points)	Graduate prospects	Overall score
1 Warwick	96.6%	91.8%	52.9%	156	—	100.0
2 University College London	75.3%	71.1%	48.7%	194	88.4%	99.3
3 King's College London	68.0%	57.8%	45.7%	184	75.2%	91.3
4 Exeter	73.8%	68.6%	42.7%	163	80.9%	91.0
5 Leeds	86.8%	78.1%	38.3%	181	—	90.3
6 Birmingham	74.9%	73.5%	41.8%	173	73.5%	90.2
7 Royal Holloway	77.2%	67.9%	44.5%	127	70.9%	86.5
=8 Nottingham	80.3%	65.8%	42.0%	151	—	86.1
=8 Bristol	66.3%	49.6%	38.6%	170	76.7%	86.1
10 Dundee	78.2%	74.8%	36.3%	174	63.7%	85.9
11 East Anglia	—	—	39.2%	144	68.2%	84.1
12 Essex	68.2%	60.7%	38.1%	111	70.7%	79.7

Linguistics

Aberdeen has taken the lead in our Linguistics table, with Oxford – formerly the regular incumbent at the top – settling for fourth place this year. Aberdeen performs strongly across the measures in our ranking without coming first in any individually. Its students gave some of the most positive feedback for both teaching quality and the wider undergraduate experience in the National Student Survey (NSS), and the university ranks in the top six for research and for entry standards. University College London (UCL) has also improved its ranking, rising from eighth place to sit second, boosted by achieving the top scores for each of the student satisfaction measures.

Edinburgh received the best results in the Research Excellence Framework while the highest entry standards in 2020's admissions round were at Cambridge, where students averaged 212 UCAS tariff points, ahead of Oxford's 189.

Linguistics analyses how language is put together and how it functions, involving its form and meaning as well as how it works in context. The degree can lead to careers in speech therapy, or in the growing field of teaching English as a foreign language. Almost 70 universities are offering linguistics in 2022–23 and both applications and enrolments in the subject have remained stable across the past decade, but without attracting huge numbers.

Jobs-wise, linguistics ties with archaeology and forensic science at 53rd in our employment ranking. A fairly high proportion (17%) were in postgraduate study 15 months after their course, 37% were working in high-skilled jobs and 3% were juggling both. But 11% were unemployed, 30% were in "low-skilled" jobs and 2% were in such jobs and studying.

Linguistics	Teaching quality	Student experience	Research quality	Entry standards (UCAS points)	Graduate prospects	Overall score
1 Aberdeen	84.7%	80.1%	46.3%	178	—	100.0
2 University College London	86.2%	83.2%	43.7%	165	73.2%	97.8
3 Warwick	84.7%	76.6%	45.2%	154	—	96.5
4 Oxford	—	—	41.3%	189	—	96.4
5 Cambridge	—	—	54.0%	212	85.7%	96.3
6 Edinburgh	71.8%	65.6%	57.7%	182	71.3%	95.8
7 Durham	82.0%	66.2%	34.6%	—	82.3%	94.5
8 King's College London	77.4%	74.2%	42.1%	159	75.6%	94.3
9 Southampton	83.8%	78.1%	42.7%	—	65.9%	93.3
10 Lancaster	76.4%	70.4%	47.0%	139	76.1%	93.0
11 Sheffield	78.0%	76.7%	42.2%	138	—	91.7
12 Leeds	78.9%	74.1%	30.6%	141	76.7%	91.2
13 Manchester	74.5%	65.8%	48.9%	163	61.1%	90.6
14 Kent	82.4%	76.1%	41.9%	118	68.3%	90.5
15 York	75.9%	74.3%	37.3%	141	66.9%	89.2
16 Newcastle	73.5%	66.4%	36.3%	156	64.4%	88.1
17 Queen Mary, London	76.3%	71.8%	50.3%	122	58.7%	88.0
18 Huddersfield	81.5%	65.9%	29.9%	109	—	84.7
19 Swansea	81.0%	73.9%	22.8%	115	—	84.6
20 Cardiff	71.6%	66.9%	35.1%	122	—	84.3

21 Reading	70.8%	69.7%	25.8%	123	66.7%	83.6
=22 Bangor	73.7%	64.9%	39.6%	103	61.3%	83.5
=22 Essex	69.6%	68.1%	36.0%	117	—	83.5
24 West of England	80.9%	80.8%	9.5%	117	—	82.2
25 Roehampton	80.4%	69.9%	21.8%	94*	—	81.2
26 Hertfordshire	83.2%	71.3%	—	100*	58.1%	77.7
27 Nottingham Trent	77.6%	68.7%	10.0%	101	56.3%	77.5
28 Manchester Metropolitan	69.3%	61.9%	29.0%	112	46.4%	76.8
29 York St John	70.1%	61.4%	9.7%	100	61.8%	76.1
30 Ulster	60.2%	61.2%	22.4%	116	50.0%	74.3
31 Brighton	67.3%	48.5%	16.2%	90	—	71.5

Employed in high-skilled job	37%	Employed in lower-skilled job	30%
Employed in high-skilled job and studying	3%	Employed in lower-skilled job and studying	2%
Studying	17%	Unemployed	11%
High skilled work (median) salary	£24,000	Low/medium skilled salary	£19,000

Materials Technology

The Oxbridge universities share first place in our Materials Technology table, Oxford having closed the gap on Cambridge. Both have high entry standards, though the 221 UCAS tariff points averaged by entrants to the Cambridge course in 2020 eclipsed the 207 averaged at Oxford. But the best-employed graduates were from Oxford, at the time of the most recent Graduate Outcomes survey, which found 100% to be in professional employment and/or postgraduate study 15 months after finishing their degrees.

Courses in this table cover four distinct areas: materials science, mining engineering, textiles technology and printing, and marine technology. These highly specialised subjects attract relatively small student numbers. The prominent research-led universities require maths and physics at A-level, or equivalent, for entry and high grades are the norm.

The hard work pays off jobs-wise, with materials technology graduates commanding £27,500 starting salaries on average in professional jobs – earning the subjects 16th place in our salaries ranking. They place 19th in our employment index, with 78.6% of graduates in high-skilled jobs and/or further study; of these 22% were pursuing postgraduate study – among the higher proportions of the 67 subjects in our jobs table.

Materials Technology	Teaching quality	Student experience	Research quality	Entry standards (UCAS points)	Graduate prospects	Overall score
=1 Oxford	90.0%	87.3%	70.8%	207	100.0%	100.0
=1 Cambridge	—	—	78.3%	221	—	100.0
3 Imperial College London	73.2%	78.7%	62.3%	177	92.0%	90.4
4 Loughborough	86.9%	87.6%	41.8%	152	88.9%	88.7
5 Sheffield	77.1%	78.6%	41.0%	157	94.2%	87.6
6 Exeter	85.8%	85.6%	36.4%	144	—	86.5

	Teaching quality	Student experience	Research quality	Entry standards (UCAS points)	Graduate prospects	Overall score
7 Birmingham	78.8%	79.5%	49.3%	144	87.7%	86.3
8 Swansea	83.3%	82.1%	45.5%	122	76.6%	82.3
9 Manchester	68.4%	69.2%	36.4%	151	76.6%	79.0
10 Queen Mary, London	61.9%	66.3%	40.0%	139	76.0%	76.9
11 Huddersfield	76.2%	62.0%	10.2%	137	—	75.9
12 Sheffield Hallam	71.7%	65.0%	17.8%	96*	—	72.4

Employed in high-skilled job	53%	Employed in lower-skilled job	12%
Employed in high-skilled job and studying	3%	Employed in lower-skilled job and studying	0%
Studying	22%	Unemployed	9%
High skilled work (median) salary	£27,500	Low/medium skilled salary	—

Mathematics

Maths experienced an upsurge in both applications and enrolments in the 2020 admissions cycle, making up for its dip in demand the year before. It also attracted some exceptionally well-qualified students – nine universities averaged more than 200 UCAS tariff points among their intakes, four of them 210 or more, led by St Andrews with a staggering 241.

But it is Oxford that takes the overall lead in our table this year, swapping with Cambridge. Oxford has the top-rated research, and with 94.7% of its maths graduates in high-skilled jobs or postgraduate study 15 months on from their degrees it also comes top for graduate prospects. QS puts Cambridge and Oxford fourth and fifth respectively in its world ranking for maths.

The best rates of student satisfaction are spread more widely, with Stirling (seventh in the main table) leading for both teaching quality and the wider experience – measures that are derived from the National Student Survey. South Wales (26th overall) is second for teaching quality and Aberystwyth, (=35th), is second for the wider experience.

The leading universities will usually look for extra maths as well as maths at A-level, or equivalent. Courses tend to combine pure and applied maths, but some universities allow for specialisation in one or the other.

Maths adds up to a promising career for most. Average starting salaries of £28,000 for high-skilled jobs rank the subject 13th out of 67, while it is comfortably inside the top 20 of our employment index, with 78.9% of graduates in professional employment or postgraduate study 15 months after finishing their degrees.

Mathematics	Teaching quality	Student experience	Research quality	Entry standards (UCAS points)	Graduate prospects	Overall score
1 Oxford	87.7%	79.0%	67.5%	208	94.7%	100.0
2 Cambridge	—	—	60.7%	221	93.9%	97.4
3 St Andrews	85.9%	84.4%	44.2%	241	86.4%	96.3

4	Imperial College London	81.3%	82.3%	59.7%	204	87.0%	95.4
5	Warwick	76.7%	73.6%	55.8%	201	88.6%	93.2
6	Durham	74.1%	72.2%	44.0%	204	90.2%	91.5
7	Stirling	94.7%	94.9%	14.0%	177	—	91.4
8	Heriot-Watt	79.1%	75.3%	42.3%	188	88.0%	91.0
9	University College London	73.6%	73.3%	42.0%	184	91.0%	90.2
10	Bristol	74.7%	69.7%	57.3%	175	84.5%	89.8
11	Glasgow	75.2%	72.8%	41.4%	210	80.9%	89.0
12	Bath	75.3%	73.4%	35.7%	185	88.0%	88.9
13	Strathclyde	75.2%	75.0%	34.6%	202	83.2%	88.4
14	Lancaster	78.2%	77.5%	45.8%	156	82.4%	87.9
15	Edinburgh	71.0%	68.7%	43.7%	210	79.1%	87.5
16	Loughborough	83.3%	84.6%	31.0%	157	80.8%	87.2
17	Manchester	68.8%	63.5%	44.3%	178	86.9%	86.9
18	King's College London	—	—	37.1%	173	80.2%	86.8
19	Nottingham	71.5%	67.6%	44.8%	172	83.1%	86.5
20	London School of Economics	69.2%	61.9%	28.7%	172	92.2%	85.8
21	Southampton	74.2%	71.0%	41.9%	162	80.6%	85.7
22	Exeter	74.6%	71.5%	37.9%	152	82.2%	85.1
23	Surrey	78.4%	77.1%	31.5%	138	82.8%	85.0
24	York	80.0%	74.5%	27.0%	150	82.1%	84.9
25	Birmingham	73.4%	71.3%	34.1%	166	81.2%	84.8
26	South Wales	88.8%	74.9%	10.1%	99	92.7%	84.5
27	East Anglia	71.1%	72.0%	33.7%	138	86.5%	84.3
28	Aberdeen	70.6%	74.1%	32.0%	166	—	84.2
29	Liverpool	78.3%	77.7%	29.8%	141	78.1%	83.5
=30	Queen's Belfast	70.4%	64.6%	25.0%	163	84.9%	83.1
=30	Northumbria	81.2%	79.5%	16.7%	136	81.3%	83.1
=30	Dundee	66.5%	64.2%	48.2%	186	71.7%	83.1
=33	Reading	76.2%	63.1%	35.3%	122	81.2%	82.1
=33	Leeds	64.0%	61.5%	42.0%	161	79.0%	82.1
=35	Kent	77.5%	73.9%	28.2%	126	77.5%	81.7
=35	Aberystwyth	85.8%	85.0%	19.4%	132	70.7%	81.7
37	Lincoln	81.8%	80.4%	—	117	87.1%	81.5
=38	Aston	70.8%	68.0%	21.7%	113	87.5%	80.9
=38	Sheffield	66.7%	64.2%	34.0%	141	80.1%	80.9
=40	Leicester	65.8%	63.1%	25.0%	128	86.8%	80.5
=40	Cardiff	63.6%	62.2%	31.6%	141	83.2%	80.5
=40	Royal Holloway, London	75.0%	71.7%	35.5%	132	71.2%	80.5
43	Wolverhampton	87.4%	82.2%	—	101	81.5%	80.3
44	Central Lancashire	76.4%	71.7%	19.8%	129	—	80.2
45	Keele	81.7%	80.2%	19.5%	117	71.9%	79.8
46	Queen Mary, London	69.4%	69.3%	30.3%	138	74.5%	79.6
=47	Newcastle	65.6%	64.9%	32.0%	139	77.2%	79.5
=47	Swansea	76.8%	71.0%	20.7%	139	72.7%	79.5
49	Plymouth	78.9%	73.6%	9.3%	130	77.3%	79.4

		Teaching quality	Student experience	Research quality	Entry standards (UCAS points)	Graduate prospects	Overall score
50	Derby	82.2%	75.6%	5.0%	118	78.3%	79.3
51	Liverpool John Moores	79.8%	78.1%	3.2%	122	78.0%	78.9
52	Coventry	78.6%	74.7%	9.4%	107	78.9%	78.6
=53	Nottingham Trent	73.7%	69.6%	18.4%	108	78.3%	78.1
=53	City	70.6%	71.2%	30.2%	111	73.2%	78.1
55	Hull	79.7%	70.3%	24.2%	114	69.4%	78.0
56	Greenwich	82.2%	75.9%	5.1%	99	77.1%	77.9
=57	Brighton	72.3%	69.5%	6.4%	100	79.4%	76.0
=57	Salford	71.7%	72.1%	4.4%	129	—	76.0
59	West of England	78.5%	76.1%	10.6%	110	67.6%	75.7
60	Liverpool Hope	75.8%	66.1%	8.8%	106	—	75.3
61	Sheffield Hallam	66.8%	63.5%	17.8%	101	77.1%	75.2
62	Chester	65.3%	61.9%	7.1%	120	79.5%	75.1
63	Manchester Metropolitan	78.6%	73.0%	5.6%	114	66.7%	74.6
64	Sussex	67.2%	65.8%	28.5%	138	60.9%	74.5
65	Portsmouth	74.9%	68.1%	11.2%	100	70.3%	74.4
66	Hertfordshire	76.7%	69.4%	20.2%	91	65.6%	74.3
67	Kingston	76.8%	73.1%	—	73	77.1%	74.1
68	Essex	60.8%	60.1%	34.3%	118	64.7%	73.3
69	Brunel	57.5%	53.8%	25.8%	108	70.2%	71.8

Employed in high-skilled job	57%	Employed in lower-skilled job	13%
Employed in high-skilled job and studying	7%	Employed in lower-skilled job and studying	1%
Studying	14%	Unemployed	8%
High skilled work (median) salary	£28,000	Low/medium skilled salary	£20,500

Mechanical Engineering

Cambridge and Imperial have shared the top spot in our Mechanical Engineering table previously and there is little between them this year, second-placed Imperial having closed the gap on Cambridge. The top research rating and highest entry standards secure Cambridge's lead, while Imperial – winner of our University of the Year award – scores well across all measures, including student satisfaction, without topping any. The remainder of the top ten features a reshuffle of last year's incumbents – except for Aberdeen, which has risen 19 places to sit 10th.

Robert Gordon is the leading post-1992 university, in 27th position. London South Bank, another modern institution in 39th place, is top on both measures of student satisfaction: teaching quality and the wider undergraduate experience for the third successive year, a remarkable achievement. Imperial College London and Bath – in third place overall – also do well in these areas. Entry standards vary greatly, three universities averaged more than 200 UCAS tariff points among their 2020 intake of students and seven averaged less than 100.

Mechanical engineering is the most in demand strand of engineering by some distance.

Applications and enrolments increased in 2020 and student numbers have stayed consistently buoyant across the past decade. There is stability careers-wise too; with graduates in professional jobs commanding £28,000 salaries mechanical engineering ranks 12th for pay (above civil engineering and bioengineering but behind the other strands of the discipline). It sits a respectable 23rd in our employment ranking – although this is a decline from 18th last year.

Mechanical Engineering	Teaching quality	Student experience	Research quality	Entry standards (UCAS points)	Graduate prospects	Overall score
1 Cambridge	—	—	67.0%	230	94.9%	100.0
2 Imperial College London	81.7%	82.2%	59.6%	216	92.5%	98.7
3 Bath	80.1%	82.7%	37.4%	184	95.3%	93.2
4 Strathclyde	68.8%	75.1%	37.2%	214	89.5%	90.8
=5 Southampton	72.7%	69.7%	52.3%	168	90.7%	90.1
=5 Bristol	70.3%	71.1%	52.3%	183	87.8%	90.1
7 Loughborough	78.6%	80.8%	41.8%	151	89.9%	89.4
8 Leeds	70.7%	70.6%	40.9%	180	88.4%	88.3
9 Sheffield	78.2%	81.3%	36.0%	157	86.5%	87.9
10 Aberdeen	76.6%	76.8%	28.4%	182	84.3%	87.3
11 Edinburgh	57.6%	61.1%	50.3%	187	90.8%	87.2
12 Heriot-Watt	67.6%	72.7%	47.8%	169	79.8%	85.9
13 Glasgow	63.4%	68.1%	47.2%	198	76.0%	85.6
=14 Lancaster	72.0%	70.7%	41.6%	140	88.1%	85.5
=14 University College London	64.6%	65.4%	44.6%	184	81.3%	85.5
16 Queen's Belfast	68.8%	71.4%	36.7%	146	89.6%	85.0
=17 Exeter	66.9%	66.6%	36.4%	152	89.6%	84.5
=17 Swansea	75.5%	73.9%	45.5%	129	81.3%	84.5
19 Manchester	67.9%	68.1%	35.1%	168	82.3%	84.0
20 Liverpool	76.3%	79.8%	32.1%	136	80.9%	83.7
21 Birmingham	67.1%	67.2%	37.7%	151	84.5%	83.4
22 Nottingham	66.2%	66.1%	40.8%	144	83.7%	82.8
23 Ulster	72.6%	69.8%	22.8%	126	92.4%	82.7
24 Cardiff	65.0%	68.7%	30.2%	140	83.0%	80.8
=25 Sussex	66.2%	72.0%	24.0%	132	86.4%	80.7
=25 Surrey	69.6%	73.9%	30.8%	128	80.3%	80.7
27 Robert Gordon	74.4%	74.6%	8.8%	143	83.9%	80.5
28 Queen Mary, London	58.0%	65.3%	46.7%	135	76.5%	79.4
29 Aston	70.5%	66.4%	20.6%	132	80.5%	78.8
30 Dundee	54.3%	53.0%	34.1%	175	76.6%	78.5
31 Hull	75.6%	72.9%	16.5%	114	79.6%	78.3
=32 Coventry	75.3%	76.2%	10.3%	117	79.9%	78.0
=32 Northumbria	64.7%	58.1%	30.7%	136	78.3%	78.0
34 Solent, Southampton	81.3%	75.9%	—	126*	78.0%	77.8
35 Newcastle	57.3%	56.0%	30.2%	131	85.3%	77.7
36 Liverpool John Moores	76.7%	76.5%	4.7%	125	78.2%	77.6

Mechanical Engineering cont.

		Teaching quality	Student experience	Research quality	Entry standards (UCAS points)	Graduate prospects	Overall score
37	Huddersfield	76.6%	74.9%	10.2%	103	81.6%	77.4
38	Teesside	79.6%	78.5%	5.8%	120	74.6%	77.3
39	London South Bank	88.5%	84.8%	19.6%	109	59.6%	77.0
40	Harper Adams	79.0%	79.5%	—	116	77.5%	76.8
41	Greenwich	72.0%	69.1%	29.5%	116	69.4%	76.6
42	Plymouth	71.2%	67.4%	15.7%	122	76.4%	76.5
43	West of Scotland	80.9%	79.9%	9.0%	128*	63.6%	75.9
44	Wales Trinity St David	86.9%	76.3%	1.0%	121*	64.6%	75.2
45	Derby	73.7%	70.9%	6.7%	114	75.4%	75.1
46	Sheffield Hallam	62.5%	56.6%	17.8%	112	83.5%	75.0
47	Lincoln	71.4%	73.9%	—	111	80.0%	74.9
48	West of England	65.6%	59.9%	10.6%	136	73.7%	74.1
49	Portsmouth	66.9%	65.7%	9.1%	110	78.5%	74.0
=50	Manchester Metropolitan	67.5%	64.4%	16.3%	125	69.4%	73.9
=50	Chester	74.3%	71.6%	7.1%	103*	—	73.9
=52	Birmingham City	69.4%	62.8%	—	116	79.1%	73.5
=52	Glasgow Caledonian	69.6%	69.1%	4.7%	150	63.9%	73.5
54	Sunderland	82.3%	79.0%	8.8%	98*	62.5%	73.4
55	De Montfort	70.1%	71.0%	12.5%	98	72.3%	73.2
56	Brunel	56.8%	53.5%	23.7%	131	71.8%	72.7
57	Bradford	65.9%	67.1%	7.7%	114	71.4%	72.2
58	Oxford Brookes	59.5%	60.8%	13.9%	93	80.9%	72.0
59	Hertfordshire	63.3%	61.0%	16.5%	93	75.2%	71.7
60	Brighton	67.2%	64.3%	7.4%	94	71.6%	70.6
61	Salford	58.9%	64.4%	4.4%	138	66.3%	70.4
62	Staffordshire	81.6%	75.9%	5.7%	101	51.3%	69.7
63	Central Lancashire	62.5%	59.0%	7.1%	99	72.1%	69.5
64	Bournemouth	58.9%	62.0%	8.5%	106	—	68.9
65	Northampton	66.5%	71.2%	4.1%	72	—	67.9
66	City	47.6%	50.9%	23.1%	110	65.6%	67.2
67	Kingston	73.0%	67.0%	2.9%	103	51.8%	66.8
68	Anglia Ruskin	50.3%	53.2%	9.1%	107*	—	65.6

Employed in high-skilled job	64%	Employed in lower-skilled job	14%
Employed in high-skilled job and studying	3%	Employed in lower-skilled job and studying	0%
Studying	8%	Unemployed	10%
High skilled work (median) salary	£28,000	Low/medium skilled salary	£23,000

Medicine

The pandemic has triggered a boom in the numbers wanting to study medicine. The number of applicants has soared 21% from 23,720 in 2020 – the year on which our rankings are based – to 28,690 for courses starting in 2021. The NHS has never been more highly valued by the public and its central role in fighting the coronavirus has polished its careers appeal for school-leavers. Overall, the numbers wanting to study medicine are up 49% since 2017.

The surge in applications has coincided with the opening of several new medical schools since 2019 at Sunderland, Lincoln, Edge Hill, Kent/Canterbury Christ Church and Anglia Ruskin. However, even this expansion has not been enough to meet demand for places. A matter of days before A-level results were published in 2021, as medical schools faced the risk of serious over-recruitment, the government lifted the cap on numbers at those schools that could cope with extra capacity, increasing places from 7,500 in 2020 to about 9,000. To reduce the pressure, some medical schools offered students £10,000 and a year of free accommodation to defer entry until 2022, or to switch to medical schools with more space.

While part of that pressure comes from the increased application rate, the rest comes from two years without A-level exams, leading to a sharp rise in the number of top grades achieved by school-leavers. The entry standards measure in our ranking is dominated by Scottish institutions. Dundee (which ranks equal seventh in the overall table) and Aberdeen (equal tenth) come top with an average of 241 UCAS points gained by entrants, followed by Glasgow with 237 points, Edinburgh with 227 and St Andrews with 213.

Oxford, which has topped the medicine ranking for the past decade, is comfortably No 1 again, well clear of Glasgow, which retains second place.

Medicine is unique among our 70 subjects for offering a guarantee of employment at the end of the course, unless unusually, a medicine graduate elects to do something other than go straight to work or study. Five medical schools – Aberdeen, Brighton and Sussex, Cardiff, Lancaster and Sheffield – report 100% graduate employment, and St Andrews, with the lowest rate, still reports 95.7% of medicine graduates in high-skilled jobs or further study after 15 months. The consistency of graduate prospects means we do not use the measure to help calculate our rankings to avoid small differences distorting positions (although the percentages are shown for guidance).

In such a compressed ranking, with just six medical schools scoring less than 80 points overall, success in the other four metrics is spread around. Brighton and Sussex, ranked equal tenth overall, leads both measures derived from the National Student Survey (NSS), tracking student satisfaction with teaching quality and the wider student experience. Its scores for both exceed 90% – remarkable in a year of considerable disruption on campuses nationwide – and perhaps reflecting the role final-year medical students felt able to play at a time of crisis in the NHS. Bristol is second; Keele is third; St Andrews fourth and Leicester is fifth for teaching quality. Brighton and Sussex also topped the rankings for teaching quality in 2020.

The research element in our medicine ranking is more important than in some subjects, given the higher proportion of medical graduates who pursue research as a career. New ratings are due to be published in spring 2022, but for now we rely on the outcomes of the 2014 Research Excellence Framework. Using the *Good University Guide* methodology, looking at both quality and quantity of world-leading and internationally excellent research, Lancaster comes out on top with a score of 55.2%, narrowly ahead of Imperial College London (54.6%). Three more universities clear the 50% threshold: University College London, Cambridge and Keele.

Medicine

		Teaching quality	Student experience	Research quality	Entry standards (UCAS points)	Graduate prospects	Overall score
1	Oxford	—	—	48.9%	207	99.2%	100.0
2	Glasgow	82.3%	79.9%	42.3%	237	98.2%	96.6
3	Edinburgh	75.9%	73.5%	49.8%	227	99.1%	94.2
4	Imperial College London	80.8%	84.0%	54.6%	191	98.7%	94.1
5	Bristol	87.9%	85.3%	47.5%	181	99.2%	93.3
6	Keele	86.4%	83.7%	50.0%	172	99.3%	91.8
=7	Cambridge	—	—	52.0%	212	98.1%	90.5
=7	Dundee	79.9%	79.9%	25.1%	241	96.4%	90.5
9	Queen Mary, London	81.0%	80.6%	40.2%	195	98.8%	89.3
=10	Aberdeen	81.8%	76.6%	20.2%	241	100.0%	89.1
=10	Brighton and Sussex Medical School	91.8%	90.9%	34.3%	167	100.0%	89.1
12	Swansea	80.6%	71.6%	44.7%	—	98.7%	89.0
13	St Andrews	85.9%	87.4%	19.8%	213	95.7%	88.3
14	Exeter	81.2%	79.4%	41.6%	185	99.0%	88.2
15	Lancaster	79.1%	74.3%	55.2%	161	100.0%	87.7
16	University College London	71.6%	69.2%	53.3%	188	97.2%	87.2
17	Newcastle	80.3%	74.2%	44.8%	174	99.1%	86.5
=18	Cardiff	77.5%	77.1%	34.5%	187	100.0%	84.4
=18	Leicester	83.8%	83.5%	33.3%	166	99.6%	84.4
20	Leeds	81.9%	76.6%	32.1%	181	98.4%	84.3
21	East Anglia	82.7%	84.1%	31.8%	168	98.8%	83.8
=22	Queen's Belfast	77.5%	74.1%	34.6%	185	99.1%	83.7
=22	King's College London	72.6%	67.7%	48.3%	174	98.9%	83.7
24	Liverpool	81.1%	82.1%	31.7%	169	99.7%	83.0
25	Southampton	76.6%	76.8%	35.6%	166	99.6%	81.3
26	Sheffield	76.6%	70.0%	36.5%	171	100.0%	81.2
27	Warwick	81.4%	75.1%	26.2%	—	98.9%	81.1
28	Hull-York Medical School	78.9%	74.5%	36.2%	158	99.4%	80.8
29	Manchester	70.8%	64.7%	34.6%	180	98.4%	78.8
30	Plymouth	76.8%	79.9%	23.1%	165	98.9%	77.5
31	Birmingham	69.9%	68.3%	31.5%	174	98.6%	77.2
32	Nottingham	65.7%	55.5%	36.8%	165	99.4%	74.0
33	St George's, London	65.3%	60.2%	22.4%	176	99.3%	71.4
34	Central Lancashire	72.0%	67.3%	8.3%	129	—	63.5

Employed in high-skilled job	89%	Employed in lower-skilled job	0%
Employed in high-skilled job and studying	7%	Employed in lower-skilled job and studying	—
Studying	3%	Unemployed	0%
High skilled work (median) salary	£35,000	Low/medium skilled salary	—

Middle Eastern and African Studies

The small student numbers on Middle Eastern and African Studies courses make for big swings in the statistics and plenty of movement in our table. Only Oxford, Edinburgh and SOAS inhabit the same ranks this year as last. St Andrews returns to first position from third, Cambridge drops to second and Durham has risen from fifth to third place.

Students at St Andrews expressed the greatest satisfaction with teaching quality and the wider undergraduate experience in the National Student Survey (NSS). Birmingham also received positive feedback from its students and holds the top research ratings. Led by Cambridge with 200 UCAS tariff points, entry standards are high, only Birmingham and Westminster average less than 144 points, equivalent to AAA at A-level. Our table gains an extra university this year in 11th place, Warwick.

Student numbers on single honours degrees are tiny and continuing to decline; 50 undergraduates began Middle Eastern studies courses in 2020 and none enrolled on single honours African studies degrees. But modules from courses in this grouping will have been taken by many as part of broader degrees. The subjects are afforded some official protection because they are of national importance and considered vulnerable.

Graduate prospects scores are often absent because student cohorts are insufficient to meet the response threshold for our employment ranking. However, the subjects tie with social work in 28th place of our jobs table. They do better in our earnings ranking – placing ninth out of 67 subject areas, with graduates in high-skilled jobs commanding £29,000 salaries, on average.

Middle Eastern and African Studies	Teaching quality	Student experience	Research quality	Entry standards (UCAS points)	Graduate prospects	Overall score
1 St Andrews	85.7%	86.1%	46.7%	187*	—	100.0
2 Cambridge	—	—	45.0%	200	—	96.5
3 Durham	79.0%	72.7%	34.6%	196	—	95.3
4 Birmingham	81.4%	78.8%	50.9%	138*	—	95.0
5 Exeter	77.8%	73.1%	36.0%	145	—	90.8
6 Manchester	71.9%	60.8%	48.9%	152	72.1%	90.6
7 Oxford	—	—	36.2%	189	—	89.4
=8 Edinburgh	70.4%	62.6%	30.1%	160	—	88.3
=8 Leeds	72.3%	64.6%	30.6%	151	—	88.3
10 SOAS, London	58.7%	52.6%	26.3%	145	78.2%	87.1
11 Warwick	81.9%	71.2%	—	165	72.2%	85.4
12 Westminster	69.3%	61.6%	11.3%	96	—	78.0

Employed in high-skilled job	54%	Employed in lower-skilled job	13%
Employed in high-skilled job and studying	5%	Employed in lower-skilled job and studying	1%
Studying	14%	Unemployed	13%
High skilled work (median) salary	£29,000	Low/medium skilled salary	—

Music

Durham's strength in undergraduate music provision remains the most eminent this year. The university is a regular at the top of our table, buoyed by convincing performances across all measures without leading in any individually. Of the six specialist institutions, the Royal Conservatoire of Scotland and the Royal Academy of Music perform best, sitting 20th in the table. Entry standards tip over the 200 UCAS tariff point mark at Glasgow and Edinburgh, while third-ranked Southampton achieves the top research ratings.

As in many of our subject tables, the best rates of student satisfaction are found at post-1992 universities further down the rankings – in music's case at East London (46th), where students regarded the teaching quality more highly than those at any other university, and at Edinburgh Napier (15th), which was top for the wider undergraduate experience.

Reflecting music's many contrasting genres, courses vary in style and content – from the practical and vocational programmes in conservatoires to the more theoretical degrees in older universities, via sonic arts, creative sound design and everything in between.

Music ranks above the other performing arts in our employment table, although it is still in the bottom 15, with nearly three in ten graduates employed in work classed as "low-skilled" 15 months after finishing their degrees and one in ten unemployed. Postgraduate study accounts for only 8% but 49% were in graduate-level occupations when surveyed – a respectable proportion compared with other subjects. Music places in the bottom five in the earnings table, however.

Music	Teaching quality	Student experience	Research quality	Entry standards (UCAS points)	Graduate prospects	Overall score
1 Durham	86.7%	76.3%	64.9%	198	78.6%	100.0
2 Cambridge	84.0%	73.1%	48.0%	191	90.0%	98.6
3 Southampton	85.5%	84.4%	70.7%	170	78.7%	98.4
4 Oxford	79.3%	67.5%	66.3%	187	83.8%	97.9
5 Royal Holloway, London	82.7%	75.3%	55.0%	172	89.6%	97.4
6 Glasgow	83.6%	77.1%	46.0%	203	76.4%	96.3
7 Edinburgh	69.3%	62.2%	48.0%	202	84.6%	94.3
8 Manchester	71.6%	64.1%	56.3%	196	74.6%	93.0
9 Leeds	80.6%	75.2%	44.2%	179	75.2%	92.2
10 Sheffield	79.0%	74.5%	60.0%	161	72.6%	91.7
11 Bristol	80.9%	69.4%	48.0%	163	77.4%	91.2
12 Birmingham	69.1%	60.5%	50.7%	174	81.0%	90.5
13 Cardiff	82.9%	82.5%	47.0%	153	71.2%	89.9
14 Nottingham	76.1%	66.0%	55.4%	136	77.2%	87.8
15 Edinburgh Napier	89.1%	87.8%	—	188	69.8%	87.7
16 Aberdeen	80.4%	72.7%	32.0%	172	68.5%	87.5
17 York	80.5%	75.3%	37.1%	150	71.2%	86.8
18 King's College London	72.6%	66.8%	43.5%	157	73.0%	86.7
19 Bangor	82.3%	75.2%	24.7%	126	85.2%	86.1
=20 Royal Conservatoire of Scotland	70.8%	66.7%	11.3%	165	88.5%	85.9
=20 Royal Academy of Music	79.5%	75.1%	23.9%	128	86.8%	85.9

=22	Goldsmiths, London	72.9%	56.8%	51.1%	136	77.7%	85.7
=22	Surrey	80.8%	76.7%	27.2%	150	72.6%	85.7
24	Newcastle	70.8%	62.1%	40.8%	155	72.6%	85.0
25	Guildhall School of Music and Drama	78.5%	75.2%	12.7%	141	84.6%	84.9
26	Sussex	82.9%	71.0%	30.2%	138	71.9%	84.6
27	Birmingham City	86.0%	74.2%	11.6%	138	78.4%	84.2
28	Liverpool	83.1%	73.5%	31.4%	155	59.4%	83.8
29	City	73.8%	65.2%	34.0%	149	—	83.7
30	Ulster	74.7%	72.8%	40.0%	117	77.0%	83.6
31	Trinity Laban	78.2%	69.0%	28.7%	122	79.6%	83.4
32	Plymouth	90.5%	83.2%	20.2%	117	—	82.9
33	Salford	78.7%	69.7%	7.2%	145	78.8%	82.4
34	Royal Northern College of Music	70.7%	73.3%	12.3%	129	84.6%	81.7
35	Royal College of Music	84.5%	80.5%	10.9%	122	74.7%	81.6
36	Oxford Brookes	83.9%	80.2%	30.2%	106	—	81.1
37	Huddersfield	76.2%	69.0%	28.0%	122	69.1%	80.1
38	Bedfordshire	86.0%	79.2%	5.6%	128	—	79.6
39	Westminster	74.3%	70.7%	22.5%	127	66.7%	79.0
40	Queen's Belfast	51.9%	50.7%	38.3%	149	72.6%	78.9
41	Hull	82.6%	77.8%	11.2%	125	65.2%	78.8
42	Sunderland	82.9%	74.6%	4.2%	—	66.7%	78.5
43	Derby	85.9%	80.5%	6.7%	116	—	78.2
=44	South Wales	80.8%	74.4%	6.4%	124	66.9%	77.8
=44	Manchester Metropolitan	86.1%	76.6%	7.5%	—	59.3%	77.8
46	East London	91.2%	83.1%	11.2%	123	52.2%	77.6
=47	Chichester	79.8%	75.1%	9.7%	136	58.9%	77.5
=47	Coventry	76.7%	76.8%	18.1%	115	—	77.5
49	Chester	85.7%	72.1%	4.3%	140	53.4%	76.5
50	Hertfordshire	84.2%	73.5%	5.3%	109	65.7%	76.2
51	York St John	87.1%	78.7%	10.5%	104	60.0%	76.1
52	West of Scotland	72.2%	57.0%	11.3%	147	59.5%	75.7
53	De Montfort	77.5%	67.2%	14.5%	118	61.5%	75.6
=54	Leeds Conservatoire	76.4%	66.9%	—	137	62.7%	75.5
=54	Bath Spa	79.2%	73.2%	10.7%	117	60.7%	75.5
=56	Gloucestershire	81.4%	70.7%	—	126	61.9%	75.4
=56	West of England	86.1%	77.6%	—	112	61.7%	75.4
=56	Wolverhampton	83.0%	75.6%	—	121	60.6%	75.4
59	London South Bank	82.8%	64.6%	12.8%	107	—	75.2
=60	Greenwich	79.2%	66.0%	—	134	60.2%	74.9
=60	Lincoln	81.5%	67.0%	6.5%	114	—	74.9
62	Brunel	62.5%	60.5%	32.6%	116	—	74.6
63	Middlesex	70.4%	65.2%	16.1%	96	72.1%	74.4
64	Leeds Beckett	73.8%	61.9%	1.7%	111	71.1%	73.9
65	Bournemouth	73.5%	52.6%	15.0%	104	68.6%	73.7
66	Winchester	81.1%	73.8%	11.2%	119	50.0%	73.6
=67	Kingston	69.0%	53.6%	—	119	70.8%	72.7

Music cont.	Teaching quality	Student experience	Research quality	Entry standards (UCAS points)	Graduate prospects	Overall score
=67 Canterbury Christ Church	74.2%	60.6%	15.2%	98	64.0%	72.7
69 West London	68.1%	60.7%	2.3%	127	62.1%	72.3
70 Falmouth	79.1%	72.5%	6.2%	105	52.5%	71.3
71 Liverpool Hope	66.2%	56.2%	15.5%	115	56.3%	70.6
=72 Kent	39.5%	37.1%	44.3%	119	63.6%	70.2
=72 Central Lancashire	67.0%	58.8%	3.9%	123	56.6%	70.2
74 Brighton	67.1%	51.4%	13.1%	108	—	69.4
75 Solent, Southampton	71.3%	65.7%	—	111	51.5%	68.5
76 Anglia Ruskin	54.4%	48.2%	16.9%	112*	54.9%	66.9
77 Staffordshire	70.1%	63.7%	—	121	34.6%	64.8
78 Cumbria	61.1%	52.0%	—	116	45.8%	64.1
79 Edge Hill	52.0%	53.7%	3.8%	131	42.1%	63.8
80 Plymouth Marjon	43.1%	34.4%	—	120	58.1%	62.4

Employed in high-skilled job	49%	Employed in lower-skilled job	29%
Employed in high-skilled job and studying	4%	Employed in lower-skilled job and studying	1%
Studying	8%	Unemployed	10%
High skilled work (median) salary	£21,493	Low/medium skilled salary	£18,000

Natural Sciences

One of three new subject rankings to join our *Guide* this year, the inaugural Natural Sciences table has a clear winner in Cambridge – which was by far the top scorer in the Research Excellence Framework and where entrants averaged 221 UCAS points in 2020. Cambridge's natural sciences graduates were also the best employed when surveyed 15 months after their degrees, with almost nine in ten working in professional-level jobs or engaged in postgraduate research.

Runner-up York has the best rates of student satisfaction with teaching quality and the second-highest scores for the broad undergraduate experience, but it is Loughborough that does best on this measure. For research University College London (UCL) finishes second to Cambridge. Entry standards are high almost throughout the table, with all but one university (London Metropolitan) averaging over 148 UCAS points – where 144 points is equivalent to AAA at A-level.

Natural sciences degrees give students the benefit of studying across different disciplines as well as the flexibility to specialise in areas of specific interest as programmes progress. The subject's interdisciplinary approach should provide graduates with a breadth of knowledge and practical skills that will stand them in good stead for future careers in industry or for postgraduate research. Some universities offer the opportunity to transfer to a single science after a year, if a student decides their interests lie in a particular direction.

All universities in our table that we have employment data for did well; none achieving lower than London Met's 76.1% of graduates in high-skilled professions or furthering their studies while the majority scored over 80% in this measure. Natural Sciences is not yet in our subject-by-subject employment or salaries rankings.

Natural Sciences	Teaching quality	Student experience	Research quality	Entry standards (UCAS points)	Graduate prospects	Overall score
1 Cambridge	—	—	58.5%	221	89.8%	100.0
2 York	85.6%	81.4%	41.3%	185	82.5%	89.0
3 Exeter	85.3%	81.4%	41.2%	173	82.1%	87.8
4 University College London	66.2%	61.6%	52.3%	179	86.1%	86.5
5 Bath	73.1%	73.7%	40.0%	186	83.3%	85.8
6 Durham	76.3%	70.6%	42.5%	206	—	84.7
7 Lancaster	82.3%	76.5%	45.4%	165	—	83.7
8 Birmingham	76.4%	77.5%	38.1%	148	78.5%	82.1
9 Loughborough	84.2%	86.6%	21.7%	164	80.1%	82.0
10 East Anglia	63.9%	60.3%	39.0%	166	78.9%	79.9
11 Nottingham	77.2%	72.9%	36.1%	174	—	79.8
12 Leeds	67.9%	60.7%	40.3%	180	—	77.9
13 London Metropolitan	76.2%	77.7%	—	104	76.1%	68.5

Nursing

More than any other subject, nursing has experienced a boom in applications off the back of the pandemic. A gentle rise in the number of applicants in 2020 from 42,820 to 45,430 became a torrent in the following 12 months. When UCAS published its applicant data for the intake due to start courses in September 2021, numbers had surged to 60,130, a rise of 32% and a new high.

The subject's growing popularity among school-leavers has contributed to the uplift. School-age applicant numbers are up 27% this year to 16,560 as the pandemic has highlighted the central place the National Health Service has in the tapestry of British life.

Edinburgh and Glasgow top the nursing rankings for the third successive year, the Scottish rivals well clear of their closest competitors. Their dominance comes from high performance in each of the measures that make up our subject ranking.

Elsewhere, our top five has experienced something of a shake-up with Southampton rising from 17th place last year to sit third. It tops our research measure in the subject. Surrey and Cardiff move up to fourth and fifth, having been eighth and seventh respectively last year. Queen Margaret, York and Manchester drop out of the top five this year, although all remain in the nursing top 20.

In other subject rankings, it is often the modern universities that lead scores for student satisfaction with teaching quality and the wider university experience, but in nursing there is a healthy mix of Russell Group and modern universities succeeding in these areas. Based on the outcomes of the National Student Survey (NSS), Glasgow comes top for satisfaction with teaching quality with fellow Russell Group members Liverpool and Edinburgh fourth and fifth. Edinburgh's achievement is particularly noteworthy, as it remains a serial underperformer in the annual NSS more generally, ranking =120th this year for satisfaction with teaching quality across all subjects.

The modern university sector is represented by Scottish universities again; Queen Margaret, Edinburgh and Edinburgh Napier ranking second and third for teaching quality and =15th and 14th respectively for nursing overall. Celtic institutions more widely monopolise the top of the ratings for student experience, with a top five split entirely between Scotland (Queen Margaret, Glasgow and Edinburgh Napier) and Northern Ireland (Ulster and Queen's Belfast).

The surge in interest in nursing has carried applications beyond the levels last seen when bursaries were available for students. With the scrapping of bursaries in favour of loans in 2017 (bringing nursing students in line with others), applications dropped around 30% across two years, though enrolments remained steady.

There is a near-guarantee of employment on graduation. With the exception of nursing students at Bolton, where curiously just 69.9% go into high-skilled jobs or postgraduate study, a minimum of 92.2% achieve this outcome. Three universities – Liverpool, Queen Margaret and Essex – record a perfect score, 11 having done so in our previous edition.

Nursing	Teaching quality	Student experience	Research quality	Entry standards (UCAS points)	Graduate prospects	Overall score
1 Edinburgh	84.3%	79.7%	53.4%	189	—	100.0
2 Glasgow	89.9%	83.7%	42.3%	211	92.3%	96.3
3 Southampton	79.7%	70.9%	65.7%	147	97.4%	92.6
4 Surrey	77.7%	74.8%	37.5%	149	99.3%	90.7
5 Cardiff	73.4%	61.2%	36.8%	171	98.1%	90.5
6 Liverpool	84.4%	78.1%	35.3%	129	100.0%	90.2
=7 Manchester	70.2%	61.4%	57.1%	144	98.2%	89.6
=7 York	78.7%	74.2%	40.2%	138	98.1%	89.6
=9 Ulster	84.1%	83.2%	27.7%	133	98.0%	89.3
=9 Queen's Belfast	81.7%	80.3%	34.7%	133	97.7%	89.3
11 Bangor	75.4%	62.6%	34.7%	148	98.8%	89.0
12 Keele	80.1%	73.6%	20.9%	141	98.9%	88.4
13 Swansea	76.5%	68.7%	14.5%	159	97.2%	87.7
14 Edinburgh Napier	85.8%	82.1%	5.3%	133	99.0%	87.6
=15 Queen Margaret, Edinburgh	87.2%	84.7%	1.5%	122	100.0%	87.0
=15 Leeds	67.4%	59.9%	31.7%	148	98.5%	87.0
17 King's College London	69.0%	59.1%	34.6%	140	98.5%	86.8
18 Nottingham	70.8%	60.0%	31.4%	137	98.8%	86.7
19 Derby	78.2%	71.0%	7.3%	141	98.9%	86.6
=20 Hull	72.6%	63.3%	16.7%	142	99.7%	86.4
=20 Stirling	71.7%	65.5%	34.1%	129	98.1%	86.4
22 East Anglia	72.9%	63.4%	24.9%	131	99.4%	86.3
23 Dundee	77.3%	72.3%	22.1%	127	97.6%	86.2
24 Bradford	78.8%	70.5%	9.5%	139	97.4%	86.0
25 City	79.5%	71.6%	20.5%	139	94.2%	85.9
=26 Plymouth	76.1%	68.6%	9.5%	142	97.7%	85.8
=26 Birmingham	67.8%	56.4%	37.0%	145	95.4%	85.8
28 Lincoln	71.8%	62.7%	22.6%	135	98.2%	85.7
29 Coventry	80.1%	74.7%	4.5%	132	97.9%	85.6
=30 Manchester Metropolitan	73.7%	63.4%	12.0%	135	99.5%	85.5
=30 Northumbria	73.6%	64.8%	14.0%	141	97.5%	85.5

32	West of Scotland	72.5%	61.7%	29.0%	142	94.1%	85.3
33	Robert Gordon	81.1%	76.1%	4.9%	127	96.1%	84.7
34	West London	83.2%	78.2%	2.5%	140	92.3%	84.5
35	Glasgow Caledonian	68.6%	67.4%	8.1%	137	98.6%	84.4
=36	Essex	81.8%	74.2%	—	110	100.0%	84.2
=36	Northampton	74.2%	64.8%	1.6%	138	97.9%	84.2
38	Kingston/St George's, London	79.3%	71.9%	2.6%	124	97.1%	84.0
39	South Wales	69.3%	59.5%	2.2%	148	97.5%	83.9
40	Greenwich	82.4%	74.0%	2.2%	107	98.5%	83.7
41	Liverpool John Moores	69.2%	62.9%	6.0%	150	95.0%	83.6
=42	Staffordshire	77.3%	66.5%	—	121	98.9%	83.5
=42	Bedfordshire	69.7%	58.5%	25.1%	120	97.2%	83.5
44	Portsmouth	65.3%	59.6%	24.3%	129	96.8%	83.4
45	East London	79.8%	70.2%	7.6%	115	—	83.2
=46	Birmingham City	74.0%	65.3%	1.5%	129	97.0%	83.1
=46	Hertfordshire	80.2%	69.7%	4.0%	112	97.0%	83.1
48	Middlesex	79.2%	73.8%	10.0%	108	96.0%	83.0
=49	Brighton	72.3%	59.7%	4.8%	125	98.3%	82.9
=49	Chester	69.3%	58.8%	12.0%	124	98.1%	82.9
=49	Wolverhampton	65.7%	55.2%	11.0%	135	97.8%	82.9
=49	Oxford Brookes	72.9%	63.8%	3.0%	127	97.4%	82.9
=49	London South Bank	73.6%	61.6%	13.7%	118	96.8%	82.9
54	West of England	68.3%	58.8%	8.2%	130	97.9%	82.8
55	Salford	67.0%	56.5%	3.8%	141	97.1%	82.7
56	Worcester	73.1%	66.3%	2.6%	120	97.7%	82.6
=57	Suffolk	75.5%	65.5%	—	118	97.9%	82.5
=57	Anglia Ruskin	72.3%	64.9%	3.1%	123	97.4%	82.5
=59	Huddersfield	59.3%	56.7%	13.2%	133	98.3%	82.2
=59	De Montfort	64.0%	58.3%	13.0%	124	98.1%	82.2
61	Bournemouth	71.1%	62.8%	4.7%	110	99.0%	81.8
62	Sheffield Hallam	64.5%	56.6%	3.7%	127	98.9%	81.7
=63	Canterbury Christ Church	69.2%	55.7%	2.2%	126	97.3%	81.5
=63	Sunderland	69.0%	63.2%	7.5%	126	—	81.5
65	Teesside	66.4%	55.6%	2.4%	124	98.1%	81.3
66	Roehampton	74.1%	72.4%	20.6%	91	—	81.1
67	Edge Hill	69.2%	61.2%	2.0%	139	92.2%	80.9
68	Cumbria	68.4%	61.4%	0.7%	127	94.8%	80.7
69	Leeds Beckett	66.4%	59.6%	3.5%	121	96.3%	80.6
70	Central Lancashire	59.5%	51.4%	8.3%	140	94.8%	80.5
71	Buckinghamshire New	75.0%	68.4%	1.0%	104	94.2%	79.9
72	Bolton	79.1%	74.5%	—	147	69.9%	74.6

Employed in high-skilled job	94%	Employed in lower-skilled job	2%
Employed in high-skilled job and studying	3%	Employed in lower-skilled job and studying	0%
Studying	1%	Unemployed	1%
High skilled work (median) salary	£24,500	Low/medium skilled salary	£20,400

Pharmacology and Pharmacy

Strathclyde has taken over from Cambridge at the head our Pharmacology and Pharmacy table. The Scottish university averaged the highest entry standards in 2020 and is in the top five for research and top ten for graduate prospects, along with good rates of student satisfaction. Strathclyde offers degrees in all three subjects encompassed in this grouping: pharmacology – which is a branch of medicine concerned with drugs, their uses, effects and how they interact with the body; pharmacy – which trains and licenses individuals to dispense prescription medicines – and toxicology, which is similar to pharmacology but focuses on the toxic rather than healing properties of venoms, poisons and drugs.

The disciplines of pharmacology and pharmacy lead to separate careers. Most English universities offer only one or the other, and courses are evenly split among institutions. The four-year MPharm degree is a direct route to professional registration as a pharmacist and the most popular option, or students can study three-year degrees in pharmaceutical science or as part of a broader degree. Pharmacology is available as a three-year BSc or as an extended course.

Solid career prospects await graduates. The subjects rank third in our earnings table, after dentistry and medicine, with average starting salaries of £31,040 in professional-level jobs. The latest data showed 85.7% of graduates were in high-skilled jobs and/or postgraduate study 15 months after finishing their degrees.

Students at 17th-ranked Sussex were the most satisfied with teaching quality on their courses, results of the National Student Survey (NSS) showed, giving an exceptionally high 95.4% score. Ulster did best on the NSS sections relating to the wider undergraduate experience and also scored over 90% for teaching quality.

Pharmacology and Pharmacy	Teaching quality	Student experience	Research quality	Entry standards (UCAS points)	Graduate prospects	Overall score
1 Strathclyde	74.0%	78.7%	52.2%	223	93.5%	100.0
2 Dundee	76.5%	72.1%	55.4%	201*	—	99.6
3 Queen's Belfast	82.8%	86.5%	60.0%	153	98.2%	99.5
4 Ulster	91.5%	91.8%	42.5%	143	96.7%	98.4
5 Nottingham	81.0%	80.8%	51.2%	146	95.7%	96.2
6 Bath	80.9%	88.7%	56.2%	140	92.4%	95.8
7 Queen Mary, London	86.3%	86.7%	40.2%	143	—	95.3
8 Cardiff	80.4%	79.5%	36.8%	157	95.2%	94.9
9 University College London	78.9%	78.1%	51.3%	157	86.1%	93.0
10 Manchester	72.2%	70.6%	57.1%	151	89.9%	92.5
11 Queen Margaret, Edinburgh	89.7%	80.2%	1.5%	—	96.2%	92.3
=12 East Anglia	81.5%	75.3%	38.1%	126	94.7%	92.2
=12 Robert Gordon	79.7%	75.4%	4.9%	192	91.9%	92.2
14 Glasgow	72.5%	80.0%	33.4%	194	82.9%	91.6
15 King's College London	77.8%	74.0%	46.8%	145	86.5%	91.1
16 Newcastle	80.2%	71.5%	47.8%	137	86.7%	90.8
17 Sussex	95.4%	85.0%	8.0%	125*	—	90.6
18 Keele	80.6%	82.6%	20.9%	136	90.8%	90.2

19 Birmingham	81.4%	79.9%	19.2%	132	90.3%	89.4
20 Sunderland	78.7%	78.8%	7.5%	129	96.6%	89.3
21 Aberdeen	85.5%	81.0%	34.7%	151	77.4%	89.1
22 Leeds	70.2%	61.1%	40.9%	149	86.7%	88.1
23 Reading	71.1%	68.7%	34.2%	119	92.5%	87.8
24 Bristol	80.3%	75.9%	47.0%	149	73.7%	87.6
25 Huddersfield	73.8%	73.3%	13.2%	130	93.3%	87.4
=26 Liverpool	73.4%	67.0%	31.7%	148	84.1%	87.1
=26 Swansea	62.2%	71.5%	44.7%	137	—	87.1
28 Bradford	79.9%	78.2%	9.5%	135	87.2%	87.0
29 Westminster	82.6%	74.3%	21.2%	112	—	86.6
30 Glasgow Caledonian	71.7%	73.0%	8.1%	158	87.0%	86.4
31 Liverpool John Moores	74.0%	70.2%	6.0%	133	91.9%	86.1
=32 Lincoln	63.9%	61.3%	22.6%	123	94.9%	85.4
=32 De Montfort	74.8%	74.0%	13.0%	106	92.2%	85.4
34 Portsmouth	77.2%	76.9%	24.3%	102	85.0%	84.7
35 Aston	70.3%	69.7%	39.1%	115	82.3%	84.4
36 Kingston	79.4%	78.9%	2.6%	113	84.6%	83.4
37 Nottingham Trent	73.6%	70.6%	24.1%	102	—	83.2
38 Greenwich	81.2%	72.4%	2.7%	119	83.0%	83.1
39 Hertfordshire	80.3%	80.0%	10.9%	109	79.0%	82.4
40 Brighton	69.5%	68.9%	4.8%	116	87.9%	82.2
41 St George's, London	64.1%	58.8%	20.0%	117	—	80.1
42 East London	76.3%	70.0%	7.6%	88	—	79.7
43 Wolverhampton	67.6%	61.0%	11.0%	119	79.5%	79.1
44 Central Lancashire	62.1%	62.9%	8.3%	136	79.0%	79.0
45 Chester	69.0%	60.3%	12.0%	102*	—	78.8

Employed in high-skilled job	68%	Employed in lower-skilled job	6%
Employed in high-skilled job and studying	7%	Employed in lower-skilled job and studying	0%
Studying	10%	Unemployed	9%
High skilled work (median) salary	£31,040	Low/medium skilled salary	£20,000

Philosophy

Does God exist? Is what we see just an illusion? Are there such things as right and wrong? Students of philosophy confront big questions on topics that include ethics, metaphysics and the mind, examining the arguments of great thinkers and expressing their own ideas. In 2022, 83 universities and colleges offered more than 1,400 courses in philosophy – as single honours degrees and as part of joint honours courses.

St Andrews holds on to the lead in our table that it took last year, buoyed by good rates of student satisfaction and the second-highest entry standards. The London School of Economics (LSE) is up four places to rank second. It has the best-employed philosophy graduates – with only 6.3% failing to have secured professional-level jobs or postgraduate study 15 months after their degrees.

Oxford – which continues to boycott the National Student Survey – takes third place, with the top score for research and the highest entry standards; it was the only university to average over 200 UCAS points among its 2020 intake. Relatively few philosophy undergraduates took the subject at A-level, and some departments actively discourage it. Degrees involve more maths skills than many candidates expect, especially when the syllabus has an emphasis on logic.

Gloucestershire, in =22nd place overall, outdoes all others for student satisfaction for both teaching quality and the wider undergraduate experience. West of England, which achieved the same feat in our previous edition, ranks second in these measures.

Starting salaries of £25,000 for professional-level jobs or £19,000 in work deemed "medium-skilled", rank philosophy 30th in our pay table. The subject sits in the lower half of our jobs ranking however, tying with Iberian Languages in 43rd place, with 65.7% of graduates in high-skilled jobs or furthering their studies when surveyed 15 months after their degrees.

Philosophy	Teaching quality	Student experience	Research quality	Entry standards (UCAS points)	Graduate prospects	Overall score
1 St Andrews	82.3%	78.8%	52.7%	198	—	100.0
2 London School of Economics	80.6%	74.6%	48.6%	184	93.7%	99.6
3 Oxford	—	—	61.3%	201	87.0%	98.5
4 Warwick	81.8%	76.7%	47.7%	171	80.8%	95.4
5 Cambridge	—	—	51.6%	197	75.7%	94.9
6 King's College London	75.0%	67.9%	53.9%	175	82.4%	94.5
7 University College London	70.2%	62.4%	55.6%	178	81.4%	93.1
8 Dundee	83.5%	72.7%	27.7%	172	—	91.2
9 Durham	70.5%	62.7%	30.1%	183	86.4%	90.7
10 Birmingham	75.6%	64.5%	52.8%	144	77.7%	90.4
11 Sheffield	81.4%	76.6%	48.3%	146	68.6%	90.1
12 Edinburgh	69.4%	59.0%	49.7%	168	78.7%	90.0
13 Lancaster	75.4%	66.6%	53.0%	140	76.0%	89.9
14 Royal Holloway, London	83.7%	75.4%	30.5%	125	81.2%	89.4
15 Bristol	72.5%	59.6%	40.9%	160	79.1%	88.9
16 Exeter	70.9%	66.8%	41.0%	162	75.6%	88.5
17 Newcastle	70.9%	53.2%	54.3%	131	81.3%	88.2
18 Sussex	78.6%	72.4%	34.2%	131	72.8%	86.6
19 Aberdeen	68.7%	60.2%	39.1%	165	—	86.4
20 York	75.7%	67.2%	30.7%	139	76.3%	86.3
21 Southampton	80.0%	75.6%	31.7%	139	66.9%	86.0
=22 Glasgow	76.7%	74.7%	18.9%	166	68.2%	85.5
=22 Gloucestershire	95.7%	87.2%	6.9%	103*	—	85.5
24 Hertfordshire	84.7%	72.4%	32.9%	97	—	84.8
25 Reading	75.2%	67.9%	28.6%	118	76.3%	84.3
26 Leeds	67.8%	61.9%	39.5%	151	67.2%	83.8
27 West of England	90.6%	83.3%	18.6%	107	63.2%	83.6

28 Queen's Belfast	66.1%	59.0%	40.3%	143	—	83.3
=29 Nottingham	72.4%	59.3%	28.2%	134	73.4%	83.1
=29 Manchester	68.1%	57.5%	31.9%	160	68.0%	83.1
31 Essex	69.8%	63.0%	44.0%	109	70.7%	82.7
32 Liverpool	71.5%	63.9%	28.4%	130	71.1%	82.5
33 Kent	79.4%	73.4%	31.0%	108	63.5%	82.0
34 Cardiff	70.1%	64.1%	36.3%	128	66.2%	81.9
35 Stirling	74.0%	67.2%	22.7%	129	—	81.7
36 East Anglia	70.0%	59.4%	28.6%	123	67.2%	80.0
37 Oxford Brookes	82.5%	71.9%	8.4%	98	65.4%	78.6
38 Brighton	82.6%	66.1%	13.1%	100*	63.3%	78.4
39 Keele	77.3%	71.1%	23.7%	109	56.6%	78.3
40 Nottingham Trent	81.6%	65.1%	10.0%	115	54.2%	76.3
41 Hull	70.3%	64.3%	10.5%	114	—	75.8
42 Manchester Metropolitan	69.4%	56.2%	12.5%	104	61.2%	73.7

Employed in high-skilled job	44%	Employed in lower-skilled job	23%
Employed in high-skilled job and studying	4%	Employed in lower-skilled job and studying	1%
Studying	16%	Unemployed	11%
High skilled work (median) salary	£25,000	Low/medium skilled salary	£19,000

Physics and Astronomy

Physicists and astronomers from Galileo to Marie Curie, Albert Einstein to Stephen Hawking, have helped earn the subjects a reputation for being the rarefied preserves of boffins. But application and enrolment figures have increased over the past decade, a trend credited to the "Brian Cox effect" – with the Manchester University particle physicist's popular television shows making them seem cooler and more accessible.

Even so, entry standards remain among the highest in our *Guide* – with seven universities averaging over 200 points in the UCAS tariff and only 14 out of 46 averaging less than 146 (when 144 points is equal to AAA at A-level). St Andrews has returned to the top of our table, having been limited to second place by Cambridge last year. It has the highest entry standards while also ranking second for teaching quality, as derived from the National Student Survey (NSS).

Cambridge leads on research ratings. Third-placed Oxford has the best-employed graduates with more than 96% in professional-level work and/or postgraduate study 15 months on from their degrees. Leicester outdoes all others for student satisfaction, topping both NSS-derived measures: teaching quality and the wider undergraduate experience.

The subjects translate into positive job and salary outcomes. Fifty per cent of graduates were working in professional-level jobs 15 months after their degrees, the latest data shows, 28% had stayed on to study further and 3% were combining both – only 12 subjects do better in our employment ranking. They sit 14th for salaries.

Physics and Astronomy

		Teaching quality	Student experience	Research quality	Entry standards (UCAS points)	Graduate prospects	Overall score
1	St Andrews	88.0%	85.2%	51.0%	223	89.6%	100.0
2	Cambridge	—	—	55.7%	221	—	98.9
3	Oxford	76.7%	68.5%	52.1%	214	96.2%	97.2
4	Durham	81.4%	74.9%	46.2%	210	89.5%	95.8
5	Edinburgh	70.5%	67.1%	48.7%	209	94.7%	94.3
6	Warwick	81.0%	75.0%	46.1%	185	89.2%	94.1
7	Imperial College London	66.2%	65.1%	49.6%	213	92.7%	92.9
8	Heriot-Watt	84.5%	88.2%	44.1%	165	80.8%	92.3
9	Lancaster	84.5%	76.6%	37.6%	161	88.6%	91.9
10	Leicester	89.7%	89.9%	40.8%	133	83.1%	91.8
11	Glasgow	74.3%	75.0%	42.0%	212	81.7%	91.4
12	Manchester	71.6%	66.0%	44.9%	192	89.8%	91.3
=13	Surrey	83.0%	80.3%	39.6%	138	88.7%	90.9
=13	Queen's Belfast	78.6%	75.3%	44.4%	166	84.7%	90.9
=15	Birmingham	74.0%	74.4%	33.8%	187	90.6%	90.7
=15	University College London	71.6%	73.4%	45.1%	169	89.4%	90.7
17	York	80.6%	77.4%	35.8%	153	89.8%	90.6
18	Nottingham	78.4%	74.8%	48.3%	164	81.3%	90.4
19	Bath	73.9%	76.9%	40.0%	173	85.8%	89.9
20	Aberdeen	79.2%	86.7%	32.0%	164	—	89.8
21	Strathclyde	76.1%	72.1%	45.3%	187	77.2%	89.3
22	Dundee	80.7%	70.8%	34.1%	171	—	89.1
23	Southampton	75.2%	70.5%	44.1%	150	86.5%	89.0
24	Bristol	72.7%	67.5%	43.7%	171	83.2%	88.5
25	Cardiff	77.6%	76.6%	34.9%	151	85.3%	88.3
26	Leeds	74.8%	71.8%	41.8%	158	82.8%	88.2
27	Sheffield	78.9%	74.7%	36.8%	147	83.5%	88.0
28	Swansea	85.3%	80.9%	33.0%	138	77.0%	87.1
29	Exeter	69.7%	66.4%	42.4%	168	81.9%	86.9
30	Sussex	78.8%	73.0%	24.7%	146	85.8%	86.3
31	Royal Holloway, London	73.7%	67.1%	31.5%	139	86.4%	85.4
32	Loughborough	79.5%	80.0%	19.0%	146	80.5%	84.7
=33	Liverpool	69.5%	69.5%	31.5%	137	85.6%	84.4
=33	Hull	85.5%	77.6%	24.2%	110	79.9%	84.4
35	Kent	73.4%	72.6%	30.7%	126	78.8%	82.9
36	West of Scotland	76.2%	72.2%	19.1%	150	—	82.6
37	Nottingham Trent	83.2%	76.2%	20.1%	109	77.9%	82.3
38	Keele	74.4%	66.0%	31.8%	124	77.3%	82.1
39	Northumbria	77.6%	80.1%	30.7%	149	62.7%	81.6
40	King's College London	58.8%	57.5%	35.8%	157	77.6%	80.5
41	Queen Mary, London	72.1%	70.1%	27.6%	138	69.3%	79.9
42	Central Lancashire	76.7%	71.6%	19.8%	—	71.4%	79.6

43 Aberystwyth	80.2%	78.5%	12.4%	112	72.0%	79.1
44 Salford	77.1%	75.1%	4.4%	124	76.5%	78.6
45 Portsmouth	71.9%	64.4%	21.8%	97	72.5%	76.7
46 Hertfordshire	71.6%	64.3%	20.2%	95	68.9%	75.2

Employed in high-skilled job	50%	Employed in lower-skilled job	9%
Employed in high-skilled job and studying	3%	Employed in lower-skilled job and studying	0%
Studying	28%	Unemployed	9%
High skilled work (median) salary	£28,000	Low/medium skilled salary	£20,000

Physiotherapy

Our Physiotherapy table is now in its ninth year, having been extracted from the "Subjects Allied to Medicine" grouping. It is topped again by Southampton, which has the best research score and is one of 11 universities with a perfect graduate prospects score. Across all institutions, 95% of physiotherapy graduates were employed in professional-level jobs 15 months after finishing their degrees, the latest Graduate Outcomes survey data shows. A further 2% were combining such work with postgraduate study and 1% were furthering their studies full-time – adding up to the subject finishing second only to medicine in our employment table, tied with nursing. Salaries rank further down the pay index, in 34th place, with graduates earning £24,907 on average in professional roles.

Student satisfaction rates are generally high, led by Wolverhampton (=8th) for teaching quality and Robert Gordon (=2nd) for the wider experience. Liverpool, tied for second place overall, is one of seven universities to score over 90% in the sections of the National Student Survey relating to teaching quality. Led by Glasgow Caledonian with 206 points in the UCAS tariff, entry standards are also consistently strong throughout the table, with no university averaging less than 119 UCAS points. The post-1992 universities feature prominently in our physiotherapy ranking, four of them in the top ten.

Applications and enrolments increased by a clear margin in 2020, and almost 70 universities and colleges are offering physiotherapy – or a related subject such as osteopathy or chiropractic – in 2022.

Physiotherapy	Teaching quality	Student experience	Research quality	Entry standards (UCAS points)	Graduate prospects	Overall score
1 Southampton	86.5%	80.5%	65.7%	152	100.0%	100.0
=2 Liverpool	94.7%	87.5%	35.3%	152	100.0%	98.5
=2 Robert Gordon	95.8%	96.5%	4.9%	196	97.9%	98.5
4 Birmingham	68.4%	64.6%	63.7%	169	98.0%	97.4
5 Glasgow Caledonian	84.1%	83.7%	8.1%	206	96.2%	96.8
6 Cardiff	86.4%	83.8%	36.8%	162	97.0%	96.6
7 Nottingham	82.3%	72.4%	40.6%	142	100.0%	96.3
=8 Bradford	93.7%	91.0%	9.5%	145	97.1%	94.2
=8 Wolverhampton	96.3%	86.3%	11.0%	135	—	94.2
=10 Oxford Brookes	86.2%	79.3%	3.0%	142	100.0%	93.9

Physiotherapy cont.	Teaching quality	Student experience	Research quality	Entry standards (UCAS points)	Graduate prospects	Overall score
=10 Brunel	87.5%	85.5%	18.2%	130	98.7%	93.9
=12 Central Lancashire	79.2%	72.1%	8.3%	148*	100.0%	93.8
=12 Salford	88.2%	81.2%	3.8%	136	100.0%	93.8
=12 Worcester	90.2%	88.5%	2.6%	131	100.0%	93.8
15 Leeds Beckett	84.3%	81.0%	3.5%	159	97.1%	93.4
16 Brighton	84.9%	83.3%	4.8%	131	100.0%	93.3
=17 Coventry	81.3%	76.6%	4.5%	139	100.0%	93.2
=17 Manchester Metropolitan	74.8%	73.2%	12.0%	150	98.8%	93.2
19 West of England	75.4%	74.2%	8.2%	150	99.0%	93.1
20 East London	92.7%	92.6%	7.6%	142	94.7%	92.3
21 Ulster	81.2%	74.8%	27.7%	143	94.7%	92.2
22 King's College London	67.5%	61.2%	34.6%	162	94.4%	92.1
=23 Northumbria	75.0%	68.7%	14.0%	142	97.9%	92.0
=23 Plymouth	81.8%	77.7%	9.5%	148	96.0%	92.0
25 Hertfordshire	89.9%	83.4%	4.0%	122	98.1%	91.9
26 York St John	81.5%	73.9%	1.9%	142	97.7%	91.8
27 Bournemouth	94.2%	88.4%	4.7%	119	96.8%	91.5
28 Sheffield Hallam	75.0%	72.0%	3.7%	147	97.3%	91.3
29 East Anglia	69.4%	68.4%	24.9%	166	93.1%	91.2
30 Huddersfield	71.5%	60.9%	13.2%	134	98.2%	90.8
31 Teesside	64.7%	65.8%	2.4%	135	100.0%	90.7
32 Cumbria	73.4%	59.5%	0.7%	128	100.0%	90.6
33 St George's, London	72.6%	61.2%	—	155	94.8%	89.4
34 Keele	72.1%	68.3%	20.9%	151	91.5%	89.1
35 London South Bank	62.8%	45.0%	13.7%	120	—	86.3

Employed in high-skilled job	95%	Employed in lower-skilled job	2%
Employed in high-skilled job and studying	2%	Employed in lower-skilled job and studying	–
Studying	1%	Unemployed	1%
High skilled work (median) salary	£24,907	Low/medium skilled salary	–

Politics

For the third successive year St Andrews takes the No 1 spot in our Politics ranking, leading a top four that remains unchanged – save for Warwick and the London School of Economics (LSE) tieing in third place, a one-place rise for Warwick. St Andrews outdoes all other universities on student satisfaction, coming top in both measures derived from the National Student Survey, in which it achieved a remarkable 90.1% for teaching quality and 85.8% for the wider experience. The glowing reviews from students are noteworthy given that satisfaction rates are often a nagging issue for the prominent research-intensive universities such as St Andrews – which also averaged the highest entry standards in 2020.

Essex, in =16th position overall, was the top scorer in the Research Excellence Framework, while the LSE is unbeaten on graduate prospects, with 91.9% of its politics graduates employed in professional-level jobs and/or furthering their studies when the government's Graduate Outcomes survey took its census.

Taking in how governments work, political ideas, policy-making and international relations, the study of politics has grown in popularity over the past decade, attracting 20% more new students in 2021 than it did in 2011. There are 120 universities and colleges offering more than 1,700 courses in 2022, and entry standards cater for a wide range of candidates.

Salaries are promising, the £25,800 median rates earned by graduates in professional jobs ranks politics 20th out of 67 subjects. Job prospects fare less strongly in comparison to other fields, with politics placing 42nd.

Politics	Teaching quality	Student experience	Research quality	Entry standards (UCAS points)	Graduate prospects	Overall score
1 St Andrews	90.1%	85.8%	38.4%	207	81.1%	100.0
2 Oxford	—	—	61.1%	205	89.8%	97.8
=3 London School of Economics	74.9%	66.9%	54.6%	170	91.9%	96.5
=3 Warwick	81.5%	75.1%	52.7%	169	82.9%	96.5
5 Cambridge	—	—	38.2%	192	87.7%	94.0
6 University College London	66.7%	61.8%	57.0%	182	86.0%	93.6
7 Lancaster	76.0%	71.1%	53.0%	144	79.5%	92.0
8 Strathclyde	78.1%	74.2%	41.6%	194	67.6%	91.8
9 Bath	74.3%	73.9%	27.4%	156	88.9%	90.6
10 King's College London	70.5%	60.1%	29.0%	186	87.3%	90.2
11 Stirling	80.6%	69.5%	33.8%	172	72.4%	90.1
12 Durham	71.2%	60.0%	27.0%	175	89.7%	89.8
13 Aberystwyth	88.1%	82.7%	40.2%	117	67.1%	89.2
14 Sheffield	75.5%	64.0%	48.3%	150	70.1%	88.4
15 Glasgow	71.5%	65.5%	30.5%	198	70.5%	88.3
=16 York	73.8%	65.7%	36.9%	146	79.8%	88.2
=16 Essex	70.5%	64.8%	69.6%	109	71.8%	88.2
18 Edinburgh	62.5%	54.7%	44.5%	184	76.0%	87.3
19 Surrey	83.9%	80.8%	12.5%	121	82.5%	87.1
20 SOAS, London	75.7%	73.4%	30.5%	162	68.3%	87.0
21 Exeter	70.9%	65.4%	29.8%	154	80.0%	86.9
=22 Aston	74.9%	70.8%	38.6%	113	79.1%	86.7
=22 Nottingham	74.5%	64.2%	30.8%	145	78.1%	86.7
24 Bristol	69.8%	56.5%	30.4%	167	79.7%	86.6
25 Aberdeen	76.1%	71.7%	18.4%	174	69.5%	86.0
26 Chichester	89.6%	79.9%	15.8%	106*	—	85.7
27 Cardiff	74.0%	64.4%	30.4%	134	77.6%	85.6
28 Leeds	72.9%	65.1%	25.1%	154	75.7%	85.5
29 Loughborough	79.1%	76.6%	22.5%	136	69.0%	85.0
30 Manchester	68.0%	57.4%	28.4%	157	77.4%	84.6

Politics cont.

	Teaching quality	Student experience	Research quality	Entry standards (UCAS points)	Graduate prospects	Overall score
31 Queen's Belfast	69.7%	62.9%	35.0%	138	72.2%	84.1
=32 Southampton	64.3%	58.3%	37.0%	136	78.6%	83.9
=32 Queen Mary, London	71.7%	62.3%	28.1%	142	73.2%	83.9
=32 Royal Holloway, London	75.0%	66.4%	30.5%	124	71.5%	83.9
35 East Anglia	73.9%	69.1%	35.5%	120	68.8%	83.8
36 Sussex	72.6%	65.7%	33.6%	137	67.6%	83.7
37 West of England	81.8%	77.5%	13.8%	105	73.8%	83.1
38 Keele	79.6%	74.1%	24.0%	106	69.7%	83.0
39 City	76.3%	69.3%	24.6%	115	71.5%	82.8
40 Swansea	77.7%	75.6%	18.5%	114	69.8%	82.4
41 Canterbury Christ Church	86.7%	72.8%	3.2%	84	78.8%	81.6
42 Birmingham	63.7%	53.3%	31.1%	146	72.7%	81.5
43 Coventry	81.3%	77.0%	5.6%	93	76.6%	81.2
44 East London	87.0%	76.7%	13.7%	80	—	81.1
45 Huddersfield	82.1%	75.2%	9.5%	106	—	80.9
46 Reading	66.8%	66.1%	37.0%	119	64.9%	80.8
47 Kent	71.7%	63.7%	27.8%	110	69.9%	80.7
=48 Bradford	72.7%	69.2%	12.7%	117	74.2%	80.6
=48 Newcastle	66.6%	58.1%	22.0%	139	72.2%	80.6
50 Dundee	68.6%	62.7%	10.8%	187	59.8%	80.4
51 Hull	80.4%	73.7%	10.8%	115	64.1%	80.2
52 Sheffield Hallam	83.5%	72.6%	14.4%	101	62.5%	80.1
53 Leicester	73.0%	63.7%	20.0%	119	67.5%	79.9
54 Brunel	76.7%	69.0%	32.4%	89	61.1%	79.7
55 Oxford Brookes	72.7%	60.4%	17.8%	101	74.7%	79.4
56 Ulster	85.7%	76.5%	20.9%	105	48.8%	79.2
57 Plymouth	75.3%	62.2%	25.8%	103	63.2%	79.0
58 London Metropolitan	86.9%	73.7%	1.2%	76	69.6%	78.6
59 Derby	73.8%	71.3%	13.5%	105	—	78.3
60 Portsmouth	70.3%	63.1%	32.2%	99	60.3%	77.9
61 Northumbria	71.1%	58.0%	12.7%	125	—	77.2
=62 Lincoln	76.3%	72.6%	7.7%	104	61.8%	77.1
=62 Greenwich	74.1%	73.1%	8.6%	101	—	77.1
64 Leeds Beckett	83.1%	75.6%	—	87	63.6%	77.0
65 Manchester Metropolitan	75.9%	61.2%	18.0%	111	56.1%	76.6
66 Bournemouth	70.9%	65.0%	15.1%	103	—	76.4
67 Westminster	75.2%	67.4%	14.3%	107	53.8%	75.7
68 Liverpool	67.9%	58.5%	12.0%	130	57.1%	74.9
69 De Montfort	71.1%	60.0%	10.7%	95	64.6%	74.8
70 Salford	74.7%	67.5%	4.8%	101	57.9%	74.4
71 West of Scotland	71.1%	59.4%	—	128	59.4%	74.2
=72 Nottingham Trent	76.7%	64.3%	5.1%	101	55.5%	74.1

=72 Middlesex	69.6%	59.9%	14.9%	92	—	74.1
74 Goldsmiths, London	63.9%	55.4%	16.8%	106	62.4%	73.8
75 Central Lancashire	66.3%	53.5%	12.0%	112	—	73.3
76 Chester	70.2%	57.6%	—	99	62.1%	72.1
77 Kingston	77.1%	67.7%	—	88	45.9%	70.4
78 Winchester	63.2%	52.4%	—	95	61.3%	69.2
79 Liverpool Hope	64.2%	52.4%	7.0%	107	40.0%	66.5

Employed in high-skilled job	45%	Employed in lower-skilled job	24%
Employed in high-skilled job and studying	5%	Employed in lower-skilled job and studying	1%
Studying	15%	Unemployed	10%
High skilled work (median) salary	£25,800	Low/medium skilled salary	£21,000

Psychology

Psychology remains one of the most popular subjects offered by British universities with 116 institutions represented in this year's subject ranking. Applications for admission in October 2020 hit 133,160, up 3.4% on the previous year, while the number of places available grew by nearly 2,000 to 26,200, up 7.4% year-on-year and 62% since 2012. With psychology A-level popular in sixth forms, this trend is unlikely to be reversed any time soon.

The top of the psychology table is stable this year with Oxford in first place for the sixth successive year, and the top five from last year all featuring again albeit in a different order. Bath moves up to second from fourth; University College London (UCL) stands third, up from fifth; while St Andrews drops to fourth from third, and Cambridge is down to fifth from second. Overall scores are tightly bunched so the smallest change in any of the five components that make up our ranking has an impact on standings.

The popularity of a psychology degree is not down to the career prospects or income it promises. A median starting salary of £22,500 is modest, with King's College London graduates securing the best at £27,000 and those from Derby and Solent making do with £10,000 less. While salaries don't count towards our rankings, graduate prospects do – and 14 universities have half or fewer of their psychology graduates in high-skilled jobs or postgraduate study 15 months after leaving, most of them featuring near the foot of the ranking. Just three universities – UCL, Bristol and King's College London – have more than four in five graduates in high-skilled jobs or further study.

Research outcomes show the strongest correlation with overall standings in the table. Loughborough, eighth overall, tops our research rating based on the amount of world-leading or internationally excellent work submitted to the most recent Research Excellence Framework. Its score of 62.3% puts it comfortably ahead of Oxford (58.6%) and Cambridge (57.5%) in second and third. UCL and Bath complete the research top five.

Although some of the top universities for psychology overall feature prominently in our two measures based on the National Student Survey (NSS) – for student satisfaction with teaching quality and the wider experience – several placed further down the ranking do well, led by Cumbria and Glasgow Caledonian, which rank =28th and 31st overall but take the top two places for teaching quality. Buckingham (46th) ties for second on this measure.

Among the leading universities in the table, only St Andrews makes the top five for teaching quality. These ratings are notable also for Durham's appearance in second last place. Allied with its appearance in the bottom ten for student experience, Durham drops 11 places in the overall psychology ranking this year from 12th to 23rd.

Cumbria also tops the NSS scores for student experience, narrowly ahead of Chichester. The small south coast university ranks =43rd overall for psychology. St Andrews (again) and Bath from our subject top five also make the top five for student experience.

Psychology	Teaching quality	Student experience	Research quality	Entry standards (UCAS points)	Graduate prospects	Overall score
1 Oxford	—	—	58.6%	190	75.9%	100.0
2 Bath	78.7%	83.4%	56.2%	185	77.8%	98.2
3 University College London	77.1%	74.7%	57.0%	181	82.9%	98.1
4 St Andrews	86.4%	85.5%	45.4%	196	70.9%	97.8
5 Cambridge	—	—	57.5%	182	75.8%	96.4
6 King's College London	73.7%	70.6%	54.1%	179	80.3%	95.5
7 Glasgow	77.5%	80.9%	52.9%	200	64.8%	94.8
8 Loughborough	77.3%	82.1%	62.3%	153	69.2%	93.2
9 York	83.7%	80.1%	46.7%	153	71.4%	92.9
10 Bristol	72.4%	70.1%	49.4%	157	80.7%	92.5
11 Cardiff	73.3%	68.8%	55.7%	164	73.9%	92.3
12 Warwick	81.9%	77.0%	43.1%	150	73.2%	91.8
13 Edinburgh	67.8%	64.8%	52.8%	190	67.5%	90.7
14 Exeter	69.6%	71.7%	43.3%	164	76.5%	90.5
=15 Royal Holloway, London	80.7%	78.5%	37.8%	138	73.8%	89.9
=15 Aberdeen	77.5%	74.4%	38.7%	172	66.3%	89.9
17 Birmingham	64.6%	63.6%	55.8%	150	77.1%	89.2
=18 Stirling	77.5%	76.3%	40.1%	165	63.5%	88.8
=18 Strathclyde	79.3%	79.7%	23.5%	192	60.3%	88.8
20 Newcastle	68.8%	66.5%	50.0%	152	71.6%	88.3
21 Southampton	76.3%	73.5%	47.8%	144	66.2%	88.2
22 Surrey	81.0%	81.6%	22.0%	131	75.3%	87.8
23 Durham	59.6%	56.9%	37.1%	172	78.9%	87.2
=24 Leeds	68.7%	66.8%	33.0%	154	74.5%	86.8
=24 Sussex	70.7%	68.6%	42.3%	141	71.7%	86.8
26 Manchester	70.9%	66.3%	44.9%	153	65.9%	86.5
27 Queen's Belfast	76.7%	76.6%	40.2%	150	57.9%	85.7
=28 Nottingham	68.1%	64.4%	36.4%	148	70.3%	85.2
=28 Cumbria	91.6%	88.6%	—	121	69.6%	85.2
=28 Aston	74.6%	72.7%	39.1%	122	69.2%	85.2
31 Glasgow Caledonian	87.3%	85.2%	8.1%	173	52.6%	85.0
=32 Kent	70.4%	72.5%	38.8%	138	66.3%	84.8
=32 Sheffield	74.0%	67.0%	38.8%	139	64.7%	84.8
34 Heriot-Watt	77.8%	76.9%	26.9%	157	55.7%	84.1
35 Lancaster	69.2%	68.9%	38.5%	145	63.3%	83.8
=36 East Anglia	70.9%	70.1%	33.2%	131	67.8%	83.6

=36	Swansea	68.6%	63.3%	44.7%	126	67.6%	83.6
38	Wales Trinity St David	85.0%	75.7%	—	128	69.8%	83.0
39	Bangor	77.9%	73.5%	32.0%	116	63.4%	82.8
40	Liverpool	71.7%	66.9%	34.6%	139	60.9%	82.5
41	Dundee	72.0%	68.7%	22.7%	174	54.2%	82.4
42	Abertay	81.8%	80.0%	15.1%	138	54.2%	81.4
=43	Chichester	84.0%	87.4%	10.3%	103	62.7%	81.1
=43	Hull	77.0%	73.5%	26.8%	115	61.4%	81.1
45	Reading	62.0%	58.9%	42.3%	127	66.2%	80.9
46	Buckingham	87.3%	80.8%	—	107	64.8%	80.6
=47	Plymouth	70.7%	65.4%	33.8%	121	61.9%	80.5
=47	Essex	70.3%	70.8%	41.0%	115	58.3%	80.5
49	Edge Hill	75.2%	73.6%	18.8%	130	57.6%	79.9
50	Leicester	67.4%	66.7%	29.6%	125	62.6%	79.8
=51	Northumbria	73.6%	66.2%	18.7%	135	58.1%	79.4
=51	Ulster	72.2%	73.6%	23.2%	125	57.8%	79.4
53	Sunderland	86.3%	80.6%	7.5%	109	56.1%	79.3
=54	Central Lancashire	71.4%	69.3%	12.2%	128	63.9%	79.2
=54	Queen Mary, London	65.8%	65.6%	26.1%	143	57.7%	79.2
56	City	64.6%	66.4%	24.1%	136	61.8%	79.1
57	Greenwich	70.7%	71.0%	6.7%	111	71.9%	79.0
=58	Staffordshire	85.4%	77.3%	8.2%	106	57.4%	78.8
=58	Derby	82.5%	77.4%	8.4%	114	56.9%	78.8
60	Portsmouth	74.3%	67.9%	21.0%	117	58.8%	78.6
61	Gloucestershire	84.3%	79.0%	—	115	58.0%	78.5
62	Lincoln	73.6%	73.9%	7.9%	123	60.8%	78.2
63	West of England	79.2%	75.6%	8.2%	118	56.4%	78.1
=64	Birmingham City	82.6%	75.7%	—	108	59.5%	77.6
=64	Queen Margaret, Edinburgh	70.8%	70.6%	8.6%	159	50.0%	77.6
66	Nottingham Trent	73.0%	65.3%	19.3%	115	58.6%	77.5
67	Kingston	75.8%	69.2%	6.5%	96	67.6%	77.4
68	Liverpool John Moores	71.5%	65.9%	7.8%	137	57.1%	77.1
69	Bolton	74.7%	69.3%	3.6%	120	59.5%	76.8
70	Goldsmiths, London	61.7%	56.2%	40.4%	115	57.5%	76.6
71	Edinburgh Napier	74.0%	71.7%	5.3%	159	44.9%	76.5
72	Chester	79.6%	68.4%	7.9%	115	54.1%	76.4
73	St Mary's, Twickenham	71.1%	72.2%	4.8%	104	64.5%	76.2
74	Suffolk	70.6%	56.7%	—	97	74.6%	76.1
=75	Teesside	67.9%	59.6%	15.0%	104	65.6%	76.0
=75	Aberystwyth	76.3%	75.7%	—	118	55.9%	76.0
=75	West London	76.9%	71.6%	7.6%	110	55.4%	76.0
=78	Keele	67.2%	67.6%	17.7%	109	59.8%	75.8
=78	York St John	81.0%	74.5%	11.0%	110	48.6%	75.8
80	London Metropolitan	84.4%	79.7%	—	83	58.0%	75.6
81	Winchester	70.9%	66.6%	6.5%	105	62.0%	75.2
82	Anglia Ruskin	76.7%	71.6%	12.6%	95	55.1%	75.1

Psychology cont.

		Teaching quality	Student experience	Research quality	Entry standards (UCAS points)	Graduate prospects	Overall score
83	Salford	69.9%	66.0%	3.8%	115	60.5%	75.0
84	Coventry	66.9%	63.8%	7.8%	109	62.8%	74.8
85	Brunel	61.7%	55.2%	26.6%	106	60.9%	74.5
86	Roehampton	69.4%	65.3%	26.4%	98	51.7%	74.1
87	Manchester Metropolitan	67.0%	56.9%	12.0%	120	56.4%	74.0
=88	Bournemouth	62.7%	57.6%	13.0%	105	62.9%	73.5
=88	Hertfordshire	71.8%	69.7%	6.0%	99	56.4%	73.5
90	West of Scotland	70.1%	63.3%	9.4%	130	46.6%	73.1
=91	Liverpool Hope	72.1%	64.9%	5.5%	108	53.1%	73.0
=91	Oxford Brookes	64.6%	61.5%	18.1%	117	51.5%	73.0
93	Leeds Beckett	76.4%	70.3%	6.5%	99	48.9%	72.6
=94	Huddersfield	65.7%	56.3%	9.5%	113	56.1%	72.5
=94	Bradford	71.6%	74.9%	9.5%	112	45.0%	72.5
96	Worcester	70.7%	70.0%	7.1%	110	49.3%	72.4
=97	Westminster	61.4%	57.3%	9.3%	109	60.5%	72.3
=97	Sheffield Hallam	66.6%	61.2%	3.7%	108	57.6%	72.3
99	Buckinghamshire New	83.7%	79.4%	—	81	47.2%	72.2
100	East London	66.7%	60.0%	8.3%	102	56.9%	72.1
101	De Montfort	67.8%	61.0%	11.2%	98	54.9%	71.9
102	Northampton	70.3%	62.6%	0.4%	107	53.5%	71.6
103	South Wales	68.9%	58.3%	0.9%	110	54.3%	71.4
104	Cardiff Metropolitan	63.3%	61.4%	—	115	56.1%	71.1
105	Bishop Grosseteste	68.0%	55.3%	—	97	59.6%	71.0
106	Bedfordshire	63.6%	57.1%	25.1%	104	47.4%	70.9
=107	Bath Spa	63.1%	60.3%	—	98	59.3%	70.3
=107	Middlesex	61.3%	57.3%	7.6%	101	57.0%	70.3
=109	Leeds Trinity	68.3%	61.1%	—	102	50.9%	69.7
=109	Newman, Birmingham	71.8%	67.5%	0.8%	93	48.5%	69.7
111	London South Bank	61.7%	52.7%	8.6%	103	54.4%	69.6
112	Canterbury Christ Church	66.0%	56.3%	2.2%	103	50.7%	68.9
113	Solent, Southampton	65.3%	61.8%	—	106	46.4%	68.1
114	Wolverhampton	69.0%	63.2%	—	94	39.2%	65.9
115	Glyndŵr	67.0%	48.6%	3.6%	—	45.2%	65.7
116	Brighton	55.0%	41.1%	12.4%	104	42.8%	64.0

Employed in high-skilled job	32%	Employed in lower-skilled job	38%
Employed in high-skilled job and studying	4%	Employed in lower-skilled job and studying	3%
Studying	14%	Unemployed	8%
High skilled work (median) salary	£22,500	Low/medium skilled salary	£18,258

Radiography

Leeds returns to the top of our Radiography table this year, its status sealed by a perfect graduate prospects score, together with strong performances across the board. Robert Gordon, last year's winner, slips to fourth. But it is seventh-placed Keele that scored most highly with its students in the National Student Survey, who returned stellar, unbeaten scores for both their teaching quality and the wider undergraduate experience. Exeter is in front for research by a clear margin, and places sixth overall.

This is the ninth year we have published a ranking for radiography degrees, which were previously listed among "Subjects Allied to Medicine" in the *Guide*. Diagnostic courses usually involve two years of studying anatomy, physiology and physics followed by further training in oncology, psycho-social studies and other modules. Candidates need at least one science A-level, or equivalent, usually biology. Entry grades are led by Glasgow Caledonian, which averaged 176 points in the UCAS tariff, and no university averaged less than 105 points.

Graduates can feel confident that they will find professional-level work soon after university, with radiography finishing fifth in our employment ranking – up from sixth last year. Salford (9th) and Teesside (21st) matched Leeds in having every one of their radiography graduates employed in good jobs and/or postgraduate study 15 months on from their degrees. Average starting salaries of £24,995 for those in professional-level jobs rank radiography 32nd out of the 67 subject areas in our pay index.

Radiography	Teaching quality	Student experience	Research quality	Entry standards (UCAS points)	Graduate prospects	Overall score
1 Leeds	88.1%	83.2%	31.7%	152	100.0%	100.0
2 Liverpool	85.9%	81.0%	35.3%	131	98.7%	97.2
3 Cardiff	74.2%	75.3%	36.8%	145	97.5%	96.6
4 Robert Gordon	85.3%	87.5%	4.9%	163	—	96.4
5 Glasgow Caledonian	88.2%	87.6%	8.1%	176	93.3%	96.1
6 Exeter	76.4%	74.7%	42.4%	137	96.2%	96.0
7 Keele	93.6%	94.8%	20.9%	127	—	95.8
8 Bangor	44.8%	34.9%	34.7%	166*	96.7%	92.6
9 Salford	70.0%	60.1%	3.8%	147	100.0%	92.4
=10 Ulster	81.8%	86.7%	27.7%	140	89.5%	92.0
=10 Plymouth	80.1%	78.5%	9.5%	137	—	92.0
12 West of England	74.4%	71.6%	8.2%	126	98.7%	91.2
13 Birmingham City	68.7%	62.3%	1.5%	135	99.1%	90.3
14 Cumbria	81.8%	71.8%	0.7%	131	95.2%	89.8
15 Derby	76.0%	73.7%	—	136	95.7%	89.7
16 Bradford	65.0%	62.2%	9.5%	145	94.6%	89.6
17 Sheffield Hallam	68.6%	65.7%	3.7%	138	96.3%	89.5
18 Portsmouth	73.4%	59.5%	24.3%	121	93.8%	89.4
=19 Suffolk	82.8%	76.4%	—	110	96.8%	88.6
=19 London South Bank	75.4%	62.2%	13.7%	133	91.7%	88.6
21 Teesside	64.0%	65.0%	2.4%	117	100.0%	88.5

Radiography cont.	Teaching quality	Student experience	Research quality	Entry standards (UCAS points)	Graduate prospects	Overall score
22 Canterbury Christ Church	80.4%	69.8%	2.2%	113	95.8%	88.1
23 Hertfordshire	85.2%	78.3%	4.0%	105	94.7%	87.8
24 Kingston/St George's, London	66.5%	62.1%	2.6%	124	95.0%	86.8
25 City	80.9%	72.2%	20.5%	123	85.9%	86.5

Employed in high-skilled job	91%	Employed in lower-skilled job	1%
Employed in high-skilled job and studying	3%	Employed in lower-skilled job and studying	–
Studying	1%	Unemployed	3%
High skilled work (median) salary	£24,995	Low/medium skilled salary	–

Russian and Eastern European Languages

Cambridge's lead in the Russian and Eastern European Languages table is secure for a seventh consecutive year. It top-scored in the Research Excellence Framework and its graduates were the second-best employed at the time of the most recent Graduate Outcomes Survey. Cambridge also has the edge in entry standards, just, within a tightly packed grouping that goes from its 189 UCAS tariff points to a still buoyant 130 points at Queen Mary, London. Most undergraduates learn Russian or another Eastern European language from scratch, and while there are no required subjects for entry, a language is useful.

Bristol has moved up from seventh to third place, boosted by the top scores for both measures of student satisfaction – teaching quality and the broad undergraduate experience – drawn from the National Student Survey. Durham is up one place to rank second, and with 86.6% of its graduates in professional-level jobs or furthering studies 15 months after their degrees it comes out top for prospects.

Unusually among our subject rankings, no post-1992 universities feature in Russian and Eastern European Languages. The subjects attract tiny cohorts – just 30 undergraduates have started courses in each of the past three academic years (one-third of numbers a decade earlier), while applications have continued to shrink with each admissions round. Just 175 candidates applied in 2020. Only 24 providers are offering programmes in Russian in 2022, even as part of broader modern language degrees, and six are advertising courses that include Eastern European languages.

The subjects occupy middling positions in both our jobs and salaries tables.

Russian and Eastern European Languages	Teaching quality	Student experience	Research quality	Entry standards (UCAS points)	Graduate prospects	Overall score
1 Cambridge			54.0%	189	84.1%	100.0
2 Durham	79.0%	72.7%	34.6%	181	86.6%	95.4
3 Bristol	82.5%	77.6%	36.0%	164	–	94.1
4 Oxford	–	–	41.3%	187	–	93.9
5 Warwick	81.9%	71.2%	45.2%	165	72.9%	92.7

	Teaching quality	Student experience	Research quality	Entry standards (UCAS points)	Graduate prospects	Overall score
6 Manchester	75.1%	58.9%	48.9%	155	—	92.2
7 University College London	71.0%	65.8%	43.7%	165	79.8%	91.5
8 Exeter	75.3%	73.3%	35.1%	144	78.6%	89.2
9 Leeds	77.2%	70.9%	30.6%	156	—	89.1
10 Glasgow	70.8%	65.5%	26.3%	185	—	88.7
11 Nottingham	75.0%	66.0%	39.4%	133	—	87.7
12 Queen Mary, London	76.2%	68.7%	35.1%	130	—	86.8
13 Edinburgh	65.8%	55.4%	30.3%	173	—	85.5
14 Birmingham	69.0%	64.0%	33.7%	146	73.1%	85.1

Employed in high-skilled job	45%	Employed in lower-skilled job	19%
Employed in high-skilled job and studying	8%	Employed in lower-skilled job and studying	1%
Studying	15%	Unemployed	12%
High skilled work (median) salary	£25,000	Low/medium skilled salary	—

Social Policy

Social policy students learn about how societies meet the basic human needs of citizens. Degrees involve analysing governments' provision for education, health and wellbeing, security and employment, and addressing solutions to the inequalities that are driven by social, demographic and economic factors.

The London School of Economics (LSE) offers the top-ranked degree in the subject, as it did last year and many times before that. It was by far the top scorer in the Research Excellence Framework and comes second only to Bath (in fourth place) for graduate prospects. Strathclyde, which topped the table two years ago, takes second. The highest entry standards were at Glasgow, the only cohort to average more than 200 UCAS tariff points. With entry standards as low as 71 UCAS points at East London, there are courses for a broad range of candidates.

Salford (10th) was the only university to score over 90% in the sections of the National Student Survey related to teaching quality. Loughborough, sixth, leads on student satisfaction with the broad undergraduate experience, and Staffordshire (25th) places second in both metrics.

Not all social policy graduates progress immediately into top careers, and the 37% who were in jobs classed as "low-skilled" 15 months on from their degrees confines the subject to 61st place in our employment ranking. The same proportion had secured professional-level jobs. Salaries averaging £24,000 for highly-skilled work rank social policy 48th.

Many students take joint honours degrees – such as pairings with politics or modern languages. Applications and enrolments have remained remarkably steady over the past decade.

Social Policy	Teaching quality	Student experience	Research quality	Entry standards (UCAS points)	Graduate prospects	Overall score
1 London School of Economics	78.3%	73.7%	74.9%	157	87.1%	100.0
2 Strathclyde	79.1%	73.5%	31.9%	193	—	94.8
3 Edinburgh	75.1%	65.9%	53.4%	175	—	94.7
4 Bath	80.0%	71.5%	43.4%	149	87.9%	93.9

Social Policy cont.

	Teaching quality	Student experience	Research quality	Entry standards (UCAS points)	Graduate prospects	Overall score
5 Glasgow	75.1%	70.6%	41.8%	202	62.5%	92.6
6 Loughborough	85.9%	85.9%	40.6%	140*	—	92.1
7 Bristol	75.7%	66.3%	47.9%	143	76.8%	89.7
8 Leeds	73.3%	63.5%	47.6%	151	75.5%	89.5
9 Queen's Belfast	79.2%	75.0%	26.2%	151	—	87.0
10 Salford	93.8%	85.3%	27.7%	99	67.6%	84.6
11 Kent	73.2%	65.9%	59.0%	106	—	84.3
12 Swansea	84.8%	69.9%	22.7%	130	—	83.8
13 Stirling	66.9%	56.5%	33.8%	152	—	82.8
14 Birmingham	64.0%	49.5%	40.1%	142	71.7%	82.6
15 Cardiff	76.3%	75.8%	30.8%	118	—	82.0
=16 Ulster	83.6%	71.7%	39.2%	109	58.1%	81.8
=16 Sheffield	72.9%	68.8%	26.8%	135	—	81.8
18 Aston	73.2%	62.5%	38.6%	120	—	81.4
19 Bangor	63.6%	58.8%	39.6%	139	—	81.3
20 York	65.5%	57.6%	47.5%	133	58.1%	80.6
21 Bolton	86.2%	78.8%	1.0%	130	—	80.3
22 Liverpool Hope	86.6%	81.1%	8.6%	117*	58.7%	79.2
23 Nottingham Trent	75.5%	64.6%	5.1%	134	—	76.9
24 Nottingham	59.2%	44.7%	43.5%	125	—	76.7
25 Staffordshire	89.6%	85.6%	—	94	58.3%	76.0
26 Chester	71.2%	59.9%	0.3%	123*	68.3%	75.2
27 Edge Hill	70.5%	66.0%	5.7%	126	—	74.4
28 Bedfordshire	83.2%	78.8%	16.3%	102	44.3%	74.2
29 West of Scotland	68.9%	60.2%	9.4%	127	—	74.1
30 De Montfort	59.7%	55.3%	11.2%	113	71.8%	73.8
31 Middlesex	63.5%	62.5%	14.9%	116*	—	72.4
32 Central Lancashire	70.6%	60.4%	11.8%	110	55.3%	72.3
33 Wales Trinity St David	68.8%	53.3%	—	134	54.1%	71.8
34 Plymouth	62.4%	57.4%	16.0%	116	—	71.6
35 Lincoln	70.6%	65.1%	5.8%	104	—	70.8
36 London Metropolitan	74.5%	65.5%	8.8%	97*	50.4%	70.4
37 South Wales	62.9%	59.3%	15.4%	107	—	70.3
38 Anglia Ruskin	70.6%	67.1%	5.4%	95*	—	69.5
=39 Brighton	58.2%	46.9%	12.4%	108	57.9%	68.7
=39 Liverpool	50.6%	36.3%	24.5%	125	—	68.7
41 Wolverhampton	77.6%	68.4%	—	90	42.4%	67.0
42 East London	72.2%	60.7%	10.6%	71	—	66.5

Employed in high-skilled job	37%	Employed in lower-skilled job	37%
Employed in high-skilled job and studying	4%	Employed in lower-skilled job and studying	2%
Studying	11%	Unemployed	10%
High skilled work (median) salary	£24,000	Low/medium skilled salary	£19,595

Social Work

In a table characterised by shifting rankings, Lancaster moves into first place this year, from third. It performs strongly across the board and, jointly with the West of England, tops the graduate prospects with an outstanding 100% achieving the top outcomes of professional jobs and/or postgraduate study 15 months on from their degrees. Entry standards are highest at runner-up Edinburgh, which topped the table last year, while Kent (fourth overall) was top in the Research Excellence Framework.

Bedfordshire (10th) received exceptionally high and unbeaten scores in the sections of the National Student Survey relating to teaching quality (95.3%) and for the broad undergraduate experience (90.3%). Bournemouth is not far behind.

Social work is a graduate career, and although the Frontline programme aims to attract graduates of other subjects to train in the profession and degree apprenticeships have been developed (though are not profiled here), social work degrees are still the main route into careers. A 12% increase in enrolments in 2020 and a 4% uplift in applications has halted a downward trend in numbers, although they are still around 20% lower than in 2014 – their highest point in the past decade.

The subject maintains its top ten rank in our salaries index, with average pay of £29,000 placing social work eighth, one position below economics. It places =28th in our employment table, with more than six in ten graduates in professional jobs 15 months on from their degrees and 10% furthering their studies or combining study with a good job.

Social Work	Teaching quality	Student experience	Research quality	Entry standards (UCAS points)	Graduate prospects	Overall score
1 Lancaster	76.1%	72.5%	51.4%	155	100.0%	100.0
2 Edinburgh	74.4%	71.0%	53.4%	173	82.7%	99.2
3 Strathclyde	83.6%	77.6%	31.9%	172	81.9%	98.3
4 Kent	85.6%	69.4%	59.0%	130	87.7%	96.7
5 Queen's Belfast	82.2%	73.0%	39.3%	143	93.5%	96.4
6 Nottingham	80.5%	71.9%	43.5%	137	91.4%	95.2
7 Bournemouth	94.4%	86.3%	4.7%	140	94.7%	94.9
8 Robert Gordon	84.2%	78.8%	18.0%	150	89.9%	94.5
9 Bath	79.2%	72.6%	43.4%	135	88.1%	94.1
10 Bedfordshire	95.3%	90.3%	16.3%	115	96.6%	93.8
11 Dundee	76.2%	75.6%	31.1%	138	95.0%	93.6
12 East Anglia	74.5%	57.4%	45.8%	133	96.6%	93.0
13 Glasgow Caledonian	87.0%	84.8%	8.1%	133	94.6%	92.5
14 York	69.9%	64.8%	47.5%	126	96.2%	92.1
15 Huddersfield	94.2%	78.4%	9.5%	133	82.1%	91.1
16 Hull	82.9%	76.6%	14.3%	140	83.6%	90.6
17 Hertfordshire	81.4%	76.7%	4.0%	139	92.3%	90.3
18 Salford	79.1%	70.5%	27.7%	134	82.3%	90.1
19 London South Bank	86.6%	67.5%	20.1%	117	92.6%	89.6
=20 Plymouth	77.8%	65.9%	16.0%	135	91.9%	89.5

Social Work cont.

		Teaching quality	Student experience	Research quality	Entry standards (UCAS points)	Graduate prospects	Overall score
=20	Lincoln	83.5%	78.6%	5.8%	128	91.7%	89.5
22	Birmingham	62.9%	57.0%	40.1%	139	89.2%	89.1
23	Ulster	73.3%	72.8%	39.2%	118	82.9%	88.6
24	Sheffield Hallam	79.2%	72.0%	—	143	88.3%	88.5
25	West of England	64.9%	63.1%	10.9%	141	100.0%	88.0
=26	Teesside	75.1%	66.6%	15.0%	124	93.4%	87.5
=26	Middlesex	78.7%	74.9%	14.9%	119	89.3%	87.5
28	Coventry	85.4%	71.3%	5.6%	127	83.5%	87.2
29	Cumbria	88.3%	71.9%	—	126	84.4%	87.1
30	Staffordshire	82.6%	77.3%	—	122	90.4%	87.0
31	Northumbria	79.2%	69.2%	12.7%	152	64.1%	86.8
32	Manchester Metropolitan	81.3%	71.0%	6.9%	142	72.5%	86.7
33	Worcester	88.4%	81.0%	—	126	76.6%	86.6
34	Swansea	77.1%	71.6%	22.7%	121	79.1%	86.5
35	Sussex	71.5%	61.7%	27.9%	140	71.7%	86.4
36	East London	77.5%	70.3%	10.6%	111	96.2%	86.2
37	Central Lancashire	78.6%	69.3%	11.8%	128	80.2%	86.1
=38	Anglia Ruskin	78.0%	75.5%	5.4%	116	90.6%	85.8
=38	Solent, Southampton	85.0%	79.1%	—	113	87.3%	85.8
=40	West of Scotland	72.7%	57.6%	9.4%	140	83.7%	85.6
=40	Leeds	53.0%	49.2%	47.6%	139	—	85.6
=42	Liverpool Hope	72.1%	64.3%	8.6%	122	94.3%	85.4
=42	Liverpool John Moores	74.8%	73.6%	5.8%	132*	—	85.4
44	Chester	86.1%	82.2%	0.3%	125	72.0%	85.3
45	De Montfort	81.8%	80.0%	11.2%	111	—	85.2
46	Glyndŵr	89.5%	77.4%	—	101	89.7%	85.1
47	Portsmouth	70.4%	60.4%	12.1%	121	93.0%	84.8
48	Winchester	82.5%	75.0%	—	117	83.7%	84.7
49	Birmingham City	79.9%	72.1%	3.8%	111	89.7%	84.6
50	London Metropolitan	85.7%	80.4%	8.8%	112	72.4%	84.5
=51	Bradford	71.1%	74.8%	10.6%	148	61.7%	84.4
=51	Greenwich	85.1%	66.4%	2.2%	149	57.5%	84.4
53	Brighton	70.9%	61.1%	12.4%	114	93.5%	84.0
54	Cardiff Metropolitan	80.7%	73.1%	—	115	83.9%	83.9
55	Kingston	81.7%	74.7%	—	111	83.3%	83.5
56	Gloucestershire	79.1%	76.8%	—	116	80.0%	83.3
57	South Wales	81.0%	69.6%	15.4%	113	71.9%	83.2
58	Oxford Brookes	71.7%	68.9%	—	111	96.0%	83.1
59	Goldsmiths, London	76.3%	66.8%	13.5%	108	81.7%	82.8
60	Chichester	84.6%	79.7%	—	98	80.7%	82.2
61	Keele	60.4%	64.3%	25.0%	124	—	82.1
=62	Leeds Beckett	73.9%	70.3%	6.4%	105	83.1%	81.3

=62	Derby	76.2%	68.5%	5.6%	120	70.5%	81.3
64	Edge Hill	70.6%	60.8%	5.7%	130	67.5%	80.2
=65	Buckinghamshire New	73.4%	65.7%	—	97	85.0%	78.9
=65	Sunderland	78.0%	73.1%	1.9%	117	58.1%	78.9
67	Northampton	65.9%	60.6%	—	110	84.2%	78.5
68	Nottingham Trent	76.1%	68.1%	5.1%	112	56.1%	77.2
69	West London	70.4%	67.7%	—	108	68.3%	76.9
70	Canterbury Christ Church	68.7%	65.3%	2.2%	101	69.9%	75.9
71	Newman, Birmingham	75.9%	74.4%	2.2%	104	44.1%	73.8
72	Wolverhampton	70.1%	62.4%	—	104	56.6%	73.4
73	Bangor	72.4%	68.2%	—	110	45.5%	73.2

Employed in high-skilled job	63%	Employed in lower-skilled job	20%
Employed in high-skilled job and studying	5%	Employed in lower-skilled job and studying	1%
Studying	5%	Unemployed	6%
High skilled work (median) salary	£29,000	Low/medium skilled salary	£19,000

Sociology

The study of human social relationships and institutions is an increasingly interesting area for undergraduates, as evidenced by 2020's admissions round in which applications and enrolments for sociology degrees increased for the eighth year running. Our subject table is only four universities shy of 100 this year and with entry standards ranging from 194 UCAS tariff points – the average for Glasgow's 2020 intake – to 88 at Roehampton, there are options for a broad church of candidates.

Courses cover topics such as gender roles, multiculturalism, media and culture and can include options to study criminology or social policy. The subject's academic breadth may be the source of its popularity, as graduate prospects offer little pulling power; sociology ranks third from bottom in our employment table and 54th for salaries. The latest data shows more students in lower-skilled jobs (40%) than in professional-level jobs (35%) 15 months on from their degrees.

With much improved student satisfaction rates and the second-best graduate prospects, Bath has risen seven places to rank second this year, behind Cambridge by only the narrowest of margins. Cambridge had the best-employed graduates 15 months after their degrees and its entry standards are only two UCAS points behind those at Glasgow. Kent achieved the best scores in the Research Excellence Framework – although weaker performance in measures of student satisfaction confine it to 23rd place overall.

Sunderland (38th) received the best scores in the sections of the National Student Survey relating to teaching quality and Queen Margaret, Edinburgh did best for the broad undergraduate experience. However, the subject attracted lukewarm feedback from students in the pandemic-hit NSS and at some universities was highly critical – at De Montfort and East Anglia, scores for both measures were under 50%.

Sociology

	Teaching quality	Student experience	Research quality	Entry standards (UCAS points)	Graduate prospects	Overall score
1 Cambridge	—	—	39.2%	192	87.7%	100.0
2 Bath	82.3%	81.1%	43.4%	152	85.0%	99.9
3 Glasgow	78.6%	68.0%	41.8%	194	63.5%	95.7
4 London School of Economics	75.9%	70.7%	45.2%	153	73.5%	94.4
5 Durham	79.9%	70.7%	28.7%	162	75.7%	94.1
6 King's College London	76.9%	71.0%	42.2%	147	73.8%	93.5
7 Bristol	71.6%	64.6%	46.7%	148	73.3%	92.3
8 Edinburgh	70.5%	61.3%	48.8%	182	61.0%	92.1
9 Leeds	71.7%	65.1%	47.6%	145	69.9%	91.2
10 Lancaster	74.1%	71.8%	51.4%	148	61.3%	91.1
11 Loughborough	83.4%	82.8%	40.6%	133	61.3%	91.0
12 Glasgow Caledonian	84.8%	74.5%	12.7%	179	60.6%	90.5
13 Warwick	74.7%	70.3%	31.7%	147	70.5%	90.1
14 Nottingham	70.8%	64.9%	43.5%	130	74.6%	89.9
15 Exeter	70.2%	66.2%	41.0%	149	68.1%	89.7
16 Aberdeen	76.0%	68.4%	31.0%	181	55.4%	89.5
=17 Surrey	75.6%	69.7%	30.2%	130	74.5%	89.4
=17 Manchester	68.1%	56.7%	50.4%	151	66.1%	89.4
19 Aston	73.8%	70.1%	38.6%	118	71.2%	88.2
20 Stirling	68.9%	62.0%	33.8%	169	61.8%	88.1
21 Southampton	67.0%	60.5%	52.8%	137	64.3%	87.9
22 Newcastle	69.4%	61.3%	30.3%	138	72.2%	87.1
23 Kent	68.6%	61.6%	59.0%	116	60.8%	86.3
24 Sheffield	73.5%	68.8%	26.8%	134	63.4%	85.5
=25 Suffolk	82.1%	73.4%	—	120	74.7%	85.3
=25 Essex	66.4%	58.6%	44.3%	123	66.7%	85.3
27 York	62.3%	58.7%	45.1%	136	63.4%	85.0
28 Sussex	69.2%	61.0%	29.7%	137	63.3%	84.3
29 Edinburgh Napier	80.8%	74.2%	5.3%	147	57.9%	84.1
30 Queen's Belfast	77.2%	70.0%	26.2%	135	54.2%	83.8
31 Swansea	77.7%	75.6%	—	132	66.7%	83.4
32 Queen Margaret, Edinburgh	82.7%	83.5%	—	147	53.4%	83.3
33 Cardiff	64.2%	56.5%	30.8%	139	63.7%	83.1
34 Leicester	75.8%	70.6%	18.4%	118	62.9%	82.9
35 Abertay	81.6%	70.9%	5.0%	146	50.0%	81.5
36 Salford	77.1%	67.8%	27.7%	104	56.5%	81.1
37 Northumbria	76.9%	65.0%	12.7%	136	52.4%	80.6
38 Sunderland	85.6%	78.7%	1.9%	107	57.2%	80.5
39 Liverpool	59.2%	52.9%	24.5%	127	67.6%	80.3
=40 Derby	77.3%	73.0%	13.5%	105	58.6%	80.1
=40 Newman, Birmingham	84.1%	76.8%	2.2%	107*	—	80.1
42 Royal Holloway, London	77.8%	71.5%	—	112	62.4%	79.6

43 Portsmouth	70.9%	61.3%	32.2%	97	58.4%	79.5
44 Ulster	74.6%	65.4%	39.2%	106	45.7%	79.4
45 Bangor	66.5%	56.6%	39.6%	118	50.2%	79.1
46 West of England	76.5%	68.5%	10.9%	112	55.9%	78.9
=47 Bedfordshire	73.3%	67.4%	16.3%	114	54.7%	78.8
=47 City	67.0%	66.5%	20.8%	123	54.3%	78.8
49 Robert Gordon	78.9%	72.1%	4.9%	146	41.4%	78.5
50 Birmingham	64.4%	49.2%	31.1%	145	47.2%	78.3
=51 Sheffield Hallam	73.0%	64.9%	14.4%	107	57.3%	78.2
=51 Anglia Ruskin	70.4%	59.6%	26.4%	112	52.8%	78.2
53 Chester	69.9%	57.4%	6.4%	114	64.5%	78.0
54 Coventry	74.7%	70.3%	5.6%	96	62.3%	77.9
55 Worcester	79.6%	74.0%	—	104	56.6%	77.8
56 Goldsmiths, London	65.9%	49.2%	33.4%	115	53.7%	77.7
57 Bournemouth	71.2%	62.2%	4.7%	106	64.0%	77.6
58 Edge Hill	72.8%	70.7%	5.7%	111	56.8%	77.5
=59 Plymouth	68.3%	62.9%	16.0%	102	59.8%	77.2
=59 Nottingham Trent	75.1%	63.6%	5.1%	109	57.4%	77.2
=61 London South Bank	68.0%	55.0%	20.1%	98	61.7%	77.1
=61 Greenwich	76.7%	70.8%	—	106	56.8%	77.1
63 Lincoln	75.3%	71.4%	—	112	55.3%	77.0
64 Liverpool John Moores	70.2%	62.0%	5.8%	120	56.1%	76.8
65 Central Lancashire	68.6%	61.7%	11.8%	117	55.3%	76.7
66 Hull	68.5%	66.0%	14.3%	112	53.4%	76.6
67 Staffordshire	71.9%	57.2%	—	113*	61.6%	76.5
68 Gloucestershire	75.9%	70.1%	14.5%	112	44.1%	76.2
69 York St John	81.5%	73.5%	—	99	51.2%	76.1
70 London Metropolitan	81.5%	68.2%	—	87*	56.9%	75.9
=71 Roehampton	67.9%	63.3%	24.9%	88	53.6%	75.4
=71 Oxford Brookes	73.3%	63.8%	17.8%	103	47.2%	75.4
73 Birmingham City	72.2%	64.0%	3.8%	111	53.0%	75.3
74 East Anglia	47.7%	45.2%	45.8%	119	—	75.2
=75 Manchester Metropolitan	67.6%	57.3%	14.9%	115	50.4%	75.0
=75 Keele	63.2%	59.6%	25.0%	109	49.8%	75.0
=75 Buckinghamshire New	77.4%	68.0%	—	122*	43.9%	75.0
78 Kingston	75.9%	67.9%	—	93	55.9%	74.8
=79 Bradford	65.8%	59.1%	10.6%	108*	54.8%	74.5
=79 Liverpool Hope	75.2%	65.2%	8.6%	113	43.8%	74.5
81 Canterbury Christ Church	75.0%	67.7%	—	95	54.8%	74.4
82 Huddersfield	69.5%	59.7%	9.5%	110	50.7%	74.3
83 Teesside	62.6%	49.0%	15.0%	103	59.8%	74.2
=84 Brunel	60.7%	55.2%	26.0%	104	50.4%	73.7
=84 Westminster	74.2%	66.6%	—	103	50.0%	73.7
86 Winchester	65.5%	61.9%	4.4%	107	54.5%	73.5
87 West of Scotland	65.8%	57.3%	9.4%	114*	50.0%	73.3
88 East London	67.5%	56.0%	13.7%	90	53.8%	72.9

Sociology cont.	Teaching quality	Student experience	Research quality	Entry standards (UCAS points)	Graduate prospects	Overall score
89 Leeds Beckett	68.9%	60.2%	6.4%	97	51.4%	72.5
90 Middlesex	64.8%	60.6%	14.9%	90	48.2%	71.3
91 Bath Spa	68.1%	55.6%	13.9%	94	43.6%	70.5
92 South Wales	62.6%	59.2%	—	98	52.6%	70.2
93 Brighton	56.9%	45.0%	12.4%	100	52.8%	69.6
94 Northampton	64.8%	50.6%	—	93	49.1%	68.2
95 St Mary's, Twickenham	63.6%	51.6%	—	94*	45.0%	67.0
96 De Montfort	48.5%	44.6%	11.2%	—	51.2%	65.2

Employed in high-skilled job	35%	Employed in lower-skilled job	40%
Employed in high-skilled job and studying	3%	Employed in lower-skilled job and studying	2%
Studying	11%	Unemployed	9%
High skilled work (median) salary	£23,000	Low/medium skilled salary	£19,000

Sports Science

Great sports facilities do not always equate to great outcomes in the academic discipline of sport science – but they can help. The best come equipped with the laboratories in which performance, endurance and recovery are closely monitored to help extract those extra hundredths of a second that could make the difference between a medal, or not.

The leading university for sport in the UK and our Sports University of the Year – Loughborough – is a case in point. It ranks fourth in this year's sports science academic ranking after an Olympic Games in Tokyo where Loughborough-linked athletes would have ranked 23rd, just above Sweden and Switzerland, as a collective in the medal table. Its sports facilities are the finest this side of the Atlantic and such is the competitive nature of the institution on all things sporting, fourth place in this ranking will be a disappointment. It does "podium" in our ranking measure for graduate prospects, taking third place for the proportion of graduates (81.4%) who are in high-skilled jobs or postgraduate study within 15 months of leaving. It also ranks fourth for research and fifth for student satisfaction.

Sports science is one of our more competitive subject rankings, with the lead changing hands regularly in recent years. Since 2017, the table has been led by Birmingham, Bath (twice), Exeter, Loughborough and now, for a second successive year, Glasgow. Our Scottish University of the Year tops the measure for entry standards with an average of 219 UCAS tariff points. The course does not disappoint, with Glasgow ranking second for student satisfaction with the university experience.

Bath ranks second, also for the second successive year. Outstanding sports facilities provide the physical surroundings in which much world-leading and internationally excellent research takes place, Bath ranking third on this measure.

Top for research, but taking a dip down the subject ranking this year, is Birmingham. Its score of 63.7% gives it a win by several lengths, but it is pulled down the ranking to 15th overall as a result of poor scores for student satisfaction, where it ranks third bottom (64.3%) for teaching quality and fourth bottom (62%) for student experience.

Nottingham, another university to benefit from huge recent investment in sports facilities in the £40million David Ross Sports Village, also suffered in pandemic year. Students rated it bottom for teaching quality and fifth-bottom for student experience, triggering a slide from ninth in our sports science ranking to 63rd.

Bolton, ranked 18th overall, puts in the strongest performance for student satisfaction, coming top for teaching quality and third for student experience, closely pursued by Strathclyde, ranked 12th overall and placing fourth for teaching quality and first for student experience.

Sports science is one of the subject areas where the modern universities compete on a level playing field with their older counterparts. For student satisfaction, Anglia Ruskin, Central Lancashire and Kingston join Bolton in the top five for teaching quality, and Worcester makes the top five for satisfaction with student experience.

Anglia Ruskin, Bolton, Liverpool John Moores and Chichester all make the top 20 of the subject ranking overall, in 17th to 20th place respectively.

Applications for sports science bounced back in 2020 after four successive years of decline, the 66,235 applications representing a rise of 3.5% over 2019. While the number of applications was still 7% down on the peak recorded in 2015, the number of places available, 15,555, was a record.

Sports Science	Teaching quality	Student experience	Research quality	Entry standards (UCAS points)	Graduate prospects	Overall score
1 Glasgow	82.5%	83.8%	42.3%	219	—	100.0
2 Bath	83.7%	81.4%	54.0%	159	79.9%	94.7
3 Aberdeen	77.9%	78.5%	34.7%	198	—	94.2
4 Loughborough	78.0%	82.2%	52.1%	154	81.4%	93.4
5 King's College London	80.6%	70.0%	55.2%	161	—	92.8
6 Exeter	72.3%	69.7%	50.8%	163	79.7%	90.9
7 Edinburgh	79.3%	78.9%	26.1%	189	72.5%	90.5
8 Durham	83.0%	74.2%	28.7%	167	76.6%	90.4
9 Leeds	75.7%	77.5%	50.5%	145	74.2%	89.2
10 Stirling	82.4%	80.1%	33.6%	168	66.1%	88.7
11 Surrey	81.4%	79.3%	33.6%	136	—	88.1
12 Strathclyde	85.6%	86.3%	—	189	66.7%	87.9
13 East Anglia	79.9%	77.1%	27.2%	139	76.5%	87.4
14 Essex	74.9%	71.8%	25.8%	138	82.4%	87.2
15 Birmingham	64.3%	62.0%	63.7%	145	75.6%	87.1
16 Swansea	76.9%	74.2%	38.8%	134	75.1%	87.0
17 Anglia Ruskin	87.9%	81.7%	—	112	81.7%	85.6
18 Bolton	91.4%	83.2%	—	118	76.1%	85.4
19 Liverpool John Moores	73.8%	71.3%	45.3%	158	61.1%	84.9
20 Chichester	81.5%	79.8%	15.2%	125	74.4%	84.8
21 Central Lancashire	85.9%	82.0%	5.1%	127	72.9%	84.5
22 Ulster	72.3%	68.6%	31.0%	142	72.2%	84.4
23 Robert Gordon	75.9%	71.0%	4.9%	159	73.3%	84.0
24 Buckinghamshire New	83.5%	80.7%	0.9%	115	77.1%	83.6
25 Brunel	67.2%	62.3%	46.4%	131	72.1%	83.5

Sports Science cont.	Teaching quality	Student experience	Research quality	Entry standards (UCAS points)	Graduate prospects	Overall score
26 Oxford Brookes	84.2%	79.5%	3.0%	121	73.1%	83.3
27 Greenwich	76.6%	71.1%	7.4%	128	77.8%	83.1
=28 Coventry	80.2%	75.8%	4.5%	132	72.9%	83.0
=28 Worcester	82.3%	82.8%	4.9%	119	72.5%	83.0
=30 Chester	76.7%	74.3%	6.6%	133	74.7%	82.9
=30 Roehampton	80.8%	78.5%	20.6%	102	73.0%	82.9
32 Aberystwyth	75.9%	72.9%	23.5%	125	—	82.6
33 Bedfordshire	77.4%	74.7%	6.7%	110	77.7%	82.0
34 Gloucestershire	78.9%	76.5%	6.0%	124	71.3%	81.9
35 Manchester Metropolitan	79.1%	77.1%	12.0%	137	64.2%	81.7
36 Staffordshire	80.2%	74.3%	19.1%	117	66.9%	81.6
37 York St John	75.6%	72.3%	5.5%	124	74.6%	81.5
=38 Middlesex	83.0%	76.3%	10.0%	121	66.0%	81.4
=38 Abertay	79.7%	73.2%	8.9%	153	60.8%	81.4
40 Edge Hill	76.8%	73.8%	7.7%	143	65.6%	81.3
=41 Lincoln	77.8%	73.8%	11.4%	123	69.0%	81.2
=41 Bangor	71.1%	69.9%	30.6%	125	66.7%	81.2
43 Cardiff Metropolitan	72.2%	69.6%	7.7%	136	71.6%	80.9
=44 Leeds Beckett	73.7%	71.3%	12.6%	113	74.0%	80.8
=44 Kent	77.3%	68.6%	21.0%	137	61.9%	80.8
46 Northumbria	75.3%	70.9%	4.4%	150	65.0%	80.6
47 West of Scotland	74.1%	72.0%	9.1%	140	66.3%	80.5
=48 Brighton	74.4%	65.2%	10.9%	117	74.0%	80.4
=48 Plymouth Marjon	82.2%	78.5%	—	120	66.8%	80.4
50 Salford	71.5%	70.0%	3.8%	136	71.4%	80.3
=51 Portsmouth	74.6%	69.8%	8.1%	122	71.3%	80.2
=51 Kingston	85.1%	80.7%	2.6%	108	65.4%	80.2
=53 Nottingham Trent	75.3%	66.8%	7.3%	128	69.6%	80.0
=53 South Wales	80.2%	76.9%	10.8%	110	66.1%	80.0
55 East London	78.6%	76.4%	7.6%	104	70.2%	79.9
56 Teesside	75.6%	67.6%	2.4%	135	68.7%	79.8
57 Hertfordshire	81.1%	80.1%	0.9%	108	68.1%	79.7
58 St Mary's, Twickenham	76.4%	74.3%	4.8%	113	69.9%	79.6
59 Sheffield Hallam	75.8%	71.3%	8.5%	124	66.5%	79.5
=60 Northampton	76.2%	68.6%	—	104	75.3%	79.1
=60 Derby	80.8%	76.4%	1.7%	118	64.0%	79.1
=60 Hull	72.2%	67.8%	14.2%	143	61.5%	79.1
63 Nottingham	58.3%	62.3%	31.4%	140	—	79.0
64 Sunderland	80.1%	69.3%	2.4%	120	65.3%	78.8
65 Wolverhampton	80.1%	75.0%	5.6%	108	65.1%	78.7
66 Winchester	65.0%	66.4%	4.4%	108	79.8%	78.6
=67 Leeds Trinity	68.3%	60.5%	0.8%	111	79.6%	78.4

=67	Newman, Birmingham	76.6%	76.6%	2.8%	104	68.2%	78.4
69	Cumbria	71.3%	71.9%	3.2%	106	73.3%	78.3
70	Wales Trinity St David	75.7%	68.0%	—	138	62.1%	78.0
=71	Liverpool Hope	66.8%	65.0%	10.9%	119	70.7%	77.9
=71	London South Bank	68.6%	60.4%	35.0%	102	—	77.9
73	Solent, Southampton	73.1%	67.0%	0.6%	123	68.1%	77.8
74	Canterbury Christ Church	75.2%	67.8%	19.0%	92	67.1%	77.7
75	Bournemouth	65.2%	61.9%	9.0%	118	70.9%	77.0
=76	Suffolk	64.6%	67.9%	—	116	72.2%	76.6
=76	Hartpury	75.6%	71.8%	—	121	60.8%	76.6
=78	London Metropolitan	71.3%	64.2%	—	109	69.1%	76.2
=78	Huddersfield	73.7%	68.5%	—	132	58.7%	76.2
80	Edinburgh Napier	69.9%	71.2%	5.3%	153	49.5%	75.4
81	Bradford	58.8%	62.4%	9.5%	—	69.6%	74.4
82	Glyndŵr	73.4%	70.0%	3.6%	105	40.8%	69.2

Employed in high-skilled job	43%	Employed in lower-skilled job	32%
Employed in high-skilled job and studying	5%	Employed in lower-skilled job and studying	1%
Studying	12%	Unemployed	6%
High skilled work (median) salary	£23,000	Low/medium skilled salary	£18,005

Subjects Allied to Medicine

For the sixth consecutive year, Strathclyde tops the table for the broad group of "subjects allied to medicine". They include audiology, complementary therapies, counselling, health services management, health sciences, nutrition, occupational therapy, optometry, ophthalmology, orthoptics, osteopathy, podiatry and speech therapy. Physiotherapy and radiography are ranked independently. Not all the universities in this table offer all these subjects, of course, and performance in our ranking reflects the specialisms that are offered.

Degrees in speech and language pathology, prosthetics and orthoptics are offered at Strathclyde – which enjoys consistently strong scores in measures derived from the National Student Survey, placing first for the wider undergraduate experience and beaten only by Nottingham for teaching quality. Southampton was the star performer in the Research Excellence Framework and ties for third place overall with University College London. Its position fuelled by much the highest entry standards, Cambridge manages second place in our table even without a score for research, as it did not enter the Research Excellence Framework in the relevant category. Glasgow Caledonian is the top-ranked post-1992 institution.

Subjects allied to medicine did not experience the same boom in applications that nursing and medicine did as a consequence of the pandemic, but numbers went up in 2020 all the same. Career prospects are solid: the grouping shares 10th place in our employment table with chemistry, and 65% of graduates were working in professional-level jobs 15 months after finishing their studies. Salaries do less well, ranking 37th out of 67 subject areas.

Subjects Allied to Medicine

		Teaching quality	Student experience	Research quality	Entry standards (UCAS points)	Graduate prospects	Overall score
1	Strathclyde	91.5%	90.9%	52.2%	189	96.2%	100.0
2	Cambridge	—	—	—	228*	89.8%	91.5
=3	Southampton	78.4%	74.6%	65.7%	133	93.9%	91.2
=3	University College London	74.2%	76.7%	48.4%	170	90.4%	91.2
5	Glasgow	81.0%	79.2%	42.3%	206	69.3%	90.2
6	Lancaster	80.9%	79.7%	55.2%	136	90.2%	89.9
7	Surrey	83.8%	77.5%	37.5%	154	90.1%	89.6
8	Manchester	71.3%	71.7%	57.1%	150	90.1%	89.2
9	Glasgow Caledonian	82.4%	78.8%	8.1%	183	91.4%	88.9
10	Reading	79.2%	81.1%	42.3%	142	91.4%	88.8
11	Newcastle	87.6%	78.1%	47.8%	161	74.5%	88.6
12	Cardiff	72.8%	66.9%	36.8%	155	95.2%	88.0
13	Swansea	84.8%	76.5%	44.7%	135	85.7%	87.5
14	East Anglia	77.8%	76.3%	24.9%	142	98.0%	87.3
15	Aston	76.6%	73.4%	39.1%	131	95.7%	87.0
16	Queen Mary, London	83.0%	79.0%	48.3%	145	77.1%	86.7
17	Nottingham	93.1%	81.0%	31.4%	142	78.3%	86.4
18	Ulster	85.1%	83.3%	27.7%	141	85.4%	86.3
19	Queen Margaret, Edinburgh	83.6%	80.5%	6.7%	162	89.0%	86.0
20	Leeds	76.7%	73.1%	31.7%	147	—	85.9
21	Robert Gordon	80.1%	71.1%	4.9%	163	92.5%	85.3
22	City	79.2%	75.1%	20.5%	132	94.0%	84.7
23	Liverpool	72.1%	71.5%	35.3%	129	93.6%	84.6
24	Northumbria	73.8%	66.6%	14.0%	152	95.5%	84.5
25	Dundee	77.2%	75.6%	31.3%	—	82.9%	84.1
26	Sheffield	77.3%	75.7%	38.3%	143	77.4%	83.7
=27	Cumbria	81.3%	75.4%	0.7%	135	97.8%	83.6
=27	King's College London	76.9%	71.0%	34.6%	151	77.4%	83.6
29	Plymouth	76.4%	71.6%	9.5%	134	97.0%	83.2
=30	Bristol	80.4%	76.5%	—	175	79.7%	83.0
=30	Hull	80.3%	75.0%	16.7%	140	—	83.0
32	Northampton	81.1%	73.6%	1.6%	127	98.7%	82.9
33	Birmingham	69.4%	71.1%	31.5%	149	82.3%	82.8
34	Exeter	68.2%	66.4%	41.1%	148	79.6%	82.7
35	Warwick	75.0%	59.5%	25.3%	151*	82.8%	82.3
=36	Cardiff Metropolitan	76.4%	69.6%	3.6%	147	90.4%	81.9
=36	Huddersfield	82.9%	77.4%	13.2%	129	85.6%	81.9
38	Portsmouth	73.7%	62.3%	24.3%	136	87.5%	81.8
39	Coventry	79.3%	77.6%	4.5%	128	89.3%	80.8
40	Bradford	73.7%	68.5%	9.5%	144	85.5%	80.4
41	West of England	75.9%	69.4%	8.2%	144	83.6%	80.3
=42	Brighton	72.6%	62.2%	4.8%	124	95.8%	79.6

=42	Liverpool John Moores	73.3%	70.3%	6.0%	150	81.6%	79.6
44	Greenwich	76.7%	64.8%	2.2%	118	95.6%	79.5
=45	Oxford Brookes	69.9%	68.0%	3.0%	124	96.6%	79.4
=45	Lincoln	80.9%	70.0%	22.6%	146	67.7%	79.4
47	Leicester	91.5%	87.0%	—	118	78.3%	79.3
48	Derby	89.4%	86.0%	7.3%	128	71.1%	79.0
49	Hertfordshire	80.8%	75.7%	4.0%	119	85.3%	78.8
=50	Kingston/St George's, London	74.1%	73.2%	—	137	85.1%	78.7
=50	London South Bank	85.0%	77.4%	13.7%	122	74.5%	78.7
=52	Birmingham City	76.5%	69.1%	1.5%	120	90.9%	78.6
=52	Sheffield Hallam	75.0%	69.8%	3.7%	128	86.8%	78.6
54	Teesside	71.7%	61.0%	2.4%	130	90.6%	78.2
55	South Wales	82.5%	75.2%	2.2%	128	78.7%	78.1
56	Brunel	65.0%	52.2%	18.2%	123	90.8%	77.8
57	York St John	77.5%	76.7%	1.9%	117	84.9%	77.7
58	Glyndŵr	85.9%	80.5%	3.6%	110*	77.8%	77.2
59	West of Scotland	81.5%	77.4%	29.0%	122*	62.9%	77.1
60	Roehampton	74.0%	74.6%	20.6%	104	—	76.8
61	St Mary's, Twickenham	80.5%	84.5%	4.8%	121	72.6%	76.5
62	Sussex	74.1%	70.4%	8.0%	140	72.1%	76.4
63	Anglia Ruskin	72.1%	65.5%	3.1%	109	88.2%	75.8
=64	Salford	75.7%	65.6%	3.8%	125	78.1%	75.7
=64	Wolverhampton	75.9%	68.6%	11.0%	126	72.7%	75.7
66	Essex	79.9%	76.0%	—	122	74.7%	75.6
67	Edge Hill	71.2%	60.4%	2.0%	132	—	74.9
68	Suffolk	52.6%	46.5%	—	134	95.7%	74.7
69	Chester	69.8%	63.3%	12.0%	114	78.6%	74.4
70	Bournemouth	65.8%	56.2%	4.7%	110	86.8%	73.7
71	Sunderland	66.5%	54.3%	7.5%	128	—	73.5
72	Manchester Metropolitan	64.1%	54.1%	12.0%	129	75.8%	73.4
73	Bedfordshire	67.7%	64.3%	25.1%	120	65.9%	73.2
74	Worcester	73.0%	69.5%	2.6%	128	68.4%	73.0
75	Leeds Beckett	66.3%	59.9%	3.5%	117	80.2%	72.9
76	Middlesex	68.1%	63.2%	10.0%	109	76.6%	72.7
77	Canterbury Christ Church	57.2%	44.8%	2.2%	123	88.6%	72.6
78	Central Lancashire	65.7%	61.2%	8.3%	142	64.8%	72.3
79	East London	71.3%	60.3%	7.6%	102	75.6%	71.6
80	De Montfort	66.5%	63.5%	13.0%	106	72.0%	71.2
81	Buckinghamshire New	75.3%	68.6%	1.0%	94	—	71.1
82	Gloucestershire	35.4%	36.6%	6.0%	115	—	61.1

Employed in high-skilled job	65%	Employed in lower-skilled job	13%
Employed in high-skilled job and studying	4%	Employed in lower-skilled job and studying	1%
Studying	13%	Unemployed	5%
High skilled work (median) salary	£24,900	Low/medium skilled salary	£18,200

Theology and Religious Studies

The top five of our Theology and Religious Studies table features the same universities as last year. Oxford has moved up from fourth to tie in second with Durham, Edinburgh has shifted one place to rank fourth and St Andrews has gone from third to fifth. Cambridge remains at the top, and Durham, has the best research score.

The Oxbridge universities averaged the same entry tariff in 2020 of 185 UCAS points – the joint highest. But as in many other subject tables it is post-1992 universities that do better on measures of student satisfaction; Newman, Birmingham (=15th) achieved exceptionally high scores for both teaching quality (96.2%) and the wider undergraduate experience (91.9%) in the National Student Survey, followed by 17th-placed Gloucestershire in each.

Looking at how different beliefs have influenced society historically and their roles within the contemporary world, theology and religious studies courses draw on students' critical thinking and textual analysis. A career within a religious organisation is not the only career option, although vocations help maintain relatively healthy graduate prospects, along with roles in the civil service, law, international development, the arts, banking, investment, teaching, research, the media and communications. Oxford has the lead over Cambridge on graduate prospects, by a whisker, with almost nine in ten graduates employed in professional jobs and/or postgraduate study 15 months after their degrees. Theology and religious studies rank 39th out 67 subject areas in our employment index, and 44th for salaries.

Theology and Religious Studies	Teaching quality	Student experience	Research quality	Entry standards (UCAS points)	Graduate prospects	Overall score
1 Cambridge	—	—	44.6%	185	88.7%	100.0
=2 Oxford	—	—	46.7%	185	88.9%	96.4
=2 Durham	79.4%	70.6%	56.6%	158	84.3%	96.4
4 Edinburgh	80.8%	72.5%	43.2%	157	84.1%	94.6
5 St Andrews	88.3%	85.0%	28.9%	155	—	94.5
6 Lancaster	80.6%	74.1%	53.0%	134	—	93.1
7 Exeter	79.9%	75.9%	38.9%	135	86.1%	92.5
8 Manchester	88.0%	73.1%	37.2%	146	74.2%	92.1
9 Leeds	78.5%	74.0%	44.4%	131	75.9%	89.9
10 Birmingham	74.4%	63.9%	36.2%	140	77.5%	87.8
11 Glasgow	75.3%	68.3%	21.4%	164	—	87.6
12 Queen's Belfast	91.2%	84.8%	—	149*	71.1%	87.5
13 King's College London	72.9%	62.2%	37.1%	145	74.5%	87.1
14 Bristol	71.9%	61.3%	36.0%	142	77.1%	87.0
=15 Kent	77.3%	59.0%	44.1%	129	71.7%	86.8
=15 Newman, Birmingham	96.2%	91.9%	3.5%	109	—	86.8
17 Gloucestershire	95.7%	87.2%	6.9%	103*	—	86.0
18 Nottingham	71.3%	64.5%	43.9%	128	71.0%	85.6
19 St Mary's, Twickenham	79.5%	73.3%	9.4%	107*	82.7%	83.8
20 Cardiff	73.2%	57.5%	33.5%	129	63.8%	82.0
21 Chester	88.0%	82.7%	11.1%	102	61.5%	81.5

22 Winchester	82.3%	69.9%	18.0%	99	—	81.2
23 Leeds Trinity	87.7%	67.6%	9.9%	94	—	80.2
24 Liverpool Hope	75.9%	67.3%	17.7%	110	—	80.0
25 Roehampton	81.0%	67.3%	24.3%	93	59.5%	79.0
26 Canterbury Christ Church	84.3%	76.2%	16.3%	98	55.6%	78.9
27 York St John	88.1%	79.6%	4.8%	90	56.4%	77.8
28 Bath Spa	80.0%	68.9%	8.3%	91	—	77.2

Employed in high-skilled job	47%	Employed in lower-skilled job	26%
Employed in high-skilled job and studying	5%	Employed in lower-skilled job and studying	1%
Studying	14%	Unemployed	6%
High skilled work (median) salary	£24,400	Low/medium skilled salary	£17,775

Town and Country Planning and Landscape

Almost two-thirds of graduates of the various courses encompassed within the planning and landscape grouping had secured professional-level jobs when surveyed 15 months after finishing their degrees, helping to place the subjects 15th in the employment table. They are also in the top 25 for starting salaries, with graduates in professional-level work earning £25,000 on average. At eighth-placed Newcastle, which comes top for graduate prospects, 94.1% had secured professional work or postgraduate study and none of the 11 institutions that we have employment data for drop below 71% on this measure.

Recruitment numbers for urban and rural planning degrees have been robust over the past decade, with applications 37% higher in 2020 than in 2011 and enrolments up 7%. Landscape and garden design courses attract smaller numbers and have experienced declines of 24% and 30% in applications and enrolments respectively over the same period.

Our table is led by Cambridge for the second year running – boosted by its ever-high entry standards, with former No 1 University College London in second place. Loughborough, in sixth place overall, was the top scorer in the Research Excellence Framework. The National Student Survey revealed Ulster's students to be the most satisfied with the quality of teaching and with the broader student experience.

Town and Country Planning and Landscape	Teaching quality	Student experience	Research quality	Entry standards (UCAS points)	Graduate prospects	Overall score
1 Cambridge	—	—	49.0%	192	—	100.0
2 University College London	67.0%	65.1%	54.1%	171	—	96.1
3 Edinburgh	74.3%	68.3%	35.1%	174	—	95.4
4 Ulster	83.3%	88.5%	28.6%	134	—	94.2
5 Sheffield	80.5%	75.7%	36.6%	150	84.0%	94.0
6 Loughborough	76.6%	74.7%	58.3%	133	80.0%	93.2
7 Reading	77.1%	63.8%	40.0%	145*	—	93.1
8 Newcastle	66.8%	60.5%	43.7%	125	94.1%	92.3
9 Birmingham	71.3%	67.8%	42.0%	131	—	90.6

Town and Country Planning and Landscape cont.	Teaching quality	Student experience	Research quality	Entry standards (UCAS points)	Graduate prospects	Overall score
10 Leeds	74.4%	64.8%	32.0%	139	—	90.1
11 West of England	82.7%	80.1%	10.6%	125	86.9%	90.0
12 Liverpool	76.9%	75.8%	26.3%	123	—	89.1
13 Manchester	58.7%	59.5%	36.5%	157	85.0%	88.9
14 Cardiff	66.7%	65.7%	36.8%	137	83.3%	88.8
15 Queen's Belfast	74.1%	64.1%	35.2%	131	80.6%	88.4
16 Heriot-Watt	70.8%	67.0%	38.1%	167	71.4%	88.2
17 Glasgow Caledonian	69.7%	67.4%	9.1%	160*	—	87.2
18 Oxford Brookes	67.9%	66.7%	17.6%	124	86.3%	86.3
19 Leeds Beckett	74.3%	71.3%	5.6%	109	88.5%	85.9
20 Birmingham City	74.3%	65.6%	2.7%	101*	—	80.0
21 Westminster	65.3%	63.3%	10.7%	96	—	78.1
22 Gloucestershire	55.2%	42.5%	20.6%	106*	78.3%	77.3

Employed in high-skilled job	64%	Employed in lower-skilled job	11%
Employed in high-skilled job and studying	6%	Employed in lower-skilled job and studying	1%
Studying	9%	Unemployed	8%
High skilled work (median) salary	£25,000	Low/medium skilled salary	£20,000

Veterinary Medicine

Veterinary medicine averaged higher entry standards than its human peer subject in 2020, when successful candidates gained 186 points in the UCAS tariff, versus medicine's 185. Some schools demand high grades in chemistry and biology, while others require chemistry and one or two additional science subjects, such as biology, maths or physics. Cambridge also sets an admissions test and all vet schools require some evidence of relevant work experience. The deadline for applications is October 15th, to allow extra time to process the high demand for courses. There were around seven applications per place in the 2020 cycle.

The norm for veterinary science degrees is five years, but the Cambridge course takes six years and both Bristol and Nottingham offer a gateway year. Edinburgh and the Royal Veterinary College also run four-year courses for graduates. The subject is offered by very few universities and student numbers are centrally controlled. Although not featured in our table yet, as there is not enough data to include it, Surrey opened the UK's eighth vet school in 2013. A ninth launched in 2020, a joint venture between Keele and Harper Adams, will also be included once it has sufficient statistics.

The table looks very similar to last year's, except for Liverpool and Bristol swapping places and Cambridge ousting Nottingham from third place. Edinburgh, which has the top score in the Research Excellence Framework, remains No 1. Nottingham has the most satisfied students, achieving exceptionally high scores for teaching quality and the broad student experience in the National Student Survey.

Employment rates in veterinary medicine are so tightly bunched that they do not form part of the calculations which determine universities' positions, although they are still shown in our table. Veterinary medicine is in the top four subjects for employment and earnings.

Veterinary Medicine	Teaching quality	Student experience	Research quality	Entry standards (UCAS points)	Graduate prospects	Overall score
1 Edinburgh	85.6%	81.3%	46.8%	214	97.7%	100.0
2 Glasgow	80.7%	82.8%	42.3%	216	95.5%	96.1
3 Cambridge	77.7%	74.2%	43.1%	201	95.1%	92.2
4 Nottingham	96.2%	94.3%	36.4%	155	97.1%	91.7
5 Royal Veterinary College	79.7%	75.2%	40.8%	177	96.3%	88.6
6 Liverpool	84.2%	80.6%	32.9%	173	98.1%	85.7
7 Bristol	83.3%	78.5%	33.2%	169	97.7%	84.8

Employed in high-skilled job	95%	Employed in lower-skilled job	1%
Employed in high-skilled job and studying	1%	Employed in lower-skilled job and studying	0%
Studying	1%	Unemployed	1%
High skilled work (median) salary	£31,000	Low/medium skilled salary	—

13 Applying to Oxbridge

Collectively known as Oxbridge, the two ancient universities of Oxford and Cambridge met a curveball in our academic rankings this year – where they were pipped to the top spot by St Andrews. It is the first time either Oxford or Cambridge has not filled the No 1 position in the history of our *Guide*. In another shift, after an eight-year run at the top of our ranking, Cambridge dropped behind Oxford, to sit third. On the international stage Oxbridge's prowess remains unchallenged by other UK institutions, with each placing among the top three global institutions in 2022's QS world rankings, and the top five of *Times Higher Education's* global league table.

Their academic clout is not why Oxford and Cambridge merit their own chapter, however. This is due to their admissions arrangements, which are different to those in the rest of the higher education system. Both universities are part of the UCAS system, but they have three significant distinctions:

1. The deadline for applications is October 15 at 6pm – three months earlier than for other universities for entry in 2023 or deferred entry in 2024.
2. You can only apply to one or the other university in the same year, so you need to choose between the two.
3. Selection is in the hands of the colleges rather than the university centrally. Most candidates apply to a specific college, although open applications can be made if you are happy to go to any college.

What are the chances of getting in?

For anyone with Oxbridge in their sights this is one of the major questions. The potted answer is that Cambridge typically receives five applications per place on average across all subjects, and Oxford receives around six applications per place. Naturally, these ratios vary between courses, as the tables on pages 285–287 overleaf show.

In the 2020 admissions cycle Cambridge received 20,426 applications and accepted 3,997 new undergraduates – over 450 more than usual owing to the exceptional circumstances of the Covid-19 pandemic and the ensuing A-level marking fiasco. Overall application numbers to Oxford have risen by 22.2% since 2016, including 2020's unusually large intake of 3,695 new students out of 23,414 applications.

Entry standards are famously formidable. While three A grades is Oxford's minimum standard offer, many courses – particularly in the sciences – require at least one A* grade. More than 70% of 2020's home applicants and over 90% of admitted students were awarded A*AA or better at A-level. The picture is very similar at Cambridge, where the typical conditional A-level offer is A*AA or A*A*A. Of UK students accepted in 2020, 98.6% achieved the equivalent of A*AA or better.

Such statistics should not put talented, academically driven students off from applying. Some other less prestigious universities have even more applicants per place than Oxbridge and admissions tutors are always looking to broaden the range of schools and colleges they recruit from. What is the worst that can happen? One wasted option out of five on a UCAS form, perhaps. One caveat is that selectors have to be confident that applicants will cope with the demands of an undergraduate course at Oxbridge.

Student satisfaction?

Unfortunately, there is no up-to-date information on how students feel about their time at Oxbridge because both universities boycott the National Student Survey (NSS). But going by a report by the Higher Education Policy Unit, published in 2018 and based on six years of survey results, Oxbridge students were more content with university life than their Russell Group peers. The analysis found Oxbridge students were more satisfied with their courses, believed that they got better feedback and enjoyed greater well-being than those at other Russell Group institutions, although they studied for longer hours.

Job prospects for those with Oxbridge degrees are reliably promising. Oxford ranks fourth this year for graduate prospects, with 89.2% of graduates employed in high skilled jobs or engaged in postgraduate study 15 months on from their degrees. It is followed by Cambridge in fifth place – by a hair's breadth – with 88.5% of graduates having achieved these most desired outcomes.

Cambridge: The Tompkins Table 2019

College	2019	2018	2017	2016	College	2019	2018	2017	2016
Christ's	1	1	2	3	Gonville & Caius	16	14	11	19
Trinity	2	3	1	1	Fitzwilliam	17	19	21	23
Pembroke	3	2	4	2	Magdalene	18	18	16	9
Peterhouse	4	4	10	8	Murray Edwards	19	26	29	25
Churchill	5	7	5	11	Girton	20	23	24	27
Queens'	6	13	7	6	Robinson	21	24	25	22
Emmanuel	7	9	6	4	Newnham	22	22	23	21
Selwyn	8	11	9	15	Downing	23	20	20	12
St Catharine's	9	10	19	17	Clare	24	16	13	18
Trinity Hall	10	12	15	13	Hughes Hall	25	25	26	29
Corpus Christi	11	15	12	10	Homerton	26	27	28	24
King's	12	5	8	14	Wolfson	27	29	27	20
Sidney Sussex	13	17	17	16	St Edmund's	28	21	22	28
Jesus	14	6	14	7	Lucy Cavendish	29	28	18	26
St John's	15	8	3	5					

*Published by Varsity. Based on degree classifications: 1st=5pts; 2:1=3pts; 2:2=2pts; 3rd=1pt.
•The Tompkins Table was not published in 2020 or 2021 because of the pandemic

Diversity

Progress to widen access to Oxbridge is accelerating, as both universities attempt to shake off their exclusive image. Sixth formers who aren't sure they will fit in socially or academically should be reassured to learn that in 2020 at Oxford the proportion of students joining from state schools was 68.6%, up from 58% five years earlier. Our social inclusion ranking confirms this dynamic, although we look at admissions from non-selective state schools only, which stood at 45.6% in the latest data, up from 39.4% in 2018 when we first launched our social inclusion index. The proportion of students from ethnic minorities (23.8%) ranks Oxford 63rd out of 132 universities and is up from 17.6%. Oxford's black achievement gap – which measures the difference between the proportion of firsts and 2:1 degrees gained by black students compared with white students is -4.1%, the fourth best among British universities.

The social and cultural diversity of Oxford students is broadening. Over the past five years the proportion of black and minority ethnic students has risen from 15.82% to 23.6%, while the number of students from socio-economically disadvantaged areas almost doubled from 8.2% to 15.9%. The proportion who come from areas of low progression to higher education has gone from 11.4% to 15.6% over the same period. The proportion of disabled students has gone from 7.2% to 10.4% of the intake and women represented 54.2% of 2020's intake, up from 48.6% five years earlier.

Cambridge is also working hard to diversify its student community. The new free and fully-funded foundation year for study in the arts, humanities or social sciences is potentially game-changing. It is open to 50 students who have experienced considerable educational disadvantage. Unlike the rest of Cambridge's undergraduate applicants, the deadline for foundation year candidates is January 26 and the stipulated UCAS tariff score is 120 points – equivalent to BBB at A-level. No tuition fees are charged for the foundation year and a scholarship is being provided to cover accommodation and living costs.

Oxford: The Norrington Table 2020

College	2020	2019	2018	2017	College	2020	2019	2018	2017
New College	1	2	5	1	Balliol	16	9	9	10
St Catherine's	2	4	3	26	St Hilda's	17	18	=13	28
Queen's	3	7	19	5	Jesus	18	10	6	18
St Peter's	4	25	16	29	Pembroke	19	17	25	3
Merton	5	1	4	2	Magdalen	20	3	2	11
Wadham	6	20	8	13	Harris Manchester	21	11	30	27
Brasenose	7	16	7	7	St Anne's	22	28	24	19
St John's	8	6	1	6	Corpus Christi	23	12	15	16
Oriel	9	8	12	20	Keble	24	23	23	12
Lincoln	10	21	26	30	St Edmund Hall	25	29	29	24
Hertford	11	14	27	22	Exeter	26	19	18	25
Trinity	12	26	10	9	Lady Margaret Hall	27	27	21	14
University	13	13	17	8	Christ Church	28	15	11	17
Worcester	14	24	=13	4	Mansfield	29	5	20	15
St Hugh's	15	30	28	21	Somerville	30	22	22	23

*Based on degree classifications: 1st=5pts; 2:1=3pts; 2:2=2pts; 3rd=1pt.

Oxford applications and acceptances by course

Arts	Applications			Acceptances			Success rate %		
	2020	2019	2018	2020	2019	2018	2020	2019	2018
Ancient and modern history	100	94	104	19	24	18	19	26	21
Archaeology and anthropology	113	103	108	30	22	26	27	21	24
Classical archaeology and ancient history	84	110	88	28	17	22	33	15	25
Classics	278	278	308	119	115	115	43	41	37
Classics and English	35	40	38	16	12	10	30	26	46
Classics and modern languages	20	9	28	7	3	6	33	38	35
Computer science and philosophy	175	149	121	16	13	12	9	9	10
Economics and management	1,540	1,529	1,449	93	85	90	6	6	6
English	901	1,058	983	247	223	236	27	21	24
English and modern Languages	117	104	132	31	24	32	26	23	24
European and Middle Eastern languages	39	51	42	14	18	13	36	35	31
Fine art	219	231	23	29	26	27	13	11	12
Geography	448	538	32	97	84	81	22	16	25
History	1.078	1,127	1,036	278	223	231	26	23	22
History and economics	167	168	121	15	19	16	9	11	13
History and English	112	110	91	13	13	14	12	12	15
History and modern languages	113	98	109	27	19	19	24	19	21
History and politics	415	403	38	51	36	44	12	9	11
History of art	119	131	138	18	14	12	15	11	9
Law	1,611	1,566	1,541	234	178	202	15	11	13
Law with law studies in Europe	274	303	33	29	30	31	11	10	9
Mathematics and philosophy	120	137	142	21	13	18	18	9	13
Modern languages	406	414	423	170	156	157	42	38	37
Modern languages and linguistics	77	96	79	31	32	29	40	33	37
Music	185	198	204	87	70	75	47	35	37
Oriental studies	150	205	177	45	40	40	30	20	23
Philosophy and modern languages	66	78	62	21	23	22	32	29	35
Philosophy and theology	140	149	155	29	30	28	21	20	18
Physics and philosophy	182	179	156	15	17	13	8	9	8
Philosophy, politics and economics (PPE)	2,233	2,338	2,219	256	242	239	11	10	11
Theology	133	92	110	56	35	37	42	38	34
Theology and oriental studies	9	7	8	2	2	4	22	29	50
Total Arts	**11,659**	**12,093**	**11,388**	**2,144**	**1,858**	**1,919**	**18.4**	**15.4**	**16.6**

The foundation year is one of hundreds of outreach activities undertaken by Cambridge, which still sits no higher than 116th in our social inclusion ranking, just below Oxford at 115th. Evidently, while Oxbridge is making progress against widening participation objectives, the independent school sector still achieves a level of success at winning places that is out of proportion to its 7% share of the school population.

Oxford applications and acceptances by course cont.

Sciences	Applications			Acceptances			Success rate %		
	2020	2019	2018	2020	2019	2018	2020	2019	2018
Biochemistry	707	752	689	114	96	101	16	13	15
Biological sciences	739	700	575	122	110	109	17	16	19
Biomedical sciences	449	418	438	49	39	41	11	9	9
Chemistry	774	637	585	220	179	179	28	28	31
Computer science	682	693	592	42	44	36	6	6	6
Earth sciences (Geology)	142	116	127	40	35	38	28	30	30
Engineering sciences	1,159	1,040	1,055	189	174	169	16	17	16
Experimental psychology	496	427	395	68	56	53	14	13	13
Human science	220	186	159	39	30	31	18	16	19
Materials science	147	188	148	47	47	40	32	25	27
Mathematics	1,829	1,656	1,567	196	184	177	11	11	11
Mathematics and computer science	502	424	371	36	40	46	7	9	12
Mathematics and statistics	232	225	202	8	12	13	3	5	6
Medicine	1,768	1,795	1,667	165	161	150	9	9	9
Physics	1,646	1,405	1,324	181	185	181	11	13	14
Psychology and philosophy (PPL)	263	265	233	35	30	26	13	11	11
Total Sciences	**11,755**	**10,927**	**10,127**	**1,551**	**1,422**	**1,390**	**13.2**	**12.9**	**13.9**
Total Arts and Sciences	**23,414**	**23,020**	**21,515**	**3,695**	**3,280**	**3,309**	**16**	**14.1**	**15.2**

Choosing the right college

Undergraduates at Cambridge are admitted to 29 colleges, each with its own distinctive history, atmosphere and location. It is worth visiting Cambridge before applying to help you decide on a college that most appeals, though it is possible to make an open application. Oxford has 30 colleges that accept undergraduates, and applicants should research the varying academic strengths and social vibes among them to give themselves the best chance of winning a place and finding an environment where they can thrive. Thorough research is essential, as is personal contact – even within colleges, different admissions tutors may have different approaches.

That said, choosing a college is not as important as it used to be. Both universities assess candidates' strengths and will find a college for those who either make an open application or who are not taken by their first choice. At Oxford, subject tutors from around the university put candidates into bands, using the results of admissions tests as well as exam results and references. Applicants are spread around the colleges for interview and may not be seen by their preferred college if the tutors think their chances are better elsewhere.

The "pool" at Cambridge gives the most promising candidates a second chance if they were not offered a place at the college they applied to. Those placed in the pool are invited back for a second interview early in the New Year. Cambridge still interviews around 80% of applicants, whereas the system at Oxford means the university rejects a greater number of applicants immediately and interviews around 40–45% of applicants.

Cambridge applications and acceptances by course

Arts, Humanities and Social Sciences	Applications			Acceptances			Success rate %		
	2020	2019	2018	2020	2019	2018	2020	2019	2018
Anglo-Saxon, Norse and Celtic	44	60	47	26	19	17	59.1	31.7	36.2
Archaeology	57	58	51	24	22	18	42.1	37.9	35.3
Architecture	471	455	438	51	53	35	10.8	11.6	8.0
Asian and Middle Eastern studies	117	143	133	51	43	47	43.6	30.1	35.3
Classics	138	134	141	73	66	63	52.9	49.3	44.7
Classics (4 years)	66	57	54	33	21	20	50.0	36.8	37.0
Economics	1,364	1,143	1,094	165	156	167	12.1	13.6	15.3
Education	140	153	112	44	42	34	31.4	27.5	30.4
English	730	766	780	232	189	187	31.8	24.7	24.0
Geography	351	297	241	116	93	95	33.0	31.3	39.4
History	632	616	576	217	174	176	34.3	28.2	30.6
History and Mod Lang	94	92	78	33	25	23	35.1	27.2	29.5
History and Politics	261	223	210	62	41	44	23.8	18.4	21.0
History of art	105	122	120	25	26	30	23.8	21.3	25.0
Human, social and political sciences	1,075	1,089	932	210	185	167	19.5	17.0	17.6
Land economy	363	314	312	69	50	58	19.0	15.9	18.6
Law	1,537	1,498	1,357	262	221	202	17.0	14.8	14.9
Linguistics	98	100	112	40	24	31	40.8	24.0	27.7
Modern and medieval languages	378	417	408	187	159	158	49.5	38.1	38.7
Music	138	172	157	70	65	63	50.7	37.8	40.1
Philosophy	222	251	275	49	47	46	22.1	18.7	16.7
Theology and religious studies	131	124	99	55	39	35	42.0	31.5	35.4
Total Arts, Humanities and Social Sciences	8,512	8,284	7,746	2,094	1,760	1,716	24.6	21.2	22.2

Sciences	2020	2019	2018	2020	2019	2018	2020	2019	2018
Computer science	1,465	1,330	1,157	119	116	133	8.1	8.7	11.5
Engineering	2,518	2,250	2,299	363	329	330	14.4	14.6	14.4
Mathematics	1,633	1,518	1,597	251	253	234	15.4	16.7	14.7
Medicine	1,817	1,584	1,474	295	281	265	16.2	17.7	18.0
Medicine (graduate course)	485	552	–	37	43	–	7.6	7.8	–
Natural sciences	3,042	2,922	2,810	663	608	611	21.8	20.8	21.7
Psych and behavioural sciences	547	527	461	96	71	69	17.6	13.5	15.0
Veterinary medicine	407	392	357	79	67	71	19.4	17.1	19.9
Total Science and Technology	11,914	11,075	10,155	1,903	1,768	1,713	16.0	16.0	16.5
Total	20,426	19,359	17,901	3,997	3,528	3,429	19.6	18.2	18.9

Note: the dates refer to the year in which the acceptances were made.
Mathematics includes mathematics and mathematics with physics.

The tables in this chapter give an idea of the relative strengths of the colleges, as well as the varying levels of competition for a place in different subjects. But only individual research will help you uncover where you will feel most at home.

The application process

Both universities have made concerted efforts to demystify the application process by making it more user-friendly, thus opening the field more fairly to applicants without school or family experience of Oxbridge.

Cambridge requires most applicants to take a written pre-interview admission assessment at the beginning of November, usually at their school or college, or other authorised centre. Some subjects administer tests at interview – which everyone with a realistic chance of being offered a place is invited to attend (online or in-person, pandemic allowing). Some applicants to Cambridge are also asked to submit examples of their written work. The Cambridge website lists the subjects setting the pre-interview assessments, which may include a reading comprehension, problem-solving test, or thinking skills assessment, in addition to a paper on the subject itself.

Applicants to Oxford must also take an admissions test for many of its courses, and written work may be a requirement – depending on the course. Those who are shortlisted are invited to interview in early to mid-December.

Applicants to Cambridge must also complete an online Supplementary Application Questionnaire (SAQ) by 22 October in most cases. However, there is an earlier deadline of 27 September for international applicants wishing to be considered for interview in October with the international interview team.

In previous years, in-country interviews have taken place in some locations for international applicants, and in-college interviews were the norm for everyone else. The pandemic has meant that all Oxbridge interviews were held online for 2022 entry (or deferred 2023 entry). At the time of writing neither university was able to say which format would be likely for those applying for 2023 entry (or deferred entry in 2024). Applicants receive either a conditional offer or a rejection in the New Year.

For more information about the application process and preparation for interviews, visit **www.undergraduate.study.cam.ac.uk/** or **www.ox.ac.uk/admissions/undergraduate**.

Oxford College Profiles

Balliol

Oxford OX1 3BJ   01865 277788   www.balliol.ox.ac.uk
Undergraduates: 374   Postgraduates: 377   undergraduate@balliol.ox.ac.uk

The current Master of Balliol, Dame Helen Ghosh, is working to raise awareness about the climate crisis, and the college's governing body has voted to reduce its endowment's fossil fuel exposure. Balliol has maintained its reputation since 1263 as the oldest academic site in the English-speaking world that was co-founded by a woman. The college was named after John de Balliol, who was ordered by Henry III to perform a substantial act of charity, following a row with the Bishop of Durham. He founded the "House of the Scholars of Balliol"; its continuation after his death was guaranteed by endowments established by his wife, Dervorguilla. Exhibitions at the college's Historic Collections have included "Slavery in the Age of Revolution" lately, as part of the "Balliol & Empire" project, launched in 2019 and designed to re-examine the college's complex ties with colonialism. Balliol ranks sixteenth on the 2019–20 Norrington table, though it more often sits in the top ten. Alongside its academic focus, it is the only Oxford college to boast the triple "threat" (to study) of a student-run bar, popular café and excellent theatre – the Michael Pilch Studio. The college has surprisingly spacious grounds for its Broad Street location, with elegant traditional buildings and the occasional concrete block. Undergraduates are guaranteed accommodation for their first and final years, while graduate students are typically lodged in beautiful Holywell Manor. The impressive medieval library hosts 70,000 books and periodicals.

Brasenose

Oxford OX1 4AJ   01865 277510   www.bnc.ox.ac.uk
Undergraduates: 375   Postgraduates: 239   admissions@bnc.ox.ac.uk

Brasenose looks onto the beautiful Radcliffe Camera library. Student wellbeing is a particular focus and support offered includes an onsite counsellor, yoga classes, welfare walks, sexual health advice and trained peer supporters. Diversity is also a priority: there has been a female majority in the undergraduate population for the last five years, while freshers' events feature LGBTQ+ and CRAE (campaign for racial awareness and equality) workshops. Unusually, college accommodation is guaranteed for all undergraduates in the city centre – with first and third-years housed in college; and second and fourth-years in either the Frewin or Hollybush Row annexes nearby. Placed seventh in the latest Norrington Table, law, Philosophy, Politics and Economics (PPE), and history are traditional strengths at Brasenose and academic results are on the rise, with 2021 seeing an impressive 47 first class awards out of 97. Food at Brasenose is delicious and affordable, served in the beautiful sixteenth-century dining hall. The Brazen Nose door knocker, after which the college is named, was placed on the wall in 1890 and hangs above the high table. Popular extracurriculars include history and debating societies, as well as the Brasenose Green Group in which students draft sustainable strategies for review by the college. The sporting community is equally thriving and includes Brasenose's prestigious boat club – one of the oldest in the world. The annual sports day involves both staff and students, while Arts Week attracts undergraduates and graduates from across the university.

Christ Church

Oxford OX1 1DP   01865 286583   www.chch.ox.ac.uk
Undergraduates: 462   Postgraduates: 256   admissions@chch.ox.ac.uk

Boasting the largest quad in Oxford, its impressive scale, beautiful meadow and religious foundations continue to attract students, academics and tourists to "ChCh" – as Christ Church is known. One of the largest and most traditional Oxford colleges, in 2021 Christ Church's Junior Common Room student body disaffiliated from the students' union – a move colloquially referred to as "ChChexit". Higher profile travails have also beleaguered Christ Church over recent years, in the form of well-publicised and costly employment tribunals with its dean, the Very Rev Martyn Percy, who at the time of writing remained in post. Founded by Cardinal Wolsey in 1525, Christ Church remains one of the most imposing sites in the university. It is also the Cathedral of the Oxford diocese. Bowler-hatted porters, a listed eighteenth-century library, daily formal dining and wooden-panelled shared sets (double rooms), still characterise the overall feel of student life here. Accommodation ranges from the Blue Boar 1960s concrete block (for first-years), to the beautiful rooms in Peck quad (the domain of second-years) and the impressive Meadows and Old Library rooms (mostly for third- and fourth-years). Offsite options are ten minutes from college. The infamous "Harry Potter" hall hosts two servings every evening, one informal and one formal. Students choose between two student bars, The Buttery, open daily, and The Undie from Wednesday to Saturday. The summer months see students strolling along the riverbank beside rowing teams, local walkers and a herd of English Longhorn cows. Extracurriculars are a notable feature of college life, with an impressive choir, music and drama societies.

Corpus Christi

Oxford OX1 4JF · 01865 276693 · www.ccc.ox.ac.uk
Undergraduates: 279 · Postgraduates: 91 · admissions.office@ccc.ox.ac.uk

As one of the smallest colleges, Corpus Christi's tight-knit community and friendly atmosphere are nurtured within beautiful buildings between Christ Church meadow and the High Street. The college provides one of Oxford's most generous bursary schemes which bestows travel, book and vacation grants. Quirky extracurriculars are a strong part of college life: the cheese society and annual tortoise race are particularly popular amongst undergraduates. The large and modern Al-Jaber Auditorium is used for music, drama, art exhibitions and film screenings. Corpus's drama club, The Owlets, is highly regarded. Academic expectations are high; medicine, English, classics and PPE are especially well-established. The college was founded in 1517 by Richard Fox, Bishop of Winchester, and at its heart is an impressive sixteenth-century library. The original bookstacks sit alongside more modern reading rooms, which contain 70,000 volumes. Bishop Fox's focus on humanist learning had a strong influence on the former trilingual library (Latin, Greek and Hebrew), and recent exhibitions have showcased Corpus's very own Magna Carta and King James Bible manuscripts. The nearest watering hole is The Bear – the oldest pub in Oxford.

Exeter

Oxford OX1 3DP · 01865 279668 · www.exeter.ox.ac.uk
Undergraduates: 366 · Postgraduates: 266 · admissions@exeter.ox.ac.uk

Hosting essay competitions for prospective undergraduates, Exeter retains its focus on academic merit while emphasising the importance of potential in its applicants. The recent formation of the South West Consortium, a joint outreach programme between Exeter, Lady Margaret Hall and Merton colleges, focuses on Bristol and the southwest of England. The college also gains an international feel via its Williams at Exeter Programme, which links it to Williams College, Massachusetts and gives 26 American students full college membership. Exeter is situated in the heart of town on Turl Street, between the High Street and Broad Street, and has occupied its current site since 1315 – one year after it was founded. It counts many prominent twentieth-century writers among its alumni including Martin Amis, Alan Bennett, Phillip Pullman and JRR Tolkien. Arts-based extracurriculars are strong, particularly the annual Arts Festival, in partnership with neighbours Lincoln and Jesus, which provides a week of live music, theatre and poetry. One of Exeter's many enviable features is its spectacular view from the Fellows' Garden, which overlooks the beautiful Radcliffe Camera and impressive All Souls' College. Most undergraduates are guaranteed in-college accommodation, though many second-years choose to live out. The 2017 Cohen Quad development, located on Walton Street and nearer Worcester college, provides 90 en-suite bedrooms in a modern building.

Harris Manchester

Oxford OX1 3TD   01865 271009   www.hmc.ox.ac.uk

Undergraduates: 113   Postgraduates: 212   admissions@hmc.ox.ac.uk

The only college solely for mature students aged over 21, Harris Manchester is known for its inclusivity and openness and attracts students from across the globe. The college was originally founded in Manchester in 1786 to provide education for non-Anglican students; and after stints in both York and London it finally settled in Oxford in 1889, moving to its current central site in 1996 where it enjoys beautiful buildings and grounds just off Holywell Street. The college's Principal, Jane Shaw, fosters a vision for an internationally and ethnically diverse community, erasing age barriers so that students can gain a first, second or third chance at higher education. All members of the MCR (middle common room) are also members of the JCR (junior common room), which creates a close-knit community. Close to the Bodleian, Harris Manchester's own library is excellent, and boasts the best student-to-book ratio of any college. Its small size, however, means degree course offerings are relatively limited, and many sports teams join other colleges. All accommodation is on the main site: the 2017 student building provides additional en-suite rooms, a lecture hall, music practice rooms and a gym. The college hosts a range of extracurriculars centred around diversity, including weekly language nights over dinner; a liberations working group relating to BAME, LGBTQ+, women and disability communities. A refugee language programme provides tutoring and companionship to Syrian families.

Hertford

Oxford OX1 3BW   01865 279404   www.hertford.ox.ac.uk

Undergraduates: 416   Postgraduates: 251   undergraduate.admissions@hertford.ox.ac.uk

Known as "the college with the bridge", Hertford prides itself not only on the breathtaking Bridge of Sighs – which links two of its buildings opposite the Bodleian Library – but building bridges for prospective students regardless of their backgrounds. With its new project, Hertford 2030, the college has announced a period of transformational change. The new Porter Centre for Diplomacy will support scholarships, research and peace-making. With partners the John Porter Charitable Foundation and a donation of £25million, the college will also build the John Porter Graduate Centre, prioritising carbon neutrality and biodiversity. In October 2021, a 3.5m tall puppet called Little Amal visited the bridge to represent Hertford's support of displaced child refugees of the world. Granted full college status in 1740, Hertford provides means-tested bursaries to UK undergraduates studying for a first degree. It also partners with Opportunity Oxford, which supports talented offer-holders from underrepresented backgrounds. The college provides accommodation across all years: first-years live on the main site, while second- and third-years are in catered halls near Folly Bridge or spacious house shares in north Oxford. Hertford's strong music scene includes a jazz band, wind band, choir and orchestra. In a new literary podcast, The Hertford Bookshelf, English Professor Emma Smith chats to Hertford alumni authors.

Jesus

Oxford OX1 3DW   01865 279721   www.jesus.ox.ac.uk

Undergraduates: 389   Postgraduates: 243   admissions.officer@jesus.ox.ac.uk

Tucked away on a small site off Turl Street, Jesus boasts a 24-hour library, music rooms and a bar with a friendly atmosphere. The new Cheng Yu Tung Building, visible from central Cornmarket

Street, contains 64 en-suite rooms, a ground floor retail space and the Tower Room for events and exhibitions. The lower ground floor houses a NHS Primary Care Centre. The college maintains strong links with Wales, having been founded by Elizabeth I at the request of a Welsh churchman in 1571. Welsh dragons sit proudly at the entrances to staircases in Second Quad. A new access partnership announced in 2021 has received £120,000 in support of its outreach programme across Wales and runs a flagship summer school programme to encourage Welsh state school students to apply. A new geography scholarship will support UK black and mixed-black postgraduate research, while students of African and Caribbean heritage shared their experiences as part of college-based Black history month. A generous range of financial support includes book and vacation grants. Offsite, Jesus has squash courts and extensive playing fields with hockey, cricket, football and rugby pitches, grass tennis courts, netball courts, a boathouse and a sports pavilion. It holds a shared ball with Somerville every three years.

Keble

Oxford OX1 3PG   01865 272708   www.keble.ox.ac.uk
Undergraduates: 449   Postgraduates: 466   admissions@keble.ox.ac.uk

Keble is one of the largest and most distinctive colleges, with an impressive Victorian Gothic polychromatic brick façade that looks onto University Parks. The "holy zebra" stripy brickwork was intended to mark the college from its predecessors and attract attention and funding. Its dining hall is said to be the longest in Oxford – reflecting Keble's 1870s foundational premise that students should eat together regularly. Aside from a formal and informal hall, Café Keble is open all day – as is the Red Brick Oven, the college pizza bar. Student productions run from the O'Reilly Theatre every fortnight during term, making Keble one of the best places for drama. Alumni have set up the Keble Association to provide study grants for arts and humanitarian projects, while both students and alumni are volunteering as tutors for Keble's new partnership with the Access Project, an intensive programme of free support for Year 10 students from disadvantaged backgrounds in the West Midlands. *Strangeway*, a new student magazine, celebrates undergraduate literature and writing. Undergraduates are offered college accommodation for three years, and some live out in their second or fourth year. The graduate community is based a short distance from the main site at the HB Allen Centre, which opened in 2019 with 250 rooms. Keble's sporting facilities and record are exemplary, with a sports ground for football, cricket and tennis 15 minutes away, as well as shared squash courts and a boat house. The annual Keble Ball is arguably the most popular black-tie event in Oxford.

Lady Margaret Hall

Oxford OX2 6QA   01865 274310   www.lmh.ox.ac.uk
Undergraduates: 422   Postgraduates: 292   admissions@lmh.ox.ac.uk

Situated just north of the city centre, Lady Margaret Hall (LMH) has an enviable expanse of green space compared to more central colleges. Beautiful gardens back onto the Cherwell River and the grounds include a punt house and tennis courts. Its comparative isolation and large undergraduate population create a strong community feel. Originally Oxford's first women-only college, established in 1879, LMH has been co-educational since 1978. It was the first Oxbridge college to establish a foundation year to encourage access by students from underrepresented groups and paved the way for Foundation Oxford, a new university-wide scheme. LMH launched the Oxford Pakistan Programme in September 2021 with speeches from its new Principal, Professor Christine Gerrard; former Principal Alan Rusbridger and alumnus Malala

Yousafzai. The college has a strong reputation in PPE (philosophy, politics and economics) with Malala among its 2020 PPE graduates. LMH's arts scene is supported by its library's extensive collections in the arts and humanities. Accommodation is guaranteed for first, second and third-year students in the Pipe Partridge, a graceful neo-classical building with 64 en-suite bedrooms, the theatre and JCR.

Lincoln

Oxford OX1 3DR   01865 279836   www.lincoln.ox.ac.uk
Undergraduates: 323   Postgraduates: 398   admissions@lincoln.ox.ac.uk

Lincoln prides itself on being a warm, friendly and dynamic college with both academic and extracurricular focus. It is one of Oxford's smaller colleges, located centrally on Turl Street – next to Exeter and Jesus. Largely comprised of ivy-covered medieval buildings, Lincoln is home to arguably the most beautiful library in Oxford, a converted Queen Anne Church. Its supportive environment includes a welfare team, cookie fairies and tutors renowned for checking in on wellbeing. The college has generous subsidies for food and accommodation, with a large number of bursaries and hardship awards. Lincoln also rewards undergraduates who perform well in examinations and has one of the largest number of scholarships available for graduates. City centre accommodation is provided for all undergraduates, while graduate students are housed nearby in Bear Lane or Little Clarendon Street. College food is excellent; the dining hall serves three meals a day during term time – a rarity amongst older colleges. Deep Hall, the college bar, is popular with students and serves lighter food. At the close of Michaelmas term, the fire is lit in hall and the Christmas tree decorated for various "Oxmas" celebrations. Drama and music are popular: the Oakeshott room in the recently refurbished Garden Building is a well-used venue for screenings and performances – especially during the Turl Street Arts festival.

Magdalen

Oxford OX1 4AU   01865 276063   www.magd.ox.ac.uk
Undergraduates: 435   Postgraduates: 174   admissions@magd.ox.ac.uk

Magdalen rivals Christ Church in terms of fame, scale and breath-taking grounds – which are thought to have inspired CS Lewis's depiction of Narnia as he strolled around them. Renowned for its stunning bell tower, from which choir boys sing to mark May Day, the college has its own deer park and riverside walkway. All undergraduates have access to beautiful in-college rooms over their course. More than a quarter of students receive some sort of financial support – from travel grants to funding for creative projects. Although twentieth in the most recent Norrington table, Magdalen more commonly sits within the top five and tends to attract students who have rarely dropped a grade. Tutors are known for their worldwide research and encourage applicants with a strong interest in their chosen subject and excellent academic ability. Magdalen's renown can lead to feelings of "imposter syndrome" for some students, with traditionally stern porters guarding strict visitor's hours. Its current diversity initiatives include funding and packages for care-experienced students, as well as financial grants and welfare support, including counselling and mentoring. The punting house is popular with tourists and students alike during the summer months. The Magdalen Players also host a production in the gardens every summer, and the Florio Society (poetry) and Atkin Society (Law) are among varied extracurricular options.

Mansfield

Oxford OX1 3TF   01865 282920   www.mansfield.ox.ac.uk
Undergraduates: 255   Postgraduates: 206   registrar@mansfield.ox.ac.uk

Mansfield welcomes students from a wide variety of social and educational backgrounds from around the world, taking around 80 undergraduates per year. Due to its smaller size and inclusive ethos, it has a well-deserved reputation as a friendly college and is proud to recruit the biggest intake of students from the state sector. Opened in Oxford in 1886, Mansfield was previously known as Spring Hill College and located in Birmingham. Its original purpose – to provide educational training to nonconformist ministers – is echoed in its current ethos: to champion equality, diversity and access, while fostering academic excellence. Undergraduates live in throughout their degree, either onsite in Victorian buildings or in an East Oxford annexe. With four 24-hour libraries, the popular Crypt Café and the sun terrace open during Trinity term, Mansfield has extensive facilities for its size. The new Hands Building is home to the Law faculty's Bonavero Institute of Human Rights. It also provides a new lecture space and additional accommodation with 73 en-suite rooms. Proximity to University Parks encourages sporting enthusiasm. The JCR committee, called the Bench, is responsible for running social events and welfare provision. The "entz reps" (entertainment officers) coordinate a full timetable of open mic and comedy nights, sports days and charity auctions. There are designated tutors for women, students with disabilities, LGBTQ+ and BAME students.

Merton

Oxford OX1 4JD   01865 286316   www.merton.ox.ac.uk
Undergraduates: 321   Postgraduates: 225   undergraduate.admissions@merton.ox.ac.uk

Founded in 1264 by Walter de Merton, Lord Chancellor of England, Merton is one of Oxford's most ancient and prestigious colleges. It houses Europe's oldest academic library in continuous use and academic excellence is a priority. Merton's wide range of subjects goes some way to explaining its breadth of achievement. Its luminous roll of alumni includes Nobel Prize winners the poet T. S. Eliot, physicist Sir Antony Leggett, zoologist Nikolaas Tinbergen and the chemist Frederick Soddy. This is also where the Emperor of Japan, Naruhito studied; and creator of Lord of the Rings, JRR Tolkien was an English professor. Some of the cheapest accommodation across Oxford colleges is guaranteed for all three years of study, alongside generous bursaries and grants. Although dubbed as the college "where fun goes to die" by its own undergraduates, Merton's extracurriculars hold a growing reputation and include the Merton Floats drama society and the Bodley Club for literary speakers. Team LevelUp, who represented Merton in a university-wide entrepreneurial competition, were the winners of the best undergraduate idea in 2021. Merton's Winter Ball is popular across the university.

New College

Oxford OX1 3BN   01865 279272   www.new.ox.ac.uk
Undergraduates: 421   Postgraduates: 329   admissions@new.ox.ac.uk

Despite its academic prestige, New College has a more fun and relaxed community than some of its rivals in the Norrington Table – in which it ranked top in the latest edition. The college has recently embarked on an ambitious scheme to redevelop its Gradel Quadrangles on the Savile Road site to create 99 new student rooms, a flexible study and working space and a multi-purpose arts and performance area. New already has one of the largest sites in central Oxford, though its expansive buildings are essentially hidden from view. Founder William of Wykeham was the first to build a college as an integrated complex in 1379 – set with Hall, Chapel, Library and Muniment Tower – and New became a model for the Oxford college layout. Well-preserved thirteenth-century city walls enclose the garden, with a famous ornamental mound. One of the few colleges with its own sports ground and pavilion, New has football, rugby and hockey pitches, as well as all-weather netball and basketball courts. Both music and drama are prominent, aided by practice music rooms, a well-equipped band room and a 120-seat, fourteenth-century performance space, the Long Room. Since completion in 2019, the Clore Music Studios on Mansfield Road have been used by the orchestra, chamber groups and a world-class male choir which sings a Choral Evensong six nights a week during term. In Michaelmas term, the antechapel holds opera performances, and in Trinity term productions take place in the ancient cloisters – which featured in *Harry Potter and the Goblet of Fire*.

Oriel

Oxford OX1 4EW   01865 276555   www.oriel.ox.ac.uk
Undergraduates: 338   Postgraduates: 191   admissions@oriel.ox.ac.uk

Oriel's beautiful surroundings continue to attract tourists and students alike. The college's central location and unusual portico, which leads directly to the immaculate main quad, are particular favourites. Following Oriel's decision not to remove the controversial Cecil Rhodes statue from its domineering position overlooking the High Street, the college is now offering a full scholarship for a black or mixed-black UK graduate student and it celebrated Black history month 2021 with a collection of new books on black heritage and culture. Oriel undergraduates have maintained a strong presence in the Union and Conservative Association over the years. Formal dinner in the college's small yet impressive medieval hall is a popular feature of the undergraduate experience, with Latin grace providing a traditional atmosphere. Facilities include a sports ground, multiple gyms, a boathouse and squash courts. The infamous Tortoise Club crew recently qualified to race for the Thames Challenge Cup at Henley. Accommodation is guaranteed for the duration of study, graded from A* to D, with varying rents. Graduate housing is off the popular Cowley Road a mile away and includes several recently renovated flats. The college usually appears at the upper end of the Norrington Table and remained in the top ten in the most recent rankings.

Pembroke

Oxford OX1 1DW   01865 276412   www.pmb.ox.ac.uk
Undergraduates: 400   Postgraduates: 235   admissions@pmb.ox.ac.uk

Pembroke promotes a supportive and down-to-earth approach to college life, enriched by the contributions of each member of its medium-sized community. Located just off St Aldates, Pembroke sits opposite Christ Church in a quieter part of the city centre. It was founded by King James I in 1624 and the current site is based around four quads: Old, Chapel, North and The Rokos. There are five recently developed buildings and two new quadrangle spaces, with a footbridge linking Chapel Quad with the new area. Lively and ambitiously intellectual, Pembroke offers a range of joint honours undergraduate courses – from PPL (psychology, philosophy and linguistics) to European and Middle Eastern languages. History is a strong suit and there are tributes to the Pembroke fallen such as war memorial plaques in the Damon Wells Chapel and just outside it a three-figure sculpture, the Mourning Women. Two study skills tutors offer a range of support, providing sessions for incoming freshers and tips for revision planning and critical thinking. Applicants from disadvantaged and non-traditional backgrounds are encouraged to apply; Pembroke's outreach work targets London and northwest England. The McGowin Library is open 24/7 and its special collections include works by alumnus Samuel Johnson. Rowing is strong, as are talks and panels by high-profile media figures. Living onsite requires pre-payment for a minimum of six dinners a week.

Queen's

Oxford OX1 4AW   01865 279161   www.queens.ox.ac.uk
Undergraduates: 360   Postgraduates: 192   admissions@queens.ox.ac.uk

Queen's describes its community as both supportive and stimulating. Its page of student ambassadors, with realistic depictions of student life published online and through Instagram, is its showcase. The new Queen's Access Podcast provides first-hand information about applications, teaching, welfare and sport. Located just off the High Street, Queen's neo-classical buildings and bell tower create an imposingly beautiful entrance. Facilities are excellent, with accommodation offered throughout undergraduate courses – some in annexes around central Oxford and a third on the main site, mostly en-suite. The lecture theatre is used for concerts and screenings, while two refurbished squash courts are said to be the best in Oxford. Sport, drama and music are all important parts of the community, particularly the Trinity Term garden play. A budget of £90,000 is set aside each year for student support, with grants and loans awarded by a student finance committee. Music awards (including choral, organ and instrumental) are given annually to offer-holders following auditions. The beer cellar is popular and JCR facilities are extensive; afternoon tea is a daily highlight. The college is fully catered, providing three subsidised meals a day. The Upper Library is one of the most beautiful reading rooms in Oxford and there is an impressive New Library.

St Anne's

Oxford OX2 6HS   01865 274840   www.st-annes.ox.ac.uk
Undergraduates: 452   Postgraduates: 367   admissions@st-annes.ox.ac.uk

St Anne's has focused on widening access since 1879, when it was founded as the Society of Oxford Home-Students to allow women to study in affordable halls around Oxford – without having to pay for college membership. It gained full college status in 1952. It hosted the university's 2021 celebration of LGBT+ members with a series of lectures named after St Anne's alumnus Michael Dillon – the first person known to have medically transitioned from female to male in the UK. Like its motto, "consulto et audacter" (purposely and boldly), St Anne's purpose-built complex is boldly modern. Rooms are decided by ballot and accommodation is guaranteed over three-year courses. With 2,000 books added every year, the new library and academic centre on Woodstock Road is a point of pride. The college is particularly strong for music, with a student-led society encompassing various ensembles. The termly showcase gives students of every level a chance to perform. St Anne's Swingers perform jazz, swing and soul. The college Arts Week, held in Trinity term, includes drama, talks, film and even dance classes. Although closer to the suburb of Jericho north of the city than central Oxford, the college is conveniently near University Parks. Many students cycle to the university sports ground, though there is an onsite gym and nearby sports field with rugby, hockey, football and cricket pitches.

St Catherine's

Oxford OX1 3UJ   01865 271703   www.stcatz.ox.ac.uk

Undergraduates: 528   Postgraduates: 385   admissions@stcatz.ox.ac.uk

"Catz" is the youngest, and contains the most undergraduates, of any Oxford college. Within its spacious site just outside the city centre – right by the English, law and social science faculties – it is characterised by a laid-back atmosphere. Its students come from more than 50 nations. Established in 1962, its modern design and progressive JCR appeal to those who prefer a less traditional experience. Facilities include a theatre, onsite boathouse, squash courts, gym (free after a one-off £3 induction) and car park – a rare feature among Oxford colleges. The large grounds include a water garden and amphitheatre. Catz offers 36 undergraduate subjects and houses more than 60,000 books in its modern and spacious library. With the largest bar in Oxford, it has a sociable reputation and hosts popular "bops" four times a term. Increased welfare support in recent years has seen the appointment of a college counsellor and a fund for transgender students. Catz's student numbers brings strength in extracurriculars – particularly in men's rugby, women's football and drama. Extensive sporting funds mean Catz is the college of choice for many athletes. Catz students also take active roles in writing, directing and acting. The annual Cameron Mackintosh Chair of Contemporary Theatre has seen visiting Professorships held by Tim Rice, Arthur Miller, Sir Ian McKellen and Sir Tom Stoppard. Rooms are small but tend to be warmer than in older colleges – and are now available onsite for first, second and third-years.

St Edmund Hall

Oxford OX1 4AR   01865 279009   www.seh.ox.ac.uk

Undergraduates: 394   Postgraduates: 326   admissions@seh.ox.ac.uk

Teddy Hall is among the oldest Oxford colleges, dating back at least to 1317 – and likely to the 1190s when St Edmund of Abingdon, taught on the site. Its library is in a converted church, complete with stained-glass windows and a book-filled tower. The undergraduate community is known for being tight-knit, lively and social – a place where no one takes themselves too seriously. Its sporting culture is renowned; the college has enjoyed repeated successes in the cuppers basketball and rugby tournaments. Located just off the High Street on the quieter Queen's Lane, students can easily access university facilities. The college is currently focusing on improving the experience of students with disabilities, with support from librarians and tutors for those with learning difficulties. Although often at the lower end of the Norrington Table, Teddy Hall offers a wide range of scholarships and prizes – from volunteering and travel bursaries, to academic scholarships and an annual personal academic expense grant. Exchange partnerships with Lingnan University, China, provide opportunities for international study. With a burgeoning reputation for creative writing, Teddy Hall hosts a writer in residence, journalism prizes, weekly student-run writers' workshops and an annual publication. The two-part college bar houses the Buttery, a meeting place for sports teams or societies, and the lively Well Bar – known for its darts matches. Undergraduate accommodation is offered for two years; offsite rooms are at Norham Gardens, close to the University Parks. All first-years live in the medieval college quads, minutes from the Bodleian library. Food is excellent, though fairly expensive.

St Hilda's

Oxford OX4 1DY   01865 286620   www.st-hildas.ox.ac.uk
Undergraduates: 416   Postgraduates: 201   admissions@st-hildas.ox.ac.uk

St Hilda's excellent facilities include an exceptionally well-stocked library, one of the busiest JCR-run student bars, and beautiful gardens – instead of the more typical Oxford quads – which lead straight onto the River Cherwell. The riverside setting is ideal for punting season, during which students can use St Hilda's own punts. Its location just beyond Magdalen bridge, towards Cowley, contributes to its campus feel. Hilda's sporting reputation is particularly strong, with excellent hockey (on land and underwater), football, and cross-country teams gaining wins over recent cuppers tournaments. Founded in 1893 as an all-female college, St Hilda's started admitting men in 2006 and now has an equal gender split. The college prides itself on an inclusive atmosphere, introducing the post of "class liberation officer" to represent those who self-identify as being from working class backgrounds. It has its own multi-faith room. The college also has a purpose-built music building and recording studio, and the drama society puts on termly plays in the theatre. Named after a former principal of St Hilda's, the annual Lady English lecture featured Joan Bakewell discussing social mobility in 2021. The Hilda's ball is Oxford's most affordable. Second-year students typically live out, but onsite undergraduate accommodation is now available for the full three years. The Anniversary Building, completed in 2021, includes 52 student bedrooms.

St Hugh's

Oxford OX2 6LE   01865 274900   www.st-hughs.ox.ac.uk
Undergraduates: 452   Postgraduates: 440   admissions@st-hughs.ox.ac.uk

Extensive on-site facilities and 14 acres of green space makes the cycle to St Hugh's from the city centre worthwhile. Like St Hilda's, it has more of an independent campus feel than that of a traditional Oxford college – and was also women-only at its foundation in 1886, though now maintains an equal ratio of men and women. Listed red-brick Edwardian buildings combine with more recent additions, such as the Maplethorpe building. The food is excellent and hall costs are subsidised; brunch at weekends is popular and there is also a café. Other Hugh's highlights include themed formal dinners on special occasions, a croquet lawn and tennis courts, as well as areas for frisbee and football. Undergraduate accommodation is guaranteed; the new Dickson Poon building houses 63 graduates in en-suite bedrooms. Also functioning as the University's China Centre, the Dickson Poon has five spacious floors, 60,000 volumes, a lecture theatre, language laboratory and an ecologically efficient roof terrace. St Hugh's Howard Piper Library is one of the best in Oxford, containing seven reading rooms and more than 70,000 books. The college's relaxed approach to academia means it often falls towards the bottom of the Norrington Table, though in the latest it sits in the middle. It is convenient for the Science and Maths departments. A new academic feedback form encourages dialogue about aspects of academic provision.

St John's

Oxford OX1 3JP   01865 277317   www.sjc.ox.ac.uk
Undergraduates: 416   Postgraduates: 260   admissions.2021@sjc.ox.ac.uk

The wealthiest Oxford college (which equals cheaper rent and food for students), St John's has a reputation for academic and sporting success. Its Inspire Programme has worked with 1,500 school pupils in the last year, divided into pre- and post-GCSE support for potential applicants.

The college provides generous academic prizes and book grants, while the unique St John's discount scheme is the envy of other colleges and gives students money off at many nearby eateries. It has recently funded the re-opening of the historic Lamb & Flag pub, whose former patrons include JRR Tolkien and CS Lewis. The college enjoys a prime spot – a few minutes' walk from the Bodleian and the High Street. Founded by London merchant tailor, Sir Thomas White, in 1555, the college traditionally produced Anglican clergymen. Its early history prioritised medicine and law, though it has expanded into the arts and humanities over the last half-century. Subsidised accommodation is guaranteed over undergraduate degrees and for first-year graduate students. The college buildings combine traditional limestone quadrangles (the Front and Canterbury Quads) with modern accommodation blocks (Kendrew Quad) and the spacious new Library and Study Centre – which doubled seating and shelving capacity when it opened. Women's rowing is a particular sporting strength. Other extracurriculars include a chapel choir, drama society and orchestra. St John's ranked eighth in the most recent Norrington Table.

St Peter's

Oxford OX1 2DL   01865 278863   www.spc.ox.ac.uk
Undergraduates: 374   Postgraduates: 232   admissions@spc.ox.ac.uk

A medium-sized college, St Peter's is small enough to create an intimate and caring environment, though large enough to be diverse. The college takes an equal number of undergraduates and graduates every year (about 100 of each), with 20 visiting students who make up a significant part of the international community. Its buildings are an eclectic mix of medieval, Georgian and nineteenth-century styles. Close to the new Westgate shopping centre, it is centrally located and near libraries, shops and the railway station. It was founded as St Peter's Hall in 1929 to offer an Oxford education to students with limited financial means. Granted college status in 1961, it has since fostered an open community, averse to pomposity and stuffiness. Peter's still dabbles in more typical Oxford traditions from time to time – including formal hall, held twice a week. It generally sits in the middle of the Norrington Table but climbed to fourth position in 2020. Facilities are impressive, although it has one of the smaller endowments. The recently renovated JCR and popular student-run bar are favourite haunts. Undergraduate accommodation is available for first and third years and ranges from traditional to purpose-built rooms – the latter a few minutes' walk away. Music is well represented, with a tuneful college choir. The JCR host popular open mic nights every two weeks. Rugby and rowing contribute to Peter's growing sporting reputation.

Somerville

Oxford OX2 6HD   01865 270619   www.some.ox.ac.uk
Undergraduates: 437   Postgraduates: 235   academic.office@some.ox.ac.uk

Progressive values, fierce intelligence and empathy are said to unite Somervillians across the years. Named after Mary Somerville, the astronomer and pioneering academic, Somerville was one of the first two Oxford colleges (along with Lady Margaret Hall) founded in 1879 to admit women – and also, in Somerville's case, students of diverse beliefs. It remains one of the most international colleges, located just off St Giles and close to the Ashmolean Museum and the beautiful Taylor Institution language library. Somerville's status as a College of Sanctuary, with Sanctuary Scholarships and a new visiting scholarship for BAME early-career academics, shows evidence of its commitment to promoting greater inclusivity. Its Twitter page demystifies the undergraduate application process and encourages state school applicants, focusing particularly on students from the southeast. The atmosphere is friendly and fun, with strong extracurriculars including an excellent chapel choir, a baking society and boat club. The arts budget funds creative projects, including one of the best Arts Week programmes in Oxford. Somerville students are prominent in both journalism and drama. Food is particularly good value and there are independent student kitchens in all buildings. College rooms are provided for three years to most undergraduates and all first-year postgraduates. Somerville typically falls towards the lower half of the Norrington table, although it has one of the largest libraries with over 100,000 volumes.

Trinity

Oxford OX1 3BH   01865 279860   www.trinity.ox.ac.uk
Undergraduates: 298   Postgraduates: 131   admissions@trinity.ox.ac.uk

Located on Broad Street – minutes from the Bodleian Library, Radcliffe Camera, High Street and Cornmarket – Trinity is in the heart of the city, though its long drive and expansive green spaces make it a peaceful haven with the highest student-to-grass ratio in Oxford. Underpinning the future of Trinity is the new Levine Building, with an auditorium, five new teaching rooms, 46 student bedrooms and an informal study space and café. The tight-knit and friendly community is reinforced by welcoming and helpful porters. Under the leadership of Dame Hilary Boulding, access and outreach have gained momentum to counterbalance Trinity's traditionally high public-school intake. Strong biochemistry, maths, English and history departments create an academic focus – though extracurriculars are also strong. During Trinity term, the beautiful lawns off Garden Quad fill with students from across the university, along with croquet players practising for the cuppers tournament. The Trinity Players stage a garden play every summer; the boat club and the chapel choir are the largest societies. Trinity Arts Week has gained momentum over recent years. First and second-years live in college, with second-year "sets" (double rooms) popular due to their views over Garden Quad. Third and fourth years mostly live out, either in "Stav" on Woodstock Road or in privately rented Cowley properties. The food is renowned – especially Monday's steak and brie night and weekend brunches. Formal Hall is held three times a week. Trinity's big budget Commemoration Ball, held every third year, sells out in minutes.

University

Oxford OX1 4BH   01865 276601   www.univ.ox.ac.uk
Undergraduates: 425   Postgraduates: 221   admissions@univ.ox.ac.uk

Baroness Valerie Amos, the Labour life peer and former UN official, became Oxford's first Black head of house when she was appointed Master of "Univ" in 2019. Her message to students at the start of the 2021–22 academic year encouraged them to make the most of what Oxford has to offer – from academia and debate, to sport, music and a buzzing social life. Its High Street location, musical talent and recent focus on access are central to Univ's identity. The generally accepted legend that Univ was founded by King Alfred in 872 makes it the oldest Oxford college – although, more likely, its origins lie with William of Durham who died halfway through the thirteenth century. It began with small funds; only enough to support four theologians. Univ's intellectual activity has grown since the eighteenth century and it remains one of the largest and most academic colleges. Strong across the board, it excels in the sciences, PPE and law. A generous bursary scheme includes travel grants for study trips abroad, while 10% of undergraduate spaces are reserved for applicants from low-income backgrounds. First and third-years live in college, with second-years housed in a comfortable annexe near Summertown. Both men's and women's rowing have excelled in recent years. College members have access to a chalet in the foothills of Mont Blanc. Multiple 24-hour libraries and proximity to the Bodleian make Univ ideal for book lovers. Beyond the libraries, the chapel choir is excellent, and students put on a popular Comedy Revue every Hilary Term.

Wadham

Oxford OX1 3PN   01865 277545   www.wadham.ox.ac.uk
Undergraduates: 484   Postgraduates: 243   admissions@wadham.ox.ac.uk

Wadham's new warden, Robert Hannigan, was previously a cybersecurity specialist and senior British civil servant. Supporting Target Oxbridge, Wadham is funding ten places for talented black students in the 2021–22 academic year. Known for its overt leftist politics and activism (the sincerity of which is questioned by some), the college prides itself on a liberal, buzzing and laid-back atmosphere. With a large intake, Wadham occupies an imposing and attractive site opposite Trinity on Parks Road and offers more languages than any other college. The JCR has rebranded itself as a student union (combining the JCR and MCR) and prioritises welfare for minority groups. Partly due to its successful student ambassador scheme, the college has a strong state school intake. Queerfest – a celebration of LGBTQ+ culture, where all attendees wear outrageously colourful outfits – is a highlight of Wadham's social calendar. Likewise, Wadstock – its open-air music festival in Hilary (spring) term – has become a university-wide event. The Holywell Music Room is the oldest purpose-built European music room, while the Sir Claus Moser Theatre stages student plays and the beautiful gardens host Shakespeare performances in summer. Wadham's chapel choir recently sang at St Paul's Cathedral. Weekday dinners are served in the seventeenth-century hall, although Wadham is the only college with no gowned formal sittings. Undergraduates are guaranteed onsite rooms in their first and final years; other years are offered modern accommodation in two college-owned complexes about a mile away.

Worcester

Oxford OX1 2HB   01865 278391   www.worc.ox.ac.uk
Undergraduates: 455   Postgraduates: 192   admissions@worc.ox.ac.uk

New provost (head of college) David Isaac CBE is working to build back Worcester's supportive and flourishing academic community following the pandemic, with the aim to create a forward-looking institution based on academic excellence. Of 2021's UK offer-holders, 83% came from state schools and 35% from disadvantaged groups. As one of Oxford's most popular colleges, Worcester maintains beautiful grounds and a strong academic reputation. Its horticulture is the subject of a blog by its gardeners, and croquet on the extensive lawns is popular. The college has its own lake, which the new Sultan Nazrin Shah Centre (containing lecture theatres and rehearsal spaces) looks over. College architecture ranges from medieval cottages to Baroque and modern buildings. With its sports grounds uniquely in college, Worcester attracts many athletes. Arts and humanities lovers enjoy its popular Arts Week and annual summer Shakespeare performances by the Buskins dramatic society. Accommodation is guaranteed across all three years and is uniquely close to the heart of college – either within the grounds or close by in comfortable rooms with kitchen access. Good food is served at the nightly formal hall, where students stand at the entrance and exit of tutors, accompanied by Latin grace. The college hosts a popular Commemoration Ball every three years.

Cambridge College Profiles

Christ's

Cambridge CB2 3BU   01223 334900   www.christs.cam.ac.uk

Undergraduates: 442   Postgraduates: 262   admissions@christs.cam.ac.uk

Students at Christ's can have the best of both worlds, enjoying tranquil gardens just a stone's throw from the city centre's attractions. Accommodation is also in line for a significant upgrade, with the King Street development adding 64 en-suite rooms, some expected to be ready for October 2022. In the longer term, Christ's is planning to build a new library with exhibition space and glass-roofed café and walkway. Most undergraduates live in college, although a few are in row houses on King's Street and Jesus Lane. About 40% of rooms are en-suite. This includes small, single bedrooms in the Modernist "Typewriter" building (New Court) and large, double bedrooms in Second Court. More traditional rooms and sets (a study room and bedroom) are in First Court. There is plenty to keep student life vibrant, from the Yusuf Hamied Theatre, which hosts student productions, to Christ's Cinema, and an art society. Students can also borrow art for their rooms through the Picture Loan Scheme. Christ's has plenty of its own sports clubs from rowing to mixed lacrosse, while some sports share teams with other colleges. Nearly three-quarters of Christ's 2020 intake came from state schools – placing it in the top half of colleges for such admissions. The Bridging Programme, launched in 2020, provides new students from underrepresented backgrounds with academic support and an introduction to university life. In recent years the college has had a reputation for being academically intense.

Churchill

Cambridge CB3 0DS   01223 336000   www.chu.cam.ac.uk

Undergraduates: 523   Postgraduates: 356   admissions@chu.cam.ac.uk

Being a "hill college" outside of the city centre has its perks for Churchill: it enjoys a 42-acre site, the largest college campus. Around three quarters of undergraduate Churchillians study STEM subjects, which is the highest proportion in Cambridge. It offers a quick commute to the West Cambridge site, where many science departments are based. Churchill is famous for its brutalist architecture, and its campus also houses a gym, theatre, music centre, squash and tennis courts and grass pitches. College sport is popular and before pandemic disruption, Churchill was a force to be reckoned with. In 2019 teams in badminton, rugby, lacrosse and netball all made it to the finals of intercollegiate cuppers. Accommodation is not bad either: students are promised on-site rooms for the entirety of their undergraduate degrees. Around 40% of them are en-suite. Cowan Court offers some of the most luxurious accommodation, complete with double beds. Churchill is one of the least traditional colleges: students are welcome to walk on the grass and they do not wear academic gowns to formal dinners. Churchill often has one of Oxbridge's highest state undergraduate intakes – over 75% in 2020 and 79% in 2021. The college has also achieved a more even gender split in the last few years, with 48% of 2021's intake female. Developments in the pipeline include a new art and design space in the old boiler rooms.

Clare

Cambridge CB2 1TL   01223 333200   www.clare.cam.ac.uk

Undergraduates: 531   Postgraduates: 283   admissions@clare.cam.ac.uk

Clare is Cambridge's second-oldest college, dating from 1326, and offers delightful garden views leading out onto the Backs. Much of Clare has been a construction site in recent years, however, as the College has been transforming Old Court by refurbishing existing rooms and building new bathrooms. It is also building a River Room Café, which will feature a terrace by the Cam and space for students to meet. Music is big at Clare, with a renowned choir and music recitals, as well as intimate gigs in the popular and atmospheric underground Clare Cellars bar. Rooms in Old Court offer a traditional experience, while Memorial Court, across the river, is close to the University Library and both humanities and science departments. Students in their second year often live at "Clare Colony", closer to the boathouse on the slopes of Castle Hill. The Colony's large, old houses and more modern buildings are around a 13-minute walk from the main site. All freshers live in Memorial, Thirkill or Lerner Court. The college has an enthusiastic boat club and very good sports facilities just beyond the botanic garden – a ten-minute cycle ride away. There is also a popular, non-partisan Politics Society, drawing high-profile speakers and a student-run newsletter, *Clareification*.

Corpus Christi

Cambridge CB2 1RH   01223 338056   www.corpus.cam.ac.uk
Undergraduates: 323   Postgraduates: 241   admissions@corpus.cam.ac.uk

Corpus Christi is a gem in the heart of Cambridge, as a small bustling college with a welcoming feel. Tourists flock to its famous clock, displayed on the outside of the Taylor Library in Kwee Court. Some students are housed in ancient rooms, others are accommodated away from, but close to, the main site, in the Beldam, Bene't Street and Botolph Court buildings. The college has its own gym, playing fields and an open-air swimming pool, located at Leckhampton, just over a mile away. There is also a cosy underground bar for socialising. All undergraduates are guaranteed accommodation with a "ballot" for selecting rooms after first year, although some "prize rooms" are allocated based on exam results. The renovations to the medieval Old Hall were shortlisted for a RIBA award. To expand the sports offering, Corpus joins with King's and Christ's Colleges to form collaborative "CCK" teams. Its small but much-used theatre, the Corpus Playroom, is where students university-wide stage plays and comedy nights. Student numbers rose from under 300 in 2019 to 323 in 2020. Alongside a small increase in students due to the Covid-19 A-level disruption, it is also part of the College's plan to add 30 new undergraduate places a year for students from underrepresented backgrounds, which will be complete in 2022. In 2020 Corpus began offering a three-week "bridging course" for these students before they matriculate.

Downing

Cambridge CB2 1DQ   01223 334826   www.dow.cam.ac.uk
Undergraduates: 482   Postgraduates: 434   admissions@dow.cam.ac.uk

Downing has a different appearance to any other college, as it was built in a neo-classical style in the nineteenth century. Grand buildings open on to the Paddock lawn – a popular spot for relaxing in the post-exam period. Students at Downing throw themselves into plenty of extra-curriculars. On the sports front it is known as a fearsome opponent on both the rugby pitch and the river. It has also been strong in football, badminton, netball and tennis. For arts and culture there is the 160-seat Howard Theatre, a vibrant drama society that hosts a festival of student writing each year, and the 2016-opened Heong Gallery – dedicated to modern and contemporary art. Downing has some plush accommodation with double beds, and more than half of rooms are en-suite, although these can be relatively expensive. Students either live on-site or in a house bordering the college. Downing also has its own termly student-run magazine, *The Griffin*.

A lively social scene centres on the comfy Butterfield Café and Bar, which hosts pub quizzes and live music in the evenings and makes a casual study space during the day. The college was originally founded for the study of law and natural sciences, and while it is still popular with scientists, lawyers and geographers thanks to its fall-out-of-bed-and-into lectures proximity to their faculties, it is now home to an eclectic body of students studying all subjects.

Emmanuel

Cambridge CB2 3AP   01223 334290   www.emma.cam.ac.uk
Undergraduates: 521   Postgraduates: 217   admissions@emma.cam.ac.uk

Visit Emmanuel and you might spot some of the college ducks among the students in the beautiful gardens. Nicknamed "Emma", students love the college for its central location, friendly atmosphere and the weekly load of laundry included in their rent. The large Paddock lawn is a space to study and socialise, while the open-air swimming pool is a boon in the summer. Extensive renovations are underway at Emma, as it builds a new court with 50 rooms, with the aim that all undergraduates may be accommodated on-site throughout their degrees. Students currently move into off-site houses in second and third years. Emma is also building a stylish new bar and lounge in Furness Lodge while turning the old bar into a new "Hub" workspace. Founded by Puritans in the 1580s, Emma strives to maintain a forward-thinking and egalitarian atmosphere. Just under 70% of 2020's new students came from state schools. At last count, around 67% of students studied STEM subjects. Societies and sports focus more on inclusion than competition and activities are diverse. The elegant Christopher Wren chapel hosts concerts organised by the music society. As one of the better-endowed colleges, Emmanuel offers several bursaries and scholarships.

Fitzwilliam

Cambridge CB3 0DG   01223 332030   www.fitz.cam.ac.uk
Undergraduates: 498   Postgraduates: 441   admissions@fitz.cam.ac.uk

Do not be surprised if you see the occasional goat figurine or drawing around college: the billy goat is the Fitzwilliam mascot. Many "Fitzbillies" enjoy the quieter surroundings of their Castle Hill locale and the camaraderie of the ten-minute walk into town. Fitzwilliam has a strong commitment to widening access. Nearly 80% of its intake came from the state sector in 2020 – one of the highest proportions in Cambridge. It participates in the Foundation Year programme for students from disadvantaged backgrounds. A friendly feel is enshrined at the busy café-bar. While Fitzwilliam lacks the archetypal ancient architecture, its gardens are beautiful, and its dining hall boasts an eye-catching brutalist lantern roof. Students are accommodated throughout their degrees in one of 408 rooms or in houses minutes from the campus. All first-year rooms are semi en-suite, equipped with a shower and washbasin, and most student kitchens include ovens. Good facilities also extend to an auditorium, a two-storey gym, a modern library and squash courts. While there are sports clubs to cater to all levels, the standards can also be high at Fitzwilliam, where the men's football team won the inter-college Cuppers for the fifth year in a row in 2021. The college's cultural life is also rich. Fitzwilliam opens its Chapel every two weeks for students to gather and work on art projects. As well as a choir, there are two *a cappella* singing groups, an opera company and the long running Fitz Swing band.

Girton

Cambridge CB3 0JG   01223 338972   www.girton.cam.ac.uk
Undergraduates: 524   Postgraduates: 303   admissions@girton.cam.ac.uk

Girton has a storied history since its inception in 1869 as the first residential college offering higher education to women in the UK. Now co-educational, it is home to a dynamic community of scholars. Girton students tend to be well-acquainted with the cycle or bus route into town as their college is the furthest from the city centre. Many students still enjoy the quiet surrounds of Girton village, however, and take advantage of extensive grounds and gardens. The top-notch facilities include three gyms and various hard courts as well as football, rugby and cricket pitches, and the only indoor heated pool of any college. A new "Social Hub" café-bar was opened in 2019 and there is another cellar bar that plays host to JCR events. Girton students can live in rooms that range from atmospheric Victorian to modern en-suites in Ash Court. Off-site accommodation is in college-owned houses or the recently opened Swirles Court (for graduates), located on the university's new development at Eddington. Just over a third of the undergraduate rooms are en-suite. One accommodation corridor is reserved for women and non-binary students in the main building. Girton has its own museum and an artsy extra-curricular scene – supported by a dark room for photography and permanent Peoples' Portraits exhibition. More than three quarters of Girton's 2020 intake came from state schools, and the college now participates in the Foundation Year programme for students from disadvantaged backgrounds, starting with the 2022 admissions round.

Gonville & Caius

Cambridge CB2 1TA   01223 332413   www.cai.cam.ac.uk
Undergraduates: 618   Postgraduates: 252   admissions@cai.cam.ac.uk

Students at Caius (pronounced "keys") are recognisable by their blue gowns as they file into hall for dinner. Founded as Gonville Hall in 1348, Caius is one of the oldest colleges and its undergraduate population is among the largest. Its main site, Old Courts, features five peaceful courtyards in the heart of town. Unlike other colleges, Caius serves a three-course meal, six nights a week. There are two sittings: the first at 6pm is fairly brisk, while the second requires students to wear their formal gowns – often with jeans or sports kit underneath. A unique dining policy obliges undergraduates to pay for 31 dinners a term in advance. Unpopular though this practice is with some, it encourages students to return to the main site and dine together. There is plenty to get involved with – the college has 45 clubs and societies. Most freshers live on West Road by the Sidgwick Site, which houses many humanities departments. This includes the Stephen Hawking Building, which offers 75 modern, en-suite rooms. There is also Harvey Court, a brutalist building with its own JCR, where some rooms have their own balconies. Many second-years live in rooms overlooking shops in the city centre or in houses near the Fenners cricket ground. More traditional rooms and sets are in the Old Courts, and these often host third-years. Caius also has a boathouse and gym. Caius has in the past had some of the lowest state school intakes (only 57% in 2020) but appears to have turned a corner, with that figure rising to 73% in 2021.

Homerton

Cambridge CB2 8PH   01223 747252   www.homerton.cam.ac.uk
Undergraduates: 632   Postgraduates: 711   admissions@homerton.cam.ac.uk

There is plenty to keep students busy within the Homerton grounds – sometimes lending the impression that it could be its own university campus. Homerton is one of the furthest colleges from the city centre, and it is also the biggest – with 632 undergraduates. Homerton officially became a college in 2010, making it Cambridge's youngest, although it was founded more than 250 years ago. Close to the railway station, a 15-minute cycle ride brings students into town. The benefit of space means accommodation is mainly en-suite study bedrooms of a high standard.

There is an orchard and extensive lawns that may be walked upon – contributing to the friendly and unpretentious atmosphere. Plenty of facilities have been upgraded recently. The college has just built new sports grounds nearby with floodlit pitches and specialist equipment. A striking new £8million dining hall, which will also hold kitchens and a buttery, is under construction. There is also an on-site gym. A new auditorium and 18 en-suite bedrooms in North Wing are recent additions. There is more to come in the form of a new lantern-shaped Porter's Lodge and library extension. Homerton has many education Tripos students, in line with its history as a teacher training college. The arts abound, including amateur dramatic performances throughout the year.

Hughes Hall

Cambridge CB1 2EW   01223 334898   www.hughes.cam.ac.uk
Undergraduates: 178   Postgraduates: 745   ugadmissions@hughes.cam.ac.uk

It is the oldest graduate college at Cambridge, but Hughes Hall also welcomes a small number of undergraduates aged over 21. With 57% of those entrants hailing from outside the UK, Hughes Hall has the most international undergraduate population of any college. Nearly 54% of undergraduates study arts and humanities subjects – also the highest proportion at Cambridge. The college enjoys commanding views over the Fenners cricket ground from its roof terraces, and sits alongside Mill Road, known for its independent businesses. Hughes Hall has a strong record on the sports pitch and the river, with its rowing club historically performing very well in the intercollegiate "Bumps" competition. It guarantees undergraduates single accommodation throughout their degrees. First-years are generally given rooms in the central college site. There are also more traditional rooms in college, as well as off-site houses. Some students can live in couples' flats, which tend to be in high demand. In 2016, 85 single en-suite rooms were built along with a bike store and study rooms in the new Gresham Court building.

Jesus

Cambridge CB5 8BL   01223 339455   www.jesus.cam.ac.uk
Undergraduates: 538   Postgraduates: 416   undergraduate-admissions@jesus.cam.ac.uk

In 2020 Jesus recruited more than 80% of its UK students from state schools – the highest proportion of all Cambridge colleges and a statistic it will no doubt take pride in. Jesus enjoys 33 acres of picturesque grounds close to the city centre as well as the open green space of Jesus Green. Many of its red brick buildings date back to its foundation in the 1500s, while the twelfth-century chapel outdates the college by 350 years. There are modern facilities too, such as the West Court development which has student common rooms, a games room, a swanky café that doubles as a popular bar in the evenings and a terrace. The West Court Gallery often hosts impressive exhibitions. Jesus also has on-site pitches for football, rugby and cricket, as well as squash and tennis courts. It is home to an eclectic student population known for being as strong in sports as in music and art. All undergraduates are accommodated for every year of their degree, not just the first three – a feature especially welcome for medical students. Jesus's current master, former media executive Sonita Alleyne, is the first Black woman to lead an Oxbridge College. The much-loved grounds are often punctuated by modern sculpture exhibitions, and the college's own collection contains work by Antony Gormley and John Bellany, among others. Students are permitted to roam on most – but not all – of the grass. The May Ball is glamorous and usually popular.

King's

Cambridge CB2 1ST   01223 330164   www.kings.cam.ac.uk
Undergraduates: 457   Postgraduates: 293   undergraduate.admissions@kings.cam.ac.uk

King's Chapel is one of the biggest draws for visitors to Cambridge – an iconic landmark, the grandeur of its scale and vaulted ceilings rivals many cathedrals. Students and parents often snap up tickets to the recordings of the choir's famous carols, weeks before they are broadcast on television. College life is less staid than the imposing surroundings would suggest. King's has a modern outlook, and the student community can be quite alternative, as evidenced by the King's Affair May Week event, which typically features techno music and avant-garde fancy dress. King's state school intake in 2020 (78%) was the fourth highest in Cambridge. The college is aiming to raise £100million to preserve its buildings and build on access efforts. A bridging programme before term starts, provides support for students from schools in disadvantaged areas. King's has punts for students to rent and art studio space for them to use. Accommodation ranges from the archetypal Cambridge rooms in old buildings to en-suite rooms in newer hostels off-site. First years tend to live on the main site in the more modern Keynes building or older Webb's Court, and in the Spalding hostel by Market Square. The gym is in the vault of Bene't Street Hostel. Garden Hostel, beside the Fellows' Garden on the other side of the river, has been renovated to provide 70 contemporary en-suite rooms. King's recently unveiled its new bar as it redevelops Chetwynd Court, and plans to add a new auditorium.

Lucy Cavendish

Cambridge CB3 0BU   01223 332190   www.lucy.cam.ac.uk
Undergraduates: 157   Postgraduates: 371   admissions@lucy.cam.ac.uk

Historically a college only for mature, female students, Lucy Cavendish has firmly entered a new chapter and welcomed its first mixed-gender intake in 2021. The college now also accepts students from age 18 and takes widening access seriously: more than 82% of UK undergraduates admitted in 2021 attended state schools, with many from disadvantaged and underrepresented backgrounds. Accommodation is provided for all for at least three years, subject to availability. Housing is either in college or in nearby houses, close to those of fellow "hill" colleges, St Edmunds and Fitzwilliam. There is also an attractive apartment complex in Histon Road. Students can stay in women-only accommodation sets if preferred for religious or cultural reasons. There are also some flats for couples. Lucy Cavendish has new accommodation in the works, which will provide 72 en-suite bedrooms and a ground floor café in a building meeting top sustainability standards. It is also set to gain a new courtyard. In 2021, Lucy Cavendish held a free bridging week for all its new undergraduate intake to help them adjust to Cambridge, with sessions on academic support and university life. The college's Fiction Prize, in its twelfth year in 2022, has helped launch the publishing career of many successful authors, including Gail Honeyman and Laura Marshall. Many students participate in university-level sports clubs, while Lucy has its own boat club and shares badminton, football and netball teams with other colleges.

Magdalene

Cambridge CB3 0AG   01223 332135   www.magd.cam.ac.uk
Undergraduates: 402   Postgraduates: 212   admissions@magd.cam.ac.uk

Old and new rub shoulders at Magdalene, whose historic courts are situated alongside the River Cam. Tradition means the college still hosts one of the university's few white tie summer balls every other year, while its modern outlook makes Magdalene a firmly 21st-century seat of learning. It unveiled its airy new library in 2021, which features study spaces for 90 as well as an archive centre and art gallery. The college's most famous alumnus, Samuel Pepys, is immortalised in the Pepys Building that houses a collection of 3,000 of the diarist's books and manuscripts. Magdalene has the longest river frontage of any college, which gives students plenty of space to enjoy the Backs. It also has one of the cheaper formal halls in Cambridge which keeps it popular for social occasions. The sports pitches are shared with St John's (both colleges have a sporty reputation) and Magdalene also has its own Eton fives court. Students live either in the main courts, in the village on the other side of Magdalene Street, or in college-owned houses a few minutes' walk away. Students from different year groups are housed together. Accommodation quality varies – some rooms have been recently renovated and there are en-suite options, as well as sets (with a bedroom and a study room) at several different sites.

Murray Edwards

Cambridge CB3 0DF   01223 762229   www.murrayedwards.cam.ac.uk
Undergraduates: 396   Postgraduates: 192   admissions@murrayedwards.cam.ac.uk

"Dome is home" is a refrain among students at Murray Edwards – often referred to as "Medwards". Students at the women's college enjoy the supportive atmosphere at its architecturally brutalist campus on Castle Hill, as well as the brunch served at weekends in hall, whose roof is the dome in question. Murray Edwards is also home to the second largest collection of women's art in the world, including work by Barbara Hepworth, Tracey Emin and Paula Rego. Women's achievements are encouraged, and the Gateway programme provides workshops on academic leadership and career development. Fifty-three per cent of undergraduates study STEM subjects, which helps address the gender imbalances in these courses. The college is participating in the university's Foundation Year scheme, which will allow students from disadvantaged backgrounds to study at Cambridge for a year before starting their degree. The laid-back feel extends to the gardens where students can grow herbs and vegetables in their allotments, as well as walk on the grass – a rare privilege among Cambridge colleges. Sport is strong and everything from badminton to hockey is catered for. The college often provides Blues players to the university teams. Rents can be high, however, which has been a subject of student criticism.

Newnham

Cambridge CB3 9DF   01223 335783   www.newn.cam.ac.uk
Undergraduates: 430   Postgraduates: 325   admissions@newn.cam.ac.uk

Newnham, which has sought to champion women's academic success and help them to realise their potential since 1871, celebrated its 150th anniversary as an all-women's college in 2021. The idyllic grounds stretch across 18-acres and feature sports pitches, tennis courts and beautiful gardens. For arts students, Newnham is ideally located for the Sidgwick Site. Upgrades to the estate mean that Newnham students can now enjoy 90 new en-suite rooms, as well as a new porters' lodge, gym, café, and some of the plushest student kitchens in Cambridge. Rooms for conferences and supervisions are in the Dorothy Garrod building, named after Cambridge's first female professor. The Iris café-bar is a light-filled space whose popular sandwiches create a daily lunchtime rush of students, fellows and visitors from other colleges. There is also a well-stocked art room open to students. Newnham also has many of its own sports clubs, including badminton, football, netball and lacrosse. Alumni include Mary Beard, who is a fellow, Sylvia Plath, Diane

Abbott and Emma Thompson. One criticism levelled against Newnham is that rents can be expensive, given that all rooms cost the same despite their varying quality. The college has introduced rent bursaries for students from lower income backgrounds.

Pembroke

Cambridge CB2 1RF   01223 338154   www.pem.cam.ac.uk
Undergraduates: 486   Postgraduates: 305   admissions@pem.cam.ac.uk

Pembroke has remained in its original location (on what is now Trumpington Street) for centuries, having been founded by Marie St Pol on Christmas Eve of 1347. Pembroke is Cambridge's third-oldest college, and within its walls there are tranquil gardens including a wild orchard, and Christopher Wren's first chapel. Its food is popular – particularly brunch – and formal dinner is traditionally served every night. Alumni include Ted Hughes, and the actors Naomie Harris and Tom Hiddleston. Renovations to the Mill Lane site across the road, due to complete by 2023, will enlarge the college's footprint by a third. The development will create 110 bedrooms, so fewer students will have to live further afield. The college is also gaining a new café, auditorium and gathering spaces as part of the Mill Lane project. Most first-years live in the modern Foundress Court and in New Court and should be prepared to share bathrooms as en-suites are uncommon. Currently, many second-years tend to move away to Selwyn Gardens behind the Sidgwick Site, or to Lensfield Road near the station, while some move as far as Grantchester Meadows. Many desirable third-year rooms are in terraced houses on Fitzwilliam Street. Pembroke students make the most of an arty extra-curricular scene, including the Pembroke Players, one of the largest college drama societies. Other clubs include the Music Society, the Stokes Scientific Society and Pembroke Politics. There are plenty of sports teams, an on-site gym and sports grounds 10 minutes away by bicycle.

Peterhouse

Cambridge CB2 1RD   01223 338223   www.pet.cam.ac.uk
Undergraduates: 311   Postgraduates: 187   admissions@pet.cam.ac.uk

As Cambridge's oldest college and one of its smallest, Peterhouse retains some traditional idiosyncrasies. It hosts a white tie ball every other year and formal hall dinners glow atmospherically by candlelight. It is one of the wealthier colleges and as such can offer travel grants, academic awards and high-standard accommodation. Students are housed either on site or not more than five minutes away for all years of their degree. Rooms are allocated on a points-based system that rewards both academic and extra-curricular achievements. Most freshers live in St Peter's Terrace – grand Georgian houses on Trumpington Street, or in the William Stone building, an eight-floor high-rise dating from the 1970s. Though it shares sports grounds with Pembroke, Peterhouse has its own squash court and a modern gym. It also has one of Cambridge's wilder outdoor spaces, known as the Deer Park – where no deer but plenty of students roam in summer. It is well located for both the science and arts faculties and is particularly strong in the arts. Two libraries, the Perne and the Ward, provide plenty of quiet learning space away from the busier faculty libraries. Rooms in Fitzwilliam Street were renovated in summer 2021, while Peterhouse is planning picturesque new gardens in Cosin Court. It has converted its old brewhouse into a music facility.

Queens'

Cambridge CB3 9ET   01223 335540   www.queens.cam.ac.uk
Undergraduates: 552   Postgraduates: 464   admissions@queens.cam.ac.uk

Walking through Queens' provides a quick course in architectural history via buildings that hail from every era since its 1448 foundation. The campus sits on both sides of the River Cam, and is connected by the striking, wooden Mathematical Bridge – as featured on many a postcard. A lively, outgoing atmosphere is especially felt in the new courts. The active BATS dramatic society puts drama centre stage. Sport is also strong – Queens' tends to field several Blues team players and its own clubs cover everything from chess to water polo, with strong men's and women's football teams. Its biennial May Ball is a popular fixture that welcomes big-name bands. An annual Arts Festival features student work and a range of events. Most first-year students are housed in the modern Cripps Building, while second and third-years are allocated accommodation through a ballot system. Queens' is also one of the few colleges to host all undergraduates onsite for three years. Students have the option of sharing a set of rooms, rather than having their own single bedsit, which can prove awkward if they have to pass through another's room to reach their own. Queens' is strong in the sciences, and around 63% of undergraduates study STEM subjects.

Robinson

Cambridge CB3 9AN   01223 339143   www.robinson.cam.ac.uk
Undergraduates: 426   Postgraduates: 227   apply@robinson.cam.ac.uk

Robinson's 1970s architecture might not fit the traditional Cambridge stereotype, but within the "red-brick fortress" there are beautiful gardens – that have the added bonus of students being allowed to walk on the grass – and a buzzing social life. The college is next to the university library and the city centre is a few minutes away by bicycle. Most humanities and science departments are also within easy reach. Robinson has a good standard of housing: around half of undergraduate accommodation is en-suite. Freshers tend to live in the centre of college while in later years they can opt to live in houses bordering the campus. The college also takes pride in serving delicious food in the Garden restaurant, along with the Red Brick café-bar. It hosts weekly "bop" parties and boasts an ideal location for student athletes. The sports grounds, shared with Queens', Selwyn and King's, are a ten-minute walk away. The college is also close to the university rugby ground and the sports ground. Robinson teams frequently do well: returning to the pre-pandemic swing of things, Robinson won the 2021 intercollegiate athletics cuppers between its men and women's teams. It has faced criticism for low intakes of students from state schools, however. In 2020 it was the only Cambridge college to admit less than half of undergraduates (48%) from the state sector.

Selwyn

Cambridge CB3 9DQ   01223 767839   www.sel.cam.ac.uk
Undergraduates: 438   Postgraduates: 270   admissions@sel.cam.ac.uk

Selwyn is in an ideal location for humanities students who value a short commute, given the Sidgwick Site is practically the college's back garden. West Cambridge is also a quick cycle away for STEM students. Selwyn enjoys an impressive range of recently renovated facilities after extensive fundraising. It has completed Ann's Court with a new building featuring a 140-seat auditorium, allowing it to work as a concert venue, and the Bartlam library has also opened recently. The sleek, recently renovated café-bar buzzes in the evenings and makes a popular study space during the day. Selwyn has one of the highest intakes of home students from state schools, 80% in 2021. All students are accommodated for every year of their undergraduate degree in what is likely to be an en-suite room. First-years tend to live together in Cripps Court. Selwyn has a strong musical tradition, and the chapel choir has recorded numerous albums and toured the world. The arts have a strong showing with the Selwyn Mighty Players, which helps fund and produce student theatre both in and out of college. Long-standing sports clubs known as the Hermes and Sirens fund grants for various teams. Selwyn shares sports and tennis grounds around a mile away. It also shares its boathouse with King's and Churchill.

Sidney Sussex

Cambridge CB2 3HU   01223 338872   www.sid.cam.ac.uk
Undergraduates: 394   Postgraduates: 229   admissions@sid.cam.ac.uk

Study snacks are never far from reach at Sidney, which has the distinction of neighbouring the city centre's main supermarket (a fact valued by undergraduates). Sidney is also just steps from the ADC student theatre and a five-minute walk from the natural sciences departments. It is one of the smaller colleges by population, and its bijou grounds mean many students are housed off-site. Some are in buildings nearby, around King Street, the furthest away have a 15-minute walk. A bridge over the shops of Sussex Street connects the college to Sussex House accommodation. However, there are some atmospheric rooms to be had in the main buildings, a few of which even include en-suite facilities. Sidney is a musical college with an award-winning chapel and a recently inaugurated organ. More bizarrely, it is also where the head of Oliver Cromwell is buried, given he was among the college's first students. The bar is a social hub, thanks to its affordability and rowdy "bops" – which are cheesy dance nights held every other Friday in term time. The extensive grounds make it a popular choice for May Week garden parties. Sports teams are more enthusiastic than wildly competitive, and grounds are shared with Christ's, a ten-minute cycle ride away.

St Catharine's

Cambridge CB2 1RL   01223 338319   www.caths.cam.ac.uk
Undergraduates: 494   Postgraduates: 299   undergraduate.admissions@caths.cam.ac.uk

One of the quintessential Cambridge sights is the flock of cyclists flying past St Catharine's on Trumpington Street on the way to their 9am lectures. Students at "Catz" can take advantage of a central location and thriving community. Mid-size Catz has two libraries, having been founded by benefactor Robert Woodlark in 1473 with a library of 84 manuscripts and three printed books. Renovations are underway to update college spaces such as the hall, as well as creating a new atrium connecting existing buildings. Catz students live on-site in their first year before moving out to the popular St Chad's complex, where accommodation is split into flats with octagonal bedrooms. St Chad's is near the Sidgwick Site – useful for arts students looking to wake up as late as possible before lectures. There is also the McGrath Centre, which houses an auditorium, junior common room and bar, plus a refurbished boathouse and hockey pitch. Its students are enthusiastic on the extra-curricular front. There are strong rowing and hockey teams and the literary society, the Shirley Society, is Cambridge's oldest. Catz holds a May Ball every other year, and students can attend one at Corpus during the "off" years. The David and Claudia Harding Foundation made a £25m donation to Catz in 2019 – one of the largest in Cambridge's history – which will support postgraduates and encourage applications by students from underrepresented backgrounds. In the 2020 application cycle around 72% of UK students came from the maintained sector, placing it in the top half of colleges for this measure.

St Edmund's

Cambridge CB3 0BN   01223 336086   www.st-edmunds.cam.ac.uk
Undergraduates: 126   Postgraduates: 510   admissions@st-edmunds.cam.ac.uk

"Eddies", as St Edmund's is affectionately known, is a home to graduates and mature undergraduates from all over the world (more than 80 countries at last count). Students bring a broad range of backgrounds and experiences with them, adding to a convivial and laid-back atmosphere on the hill away from the centre of town, with an average student age of 23. Eddies also participates in the university's Foundation Year programme, which provides a fully funded year of study (before starting a degree) for students from less-advantaged backgrounds. The college's cheap and cosy bar, which remains entirely student-run, is a popular choice for socialising. Many of the university's top athletes go to Eddies. The college aims to be particularly supportive of student parents through its St Teddy's Club, featuring family lunches and gatherings. Accommodation and food can be pricey, as St Edmund's does not enjoy the big endowments of some of the larger colleges. The new Mount Pleasant halls opened in September 2019 with 136 comfortable en-suite bedrooms and 64 studio flats. St Edmund's is unique among Cambridge colleges for having a catholic chapel and takes a relaxed approach to traditions. There is no Fellows' high table in hall, and students and academics at all stages of their careers are encouraged to mingle.

St John's

Cambridge CB2 1TP   01223 338703   www.joh.cam.ac.uk
Undergraduates: 658   Postgraduates: 312   admissions@joh.cam.ac.uk

With the River Cam snaking under the Bridge of Sighs, past grand ivy-covered buildings, few campuses anywhere can rival the fairy tale setting of St John's. Inside the stunning buildings, however, the college hosts a vibrant community with myriad sporting and cultural activities. Notably St John's offers some of the most generous financial support to its students of any institution in the country. From 2023, the Free Places programme will completely cover the costs of up to 40 low-income undergraduates at a time (including all tuition fees, accommodation and living expenses). In the meantime, the "Studentships" grants will top up financial support provided by the Cambridge Bursary. While the college's state school intake was 65% in 2020 (among the lowest five colleges by this measure), it represents a significant improvement on 2017's 48%. A large and wealthy college, St John's is renowned for its prowess on the sports field. The "Red Boys" team is strong in inter-college rugby – they won the league for the fourth time in five years in 2018 – and "Maggie", as the boat club is known, is another force to reckon with. The women's hockey and netball teams have also enjoyed success in recent years. The Picturehouse is the college's student-run cinema, with weekly screenings. Accommodation is generally good, with some truly enviable rooms on offer. Food in the buttery is delicious and well subsidised. St John's May Week Ball is known as one of the most fabulous. On the night, punts fill the river to watch the legendary fireworks display.

Trinity

Cambridge CB2 1TQ   01223 338422   www.trin.cam.ac.uk
Undergraduates: 744   Postgraduates: 335   admissions@trin.cam.ac.uk

Trinity is arguably Cambridge's most famous college, with its vast grounds on the Cam and an alumni list that ranges from Sir Isaac Newton to Eddie Redmayne. It has retained some of its quirkier traditions, including the Great Court Run, where students try to run around the court faster than the clock can strike twelve (made famous by *Chariots of Fire*). Trinity has by far the largest undergraduate population in Cambridge and is the richest college, which is reflected in the resources (including bursaries) and high-quality accommodation available. At last count around 63% of its undergraduates were studying STEM subjects. The Tudor-Gothic buildings of New Court have been renovated to provide 169 student rooms, and nearly half the accommodation is now en-suite. A two-storey gym is minutes from the main gate, along with pitches for netball, football, rugby and cricket. Their proximity makes it easy to enjoy sport, and there are also hockey pitches and courts for badminton, tennis and squash. The punts are popular on summer afternoons. The famed chapel choir has toured extensively and hopes to return to Australia in 2023. The JCR takes up two floors and is a popular space for socialising and watching films. There is a bar that serves as a café during the day. Trinity also hosts candlelit formals in its stunning Hall. The college takes on a studious atmosphere in exam term. It accepted 62% of its UK undergraduate intake from the state sector in 2020, one of the lowest figures in Cambridge.

Trinity Hall

Cambridge CB2 1TJ   01223 332535   www.trinhall.cam.ac.uk
Undergraduates: 408   Postgraduates: 224   admissions@trinhall.cam.ac.uk

Trinity Hall (nicknamed "Tit Hall") is compact, with plenty of charm, and should not be mistaken for its larger neighbour Trinity. Home to Cambridge's smallest college chapel, year groups are also relatively small which creates a friendly atmosphere. The Jerwood Library has enviable views of the River Cam, while it is only a short walk across Garrett Hostel Bridge to access the Sidgwick site and the university library. Market Square is also just a few minutes away. All first-years are housed on the central site, where the cafeteria, coffee shop, bar, library, chapel and main music room are also located. The Thompson's Lane off-site accommodation is also central. There are en-suite rooms in WYNG Gardens, while there are also more affordable single rooms in Bishop Bateman Court. Many students live at the Wychfield site further afield, which has extensive gardens and more single as well as en-suite rooms. The chapel choir's recordings are well-received, and off-site there are squash and tennis courts, plus football, hockey, rugby, cricket and netball facilities. Alumni include the scientists Stephen Hawking and David Thouless, actress Rachel Weisz and Olympic medal-winning cyclist Emma Pooley.

Wolfson

Cambridge CB3 9BB   01223 335918   www.wolfson.cam.ac.uk
Undergraduates: 194   Postgraduates: 839   ugadministrator@wolfson.cam.ac.uk

Mature students would do well to consider Wolfson, a forward-thinking and welcoming college. Wolfson has a small intake of undergraduates annually (it accepted 21 in 2021), and its postgraduate-heavy balance creates a more international and grown-up feel to social life. It does not shy away from breaking some Cambridge conventions, with no "high table" – meaning academics and students share their dinners. The college was originally founded in 1965, and at the time was unique in Cambridge in accepting both women and men as part of the fellowship and the student body. Wolfson may not have the medieval buildings of many central colleges, but it boasts serene gardens and a fast commute to the Sidgwick Site and the university library. Wolfson's Howler comedy nights (back after a pandemic hiatus) draw an audience from across Cambridge to catch professional and student stand-up at its lively bar. Undergraduates are guaranteed accommodation on the College campus for their first three years. Wolfson has one of the university's best gyms as well as a court for basketball and tennis. It raised £7million in donations when it celebrated its 50th anniversary in 2015, and students have seen the benefits in some refurbished facilities.

14 University Profiles

A year of pandemic disruption on campuses caused universities to rise to a unique set of challenges. Within the Covid-19 landscape, "blended learning" – hitherto unfamiliar territory for most of us – rocketed into common parlance and into every student's reimagined university experience, as they adapted to learning through a combination of online and face-to-face teaching. What had been a steady stream of technology-enhanced learning in higher education pre-2020 became a necessary torrent, as institutions scrambled to provide degrees remotely.

A *Good University Guide* analysis compared 2021's National Student Survey (NSS) results with those from 2020 and found that all but two universities (Imperial College London and Surrey) saw their ratings fall, some by huge margins, as students delivered an often-damning verdict on how institutions had handled the pandemic. The findings have had a significant impact on our overall rankings because the NSS results account for two of the eight measures in our academic league table: teaching quality and student experience.

For prospective students applying for entry in 2023 the findings remain relevant, because "blended learning", to one extent or another, is here to stay. While the recording of lectures for playback later has had widespread uptake sector-wide, some universities have used the enforced pivot to a blended approach as a springboard for diving into a more all-encompassing, technology-rich mode of delivery. For some students, the ability to access teaching content online at times that suit them may be a vital tool that frees them from timetable tyranny, making juggling a degree with work and family commitments possible. Others – typically school-leavers – will want as much on-campus teaching as possible, to get the most out of both the academic and social sides of university life.

This chapter provides profiles of all 132 universities that feature in *The Times and Sunday Times* league table. It also has profiles of the Open University, which supplies the country's most part-time degrees; Birkbeck, University of London, which specialises in evening courses; and the University of the Highlands and Islands. Because of their special course or geographical circumstances, none of these appear in our main ranking. University College Birmingham withheld data for our table and is therefore not profiled, although it is listed at the end of the book.

Specialist colleges, such as the Royal College of Music (**www.rcm.ac.uk**) or institutions that only offer postgraduate degrees, such as Cranfield University (**www.cranfield.ac.uk**), are omitted. This is not a reflection on their quality, it is simply due to their particular roles. A number of additional institutions with degree-awarding powers are listed at the end of the book with their contact details.

Dating back to 1836, the University of London (**www.london.ac.uk**) is Britain's biggest conventional higher education institution by far, with more than 120,000 students. A federal university it consists of 17 self-governing colleges, and most of its students are based in the capital. Further afield it also offers degrees at the Institute in Paris, and its global prestige attracts more than 50,000 students in 190 countries to take University of London degrees via distance learning. Its School of Advanced Study comprises nine specialist institutes for research and postgraduate education (**details at www.sas.ac.uk**).

The following University of London colleges have their own entries in this chapter: Birkbeck, City, Goldsmiths, King's College London, London School of Economics and Political Science, Queen Mary, Royal Holloway, SOAS, St George's and University College London. Contact details for its other constituent colleges are given on page 586.

Guide to the profiles

Our extensive survey of UK universities provides detailed, up-to-date information for their profiles. The latest campus developments, results from the National Student Survey, trends in application and social data, financial help available to undergraduates, research reputation and findings from the government's Teaching Excellence Framework inform their content. You can also find contact details for admission enquiries along with postal addresses. In the light of social distancing measures open days have had to go online and any physical dates are liable to change. So, we recommend prospective students consult a university's website for the most recent and relevant information on how best to visit – virtually or in person.

We also include data under the heading "Where do the students come from?" This is taken from our revamped table on social inclusion that gives details of student recruitment and the socio-economic and ethnic mix of each institution. The methodology for its data can be found on pages 92–96.

In addition, each profile provides information under the following headings:

» **The Times and Sunday Times rankings:** For the overall ranking, the figure in bold refers to the university's position in the 2023 *Guide* and the figure in brackets to the previous year. All the information listed below the heading is taken from the main league table. (See chapter 1 for explanations and the sources of the data).
» **Undergraduates:** The number of full-time undergraduates is given first followed by part-time undergraduates (in brackets). The figures are for 2019–20 and are the most recent from the Higher Education Statistics Agency (HESA).
» **Postgraduates:** The number of full-time postgraduates is given first followed by part-time postgraduates (in brackets). The figures are for 2019–20 and are the most recent from HESA.
» **Mature students:** The percentage of undergraduate entrants who were 21 or over at the start of their studies in 2020. The figures are from UCAS.
» **International students:** The number of undergraduate overseas students (both EU and non-EU) as a percentage of full-time undergraduates. The figures are for 2019–20 and are from HESA.
» **Applications per place:** The number of applications per place for 2020, from UCAS.
» **Accommodation:** The information was obtained from university accommodation services, and their help is gratefully acknowledged.

Tuition fees

Details of tuition fees for 2022–23 are given wherever possible. At the time of going to press, a number of universities had not published their international fees for 2022–23. In these cases, the fees for 2021–22 are given. Please check university websites to see if they have updated figures.

It is of the utmost importance that you check university websites for the latest information. Every university website gives details of the financial and other support available to students, from scholarships and bursaries to study support and hardship funds. Some of the support will be delivered automatically but most will not, and it is up to applicants to explore the details on university websites, including methods of applying and deadlines, to get the greatest benefit. In addition, in England the Office for Students (**www.officeforstudents.org.uk**) publishes "Access Agreements" for every English university on its website. Each agreement outlines the university's plans for fees, financial support and measures being taken to widen access to that university and to encourage students to complete their courses.

University of Aberdeen

Students joining Aberdeen in 2022 will benefit from the newest addition to this five-centuries-old university: a £37.5million science teaching hub. Opening at the beginning of the year, the hub will feature fully digitised, paperless teaching spaces alongside flexible laboratory areas for specialist teaching and multifunction spaces.

Teaching is organised across 12 schools at Aberdeen, which dates back to 1495 and won our Scottish University of the Year award in 2019. The Old Aberdeen campus houses the imposing and historic King's buildings. At Foresterhill, life sciences and medical students share Europe's largest health campus, run by the university and NHS Grampian.

The opportunity to follow a special interest is built in to degrees at Aberdeen, allowing students to add contrasting courses to their main subject area. The Aberdeen Employability Boost Award for students and graduates has been introduced to enhance readiness for work, offering live workshops and employer-led sessions to find out how to stand out in job applications.

Two new work experience programmes – the ABDN Connect Internship Programme and ABDN Community Volunteering Programme – help students to find their feet in participating businesses, charities and not-for-profit organisations. Studying abroad is encouraged too, through the European or international exchange programmes. Academic credits gained overseas count towards an Aberdeen degree.

AFG College with the University of Aberdeen is the first campus to open in Qatar in partnership with a UK institution. It offers bachelor's degrees in accounting and finance and business management. Aberdeen also has partnerships in Sri Lanka and an alliance with Curtin University in Western Australia.

The university's research pedigree is burnished by association with five Nobel laureates in the fields of chemistry, medicine, physics and peace. In the most recent Research Excellence Framework, three-quarters of the work submitted by Aberdeen was rated world-leading or internationally excellent. For environmental and soil science the university was top in the UK, and it was ranked in the top three for psychology and English.

To aid the Covid-19 relief effort, space scientists based in the School of Geosciences developed a ventilator inspired by the life-support systems for manned space missions. The user-friendly device, known as ATMO-Vent, was built using low-cost components.

Aberdeen remains Europe's energy capital and the university has strong links with the oil and gas industries. Moving with the times, the university has developed expertise in offshore oil and gas decommissioning and

King's College
Aberdeen AB24 3FX
01224 272 000
study@abdn.ac.uk
www.abdn.ac.uk
www.ausa.org.uk
Open days:
see website

ABERDEEN
Edinburgh
Belfast
London
Cardiff

The Times and *The Sunday Times* **Rankings**
Overall Ranking: 20 (last year: 27)

Teaching quality	77.5%	=31
Student experience	76%	12
Research quality	29.9%	43
Entry standards	184	8
Graduate prospects	77.3%	31
Good honours	88.2%	14
Expected completion rate	88.5%	43
Student/staff ratio	15.7	=63
Services and facilities	£2,624	60

houses the National Decommissioning Centre. At the Oceanlab research facility, just north of Aberdeen, engineers test subsea equipment.

Even before the pandemic, a lecture-capture facility gave students the option to watch later online. An evaluation of blended learning post-Covid is under way and a joint assessment by the university and students' union found that great communication with students was among the highlights of distance learning during the pandemic. This is reflected in our analysis of the latest National Student Survey, in which Aberdeen was ranked 13th in the UK for the quality of its Covid response.

Aberdeen's bursaries and scholarships are tailored to undergraduates depending on where they come from: Scotland, the rest of the UK or abroad. It is worth checking out the university's website to explore what's on offer, from means-tested access scholarships to merit-based awards for those entering with top grades. Contextual offers are made to students who meet one or more of the university's widening access criteria, which include those estranged from their parents, who have been in the care system or who come from areas of deprivation and/or with typically low rates of participation in higher education. Aberdeen ranks 11th for social inclusion among Scotland's 15 universities.

The Olympic-standard Aberdeen Sports Village attracts high-profile events and recently hosted the 2020 European Junior Swimming Championships. The university has extra facilities in and around the city including the rowing club boathouse on the River Dee and a climbing bothy in Royal Deeside. Archery and weightlifting feature among more than 220 sports clubs and societies and the university's sports scholarships attract elite student athletes.

All new students who apply by the deadline are guaranteed one of 2,181 rooms around the King's Head campus, Hillhead Student Village and the city centre. Only a small number of catered places are available.

Mental health support is wide-ranging and students have access to free counselling, therapy pets and free mindfulness sessions.

Aberdeen's northerly latitude means long days in the summer stretching beyond 11pm, and in winter there's a good chance of seeing the Northern Lights. Skiers and snowboarders can head to the nearby Glenshee Ski Centre and getting away from it all to reconnect with nature is not a problem with the Cairngorms National Park, 150 miles of coastline and lochs on the doorstep.

Tuition fees

»	Fees for Scottish students	£0–£1,820
	RUK fees	£9,250
»	Fees for International students 2022–23	£18,000–£20,700
	Medicine	£46,000
»	For scholarship and bursary information see www.abdn.ac.uk/study/undergraduate/finance.php	
»	Graduate salary	£25,251

Student numbers

Undergraduates	9,510	(615)
Postgraduates	3,205	(1,855)
Applications/places	18,710/2,485	
Applications per place	7.5	
Overall offer rate	68.5%	
International students – EU	22.4%	
Non-EU	7.4%	

Accommodation

University provided places: 2,181
Catered costs: £147 per week
Self-catered: £90–148 per week
First years guaranteed accommodation
www.abdn.ac.uk/accommodation

Where do the students come from?

State schools (non-grammar)	79.2%	Deprived areas	8.6%	
Grammar schools	3.1%	All ethnic minorities	14.5%	
Independent schools	17.7%	White working-class males	7.6%	
First generation students	30%	Black achievement gap	-12.3%	

Social inclusion ranking (Scotland): 11

Disabled	5.1%	
Mature (over 21)	15.6%	

Abertay University

Abertay is one of the partners in a project bringing Scotland's first esports arena to Dundee – further cementing the reputation of the university and the city as an international hub for the gaming industry. It will have a prime location next to the V&A Dundee Museum of Design, widely regarded as an architectural triumph and the centrepiece of the regeneration of Dundee's waterfront. The university plans to make the most of the new gaming complex by developing new academic programmes related to the lucrative esports industry.

Promising a more personal undergraduate experience than bigger universities can offer, Abertay has fewer than 4,000 students in Scotland's fourth-largest city. It packs a big punch in new technologies: it was the first university to offer degrees in ethical hacking and its cyberQuarter hub, opened in 2020, provides a bridge between academia and industry in the field of cybersecurity. A new 5G Innovation Hub is on the way, opening in partnership with the Scotland 5G Centre, which will boost employment and investment in the Tay Cities region.

Abertay's superb record in the National Student Survey (NSS) earned it University of the Year for Teaching Quality in our previous *Guide*. However, the pandemic has taken a toll on student satisfaction scores. Only 29 universities have had a bigger year-on-year fall in scores for teaching quality and the wider student experience.

In the most recent Teaching Excellence Framework, in 2017, Abertay was awarded silver, commended for embedding employability within the curriculum after reform to include more choice and flexibility throughout the institution. The panel also highlighted course design and assessment, which provides scope for students to be stretched, and teaching that encourages them to be engaged and committed to their studies.

Abertay's School of Design and Informatics introduced a new master's degree in applied artificial intelligence and UX, which began recruiting in September 2021. The faculty houses the Emergent Technology Centre for teaching and research into mixed-reality technologies, using PlayStation development tools in its labs, forging closer links with Sony, which chose Abertay as the site for the largest teaching laboratory in Europe for PlayStation consoles.

Abertay also hosts the national Centre for Excellence in Computer Games Education. All games students become members of UKIE (UK Interactive Entertainment) and gain access to a bespoke programme of mentorship and support. David Jones, creator of *Grand Theft Auto*, is an Abertay graduate.

While tech is a standout specialism, Abertay is a multi-faculty university offering a wide range of degrees. Most include a work placement and there are mandatory interdisciplinary courses

Kydd Building
Bell Street
Dundee DD1 1HG
01382 308 080
sro@abertay.ac.uk
www.abertay.ac.uk
www.abertaysa.com
Open days:
see website

DUNDEE
Edinburgh
Belfast
London
Cardiff

The Times and The Sunday Times Rankings
Overall Ranking: =94 (last year: =80)

Teaching quality	78.3%	=18
Student experience	71.7%	43
Research quality	5.1%	=91
Entry standards	144	=38
Graduate prospects	68.5%	=73
Good honours	78.5%	62
Expected completion rate	73.6%	124
Student/staff ratio	22.4	129
Services and facilities	£1,780	120

for all undergraduates, plus Scotland's first accelerated degrees – which take three years, rather than the usual four. Ten new standard degree courses took their first students in September 2021, including accounting and finance with people management, digital marketing with events management and business management with law.

Remote learning continues to have a role across Abertay's schools. The experience of the pandemic proved that larger lectures can be delivered effectively online (although not, as yet, with a lecture-capture facility). As part of a bespoke approach to course delivery, collaborative and interactive activities are the focus of in-person teaching.

Abertay tops our Scottish social inclusion ranking for the second successive year. It was the first north of the border to implement access thresholds – using a contextual admissions policy that allows applicants from disadvantaged educational backgrounds to be offered places with lower than standard tariff requirements. The university also offers extensive pathways from further education colleges, as well as its own part-time access programme with evening classes for those without formal qualifications. About half its students qualify for some form of scholarship or bursary.

Sports science research scholarships enable students and staff to work with clubs such as Dundee United Football Club, Fife Flyers Hockey Club and the World Karate Federation. Two scholarships are available to students through a link with the leading mobile games company Ninja Kiwi Europe, which also supports Abertay's games design competition. The university also has a strong relationship with Santander, which supports student enterprise, and Heineken, which runs a marketing challenge for students at the School of Business, Law and Social Sciences.

Places in about 300 twin study rooms are available from £65 per week. New joiners who apply by the deadline are guaranteed a room.

Freshers week includes a new compulsory training module (very rare in British higher education) to help students to understand sexual consent and what is acceptable and unacceptable during their time at university, as well as a live session on diversity and inclusivity. The counselling and mental health service is free and confidential for all students, offering self-help resources, one-to-one therapy and seminars. A focus on managing anxiety, overcoming procrastination, and mindfulness helps students keep on top of their wellbeing.

Tuition fees

»	Fees for Scottish students	£0–£1,820
	RUK fees	£9,250
»	Fees for International students 2022–23	£14,000–£15,500
»	For scholarship and bursary information see www.abertay.ac.uk/study-apply/money-fees-and-funding/	
»	Graduate salary	£23,000

Student numbers

Undergraduates	3,665	(170)
Postgraduates	220	(225)
Applications/places	4,905/1,130	
Applications per place	4.3	
Overall offer rate	84%	
International students – EU	11.4%	
Non-EU	0.9%	

Accommodation

University provided places: 400
Self-catered: £65–£133 per week
www.abertay.ac.uk/accommodation

Where do the students come from?

State schools (non-grammar)	96.4%	Deprived areas	16.3%	Disabled	6.2%
Grammar schools	0.1%	All ethnic minorities	9.5%	Mature (over 21)	35.6%
Independent schools	3.4%	White working-class males	11.3%		
First generation students	47.5%	Black achievement gap	n/a		

Social inclusion ranking (Scotland): 1

Aberystwyth University

A serial winner in our awards – the 2018 and 2019 University of the Year for Teaching Quality and the 2020 Welsh University of the Year – Aberystwyth continues to flourish in a number of our key performance measures. This year it ranks third for teaching quality and sixth for student experience, even after one of the toughest years that students and universities have known.

Although students did not rate Aberystwyth especially highly for its response to the pandemic (with 69 universities recording smaller drops in their teaching and student experience scores in the 2021 National Student Survey when compared with 2020), Aberystwyth had been at the top of our rankings for teaching quality and student experience pre-pandemic, so the impact was less than it might have been. It remains the top Welsh university for student satisfaction.

While the university intends to get back to predominantly campus-based learning, it will continue to blend remote learning with traditional course delivery. It was in a better position than many when the pandemic hit to shift to online course delivery. Lecture capture was introduced in 2016 and Aberystwyth supports students with equipment or connectivity issues. All staff have been trained in the technical and pedagogical use of online teaching tools.

As a more recognisable university life resumes, Aberystwyth will welcome the first students to its new School of Veterinary Science, delivering a bachelor of veterinary science (BVSc) degree in collaboration with the Royal Veterinary College. Students will spend the first two years of the five-year course in Aberystwyth before transferring to the RVC's Hawkshead campus in Hertfordshire to complete their degree.

It is the first veterinary school in Wales, and one of only ten across the UK. Work has been completed on an EU-backed veterinary hub containing high-specification laboratories and office space. The Centre of Excellence for Bovine Tuberculosis will be based at the facility.

Also completed during lockdown was the Aberystwyth Innovation and Enterprise Campus (AberInnovation), a £40.5million facility providing world-leading facilities in food, biorefining and agric-tech. Based on the university's Gogerddan campus, it will forge collaborations between academia and business.

In September 2022, Aberystwyth will introduce nursing degrees for the first time, reflecting the huge expansion in nursing provision and the surge in applications UK-wide. Specialisms in adult nursing and mental health will be offered. There will be a chance to study up to half of the degree in the Welsh language. The introduction of such popular options should help Aberystwyth to regain some lost ground, with the number of accepted applicants down

Penglais Campus
Aberystwyth SY23 3FL
01970 622 021
ug-admissions@aber.ac.uk
www.aber.ac.uk
www.abersu.co.uk
Open days:
see website

Edinburgh
Belfast
ABERYSTWYTH
London
Cardiff

The Times and The Sunday Times Rankings
Overall Ranking: 38 (last year: 42)

Teaching quality	81.8%	3
Student experience	77.9%	6
Research quality	28.1%	45
Entry standards	118	=79
Graduate prospects	65%	=96
Good honours	72.8%	=106
Expected completion rate	85%	=61
Student/staff ratio	16	=70
Services and facilities	£3,277	20

45% since 2011. Applications have fallen by almost a third over the same period.

Student endorsement of teaching quality through the annual NSS is backed up by the verdict of the Teaching Excellence Framework (TEF), which awarded gold status to Aberystwyth. The TEF panel found "outstanding levels of stretch" ensuring that all students were significantly challenged to achieve their full potential. Substantial investment in e-learning was another plus point, as was the integrated approach to Welsh-language teaching. Just under a third of existing students come from Wales and Welsh-medium teaching is flourishing.

The Hugh Owen Library on the Penglais campus has been refurbished and the campus is also home to the National Library of Wales, one of the UK's copyright libraries.

Scores in the 2014 Research Excellence Framework showed improvement, with the best scores in international politics, geography and earth science. There was also recognition for the Institute of Biological, Environmental and Rural Sciences, which serves 1,500 undergraduate and research students, and offers the UK's widest range of land-related courses.

The university has jumped almost 50 places in this year's social inclusion ranking, to stand in the top 40 among English and Welsh universities. The introduction of a new measure for the recruitment of white working-class males – for which Aberystwyth ranks ninth – has contributed significantly to the improved standing. It also ranks in the top 50 for the proportion of students recruited from areas with the lowest participation rates in higher education.

To further diversify the student intake, the university runs a contextual offers scheme that typically reduces the offer by eight UCAS points, equivalent to one grade at A-level.

The attractive seaside location remains a draw, although travel to other parts of the UK is slow. However, the rewards – and sunsets – on arrival are great and students are immensely loyal to their university. The Penglais and Gogerddan campuses are about a mile apart, with teaching facilities and residential accommodation within walking distance of each other. All first years are guaranteed accommodation.

Sports facilities are excellent, with 48 acres of pitches. A pool and saunarium is complemented by a new outdoor sun deck (just to confound those who say it rains all the time). The sea, rivers and mountains nearby provide plenty of outdoor opportunities, while the university is unusual in offering stabling for students' horses.

Tuition fees
» Fees for UK students   £9,000
» Fees for International students 2022–23   £14,300–£16,300
» For scholarship and bursary information see www.aber.ac.uk/en/study-with-us/fees/
» Graduate salary   £20,369

Student numbers

Undergraduates	5,470	(1,135)
Postgraduates	590	(520)
Applications/places	8,550/1,575	
Applications per place	5.4	
Overall offer rate	96.6%	
International students – EU	12.8%	
Non-EU	5.6%	

Accommodation
University provided places: 3,145
Catered costs: £167 per week
Self-catered: £85–£147 per week
First years guaranteed accommodation
www.aber.ac.uk/en/accommodation

Where do the students come from?

State schools (non-grammar)	90.4%	Low participation areas	14.1%	Disabled	12.1%
Grammar schools	4.3%	All ethnic minorities	7.2%	Mature (over 21)	16.2%
Independent schools	5.2%	White working-class males	9.9%		
First generation students	39.1%	Black achievement gap	n/a		

Social inclusion ranking: 36

Anglia Ruskin University

Applications are open for courses at ARU Peterborough, a new outpost of Anglia Ruskin University. The £30million purpose-built facility will welcome its first cohort of undergraduates in September 2022 and aims to have 12,500 students by 2030. Located in an area with lower progression to higher education than the national average, ARU Peterborough offers employment-based degrees and degree apprenticeships delivered through a mixture of on-campus, remote and work-based learning.

In keeping with the university's focus on employability, courses at ARU Peterborough have been created in co-operation with regional organisations to meet local demand for skills. They span business, marketing and finance, computing and games development, education, engineering, agri-technology and environment, health and social care, and nursing and midwifery.

Anglia Ruskin has larger sites in Cambridge and Chelmsford. Healthcare courses are based in Cambridge, where the Young Street Building was lit in blue during the pandemic to pay tribute to NHS workers. As the biggest provider of health, social care and education courses in the east of England, ARU has a strong record for training key staff including social workers, operating

department practitioners and teachers. It was chosen to develop a new facility for nursing training by the North Anglia NHS Foundation Trust and has been shortlisted by the *Nursing Times* for its Pre-registration Provider of the Year Award in 2019 and 2020.

In Chelmsford, ARU opened its School of Medicine in 2018. The university also has a base in the City of London, mainly for business and law students.

Widening access is part of ARU's mission, and the university made 73 contextual offers to applicants hoping to study medicine in 2020, who qualified for the lower-than-standard grade according to indices of disadvantage. Care leavers and applicants with disabilities are a particular focus of ARU's outreach work to widen participation. The university does well on recruiting students from a range of underrepresented backgrounds, once again achieving a place in the top 20 in our social inclusion ranking. More than two-thirds of entrants in 2019 were aged over 21 when they began their course, while 54% are among the first generation in their immediate family to attend university.

The university takes a holistic view of applications, considering not only entry qualifications but also whether the applicant has demonstrated a genuine interest in their subject and motivation to learn. Relevant volunteering or part-time employment also boosts the chances of success. At ARU College,

Bishop Hall Lane
Chelmsford CM1 1SQ
01245 686 868
answers@aru.ac.uk
www.aru.ac.uk
www.angliastudent.com
Open days:
see website

The Times and The Sunday Times Rankings		
Overall Ranking: 115 (last year: 117)		
Teaching quality	76.3%	=46
Student experience	71.3%	=45
Research quality	5.4%	=89
Entry standards	109	=111
Graduate prospects	71.3%	63
Good honours	76.2%	=83
Expected completion rate	79.9%	102
Student/staff ratio	20	118
Services and facilities	£1,596	126

formerly Cambridge Ruskin International College, students develop study skills during a foundation year. Courses in computing and digital technology, business, animal sciences, health and medical sciences, art and design, psychology and nursing all offer a foundation year.

Awarded silver in the Teaching Excellence Framework, ARU was commended for its strong support for students at risk of dropping out. Its projected dropout rate is 14.6%, well below the expected level of 18.2% taking account of the course and subject mix. The university identifies those who may need extra support once they have started their degree and provides tailored assistance including advice on money matters. Students have access to a personal tutor and mentors.

Students sign up for work placements of up to a year with local and national businesses to get ready for the workplace. Ruskin Modules were incorporated into most degree courses from September 2021, teaching skills such as problem-solving, teamwork and creative thinking. ARU has also introduced the Graduate Capitals programme, integrated into course design and the personal develop tutor programme, which helps students to hone employability skills in six key areas.

ARU is one of the UK's leading providers of degree apprenticeships, offering courses across policing, business and management, building, digital, data and technology, and nursing and healthcare. In partnership with more than 330 employers, the university operates 20 programmes and expects to have about 3,000 students enrolled by September 2022.

Financial support in the form of scholarships and bursaries is inclusive by design. Undergraduates from low-income households qualify for the ARU bursary of up to £300, and the university offers £1,000 merit scholarships for those who arrive with BBB or better at A-level or equivalent qualifications. Tuition fees for international students are lower than those of many other UK universities.

The university's Welcome Buddy scheme links freshers with existing students who help them settle in. Accommodation in Cambridge and Chelmsford is guaranteed for all first-years who apply by the July deadline. The Chelmsford campus now has the Old Factory gym, featuring fitness mod cons including sled tracks and a spin studio. The Cambridge campus has a gym, fitness studio and tennis court. Students also get discounted membership at the Kelsey Kerridge Sports Centre nearby.

Tuition fees
- » Fees for UK students £9,250
- » Fees for International students 2022–23 £14,300–£15,000
- » For scholarship and bursary information see www.aru.ac.uk/student-life/help-with-finances
- » Graduate salary £24,214

Student numbers

Undergraduates	19,000 (2,280)
Postgraduates	2,615 (2,825)
Applications/places	14,795/2,695
Applications per place	5.5
Overall offer rate	67.4%
International students EU	8.4%
Non-EU	5.5%

Accommodation
University provided places: 2,106
Self-catered: £108–£205 per week
www.aru.ac.uk/student-life/accommodation

Where do the students come from?

				Social inclusion ranking: 17	
State schools (non-grammar)	92.3%	Low-participation areas	16.1%	Disabled	5.4%
Grammar schools	4.4%	All ethnic minorities	36.6%	Mature (over 21)	67.8%
Independent schools	3.4%	White working-class males	4.5%		
First generation students	53.9%	Black achievement gap	-15%		

Arts University Bournemouth

The latest Arts University Bournemouth (AUB) prospectus was published on Instagram only. Its shift to the picture-led social media platform chimes with the south coast university's art, design, media and performance specialisms.

Located on the coast between Bournemouth and Poole, the campus benefits from modern and architecturally striking buildings, housing industry-standard technology. New addition Campus Halls features student artworks in communal spaces.

Access to the institution's rich digital and creative environment has been the focus of investment for students, who benefit from software such as Adobe Creative Cloud Suite and access to LinkedIn learning courses. Digital capability is assessed at the start of the academic year, to ensure that everyone is fully equipped for their courses. Those in digital hardship receive support such as long-term laptop loans and financial help.

However, only Leeds Arts and nearby Bournemouth universities fared worse in our analysis of 2021's pandemic-impacted National Student Survey results. AUB suffered huge falls in student satisfaction, notably with learning resources (down 20.6 percentage points), overall satisfaction (down 15.4 percentage points), and academic support and course organisation and management (both down 13.7 percentage points) in a damning assessment of students' pandemic experience.

Banksy expert Professor Paul Gough, the vice-chancellor since 2020, has set out plans to rebuild the curriculum to better embed equality, diversity and inclusion as well as the United Nations sustainability goals. His vision will be incorporated into 20-plus undergraduate degrees, spanning architecture, dance and event management along with art and design, acting and film subjects.

Practical elements to give students a career edge are also incorporated into courses, such as live briefs for local and national businesses. Many practising artists and creative professionals contribute to teaching and the curriculum earned a gold award from the Teaching Excellence Framework panel.

AUB is home to the largest film school outside London. Founded more than 50 years ago, Bournemouth Film School (BFS) offers courses covering all aspects of film-making. Its partnership with Crowdfunder is in its fifth year – an alliance that shows students how to source funding and that also boosts their own graduate film budgets. In 2020 its 11 graduate films raised £68,000. The school's guest Q&A series has included Russell T Davies (*It's a Sin*, *Queer as Folk*, *Doctor Who*) and actress T'Nia Miller (*The Haunting of Bly Manor*).

In line with its strategic plan to promote community and civic responsibility, the university is restoring the Palace Court Theatre

Wallisdown
Poole BH12 5HH
01202 363 228
admissions@aub.ac.uk
www.aub.ac.uk
www.aub.ac.uk/life-aub/
students-union
Open days: see website

The Times and The Sunday Times Rankings
Overall Ranking: =79 (last year: 54)

Teaching quality	75.4%	=58
Student experience	68.8%	=75
Research quality	2.4%	118
Entry standards	145	=36
Graduate prospects	53.5%	130
Good honours	69%	119
Expected completion rate	88.4%	=44
Student/staff ratio	14.3	=33
Services and facilities	£1,806	118

in Bournemouth town centre. It will renovate the art deco venue to include a teaching space with its 400-seat auditorium, interval bar and rehearsal studio – providing an outpost less than five-minutes' walk from the beach.

With about 3,300 undergraduates, the university is a small institution and everything takes place on its single site. Facilities include the CRAB drawing studio, the first to be built at an art school for more than a century and designed by alumnus Sir Peter Cook. The Photography Building has flexible teaching spaces and IT suites, and TheGallery is AUB's own exhibition space, where the work of students and other contemporary artists is showcased. The library's Museum of Design in Plastics showcases more than 12,000 examples of mass-produced design icons.

Only 12 staff were entered for the 2014 Research Excellence Framework, but 43% of their work was rated as world-leading or internationally excellent.

Applications are buoyant, edging upwards for the second year running in the 2020 cycle. About 70% of students receive some form of financial help, which includes £300 final-year bursaries. Applicants from low-participation neighbourhoods and care backgrounds are flagged in the admissions process, and the information is taken into account when assessing portfolios, auditions and applications. However, the university does not make lower offers based on contextual information.

AUB Open launched in 2021, offering short courses, industry-recognised qualifications and credentials and improved access to creative degrees to students at outreach schools and colleges.

More than 200 staff have been trained in mental health first aid, and the students' union runs The Small Things Matter, offering mindful self-care tools which during the pandemic provided advice on issues such as embracing "oneliness", managing isolation and keeping calm. All students and staff have free access to the Headspace app, while drop-in and scheduled support is offered through the university's wellbeing and counselling service. Its Report and Support channel is a pathway for students and staff to report abusive behaviour.

AUB does not have its own sports facilities. Instead, a subsidy allows students to share the neighbouring University of Bournemouth's extensive gym, courts, pitches and fitness studios. With the new halls of residence there are now 1,131 study bedrooms first-year full-timers can live in.

Tuition fees
»	Fees for UK students	£9,250
	Foundation years	£5,421
»	Fees for International students 2022–23	£17,950–£19,950
»	For scholarship and bursary information see www.aub.ac.uk/fees/undergraduate	
»	Graduate salary	£20,000

Student numbers
Undergraduates	3,270	(0)
Postgraduates	100	(75)
Applications/places	6,720/1,260	
Applications per place	5.3	
Overall offer rate	51.8%	
International students – EU	7%	
Non-EU	9%	

Accommodation
University provided places: 1,131
Self-catered: £115–£219 per week
First years guaranteed accommodation
www.aub.ac.uk/accommodation

Where do the students come from?
State schools (non-grammar)	92.9%	Low-participation areas	11.1%	**Social inclusion ranking: 94**		
Grammar schools	2.9%	All ethnic minorities	13.2%	Disabled	9%	
Independent schools	4.2%	White working-class males	4.5%	Mature (over 21)	12.3%	
First generation students	39.3%	Black achievement gap	-38.5%			

University of the Arts London

A new president and vice-chancellor, James Purnell, took over from Sir Nigel Carrington at University of the Arts London in March 2021. Purnell, who served as work and pensions secretary and culture secretary in Gordon Brown's government, was until recently the BBC's director of radio and education.

"UAL is already one of the world's great creative institutions, so I will start by listening to what students, staff, governors and stakeholders seek from the next phase in our growth," he said when he took the job, adding, "I am especially alert to student wellbeing as Covid reshapes their teaching and personal experience." He will be doing a lot of listening after results from the National Student Survey in summer 2021 showed UAL to be one of the 20 universities whose results took the biggest hit after a year of pandemic.

Pre-pandemic, UAL students often worked online, especially for group projects. The university's "new normal" approach will combine the best of online delivery with access to physical spaces and teaching.

UAL is one institution comprised of six distinct colleges that retain unique identities and specialisms: Camberwell College of Arts, Central St Martins College of Art and Design, Chelsea College of Arts, London College of Communication, London College of Fashion,

and Wimbledon College of Arts.

All the colleges were founded in the 19th or early 20th centuries and UAL has established a reputation for innovation across the creative fields since becoming a university in 2004 and has produced more than half of the nominees for the Turner prize since it was first awarded in 1984. The artist Grayson Perry, who won the Turner prize in 2003, is UAL's chancellor and showcases designs by students from the London College of Fashion.

For the third year in a row, UAL is ranked by QS as second in the world for art and design, behind the Royal College of Art, a postgraduate institution, and once again leads our rankings for arts universities. In the latest Teaching Excellence Framework, UAL won silver, drawing praise for its "immersive, inquiry-led curriculum with opportunity for work placements and employer involvement via live briefs".

St Martins' award-winning £200million campus at King's Cross is a defining feature in the area's regeneration, and students benefit from modern facilities opening on to the fountains on Granary Square. The London College of Fashion is set to relocate its campuses across the city, from Shoreditch to Oxford Circus, to a new site at Queen Elizabeth Olympic Park in Stratford, east London. Building work has been delayed by the pandemic, but eventually the college will join creative organisations including the BBC,

272 High Holborn
London WC1V 7EY
020 7514 6000
www.arts.ac.uk/contact-us
www.arts.ac.uk
www.arts-su.com
Open days:
see website

Overall Ranking: =52 (last year: =83)

Teaching quality	70.9%	=115
Student experience	56.7%	129
Research quality	8.0%	72
Entry standards	140	=43
Graduate prospects	58.2%	123
Good honours	76.8%	75
Expected completion rate	85.5%	=57
Student/staff ratio	12.8	=9
Services and facilities	£3,566	13

Sadler's Wells and the V&A at London's new East Bank hub.

UAL published an anti-racism action plan in 2021, which pledges that 30% of its staff in every college and department will be from black, Asian and minority ethnic backgrounds within three years. Shades of Noir, an action group on race and diversity within higher education, the creative and cultural sectors, has also formally joined the university as its Centre for Race and Practice-Based Social Justice. The university sits in the middle reaches of our social inclusion ranking after achieving a top-30 place in the previous edition. Nine out of ten students are state-educated and one in six are in receipt of disability support allowance, the third-highest rate in the country.

In the most recent Research Excellence Framework, 83% of work submitted by UAL academics was judged to be world-leading or internationally excellent. The university's Social Design Institute is contributing to pioneering research on behalf of the Design Council to explore the social and environmental value of design in the UK as well as its economic impact.

Three new degrees will be introduced in September 2022: fashion consumer behaviour at the London College of Fashion; art, politics, philosophy and economics at Chelsea, Camberwell and Wimbledon; and game arts at the London College of Communication.

Scholarship and bursary provision is extensive, often specific to course or entry pathway. Graduates of the Lilian Baylis Technology School in south London can apply for a £5,000 bursary and the same amount is offered to a St Martins student through the Les Visionnaires scholarship fund. The UAL Bursary (£1,000) is awarded to all those with home status who are in receipt of the full maintenance grant.

A new recruitment service, UAL Arts Temps Ltd, finds temporary jobs for UAL students in the creative and non-creative sectors through a partnership with employers. A six-month start-up accelerator programme for creative graduates is offered in partnership with Google.

Excellent provision for mental healthcare includes 21 full-time professionals whose diversity reflects the student body, as well as 80 staff trained in mental health first aid. Tell Someone is UAL's service for students to report concerns and discuss formal and informal resolutions, anonymously if they like.

Tuition fees

»	Fees for UK students	£9,250
	Foundation courses from	£5,420
»	Fees for International students 2022–23	£23,610
»	For scholarship and bursary information see www.arts.ac.uk/study-at-ual/student-fees-funding	
»	Graduate salary	£22,000

Student numbers

Undergraduates	15,705	(25)
Postgraduates	3,650	(580)
Applications/places	27,355/4,825	
Applications per place	5.7	
Overall offer rate	45.5%	
International students – EU	13.3%	
Non-EU	36.6%	

Accommodation

University provided places: 3,196
Self-catered: £150–£440 per week
No accommodation guarantee
www.arts.ac.uk/study-at-ual/accommodation

Where do the students come from?

State schools (non-grammar)	90%	Low-participation areas	7.2%	**Social inclusion ranking: 50**		
Grammar schools	2%	All ethnic minorities	31.7%	Disabled	17%	
Independent schools	8%	White working-class males	4%	Mature (over 21)	18%	
First generation students	38.2%	Black achievement gap	-23.4%			

Aston University

A campus experience within a big city greets students at Aston University. Based on a self-contained 60-acre site not far from the centre of Birmingham, the multi-faculty institution is renowned for its strength in engineering and the sciences and its accent on work-ready skills.

From beginnings as a college of advanced technology, Aston has expanded to encompass five schools: business, medicine, engineering and applied science, life and health sciences, and languages and social sciences.

The Teaching Excellence Framework panel awarded Aston gold, highlighting the way that employability skills are embedded in degrees, as well as the involvement of professional bodies and employers in course design and delivery. The university also drew praise for outstanding personalised provision, featuring bookable personal tutoring sessions.

Every Aston degree has work-based modules or a placement year. Most students choose integrated placements, organised by a university team, in the UK or abroad. Alternatively, students can set up and run their own business. Placement years may also be used to study overseas at one of Aston's partner universities, or undergraduates can create a combination of options for a 12-month tailor-made experience. Students on some courses – pharmacy and optometry,

for example – take a pre-registration year to gain work experience.

Aston has forged productive partnerships with local and global small and medium-size enterprises as well as strong links with large organisations such as BMW, HSBC, Greater Birmingham Chambers of Commerce, the National Crime Agency and Public Health England. This all pays off in a strong showing in the new Graduate Outcomes survey, first published in 2020: Aston has finished in the UK top 30 in successive years for the proportion of graduates in high-skilled or graduate-level jobs within 15 months of leaving university.

Aston is among the top-performing pre-1992 universities in our social inclusion index, a position supported by having the highest proportion – 99.5% – of students recruited from non-selective comprehensive state schools. It also has the UK's highest proportion – almost 85% – of students drawn from ethnic minority backgrounds.

The university's modern teaching facilities include a redeveloped library and an up-to-date home for the highly rated business school, the base for almost half of all Aston's students. Extra social learning spaces have been added and a new students' union opened at the heart of the campus in 2019. There are many pockets of greenery where students can relax: the campus is dotted with outdoor sculptures and there are geese to watch on the redesigned Chancellor's Lake.

Aston Triangle
Birmingham B4 7ET
0121 204 3030
ugadmissions@aston.ac.uk
www.aston.ac.uk
www.astonsu.com
Open days:
see website

The Times and The Sunday Times **Rankings**
Overall Ranking: 45 (last year: 43)

Teaching quality	72.3%	=98
Student experience	69.9%	=62
Research quality	25.8%	48
Entry standards	126	=60
Graduate prospects	77.4%	=28
Good honours	83.3%	33
Expected completion rate	90.1%	36
Student/staff ratio	15.8	=65
Services and facilities	£2,234	87

Aston's response to the challenges of Covid-19 won broad student approval in the National Student Survey. Our analysis comparing the outcomes in 2020 and 2021 put Aston in the top 70 in the UK. Its strongest results were for course organisation and management: scores fell just 2.1% year-on-year, while other institutions shed up to 13.7 percentage points as students passed judgment on their pandemic performance.

The pioneer of degree apprenticeships in the UK, Aston offers 18 programmes across the IT, business, technology, transport, science and healthcare sectors. By September 2022 new programmes will be introduced including digital marketing, business-to-business sales, research science, and leadership and management courses covering healthcare, supply chains and engineering.

In the latest Research Excellence Framework in 2014, life and health sciences produced Aston's best results and the proportion of work placed in the top two categories (rated world-leading or internationally excellent) doubled to nearly 80%. New research centres in enterprise, healthy ageing, Europe, and neuroscience and child development have proved their worth. Pharmacy, another of the university's strengths, was awarded a prestigious Regius Professorship to celebrate the Queen's 90th birthday in 2016.

Aston achieved a new record for the number of applications in the 2020 recruitment cycle, up 9% on the year before. Enrolments have remained steady since 2015, however, which implies a smaller chance of being offered a place.

There is a women-only gym alongside other facilities at the Sir Doug Ellis Woodcock Sports Centre on campus, such as a swimming pool and sports hall with indoor courts. Six miles away, the Outdoor Recreation Centre has pitches for football, cricket and hockey.

Birmingham is one of the country's leading student cities with something to suit every undergraduate tribe. First-years are guaranteed accommodation on campus.

Tuition fees

» Fees for UK students	£9,250
» Fees for International students 2022–23	£16,300–£20,200
Medicine	£43,650
» For finance information see www2.aston.ac.uk/study	
» Graduate salary	£25,000

Student numbers

Undergraduates	10,800	(1,135)
Postgraduates	1,285	(2,115)
Applications/places		18,730/2,610
Applications per place		7.2
Overall offer rate		81%
International students – EU		2.3%
Non-EU		6.8%

Accommodation

University provided places: 1,150
Self-catered: £141–£147 per week
First years guaranteed accommodation
www2.aston.ac.uk/accommodation/

Where do the students come from?

State schools (non-grammar)	99.5%	Low-participation areas	10.8%
Grammar schools	0.2%	All ethnic minorities	84.7%
Independent schools	0.2%	White working-class males	2.1%
First generation students	53.1%	Black achievement gap	-16.2%

Social inclusion ranking: =57

Disabled	3.2%
Mature (over 21)	5.4%

Bangor University

Bangor's scenic setting, with the mountains of Snowdonia on one side and the Menai Strait on the other, is hard to beat.

The university – based in Gwynedd, the county with more Welsh speakers than any other – also holds its own on teaching quality, the only one in Wales to gain gold in the most recent Teaching Excellence Framework. The panel commended its bilingual learning in Welsh and English as well as the personalised support for students and strategic approach to assessment, coupled with very good physical and virtual learning resources. No university has more students who study through the medium of Welsh. Others can opt for Welsh language modules alongside an English-medium degree.

The historic institution was set up in an old coaching inn in 1884, funded by quarrymen and farmers who wanted higher education for local people. Today it has 14 academic schools and a wide-ranging curriculum across the arts, humanities and sciences.

As part of a drive to boost employability and personal development, students can choose to do a year's work placement in an organisation relevant to their field of study at the end of their second year as part of almost all undergraduate degrees. For those taking up a placement, tuition fees for UK students are reduced to £1,350 that year. Undergraduates can also choose to study abroad for a year or take advantage of opportunities to volunteer.

The Bangor Employability Award accredits activities that are valued by employers such as volunteering, learning a new language and part-time work. Graduates can take paid internships within the university's academic schools and services.

The university has a campus-like atmosphere, with buildings in a compact coastal hub. Radiography students and some nursing and midwifery students are based at the more urban Wrexham campus.

Bangor's scores have been consistently strong in the National Student Survey, although the pandemic cohort of final-year students in 2020–21 gave a less glowing write-up. Bangor's ranking for satisfaction with teaching quality slides from =40th to =68th, while scores for the overall student experience have fallen to =70th, down from =36th in our previous edition.

Bangor continues to expand its curriculum of joint honours degrees, and students have a wide range of new subject combinations available from September 2022. Among them are philosophy, ethics and religion; modern languages and Cymraeg; film studies and production; and English literature and journalism.

The university offers five degree apprenticeships covering cybersecurity, mechanical engineering, electrical/electronic engineering, data science and software

College Road
Bangor LL57 2DG
01248 383 717
admissions@bangor.ac.uk
www.bangor.ac.uk
www.undebbangor.com
Open days:
see website

The Times and The Sunday Times **Rankings**
Overall Ranking: 64 (last year: 62)

Teaching quality	74.8%	=68
Student experience	69.3%	=70
Research quality	27.2%	47
Entry standards	123	=67
Graduate prospects	66.3%	90
Good honours	76.1%	=85
Expected completion rate	81.4%	90
Student/staff ratio	15.9	=68
Services and facilities	£2,141	99

engineering. The first part of the course is delivered through Grŵp Llandrillo Menai, a group of local colleges. Links with further education partners across north Wales are considered a unique strength by the university, helping to build new skills and applied learning across the region.

Bangor is central to the proposed north Wales medical school. For the time being, though, it is delivering a four-year MBBCh graduate entry to medicine programme in collaboration with Cardiff University. This allows students to undertake all of their Cardiff medical degree in north Wales.

Bangor's research pedigree is to be further boosted by significant investment into low-carbon energy including nuclear, wind, solar and tidal sources. Half of Bangor's faculties were rated in the top 20 in the UK in the most recent Research Excellence Framework, led by leisure and tourism, languages and psychology.

The highly rated School of Ocean Sciences has its own research vessel, Prince Madog, while teaching and research at the School of Natural Sciences benefit from 18 hectares of botanic gardens on the shores of the Menai Strait. There is a research farm, animal care facilities, aquariums and greenhouses and a natural history museum holding 500 items collected from all over the world.

Bangor's Talent Opportunities is aimed to widen participation, reaching more than 2,000 students in years 9–11 with activities designed to raise their higher education aspirations. A "beneficial offers" scheme reduces entry tariff requirements by up to 24 points for entrants who qualify under certain indices of deprivation and in September 2020 applied to about 17% of Bangor's offers.

Both student villages, St Mary's and the larger Ffriddoedd, are within walking distance of university buildings. Bar Uno at Ffriddoedd is the main campus hangout and the beaches of Anglesey are popular with students.

The Pontio arts and innovation centre houses the students' union and links the university with the town. It has a cinema, theatre and lecture theatres plus places to eat and drink. Membership to all clubs and societies is free and there are about 200 sports and other activities to choose from.

The sports centre at Ffriddoedd – Canolfan Brailsford (named after the cycling coach Sir Dave Brailsford, who grew up nearby) – has two sports halls, three gyms, a multi-route climbing wall, outdoor grass pitches and a floodlit synthetic pitch. Gym membership is included in the fees for halls.

Tuition fees

»	Fees for UK students	£9,000
»	Fees for International students 2022–23	£15,250–£18,250
»	For scholarship and bursary information see www.bangor.ac.uk/studentfinance/Info	
»	Graduate salary	£21,000

Student numbers

Undergraduates	7,005	(230)
Postgraduates	1,995	(715)
Applications/places		7,665/1,785
Applications per place		4.3
Overall offer rate		82.6%
International students – EU		5%
Non-EU		10.9%

Accommodation

University provided places: 2,690
Self-catered: £100–£199 per week
First years guaranteed accommodation
www.bangor.ac.uk/student-life/accommodation

Where do the students come from?

State schools (non-grammar)	92%	Low participation areas	13.1%
Grammar schools	4.4%	All ethnic minorities	7.9%
Independent schools	3.6%	White working-class males	7.1%
First generation students	43.1%	Black achievement gap	-24.7%

Social inclusion ranking: =51

Disabled	10.8%
Mature (over 21)	30%

University of Bath

The doors of the University of Bath's new £70million School of Management building will open for the 2022–23 academic year. Designed to foster collaboration between students, academics and employers, facilities will include an entrepreneurship hub and behavioural research lab as well as lecture theatres and an auditorium for undergraduates studying accounting, finance, business and management.

Bath is committed to embedding the best aspects of blended teaching offered during the pandemic into its long-term, sustainable approach post-Covid at its leafy campus at Claverton Down, just outside the UNESCO World Heritage city. The "Bath Blend", is a three-pronged approach: in-person, online interactive and independent learning. Faculties and departments which offer courses in engineering, humanities, management, science and social science, are striking the right balance for their discipline and cohort with a bespoke balance of Bath Blend elements.

Lecture-capture was widely used at Bath before the pandemic and will continue. Investment in technology-enhanced learning has included appointing new instructional designer staff to train and support the transition to online learning. Bath's success in this area is reflected in a top ten national ranking in the 2021 National Student Survey, in which outcomes have been swayed by the pandemic.

The university's successful teaching methods earned gold in the most recent Teaching Excellence Framework. Bath was recognised for its high-quality physical and digital resources as well as students' engagement with developments at the forefront of research. The panel also commended its strong employment orientation.

Industry experience and professional accreditation are woven into the curriculum. A work placement scheme has links with more than 3,000 organisations around the world and two-thirds of undergraduates spend a placement year in the private, public or not-for-profit sectors. The careers service hosts up to 400 employer visits a year. Tuition fees are slashed during a work placement year (£1,850 for 2021).

Bath excelled in the latest Research Excellence Framework in 2014. Almost a third of the work submitted was assessed as world-leading and 87% was in the top two categories.

For the past 40 years Bath's automotive propulsion research team has worked with industrial partners to innovate around challenges such as engine downsizing, improved fuel consumption and cost-effective electric motors. The joint purchase of the Bristol and Bath Science Park with South Gloucester council is creating a new home for the Institute for Advanced Automotive Propulsion Systems research centre, where work to develop the next generation of ultra-low and zero emission vehicles has begun.

Claverton Down
Bath BA2 7AY
01225 383 019
admissions@bath.ac.uk
www.bath.ac.uk
www.thesubath.com
Open days:
see website

The Times and The Sunday Times **Rankings**
Overall Ranking: 9 (last year: 9)

Teaching quality	76.8%	36
Student experience	79%	4
Research quality	37.3%	24
Entry standards	167	=15
Graduate prospects	85.7%	7
Good honours	90.6%	10
Expected completion rate	96%	6
Student/staff ratio	15.1	=49
Services and facilities	£2,965	31

Bath remains a very popular choice. Applications reached their highest point yet in the 2020 cycle, up 8% since 2019, and had already gained a further 6% by the end of March in the 2021 admissions round. There were no spaces available via clearing in 2020.

Two new degree courses will begin in September 2022: structural and architectural engineering and physics with theoretical physics. Beginners' Mandarin is now offered alongside beginners' French, Spanish, Italian, German and Russian.

Financial assistance is largely targeted at students from low-income households, who have limited experience of higher education or have experienced other factors of educational disadvantage. About 300 students per year receive the Bath Bursary (although the number of awards is uncapped) worth £3,000 per year of study. The Gold Scholarship programme awards £5,000 per year of study to up to 50 students.

Any pupil who qualifies under the widening participation scheme has their application flagged up to the admissions department and each person's potential is considered within the context of their background. Contextual offers through the Access to Bath support and transition course are one A-level grade lower than the typical offer. However, the university continues to struggle in our social inclusion table, ranking in the bottom ten in the country for recruitment of students from non-selective state schools

(54.1%) and first-generation students (24.3%).

A past winner of our Sports University of the Year award, Bath has world-class facilities – matched by the quality of its sport, health and exercise science degrees. The on-campus Sports Training Village (STV) is a £35million multi-sport centre open to students, staff and the public. As well as providing a home for all clubs in Team Bath, it is a national training centre for several Olympic and Paralympic sports. The Team Bath Gym and Fitness Centre has been expanded to offer 200 workout stations and two exercise studios, hosting in-person and online daily classes.

An on-campus wellbeing service offers support for those struggling to adjust to university life, feeling panicky or having relationship problems. The counselling team offers one-to-one support as well as workshops to assist emotional wellbeing and there is 24/7 access to a confidential advice service by phone, video or live chat.

The university has 4,850 study bedrooms, enough to guarantee a space for all first-years who apply by the deadline.

Tuition fees

» Fees for UK students	£9,250
Foundation	£7,710
» Fees for International students 2022–23	£19,800-£24,500
» For scholarship and bursary information see www.bath.ac.uk/topics/tuiton-fees/	
» Graduate salary	£28,500

Student numbers

Undergraduates	13,530	(75)
Postgraduates	3,075	(1,880)
Applications/places	29,490/3,605	
Applications per place	8.2	
Overall offer rate	73.7%	
International students – EU	10.1%	
Non-EU	12.8%	

Accommodation

University provided places: 4,850
Catered costs: £190–£225 per week
Self-catered: £72–£215 per week
First years guaranteed accommodation
www.bath.ac.uk/professional-services/student-accommodation/

Where do the students come from?

State schools (non-grammar)	54.1%	Low participation areas	5.5%		
Grammar schools	17.6%	All ethnic minorities	18.3%		
Independent schools	28.2%	White working-class males	3.6%		
First generation students	24.3%	Black achievement gap	-7%		

Social inclusion ranking: 107

Disabled	5.7%
Mature (over 21)	2.9%

Bath Spa University

Students like flexibility, Bath Spa found after the rapid introduction of remote learning during the pandemic. Online learning has made engagement in some activities easier and there are plans to continue delivering some teaching sessions online, with lecture-capture available for all.

The pandemic also shone a light on the value of on-campus experience – especially for peer interaction, social learning, practical work, group seminars, lab and workshop activities. The university plans to maximise students' time on site and address the challenges of software, hardware, study space and connectivity. Overall, the university's response to the pandemic led to a favourable outcome in the latest National Student Survey of the pandemic cohort of final-year students.

Bath Spa has been expanding its curriculum in recent years. Many courses across a broad subject range were introduced from September 2021. Another seven will be added in 2022: architecture, commercial photography, international relations and politics, professional humanities, business psychology, public health and an accelerated two-year education degree.

Some of the new courses have proved highly popular – law, wildlife conservation, and acting for screen (delivered by a franchise partner) among them – and contributed to a 20%

increase in applications by the end of March in the 2021 admissions round. The increase should even out the 2020 dip in application and enrolment figures, in a year where 12% of first-years gained their places via clearing.

Work-based learning is built into courses wherever possible. The School of Humanities, for example, offers a mix of academic and applied study through partnerships with organisations such as the National Trust, the Roman Baths Museum and independent bookshops and publishers. The Music and Performing Arts School uses work placements and live briefs with industry partners such as the Bath Festival and the National Theatre to enhance students' learning and graduate prospects. The School of Sciences has links with the Yeo Valley food business and the Avon and Somerset police, and the business school with H&M and Oracle.

Despite these initiatives, Bath Spa performs poorly in our graduate outcomes measure, although its record is broadly in line with many other predominantly arts-based institutions.

The most recent Teaching Excellence Framework awarded Bath Spa silver, praising its course design and assessment practices "that provide high levels of rigour and stretch". The panel also noted the personalised teaching, the availability of a personal tutor, peer mentoring and independent study.

With grounds landscaped by Capability Brown, Bath Spa's Newton Park campus is one of the UK's most picturesque. Located

Newton Park
Newton St Loe
Bath BA2 9BN
01225 876 180
admissions@bathspa.ac.uk
www.bathspa.ac.uk
www.bathspasu.co.uk
Open days:
see website

The Times and The Sunday Times **Rankings**
Overall Ranking: =103 (last year: =104)

Teaching quality	74.4%	=78
Student experience	67%	=94
Research quality	7.9%	=73
Entry standards	106	=118
Graduate prospects	54.4%	129
Good honours	81.9%	40
Expected completion rate	84.5%	=65
Student/staff ratio	18	=103
Services and facilities	£2,135	100

four miles outside the UNESCO World Heritage city, it features an imposing Georgian manor house owned by the Duchy of Cornwall and a 14th-century gatehouse is one of the teaching facilities. Contemporary developments include the Michael Tippett concert hall and the Commons building.

The Newton Park headquarters is one of four campuses. The university's Locksbrook Road arts and design campus opened in 2019. With views over the River Avon, the city-centre building features technical workshops, flexible studio spaces and social areas in a redeveloped factory close to student accommodation.

The Sion Hill campus is within walking distance of the city centre, housing studios and workshops for fashion and textiles, and a specialist art and design library. Corsham Court, another historic manor house, is the university's postgraduate centre near Chippenham.

Bath Spa's outreach programme – Be Inspired! – aims to widen participation by engaging with children aged nine to 19 and their parents or carers. The equal-opportunity admissions process takes into account the experiences of those who may have followed non-traditional paths to higher education.

Bursaries range in value from £2,500 to £4,750 depending on students' circumstances, paid over three or four years. To qualify, household income can be up to £42,875. Talent and Excellence scholarships of £500

cash are paid in the first year to students who achieved results better than their predicted grades, or who display outstanding talent in the creative arts – and to all students who enter Bath Spa with AAB or equivalent grades.

Sports facilities including a gym, netball and tennis courts and games pitches are dotted around the campuses.

First-years who apply by the deadline are guaranteed student accommodation, which is allocated so that everyone gets the same chance of their preferred option, regardless of which stage in the cycle they applied.

The university has introduced a compulsory training module on sexual consent, racial, LGBTQ+, disability and social tolerance, drugs and alcohol. Using the Report and Support platform, students, staff and visitors can report anything they have experienced that makes them feel uncomfortable, and the platform signposts the way to helpful information or a trained adviser. Students are also asked to complete UniHeads mental health awareness training during their induction period.

Tuition fees

»	Fees for UK students	£9,250
	Foundation courses	£7,995
»	Fees for International students 2021–22	£13,910–£15,530
»	For scholarship and bursary information see www.bathspa.ac.uk/students/student-finance	
»	Graduate salary	£19,500

Student numbers

Undergraduates	6,545	(120)
Postgraduates	975	(815)
Applications/places	11,580/1,925	
Applications per place	6	
Overall offer rate	79%	
International students – EU	3.1%	
Non-EU	2.8%	

Accommodation
University provided places: 1,926
Self-catered: £122–£244 per week
First years guaranteed accommodation
www.bathspa.ac.uk/be-bath-spa/accommodation/

Where do the students come from?

State schools (non-grammar)	91.1%	Low participation areas	14.6%	
Grammar schools	2.6%	All ethnic minorities	8.7%	
Independent schools	6.3%	White working-class males	5.1%	
First generation students	42.6%	Black achievement gap	-21.9%	

Social inclusion ranking: =74

Disabled	11.4%
Mature (over 21)	29.6%

University of Bedfordshire

Students at the University of Bedfordshire felt their institution dealt with the effects of Covid-19 better than most other UK universities. Our analysis of the National Student Survey, comparing results from 2020 and 2021, which capture students' satisfaction with their institution's pandemic performance, rank Bedfordshire 22nd.

The turnaround boosted Bedfordshire's rankings for satisfaction with teaching quality and the wider experience, but not by enough to lift Bedfordshire off the foot of our overall academic ranking. Satisfaction with teaching fell just 2.2 percentage points year-on-year, a better performance than the vast majority of universities managed.

Extra support for students has been introduced through initiatives such as the Fika mental fitness app, which provides programmes designed to help students combat the challenges of remote study and the impact of the pandemic on mental health.

Bedfordshire has committed to a full return to face-to-face learning for students, which will gradually resume via a blend of in-person and online teaching. The positive elements of digital learning and technology-enhanced support will not be lost, says the university, and will be reflected in a new strategy.

Investment teaching and learning spaces across its five campuses include adding a custody suite for the new professional policing degree, which welcomed its first students in September 2021 at the Luton campus – Bedfordshire's biggest site. Luton's £40million building for Stem subjects (science, technology, engineering and maths) features 6,000 square metres of hi-tech teaching space. It has computer laboratories and workshops for automotive engineering, cybersecurity and robotics, and an outreach centre to promote Stem subjects to the community.

The Bedford campus, in a leafy setting a 20-minute walk from the town centre, houses the education and sports faculty as well as courses in performing arts, law and business management. The university is one of the UK's largest providers of training for physical-education teachers and has recently gained a sports therapy suite at the Bedford site. A specialist sensory building is also being developed to provide resources for special educational needs, early years and primary education courses.

The Aylesbury campus at the Stoke Mandeville Hospital, home of the highly regarded National Spinal Injuries Centre, is Bedfordshire's newest, opened in 2020. The three-storey building has a specialist skills room set out as a ward, complete with audiovisual technology. Healthcare students undertake the classroom element of their course at Stoke Mandeville, while gaining experience

University Square
Luton LU1 3JU
0300 330 0073
admissions@beds.ac.uk
www.beds.ac.uk
www.bedssu.co.uk
Open days:
see website

***The Times and The Sunday Times* Rankings**

Overall Ranking: 132 (last year: 131)

Teaching quality	74%	=80
Student experience	67.6%	=86
Research quality	7.0%	=77
Entry standards	106	=118
Graduate prospects	66.2%	=91
Good honours	63.8%	129
Expected completion rate	53.1%	131
Student/staff ratio	26.3	132
Services and facilities	£1,693	124

in an integrated health trust that provides specialist, acute and community services.

At the university's Milton Keynes campus, courses range from human resource management to professional social work practice. The Putteridge Bury campus, a neo-Elizabethan mansion on the outskirts of Luton, doubles as a management centre and conference venue.

Bedfordshire gained silver in the Teaching Excellence Framework, winning praise for its success in widening participation, not only by enrolling students from underrepresented groups but also in helping them to achieve good results.

Bedfordshire has a successful track record for recruiting students who are less likely to attend university, ranking =10th in our social inclusion table. In the four years that this index has been published, the university has never ranked lower than 11th. Two-thirds of students are the first in their family to enter higher education, three-quarters are mature students aged over 21 when they begin their studies, and almost all (more than 98%) went to non-selective state schools.

The financial support extended by Bedfordshire to its students is among the most inclusive in the country. Every full-time undergraduate entrant in 2021 qualified for a bursary of at least £500 per year. Merit scholarships are given to students who achieve 112 UCAS points (BBC at A-level or equivalent), and receive £2,400 over three years.

Between 2008 and 2014, the university more than doubled the number of academics it entered for the Research Excellence Framework and was rewarded with one of the biggest increases in funding for research at any university. Almost half the work submitted was placed in the top two categories (world-leading or internationally excellent). Social work and social policy, health subjects and English produced the best results.

Degrees in healthcare science, education and sociology, and early years education began in September 2021, along with top-up years for a suite of business administration courses. A physiotherapist degree apprenticeship joins the curriculum from September 2022, after the introduction of programmes in occupational therapy and operating department practice in 2021. The university hopes to increase its apprentice numbers from 250 to 350 by September 2022.

First-years are guaranteed a space in student accommodation, which is divided across the Luton and Bedford campuses.

Tuition fees

»	Fees for UK students	£9,250
	Foundation courses	£6,165
»	Fees for International students 2022–23	£12,900
»	For scholarship and bursary information see www.beds.ac.uk/howtoapply/money/fees/	
»	Graduate salary	£24,000

Student numbers

Undergraduates	11,010 (2,145)
Postgraduates	2,710 (860)
Applications/places	8,385/1,095
Applications per place	7.7
Overall offer rate	76.4%
International students – EU	15.4%
Non-EU	9.6%

Accommodation

University provided places: 1,411
Self-catered: £110–£204 per week
www.beds.ac.uk/accommodation

Where do the students come from?

State schools (non-grammar)	98.1%	Low participation areas	9%	Disabled	4.5%
Grammar schools	0.6%	All ethnic minorities	58.3%	Mature (over 21)	74.4%
Independent schools	1.3%	White working-class males	2.4%		
First generation students	65.8%	Black achievement gap	-31.9%		

Social inclusion ranking: =10

Birkbeck, University of London

Applications to Birkbeck boomed during the pandemic. The appeal of an institution where home-working plus limited time on campus has always been the modus operandi – rather than a blended learning system cobbled together in haste to cope with Covid – produced a 28.6% spike in applications at the end of March 2021 compared with the same point in the cycle in 2020.

As students struggle to cope with the pandemic elsewhere, Birkbeck has come into its own: "At other universities, students who combine study with work or other commitments are unusual. At Birkbeck, you are what we are about," says the prospectus.

Although there are plenty of conventional three-year full-time degrees after a recent expansion of Birkbeck's course portfolio, the university remains best known for its evening-class degrees taken over four years full-time or six years part-time. Founded nearly 200 years ago to provide higher education to working Londoners, Birkbeck is ideal for students combining work or childcare with their studies.

Birkbeck's founding cause is to widen access to higher education and continuing that vision, more foundation-year degree courses have been added lately. New options include creative writing, and creative writing and English with a foundation year. Others have an optional foundation year: global political economy and comparative literature and culture (also with optional international experience). A six-year part-time BSc in accounting began in September 2021 with a foundation year.

Evening classes – between 6pm and 9pm – at the Bloomsbury campus are central to the Birkbeck experience. Libraries and food outlets open late to cope with this skew to the student day.

The university has been expanding its reach across the capital, too. A partnership with the University of East London established a presence in Stratford, close to the Queen Elizabeth Olympic Park, and a new teaching facility has opened on Euston Road, a 15-minute walk from the main campus.

Birkbeck withdrew from our league table in 2019 on the grounds that our measures place a heavily part-time university at a disadvantage compared with traditional, residential institutions. We continue to include it in our listings because of its unique place in British higher education, where it sets a high bar for widening participation.

Where comparisons can be made on a level playing field, Birkbeck performs well against its peers, notably for research. The university was in the top 40 in our analysis of

Malet Street
London WC1E 7HX
020 3907 0700
studentadvice@bbk.ac.uk
www.bbk.ac.uk
www.bbk.ac.uk/su
Open days: see website

The Times and The Sunday Times Rankings
Overall Ranking: n/a
No data available

the 2014 Research Excellence Framework, which rates universities for the quality and quantity of their output. More than 80% of its eligible academics were entered and almost three-quarters of the work submitted was rated in the top two categories – world-leading or internationally excellent. Psychology and environmental science were in the top six in the country.

Birkbeck does well in the QS World University Rankings; at =332nd it is in the top 40 in the UK, and seventh in London.

The Wohl Wolfson ToddlerLab in Torrington Square is the world's first purpose-built centre for the study of brain development in toddlers as they interact with their natural environment. It will build on the globally-renowned research conducted in Birkbeck's BabyLab and hopes to advance the understanding of conditions such as autism, ADHD, Fragile X and Williams Syndrome.

Awarded silver in the Teaching Excellence Framework, Birkbeck impressed assessors with its range of initiatives to support students from diverse backgrounds to achieve their full potential.

Many Birkbeck students are already well into their careers when they enrol, so the university has always performed well on graduate employment. A string of collaborations with businesses from large corporations to small and medium-sized enterprises provide pathways to industry through career workshops, opportunities for entrepreneurship, and course programmes co-created with sector leaders such as Goldman Sachs, Facebook, Santander and Le Cordon Bleu.

The college welcomes applications from people without traditional qualifications and continues to attract non-traditional learners of all ages and backgrounds. Those who have taken A-level or equivalent qualifications recently are made offers based on the UCAS tariff, but others are assessed by the college on the basis of interviews and/or short tests. The My Birkbeck student centre brings together all the college's student support service and about 40% of students qualify for some form of financial support.

Most Birkbeck students live at home in the capital, but places are available in University of London intercollegiate halls for those who need them. A gym, swimming pool and other facilities are available at Student Central, the former University of London students' union, which is next door to the Bloomsbury campus.

Tuition fees
- » Fees for UK students £9,250
- » Fees for International students 2022–23 £14,560
- » For scholarship and bursary information see www.bbk.ac.uk/student-services/financial-support
- » Graduate salary n/a

Student numbers

Applications/places	5,220/915
Applications per place	5.7
Overall offer rate	n/a

Accommodation
www.bbk.ac.uk/student-services/accommodation

Where do the students come from?
No data available

University of Birmingham

The spotlight will be on the University of Birmingham's world-class sports facilities in 2022, when the city hosts the Commonwealth Games. The university is an official partner and will hold the hockey and squash events. Its Vale Village halls of residence are also set to house the largest of the athlete villages after plans for the Games' £500 million base at Perry Barr were delayed by the pandemic.

A member of the Russell Group of research-led universities, Birmingham's success in the 2014 Research Excellence Framework – when 80% of work was rated world-leading or internationally excellent – included its submission for sport, exercise and rehabilitation studies. The subject area was placed in the top five, as were philosophy, history, classics, theology and religion, area studies and chemical engineering.

However, Birmingham fared far less well in the eyes of its students over its operations during the pandemic. Our analysis of the 2021 National Student Survey put Birmingham – a consistent heavy hitter in our academic rankings – in 98th position, behind many less prestigious institutions. Scores for overall satisfaction fell 10.9 percentage points, reflecting discontent with Birmingham's response to the challenges of university life during Covid-19. Satisfaction with learning resources was down 12.2% and assessment and feedback suffered a 10.4% drop.

Teaching and learning were restored to campus-based, in-person delivery from September 2021, with online learning reserved as a back-up option. Lecture-capture continues, and students have been assigned an online academic tutor group – all of which should help to lift levels of satisfaction.

There are plenty of new facilities on campus. Birmingham is more than halfway through a ten-year, £600million transformation on a scale not seen since its original redbrick buildings were completed in 1909. At the 260-acre campus in leafy Edgbaston, the landmark Old Joe, said to be the world's tallest freestanding clocktower at 100 metres high, jostles for position among the new developments. Among them are a dedicated student hub, library and sports club. The Collaborative Teaching Laboratory has been designed to change the way Stem subjects (science, technology, engineering and maths) are taught, and features wet, dry and e-labs alongside learning space for 1,000 students.

In February 2021 the £46.5million School of Engineering opened, bringing engineering disciplines together over 12,000 square metres on five floors. As well as contemporary and flexible design and research spaces there is a full-size set of railway points and a test track for the university's scaled hydrogen-powered train.

Birmingham's city centre Exchange development opens in September 2021 as a hub for public engagement, regional and national

---

Edgbaston
Birmingham B15 2TT
0121 414 3344
www.birmingham.ac.uk
www.guildofstudents.com
Open days:
see website

The Times and The Sunday Times **Rankings**		
Overall Ranking: 25 (last year: 19)		
Teaching quality	68.8%	123
Student experience	64.7%	=112
Research quality	37.1%	26
Entry standards	152	25
Graduate prospects	78%	26
Good honours	89.2%	11
Expected completion rate	94.6%	10
Student/staff ratio	14.7	=40
Services and facilities	£3,854	6

policy development, and skills and leadership training. A Molecular Sciences building for the School of Chemistry is due to open in 2023, along with a Life Sciences Park in Selly Oak, a mile from the City South campus at Edgbaston. Drama is also based in Selly Oak, where the BBC Drama Village on campus offers opportunities for student placements.

Further afield, Birmingham is the first Russell Group university to open a Dubai outpost. Students take courses in business, economics, computer science, mechanical engineering and teacher training on a new campus.

Outshining several other Russell Group universities to be awarded gold in the Teaching Excellence Framework, Birmingham was praised by assessors for a strategic focus on the development and delivery of relevant, research-informed teaching which is highly valued by employers. "All student outcomes are excellent," the panel acknowledged.

Birmingham's enduring popularity with undergraduates hit new heights in the 2020 admissions round, in which almost 56,000 students applied – a 5% increase on 2019 and 30% up in a decade. Enrolments are also on the rise: places rose 13% in 2020, up 40% in a decade.

Birmingham topped the 2021 High Fliers report, which looks at the graduates most targeted by top employers. Undergraduates can build work experience through research assistant roles and summer internships, with advice from alumni mentors. Bursaries

are available to help fund internships, and scholarships may be provided to pay for travel projects that are not linked to the student's main degree, bringing opportunities to life.

A degree apprenticeship in computer science with digital technology – run in partnership with PwC – has taken the earn-as-you-learn route to the next level. The company pays apprentices' tuition fees as well as salaries throughout the four-year course.

While Birmingham outperforms ten of the 24 Russell Group universities in our social inclusion table, it is still in the bottom 20 overall in England and Wales. Its Pathways to Birmingham programmes for year 12–13 pupils encourages applications from those from underrepresented backgrounds and provides bursaries. Applicants are eligible for a contextual offer if they have spent time in care or if they come from an area with low progression to higher education.

Extensive facilities for sport include six glass-backed squash courts, a 50m swimming pool, climbing wall and multipurpose arena with bleacher seating for more than 800 people.

Tuition fees

» Fees for UK students	£9,250
» Fees for International students 2022–23	£19,740–£25,860
Medicine & Dentistry	£44,100
» For scholarship and bursary information see www.birmingham.ac.uk/undergraduate/fees/fees.aspx	
» Graduate salary	£25,700

Student numbers

Undergraduates	22,505	(650)
Postgraduates	8,155	(4,450)
Applications/places	55,935/6,630	
Applications per place	8.5	
Overall offer rate	70.8%	
International students – EU	3.1%	
Non-EU	15%	

Accommodation
University provided places: 6,268
Catered costs: £134–£200 per week
Self-catered: £89–£278 per week
First years guaranteed accommodation
www.birmingham.ac.uk/study/accommodation/Index.aspx

Where do the students come from?

State schools (non-grammar)	68.4%	Low participation areas	7.6%	Disabled	5.2%
Grammar schools	14%	All ethnic minorities	34.1%	Mature (over 21)	4.4%
Independent schools	17.5%	White working-class males	2.4%		
First generation students	30.7%	Black achievement gap	-15%		

Social inclusion ranking: 103

Birmingham City University

Birmingham City University (BCU) has begun a £5million expansion of its City South Campus in Edgbaston to provide extra teaching and training space for its 1,000 healthcare and education students.

The work is part of BCU's wider £340million development programme. The second phase is nearly complete to transform a Victorian factory into a STEAMhouse innovation centre. The £60million facility is designed to encourage collaboration within STEAM (science, technology, engineering, arts and maths) subjects, allowing start-ups to tap into the latest teaching and research.

Buildings at BCU's canalside City Centre campus look out on Eastside City Park, Birmingham's first new urban green space for more than 130 years. The campus will be close to the high-speed HS2 rail line's Curzon Street station due to be in service by the end of the decade.

The Royal Birmingham Conservatoire's 500-seat concert hall, rehearsal rooms and teaching spaces are at the City Centre campus, with student services and a library. Courses taught here include music, business, English, social sciences, acting and media.

BCU's world-renowned School of Jewellery, founded in 1890, is based in the city's Jewellery Quarter. The Birmingham Institute of Fashion and Creative Art is the university's outpost in Wuhan, China, in partnership with Wuhan Textile University.

Opened in 2020, the Sir Lenny Henry Centre for Media Diversity, a research centre named after the BCU chancellor, has published Representology: the Journal for Media and Diversity, in partnership with Cardiff University. Bringing together academics and media practitioners, the publication examines how British media represent the population they serve.

BCU managed only a relatively small submission to the Research Excellence Framework in 2014, of which 60% was judged to be in the top two categories (world-leading or internationally excellent).

Awarded silver in the Teaching Excellence Framework, BCU was recognised for its consistency in retaining students most at risk of dropping out. The panel also praised personalised learning and the use of peer mentors, including a black and minority ethnic support scheme.

BCU's curriculum gained the UK's first accounting and Islamic finance course in September 2021, filling a finance industry niche. Nine degree options will be added in 2022, including art business, fashion imaging, landscape architecture with urban design, and sport in community development. One of the courses, fire engineering, has been designed to help deal with skills shortages in fire safety exposed by the Grenfell Tower blaze.

University House
15 Bartholomew Row
Birmingham B5 5JU
0121 331 6295
admissions@bcu.ac.uk
www.bcu.ac.uk
www.bcusu.com
Open days:
see website

The Times and The Sunday Times **Rankings**
Overall Ranking: =83 (last year: =90)

Teaching quality	76.4%	=43
Student experience	69.3%	=70
Research quality	4.3%	=98
Entry standards	118	=79
Graduate prospects	69.4%	=69
Good honours	76.7%	=76
Expected completion rate	82.7%	=79
Student/staff ratio	16.5	=77
Services and facilities	£2,039	104

About 50 professional accreditations are embedded within courses, recognised by bodies such as the Nursing and Midwifery Council and the Royal Institute of British Architects. Students can also build experience through the Graduate+ range of extracurricular, employment-related activities, recorded through an online e-portfolio.

The university is one of only seven institutions to offer the new flexible online nursing course. Most of the theory component is taught online to widen access for those who may not be able to commit to full-time study. BCU also welcomed its first cohort of nursing apprentices in September 2020, bringing its portfolio of higher and degree apprenticeships to 18. At present there are about 1,000 students signed up to a wide range of apprenticeship courses, training for roles including academic professional, aerospace engineer and architect.

Almost all students (97%) were recruited from non-selective state schools in the 2020 admissions round and 56% were the first in their families to go to university, although the university falls out of our top 20 for social inclusion overall. Student mentoring, summer schools and interactive workshops under the Aimhigher scheme contribute to BCU's work to widen participation. The university also provides advice and guidance talks to pupils and parents, as well as study skills sessions. Literacy tutoring is delivered at 12 Birmingham primary schools.

Meet or Beat scholarships offer £1,000 incentives for UK students to match or exceed published entry requirements, with £850 cash and £150 credit towards course materials. The £1,000 BCU-Santander Widening Participation Bursary is aimed at supporting students from traditionally underrepresented groups. International students may qualify for a £2,000 fee reduction, based on their academic background.

As well as the modern facilities for sport and life sciences at the City South campus, students have access to an 80-station fitness suite, eight-court sports hall and workout and spinning studios at the Doug Ellis Sports Centre at Perry Barr. There is also a sports pavilion with an all-weather pitch, 12 football pitches and two rugby pitches.

Renowned for being diverse, centrally located and with lots going on, Birmingham is one of the UK's leading student cities. With 70% of 2020's entrants drawn from the West Midlands, the majority of BCU students live at home and commute, allowing the university to guarantee a space in student accommodation to all first-years and international students who apply by the deadline.

Tuition fees

» Fees for UK students	£9,250
» Fees for International students 2022–23	£13,500
» For scholarship and bursary information see www.bcu.ac.uk/student-info/finance-and-money-matters	
» Graduate salary	£24,000

Student numbers

Undergraduates	19,580 (1,360)
Postgraduates	3,705 (2,285)
Applications/places	34,775/4,975
Applications per place	7
Overall offer rate	64.4%
International students – EU	2.8%
Non-EU	6.4%

Accommodation

University provided places: 2,060
Self-catered: £119–£165 per week
First years guaranteed accommodation
www.bcu.ac.uk/student-info/accommodation

Where do the students come from?

State schools (non-grammar)	97.3%	Low participation areas	15.2%	Disabled	5.5%
Grammar schools	1.5%	All ethnic minorities	59.1%	Mature (over 21)	22.7%
Independent schools	1.1%	White working-class males	3.7%		
First generation students	56.2%	Black achievement gap	-17.1%		

Social inclusion ranking: =33

Bishop Grosseteste University

"Go small, get more," advises the prospectus for Bishop Grosseteste University (BGU), which counts fewer than 1,700 full-time undergraduates on its books. The Lincoln-based university makes an asset of the family feel engendered by its bijou size. BGU experienced the joint biggest rise – 38 places – of any university in the previous edition of the *Good University Guide,* owing to significant improvement in student satisfaction. However, outcomes from the National Student Survey in summer 2021 have reversed virtually half of the previous gains. Comparing results year-on-year, only six universities had a sharper fall in student satisfaction in the wake of the pandemic.

Named after a 13th-century bishop of Lincoln, Bishop Grosseteste was founded as an Anglican teacher-training college for women in 1862. Teaching degrees remain its focus, though it now offers a range of degrees to people of all genders, and all faiths and none.

Awarded gold in the Teaching Excellence Framework, BGU was commended for an "outstanding learning environment and a personalised approach with high-quality support maximising retention, attainment and progression". Course design and assessment were highlighted for providing outstanding levels of stretch, ensuring students are consistently challenged and engage with developments from the forefront of research, scholarship or working practice.

Although only 11 staff entered the 2014 Research Excellence Framework under three subject areas, some work was classed "world-leading" in education, history and English.

New degrees in counselling and music and musicianship joined the curriculum in September 2021 and a third degree apprenticeship will be offered from 2022 for business-to-business sales professionals. The addition will bring the number of students on degree apprenticeship courses to more than 75.

Admissions are on the rise. Applications increased by 6% in the 2020 cycle and enrolments edged up more sharply, by 9%, in a recruitment round that resulted in 22% of new undergraduates gaining places via clearing. Applications for admission in September 2021 showed a 29% uplift at the end of March compared with the same time the year before.

The leafy campus in historic Lincoln features two on-site halls of residence, one of them with modern teaching and learning facilities attached after a £2.2million extension that doubled the teaching space.

The Venue, at the heart of the campus, is used primarily as a theatre during the daytime by drama and performing arts students, then turns into a cinema by night.

Most BGU undergraduate programmes

Longdales Road
Lincoln LN1 3DY
01522 583 658
enquiries@bishopg.ac.uk
www.bishopg.ac.uk
www.bgsu.co.uk
Open days: see website

The Times and The Sunday Times **Rankings**

Overall Ranking: 82 (last year: 64)

Teaching quality	75.5%	=56
Student experience	67.3%	=90
Research quality	2.1%	120
Entry standards	107	=116
Graduate prospects	75%	=42
Good honours	72.1%	110
Expected completion rate	88.1%	=48
Student/staff ratio	19.1	116
Services and facilities	£2,200	91

will be delivered largely in-person on campus through an interactive and collaborative learning, teaching and assessment model. After the rapid introduction of remote learning during the pandemic, however, the university is now embedding online learning practice to enhance classroom delivery.

A round-the-clock mental health and wellbeing service has been introduced, linking students with counsellors over the phone or in structured sessions to help with issues such as stress and anxiety, financial wellbeing, alcohol and drug issues and legal information.

Further efforts to support students include an online resilience toolkit, which has been created by the university's Wellbeing Framework steering group to provide key information, activities, mindfulness techniques and links to other support. The chaplaincy is another source of help for many.

BGU focuses its outreach work on school students in years 9–12, providing presentations, campus visits and help with study skills. Students who complete the year 12 programme and apply to BGU qualify for a contextual offer of a reduced UCAS tariff. About half of BGU's 18-year-old applicants each year qualify for a contextual offer. They are also extended to those from low-participation backgrounds and to those who have been in care. About half of students qualify for bursaries or scholarships ranging from £800 to £3,600.

This approach pays dividends in our social inclusion ranking, where BGU scores in the top five in three of the nine indicators that make up the ranking: recruitment from areas with low take-up of higher education (27.9%, ranking fourth); recruitment of first-generation students whose parents have not attended university (63.9%, fifth); and students in receipt of Disability Support Allowance (15.8%, fourth).

All first-years are guaranteed student accommodation, though not necessarily on campus. The university has 281 spaces spread across Wickham Hall, Constance Stewart Hall and Cloud Houses.

BGU's sports facilities include a sports hall, gym and acres of outdoor fields, offering opportunities to take part in activities from fitness classes and indoor tennis to hockey, volleyball and rugby.

The campus grounds have a peace garden where students can relax in tranquillity and Lincoln's lively nightlife – helped by the presence of the much larger University of Lincoln – adds to the appeal of a friendly city with a balance of modern and historic charms.

Tuition fees

»	Fees for UK students	£9,250
	Foundation courses	£6,935
»	Fees for International students 2022–23	£12,445
»	For scholarship and bursary information see	
	www.bishopg.ac.uk/apply-now/fees-funding/	
»	Graduate salary	£24,000

Student numbers

Undergraduates	1,665	(0)
Postgraduates	410	(205)
Applications/places		1,460/610
Applications per place		2.4
Overall offer rate		94.5%
International students – EU		0.2%
Non-EU		0.4%

Accommodation

University provided places: 281
Self-catered: £113–£144 per week
First years guaranteed accommodation
www.bishopg.ac.uk/student/accommodation/

Where do the students come from?

State schools (non-grammar)	95.4%	Low participation areas	27.9%	**Social inclusion ranking: 2**	
Grammar schools	3.1%	All ethnic minorities	4.7%	Disabled	15.8%
Independent schools	1.5%	White working-class males	6%	Mature (over 21)	28.9%
First generation students	63.9%	Black achievement gap	n/a		

University of Bolton

The University of Bolton is in the midst of a boom in popularity. Record numbers of new students enrolled on degree courses in the 2020 admissions cycle in its biggest year-on-year applications spike – up 22% compared with 2019.

This Greater Manchester institution takes pride in offering students a supportive learning environment, borne out by its results in the National Student Survey. In the northwest, only Lancaster and Edge Hill achieved better ratings from the pandemic cohort of final-year students when scores are compared with the previous year.

Bolton is one of the UK's most socially inclusive universities. In the 2020 admissions round it recruited almost all (98%) of its students from non-selective state schools and 55% from families without a history of higher education. More than two in ten students came from some of the country's most deprived areas. Overall, Bolton ranks in the top 25 in the country on six out of nine social inclusion measures in our unique ranking.

The university's latest developments include the city centre Institute of Management as well as the £31million Bolton One health, leisure and research centre on the main Deane campus. Here, students have access to a multi-sports hall, climbing wall and a sports and spinal injuries clinic, as well as a 25m competition swimming pool and a therapeutic hydrotherapy pool, fitness suite and community gym.

Bolton has branched out to establish an outpost in the city of Manchester through a partnership with a training provider. In the United Arab Emirates, the university has a campus at Ras al-Khaimah with space for 700 students on undergraduate and postgraduate courses identical to those taught in Bolton.

Founded as the Bolton Mechanics Institute in 1824, the university has continued to develop options for students to progress with its 2018 merger with the local further education provider Bolton College. The university wholly owns Alliance Learning, one of the northwest's largest independent apprenticeship training providers.

Bolton's own suite of on-campus, full-time higher and degree apprenticeships has swelled to 15 courses since the addition of four new programmes in September 2021: social work, electrical and electronic engineering, mechanical engineering, and digital and technology solutions: network engineering.

Investment in the careers service has added an employer engagement team, which works with local, regional and national employers to source work placements, live project briefs and internships for students, and advertises graduate job vacancies.

Awarded silver in the Teaching Excellence

Deane Road
Bolton BL3 5AB
01204 903 394
UGadmissions@bolton.ac.uk
www.bolton.ac.uk
www.boltonsu.com
Open days:
see website

Edinburgh
Belfast
BOLTON
London
Cardiff

The Times and The Sunday Times **Rankings**
Overall Ranking: =89 (last year: 118)

Teaching quality	81.3%	5
Student experience	75.9%	13
Research quality	2.9%	114
Entry standards	116	=91
Graduate prospects	60.2%	=119
Good honours	63.7%	130
Expected completion rate	75.8%	120
Student/staff ratio	14.5	=37
Services and facilities	£2,779	48

Framework, Bolton was commended for an institutional culture that "facilitates, recognises and rewards excellent teaching", as well as providing excellent support for students from disadvantaged backgrounds. The panel blamed "the student demographic and the challenging local employment context" for the university's above-benchmark dropout rate and relatively poor graduate employment record, and praised Bolton's initiatives to address these challenges. Such efforts appear to be bearing fruit, as the latest data shows Bolton has cut its non-completion rate to 18.6%, not far off the expected level and well down from the days when almost one in three students failed to complete their course.

Bolton's distinctive research facilities include the Centre for Islamic Finance and the National Centre for Motorsport Engineering, opened in 2017, which incorporates the renowned Centre for Advanced Performance Engineering (Cape) training base. The university helps to run a professional motor racing team in conjunction with a motorsports company and students work and learn alongside its engineers and mechanics as they study for degrees in automotive performance engineering or motorsport technology.

General engineering was one of two subject areas to have most of their work submitted to the 2014 Research Excellence Framework rated world-leading or internationally excellent. The best results were in English, and almost a third of the university's small submission reached the top two categories overall.

The focus on student support is evident in the Life Lounge, Bolton's mental health and wellbeing service, which offers extensive services including counselling, a cognitive behavioural therapy clinic and mental health advisers who attend suicide prevention meetings with Bolton council and other local organisations. Life Lounge staff are developing a "Z card" pocket-sized guide for all university staff to respond to a student in distress.

As well as Bolton One's sports facilities, students can also use the Anderton Centre, eight miles away, for outdoor adventure activities. Football pitches are found at Ladybridge FC, four miles away.

Rooms in student accommodation are allocated on a first-come, first-served basis. The Orlando Village has 381 spaces, enough so far for all first-years who want one. Many students live locally and commute.

Bolton is renowned as one of the UK's friendliest towns, and the bright lights of Manchester are only a 20-minute train ride away.

Tuition fees
» Fees for UK students   £9,250
» Fees for International students 2022–23   £12,450
» For scholarship and bursary information see www.bolton.ac.uk/student-life/fees-and-funding/
» Graduate salary   £21,000

Student numbers

Undergraduates	5,910	(765)
Postgraduates	690	(815)
Applications/places		6,250/1,015
Applications per place		6.2
Overall offer rate		50.6%
International students – EU		2.8%
Non-EU		5.1%

Accommodation
University provided places: 381
Self-catered: £99–£125 per week
https://orlandovillage.co.uk

Where do the students come from?

State schools (non-grammar)	97.7%	Low participation areas	31.3%	Disabled	10.3%
Grammar schools	0.8%	All ethnic minorities	32.7%	Mature (over 21)	66.8%
Independent schools	1.5%	White working-class males	5.4%		
First generation students	54.7%	Black achievement gap	-21.4%		

Social inclusion ranking: 5

University of Bournemouth

The option of a professional work placement – in the UK or abroad – is offered during every undergraduate degree at the University of Bournemouth. Placements range from four weeks to a year, and dedicated university staff provide advice and guidance to find the ideal match.

During a whole year in industry tuition fees are reduced to £850 and students continue to benefit from university and students' union support for the duration of their placement. The well-established scheme is a resounding success, as borne out by Bournemouth's strong record on graduate outcomes. The university is a regular in our top 50 for high-quality graduate prospects, although it ranks just outside this year. A survey in 2020 found that 24% of graduates who undertook a work placement went on to do more work for the same organisation.

Bournemouth's links with more than 70 universities worldwide facilitate study abroad too, and students have access to the university's Global Talent Programme – an extracurricular award with a focus on employer-led skills and achievements – tailored to help them shine as graduates anywhere in the world. The international links go both ways, and Bournemouth has about 1,600 overseas students from more than 140 countries.

Awarding Bournemouth silver in the Teaching Excellence Framework, the panel praised the work placement system and highlighted peer-assisted learning. All first-years are offered advice and mentoring from "student reps" who are further along in their chosen course.

The use of education technology was already a feature at Bournemouth before the pandemic. Its £6million Brightspace virtual learning environment was introduced in 2017, enabling students to study from home or the workplace and reduce their on-campus time.

However, students gave the university a resounding thumbs-down in the National Student Survey, conducted at the height of the pandemic. In a comparison of scores from 2020 and 2021, no university fell further. Bournemouth's score for overall satisfaction tumbled from 80.2% to 61.2%. The results from the 2021 survey are being widely interpreted as a measure of how well students feel their institution has coped with Covid.

The university has benefited from extensive campus developments lately, with the opening of two new Gateway Buildings – one on each of its sites. On the main Lansdowne campus, the project hosts the Faculty of Health and Social Sciences, where simulation suites replicate an operating theatre, hospital wards, a birthing room and a residential flat for at-home care practice.

Poole Gateway, on the Talbot campus, has

Fern Barrow
Talbot Campus
Poole BH12 5BB
01202 961 916
futurestudents@bournemouth.ac.uk
www.bournemouth.ac.uk
www.subu.org.uk
Open days:
see website

The Times and The Sunday Times **Rankings**

Overall Ranking: =106 (last year: 68)

Teaching quality	67%	127
Student experience	60.2%	124
Research quality	9.0%	=64
Entry standards	110	=109
Graduate prospects	72.4%	56
Good honours	80%	54
Expected completion rate	80.9%	=94
Student/staff ratio	18.6	109
Services and facilities	£2,511	67

5,000 square metres of space for industry-standard facilities for Bournemouth's flagship media courses. As well as two television studios with ultra-high-definition cameras, there is a film studio and sound stage, green screen, edit suites and a motion-capture studio for animation.

The university hosts the National Centre for Computer Animation and graduates have worked on films such as *Blade Runner 2049*, *Dunkirk*, *The Avengers* and *Solo: A Star Wars Story*. For music and sound production there are two recording studios with mixing desks, three surround-sound studios and two post-production studios. Students also have access to Games PC and Mac laboratories and a critical listening lab.

Bournemouth's performance in the 2014 Research Excellence Framework was one of the best among post-1992 universities. Sixty per cent of its entry was judged to be world-leading or internationally excellent. Its two leading departments – communication, cultural and media studies, and leisure and tourism – led the way with some of the strongest submissions. Students have the opportunity to work with academics on live research projects through an undergraduate research assistant programme.

Outreach initiatives aim to raise aspirations and attainment among disadvantaged pupils. The AccessBU contextual offer system makes allowances for applicants' personal circumstances, which may qualify them for entry at lower-than-published grades. Help with finance includes maintenance bursaries of £2,400, awarded to UK students from low-income backgrounds. Students entering with AAA grades at A-level or equivalent are automatically awarded a £1,000 academic scholarship.

Bournemouth offers more than 120 course options. Three were added in September 2021: multimedia sports journalism, photography and virtual and augmented reality. A degree in immersive media will begin in 2022.

The 65-acre Chapel Gate sports facility, near the airport, hosts football, rugby, hockey, cricket, squash, table tennis, archery and rifle shooting. Bournemouth also has fitness and spin studios, a sports hall, treatment rooms and dance studios.

Students have access to mental health advisers, who provide one-to-one support and encourage positive habits and routines to build resilience. Diversity is championed at Bournemouth, which runs an annual Pride event and holds the Athena Swan Bronze award in recognition of its work towards gender equality.

Students can select their study bedrooms from the university's 3,400 spaces, and all first-years are guaranteed a spot.

Tuition fees

» Fees for UK students		£9,250
Foundation courses		£8,200
» Fees for International students 2022–23		£15,250–£16,500
» For scholarship and bursary information see		
www.bournemouth.ac.uk/study/undergraduate/fees-funding		
» Graduate salary		£24,000

Student numbers

Undergraduates	12,735	(1,160)
Postgraduates	2,330	(1,265)
Applications/places	19,630/3,900	
Applications per place	5	
Overall offer rate	77.4%	
International students – EU	4%	
Non-EU	3.9%	

Accommodation

University provided places: 3,400
Self-catered: £129–£204 per week
First years guaranteed accommodation
www.bournemouth.ac.uk/why-bu/accommodation

Where do the students come from?

State schools (non-grammar)	90.8%	Low participation areas	11.4%	Disabled	8.3%
Grammar schools	4.1%	All ethnic minorities	14.9%	Mature (over 21)	17.7%
Independent schools	5.1%	White working-class males	7.7%		
First generation students	46.8%	Black achievement gap	-26%		

Social inclusion ranking: 67

University of Bradford

The University of Bradford has a new five-year access and participation plan, which aims to eliminate gaps in access to higher education and attainment within it. The ambitious plan galvanises a long-held commitment to social mobility at Bradford, the winner of our 2020 University of the Year for Social Inclusion award.

Underpinned by the university's wider aim to help to create fairer societies, the new strategy targets underrepresented groups. Among them are students from low-participation backgrounds, black, Asian and minority ethnic students, care leavers, white working-class males and refugees. The university has set objectives to eliminate ethnic minority achievement gaps and to significantly reduce progression gaps by 2024–25.

Bradford already performs strongly in these areas. Just two universities recruit a larger proportion of students from ethnic minority backgrounds (77.3%). The narrowness of its black achievement gap of 10.1% (79.8% of black students leave with a first or 2:1 compared with almost 90% of white students) puts Bradford in 14th place in the country. Only one university exceeds Bradford's tally of drawing two-thirds of students from households where they are the first to attend university.

Bradford was also one of the first higher education institutions to sign the Social Mobility Pledge – a coalition of 500 organisations dedicated to levelling up Britain using fair recruitment practices. It has also launched a decolonisation programme to create learning spaces free from racism and equality is at the core of the new teaching and learning strategy.

Awarded silver in the Teaching Excellence Framework, Bradford was praised for its "strategic and systematic commitment to diversity and social mobility that enables the majority of students, including a very high number from black, Asian and minority backgrounds, to achieve excellent outcomes".

The panel also commended the curriculum for stretching students to achieve their full potential and acquire the knowledge, skills and understanding valued by employers, and for its work-based learning. The physiotherapy and sport rehabilitation team was singled out for recognition with a teaching excellence award from Advance HE in 2019.

Three new degrees come on stream from September 2022: psychology and criminology, architectural technology and architectural engineering. Bradford offers five degree apprenticeships.

Work experience or placements are offered within many degrees and many courses are designed with input from industry partners such as the BBC, the NHS, Jaguar Land Rover, Amazon, the Civil Service, Wm Morrison Supermarkets, PwC and Fujitsu, helping Bradford to achieve a ranking for graduate

---

Richmond Road
Bradford BD7 1DP
01274 233 081
enquiries@bradford.ac.uk
www.bradford.ac.uk
www.bradfordunisu.co.uk
Open days:
see website

The Times and The Sunday Times **Rankings**
Overall Ranking: =89 (last year: 106)

Teaching quality	74.8%	=68
Student experience	71.4%	44
Research quality	9.2%	=62
Entry standards	123	=67
Graduate prospects	71.7%	59
Good honours	82.9%	=35
Expected completion rate	83.7%	=73
Student/staff ratio	18.7	=110
Services and facilities	£2,005	107

outcomes far above its overall position in our table. More than 70% of programmes are accredited or recognised by professional bodies such as the General Pharmaceutical Council and the Royal Society of Chemistry.

Among Bradford's specialist developments is the purpose-built Digital Health Enterprise Zone, which hosted one of the first mass Covid-19 vaccine trials and hopes to develop innovations for people with long-term conditions. The Lady Hale mock court opened in 2020, while the university's Wolfson Centre for Applied Health Research opened at Bradford Royal Infirmary in 2019 in a partnership with the University of Leeds and Bradford Teaching Hospitals NHS Foundation Trust.

The world-renowned Peace Studies and International Development department has more than 40 years' experience and collaborates with the United Nations, the UK Ministry of Defence and development banks in Africa and China. Its research was part of Bradford's submission to the Research Excellence Framework in 2014. Across all subjects, fewer than a quarter of eligible academics were entered, but almost three-quarters of the work submitted reached the top two categories to be considered world-leading or internationally excellent. Allied health, management and archaeological science led the way.

Bradford remains committed to face-to-face learning after the rapid shift to online course delivery necessitated by the pandemic.

Lecture-capture is available in some teaching rooms and the university uses technology to supplement in-person teaching, rather than to replace human interaction. Students felt the university handled the educational impact of the pandemic well. Our analysis of the 2021 National Student Survey put Bradford in the top 20 when outcomes are compared with 2020.

About 60% of students receive some form of financial assistance. More than 3,000 cash bursaries are awarded to those with household income below £30,000. More than a quarter of the 2020 intake qualified for the Bradford Progression scheme, which makes contextual offers eight UCAS tariff points lower than the published requirement.

Unique Fitness and Lifestyle on the City Centre campus has a swimming pool, climbing wall and squash courts. The campus has a multi-use games area and 3G five-a-side pitch too. Five minutes away on foot, there is a full-size football pitch at Bradford Sports Park, plus tennis courts and a conditioning suite. The Woodhall sports ground has more pitches, four miles from the city campus.

Tuition fees

» Fees for UK students	£9,250
» Fees for International students 2022–23	£17,740–£21,886
Foundation years (2021–22)	£12,800
» For scholarship and bursary information see www.bradford.ac.uk/money/fees/	
» Graduate salary	£24,000

Student numbers

Undergraduates	7,010	(470)
Postgraduates	995	(1,295)
Applications/places	11,505/1,805	
Applications per place	6.4	
Overall offer rate	80.8%	
International students – EU	3.7%	
Non-EU	8.6%	

Accommodation

University provided places: 1,014
Self-catered: £81–£101 per week
www.bradford.ac.uk/accommodation/

Where do the students come from?

State schools (non-grammar)	93.8%	Low participation areas	10.4%	Disabled	10.2%
Grammar schools	4%	All ethnic minorities	77.3%	Mature (over 21)	25.1%
Independent schools	2.2%	White working-class males	2.2%		
First generation students	66.5%	Black achievement gap	-10.1%		

Social inclusion ranking: =12

University of Brighton

The Big Build project at the University of Brighton's Moulsecoomb campus is coming to fruition. The first residents will move into 800 new study bedrooms in five halls of residence in September 2022. Shaped to reflect the undulating South Downs nearby, the halls have been built above new students' union and fitness facilities.

Moulsecoomb hosts the schools of applied sciences, architecture, technology and engineering, and business and law. Elm House is being built with flexible teaching and collaborative spaces as the new base for the School of Business and Law. Its façade of reflective tiles will suggest movement as the light changes, a design inspired by the murmurations of starlings that gather across the Brighton seafront.

The city centre campus on Grand Parade is home to Brighton's wide range of creative courses. It houses the Centre for Contemporary Arts, opened in 2019, which showcases work and research by emerging and established artists.

The university's reach extends along the south coast to its Eastbourne campus, the base for about 3,000 students taking courses in sport and exercise, events, hospitality and tourism, adult nursing and midwifery, physiotherapy and podiatry. A multi-professional skills simulation suite opened at the Eastbourne campus in 2020 to help healthcare students to develop their techniques in real-life scenarios.

The Brighton and Sussex Medical School is one of the first awarded to a post-1992 university, run in a longstanding partnership with Brighton's neighbour, the University of Sussex. Based at Falmer, the Sussex campus a few miles out of town, the school accepts 200 trainee doctors each year.

Brighton has its own Falmer campus too, where students take courses including English, criminology and nursing. Dedicated facilities – such as a curriculum centre and medical simulation suites – cater for these specialisms.

In the most recent Teaching Excellence Framework, Brighton was awarded silver, winning praise for its close working relationships with professional bodies, employers and local community groups and its personalised learning and support, particularly for first-year students.

Brighton has fallen down our league table in recent years, having been our inaugural University of the Year in 1999. Its ranking is suppressed by a dropout rate that is significantly higher than the projected level, based on its course profile and the social and academic background of its intake. More than one in six students drop out, compared with the expected figure of below one in eight. However, it has scored well in the new-style Graduate Outcomes survey, ranking in the top 60.

Work-related experience is built into all courses, from long or short placements, to

Mithras House
Lewes Road
Brighton BN2 4AT
01273 644 644
enquiries@brighton.ac.uk
www.brighton.ac.uk
www.brightonsu.com
Open days:
see website

The Times and The Sunday Times Rankings
Overall Ranking: 117 (last year: 120)

Teaching quality	69.1%	122
Student experience	59.3%	125
Research quality	7.9%	=73
Entry standards	109	=111
Graduate prospects	71.6%	=60
Good honours	72.6%	108
Expected completion rate	82.8%	78
Student/staff ratio	16.7	=80
Services and facilities	£2,462	71

assessed voluntary work and live project briefs. Step-Up, a paid internship and skills training programmed launched in 2020, places students in training and development workshops with local employers ending in a six-week paid work placement.

Brighton's continuing partnership with Santander Universities to fund awards, scholarships, internships and business grants began more than 12 years ago and students continue to benefit from the bank's investment in their education, entrepreneurship and employability.

The university runs five mentoring programmes designed to boost work-ready skills. One of them is the LGBTQ+ programme run by Uni-Amex, which links students with a mentor sharing their sexual or gender identity. Another mentoring programme is Men in Primary Education, designed to boost the numbers of male teachers.

Forced, like other universities, to rapidly adapt to online learning during the pandemic, Brighton has pledged to continue using digital technology – especially lecture-capture and playback facilities – to enhance teaching on campus. However, the university has taken one of the 15 biggest year-on-year falls in its scores in the National Student Survey for 2021.

Those applying for courses beginning in 2022 will have the option of seven new degrees, in politics, diagnostic radiography, design engineering, fashion accessories and business, strength and conditioning, team entrepreneurship and exercise, health and rehabilitation science.

Brighton's degree apprenticeship provision is continuing to expand. Six new programmes beginning in September 2021 have brought the portfolio to a total of 18 courses in diverse fields such as teaching, digital and technology solutions, podiatry, social work, environmental practice and construction site management.

Research is a strong suit for Brighton compared with its post-1992 peer institutions. In the 2014 Research Excellence Framework, two-thirds of the work submitted was placed in one of the top two categories, indicating world-class or international excellence.

The focus for support for mental health and wellbeing is on students who might feel marginalised – including those who are pregnant or have children, LGBTQ+ students and the disabled. A new Wellbeing Champions scheme offers students training to build and maintain their own wellbeing and share their knowledge with peers.

Tuition fees

- » Fees for UK students — £9,250
- » Fees for International students 2022–23 — £13,842–£15,462
  Medicine — £37,293
- » For scholarship and bursary information see www.brighton.ac.uk/studying-here/fees-and-finance/index.aspx
- » Graduate salary — £24,000

Student numbers

Undergraduates	13,535 (2,000)
Postgraduates	1,550 (1,905)
Applications/places	24,890/3,060
Applications per place	8.1
Overall offer rate	71.3%
International students – EU	4.4%
Non-EU	7.6%

Accommodation

University provided places: 2,608
Self-catered: £82–£216 per week
First years guaranteed accommodation
www.brighton.ac.uk/accommodation-and-locations/Index.aspx

Where do the students come from?

State schools (non-grammar)	89.4%	Low participation areas	12.9%	
Grammar schools	5.4%	All ethnic minorities	20.8%	
Independent schools	5.3%	White working-class males	7.1%	
First generation students	45.7%	Black achievement gap	-27.3%	

Social inclusion ranking: =74

Disabled	10.1%
Mature (over 21)	24.3%

University of Bristol

The Georgian buildings of Clifton make an attractive backdrop to undergraduate life at the University of Bristol, where a traditional subject mix, high entry standards and membership of the research-led Russell Group of universities combine to create a hugely popular institution.

The surge in student numbers experienced by Bristol since the cap was lifted is showing no signs of slowing down. There were almost seven applications per place in the 2020 admissions cycle, pushing enrolments 37% higher than in 2014 with a similar hike in admissions. In the 2021 cycle applications were already 9% higher by the end of March than they were at the same point the year before.

A degree from Bristol carries weight with employers, and the university achieved another top ten place in the latest High Fliers graduate market report.

More than 20 degree programmes offer a year in industry or professional placements as part of the course and the university belongs to a range of networks that match students with practitioners in relevant fields.

In the most recent Teaching Excellence Framework, Bristol was praised for encouraging independent learning, but low scores in the National Student Survey for assessment and feedback, and academic support resulted in a silver award.

Its performance in the 2014 Research Excellence Framework was outstanding. Bristol entered more than 90% of its eligible staff and 83% of their work was rated world-leading or internationally excellent, the top two categories. Geography, sport and exercise sciences were No 1 in the country. Bristol's submissions in clinical medicine, health subjects, economics, and sport and exercise sciences were placed in the top categories for their impact.

Bristol's research pedigree means that undergraduates benefit from a research-led curriculum and opportunities to be taught by academics at the cutting edge. A degree in data science with a year in industry joined the curriculum in 2021 and a foundation course in science, technology, engineering and mathematics has been added.

Most teaching takes place on the main campus in Clifton, where standout facilities include the £56million Life Sciences Building, opened in 2015. Its chemistry laboratories are certified as a Centre for Excellence in Teaching and Learning. Eight of Bristol's nine libraries are at the Clifton site. A new humanities hub features a lecture theatre, social learning zone, gallery space, virtual museum and cinema. The Richmond Building, a few minutes away, is home to the students' union, two theatres and one of the city's largest gig venues. Further afield in Stoke Bishop a botanic garden has more than 4,500 plant species.

Beacon House
Queens Road
Bristol BS8 1QU
0117 394 1649
choosebristol-ug@bristol.ac.uk
www.bristol.ac.uk
www.bristolsu.org.uk
Open days:
see website

The Times and The Sunday Times Rankings
Overall Ranking: 14 (last year: 13)

Teaching quality	72.9%	89
Student experience	67.4%	89
Research quality	47.3%	6
Entry standards	164	=18
Graduate prospects	79.7%	=20
Good honours	91.3%	8
Expected completion rate	95.3%	8
Student/staff ratio	13.4	19
Services and facilities	£2,704	52

The pandemic has slowed progress on Bristol's £300million Temple Quarter Enterprise Campus. The landmark development, which will focus on digital, business and social innovation, is now scheduled to open in 2025 – two years later than planned. Located near Temple Meads train station on a seven-acre site, the new car-free campus will be part of a wider city redevelopment. There will be space for 3,000 students and 800 staff as well as business and community partners. Nearly 1,000 extra study bedrooms will be provided.

New research facilities are due to open sooner – in 2022 – in existing university buildings on Avon Street.

A pioneer of contextual offers, now the norm, Bristol makes offers up to two grades lower than standard to students who come from low-achieving schools and postcodes where progression to higher education is low. In 2020, 35% of applicants qualified. There is also a generous bursary and scholarship scheme: about a quarter of the annual intake qualifies for some form of financial award.

However, these efforts to widen access have yet to make much of an impact on Bristol's social inclusion ranking. The university remains close to the bottom of the ranking overall, dropping a place this year to third last. More than four in ten students come from selective state or independent schools and the vast majority (77.1%) come from families with a history of university education, the fifth-largest proportion of any university.

Sports facilities are spread across five sites. An impressive complex with a well-equipped gym has been developed at the heart of the university precinct, featuring a sports medicine clinic. The swimming pool is five minutes away in the Richmond Building. Three miles north of the main campus is the 38-acre Coombe Dingle sports complex, the site of most training and competition.

An online toolkit, Being Well, Living Well, is designed to help students to settle in, support their friends and to get help if needed. It also includes content around drugs and alcohol use, and the importance of sexual consent.

With 8,123 study bedrooms (just under a fifth of them catered) Bristol is able to guarantee accommodation to first-years, as long as they apply by the deadline.

A diverse and cosmopolitan city, Bristol is a student hit. With job opportunities on the doorstep it makes a convincing place to settle down after graduating too.

Tuition fees

- » Fees for UK students £9,250
  Foundation years (2021–22) £5,150
- » Fees for International students 2022–23 £21,100–£25,900
  Dentistry £39,900; Medicine £36,800; Veterinary science £33,600
- » For scholarship and bursary information see www.bristol.ac.uk/study/undergraduate/fees-funding/
- » Graduate salary £28,000

Student numbers

Undergraduates	19,570	(465)
Postgraduates	6,075	(1,260)
Applications/places	52,385/6,090	
Applications per place	8.6	
Overall offer rate	71.8%	
International students – EU	5%	
Non-EU	20%	

Accommodation

University provided places: 8,123
Catered costs: £158–£262 per week
Self-catered: £90–£238 per week
First years guaranteed accommodation
www.bristol.ac.uk/accommodation/undergraduate/

Where do the students come from?

State schools (non-grammar)	59%	Low participation areas	6.1%	
Grammar schools	12.3%	All ethnic minorities	20.3%	
Independent schools	28.7%	White working-class males	2.6%	
First generation students	22.9%	Black achievement gap	-11.7%	

Social inclusion ranking: 114

Disabled	5.5%
Mature (over 21)	5.8%

Brunel University, London

Founded in 1966, Brunel University has long aimed to be the UK's leading technological university. Practical learning is embedded in all courses, taught in hands-on settings such as laboratories, the theatre or clinical simulation suites. Almost all degrees have the option of work placements and under normal circumstances students may find themselves gaining clinical experience at King's College Hospital or experiencing business life at IBM for a few weeks or up to a full academic year.

Universities, such as Brunel, with a focus on practical-based courses tend to have been judged as having responded poorly to the pandemic in the eyes of their students. Our analysis of year-on-year National Student Survey results from 2021 and 2020 bears this out, with Brunel ranked fourth from bottom nationally and seeing a collapse in student satisfaction in some areas. Scores for overall satisfaction (down 19 percentage points), learning resources (down 16.8 percentage points) and learning community (down 15.1 percentage points) had the biggest falls at Brunel in 2021 compared with the previous year.

Brunel is operating a blended approach to teaching and learning, in common with most other universities, retaining the flexibility of online delivery while giving opportunities for on-campus activities that are interactive and that add value to the academic experience. Brunel's Blackboard Learn virtual platform was established well before the pandemic hit, and gives access to recordings of lectures. The platform is also a source of information about relevant materials, learning resources and reading lists.

When awarding Brunel silver, assessors from the Teaching Excellence Framework praised the high levels of employer engagement and opportunities for work experience. Assessors highlighted the analytical approach to addressing attainment gaps within its diverse student body.

Among wide-ranging industry links is an exclusive strategic alliance with the Environment Agency, which recruits up to 30 interns from Brunel each year. The university places more than 600 students on six to 12-month placements each year, and has links with local and national businesses such as Jaguar Land Rover, Disney, L'Oréal, and Morgan Stanley.

Its self-contained Uxbridge campus, is a rarity among London universities, which are more commonly spread across several locations. Students can navigate their way from one end of the campus to the other in ten minutes, while the West End is 45-minutes away via public transport.

The university's new medical school had to postpone its planned 2021 launch. Instead, its first cohort of students will begin

Kingston Lane
Uxbridge
UB8 3PH
01895 265 265
admissions@brunel.ac.uk
www.brunel.ac.uk
https://brunelstudents.com
Open days:
see website

The Times and The Sunday Times **Rankings**		
Overall Ranking: 121 (last year: 88)		
Teaching quality	63.4%	130
Student experience	59.2%	=126
Research quality	25.4%	49
Entry standards	118	=79
Graduate prospects	67.1%	85
Good honours	77%	=72
Expected completion rate	87.4%	=52
Student/staff ratio	17	=87
Services and facilities	£1,591	127

courses in September 2022. Offering five-year undergraduate Bachelor of Medicine, Bachelor of Surgery degrees, the medical school will only be open to students from outside Britain initially, although it is keen to extend applications to UK students as soon as possible.

A suite of four electronic and electrical engineering degrees joined the curriculum in September, along with mathematics for data science, music production and journalism (communication), plus journalism (politics). Nursing (adult) and nursing (child health) are also being introduced, subject to Nursing and Midwifery Council approval. Those joining from September 2022 will also have the options of history and international relations – as either a BA or a BSc.

In partnership with the Metropolitan Police the university offers a police constable degree apprenticeship as well as a graduate-level entry programme. There are other degree apprenticeships for clinical practitioners, nurse associates and a new programme in digital technology solutions. The university expects to have more than 800 learners on degree apprenticeship programmes by 2022.

Brunel's already superb sports facilities have gained an extra artificial pitch and temporary gym – exclusively for rugby players – via a partnership with Ealing Trailfinders Rugby. Opposite the campus, the Sports Park's facilities include an FA-registered 3G pitch and a floodlit international standard rugby pitch

with natural turf and automated irrigation. There are sports scholarships for elite student athletes – and all students are encouraged to get active for fun. Brunel was the first university to introduce a sports hijab for its female Muslim students.

The university also has a multimillion-pound Indoor Athletics Centre with a 132m straight sprint, pole vault, high jump and long/triple jump facilities. A bespoke strength and conditioning gym is for elite student athletes. The rower James Cracknell (MSc sport science 1999) is among a number of Olympians who have studied at Brunel.

Brunel is among the most socially inclusive of the pre-1992 universities, ranking in the top 50 of all four of our social inclusion rankings published to date. More than three-quarters of entrants were from black and ethnic minority backgrounds in 2019 with more than half of admissions being the first members of their family to go to university.

Plentiful student accommodation includes refurbished and new rooms. First-years are guaranteed a space provided they apply and have an unconditional firm offer by September 6.

Tuition fees

- » Fees for UK students £9,250
- » Fees for International students 2022-23 £16,825–£20,450
  Medicine £41,200
- » For scholarship and bursary information see www.brunel.ac.uk/study/undergraduate-fees-and-funding
- » Graduate salary £25,000

Student numbers

Undergraduates	11,230	(230)
Postgraduates	3,100	(960)
Applications/places		18,915/2,270
Applications per place		8.3
Overall offer rate		82.4%
International students – EU		5.7%
Non-EU		15.6%

Accommodation

University provided places: 4,370
Self-catered: £121–£208 per week
First years guaranteed accommodation
www.brunel.ac.uk/life/accommodation

Where do the students come from?

State schools (non-grammar)	89.6%	Low participation areas	3.9%
Grammar schools	5.2%	All ethnic minorities	75.5%
Independent schools	5.2%	White working-class males	3.6%
First generation students	51.2%	Black achievement gap	-18.7%

Social inclusion ranking: 48

Disabled	6.3%
Mature (over 21)	11.2%

University of Buckingham

The University of Buckingham's School of Computing is expanding. Funding for a £3.2million Innovation and Incubation Hub has been secured for new lab space and hardware fit for the evolving tech landscape. It will equip students with specialist skills in artificial intelligence, cybersecurity, games development, immersive applications development and robotics. An incubation space to nurture spin-off companies will operate alongside teaching facilities.

In line with its tech innovations, the university introduced three new computing degree courses for 2021. In their second year, students specialise in AI, cybersecurity or games development and immersive technologies.

Buckingham is Britain's first – and largest – private university. It has fewer than 1,600 full-time undergraduates, but the traditional range of courses they are offered matches that of other UK universities.

Buckingham is also the pioneer of two-year undergraduate degrees, with which it first disrupted the higher education landscape more than 40 years ago. Instead of 26–30 weeks of teaching over three years – the UK norm – most Buckingham students have 40 weeks a year spread over two years. The more concentrated pattern is a big draw for students, who graduate with a year's head start on their peers in the jobs market. The university believes that condensing their learning also increases the students' focus.

An extended academic year makes the two-year degrees possible. There are four nine-week terms, and students still get plenty of time off. Degree courses begin in January or September – providing flexibility that appeals to many students, including those switching to Buckingham after being unhappy at their original choice of university. There is a cost saving too: tuition fees for subjects other than medicine are £25,200 for a two-year course – slightly less than the standard £27,750 for three years of study – and saving a year's living costs. Buckingham students on two-year courses also qualify for up to £900 extra in Student Loans support, to cover added living expenses during longer terms.

Buckingham also offers three-year degrees in the humanities, however, and other schools are beginning to follow suit.

The proportion of British students who choose Buckingham is growing, though those from overseas still account for just over half. A boom in applications in recent years halted in the 2020 cycle, with a 6% dip on 2019 figures.

With nearly four in ten UK-domiciled recruits drawn from ethnic minorities and just over four in ten mature students, Buckingham scores well in some of our social inclusion measures. However, it has the lowest proportion of white working-class male students (1.1%) of any university and

Hunter Street
Buckingham MK18 1EG
01280 820 227
admissions@buckingham.ac.uk
www.buckingham.ac.uk
Open days:
see website

The Times and The Sunday Times **Rankings**

Overall Ranking: =89 (last year: 108)

Teaching quality	79%	15
Student experience	73.4%	=29
Research quality	n/a	
Entry standards	118	=79
Graduate prospects	87.1%	6
Good honours	67.7%	124
Expected completion rate	85%	=61
Student/staff ratio	18.8	=112
Services and facilities	£1,644	125

relatively low numbers recruited from non-selective state schools (68.5%).

Buckingham's medical school is a popular choice for home and overseas students. Medical students finish their courses in a shorter time than they would elsewhere with a four-and-a-half-year MBChB – modelled on the one offered by the University of Leicester. Annual tuition fees are £37,000 for UK medical students.

The Crewe campus opened at the start of 2020, 120 miles from the university's headquarters. A joint venture with the Indian private healthcare company Apollo Hospitals, Crewe offers medicine and podiatry courses and hopes to add other medical and allied health degrees in future.

The government's Teaching Excellence Framework awarded Buckingham gold. The panel praised personalised learning, a result of teaching in small groups, and rigorous attendance monitoring, making for the best rates of retention, attainment and progression. Physical and digital resources were outstanding, the panel noted, encompassing one-to-one IT support and extensive access to online journals.

With an eye to employability, students can complete a number of Microsoft certifications for free within the School of Computing. Work experience opportunities are available through the school's partnership with Deepnet Security and links with organisations including Ten-D Innovations (Shanghai), Zizo, Vitalograph and ABB Robotics.

Law students can train as Citizens Advice volunteers. There are shadowing opportunities with law firms, barrister's chambers and in court through the Street Legal placement scheme, and an initiative with the Home Office allows law students to opt for a one-year paid work placement.

B-Enterprising, a new scheme offered by the university's careers and employability service, places students of any discipline in start-ups and small businesses for paid experience.

Students who achieve AAB or better in their A-levels or equivalent are eligible for high-achiever scholarships of £2,000. The university discounts tuition fees by £2,000 per year for students with household incomes under £25,000. In 2020, 11% of admissions received a bursary.

The leafy main campus has a bar and fitness facilities, and events are hosted at the nearby Radcliffe Centre. The halls of residence on campus provide enough spaces for all first-years who want to live in.

Tuition fees

» Fees for UK students (2-year degree)	£12,672
(3-year degree)	£8,448
» Fees for International students 2022–23 (2-years)	£20,232
(3-year degree)	£13,488
Medicine (all students 4.5-year degree)	£37,951
» For scholarship and bursary information see www.buckingham.ac.uk/admissions/fees	
» Graduate salary	£25,000

Student numbers

Undergraduates	1,590	(55)
Postgraduates	1,160	(300)
Applications/places		1,115/100
Applications per place		11.2
Overall offer rate		n/a
International students – EU		4.6%
Non-EU		36.1%

Accommodation

University provided places: 476
Self-catered: £121–£249 per week
First years guaranteed accommodation
www.buckingham.ac.uk/life/accommodation

Where do the students come from?

State schools (non-grammar)	68.5%	Low participation areas	7.8%	
Grammar schools	10.3%	All ethnic minorities	38.7%	
Independent schools	21.2%	White working-class males	1.1%	
First generation students	35%	Black achievement gap	-41.2%	

Social inclusion ranking: 111

Disabled	5.9%
Mature (over 21)	42.1%

Buckinghamshire New University

Embracing and celebrating diversity remains a key focus for Buckinghamshire New University (BNU). It created a black, Asian and minority ethnic network after the Black Lives Matter protests of summer 2020, holding a series of events during Black History Month and introduced workstreams designed to expand opportunities for students and staff from ethnic minorities.

The university has also called on fellow higher education institutions to create more inclusive environments for Gypsy, Traveller, Roma, Showman and Boater (GTRSB) students and to push for better academic and personal outcomes for them.

BNU climbs eight places in our social inclusion ranking to stand 26th overall in 2021. No university has more mature students (78%) and nearly a third of the intake is drawn from ethnic minorities. BNU's mobile interactive experience vehicle visits schools in low-participation areas, where staff encourage young people to find out about courses and careers.

However, in our academic ranking, the university remains in the lower reaches, not helped by one of the biggest falls in student satisfaction of any university during the pandemic.

Originally founded as a School of Science and Art in 1891, BNU gained university status in 2007. The main campus in High Wycombe has benefited from £100 million in site developments over the past decade and its prizewinning Gateway Building has a commanding position in the town centre. There is a second base in Uxbridge, northwest London, and a third in Aylesbury, hosting nursing and other healthcare courses.

Over the past four years almost 60 new courses have been added to BNU's curriculum, in line with its skills-based remit. Applications increased by more than 21% from 2019–20. More than one third of first-years entered via clearing in the 2020 admissions cycle.

BNU's suite of healthcare courses gained new midwifery and paramedicine programmes in September 2021 in response to growing interest in the sector during the pandemic. The healthcare additions bolster BNU's reputation as one of the southeast's leading providers of nursing qualifications.

Social work courses are professionally accredited and a new Institute for Health and Social Care was created in autumn 2020 with a remit to oversee all related activities and support the region.

For more than 15 years, BNU has worked in partnership with Thames Valley Police to deliver programmes, which include a bachelor's degree in police studies with criminal investigation, a police constable degree apprenticeship and a new pre-join

Queen Alexandra Road
High Wycombe HP11 2JZ
0330 123 2023
advice@bucks.ac.uk
www.bucks.ac.uk
www.bucksstudentsunion.org
Open days: see website

The Times and The Sunday Times Rankings

Overall Ranking: =119 (last year: 112)

Teaching quality	75.8%	=53
Student experience	68.2%	82
Research quality	1.5%	123
Entry standards	108	=113
Graduate prospects	64.6%	=99
Good honours	60.3%	132
Expected completion rate	73.1%	126
Student/staff ratio	17.4	=94
Services and facilities	£3,660	10

professional policing programme. The latter two pathways paved the way for more than 35 new police officers – aged from 19 to 44 – to join Thames Valley Police at the end of 2020.

Degree apprenticeship provision is extensive with 16 programmes and more than 800 learners on courses including nursing, healthcare, academic practice, social work, leadership and management, engineering and digital technology. Apprenticeships in midwifery, paramedicine and community and public health are planned.

The university's range of film and television degrees has the advantage of teaching on location from industry professionals at nearby Pinewood Studios, home of the James Bond films. Courses are run via BNU's partnership with Pinewood's CMS training platform. Facilities include a cinema-standard viewing room, teaching rooms and new equipment for film workshops.

Travel and aviation courses include the opportunity to study for a professional pilot's licence while working towards a degree. The International Civil Aviation Organisation chose BNU as its partner in a new aviation security master's degree introduced in 2020.

The Teaching Excellence Framework (TEF) upgraded BNU's bronze award to silver in the second round of assessments. The judging panel was impressed by small class sizes and individual action plans to support students into work, as well as active engagement with the student body, and the "live briefs" co-designed with students to address real-world problems.

Most bursaries are worth £1,000 per year of study. The university also provided a learning technology grant to 223 students during the pandemic, to contribute towards the cost of a laptop, IT accessories and wi-fi.

Sports facilities include one of only five swimming performance centres approved by Swim England.

Survive and Thrive sessions during Welcome Week raise awareness of all the support available to students. The students' union also organises mixers for international, LGBTQ+, ethnic minority and disabled students.

BNU owns or endorses 881 student bedrooms, a large proportion renting from just £80 per week. First-years who want to live in are guaranteed a space. The university funds free access to recreational and sporting activities through the students' union's Big Deal programme. Students can get involved in everything from martial arts to water sports.

Tuition fees
- » Fees for UK/EU students — £9,250
- » Fees for International students 2022–23 — £14,250
- » For scholarship and bursary information see www.bucks.ac.uk/applying-to-bucks/undergraduate/fees-and-funding
- » Graduate salary — £24,000

Student numbers

Undergraduates	11,525	(1,370)
Postgraduates	405	(775)
Applications/places		7,265/1,970
Applications per place		3.7
Overall offer rate		79.6%
International students – EU		5.8%
Non-EU		0.8%

Accommodation
University provided places: 881
Self-catered: £80–£175 per week
First years guaranteed accommodation
www.bucks.ac.uk/life/accommodation

Where do the students come from?

State schools (non-grammar)	94.7%	Low participation areas	10.7%	Disabled	2.7%
Grammar schools	1.4%	All ethnic minorities	30.4%	Mature (over 21)	78%
Independent schools	3.9%	White working-class males	5.4%		
First generation students	47.2%	Black achievement gap	-12.4%		

Social inclusion ranking: 26

University of Cambridge

After an eight-year run at the top of our academic ranking, Cambridge drops to third place this year – behind St Andrews and Oxford. It is also equal third in the latest QS World University Rankings. A student boycott of the annual National Student Survey does Cambridge no favours when satisfaction levels are so high at St Andrews. Cambridge continues to be No 1 in more of our subject rankings (23) than any other university, however.

The university is working hard to diversify its intake, launching a foundation year, to that end in 2022. In common with many of the highly selective, research-led Russell Group universities, it is under pressure to admit a more socially diverse student population. Cambridge remains anchored to the foot of our social inclusion rankings for England and Wales, and while the proportion of students from underrepresented groups is higher than in our first edition of the rankings, published in 2018, there is still work to be done. Less than half the students are recruited from non-selective state schools and it has taken a high-profile scholarship scheme from the rapper Stormzy to push the number of black students above 200 for the first time.

Potentially game-changing, the new foundation year entry will be limited to 50 students who have experienced considerable educational disadvantage. Unlike other undergraduate applicants, who have to submit their UCAS form by October 15, the deadline will be January 26 and the stipulated UCAS tariff rate is 120 points, equivalent to BBB at A-level. (The standard offer via traditional entry routes is A*A*A or A*AA.) Applicants can make an open application or express a preference for a college.

Eligibility criteria are extensive but exclude disadvantage arising from the Covid-19 disruption to schooling. Disadvantage covers personal, family and educational areas, and includes eligibility for free school meals, coming from a household where annual income is less than £25,000, the loss of a parent or carer while at secondary school, moving secondary school two or more times, and late diagnosis of special educational needs such as dyslexia, dyspraxia and autism.

There are no tuition fees for the foundation year and a scholarship is provided to cover accommodation and living costs, effectively making the year free. Foundation year students will be full members of the university and live and study alongside students admitted through the more usual routes. Subject to successfully completing the year and achieving 65% in examinations, students can then progress on to one of 18 courses in the arts, humanities or social sciences. It does not cover science subjects at present.

Cambridge Admissions Office
Student Services Centre
New Museums Site
Cambridge CB2 3BT
01223 333 308
admissions@cam.ac.uk
www.undergraduate.
study.cam.ac.uk
www.cusu.co.uk
Open days:
see website

The Times and The Sunday Times Rankings
Overall Ranking: 3 (last year: 1)

Teaching quality	n/a	
Student experience	n/a	
Research quality	57.3%	1
Entry standards	206	2
Graduate prospects	88.5%	5
Good honours	95.1%	=1
Expected completion rate	99%	2
Student/staff ratio	11.4	5
Services and facilities	£3,972	4

The university is working hard to demystify the admissions process for the majority who seek a place without a foundation year. Colleges partner with areas of the country to engage in outreach work and encourage applications from schools for whom the path to Cambridge is less well travelled. Bursaries of £3,500 a year for UK students are offered to those from homes with annual incomes of £25,000 or less, tapering to £100 for households with an income up to £62,215.

With about 20,000 undergraduates and postgraduates in all, students are admitted to one of 31 colleges of greatly differing history, atmosphere and location. While it is possible to make an open application, it pays to visit Cambridge before applying and decide on a college that appeals. Many of the colleges in the city centre are housed in historic buildings on a well-trodden tourist trail but there are more modern colleges outside the centre.

The extensive suite of admissions statistics available for applicants reveals sharply differing social and subject mixes between the colleges, although all have a long list of illustrious alumni.

College-owned accommodation is usually provided for three years (and often four where necessary), with catering available but not compulsory. What is compulsory, however, is that students are required to live during term-time within the university "precincts", defined as being within a three-mile radius of Great St Mary's Church. It is one of the many quirks and traditions with which the university is associated.

While courses proliferate elsewhere, Cambridge keeps things simple, offering just 30 undergraduate courses across about 65 subject areas. Like other universities, it moved to blended learning during the academic year 2020–21 with lectures taking place for the most part online, but supervisions (tutorials), practicals and seminars largely taking place in person. Going forward, the university warns there may continue to be exceptions where staff are unable to teach in person, or lecture theatre safety is still being evaluated or "where it improves the educational experience".

The eight-week terms are high-pressured academically – with students guided to spend between 42 and 46 hours a week on their studies – yet most find time for an extensive social life. Theatre and music societies abound. There is a thriving student media and sports facilities are outstanding, with rowing and cricket to the fore.

Tuition fees

» Fees for UK students	£9,250
» Fees for International students 2022–23	£22,227–£33,825
Medicine and Veterinary Science	£58,038
» For scholarship and bursary information see www.undergraduate.study.cam.ac.uk/fees-and-finance	
» Graduate salary	£30,100

Student numbers

Undergraduates	12,480	(385)
Postgraduates	7,060	(1,420)
Applications/places	20,695/3,905	
Applications per place	5.3	
Overall offer rate	26.5%	
International students – EU	8.8%	
Non-EU	14.2%	

Accommodation

See: http://www.undergraduate.study.cam.ac.uk/why-cambridge/student-life/accommodation
College websites provide accommodation details

See Chapter 13 for individual colleges

Where do the students come from?

State schools (non-grammar)	47.8%	Low participation areas	4.8%	
Grammar schools	21.3%	All ethnic minorities	29.3%	
Independent schools	30.9%	White working-class males	1.8%	
First generation students	15.4%	Black achievement gap	-6.6%	

Social inclusion ranking: 116

Disabled	3.9%
Mature (over 21)	4.6%

Canterbury Christ Church

Named after a pioneering female engineer from Kent, the Verena Holmes Building opened at Canterbury Christ Church University (CCCU) early in 2021. The £65million development on the city centre campus is the new home for courses in science, technology, health, engineering and medicine.

Located next to the World Heritage site St Augustine's Abbey (a few minutes from Canterbury Cathedral), it features industry-standard facilities on each floor. It has been designed as a space for research, experimentation and industry collaboration alongside teaching and learning as part of CCCU's £150million investment in its main campus.

New hi-tech engineering labs should support the university's goal of attracting 35% female engineering students to turn around the traditional male domination in the subject, and 40% from less-advantaged communities. CCCU is one of 189 universities worldwide and 18 in the UK and Ireland – to adopt the Massachusetts Institute of Technology's creative curriculum for engineering, CDIO – conceive, design, implement and operate – with the aim of producing graduates able to master those four skills in a modern team-based environment.

The Kent and Medway Medical School welcomed its second cohort of 100 student doctors in September 2021. Set up in 2020 with the University of Kent, it is working in partnership with the highly regarded Brighton and Sussex Medical School for support and quality assurance.

An increase in applications to professional health and teacher training programmes has contributed to a 15% rise in 2021 compared with the same point in the cycle the previous year. However, applications show a sharp decline since 2014, falling by 38%. Enrolments have stayed much steadier, helped by an increased offer rate. Nearly 14% of 2020's intake came via clearing, down from a quarter in 2019.

CCCU's league table ranking in 2020 suffered from a high dropout rate, with 28.4% of students failing to complete their courses – more than double the expected level. Combined with declines in student satisfaction, CCCU fell to four places off the bottom of the table. However, it has recovered some ground in this edition, despite one of the sharpest declines in student satisfaction during the pandemic. Overall satisfaction fell from 77.4% in 2020 to 65.3% in 2021, according to our analysis of National Student Survey scores.

The university continues to have a strong record for attracting students from underrepresented groups, reflected in its 93% offer rate to applicants with the highest levels of educational disadvantage in the 2020 admissions cycle – more than 10% above the national average. CCCU rises six places to

North Holmes Road
Canterbury CT1 1QU
01227 928 000
courses@canterbury.ac.uk
www.canterbury.ac.uk
https://ccsu.co.uk
Open days:
see website

The Times and The Sunday Times **Rankings**
Overall Ranking: =119 (last year: 127)

Teaching quality	72.3%	=84
Student experience	62.9%	122
Research quality	4.5%	97
Entry standards	98	131
Graduate prospects	70.4%	67
Good honours	68.9%	120
Expected completion rate	77.3%	116
Student/staff ratio	16.4	=74
Services and facilities	£2,223	89

stand =51st in our latest social inclusion ranking, assisted by a programme working with more than 50 schools and colleges in Kent and Medway to widen access to higher education.

The first academic professional degree apprentices started in September 2021, bringing the number of apprenticeship programmes to ten. Social work, registered nursing, diagnostic radiography and advanced clinical practice are among the other options. Police constable and manufacturing engineer programmes are run with external partners.

Financial support ranges from grants of up to £600 per year of study for those from low-income backgrounds to sports and choral scholarships. Travel bursaries and career-start bursaries of up to £2,500 help students to fulfil work experience placements or develop business ideas. In response to the rapid introduction of online learning during the pandemic, CCCU has extended its laptop loan scheme and introduced a new Student App Store and virtual campus PC, to address digital poverty and ensure remote access to teaching software.

While most students are based at the Canterbury campus, where CCCU has a prizewinning library and student services centre, the university also has campuses in Chatham and Broadstairs and a postgraduate centre in Tunbridge Wells. The purpose-built campus at Broadstairs offers subjects ranging from commercial music to digital media, photography and early childhood studies, while the recently expanded Medway site at Chatham's historic dockyard specialises in education and health programmes.

In addition, a life sciences industry liaison laboratory at Discovery Park in Sandwich provides students with first-class facilities, and acts as an added resource for local businesses.

Peer mentors and wellbeing advisers are part of a wide-ranging team offering support for students. The Safezone app alerts university security if a student needs urgent assistance.

A modern sports centre is close to the Canterbury campus and there are playing fields a mile away in the Kent countryside at Stodmarsh as well as Polo Farm Sports Club two miles away. The Verena Holmes Building features high specification provision for sport and exercise science.

There is enough accommodation to guarantee a place for all foundation and first-year students who apply by the end of July. The picturesque, cobbled streets of Canterbury are home to a large student population and the entertainment options are lively.

Tuition fees

» Fees for UK/EU students	£9,250
» Fees for International students 2022–23	£14,500
Medicine (2021–22)	£46,600
» For scholarship and bursary information see www.canterbury.ac.uk/study-here/fees-and-funding	
» Graduate salary	£24,000

Student numbers

Undergraduates	9,065	(1,730)
Postgraduates	1,115	(1,430)
Applications/places	10,620/2,825	
Applications per place	3.8	
Overall offer rate	82.7%	
International students – EU	3.3%	
Non-EU	0.7%	

Accommodation
Self-catered: £118–£195 per week
First years guaranteed accommodation
www.canterbury.ac.uk/study-here/student-life/accommodation

Where do the students come from?

State schools (non-grammar)	94.3%	Low participation areas	18%		
Grammar schools	3.9%	All ethnic minorities	27.5%		
Independent schools	1.8%	White working-class males	6.7%		
First generation students	59.2%	Black achievement gap	-38.5%		

Social inclusion ranking: =51

Disabled	7.8%
Mature (over 21)	37%

Cardiff University

Students arriving for the 2021–22 academic year found help with their studies, health and wellbeing or future plans at the new £50million Centre for Student Life at Cardiff, our Welsh University of the Year. It is a jewel in the institution's £600million campus upgrade – its biggest overhaul for a generation.

The new six-storey Abacws building, brings together the Schools of Computer Science and of Mathematics. Designed to foster an interdisciplinary approach to learning, key features include a simulated trading room, a cybersecurity lab, flexible lecture theatres and seminar rooms laid out to encourage interaction.

Significant refurbishment of the Bute Building boosts provision for students in the Welsh School of Architecture. The university's new social science research park, sbarc | spark, will create a stimulating environment where spinout businesses will be nurtured alongside laboratory space and creative areas at the Innovation Campus at Maindy Park in the heart of Cardiff. The entire university estate will be improved in a rolling £41million programme of investment – including the addition of lecture-capture technology in teaching rooms.

The upgrading of student services is well-timed to meet the demand for places at Cardiff. A snapshot of the 2021 recruitment cycle at the end of March revealed that applications were up 12%.

Cardiff is once again the top-ranked university in Wales, edging out Swansea and Aberystwyth, despite less than stellar results in the pandemic-affected National Student Survey (NSS) results in 2021. The NSS outcomes were disappointing, not least because internal feedback had indicated that some elements of the rapidly introduced remote learning system worked well, such as synchronised online and in-person delivery of teaching sessions.

The only Russell Group university in Wales, Cardiff was awarded silver in the Teaching Excellence Framework, thanks in part to the support that personal tutors provide and the direct engagement of students with developments at the forefront of research, scholarship and professional practice.

Most academic schools are based at Cathays Park, where the elegant pale stone buildings sit within tree-lined avenues in the city centre. The healthcare schools share a 53-acre campus at Heath Park with the University Hospital of Wales, where the £18million Cochrane Building provides teaching and learning facilities.

Cardiff achieved excellent results in the 2014 Research Excellence Framework, but entered only 62% of eligible staff – the lowest proportion at any Russell Group university. This depressed its position in our research ranking,

---

Cardiff
CF10 3AT
029 2087 4455
enquiry@cardiff.ac.uk
www.cardiff.ac.uk
www.cardiffstudents.com
Open days:
see website

The Times and The Sunday Times Rankings		
Overall Ranking: =35 (last year: 34)		
Teaching quality	71%	114
Student experience	66.2%	103
Research quality	35.0%	34
Entry standards	145	=36
Graduate prospects	80.4%	=16
Good honours	84.1%	31
Expected completion rate	91.8%	=26
Student/staff ratio	13.7	=23
Services and facilities	£2,686	54

which rewards quantity as well as quality. However, 87% of the submission was rated in the top two categories (world-leading or internationally excellent) and Cardiff was in the top three for the impact of its research and No 1 for civil and construction engineering.

The university counts two Nobel Prize winners and 15 Royal Society Fellows on staff. Research activities will gain 129,000 square feet of hi-tech laboratory space in the new Translational Research Hub from September 2022, which will house the renowned Cardiff Catalysis Institute and the Institute for Compound Semiconductors.

Cardiff's wellbeing and counselling service offers extensive pastoral provision, from workshops on managing anxiety and suicide safety to group therapy or one-to-one sessions with professional therapists. Trained student volunteers act as wellbeing champions. A disclosure response team is trained to help students affected by harassment, hate crime, sexual violence, relationship abuse and other forms of unacceptable behaviour.

Outreach activities aim to dispel negative myths about what it is like to study at an elite Russell Group university and encourage applications from diverse groups. Residential summer schools, roadshows, community-based courses and activities on campus target prospective students in areas from where few apply, as well as care leavers and those with autism.

Contextual admissions up to one grade lower than the published requirements are available on most programmes except medicine and dentistry – for which applicants may be given extra points in the interview selection process.

A new partnership with Cardiff City Football Club's House of Sport and Cardiff Council gives students access to floodlit, all-weather and grass pitches. The university has a three-floor fitness centre at Senghennydd Road and Studio 49 offers a range of fitness classes.

University accommodation is guaranteed to first-years and there is even a small number of catered and part-catered rooms, rarely found at UK universities these days. For private renters, the NatWest Student Living Index 2020 ranked Cardiff second for the lowest monthly rental costs.

The Welsh capital has lively bars and clubs, international sport at the Millennium Stadium and a vibrant arts scene – within reach of the seaside and the Brecon Beacons for a breath of fresh air.

Tuition fees

» Fees for UK students £9,000
» Fees for International students 2022–23 £19,200–£23,450
  Medicine £36,700, Dentistry £39,450 (clinical years)
» For scholarship and bursary information see
  www.cardiff.ac.uk/study/undergraduate/tuition-fees
» Graduate salary £24,630

Student numbers

Undergraduates	20,160 (3,595)
Postgraduates	6,645 (2,865)
Applications/places	39,225/5,935
Applications per place	6.6
Overall offer rate	73.4%
International students – EU	3.2%
Non-EU	13.5%

Accommodation

University provided places: 5,346
Catered costs: £155–£164 per week
Self-catered: £129–£147 per week
First years guaranteed accommodation
www.cardiff.ac.uk/study/accommodation

Where do the students come from?

State schools (non-grammar)	77.1%	Low participation areas	9.8%	Disabled	5.3%
Grammar schools	8.6%	All ethnic minorities	18.5%	Mature (over 21)	10.9%
Independent schools	14.2%	White working-class males	4.1%		
First generation students	31.4%	Black achievement gap	-18.7%		

Social inclusion ranking: 101

Cardiff Metropolitan University

Degrees in robotics engineering, virtual and augmented reality and computing with creative design welcomed their first students at Cardiff Metropolitan in 2021. The courses are among a wider suite of tech-focused subjects launched under its School of Technologies, which has now opened the third phase of a new building at the Llandaff campus. Bringing modern digital learning facilities, the school has also launched degrees in data science and computing for interaction.

Across both Llandaff and Cyncoed campuses, close to Cardiff city centre, the university has been investing in upgrades such as new learning spaces, cafés, commuter kitchens and wellbeing areas. There are more developments in the pipeline to enhance the student experience.

Winner of Welsh University of the Year in our last *Guide*, Cardiff Met's ethos is to provide practice-focused, professionally oriented education. It achieved some of the best scores for student satisfaction in 2020, but as with many of the institutions designed for hands-on learning – rendered unfeasible by social distancing – it fared less well in the most recent National Student Survey. When the 2021 results were compared with those from 2020, Cardiff Met ranked only 90th.

Students marked it down in the pandemic year for learning resources (down 17.9 percentage points), academic support and overall satisfaction (both down 8.8 percentage points).

Cardiff Met has rolled out lecture-capture technology across the university, enabling students to access recorded material on demand. It plans on continuing certain elements of remote learning – such as virtual personal tutor meetings, pre-recorded content and live virtual lectures – alongside in-person seminars, workshops and practical sessions.

Cardiff Met was one of only four Welsh universities awarded silver in the government's Teaching Excellence Framework (TEF).

The TEF panel said that course design was informed by a significant focus on employability, producing good outcomes for a range of student groups, including those from black and minority ethnic communities, disadvantaged and mature students. This is reflected in a top 25 finish in our unique social inclusion ranking.

The university succeeds in recruiting more working-class white male students than most (ranking 16th), and almost half of students are the first in their family to go to university. The "community to campus" programme opens higher education to those without traditional A-level qualifications. About a fifth of students are estimated to qualify for bursaries and scholarships.

Sport, the university's best-known feature, is based at the Cyncoed campus where facilities

200 Western Avenue
Llandaff
Cardiff CF5 2YB
029 2041 6010
askadmissions@cardiffmet.ac.uk
www.cardiffmet.ac.uk
www.cardiffmetsu.co.uk
Open days: see website

The Times and The Sunday Times **Rankings**
Overall Ranking: =79 (last year: 79)

Teaching quality	74.9%	=64
Student experience	70.2%	=56
Research quality	3.9%	107
Entry standards	123	=67
Graduate prospects	68.4%	=75
Good honours	75.4%	93
Expected completion rate	78.9%	106
Student/staff ratio	18.5	=106
Services and facilities	£2,629	59

support competitive sport as well as sports degrees. The £7million National Indoor Athletics Centre has a six-lane 140m straight and competition-standard long jump, high jump and pole vault pits as well as physiotherapy and sports medicine facilities. Cyncoed also hosts archery, tennis and fitness centres, pitches, a swimming pool and gym.

Elite sport scholarships offer tailored support worth up to £5,000 a year. The university competes at football, rugby, basketball, athletics, cricket, netball and hockey at the highest level of BUCS (British University & College Sport) competitions.

The university supports elite-level competition across leagues including men's and women's football in the Welsh Premier leagues, men's rugby in the National Championship and women's basketball in the Women's British Basketball League. All first-year students qualify for free sport and fitness membership.

Two new degree apprenticeships in applied cybersecurity and applied software engineering have joined established programme in data science, bringing apprentice numbers to about 70 by September 2022. There are also options in applied entrepreneurship and innovation management, along with a health and wellbeing degree. Another five degrees launch in September 2022: digital health; pharmaceutical science; health and wellbeing; management and leadership; and aviation management.

Via the MetHub platform, students and graduates can access help with job applications, work placements and internships. Appointments with the careers team are bookable online. Graduate start-ups are on the rise, and support is offered through the Centre for Entrepreneurship.

Researchers in Cardiff School of Art and Design have spent the past five years working on HUG, an interactive device that looks like a soft toy with a soft body and weighted arms that wrap around a person, giving the sensation of giving and receiving a hug. Electronics replicate a heartbeat and each HUG plays programmable playlists. Proven to improve life for people with dementia, HUG is now going into full-scale production, thanks to a partnership with the Alzheimers's Society accelerator programme.

Cardiff offers music, culture, sport, nightlife and proximity to the great outdoors. First-years who apply by the end of May are guaranteed student accommodation, more than half of which is catered. Before being given a key, they must complete a compulsory halls induction, which includes sections on consent, alcohol and drugs.

Tuition fees

» Fees for UK students	£9,000
» Fees for International students 2022–23	£14,500
» For scholarship and bursary information see www.cardiffmet.ac.uk/study/finance/Pages/ Undergraduate-Students.aspx	
» Graduate salary	£20,000

Student numbers

Undergraduates	7,540	(560)
Postgraduates	2,175	(645)
Applications/places		9,540/2,445
Applications per place		3.9
Overall offer rate		86.7%
International students – EU		2%
Non-EU		6.1%

Accommodation

University provided places: 1,735
Catered costs: £168–£179 per week
Self-catered: £118–£125 per week
www.cardiffmet.ac.uk/accommodation/Pages/default.aspx

Where do the students come from?

State schools (non-grammar)	94%	Low participation areas	16.7%	Disabled	10.1%
Grammar schools	1%	All ethnic minorities	14.3%	Mature (over 21)	23.9%
Independent schools	5.1%	White working-class males	8.2%		
First generation students	48.9%	Black achievement gap	-16.4%		

Social inclusion ranking: 25

University of Central Lancashire

Crowned with a rooftop garden, a £60million student centre has opened at the Preston campus. The centre houses all student services at the University of Central Lancashire (UCLan), from mental health provision to careers advice and housing assistance. A large pedestrianised public square has been developed alongside, forming a new gateway into Preston.

The latest development under the university's £200million masterplan follows the opening in 2019 of the £35million Engineering Innovation Centre, where the latest drone technology has been installed at the Lancashire Drone Command and Control Centre, a £1.4million project funded by the Lancashire Local Enterprise Partnership. The university will build on its success with a £1.8million Drone Innovation Zone where experts will flight-test new technologies in long-term collaborations with businesses to bring new products to market.

Already one of Britain's biggest universities, with nearly 16,000 undergraduates, UCLan operates on multiple sites – including the Larnaka campus in Cyprus, offering UK degrees in a Mediterranean setting. Students on a wide range of UK-based courses have the opportunity to spend a year there.

Courses based at UCLan's Burnley campus promise small class sizes, and the Pennine site has a students' union hub, a moot court and science laboratories. The Westlakes campus in West Cumbria focuses on nursing and other health subjects.

Enrolments in the 2020 admissions cycle were up with nearly 6,000 new students accepted out of more than 20,600 applications. The curriculum gained another nine courses including media management, microbiology, youth work and community practice, and enterprise management.

Awarded silver in the Teaching Excellence Framework in 2019, UCLan was commended for embedding employability skills across the curriculum and for extensive engagement with local employers. All students can take advantage of work placements and other opportunities upon graduation, through links with BAE Systems, the NHS, Lancashire Constabulary, Wigan Warriors, Hewlett Packard, IBM and other organisations.

For fashion students, a new agreement with a fashion brand has created work experience opportunities and the chance to work on live briefs during course modules.

UCLan is aiming to record all lectures, so students can listen remotely. The increased availability of online material during the pandemic proved useful for UCLan students – although the university remains committed to in-person delivery for the majority of teaching and learning.

Preston PR1 2HE
01772 892 400
cenquiries@uclan.ac.uk
www.uclan.ac.uk
www.uclansu.co.uk
Open days:
see website

The Times and The Sunday Times Rankings
Overall Ranking: 87 (last year: 75)

Teaching quality	72.8%	=90
Student experience	66.4%	=101
Research quality	5.6%	=86
Entry standards	124	=65
Graduate prospects	67.7%	82
Good honours	72.8%	=106
Expected completion rate	72.4%	127
Student/staff ratio	14.3	=33
Services and facilities	£2,428	74

Degree apprenticeships cover 33 subject areas across the fields of engineering, professional services and health and wellbeing – with more than 1,500 learners on the programmes.

Physics, maths and astronomy have longstanding research links with Nasa. UCLan scientists unveiled in December 2020 the highest-ever resolution images of the Sun from Nasa's solar sounding rocket mission.

The £5million Dental School opened in 2007, and its on-site clinic stepped in to help the NHS with emergency dental care during the coronavirus pandemic.

World-leading research was found in all 16 subject areas assessed in the 2014 Research Excellence Framework. UCLan academics have been involved in sector-leading stroke research with the Department of Health and work on nutritional science with the Bill and Melinda Gates Foundation.

More than half of UCLan students are aged over 21. The university's six-week, part-time Return to Study taster courses target the age group covering subjects including sport, medical sciences and justice. A long-term commitment to widening participation gives the option of a foundation entry year for all degree courses. Contextual offers were introduced in 2021, cutting the standard tariff requirement by eight UCAS points for disadvantaged students. The scheme helps UCLan to achieve a ranking of =44th for social inclusion. More than half of entrants in 2020 were the first in their household to go to university.

The portfolio of 14 undergraduate bursaries and scholarships includes medical scholarships – two for East Lancashire and Cumbria-based students and two for northwest students from underrepresented backgrounds – which cover all tuition fees for the duration of the five-year course. Other awards include bursaries of £1,000 a year for young people leaving care or estranged from their parents. For those from low-income households, a bursary of £2,000 is available, spread across three academic years.

Sporting life at the Preston campus centres on the Sir Tom Finney Sports Centre, and two miles away there are extra facilities at the UCLan Sports Arena, offering a 1.5km cycle circuit, floodlit international standard athletics track and all-weather pitches.

A new compulsory module on suicide awareness has been introduced for all students during the welcome programme.

Tuition fees

»	Fees for UK students	£9,250
	Foundation courses	£6,000
»	Fees for International students 2022–23	£14,250
	Foundation courses	£10,800
	Medicine	£46,000
»	For scholarship and bursary information see www.uclan.ac.uk/study/fees-and-finance	
»	Graduate salary	£22,500

Student numbers

Undergraduates	15,965 (1,870)
Postgraduates	3,420 (3,465)
Applications/places	20,605/4,470
Applications per place	4.6
Overall offer rate	70.6%
International students – EU	2.4%
Non-EU	8.4%

Accommodation

University provided places: 1,150
Self-catered: £77–£125 per week
www.uclan.ac.uk/accommodation

Where do the students come from?

State schools (non-grammar)	96.2%	Low participation areas	14.3%	Disabled	7.5%
Grammar schools	2.4%	All ethnic minorities	30.9%	Mature (over 21)	39.2%
Independent schools	1.4%	White working-class males	7%		
First generation students	51.1%	Black achievement gap	-26.8%		

Social inclusion ranking: =44

University of Chester

The University of Chester had moved to what it describes as a "student-centred digital-first" approach to teaching and learning before the pandemic hit, meaning it benefited from an established digital infrastructure. On-campus facilities include access to round-the-clock study spaces with free wi-fi and more than 2,000 specialist software-equipped computers, as well as 32,000 physical books. A laptop loan scheme supports students' flexible working and first-years are given core texts digitally, along with millions more e-books and journals via an online platform.

In addition, the "Chester Blend" teaching philosophy has been developed to deal with the challenges posed by Covid-19, placing equal priority on face-to-face and online learning, and enabling students to take part in customised sports and activities while maintaining social distancing. The university's Recap centre, meanwhile, provides students with recorded lectures on demand.

Such close attention to the student experience is reflected in the excellent scores Chester received in the 2020 National Student Survey, in which it ranked in the top 30 for teaching quality and the wider experience. This makes its disappointing rank in our analysis of the 2021 National Student Survey (NSS) results all the more surprising. The university finished in the bottom 20 when 2021's outcomes were compared with those of 2020 as the pandemic impacted scores. Learning resources (down 21.6 percentage points) and overall satisfaction (down 13.4) were the sections most severely affected. As a group, however, practical-based institutions such as Chester tended to fare relatively poorly in the most recent NSS, with a few exceptions.

Founded more than 180 years ago as a teacher-training college by William Gladstone, the future prime minister, among others, Chester predates all other English universities except Oxford, Cambridge, Durham and London. It is structured around seven faculties based at sites throughout the city of Chester and at four professionally focused centres in Birkenhead, Reaseheath, Shrewsbury and Warrington.

The original Exton Park (Parkgate Road) campus is a 32-acre site, a 10-minute walk from Chester city centre. The Queen's Park campus, once the wartime headquarters of the army's Western Command, now houses Chester Business School. At the Riverside campus, the Faculty of Health and Social Care's interprofessional simulation facility was the first used to train nursing students to join the coronavirus front line in the northwest. Courses in education and children's services are also based at Riverside, in the former county hall, and the Riverside Innovation Centre hosts business start-ups generated by Chester students and graduates. The Kingsway

Parkgate Road
Chester CH1 4BJ
01244 511 000
admissions@chester.ac.uk
www.chester.ac.uk
www.chestersu.com
Open days:
see website

The Times and The Sunday Times Rankings
Overall Ranking: 68 (last year: 69)

Teaching quality	75.4%	=58
Student experience	67%	=94
Research quality	4.1%	=101
Entry standards	117	=85
Graduate prospects	71%	=64
Good honours	74.8%	95
Expected completion rate	81.1%	=92
Student/staff ratio	14.7	=40
Services and facilities	£2,953	33

creative campus houses arts and media courses.

The expanding Warrington centre is moving from its out-of-town Padgate base into new town centre premises, where it will occupy a shopfront building in Time Square plus more spacious facilities five minutes' away in the Sarah Parker Remond building.

Elsewhere, the Faculty of Science and Engineering is moving from Thornton Science Park to the university's Exton Park site, leaving its old home to be redeveloped into a research and innovation hub. Its new home will include wet and dry labs and a design/manufacturing suite.

Eleven new degrees in 2021 included business with psychology; geography; nutrition and exercise science; and marine biology. Undergraduates joining Chester from September 2022 will have another two options: fashion marketing and communication (social media); social justice – with or without a foundation year.

The portfolio of degree apprenticeships is growing. A programme to train advanced clinical practitioners launched in 2021 to be joined from 2022 by an option for academic professionals. Other apprenticeships include healthcare assistant practitioner, police constable, registered nurse and chartered manager, bringing the total to about 1,200 learners.

Chester's silver award in the Teaching Excellence Framework (TEF) brought praise for its students' employability skills. About two-thirds of undergraduates take work-based learning modules. The TEF panel said Chester had an "embedded culture of valuing, recognising and rewarding good teaching". More than two-thirds of the academic staff hold Higher Education Academy fellowships. Evening classes in a foreign language are offered to all students.

All but one of 15 subject areas entered in the 2014 Research Excellence Framework had some research that was judged world-leading, and the university more than doubled the work submitted compared with 2008.

First-years are guaranteed student accommodation, about a third of which is fully or partially catered. Most sports facilities are near the Exton Park site, which has a sports hall, grass pitches, tennis and squash courts, a swimming pool and a fitness studio.

Small enough not to get lost but with enough to keep most students entertained, historic Chester has the attractive River Dee running through it and the bright lights of Liverpool and Manchester nearby.

Tuition fees

»	Fees for UK students	£9,250
	Foundation courses	£7,850
»	Fees for International students 2022–23	,950
	Foundation courses	£9,250
»	For scholarship and bursary information see http://www1.chester.ac.uk/finance	
»	Graduate salary	£22,500

Student numbers

Undergraduates	8,285	(945)
Postgraduates	1,690	(2,625)
Applications/places		14,865/2,220
Applications per place		6.7
Overall offer rate		75.4%
International students – EU		1.2%
Non-EU		4.8%

Accommodation

University provided places: 1,615
Catered costs: £146–£150 per week
Self-catered: £88–£149 per week
www1.chester.ac.uk/departments/accommodation-office

Where do the students come from?

State schools (non-grammar)	93.2%	Low participation areas	21.3%
Grammar schools	3.9%	All ethnic minorities	9.6%
Independent schools	2.9%	White working-class males	7.8%
First generation students	54.3%	Black achievement gap	-18.3%

Social inclusion ranking: 31

Disabled	6.9%
Mature (over 21)	33.4%

University of Chichester

The new School of Nursing and Allied Health opened to University of Chichester students in September 2021. Its first ambition is to develop hundreds of healthcare workers by 2025. Adjoining St Richard's Hospital in Chichester, the school is run in partnership with University Hospitals Sussex NHS Foundation Trust, and other regional health and social care providers.

The first three-year bachelor's degree course based at the 1,600 sq ft facility is in adult nursing, running alongside physiotherapy and alternative entry pathways including health-related degree apprenticeships. Its students will hone their clinical skills in mock wards and simulation suites.

The School of Nursing and Allied Health further broadens the academic focus at Chichester, which has long been known for its strong arts and teacher training provision. It follows the addition in 2018 of a Tech Park at the Bognor Regis campus, opened by the Duke and Duchess of Sussex on their first – and only – visit to the county of their titles.

The £35million Tech Park brings together degree courses in STEAM subjects (science, technology, engineering, arts and mathematics) and its cutting-edge facilities include a machinery workshop with welding floor, fabricating laboratory, specialist 3D printers and an engineering centre. Its department of creative digital technologies features a television production studio, a special effects room and a media operations centre.

Other new degrees include criminology, law with criminology, sociology, and sociology with criminology.

The university's portfolio of nine degree apprenticeships is set to gain at least another three from September 2022. There are 223 learners on Chichester's existing programmes, including social work, manufacturing engineering, digital marketing and senior leadership.

Chichester entered our top 50 in 2020 and has held on to that status despite a four-place fall in our ranking. It performed well during the pandemic, based on the National Student Survey outcomes in summer 2021. Although overall scores for teaching quality and student experience are down, Chichester's decline was among the 25 smallest year-on-year, and as a result it has climbed our rankings on these measures, to place in the top ten for both satisfaction with teaching quality and the wider student experience.

A three-time winner of our University of the Year for Student Retention, Chichester consistently achieves one of the lowest dropout rates in British higher education. The latest figures in 2021 show a projected dropout rate of 7.4%, far below the expected level of 12.4%.

Chichester's success at keeping students on

Bishop Otter Campus
College Lane
Chichester PO19 6PE
01243 816 002
admissions@chi.ac.uk
www.chi.ac.uk
www.ucsu.org
Open days:
see website

The Times and The Sunday Times **Rankings**
Overall Ranking: 50 (last year: =46)

Teaching quality	80.5%	7
Student experience	76.3%	=9
Research quality	6.4%	81
Entry standards	122	=72
Graduate prospects	62.9%	108
Good honours	78.4%	=63
Expected completion rate	90.5%	35
Student/staff ratio	14.9	=47
Services and facilities	£1,783	119

courses comes despite offering them relatively low rates of financial support. Bursaries of just £300 a year are awarded to students from homes with less than £25,000 annual income – less generous than at many other universities. However, just over a quarter of students benefit from some form of the financial support on offer.

Chichester has fallen more than 40 places in our latest social inclusion ranking to stand 81st overall, despite a strong showing on some indicators, having one of the better records on recruitment of students from non-selective state schools (94.4%, ranking 45th), recruitment of students from parts of the country with the lowest participation in higher education (19.5%, 18th) and recruitment of students from homes where neither parent attended university (47.6%, 51st).

Awarded silver in the government's Teaching Excellence Framework, Chichester was commended for its outstanding support for disadvantaged students. The university entered a quarter of its eligible staff for the Research Excellence Framework in 2014 and did well in music, drama and performing arts, English and sport. The Mathematics Centre has an international reputation and has become a focal point for curriculum development in England and elsewhere.

Chichester students all sign a charter committing to respect the diversity of the student community and the students' union runs engagement activities covering the importance of sexual consent, mental health support and inclusion.

The university owns and manages all of its 1,182 residential places, which are fairly equally divided between the Bognor Regis and Chichester (Bishop Otter) campuses. Unusually, a large proportion – 40% – are catered. First-years are guaranteed a room if they made the university their first choice. An intercampus bus service links Bognor and Bishop Otter, which each have students' union bars.

Students can easily access Chichester's excellent sports resources as they are all on campus. Facilities include indoor and outdoor climbing walls, a grass rugby pitch and a three-court sports dome. The sports hall has four courts and students can also use Astro pitches, a fitness suite and a multi-use games area. The university awards between 20 and 25 gifted athlete scholarships per year across three levels: elite, development and Bucs (British Universities and Colleges Sport).

Seaside attractions abound along Bognor's long stretch of coastline or in the yachting hub of Chichester.

Tuition fees

»	Fees for UK students	£9,250
	Foundation courses	£5,500
»	Fees for International students 2022–23	£14,500
»	For scholarship and bursary information see www.chi.ac.uk/study-us/fees-finance	
»	Graduate salary	£22,000

Student numbers

Undergraduates	3,940	(455)
Postgraduates	465	(680)
Applications/places		6,750/1,415
Applications per place		4.8
Overall offer rate		74.1%
International students – EU		2%
Non-EU		2%

Accommodation

University provided places: 1,182
Catered costs: £159–£177 per week
Self-catered: £104–£153 per week
First years guaranteed accommodation
www.chi.ac.uk/student-life/accommodation

Where do the students come from?

State schools (non-grammar)	94.4%	Low participation areas	19.5%	**Social inclusion ranking: 81**	
Grammar schools	1.5%	All ethnic minorities	6.8%	Disabled	10.7%
Independent schools	4%	White working-class males	6.7%	Mature (over 21)	18.7%
First generation students	47.6%	Black achievement gap	-30.7%		

City, University of London

Professor Anthony Finkelstein became president of City, University of London in 2021. Joining from his former position as the government's chief scientific adviser for national security, his academic background is in systems engineering. Upon his appointment Professor Finkelstein said he was looking forward to realising "the outstanding potential of City".

Among further developments, the university's Northampton Square base has a new home for the City Law School. The future-facing hub of legal knowledge brings together all academic and professional law programmes. A technology-led mock courtroom is one features, along with a law library and a legal advice clinic.

Rooted in the heart of the capital since its foundation more than 125 years ago, the university's career focus spans the professions. Its world-class Bayes Business School is next in line for a physical makeover. It had a recent name change from Cass, after it was found that some of the MP, merchant and philanthropist Sir John Cass's wealth had been obtained through links to the slave trade.

Bayes is set to occupy a newly acquired building on Finsbury Square, where educational and social spaces will occupy seven floors. The school's MBA has been ranked fifth in the world for entrepreneurship by the Financial Times and attracts high-profile visiting lecturers.

Journalism students are already benefiting from a dedicated new learning space, modelled on a broadcast newsroom designed for multiple digital channels with radio studios.

Investment of more than £140million since 2012 has gone into improvements to the main Northampton Square campus in Clerkenwell. A coffee shop, seating areas and exhibition space have augmented entrance area and the building has a 240-seat lecture theatre, students' union facilities, a cafeteria and multifaith area.

With more than 4,100 accepted applicants in 2020, City welcomed its largest cohort of new students for over a decade, more than a third recruited via clearing. Since 2011 enrolments have swelled by nearly 40%, and applications for 2021 were 10% higher at the end of March than at the same point the year before, due to a pandemic-influenced increase of demand for nursing and other healthcare degrees. A new degree in nutrition and food policy launches in September 2022.

City was awarded silver in the Teaching Excellence Framework thanks to strong engagement with students and the students' union and excellent assessment and feedback. The strength of this relationship is reflected in the results of the pandemic-affected 2021 National Student Survey (NSS), in which

Northampton Square
London EC1V 0HB
020 7040 8716
ugadmissions@city.ac.uk
www.city.ac.uk
www.citystudents.co.uk
Open days: see website

The Times and The Sunday Times **Rankings**

Overall Ranking: 55 (last year: 82)

Teaching quality	68.5%	124
Student experience	67.5%	88
Research quality	22.6%	51
Entry standards	131	=52
Graduate prospects	79%	=23
Good honours	77.8%	67
Expected completion rate	88.1%	=48
Student/staff ratio	17.6	=98
Services and facilities	£2,793	=42

just 22 universities outperformed City when results were compared with those from 2020. In a year when most universities suffered falls, City managed to improve its ratings for course organisation and management, helping it to gain nearly 40 places in our rankings for student experience, albeit from a low starting point.

Supporting a strong performance in our graduate prospects measure, City's mentoring service connects students with experienced industry professionals and creates about 400 such pairings per year. The City Ventures Team and Launch Lab run a three-month accelerator programme to kickstart student and graduate start-ups. Mentoring, free desk space, workshops and wi-fi are available for up to two years. The incubator has created more than 1,000 jobs and secured £13million investment.

The university entered just over half its eligible academics in the 2014 Research Excellence Framework, with three-quarters of its submission rated as world-leading or internationally excellent. The best results were in music and business.

Targeting London schools in deprived areas and with low progression rates to higher education, City's widening participation team offers maths and English tutoring to primary and secondary pupils as well as careers guidance, campus visits and taster weeks in subjects including business, health, psychology and law. A Micro-Placements programme aims to improve social mobility by arranging summer work experience for students from underrepresented backgrounds.

The university plans to launch contextual offers for 2022, which should further diversify one of the more socially inclusive institutions within the University of London. Although it has fallen 25 places this year in our social inclusion ranking for England and Wales to stand 72nd, it has the second highest proportion of UK students drawn from ethnic minorities (79.3%) and the 13th highest proportion of students from homes where neither parent attended university (58.1%).

The redeveloped sports centre, between the campus and the business school, is the largest university sports facility in central London with 3,000 square metres available to students, staff and the local community. At its heart is the Saddlers sports hall, which seats 400 spectators.

City has only 734 residential places, although this is enough to guarantee accommodation for new entrants who accept an offer by the end of June.

Tuition fees

» Fees for UK students	£9,250
» Fees for International students 2022–23	£15,460–£26,530
» For scholarship and bursary information see www.city.ac.uk/prospective-students/finance	
» Graduate salary	£27,000

Student numbers

Undergraduates	10,120	(900)
Postgraduates	6,800	(2,155)
Applications/places		25,020/2,850
Applications per place		8.8
Overall offer rate		54.8%
International students – EU		8.3%
Non-EU		20.4%

Accommodation

University provided places: 734
Catered costs: £293–£306 per week
Self-catered: £160–£232 per week
First years guaranteed accommodation
www.city.ac.uk/prospective-students/accommodation

Where do the students come from?

State schools (non-grammar)	87.8%	Low participation areas	2.1%	Disabled	3.8%
Grammar schools	5.6%	All ethnic minorities	79.3%	Mature (over 21)	13%
Independent schools	6.5%	White working-class males	2.1%		
First generation students	58.1%	Black achievement gap	-16.9%		

Social inclusion ranking: 72

Coventry University

Renowned for its go-ahead ethos, Coventry University is continuing to innovate. It has Britain's first standalone 5G network, thanks to a partnership with Vodafone – the first step to becoming a 5G campus. The network is operating in the Alison Gingell Building on the city centre campus and allows trials of virtual reality learning technologies, which will help to train students in the School of Health and Life Sciences.

The dynamic and innovative institution has been a regular winner in our University of the Year awards over the past decade. Shortlisted for our 2020 University of the Year award, Coventry was also Modern University of the Year three times between 2014 and 2016 and University of the Year for Student Experience in 2018.

The university's drive to produce job-ready graduates with industry-standard experience has been boosted by the recent addition of 53 high-tech workstations for practical electronics and physics experiments. Installed in the Faculty of Environment, Engineering and Computing's new Beatrice Shilling Building, the equipment has been provided by Tektronix, a leading electronic test and measurement equipment supplier.

In another career-focused collaboration, the university's Institute for Advanced Manufacturing and Engineering, run with the Unipart manufacturing group, is a working factory that doubles as an academic base, providing students with real-world experience and the skills to address domestic shortages while they study.

The Faculty of Arts and Humanities is a focus of redevelopment on campus, set to gain flexible and immersive media facilities and a large gallery, with modern teaching spaces. Its theatre facilities in a former art deco cinema in Coventry have also been done up.

The university was awarded gold in the Teaching Excellence Framework for "consistently outstanding" student support services, especially for those from disadvantaged backgrounds, which aid retention and progression.

As well as campuses in Coventry and Scarborough, the university's CU London operation already has a site in Dagenham and has opened a second in Greenwich. A campus in Wroclaw, in Poland, welcomed its first students in 2020 and has since opened undergraduate applications to students from outside the European Union. Degree courses include digital technology, business management and leadership, aviation management and cybersecurity. Coventry also offers training for teachers and nurses in Morocco and has hubs in Dubai, Singapore, Brussels and Egypt.

Applications from the Continent have been impacted by Brexit and the sustained

Priory Street
Coventry CV1 5FB
024 7765 2222
ukadmissions@coventry.ac.uk
www.coventry.ac.uk
www.cusu.org
Open days: see website

The Times and The Sunday Times **Rankings**
Overall Ranking: 51 (last year: =46)

Teaching quality	78%	=25
Student experience	74.4%	22
Research quality	3.8%	=108
Entry standards	113	=102
Graduate prospects	70.8%	=66
Good honours	77%	=72
Expected completion rate	80%	101
Student/staff ratio	14.2	=30
Services and facilities	£2,805	41

uncertainty of Covid-19, however, bringing the university's recent period of rapid expansion in applications and enrolments to a halt. Applications fell by 9% in 2020 and enrolments dropped more steeply – by 24%.

A raft of new degrees began in September 2021: acting for stage and screen, film production, politics and international relations, illustration, animation, and diagnostic radiography.

The university's new blended learning adult nursing degree has broken new ground, allowing students anywhere in the UK to enrol from September 2021. Half the course is practical, and half is academic content, of which 95% is online and 5% face-to-face in Coventry, Scarborough or London. Students will have access to simulators for half the practical work, and the rest will be learnt during work placements.

Coventry has one of the largest higher and degree apprenticeship programmes of any university with more than 1,800 students enrolled across programmes based in Coventry, Scarborough and London. New options are planned in public health, rail engineering, policing, senior leadership, digital and human resources.

Just 13% of the university's eligible academics were entered in the 2014 Research Excellence Framework, although 60% of the submission was rated world-leading or internationally excellent.

Coventry's Aula learning experience platform – successfully piloted pre-Covid by more than 2,000 students – was rolled out during the pandemic. It promotes a social and engaged approach to teaching and learning, and the development of learning communities. Coventry was named the world's best university for its provision of Massive Open Online Courses (MOOCs) in MoocLab's World University Rankings 2021.

The university occupies a middling position in our social inclusion index, drawing 92.6% of its intake from non-selective state secondary schools. Nearly half of first-years (45.7%) are the first in their family to go to university.

Applicants who make Coventry their firm choice are guaranteed one of the 3,016 rooms. All students can take part in a training course called "I Heart Consent", delivered in sexual health and guidance week. Support for mental wellbeing is extensive, ranging from one-to-one appointments with counsellors to a harassment reporting team.

Coventry's relatively low cost of living and student-oriented nightlife create a lively student city.

Tuition fees

» Fees for UK students	£9,250
Foundation courses	£7,900
» Fees for International students 2021–22	£15,000–£17,700
» For scholarship and bursary information see www.coventry.ac.uk/study-at-coventry/finance/	
» Graduate salary	£24,000

Student numbers

Undergraduates	28,575 (3,065)
Postgraduates	4,345 (2,440)
Applications/places	31,620/5,630
Applications per place	5.6
Overall offer rate	87.8%
International students – EU	10.8%
Non-EU	19.7%

Accommodation

University provided places: 3,016
Catered costs: £99–£125 per week
Self-catered: £99–£199 per week
First years guaranteed accommodation
www.coventry.ac.uk/life-on-campus/accommodation

Where do the students come from?

State schools (non-grammar)	92.6%	Low participation areas	12.2%	
Grammar schools	4.6%	All ethnic minorities	60.8%	
Independent schools	2.9%	White working-class males	4.1%	
First generation students	45.7%	Black achievement gap	-22.5%	

Social inclusion ranking: 56

Disabled	4.2%
Mature (over 21)	32.8%

University for the Creative Arts

Providing in-person learning and access to workshops, studios and technical facilities is central to what the University for the Creative Arts (UCA) does. The Farnham-based specialist arts university had to innovate to overcome the challenges of staff and students not being on campus during the pandemic. Among its creative solutions to remote learning was to support students by developing personalised technical instruction, as well as by supplying materials, providing licences and access to creative software and hosting an online graduate showcase.

Lecture-capture facilities across its four campuses in the southeast of England (Farnham, Epsom, Canterbury and Rochester) have made lectures accessible via students' laptops and smartphones and available to play back at any point in the academic year.

Among the UK's seven arts universities, UCA ranked third for its Covid response, our analysis of the 2021 National Student Survey (NSS) results found. While universities with a strong accent on practical courses tended to be marked down more heavily by their students, UCA fared better than most despite having a 13.6 percentage point fall in overall satisfaction in 2021.

The university achieved a gold award in the Teaching Excellence Framework, reflecting its outstanding levels of stretch for students, driving them to achieve their full potential. The TEF panel also hailed "significant contact with employers that frequently engages students in developments from the forefront of professional practice".

As part of a new employability strategy, UCA is integrating a placement and/or live industry brief opportunities into all courses, with the aim of ensuring that each student graduates with a strong online presence and portfolio. Dedicated teams co-ordinate placements, industry opportunities and careers events in each academic school.

This comes after disappointing showings in the first two Graduate Outcomes surveys. UCA has ranked bottom in the UK in both years with just 51% of graduates (down from 54.2%) in high-skilled jobs or graduate-level study in the latest figures. However, universities serving the creative industries have always struggled in graduate prospects surveys owing to the unstable and diverse nature of the destination businesses.

New halls of residence at the Farnham campus, UCA's biggest site, have added 252 spaces. More than 2,000 students are based at Farnham, where subjects range from advertising, animation and computer games technology to film production, journalism, music composition and technology. The £4million Film and Media Centre consolidates UCA's strong reputation

UCA Farnham
Falkner Road
Farnham GU9 7DS
01252 416 110
admissions@uca.ac.uk
www.uca.ac.uk
http://ucasu.com
Open days:
see website

The Times and The Sunday Times **Rankings**
Overall Ranking: 69 (last year: 71)

Teaching quality	76.6%	=38
Student experience	65.1%	=109
Research quality	3.4%	112
Entry standards	134	50
Graduate prospects	51%	132
Good honours	78.7%	59
Expected completion rate	84.5%	=65
Student/staff ratio	14.1	29
Services and facilities	£2,749	50

in the industry, borne out by Oscar and BAFTA nominations for its alumni.

Further afield, our 2019 Modern University of the Year launched the Institute of Creativity and Innovation in China in 2020, UCA's first overseas campus. Opened in partnership with Xiamen University, it offers undergraduate programmes in digital media technology, visual communication design, advertising, and environmental design. The courses are taught jointly and comply with UK higher education standards.

Courses at the Epsom campus specialise in fashion, graphics, music and business programmes. The Business School for the Creative Industries – the first of its kind in the UK – includes degrees in event and promotion management, and international buying and merchandising. At the purpose-built Rochester site a full range of art and design courses is offered covering fashion, photography, computer animation and jewellery-making. Students taking UCA's popular television production course are based at Maidstone TV Studios, the largest independent studio complex in the UK. Those on the Royal School of Needlework's hand embroidery degree, which is accredited by UCA, are based in apartments designed by Sir Christopher Wren at Hampton Court Palace.

The Canterbury School of Architecture is one of only two such faculties remaining within a specialist art and design institution – promoting collaboration between student architects, designers and fine artists. On a modern site close to the city centre, the Canterbury campus also hosts degree courses in fine art, interior design, graphic design, and illustration and animation.

Many staff are practitioners as well as academics, and UCA has plenty of successful role models among its alumni, such as the artist Tracey Emin and the fashion designers Karen Millen and Dame Zandra Rhodes, its former chancellor. New degrees include digital media and magazine publishing; fashion branding and communications; and fashion image and styling.

Most (94%) students are recruited from non-selective state schools and about one in ten receive disability support allowance – among the highest proportions in the country and helping UCA to a rank just outside the top 40 in England and Wales for social inclusion.

With 1,043 rooms across four campuses, the university makes an accommodation guarantee to all first-years. There are no sports facilities, but the students' union operates a variety of clubs.

Tuition fees

»	Fees for UK students	£9,250
	Foundation courses	£5,420
»	Fees for International students2022–23	£16,270
	Foundation courses	£14,920
»	For scholarship and bursary information see www.uca.ac.uk/study-at-uca/fees-finance/	
»	Graduate salary	£20,000

Student numbers

Undergraduates	4,465	(1,515)
Postgraduates	645	(135)
Applications/places		5,635/865
Applications per place		6.5
Overall offer rate		92.5%
International students – EU		6.8%
Non-EU		11.4%

Accommodation

University provided places: 1,043
Self-catered: £120–£180 per week
First years guaranteed accommodation
www.uca.ac.uk/study-at-uca/accommodation/

Where do the students come from?

State schools (non-grammar)	93.6%	Low participation areas	15.1%	**Social inclusion ranking: 41**	
Grammar schools	4.3%	All ethnic minorities	24.3%	Disabled	10.6%
Independent schools	2.1%	White working-class males	5.4%	Mature (over 21)	17.2%
First generation students	47.5%	Black achievement gap	-23.1%		

University of Cumbria

A foothold in east London adds to the reach of the University of Cumbria. The institution has seven campuses, from Ambleside, on Lake Windermere in the Lake District National Park – offering the UK's biggest programme of outdoor education courses plus conservation and forestry degrees – to the new one in Canary Wharf, east London, which has a programme of health, education and business courses.

Applications for 2021 entry were nearly 15% higher at the end of March than at the same point in 2020. The increase bucks a six-year trend of declining applications to study at Cumbria. Over the decade from 2011 to 2020 applications almost halved. Enrolments have declined less steeply – but still significantly – by 39% over the same period.

Cumbria was one of 11 universities awarded bronze in the Teaching Excellence Framework in 2017. It was marked down for a low graduate employment rate in high-skilled jobs but pointed out that such roles are in short supply in the northwest compared with the national average. The university has ranked in the middle reaches of our new graduate outcomes measure both in the last edition and this, beating many of its peers.

Links between the university and some of the northwest's biggest employers – such as the NHS, ambulance service, police force, military and secondary schools – provide work placements for students as well as apprenticeships.

The main campus in Lancaster is set in parkland a short walk from the city centre and caters for courses in education, health, sport and business. Its £9million Sentamu teaching and learning building has a 200-seat lecture theatre and the restaurant has panoramic views towards Morecambe Bay. The library has bookable study rooms, individual booths and laptops for loan and teaching facilities on campus include sport performance labs, ambulance simulators and teacher training rooms.

The Workington campus provides graduate courses in decommissioning, reprocessing and managing nuclear waste and has specialist facilities. The university is a partner in the National College for Nuclear and the Project Academy for Sellafield. Cumbria's base in Barrow is at Furness College, specialising in nursing and health practitioner courses. The university's Fusehill campus in Carlisle is in a former First World War military hospital and offers courses in health, science, conservation, education, business, law and policing. A second site in Carlisle, close to Hadrian's Wall, is home to the university's Institute of Arts.

The creative arts produced by far the best results in the 2014 Research Excellence

Head Office
Fusehill Street
Carlisle CA1 2HH
0808 178 7373
UoCAdmissions@cumbria.ac.uk
www.cumbria.ac.uk
www.ucsu.me
Open days: see website

The Times and The Sunday Times **Rankings**
Overall Ranking: 125 (last year: 114)

Teaching quality	73.3%	=84
Student experience	66.5%	=98
Research quality	1.2%	124
Entry standards	120	=77
Graduate prospects	68.5%	=73
Good honours	66.5%	127
Expected completion rate	81.7%	=87
Student/staff ratio	16.6	79
Services and facilities	£1,748	123

Framework, with 90% of the submission assessed as world-leading or internationally excellent, the top two categories. Overall, Cumbria is just three places off the bottom of our research ranking, having entered only 27 academics for assessment (8% of those eligible). Almost 30% of the work of this small group was placed in the top two categories, however.

The university offers ten degree apprenticeships with 565 trainees on programmes in health, business and industry. Diagnostic radiography, district nursing and midwifery are new additions. Cumbria expects growth in demand to swell student apprentice numbers to about 1,700 by September 2022.

The curriculum gained a new degree in health and social care in September 2021 and an accelerated outdoor education degree will begin in September 2022 – boosting already strong provision in this area.

More than half of Cumbria's students are the first in their family to go to university and nearly one in five come from deprived areas, helping the university to a creditable ranking of =44th in our social inclusion ranking. The university awarded 105 of its Cumbria Bursaries in the 2020–21 academic year to new recruits with household income below £25,000. The bursaries are worth £1,000 a year for full-time students and £500 for part-timers.

Sports facilities are available at the Lancaster, Carlisle and Ambleside campuses – ranging from a fitness suite, sports hall and swimming pool in Lancaster to a large sports hall and fitness facilities in Carlisle and a gym with classes and small group training in Ambleside.

A survey showed that 95% of students would recommend the university's health and wellbeing support services to their friends. Appointments with counsellors, psychotherapists and mental health practitioners are available if needed and there is free access to the online platform TogetherAll.

Stone cottages at the Ambleside campus are hard to beat for their picturesque setting and the university offers some of the UK's cheapest student accommodation, starting at just £56 a week.

Tuition fees

»	Fees for UK students	£9,250
	Foundation courses	£6,000
»	Fees for International students 2022–23	£12,800–£15,500
	Foundation courses	£10,500
»	For scholarship and bursary information see www.cumbria.ac.uk/study/student-finance	
»	Graduate salary	£24,000

Student numbers

Undergraduates	4,285 (1,690)
Postgraduates	770 (1,200)
Applications/places	4,245/955
Applications per place	4.4
Overall offer rate	73%
International students – EU	1.8%
Non-EU	1.6%

Accommodation

University provided places: 500
Self-catered: £56–£120 per week
www.cumbria.ac.uk/student-life/accommodation/

Where do the students come from?

					Social inclusion ranking: =44	
State schools (non-grammar)	95.7%	Low participation areas	18.2%	Disabled	8.8%
Grammar schools	2.3%	All ethnic minorities	13.4%	Mature (over 21)	52.6%
Independent schools	2%	White working-class males	5.2%		
First generation students	55.6%	Black achievement gap	-24.3%		

De Montfort University

De Montfort University (DMU) in Leicester has been undergoing a transformative programme of campus developments. Students admitted in 2021 were the first to use the latest improvement – the Yard – a £5.5million four-storey extension to the learning space for the Faculty of Business and Law. The new wing adds to the same faculty's teaching space in the regenerated Great Hall of Leicester Castle Business School.

A campus university in the centre of the city, DMU has invested £136million in teaching and learning spaces designed to inspire students. The flagship Vijay Patel Building has brought all art and design courses together. It includes the city's largest display space, The Gallery, as well as printmaking, casting and photographic facilities. There are also workshops for glass, ceramics and rapid prototyping. Its namesake, Dr Vijay Patel, is a graduate of DMU's Leicester School of Pharmacy. The development echoes the history of DMU, which opened in 1870 as an art school to provide education and training for workers from Leicester's booming industries.

Digital provision has also been boosted through DMU Replay, with which students can access recorded audio-visual content and revisit lectures, while a real-time digital conferencing tool enables them to take part in interactive lessons.

Despite the physical and virtual advances in its estate, DMU scored poorly with students for its Covid response, our analysis of the 2021 National Student Survey (NSS) revealed. Just 14 universities saw a greater decline in their NSS outcomes when compared to the 2020 results, with ratings for learning resources hard hit with a 20 percentage point fall year-on-year.

This has left DMU in the bottom ten nationally in our NSS-derived rankings for teaching quality and student experience, preventing any recovery from 2020's 45-place fall in our institutional academic ranking. The university, which was ranked as high as 53rd six years ago, has slipped a further seven places to 126th.

DMU's performance in the government's Teaching Excellence Framework (TEF) is much stronger, holding a gold award – the highest standard. The TEF commended "optimum" levels of contact time between students and staff and "outstanding" support for learning.

In a push to retain talent in the region, DMU is linking 1,000 of its graduates with opportunities within the county. "Leicester 1,000" offers workshops, CV help, upskilling resources and advice on landing a job.

Twenty students have also been placed at 20 local businesses via a partnership with a recruitment company. The university is working with businesses to help them recruit and retain more diverse workforces through

The Gateway
Leicester LE1 9BH
0116 270 8443
enquiry@dmu.ac.uk
www.dmu.ac.uk
www.demontfortsu.com/
Open days: see website

Edinburgh
Belfast
LEICESTER
London
Cardiff

The Times and The Sunday Times Rankings
Overall Ranking: 126 (last year: 119)

Teaching quality	67.7%	125
Student experience	61.6%	123
Research quality	8.9%	=67
Entry standards	105	=121
Graduate prospects	65%	=96
Good honours	76.1%	85
Expected completion rate	80.2%	=98
Student/staff ratio	20.2	=120
Services and facilities	£2,353	82

the £400,000 Leicester's Future Leaders project. The careers and employability service at DMU was recognised at the 2021 National Undergraduate Employability awards.

All DMU students are guaranteed work experience. Opportunities include virtual and in-person placements, internships and mentoring with organisations including Disney, ASOS, HSBC, KPMG, L'Oréal, Microsoft and the NHS. Some courses offer the chance to take part in industry showcases, such as engineering's Formula Student competition at Silverstone circuit and Graduate Fashion Week.

More than half of students are from black, Asian and ethnic minority backgrounds at DMU, which won our first University of the Year for Social Inclusion award for 2019. Just under half of students are from families where neither parent went to university. The proportion who receive a Disabled Student's Allowance is high and the university is in the top 40 overall in our social inclusion ranking.

New degree courses include: business information systems; Internet of Things; applied computing; and business data analytics. At the last count more than 500 learners were on DMU's 11 higher and degree apprenticeships. The latest programmes include data analysts, data scientists, digital and technology solutions specialists and registered nurses. Policing, architecture, digital and technology solutions, cybersecurity and hearing aid dispensing are among established options.

Almost 60% of research was rated world-leading or internationally excellent in the 2014 Research Excellence Framework. Longstanding partnerships with Hewlett-Packard and Deloitte illustrate strong links with business and industry, which feed into innovative training and research collaborations. The Stephen Lawrence Research Centre is one example, promoting social justice on a local, national and global scale.

Buses are provided to Beaumont Park, DMU's outdoor sports facilities which have undergone a £3.4million upgrade. Here, students have access to new 3G pitches for football, rugby, American football and lacrosse and a modern clubhouse. On-campus facilities include a swimming pool, sports hall, fitness suite and dance studio.

The Your DMU pre-induction course contains guidance on initiatives such as No Space for Hate – which gives practical support to students who have experienced harassment, and #NoBystanders – which encourages students to challenge inappropriate or threatening behaviour.

Tuition fees

»	Fees for UK students	£9,250
	Foundation courses	£6,165
»	Fees for International students 2022–23	£14,750–£16,336
»	For scholarship and bursary information see https://www.dmu.ac.uk/study/fees-funding/index.aspx	
»	Graduate salary	£22,500

Student numbers

Undergraduates	21,565	(1,480)
Postgraduates	3,775	(2,185)
Applications/places	23,450/4,695	
Applications per place	5	
Overall offer rate	79.3%	
International students – EU	6.1%	
Non-EU	12.8%	

Accommodation
University provided places: 4,100
Self-catered: £99–£197 per week
www.dmu.ac.uk/study/accommodation/index.aspx

Where do the students come from?

State schools (non-grammar)	95%	Low participation areas	14.7%	Social inclusion ranking: 37		
Grammar schools	2.2%	All ethnic minorities	54.2%	Disabled	10.4%
Independent schools	2.8%	White working-class males	4.9%	Mature (over 21)	15.4%
First generation students	47.9%	Black achievement gap	-24.2%		

University of Derby

Initiatives to widen participation in higher education at the University of Derby were recognised with two national awards in 2020 – University of the Year in the UK Social Mobility Awards, and best UK higher education provider in the National Education Opportunities Network (NEON) Awards.

It is a strong performer in our social inclusion ranking, rising one place to 16th in England and Wales in this edition. Its strengths lie in recruitment of students from areas with low participation in higher education (23.8% of the 2020 intake, =8th), mature students (36%, 29th) and those who receive disability support allowance (11.2%, =15th). The majority of students come from non-selective state schools (96.2%, =24th).

In response to nationwide concern about the low progression rate of white working-class males into higher education, Derby runs school programmes for year 8 pupils to help them to develop the skills and behaviours needed. Derby's proportion of white working-class male students is in the top third among UK universities.

Another successful outreach programme is Derby's Student Legal Advice Centre. Law students offer a pro bono service in partnership with the British Red Cross and Paragon Law. Their legal advice gives "life-changing" support to those in need in the city – while participating students gain valuable skills and experience.

Derby's record on teaching and learning is strong: the university was awarded gold in the government's Teaching Excellence Framework, winning praise for its personalised learning and support.

The university takes a progressive approach to feedback and assessment methods (often a bone of contention in student satisfaction surveys) and aims to lead the higher education sector in self- and peer-evaluation. All undergraduates can have one-to-one academic tutor sessions whenever they need them, and the work of the Centre for Excellence in Learning and Teaching works includes assessment and digital practice. Derby's 75.1% positive score for satisfaction with assessment and feedback in the 2021 National Student Survey puts it in the top dozen institutions in the country.

Derby has ambitious plans to develop a City Hub, where the 550-seat Derby Theatre is already part of cultural life. The centrepiece will be the new business school, due to open in 2024, a landmark building designed for net-zero carbon emissions from its construction to operation.

Students experience hands-on learning in "real world" simulation environments including a crime scene house for forensic science students, a replica crown court, a

---

Kedleston Road
Derby DE22 1GB
01332 590 500
admissions@derby.ac.uk
www.derby.ac.uk
www.derbyunion.co.uk
Open days: See website

The Times and The Sunday Times **Rankings**
Overall Ranking: =94 (last year: =94)

Teaching quality	78.2%	=21
Student experience	72.1%	=39
Research quality	2.5%	117
Entry standards	116	=91
Graduate prospects	67%	=86
Good honours	69.3%	118
Expected completion rate	78.5%	108
Student/staff ratio	14.7	=40
Services and facilities	£1,884	115

Bloomberg financial markets lab and an NHS-standard hospital ward. Hospitality courses benefit from industry-standard kitchens and a fine dining restaurant.

A shuttle bus links the university's three bases in Derby. Kedleston Road is the biggest campus, hosting most teaching subjects as well as the students' union, a multi-faith centre and the main sports facilities. The campus has a new cycling hub with showers, lockers and changing facilities.

The Markeaton Street site is the base for arts, design, engineering and technology courses, while courses including fine art and social care are based at Britannia Mill, a ten-minute walk away.

Nursing has a school of its own in the market town of Chesterfield to accommodate the growing demand. Engineering and IT are also taught in Chesterfield, where there is an innovation centre. In the spa town of Buxton, the Devonshire Dome, a former hospital, hosts courses including hospitality management.

New degrees include midwifery, international business management, environmental sustainability, biomedical science, global affairs and politics, and fashion styling and communication. Degree apprenticeships cover 19 areas including policing, aerospace engineering, senior leadership and prosthetics and orthotics. Derby hopes to have about 1,800 apprenticeship students by September 2022.

Internships are available with Microsoft, IBM, Porsche, Bentley, Rolls-Royce and Toyota, among others.

Bursaries of up to £1,000 are awarded according to a sliding scale of household income and paid as £100 e-cards for study resources plus up to £900 cash.

Only 19% of Derby's eligible academics were entered for the 2014 Research Excellence Framework, although nearly 30% of the submission was placed in the top two categories. A new "omics" laboratory, covering a range of biological sciences, extends the university's research capacity. In an example of collaborative work with a range of regional partners, students at a Derby laboratory joined a drive to develop a ten-minute Covid-19 test now used worldwide. All first-years are guaranteed accommodation after a £30million, five-year investment to offer more than 2,700 places.

The sports centre at Kedleston Road has gained a new HiPAC (high performance analysis centre) and an extra all-weather pitch. Students can also use a 70-station fitness gym, squash courts and climbing wall.

Tuition fees

- » Fees for UK students   £9,250
- » Fees for International students 2022–23   £14,045–£14,700
- » For scholarship and bursary information see www.derby.ac.uk/study/fees-and-finance/
- » Graduate salary   £23,000

Student numbers

Undergraduates	12,335	(2,990)
Postgraduates	1,605	(2,755)
Applications/places		17,505/2,790
Applications per place		6.3
Overall offer rate		80%
International students – EU		5.4%
Non-EU		4.3%

Accommodation

University provided places: 2,735
Self-catered: £113–£160 per week
First years guaranteed accommodation
www.derby.ac.uk/life/accommodation/

Where do the students come from?

State schools (non-grammar)	96.2%	Low participation areas	23.8%	
Grammar schools	1.7%	All ethnic minorities	30.2%	
Independent schools	2.1%	White working-class males	6.9%	
First generation students	53.3%	Black achievement gap	-26.5%	

Social inclusion ranking: 16

Disabled	11.2%
Mature (over 21)	36%

University of Dundee

More than 100 of Dundee's final-year medical students graduated in April 2020, two months earlier than planned, so they could start work on the NHS frontline. As part of Dundee's extensive response to Covid-19 the new graduates registered early with the General Medical Council to help allay fears that the healthcare system could be overwhelmed by the virus.

Drawing on the university's renowned strength in the life sciences, within days of the first lockdown's announcement academic partnerships had been formed to tackle Covid-19. Researchers collaborated with those at the University of Glasgow to identify 38 proteins produced by the virus SARS-CoV-2.

The university's two Thermo KingFisher Flex robots (which extract DNA from blood samples) were handed over to the Royal Navy in March 2020 for urgent transportation to a national diagnostic centre in Milton Keynes.

Elsewhere, leading lung condition authority Prof James Chalmers from Dundee's School of Medicine has led an £8.4million study into the long-term effects of Covid-19 on hospitalised patients. Collectively, since the pandemic's outbreak university staff or students have been involved in more than 50 initiatives related to researching the coronavirus or in helping those affected by it.

For its students, Dundee took steps to ensure their academic progress and degrees were assessed fairly during the pandemic. A "mitigating circumstances" policy allowed those affected by the coronavirus – either by suffering it themselves or caring for others affected – to have the context considered in relation to their academic performance.

After an initial pivot to remote learning, practical work and smaller group sessions have returned to on-campus delivery. Dundee continues to deliver lectures and similar large-scale teaching sessions for 40-plus students online in real time (and viewable later) and via pre-recorded content.

However, despite these efforts, the university's 2021 National Student Survey scores were severely impacted, recording a 8.8 percentage point drop in Dundee's score for overall satisfaction, dragging its wider ranking for student experience down by 30 places to =49th.

Dundee was one of three Scottish universities to be awarded gold by the Teaching Excellence Framework (TEF) panel. Assessors commended the opportunities students have to develop work-ready skills and knowledge, and said courses encourage ideal levels of stretch and student engagement. Students from all backgrounds achieve outstanding outcomes at Dundee, the TEF report found.

Dundee's campus has benefited from

Nethergate
Dundee DD1 4HN
01382 383 838
contactus@dundee.ac.uk
www.dundee.ac.uk
www.dusa.co.uk
Open days: see website

The Times and The Sunday Times **Rankings**
Overall Ranking: =35 (last year: =23)

Teaching quality	75.1%	=62
Student experience	71%	=49
Research quality	31.2%	41
Entry standards	177	=10
Graduate prospects	76.3%	34
Good honours	78.8%	=57
Expected completion rate	89%	41
Student/staff ratio	14.5	=37
Services and facilities	£2,718	51

about £200 million of redevelopment investment. The £50million Discovery Centre encourages interaction between disciplines. The medical school has its own 20-acre site, while nursing and midwifery students are 35 miles away in Kirkcaldy. The highly rated design courses are taught at the Duncan of Jordanstone College of Art, one of the university's ten schools.

Dundee is leading the Tay Cities Biomedical Cluster project, which has received £25 million initial funding from the Scottish government. It will feature a three-storey innovation hub adjacent to the university's main campus, for new life sciences companies and a medical device research and development facility. Building begins in 2022 and should finish by the end of 2023.

In the 2014 Research Excellence Framework Dundee was top for biological sciences, attracting students from all over the world. It also offers a joint degree with the National University of Singapore. However, excellence runs much wider: Dundee was in the top three in the UK for research in civil engineering and in the top ten for maths and general engineering.

A substantial annual spend on scholarships and bursaries includes £2 million for overseas students alone. The hefty budget funds Dundee's wide range of awards, which students may qualify for based on their financial need and/or academic merit.

Dundee's widening participation activities are designed to attract applications from students from disadvantaged backgrounds. The university's summer schools prepare access students for higher education and have helped more than 3,500 students who otherwise might not have considered university. Only four universities in Scotland recruit more students from areas of the highest deprivation, although Dundee slips three places in our latest ranking for social inclusion in Scottish universities.

Sports facilities on campus and at the Riverside sports ground on the banks of the River Tay are excellent. Scottish students who apply before June 15 are guaranteed student accommodation, and the application deadline is extended to August 31 for those from the rest of the UK or abroad.

Named the Best Place to Live by the *Sunday Times* in 2019, Dundee offers low rents, a lively social scene and a regenerated waterfront distinguished by the striking V&A museum.

Tuition fees

- » Fees for Scottish students £0–£1,820
  RUK fees £9,250
- » Fees for International students 2022–23 £19,500–£23,650
  Medicine £47,475; Dentistry £49,200 (clinical years)
- » For scholarship and bursary information see
  https://www.dundee.ac.uk/collections/tuition-fees
- » Graduate salary £24,373

Student numbers

Undergraduates	10,225	(1,410)
Postgraduates	2,420	(2,180)
Applications/places	20,125/2,685	
Applications per place	7.5	
Overall offer rate	52%	
International students – EU	6.2%	
Non-EU	6.4%	

Accommodation

University provided places: 1,587
Self-catered: £134–£163 per week
www.dundee.ac.uk/accommodation

Where do the students come from?

State schools (non-grammar)	83.5%	Low participation areas	16.2%	Disabled	4.5%
Grammar schools	5.8%	All ethnic minorities	11.5%	Mature (over 21)	26.6%
Independent schools	10.6%	White working-class males	5.5%		
First generation students	40.8%	Black achievement gap	-14.4%		

Social inclusion ranking (Scotland): 9

Durham University

Partnering with a local sixth-form centre to establish the Durham Mathematics School is one initiative by which the university aims to increase its footprint in the northeast. The new free school follows similar initiatives that have involved King's College London and the University of Exeter, creating some of the highest-attaining sixth-form colleges. The school, due to open in September 2022, is intended to provide a steady pipeline of students into the university's maths, science and engineering departments; 8.4% of Durham's intake was recruited regionally in 2020.

This local recruitment – the northeast is the English region with the lowest participation rates in higher education – should help to diversify the student population. The university stands six places off the bottom of our latest social inclusion ranking, although that is an improvement on our last edition. Durham is one of five universities where less than half the student intake is drawn from non-selective state schools, and it remains a favourite of the privately educated, who accounted for 36.5% of the intake in 2019/20, the fourth highest of any university.

A Sutton Trust summer school, supported progression, a programme to support black students, and contextual offers are all being deployed to change the student profile.

In 2020, 18% of applicants were made a contextual offer of at least one A-level grade below the standard offer for a given course. Students need to tick at least two criteria that include attending a state school, being in receipt of free school meals, living in an area with low progression rates to higher education, or one with a high rate of socio-economic disadvantage.

Durham is one of the winners in our analysis of the handling of the Covid pandemic on Britain's campuses. It ranks just outside the top 30 for having one of the smaller drops in student satisfaction when the outcomes of the pandemic-hit 2021 National Student Survey (NSS) are compared with those from 2020. So, although its scores are down year on year, the losses sustained are less than at many universities, leading to an improved ranking in our measures of teaching quality (up 33 places) and student experience (up 37 places).

It is among a relatively small number of universities to commit to a return to face-to-face teaching. "We are now exploring our curricula to ensure that best practice and digital innovations are not lost but that they are used effectively to meet the learning needs of different subject areas as we return to face-to-face teaching."

Lecture capture was available pre-pandemic and will remain, even as the university stresses the "importance of

The Palatine Centre
Stockton Road
Durham DH1 3LE
0191 334 1000
www.durham.ac.uk/study/askus
www.dur.ac.uk
www.durhamsu.com
Open days: see website

The Times and The Sunday Times **Rankings**		
Overall Ranking: 6 (last year: 6)		
Teaching quality	76.4%	=43
Student experience	70.2%	=56
Research quality	39%	16
Entry standards	182	9
Graduate prospects	84.5%	10
Good honours	93.2%	4
Expected completion rate	96.8%	4
Student/staff ratio	13.5	=20
Services and facilities	£3,846	7

opportunities for personal interaction between staff and students, and between students".

Durham has a collegiate structure similar to Oxford and Cambridge, but unlike Oxbridge, teaching takes place centrally rather than within colleges. The colleges provide an important social hub and each has its own characteristics. Applicants can choose the college that feels like the best fit, although an algorithm now allocates students to colleges with principals having a much reduced say.

University College (Castle) and Collingwood remain the most popular options, the former being part of the Cathedral and Castle UNESCO World Heritage Site at the heart of the historic peninsula ringed by the River Wear, the latter being at the heart of the hill colleges to the south and close to the science site and the main library.

Colleges can offer accommodation for all first years, with more than 7,500 places available. Despite the small size of the city, there is no shortage of private landlords and accommodation blocks to mop up the "livers out" in their second and third year of studies.

The collegiate structure leads to intense sporting rivalries and participation rates are high. Facilities are centred on the Maiden Castle sports and wellbeing park on the edge of the city, and the racecourse, close to the centre.

Durham graduates are among the most sought after and the university fares well in the graduate prospects measure. Over the past year it has facilitated 1,100 employer events, hosted 310 employer sessions and advertised more than 5,000 graduate vacancies.

A new purpose-built space for entrepreneurship – the Hazan Venture Lab – provides individual and group working areas, a bookable meeting room, a mini-library and other facilities for students or graduates working on new ventures or enterprise projects.

All new students must take a one-hour online course, called Consent matters: boundaries, respect and positive intervention. There are also sexual misconduct and violence awareness talks during induction week. These initiatives follow a number of high-profile incidents involving Durham students in recent years. It was among the top ten universities cited on the Everyone's Invited website alleging sexual violence, assault or harassment, but is now one of very few to have made a consent module compulsory for all freshers.

Tuition fees

» Fees for UK students £9,250
» Fees for International students 2022–23 £22,900–£28,500
» For scholarship and bursary information see www.dur.ac.uk/student.finance/
» Graduate salary £27,905

Student numbers

Undergraduates	14,685	(40)
Postgraduates	3,815	(975)
Applications/places	32,685/5,140	
Applications per place	6.4	
Overall offer rate	72.2%	
International students – EU	4.2%	
Non-EU	18.7%	

Where do the students come from?

State schools (non-grammar)	49%	Low participation areas	6.9%	Disabled	5.8%
Grammar schools	14.5%	All ethnic minorities	13.5%	Mature (over 21)	4%
Independent schools	36.5%	White working-class males	3%		
First generation students	23%	Black achievement gap	-8.7%		

Accommodation

University provided places: 7,552
Catered costs: £202–£215 per week
Self-catered: £142–£154 per week
First years guaranteed accommodation
www.dur.ac.uk/colleges-and-student-experience/accommodation-and-catering/costs/

Social inclusion ranking: 110

University of East Anglia

Productivity East opened in September 2021 to provide a new regional hub for engineering, technology and management at the University of East Anglia (UEA). The £7.4million development is an interdisciplinary initiative for schools such as computing, sciences, engineering, mathematics and the Norwich Business School at UEA's 320-acre campus on the edge of Norwich.

It has workshops dedicated to advanced robotics and CNC (computer numerical control), a 3D printing studio, digital design lab and studio space. Its aim is for students to work alongside researchers and businesses to discover practical solutions to challenges – existing and future – to encourage engineers to explore digital solutions and to create innovative products and services.

Alongside the £30million Science Building, opened in 2019 with four floors of cutting-edge equipment, Productivity East adds modern teaching and learning spaces to the original 1960s campus where some buildings are listed, including the iconic Denys Lasdun-designed Ziggurat accommodation blocks.

Awarded gold in the Teaching Excellence Framework, UEA drew praise for its "strategic approach to personalised learning, which secures high levels of commitment to studies". Assessors noted that investment in high-quality physical and digital resources has had a "demonstrable impact on the learning experience". These include a media suite in the arts and humanities faculty, the £19million Biomedical Research Centre and the Enterprise Centre, dedicated to supporting entrepreneurial skills.

The university's lecture-capture system began its rollout in January 2020, just weeks before the first lockdown. Since then, equipment has been installed in most bookable rooms and the software has also helped to generate learning resources. The university hopes to expand the use of recordings alongside face-to-face learning.

Despite these advances, students still marked the university down in the 2021 National Student Survey. Analysis of the post-pandemic outcomes compared with 2020 found 68 universities performed better than UEA in the eyes of their students across nine areas that contribute to our teaching quality and student experience scores.

The curriculum gained 29 fresh options for 2021, most of which added a year abroad, working in industry, or a foundation year to existing programmes. New courses included microbiology, film and television production, marine sciences and law with criminology.

Most degrees have opportunities for work experience built in and recent graduates can tap into UEA's Gateway to Growth paid internship programme, taking placements at businesses in the eastern region for between four weeks and a year.

Environmental science has long been

Norwich Research Park
Norwich NR4 7TJ
01603 591 515
admissions@uea.ac.uk
www.uea.ac.uk
www.uea.su
Open days: see website

***The Times and The Sunday Times* Rankings**
Overall Ranking: 27 (last year: 21)

Teaching quality	74.6%	72
Student experience	71.3%	=45
Research quality	35.8%	32
Entry standards	133	51
Graduate prospects	76.3%	=39
Good honours	85.5%	=24
Expected completion rate	88.6%	=42
Student/staff ratio	13.2	=16
Services and facilities	£3,087	26

recognised as UEA's flagship subject area. Its Climatic Research Unit and the Tyndall Centre for Climate Change Research, funded by a consortium of universities and the Chinese government, are among the leading investigators of the global challenge of our times. The Anglian Centre for Water Studies is a partnership with Anglian Water, contributing expertise from UEA's schools of environmental sciences, psychology and Norwich Business School to addressing the problem of using water sustainably.

In the 2014 Research Excellence Framework, social work and pharmacy led UEA's results, and 82% of all work submitted was placed in one of the top two categories.

The £75million Quadram Institute based on Norwich Research Park has opened with the remit of improving health and preventing disease through innovations in microbiology, gut health and food. The Sainsbury Centre for the Visual Arts houses a priceless collection of modern and tribal art in a building designed by Sir Norman Foster.

UK students are automatically considered for bursaries using household income information from Student Finance England. Awards are set at £800 or £1,300 a year, rising to £2,500 a year for care leavers or students estranged from their parents. Bursaries are mainly in the form of fee waivers, although accommodation discounts or cash grants are available. Bright spark scholarships of £3,000 over three years are awarded to new entrants who have gone above and beyond their entry requirements. Applicants who complete the Extended Project Qualification in the summer holidays, for example, can gain points worth up to half an A-level.

UEA's outreach programmes work with more than 50,000 prospective students each year in areas of disadvantage and under-representation in higher education. In 2020, 10% of admissions received contextual offers, reducing grade requirements. Medicine with a Gateway Year is a programme aimed at widening access to UEA's medical school.

UEA's Sportspark and Colney Lane Pavilion have extensive facilities including an Olympic-sized swimming pool and fitness centre, five sports halls, an ultimate frisbee pitch, a climbing wall and pitches for rugby, cricket and football.

A less obvious student hotspot than many, down-to-earth Norwich has enough going on to keep most undergraduates entertained. Tuesdays are student nights in the city and the café scene is recommended.

Tuition fees

» Fees for UK students	£9,250
» Fees for International students 2022–23	£18,000–£22,800
Medicine	£35,200
» For scholarship and bursary information see www.uea.ac.uk/study/fees-and-funding/	
» Graduate salary	£24,000

Student numbers

Undergraduates	12,920	(490)
Postgraduates	3,095	(1,530)
Applications/places	19,965/3,725	
Applications per place	5.4	
Overall offer rate	79.4%	
International students – EU	4.1%	
Non-EU	11.6%	

Accommodation
University provided places: 4,226
Self-catered: £83–£200 per week
First years guaranteed accommodation
www.uea.ac.uk/uea-life/accommodation

Where do the students come from?

					Social inclusion ranking: 84	
State schools (non-grammar)	78.7%	Low participation areas	11.7%		Disabled	6.5%
Grammar schools	10.9%	All ethnic minorities	21.4%		Mature (over 21)	11.3%
Independent schools	10.4%	White working-class males	6.3%			
First generation students	39.5%	Black achievement gap	-11.5%			

University of East London

The eye-catching regeneration of the University of East London's (UEL) Docklands base was described as "poetry", winning design awards after its completion in 1999 as London's first new campus for 50 years. Free buses connect the striking waterside buildings with headquarters in Stratford, where UEL has taken over the University Square Stratford development, built in partnership with Birkbeck, University of London, using the extra space to add a trading floor simulator and other facilities for the Royal Docks School of Business and Law.

UEL became a university in 1992, but traces its history back to the establishment of the West Ham Technical Institute 100 years before. With a focus on careers-led education, UEL forges local, national and global industry links. One collaboration, with Amazon Web Services, has led to the creation of the UEL Career Zone and support for the university's flagship Professional Fitness and Mental Wealth programme, which puts soft skills such as critical thinking and practical skills such as digital proficiency at the heart of every course. Achievements in the modules are recorded in a digital career passport and count towards undergraduates' final results.

Under the Vision 2028 strategy, UEL has pledged to invest in the student experience and learning outcomes. The Dual Delivery education framework, rolled out in 2020, appears to have ticked that box: UEL has found that its blended learning programme increased student engagement and retention and improved readiness for work.

Building on these gains, UEL has introduced Dual Delivery 2.0 to continue using remote learning to provide flexibility within courses, but ensuring that face-to-face opportunities allow collaboration with peers. The approach integrates academic, personal and career development and makes sure an afternoon is dedicated to scheduled sporting or other club activities.

It seems to be going down well. In the 2021 National Student Survey, UEL was among the 40 universities with the smallest drop in scores compared with 2020 as students passed judgment on their institution's handling of the pandemic. Scores for teaching, assessment and feedback, and course organisation and management performed particularly well.

UEL's career focus has yet to translate into buoyant results in the Graduate Outcomes survey, however, where it ranks =125th (out of 132 institutions) for the second successive year. Low graduate employment rates were the main stumbling block in its failed appeal to be upgraded from bronze to silver in the Teaching Excellence Framework. UEL remains one of only

---

Docklands Campus
University Way
London E16 2RD
020 8223 3333
study@uel.ac.uk
www.uel.ac.uk
www.uelunion.org
Open days: see website

The Times and The Sunday Times **Rankings**
Overall Ranking: 130 (last year: 129)

Teaching quality	74.8%	=68
Student experience	69.4%	=68
Research quality	7.2%	76
Entry standards	97	132
Graduate prospects	57.7%	=125
Good honours	73.1%	=103
Expected completion rate	76.5%	117
Student/staff ratio	21.9	=125
Services and facilities	£1,556	129

11 universities in our table with a bronze award.

The university achieves much more success with social inclusion. UEL ranks well inside the top 20 in England and Wales. Just over 70% of undergraduates are from ethnic minority populations and 56% are the first in their family to go to university. UEL achieves success at keeping the projected dropout rate low, at 10.6%, considerably below the expected rate of 18.2% according to its course mix and the academic and social background of its intake.

More than half of UEL's undergraduates are 21 or older on entry – many choosing to start their course in February rather than the autumn. The university's pre-entry programmes offer those aged 19 and above who have no formal qualifications the opportunity to convert their skills, experiences and knowledge into academic competencies during a ten-week course, accepted as an entry qualification.

The university believes the 7.5% dip in applications in the 2021 cycle at the end of March, compared with 2020, was due to the impact of Brexit on international interest as well as the destabilising effect of Covid-19 on applications by students from India. Over the past decade, applications have decreased by about 30%, as have new student enrolments.

Of 37 new course offerings from September 2021 – covering options from aeronautical engineering to fashion buying – many feature the addition of a placement or foundation year. The list also includes top-up courses in e-sports, international business management, and events and hospitality.

World-class research doubled in the 2014 Research Excellence Framework compared with the 2008 assessments: 62% of the work submitted reached the top two categories. The university was ranked equal first in England for the impact of its research in psychology.

UEL sports scholar Jona Efoloko was part of the Team GB 4x100m relay squad at the Tokyo Olympics and sports graduate Adam Gemili was in the 200m sprint squad. A scholarship worth up to £6,000 is offered to help talented sportsmen and women fulfil their potential.

Unusually for a London university, UEL has two halls of residence on campus, in standout waterside buildings. First-years who want to live in are guaranteed a room in the 1,169 spaces. Campus social life centres around the Docklands student village, while students have some of London's hippest enclaves on their doorstep.

Tuition fees

» Fees for UK students	£9,250
» Fees for International students 2022–23	£13,740
» For scholarship and bursary information see www.uel.ac.uk/undergraduate/fees-and-funding	
» Graduate salary	£24,000

Student numbers

Undergraduates	9,565	(705)
Postgraduates	3,655	(1,430)
Applications/places		15,440/1,765
Applications per place		8.7
Overall offer rate		73.1%
International students – EU		3.7%
Non-EU		7.7%

Accommodation

University provided places: 1,169
Self-catered: £148–£193 per week
www.uel.ac.uk/accommodation

Where do the students come from?

State schools (non-grammar)	96.3%	Low participation areas	8.5%	**Social inclusion ranking: 14**	
Grammar schools	1%	All ethnic minorities	70.1%	Disabled	7.2%
Independent schools	2.7%	White working-class males	3.3%	Mature (over 21)	55.2%
First generation students	56.6%	Black achievement gap	-21.5%		

Edge Hill University

Edge Hill is our Modern University of the Year, rising to its highest ever position in our rankings. It was also shortlisted for our overall University of the Year award. Originally a teacher training college, Edge Hill has expanded greatly under the stewardship of John Cater, vice-chancellor for nearly 30 years. The opening of the medical school in 2020, is the latest addition among developments which have added schools, departments and facilities in recent years.

The biosciences have been boosted by investment of nearly £250,000 at the Lancashire institution. There are new facilities for electron microscopy, used to image the surface of cells, which is valuable for research in regenerative medicine, drug development and nanomedicine. Much of the new equipment is used across a range of STEM (science, technology, engineering and mathematics) subjects.

The medical school houses the only bioethics unit in England, and health and social care students learn clinical skills in its simulation centre. The university's £13million Tech Hub has biotechnology laboratories for research into disease prevention, DNA sequencing, cloning and genetic treatments.

Edge Hill has been training teachers since the 19th century and is still one of the UK's largest providers of secondary teacher training and courses for classroom assistants. A university since 2005, it has swiftly become a consistently strong performer in our league table and one of the leading post-1992 institutions.

The main campus in 160 acres near the northwest market town of Ormskirk has been redeveloped to the tune of £300million over the past decade or so. The £27million Catalyst building opened in 2018, brought together student support services and the university library, with additional study spaces. Creative Edge, a £17million complex for the departments of media and computing, has studios for television, animation, sound, photography and radio. There is also a multimedia laboratory.

The university was one of three in the northwest of England to be awarded gold in the first round of assessment by the Teaching Excellence Framework. The panel noted that "students from diverse backgrounds achieve consistently outstanding outcomes".

Edge Hill recruits almost all its students from non-selective state schools, and almost two in every ten undergraduates come from some of the country's most educationally deprived areas. Based on the academic and social backgrounds of the intake, the

St Helens Road
Ormskirk L39 4QP
01695 650 950
admissions@edgehill.ac.uk
www.edgehill.ac.uk
www.edgehillsu.org.uk
Open days: see website

The Times and The Sunday Times **Rankings**
Overall Ranking: =58 (last year: 70)

Teaching quality	74.9%	=64
Student experience	70.5%	=52
Research quality	4.9%	=93
Entry standards	129	=55
Graduate prospects	67.4%	84
Good honours	73.5%	101
Expected completion rate	86.2%	56
Student/staff ratio	14.3	=33
Services and facilities	£2,781	=46

university's projected dropout rate (7.7%) is significantly better than its benchmark (11.9%).

A seven-week fast-track programme for adults offers an alternative route to entry, outside published UCAS course tariffs. The MBChB medicine degree has the option of an integrated foundation year for those without the requisite academic qualifications and who meet criteria for widening participation in higher education.

After the rapid acceleration of remote learning during the pandemic, the university's approach to teaching and learning will include elements of online and digital tools across all faculties. Edge Hill found the flexibility of online course delivery had profound advantages for students on professional development programmes and also benefited those studying while working in health, medicine and education services.

Full lecture-capture facilities can be accessed on mobile devices – helping students to personalise the way they study.

Edge Hill's curriculum has gained new degrees in electronic engineering, computer science and artificial intelligence, and contemporary mental health practice. For 2022 entry, the university hopes to offer courses in intelligent automation and robotics, and electrical engineering at BEng or MEng level.

Out of six subject areas submitted to the 2014 Research Excellence Framework, English, sport and media produced the best results.

Improvements were recorded in all subjects submitted, although Edge Hill is only just in our top 100 for research. Two new research centres were added in 2020: the International Centre on Racism and the Centre for Child Protection and Safeguarding in Sport.

Edge Hill's £30million sports centre has an eight-court sports hall, 25m swimming pool, 80-station fitness suite, aerobics studio and health suite with sauna and steam rooms. Outdoors, there is a trim trail with exercise stations, a competition-standard running track, rugby, hockey and football pitches, an athletics field and netball and tennis courts.

Student accommodation in the elegant 1930s-designed Main Building is being refurbished and all first-years are guaranteed a room on campus. A total of 2,495 rooms are available but only a few are catered.

Students share the campus with resident ducks who live by two lakes. La Plage is a man-made sandy beach if the real thing seems too far away, eight miles away on the coast at Southport. The bright lights of Liverpool are within easy reach.

Tuition fees

» Fees for UK students	£9,250
Foundation courses 2021–22	£6,165
» Fees for International students 2022–23	£15,000
» For scholarship and bursary information see www.edgehill.ac.uk/study/fees-and-funding/	
» Graduate salary	£23,000

Student numbers

Undergraduates	9,330	(690)
Postgraduates	1,280	(2,255)
Applications/places		15,765/3,795
Applications per place		4.2
Overall offer rate		71.7%
International students – EU		0.5%
Non-EU		0.3%

Accommodation

University provided places: 2,495
Catered £112
Self-catered: £60–£140 per week
First years guaranteed accommodation
www.edgehill.ac.uk/study/accommodation/

Where do the students come from?

State schools (non-grammar)	96.8%	Low participation areas	18.8%	Disabled	6.8%
Grammar schools	2.2%	All ethnic minorities	8.6%	Mature (over 21)	25%
Independent schools	1.1%	White working-class males	7.6%		
First generation students	55.3%	Black achievement gap	-21.5%		

Social inclusion ranking: 43

University of Edinburgh

Early intervention on mental health issues is the focus of Edinburgh's new Health and Wellbeing Centre. Opened in September 2020 near the grand McEwan Hall, the £8million centre offers health, counselling and disability services and a wellbeing lounge where students can grab a calm moment. Each student has a personal tutor, who is ready to signpost relevant services where necessary.

This ancient university, established in 1583, has many facilities with advanced technology to maintain its global edge into the future. Many of its buildings are clustered in a historic setting bordering the Old Town, but investment in improving the student experience is being pumped into all locations. A couple of miles out of the city centre at the 115-acre King's Buildings campus, the Nucleus Building is due to open in 2022–23. It will provide teaching and learning facilities including a laboratory for the College of Science and Engineering.

At the Western General Hospital campus the university has plans to extend the Institute for Genetics and Cancer, adding extra laboratories for world-leading research into cells, tissues and tumours. Edinburgh's leading research profile has helped to secure another top-20 place in the QS World University rankings. More than a quarter of undergraduates come from outside the UK and during the pandemic the university paid up to the full £1,750 for managed quarantine hotel stays for students who were coming to campus from "red list" countries.

The university has forged a strong reputation in data science. It already has the largest computing department in Europe and hosts the £79million national supercomputer, Archer2. Now, building on that expertise under the Scottish government's City Region Deal, Edinburgh is establishing five data-driven innovation hubs such as the Edinburgh Futures Institute to tackle global issues such as climate change, space exploration and food production using high-speed data analytics.

One of the hubs, the £45million Bayes Centre, is already open on the central campus and the £74million Agritech hub is planned at the Easter Bush campus, eight miles south of the city centre. The Usher Institute will apply data science to solve health and social care problems at the BioQuarter, a collaboration with public bodies.

Edinburgh completed is divestment from fossil fuel investments in early 2021 – a substantial undertaking for the university with the third-largest endowment fund of any UK institution, behind Oxbridge. It has also built a large solar farm at the Easter Bush campus, home of the Royal (Dick) School of Veterinary Studies and the Roslin Institute, to help to meet its commitment to achieve

Old College
South Bridge
Edinburgh EH8 9YL
0131 650 4360
futurestudents@ed.ac.uk
www.ed.ac.uk
www.eusa.ed.ac.uk
Open days: see website

The Times and The Sunday Times **Rankings**
Overall Ranking: 13 (last year: 17)

Teaching quality	69.6%	=120
Student experience	64.6%	114
Research quality	43.8%	10
Entry standards	187	7
Graduate prospects	79%	=23
Good honours	90.9%	9
Expected completion rate	93.3%	=17
Student/staff ratio	11.7	=6
Services and facilities	£2,466	70

net-zero carbon emissions by 2040.

Perennially popular, Edinburgh had record enrolments in the 2020 admissions cycle, surging by 15% year-on-year and up 55% in a decade. The trend is continuing, applications rose 14% at the end of March 2021 compared with the same point in 2020.

A new degree in learning in communities began in September 2021 and from 2022 the university will offer degrees in sport management, and Arabic with Islamic and Middle Eastern Studies.

Edinburgh has worked hard to lose its exclusive tag and put widening participation in the spotlight and was an early convert to contextual offers. So far, however, only one in five students are the first in their family to go to university and Edinburgh slips to the bottom of our Scottish social inclusion rankings in this edition. Outreach activities aim to raise aspirations and attainment at partner schools, and applicants in target groups may receive a contextual offer that is lower than the standard entry requirements in recognition of the hurdles many will have had to overcome.

The Access Edinburgh Scholarship provides up to £5,000 depending on circumstances and household income, to help undergraduates on their way. Financial assistance programmes are especially valued by English, Welsh or Northern Irish students facing four years of full tuition fees.

Edinburgh's sports programmes are among the best in the UK, producing past Olympic champions such as the cyclist Sir Chris Hoy and the rower Dame Katherine Grainger. The university has an outdoor centre 80 miles from Edinburgh in a beautiful setting in the southern Highlands. There is a network of student gyms in and around the city with membership packages starting at just £15 a year. Students have a choice of 65 sports clubs and can take part in the full range of fixtures from informal games to competitive tournaments.

There are 6,236 residential places reserved for undergraduates, nearly a third of which come with breakfast and evening meals included. All first-years are guaranteed a room.

Edinburgh students have enviable access to the cultural hangouts of one of the world's most exciting cities.

Tuition fees

»	Fees for Scottish students	£0–£1,820
	RUK fees	£9,250
»	Fees for International students 2022–23	£23,100–£32,100
	Medicine (clinical years)	£32,100–£49,900
	Veterinary medicine	£34,200
»	For scholarship and bursary information see www.ed.ac.uk/student-funding	
»	Graduate salary	£27,438

Student numbers

Undergraduates	22,395	(665)
Postgraduates	9,585	(2,725)
Applications/places		64,255/7,140
Applications per place		10.8
Overall offer rate		51%
International students – EU		9.3%
Non-EU		22.2%

Accommodation

University provided places: 6,236
Catered costs: £208–£217 per week
Self-catered: £90–£184 per week
First years guaranteed accommodation
www.accom.ed.ac.uk/

Where do the students come from?

State schools (non-grammar)	56.6%	Deprived areas	10.8%		
Grammar schools	6.6%	All ethnic minorities	13.1%		
Independent schools	36.8%	White working-class males	2.8%		
First generation students	20.3%	Black achievement gap	-20%		

Social inclusion ranking (Scotland): 15

Disabled	5.5%		
Mature (over 21)	7.1%		

Edinburgh Napier University

For the second year in a row, Edinburgh Napier is No 1 in the Scottish capital for student satisfaction. The results of the 2021 National Student Survey give the university the thumbs-up for its response to the pandemic and help to maintain its top position among Scotland's modern universities overall.

Edinburgh Napier's lectures are likely to continue to be live-streamed so students can access them off-campus, but the university has many applied courses for which practical experience on site will be a priority, along with small-group teaching across subjects.

Edinburgh Napier's career-driven courses are based at three campuses across the city, each with a distinct focus. Beside the 16th-century tower marking the birthplace of John Napier, the mathematician from whom the university takes its name, the Merchiston campus hosts creative arts subjects, which produced the institution's best results in the 2014 Research Excellence Framework. Screen Academy Scotland, run in partnership with Edinburgh College of Art, now part of the University of Edinburgh, also operates from the campus in trendy Bruntsfield, where facilities include soundproofed music studios and a broadcast journalism newsroom.

Computing students, also based at Merchiston, have access to the latest hardware, software and expertise through alliance schemes at the School of Computing. The 500-seat computer centre, open 24/7, has a Cyber Academy, cyberattack simulation suite and computer games laboratory.

Overlooking Edinburgh, Craiglockhart campus hosts the Business School, featuring a curved lecture theatre known as the Egg. Sighthill, 20 minutes away by tram, also has splendid views of the city. As the base for the schools of nursing, midwifery and social care, it has a large simulation and clinical skills centre with mock hospital wards and high-dependency unit. Resources for students of life, sport and social sciences include an environmental chamber and biomechanics laboratory.

Overseas, the School of Health and Social Care provides professional training and research in neonatal services in Vietnam and delivers professional training for nurses in Singapore.

Applications generally remained steady in 2021, unaffected by the withdrawal of languages programmes the previous year. Applications had edged up 4.5% by the end of March 2021 compared with the same point a year before. A new degree in music joined the curriculum in September 2021.

The university's undergraduate degree in cybersecurity and forensics was the first in the UK to be fully certified by the National Cyber Security Centre, whose parent organisation

Sighthill Court
Edinburgh EH11 4BN
0333 900 6040
ugadmissions@napier.ac.uk
www.napier.ac.uk
www.napierstudents.com
Open days:
see website

The Times and The Sunday Times Rankings
Overall Ranking: 57 (last year: 63)

Teaching quality	78.4%	17
Student experience	75%	16
Research quality	4.6%	=95
Entry standards	149	=29
Graduate prospects	76.1%	=60
Good honours	80.5%	=50
Expected completion rate	80.3%	97
Student/staff ratio	19.9	117
Services and facilities	£2,585	62

is GCHQ, the Government Communications Headquarters. Computing students can undertake a year-long work placement in their third year.

Many other courses at Edinburgh Napier include work placements of varying duration. There are opportunities for creative arts students to gain experience on projects and internships through extensive industry links, including BBC Scotland.

The university offers 11 graduate apprenticeships (known as degree apprenticeships in the rest of the UK) with 357 students enrolled on programmes in the fields of architecture, building and planning, business management, engineering, computing, and informational technology.

Edinburgh Napier's drive to increase its numbers from underrepresented groups continues with workshops and extra support for qualifying students before and during their course. Four in ten students are the first in their family to go to university and the institution regularly exceeds its benchmark on widening access.

Undergraduates from Scotland qualify for the national scheme for financial help. For students from the rest of the UK, the university offers attractive financial packages allowing students to pay tuition fees for only three years of their four-year degree course. About 83% of students from England, Wales and the island of Ireland qualify for

financial aid including bursaries up to £3,000, depending on circumstances and £1,000 merit scholarships for those who achieve at least BBB at A-level or equivalent qualifications.

All new students take the online course Consent Matters when they join the university. Those in positions of responsibility – society and sports club leaders, student representatives and resident assistants – are invited to participate in active bystander training, introduced as part of Edinburgh Napier's response to tackling sexual violence and misconduct.

Edinburgh Napier is the official training partner of four teams in Scottish Rugby's new Super6 league, as well as Cricket Scotland. The university runs an elite athlete programme to support students with funding, travel to competitions and training camps. There are 36 sports clubs for students, who use a well-equipped fitness centre and sports hall.

With 1,240 study bedrooms, the university can guarantee a space to all first-years from outside Edinburgh who apply by the deadline.

Tuition fees
» Fees for Scottish students   £0–£1,820
  RUK fees (capped at £27,750 for 4-year courses)   £9,250
» Fees for International students 2022–23   £14,170–£16,425
» For scholarship and bursary information see
  www.napier.ac.uk/study-with-us/undergraduate/
  fees-and-finance
» Graduate salary   £23,970

Student numbers

Undergraduates	9,365	(895)
Postgraduates	2,295	(1,380)
Applications/places		19,505/2,985
Applications per place		6.5
Overall offer rate		55.8%
International students – EU		10%
Non-EU		3.9%

Accommodation
University provided places: 1,240
Self-catered: £103–£179 per week
First years guaranteed accommodation
www.napier.ac.uk/study-with-us/accommodation

Where do the students come from?

State schools (non-grammar)	94.5%	Deprived areas	15.1%	Disabled	5.3%
Grammar schools	0.8%	All ethnic minorities	10.5%	Mature (over 21)	39.2%
Independent schools	4.7%	White working-class males	7.5%		
First generation students	39.7%	Black achievement gap	-2.9%		

Social inclusion ranking (Scotland): 3

University of Essex

The UK may have left the European Union, but Essex is moving firmly in the opposite direction and is one of ten universities to have formed a new alliance, the Young Universities for the Future of Europe (YUFE). The aim is to develop a new pan-European university, giving students the chance to study for a special diploma by compiling their own curriculum from all the courses offered by the alliance's partners. They include the universities of Antwerp, Maastricht, Bremen, Eastern Finland and Rijeka.

The initiative reflects the ambition of this 1960s university, where enrolments have grown by more than one third since 2014 and the number of applications has increased at almost the same rate. By 2025 it hopes to increase its student population by a third, to 20,000. It also aims to achieve a top 25 ranking in our league table, something it last managed in 2017 when it was shortlisted for our University of the Year award, although it has fallen back since and is not helped in this edition by a poor score in the most recent National Student Survey (NSS), widely regarded as a judgment on how universities have handled the pandemic.

However, an extensive programme of building and refurbishment should help student satisfaction scores in the coming years.

The iconic brutalist towers that dominate the Colchester campus are being refurbished. The new Causeway teaching centre close by has 15 teaching rooms, each with space for about 40 students. A new school of health and social care will be open at Colchester by September 2022, incorporating a therapy suite hub, a nursing skills lab, a speech and language therapy lab and two community living teaching spaces for occupational therapy students, enabling practical teaching in a realistic home environment.

At the school for sport, rehabilitation and exercise sciences, a new biomechanics lab combined with a strength and conditioning lab includes all the latest technology, while a new rehab clinic has opened in the sport centre. A £2million refurbishment of the School of Life Sciences will be complete by December 2021, extending the marine biology and aquatic sciences laboratory.

New degrees feature a foundation year or the option of a year abroad or placement year. They include a BA in curating, heritage and human rights; curating with politics; global studies with Latin American studies; history combined with drama, heritage or law; politics or linguistics with data science; global politics; and two new LLB degrees combining law with history or literature.

This fleetness of foot when it comes to refreshing the course programmes stands Essex in good stead to exploit the latest

Wivenhoe Park
Colchester CO4 3SQ
01206 873 666
admit@essex.ac.uk
www.essex.ac.uk
www.essexstudent.com
Open days: see website

The Times and The Sunday Times Rankings
Overall Ranking: 43 (last year: 40)

Teaching quality	70.7%	=117
Student experience	67.6%	=86
Research quality	37.2%	25
Entry standards	115	=96
Graduate prospects	67.6%	83
Good honours	77.6%	69
Expected completion rate	86.8%	54
Student/staff ratio	15.5	=56
Services and facilities	£4,027	3

trends in the student market and continue its expansion. Its reputation is built on its strength in the social sciences, where it is ranked in the QS global top 50 for politics and sociology.

The university achieved the best results in the 2014 Research Excellence Framework in politics and was in the top ten for economics and art history. Essex ranks in the top 25 in our research ranking, with almost 80% of its large submission rated world-leading or internationally excellent. Essex took gold in the Teaching Excellence Framework.

The student development team works with employers of all sizes to help students gain career insights, work experience and commercial awareness. An EmployerLink service connects students and graduates to employers, although the university has slipped in our graduate prospects ranking with around two-thirds of graduates being in high-skilled jobs or postgraduate study 15 months after leaving.

Essex allocates mental health advisers to students throughout their studies and it is one of a small number of universities to provide mandatory Moodle courses and flat meetings for students when they join covering consent and alcohol and drug abuse. Bystander intervention workshops are made available throughout the academic year.

The £12million Essex Sport Arena has seating for 1,655 spectators and is home to the university's professional basketball teams, the Essex Rebels. The 40-acre sports area also includes an 18-hole frisbee-golf course, all-weather tennis courts and room for five-a-side futsal.

Essex's student population is unusually diverse for a pre-1992 university and it climbs 18 places in our social inclusion ranking. About 44% of students are drawn from ethnic minorities and almost half are first-generation students. One in seven come from areas that send the fewest children into higher education.

Away from Colchester, the university has outposts in Southend-on-Sea and Loughton. The modern seaside campus offers courses in business, health and the arts, and its accommodation complex houses a gym and fitness studio. A new nursing lab is planned and further new facilities will add more than 100 additional teaching spaces for students. The East 15 Acting School has a theatre in Southend and another campus in Loughton.

Tuition fees

»	Fees for UK students	£9,250
»	Fees for International students 2022–23	£17,700–£20,650
»	For scholarship and bursary information see www1.essex.ac.uk/student/money	
»	Graduate salary	£24,000

Student numbers

Undergraduates	12,400	(506)
Postgraduates	2,345	(1,280)
Applications/places		18,345/3,375
Applications per place		5.4
Overall offer rate		71.1%
International students – EU		14.3%
Non-EU		13.7%

Accommodation
University provided places: 5,321
Self-catered: £105–£153 per week
First years guaranteed accommodation
www.essex.ac.uk/life/accommodation

Where do the students come from?

State schools (non-grammar)	91.2%	Low participation areas	13.9%	Disabled	4.7%
Grammar schools	4.9%	All ethnic minorities	43.8%	Mature (over 21)	17.5%
Independent schools	3.9%	White working-class males	5.6%		
First generation students	46.9%	Black achievement gap	-15.6%		

Social inclusion ranking: =54

University of Exeter

Exeter was the first university to offer students cash to defer entry to 2022 as its medical school grappled with the potential for over-recruitment in July 2021. A £10,000 bursary and a free year of accommodation attracted widespread headlines, but within days oversubscribed medical schools across the country had launched similar schemes encouraging students to move to those with vacancies or to defer entry.

Such measures illustrate the difficulties that many popular universities have faced in the past two summers as teacher-assessed grades have swollen the number of top A-levels. The number of accepted applicants in 2020 hit 8,200, almost double the 4,220 admitted in 2011 and 19% up on 2019.

A further £20million is being spent on improving and refurbishing facilities across the Streatham campus, much of it on the Harrison building to upgrade the delivery of engineering courses. Money is also being invested in Exeter's Cornwall campuses, notably Penryn, shared with Falmouth University, where facilities for the college of life and environmental sciences, the college of engineering, mathematics and physical sciences, and the business school will benefit from an investment of nearly £12million.

Penryn is home to the newly opened Renewable Energy Engineering Facility (Reef), which provides specialist teaching facilities for the design, building and testing of renewable projects.

The need for more accommodation will be met in large part with the completion of 1,500 new student bedrooms in the East Park, Moberly and Spreytonway developments on the Streatham campus, bringing the stock to nearly 6,000 rooms in Exeter, with a further 765 at Penryn.

A continuing £72million investment in IT infrastructure has proved to be well-timed with the pandemic-enforced shift to online learning. The university is preparing to resume more face-to-face learning.

Exeter (like many) suffered a heavy reverse in the 2021 National Student Survey (NSS), which has hit rankings for teaching quality and student experience, down 10 and 15 places respectively, after students were more critical than most about the university's pandemic efforts.

The university has climbed two places in our social inclusion ranking to stand 109th out of 116 institutions and is working to diversify its intake, barely half of whom at present come from non-selective state schools. One in six entrants in 2020 received a contextual offer and that is expected to rise after tweaking the eligibility criteria. Now, all state school-educated applicants living in postcodes among the 40% sending fewest children to

Northcote House
The Queen's Drive
Exeter EX4 4QJ
0300 555 6060
www.exeter.ac.uk/enquiry
www.exeter.ac.uk
www.exeterguild.org
Open days: see website

The Times and *The Sunday Times* Rankings
Overall Ranking: 21 (last year: 12)

Teaching quality	72.6%	94
Student experience	70.1%	59
Research quality	38%	18
Entry standards	156	23
Graduate prospects	77.4%	=28
Good honours	88.9%	12
Expected completion rate	94.5%	11
Student/staff ratio	15.1	=49
Services and facilities	£2,688	53

university, or those from state schools or colleges with more than 450 pupils living in the most deprived 40% of districts (even if the applicants don't live in those areas), will be eligible for a contextual offer, typically one A-level grade below the standard offer. A contextual offer to study medicine can come down to ABB at A-level.

There is also a generous bursary and scholarship scheme, topped by the Access to Exeter bursary worth £2,100 in the first year and £1,550 in the second year for students from homes with income below £16,000 per year, or worth £1,050 across both years where income is below £25,000.

Exeter was awarded gold in the Teaching Excellence Framework, attracting praise for "optimum" contact hours and class sizes and for involving business, industry and professional experts in its teaching.

Exeter recorded much-improved results in the 2014 Research Excellence Framework. More than 80% of its large submission was rated world-leading or internationally excellent, with the best results in clinical medicine, psychology and education.

Four new degrees are planned for 2022. They include a MSci in human sciences, a combined honours degree in Arabic and politics, a joint English and history degree, and a dual English and Chinese law degree offered with the Chinese University of Hong Kong, a four-year course that offers admission to practice in both territories. Unlike many Russell Group universities, Exeter has embraced degree apprenticeships, with 1,340 students following one of six undergraduate and nine postgraduate programmes.

The main Streatham campus, close to the centre of Exeter, has an attractive green hillside setting. Most students are based there, served by the £48million Forum building, which features an extended library, student services centre, technology-rich learning areas and auditorium.

The nearby St Luke's campus houses the medical school, which also has a health education and research centre at the Royal Devon and Exeter Hospital and a smaller base in Truro, Cornwall. The Graduate School of Education and the sport and health sciences school are also based at St Luke's.

More than £12million has been invested in sports facilities in recent years, providing some of the best in the country. The Sports Park on the main campus includes a 200-station gym, while Penryn offers sailing and surfing in one of the best locations in the UK.

Tuition fees

» Fees for UK students £9,250
» Fees for International students 2022–23 £19,500–£25,000
  Medicine £38,500
» For scholarship and bursary information see www.exeter.ac.uk/undergraduate/fees/
» Graduate salary £25,000

Student numbers

Undergraduates	19,875	(445)
Postgraduates	4,545	(2,070)
Applications/places		38,385/6,925
Applications per place		5.5
Overall offer rate		87.5%
International students – EU		5.6%
Non-EU		16.8%

Accommodation

University provided places: 6,654
Catered costs: £159–£269 per week
Self-catered: £110–£181 per week
First years guaranteed accommodation
www.exeter.ac.uk/accommodation

Where do the students come from?

State schools (non-grammar)	52.8%	Low participation areas	6.3%	**Social inclusion ranking: 109**	
Grammar schools	11.8%	All ethnic minorities	10.7%	Disabled	7.8%
Independent schools	35.5%	White working-class males	3.6%	Mature (over 21)	7.1%
First generation students	26.3%	Black achievement gap	-13.4%		

Falmouth University

Student feedback inspired the design of a new social space at Falmouth University's Penryn campus. Positioned for show stopping views down the Penryn River, the building was constructed with sustainably sourced materials and opened at the beginning of the 2021–22 academic year, providing an informal, comfortable workspace as well as a bar and café.

Feedback has also guided Falmouth's plans for post-pandemic blended learning. The intention is to continue to record lectures but to use digital advances mainly to support predominantly in-person teaching. Students gave online assessment the thumbs-up, but the university's creative arts bias and "maker culture" favours a return to campus, with access to specialist facilities.

Originally the Falmouth School of Art, founded in 1902, the university has grown into a specialist art institution with a much broader remit. Courses cover film, performance, business entrepreneurship and marketing, journalism, game development and architecture – as well as a wide range of art and design options. Collaboration between creative disciplines is part of the Falmouth experience.

Of seven new degrees added in 2021 – including post-production and visual effects, marketing communications, fashion styling and art direction, computer science, and game

development: production – two are delivered online: creative writing and visual communications. Certificate of Higher Education (level 4) courses have begun in music, popular music and creative music technology. From 2022, Falmouth will also introduce degrees in architectural design and technology, esports, interior design (online) and an integrated foundation year.

Subtropical gardens and light-filled creative spaces distinguish the campus, near the town centre and a short walk from the popular Gyllyngvase beach. The photography department has an in-house photo agency which takes on live industry projects.

The Penryn campus, shared with the University of Exeter, has been developed over the past 17 years to consolidate £100million facilities. Performing arts students have access to exceptional facilities at the Academy of Music and Theatre Arts at Penryn, such as a cinema, motion-capture studio, video-editing suites and specialist animation software, fully sprung dancefloors, rehearsal studios and theatre space. It hosts student and visiting productions.

Awarded gold in the Teaching Excellence Framework, Falmouth impressed assessors with students' personalised learning, partly through individual timetabling and a "data-driven approach to monitoring contact and teaching patterns". The panel also praised the university for stretching students and ensuring that they acquire the knowledge, skills and understanding

Woodlane
Falmouth TR11 4RH
01326 254 350
futurestudies@falmouth.ac.uk
www.falmouth.ac.uk
www.thesu.org.uk
Open days: see website

The Times and The Sunday Times Rankings
Overall Ranking: 87 (last year: =94)

Teaching quality	76.6%	=38
Student experience	69%	74
Research quality	4.6%	=95
Entry standards	123	=67
Graduate prospects	54.5%	=128
Good honours	76.5%	=79
Expected completion rate	84.6%	=63
Student/staff ratio	15.3	=54
Services and facilities	£2,042	103

most highly valued by employers.

"Doing it for real" is Falmouth's ethos. The university interviews all applicants and asks them to prove their potential via a portfolio, performance or pitch. All students have opportunities to work on real projects or live briefs in collaboration with industry partners. However, in common with most arts universities, Falmouth appears near the bottom of our graduate prospects ranking with barely half its students in high-skilled jobs or postgraduate study within 15 months of graduating.

Between 35 and 45% of students qualify for financial aid. Those from low-income households are awarded a bursary from £250 to £500 and there is further assistance for those with dependants. For Real is a scheme to help with travel and accommodation costs for trips off campus, and the Falmouth Edge Awards drive creativity with a financial incentive for exceptional projects. International students can apply for talent scholarships for a discount of £2,000 off first-year tuition fees.

Raising Aspirations, an outreach programme in schools and colleges in areas of high deprivation and low progression rates to higher education, began in September 2021. It focuses on helping pupils to overcome lost learning and reduced support during the pandemic, offering guidance, masterclasses and mock interviews.

Falmouth's best results in the Research Excellence Framework in 2014 were from music, dance, drama and the performing arts, with a third of its work rated world-leading or internationally excellent. Almost a quarter of its art and design submission was also placed in the top two categories.

The sports centre on the Penryn campus has a four-court sports hall, fitness studio and gym, as well as multi-use pitches and outdoor gym. Spinning, yoga and Zumba are some of the classes offered. Watersports on the Cornish coast are a huge part of the Falmouth student experience and part-time jobs in the tourist trade help with living costs. Accommodation is guaranteed to first-years.

Listed in the *Sunday Times* Best Places to Live in 2019, buzzing Falmouth was described as being "as close as Britain gets to the California/Barcelona city-by-the-sea lifestyle". Beerwolf Books Freehouse has the twin appeal of beer and books and there are plenty of other lively venues. It even has its own (self-styled) royalty: the comedian and actress Dawn French, a resident of Cornwall, likes to be known as the Queen of Falmouth University.

Tuition fees

»	Fees for UK students	£9,250
	for 2-year courses	£11,100
»	Fees for International students 2022–23	£17,460
	for 2-year courses	£19,570
»	For scholarship and bursary information see www.falmouth.ac.uk/study/tuition-fees	
»	Graduate salary	£19,250

Student numbers

Undergraduates	5,475	(25)
Postgraduates	175	(570)
Applications/places	5,780/1,740	
Applications per place	3.3	
Overall offer rate	64%	
International students – EU	7.9%	
Non-EU	3.1%	

Accommodation

University provided places: 2,323
Catered costs: £159–£198
Self-catered: £116–£186 per week
First years guaranteed accommodation
www.falmouth.ac.uk/accommodation

Where do the students come from?

State schools (non-grammar)	91.3%	Low participation areas	9.5%	**Social inclusion ranking: 93**		
Grammar schools	2.1%	Ethnic minorities	6.4%	Disabled	10.9%
Independent schools	6.6%	White working-class males	5.7%	Mature (over 21)	18.1%
First generation students	33.3%	Black achievement gap	-25.8%		

University of Glasgow

A £1billion ten-year development programme is underway to create "a campus fit for today and the future" at Glasgow, our Scottish University of the Year. The institution, founded in 1451, must make room for more students, with record enrolments in 2020, up 20% to nearly 6,500 undergraduates. Student numbers have soared by 57% over the past decade and applications have risen by one third to reach almost 36,500 in 2020.

The curriculum is expanding to match. In September 2021 new degrees began in finance and materials chemistry, while design and technology education replaced a withdrawn course in technological education. Students enjoy the flexibility of Glasgow's degrees in the broad areas of arts, social sciences and science, which allow them to study several subjects before choosing a specialism of one or two.

Glasgow emerges from the pandemic with student satisfaction levels just outside the top 20 in the UK, according to a comparison between scores in the 2021 National Student Survey and the outcomes a year before. The results indicate that students felt their university coped well with the teaching challenges caused by Covid-19.

Before the pandemic, Glasgow was already using pre-recorded materials in some courses. While large group lectures have worked well online, students also enjoy meeting in person for small group sessions. The university has committed to more blended learning so campus activities can focus on collaborative and interactive learning, especially for clinical and other laboratory and practical skills.

There is extra room for the growing student community in the £90.6million James McCune Smith Learning Hub, which combines flexible study and social learning areas with interactive teaching spaces for up to 500 students.

Next on the horizon is the £113million Advanced Research Centre, designed to be the creative and collaborative heart of Glasgow's Western campus. It will explore five themes: creative economies and cultural transformation, digital chemistry, international development, quantum and nanotechnology, and technology touching life.

One of only two Russell Group universities in Scotland, Glasgow secured a top-100 spot in the latest QS world rankings. It reached the top ten in the UK in 18 subjects in the most recent Research Excellence Framework, with best results in architecture, agriculture, veterinary science and chemistry. More than a quarter of undergraduates are from outside the UK and Glasgow has a branch campus in Singapore and a joint graduate school with Nankai University in northeastern China.

University Avenue, Glasgow G12 8QQ
0141 330 2000
studentenquiries@gcu.ac.uk
student.recruitment
@glasgow.ac.uk
www.glasgow.ac.uk
www.guu.co.uk
Open days: see website

GLASGOW
Edinburgh
Belfast
London
Cardiff

The Times and The Sunday Times Rankings
Overall Ranking: 12 (last year: 14)

Teaching quality	76.3%	=46
Student experience	74.2%	24
Research quality	39.9%	12
Entry standards	202	3
Graduate prospects	75.7%	=36
Good honours	86.9%	19
Expected completion rate	88.2%	=46
Student/staff ratio	13.1	=14
Services and facilities	£2,843	38

Glasgow has a proud history of innovation – the first to have a school of engineering and the first in Scotland to have a computer. Its gothic revival buildings on the Gilmorehill campus are a landmark in the city's fashionable West End, where the university has been based since 1871.

The spacious Garscube campus, four miles from Gilmorehill in the northwest of the city, hosts the veterinary school and outdoor sports pitches. Liberal arts and teaching courses are delivered in Dumfries, where more than £13million has been spent on better sporting and social facilities.

Glasgow's School of Culture and Creative Arts is Scotland's leading centre for music research and there are opportunities for student placements within the city's legendary music scene.

The university's only graduate apprenticeship is a four-year programme in software engineering designed with local employers to create a talent pipeline with skills tailored to industry needs. An internship hub connects small and medium-sized enterprises (SMEs) with motivated, proactive interns, many of whom find jobs.

Students from the rest of the UK will find their fourth-year tuition fees waived on most degree courses. There are access bursaries of £1,000 to £3,000 per year for students from England, Wales and Northern Ireland from low-income households.

Extensive scholarships target different disciplines and student cohorts. Some entrants on pre-entry programmes designed to widen participation are made lower offers, and grade adjustments are extended to students who have been in care or are carers, who have refugee status or are estranged from their family. However, most Glasgow students (74%) come from families with a history of university education and two in ten come from selective and/or independent schools. Glasgow is 13th of 15 Scottish universities in our social inclusion ranking.

There are more than 3,400 residential places, enough to guarantee accommodation for new undergraduates. Glasgow's sports union supports more than 50 clubs and activities and there are purpose-built sports facilities on the Gilmorehill and Garscube campuses. Scotland's biggest metropolis was crowned the world's friendliest and most affordable city by *Time Out* in 2019. It was also the first in the UK to be named a UNESCO City of Music.

Tuition fees

» Fees for Scottish students   £0–£1,820
RUK fees £9,250 (capped at £27,750 for 4-year courses. Cap does not apply to Medicine, Dentistry or Veterinary Surgery.)
» Fees for International students 2022–23   £20,400–£23,950
Medicine £52,000 (clinical years); Dentistry £46,950; Veterinary £32,500
» For scholarship and bursary information see https://www.gla.ac.uk/undergraduate/fees/
» Graduate salary   £25,500

Student numbers

Undergraduates	18,555	(2,615)
Postgraduates	8,730	(2,565)
Applications/places	36,455/5,330	
Applications per place	6.8	
Overall offer rate	60.5%	
International students – EU	10.4%	
Non-EU	10.4%	

Accommodation

University provided places: 3,407
Catered costs: £168–£186 per week
Self-catered: £128–£243 per week
First years guaranteed accommodation
www.gla.ac.uk/undergraduate/accommodation/

Where do the students come from?

State schools (non-grammar)	80.1%	Deprived areas	13.5%	Disabled	3.1%
Grammar schools	5.3%	All ethnic minorities	11.9%	Mature (over 21)	15.6%
Independent schools	14.5%	White working-class males	4.5%		
First generation students	25.9%	Black achievement gap	-13%		

Social inclusion ranking (Scotland): 13

Glasgow Caledonian University

A scheme to compensate for the impact of the pandemic on graduate opportunities has been so popular that Glasgow Caledonian University (GCU) has decided to make it a permanent fixture. The MINT (mentoring, internships, networking and talks) scheme surpassed expectations for participation and graduate outcomes after it was introduced in 2020, backed by honorary graduates and alumni such as the footballing legend Sir Alex Ferguson and Martin Compston, the *Call of Duty* actor.

With a strong performance in our analysis of the first two Graduate Outcomes surveys – 62nd in 2020 and =39th in 2021 – GCU will be hopeful that MINT can shield its former students from the downturn in the graduate jobs market.

GCU's stated mission is to be a "university for the common good" and its new 2030 strategy sets out a vision to be a world leader in social innovation. It is already among the top universities in the UK for social inclusion, ranking fifth among Scotland's 15 universities in 2021. In the 2020 admissions round, GCU recruited almost 23% of first-years from areas with the lowest participation rates in higher education, and had the 13th highest proportion of white working-class male students – one of the most underrepresented demographics.

Outreach initiatives target local communities and schools with a low progression rate to university, providing campus visits, skills training, careers guidance and taster days. The university's success on completion rates – with a projected dropout rate of 8.3%, below the 9.7% expected – shows that the academic, social and financial support for those at risk of giving up is bearing fruit.

GCU was the first university to be named a cycle-friendly campus by Cycle Scotland and is also a platinum award-winning eco campus. It was the top UK university for promoting gender equality according to the 2021 THE Impact rankings, which measures the success of the global higher education sector against United Nations Sustainable Development Goals.

Under the Going Digital banner, GCU has implemented digital learning across all courses. Blended learning at GCU means capitalising on new technologies to boost engagement and flexibility for students to learn off-campus. Separately it has introduced a new evaluation feature online to allow module leaders to respond to feedback as part of a drive to improve the student experience.

The Glasgow campus occupies a single site, where the centrepiece of a £32million redevelopment is the Heart of Glass building. Fashion courses are a flagship programme

Cowcaddens Road
Glasgow G4 0BA
0141 331 8630
admissions@gcu.ac.uk
www.gcu.ac.uk
www.gcustudents.co.uk
Open days:
see website

GLASGOW
Edinburgh
Belfast
London
Cardiff

The Times and The Sunday Times **Rankings**

Overall Ranking: 60 (last year: 75)

Teaching quality	74.8%	=68
Student experience	72.5%	36
Research quality	7%	=77
Entry standards	165	17
Graduate prospects	75.3%	=39
Good honours	84%	32
Expected completion rate	85.1%	60
Student/staff ratio	22.3	128
Services and facilities	£2,006	106

and GCU's British School of Fashion has had partnerships with companies including Marks & Spencer, which has a design studio at the London campus and funds scholarships. The university's purpose-built studio in Glasgow, the Fashion Factory, has industry-standard machinery for designing and making clothing.

GCU is also one of the largest providers of graduates to the NHS in Scotland and its facilities include a virtual hospital. It trains 90% of the country's eyecare specialists and is the only university offering optometry degrees.

Health was one of GCU's strengths in the 2014 Research Excellence Framework, when half its submission was rated in the top two categories. GCU was in the top 20 in the UK for allied health research and did well in social work and social policy, and the built environment.

GCU was the first Scottish university to open a campus in London, where postgraduate fashion students are based in trendy Spitalfields. Across the Atlantic in New York's SoHo, it was the first foreign university to be granted a charter to award its own degrees in fashion and business. GCU has helped to set up the African Leadership College in Mauritius, where the first students embarked on GCU degrees in 2017. It also co-founded the Grameen Caledonian College of Nursing in Bangladesh, and has links with institutions in Oman, China, India and South America.

The School of Engineering and Built Environment teaches three-quarters of Scotland's part-time construction students and the Glasgow School for Business and Society offers highly specialised degrees, having pioneered subjects such as entrepreneurial studies and risk management. It welcomed its first cohort of economic policy undergraduates in September 2021. A new degree in artificial intelligence and data sciences will begin in 2022.

Scotland's leading graduate apprenticeship provider (known as degree apprenticeships south of the border), GCU offers seven programmes and expects to have more than 700 learners by September 2022. Subject areas include business management, civil engineering and cybersecurity.

Student facilities include the Arc sports centre and 24-hour computer labs. There are only 654 residential places, with priority given to international or disabled students, and those under 19. The historic West End's red brick flats are popular for off-campus student living. Known for its friendliness and culture, Scotland's largest city has five universities and undergraduates thrive there.

Tuition fees

»	Fees for Scottish students	£0–£1,820
	RUK fees (capped at £27,750 for 4-year courses)	£9,250
»	Fees for International students 2022–23	£13,000
»	For scholarship and bursary information see www.gcu.ac.uk/study/tuitionfees/	
»	Graduate salary	£24,000

Student numbers

Undergraduates	12,185	(1,980)
Postgraduates	2,025	(1,350)
Applications/places	20,885/3,570	
Applications per place	5.9	
Overall offer rate	54.5%	
International students – EU	5%	
Non-EU	2.6%	

Accommodation

University provided places: 654
Self-catered: £100–£118 per week
www.gcu.ac.uk/study/undergraduate/accommodation/

Where do the students come from?

State schools (non-grammar)	96%	Deprived areas	22.5%	Disabled	2.4%
Grammar schools	0.4%	All ethnic minorities	13.5%	Mature (over 21)	38.8%
Independent schools	3.7%	White working-class males	8.7%		
First generation students	43.9%	Black achievement gap	-32%		

Social inclusion ranking (Scotland): 5

University of Gloucestershire

The decline of the British high street has opened up an opportunity for the University of Gloucestershire: it has bought the former Debenhams department store in Gloucester to convert it into a city campus. The first phase will open by September 2023 and the landmark 1930s building will eventually provide 20,000 square metres of space on five floors to accommodate an expanding course offering.

A far-reaching review of the curriculum resulted in the introduction of eight new degree options in September 2021, with 18 to follow in 2022. New courses for 2021 included architecture, games art and biomedical science, as well as sport coaching science. Degrees in politics, education with psychology, conservation biology, quantity surveying and occupational therapy are among the later additions.

The university also has plans to expand its portfolio of degree apprenticeships, boosting the range by half – to include social work, engineering, education, project management and finance – and bumping up apprentice numbers from 600 to 1,000 in 2022.

So far there are three campuses in Cheltenham and another in Gloucester, seven miles away. The main Park campus, a mile from the centre of Cheltenham, houses the business, education and professional studies faculty. Art and design facilities are closer to the town centre at Francis Close Hall. Hardwick, nearby, has photography and fine art studios as well as its own gallery. Facilities at the Cheltenham sites have been upgraded, with a new biomedical laboratory as well as an architecture studio and community teaching space. The purpose-built Oxstalls campus in the centre of Gloucester caters for business, healthcare, sport and exercise sciences.

Located on the edge of the Cotswolds, designated an Area of Outstanding Natural Beauty, the university has a long record of championing green issues. It won first place for sustainability in the most recent People & Planet UK university league, in 2019, and has done away with a printed prospectus, now published only online.

For teaching and learning, however, the university has a preference for in-person rather than online delivery. Responding to student feedback, Gloucestershire has promised to give face-to-face teaching priority wherever possible and will use digital methods only if they offer a better learning experience. Lecture-capture and audio recordings are uploaded to a virtual platform for flexible access.

This approach helped Gloucestershire to achieve 61st place in our analysis of the pandemic-influenced 2021 National Student

The Park
Cheltenham GL50 2RH
03330 141 414
admissions@glos.ac.uk
www.glos.ac.uk
www.uogsu.com
Open days: see website

Edinburgh
Belfast
CHELTENHAM
Cardiff
London

***The Times* and *The Sunday Times* Rankings**

Overall Ranking: =96 (last year: 109)

Teaching quality	75.8%	=53
Student experience	69.9%	=62
Research quality	3.8%	=108
Entry standards	117	=85
Graduate prospects	63.4%	106
Good honours	75.8%	=88
Expected completion rate	80.8%	96
Student/staff ratio	17.3	=91
Services and facilities	£1,930	111

Survey outcomes compared with the results from 2020, a creditable performance when many universities found their scores much more severely affected.

Gloucestershire became a university in 2001, having begun as a teacher-training college. Its primary and secondary teacher-training courses are rated "outstanding" by Ofsted. It was awarded silver in the Teaching Excellence Framework for its integrated approach to enhancing employability through volunteering and placements. Relationships with businesses such as Waitrose and the financial advisers St James's Place oil the wheels for student placements and projects.

The university offers diplomas in environmentalism, sustainability research and development projects that bring together researchers from around the world, undertaking work for agencies such as UNESCO. Its Countryside and Community Research Institute on the Oxstalls campus is the largest rural research centre in the UK and produced Gloucestershire's best results in the 2014 Research Excellence Framework. Only 20% of eligible staff took part and overall 44% of the university's submission was rated as world-leading or internationally excellent.

About half of each new cohort of undergraduates qualifies for some form of financial aid, from a work experience bursary (£300 to £1,000) to sports scholarships or the academic merit scholarship. The latter is worth £400 a year and is awarded to between 500 and 650 new students who achieve 128 UCAS tariff points or better, equivalent to at least ABB at A-level. Gloucestershire is one of the more socially diverse universities, ranking in the top 40 in our social inclusion ranking in 2020 and 2021.

A strong sporting tradition is supported by extensive facilities at Oxstalls Sports Park and in Cheltenham. Students have the run of an indoor and outdoor tennis centre, playing fields, international-standard 3G pitches for rugby and football, fitness suites, a sports hall and cricket pavilion. Sports scholarships are offered each year. The university's sporting alumni include Lizzie Yarnold, double Olympic skeleton gold medallist, and Ruaridh McConnochie, the former England rugby international.

All first-years are guaranteed housing in university halls or managed accommodation. The spa town of Cheltenham has plenty of nightlife within an attractive setting and the university supports local music festivals including Wychwood and 2000Trees.

Tuition fees

» Fees for UK students	£9,250
» Fees for International students 2022–23	£15,000
» For scholarship and bursary information see www.glos.ac.uk/finance/fees-and-loans	
» Graduate salary	£21,000

Student numbers

Undergraduates	6,040	(345)
Postgraduates	650	(885)
Applications/places	8,020/2,000	
Applications per place	4	
Overall offer rate	80.7%	
International students – EU	1.7%	
Non-EU	3.4%	

Accommodation

University provided places: 1,685
Self-catered: £115–£203 per week
First years guaranteed accommodation
www.glos.ac.uk/accommodation

Where do the students come from?

State schools (non-grammar)	92.4%	Low participation areas	13.4%	Disabled	11%
Grammar schools	4.5%	All ethnic minorities	9.7%	Mature (over 21)	28.9%
Independent schools	3.2%	White working-class males	7.4%		
First generation students	47.1%	Black achievement gap	-19.2%		

Social inclusion ranking: =33

Goldsmiths, University of London

Among Goldsmiths' celebrated alumni is Bernardine Evaristo, whose novel *Girl, Woman, Other* shared the Booker prize in 2019. The novelist graduated with a PhD in creative writing from Goldsmiths in 2013. The university's Department of English and Comparative Literature swapped the latter part of its title for "Creative Writing" in 2020, to better reflect its expertise. It houses a dedicated Writers' Centre and offers a sought-after undergraduate degree in English and creative writing, as well as postgraduate courses.

Based in New Cross, in southeast London, Goldsmiths has all undergraduate teaching and support on one site. Some of the capital's best facilities help to cement its position as one of the leading universities in the world for the creative arts. The recently opened Goldsmiths Centre for Contemporary Art is housed in the grade II listed former water tanks for the Laurie Grove public baths. The university's £2.9million performance studios and 200-seat theatre are used by the public as well as students.

Dedicated studio space is set aside for all design students, and the university has its own yarn store along with nine specialist research laboratories. There are radio and television studios for media and communications students, who also have access to digital video and audio editing hardware and software. Studios provide industry-standard equipment for those studying Goldsmiths' range of music degrees.

In the QS World University Rankings by subject, published in 2021, Goldsmiths ranks 15th in the world for art and design and in the top 50 for the performing arts. Its international stature is further bolstered by its roll call of alumni, from Mary Quant in the 1950s to numerous Turner prize winners, including Damien Hirst and *12 Years a Slave* director Steve McQueen.

Goldsmiths' degree portfolio extends beyond the creative arts, to include management, economics, politics and computing. The suite of law courses is expanding with the September 2021 addition of degrees in law with politics and human rights, and law with criminal justice and human rights. Other additions include promotional media; social and community work; music with a foundation year; history with military history, global history or public history; and a graduate diploma in art.

In the Teaching Excellence Framework (TEF) Goldsmiths managed only bronze, its accreditation dragged down by poor student satisfaction, a common problem in London, and low levels of graduate employment, which is often a challenge for arts-dominated institutions. The TEF panel acknowledged its high-quality resources and

New Cross
London SE14 6NW
020 7078 5300
Course-info@gold.ac.uk
www.gold.ac.uk
www.goldsmithssu.org
Open days: see website

The Times and The Sunday Times **Rankings**

Overall Ranking: 61 (last year: 97)		
Teaching quality	67.4%	126
Student experience	57.7%	128
Research quality	33.4%	36
Entry standards	127	=58
Graduate prospects	61.3%	=116
Good honours	82.7%	38
Expected completion rate	79.1%	105
Student/staff ratio	14.3	=33
Services and facilities	£3,120	25

said students benefited by connecting with local communities.

Last year, in our two rankings derived from the National Student Survey (NSS), Goldsmiths finished bottom for teaching quality and student experience, dragging down its overall ranking in our academic table. However, its students spared it from harsh judgment for its handling of the pandemic with scores for the 2021 NSS faring better than most other universities when compared with 2020 outcomes. Goldsmiths finished fifth bottom for teaching quality and third bottom for student experience, modest but significant improvements in such a tough year.

The university did well in the 2014 Research Excellence Framework: 70% of its submission was judged world-leading or internationally excellent, with the best results in communication and media studies. The entire submission in music had world-leading impact.

Actions to address the climate emergency and become carbon neutral by 2025 are continuing among staff and students. Beef products have long been off the menu, single-use plastic bottles and cups incur a 10p levy and in the past year the university managed to recycle 50% of its waste.

Goldsmiths does well in our social inclusion index also, once again ranking in the top 30 in England and Wales. Nine out of ten students arrive from non-selective state schools and almost half are from ethnic minority backgrounds. Students who enter via schemes to widen access are guaranteed conditional offers, and there are scholarships for students from low-participation neighbourhoods.

The Alchemy Project applies Goldsmiths' creativity to outreach initiatives. The ten-week course is for Year 9 to 11 students who are at risk of exclusion from education as a result of challenges at school, at home and on the street, providing them with expert music tuition at Goldsmiths alongside weekly one-to-one mentoring from students in the Social, Therapeutic and Community Studies department. The Alchemy cohort produces a digital mixtape of original music and live performance.

The campus is ten minutes by train from central London, although the immediate area has more fashionable enclaves such as Peckham, known for its artistic atmosphere and rooftop bars.

The university owns or endorses nearly 1,400 study bedrooms, most local and none further than a 30-minute commute. First-years are prioritised and international students who apply by the deadline are guaranteed a space.

Tuition fees

» Fees for UK students	£9,250
» Fees for International students 2022–23	£17,050–£23,870
» For scholarship and bursary information see www.gold.ac.uk/ug/fees-funding/	
» Graduate salary	£24,000

Student numbers

Undergraduates	6,330	(170)
Postgraduates	2,460	(1,130)
Applications/places	11,350/1,690	
Applications per place	6.7	
Overall offer rate	68.3%	
International students – EU	7.7%	
Non-EU	13.4%	

Accommodation

University provided places: 1,396
Self-catered: £149–£317 per week
www.gold.ac.uk/accommodation/

Where do the students come from?

State schools (non-grammar)	89.6%	Low participation areas	5.3%	Disabled	9.8%
Grammar schools	3.5%	All ethnic minorities	48.8%	Mature (over 21)	22%
Independent schools	6.9%	White working-class males	4.4%		
First generation students	45.5%	Black achievement gap	-19.7%		

Social inclusion ranking: 28

University of Greenwich

Student nurses, midwives and paramedics can train for real-life emergencies using augmented-reality technology and lifelike manikins in simulated hospital wards and consulting rooms after the redevelopment of facilities at Avery Hill, one of three campuses at the University of Greenwich. Three manikins were specially built for the university and the most complex – Lucina – blinks, breathes, has radial pulses and can even give birth.

The makeover of the Victorian mansion on the outskirts of southeast London has added three clinical skills laboratories and a new library. The facilities help to prepare healthcare students for a seamless transition to work placements in the NHS and the technology to livestream simulations is useful for debriefing and will guard against loss of learning if there are further Covid-19 lockdowns.

While many universities scrambled to get digital learning provision up to speed at the onset of the pandemic, Greenwich already had lecture-capture facilities. This allows students to listen back remotely – even if they have attended the lecture in person. Greenwich is determined to use remote learning to complement – rather than replace – face-to-face contact, especially if keeping larger lectures online enables more in-person, small group teaching on campus. Students appear to approve: Greenwich has done well to reach the top 40 in our comparison of the 2021 National Student Survey outcomes with scores from 2020.

Greenwich was awarded silver in the Teaching Excellence Framework for investing in high-quality physical and digital resources to enhance learning. Assessors also praised course design and assessment practices that stretch students.

The university's historic Dreadnought building at the Greenwich campus, which occupies a World Heritage site overlooking the Thames, completed a £23million refurbishment in 2018 that brought many services together under one roof, including the students' union, a bar, student and academic services, a gym, media suite, radio station and flexible teaching spaces.

The prizewinning Stockwell Street development, also in Greenwich, was designed partly by the university's specialists in architecture and has a landscaped roof terrace, large architecture studio, model-making workshop, and television and sound studios as well as the main library and other facilities.

At Chatham, in Kent, Greenwich shares the Medway campus with the University of Kent. The schools of pharmacy, science and engineering are based there as are nursing and some business students. The historic dockyard buildings house a student hub with study spaces as well as a restaurant, bar and nightclub.

The university's Natural Resources

Maritime Greenwich Campus
Old Royal Naval College
Park Row
London SE10 9LS
020 8331 9000
courseinfo@gre.ac.uk
www.gre.ac.uk
www.greenwichsu.co.uk
Open days: see website

The Times and The Sunday Times Rankings		
Overall Ranking: =89 (last year: 98)		
Teaching quality	74.9%	=64
Student experience	70%	=60
Research quality	4.9%	=93
Entry standards	114	=99
Graduate prospects	71%	=64
Good honours	79.5%	55
Expected completion rate	81.7%	=87
Student/staff ratio	18.5	=106
Services and facilities	£2,116	101

Institute at Medway was awarded a Queen's Anniversary Prize in 2019 for its work in developing smart solutions to tackle pests that cause plague, famine and disease.

Degrees in climate change, urban design and operation department practice are new to the curriculum as are two Elevate programmes – a bachelor's degree in management and leadership, and a law in practice LLB – which focus on flexible blended learning and employability.

The university's portfolio of degree apprenticeships has been expanded to offer 20 programmes across the faculties of engineering and science, education, health and human sciences, and liberal arts and science.

Employability is a high priority through a strategic relationship with a recruitment company on campus. High-quality internships and other opportunities are found along the way. Greenwich has fared well in the first two Graduate Outcomes surveys, ending up in the middle of the field somewhat above its overall academic ranking.

Companies such as Pfizer, Northern Trust, BAE Systems, Soho House, the Dorchester and Warner Media tap in to the university's talent stream and Greenwich has partnerships with emerging businesses including MarketAxess, Sparta Global, CloserStill Media and M3 Consulting to give students insights into the world of work.

Graduate Abiy Ahmed became prime minister of Ethiopia aged 42 in 2018, and Africa's youngest leader, winning the Nobel Peace Prize in 2019 for his efforts towards international co-operation. The university has a second Nobel laureate in the late Dr Charles Kao, who won the physics prize in 2009 for work in fibre optics. Baroness Doreen Lawrence, the mother of Stephen Lawrence, is another former student, notable for her anti-racist campaigning.

Greenwich ranks just outside the top 20 overall for social diversity on campus. With more than 56% of undergraduates from ethnic minorities, it is in the top 25 universities in the country on this measure. About half of students are the first in their family to go to university, putting Greenwich in 18th place.

There are gyms at all three campuses. Sports halls at Avery Hill and Medway are suitable for badminton, basketball, netball, futsal and volleyball. Avery Hill also has four grass football pitches, a 3G pitch for football and rugby, a hockey pitch, tennis courts, and an indoor 3G training facility that is shared with Charlton FC.

Tuition fees

»	Fees for UK students	£9,250
	Foundation courses	£6,165
»	Fees for International students 2022–23	£15,100
	Pharmacy	£21,200
»	For scholarship and bursary information see www.gre.ac.uk/finance	
»	Graduate salary	£25,000

Student numbers

Undergraduates	12,925 (1,655)
Postgraduates	2,905 (2,340)
Applications/places	27,450/3,980
Applications per place	6.9
Overall offer rate	64.6%
International students – EU	8.1%
Non-EU	10.7%

Accommodation

University provided places: 2,188
Self-catered: £118–£291 per week
First years guaranteed accommodation
www.gre.ac.uk/accommodation

Where do the students come from?

State schools (non-grammar)	92.9%	Low participation areas	6.9%	Disabled	5.8%
Grammar schools	4.8%	All ethnic minorities	56.2%	Mature (over 21)	34%
Independent schools	2.3%	White working-class males	6.1%		
First generation students	56.2%	Black achievement gap	-18.3%		

Social inclusion ranking: =22

Harper Adams University

Harper Adams University – renowned as the UK's leading specialist agricultural institution – still occupies a single site on the Shropshire country estate where it was founded in 1901. From its rural English setting it takes a global perspective on specialisms ranging from food production and processing to animal sciences, land management and sustainable business.

The university is launching the UK's first School of Sustainable Food and Farming, to help the industry reach net-zero carbon emissions. Supported by Wm Morrison supermarkets and co-partnered by research company Raft Solutions, the school will be based at the university.

The Harper and Keele Veterinary School, a joint venture with Keele University, welcomed its second cohort of students in 2021. It benefits from the new Veterinary Education Centre on campus, which features two lecture theatres, clinical teaching rooms and diagnostic facilities.

The facility is used by veterinary nursing and veterinary physiotherapy students as well as those studying for their bachelor of veterinary medicine and surgery degree. The vet school has also been gifted the Animal Health Trust Library – a valuable collection of journals, textbooks and reports.

Harper Adams has launched two gateway routes to study veterinary medicine. Undergraduates may take an extended degree in veterinary bioscience (with access to veterinary medicine) before being assessed for entry to the vet school and, more recently, outstanding performance in the first year of a range of other animal science degrees may also count as a preparatory stage before assessment.

After 23 years at Harper Adams, including 12 as its vice-chancellor, Dr David Llewellyn retired in July 2021. He led the institution through an extremely successful period, during which university status came in 2012 and teaching quality has taken centre stage. It was our 2020 Modern University of the Year and runner-up for the overall award the same year and has been our top-ranked modern university for the past six years.

The purple patch under Dr Llewellyn's leadership includes Harper Adams becoming one of only two institutions to achieve gold in successive years in the government's Teaching Excellence Framework (TEF). Having earned gold in 2017, it did not need to be reassessed – but the university wanted to test its performance against the latest measures. The TEF panel praised Harper Adams' course design, delivery and assessment practices, which stretched and challenged students to achieve their full potential, and gain knowledge and skills valued by employers.

The university has scored consistently well for teaching quality and student experience, ranking in the UK top ten in 2020 for both measures derived from the annual National

Edgmond
Newport
Shropshire TF10 8NB
01952 815 000
admissions@harper-adams.ac.uk
www.harper-adams.ac.uk
www.harpersu.com
Open days: see website

The Times and The Sunday Times Rankings
Overall Ranking: 29 (last year: 28)

Teaching quality	79.3%	14
Student experience	76.1%	11
Research quality	5.7%	85
Entry standards	121	=74
Graduate prospects	75.7%	=36
Good honours	76.5%	=79
Expected completion rate	91.8%	=26
Student/staff ratio	14.2	=30
Services and facilities	£4,101	1

Student Survey (NSS). It was hit less hard than most when it came to students passing judgment on its handling of the pandemic. There was a big fall in satisfaction with assessment and feedback, but otherwise scores were only gently down, pushing its new rankings for teaching quality and student experience down to top 20 level in both instances.

Campus facilities include the modern Bamford Library, which holds one of the largest specialist land-based collections in the UK, and the Weston teaching and learning building. Students also get to learn "in the field" at the university's 627-hectare farm. A functioning commercial farm, its livestock includes 390 dairy cows and 280 followers (young cows that will replace the milk producers), 230 sows, 70,000 hens, two sheep flocks and an intensive beef unit.

Students are offered placement years and accredited part-time programmes in industry meaning that only about half are on campus at once. Tuition fees are about a fifth of the full rate during placement years, and students usually earn a wage while also gaining work experience.

Harper Adams offers five degree apprenticeships in the areas of rural surveying, geospatial mapping (utilities pathway), food and drink engineering, food industry technical professional, and senior leader (food business management).

The new Centre for Effective Innovation in Agriculture is addressing the gap between scientific research and real-life farming experience. Its work is designed to give farmers more input into agricultural research and development.

Scholarships funded by philanthropic and industry donations totalling £525,000 are available via the university's development trust. They often have work placements included, such as a £4,500 merit-based award from the British Poultry Council. One £2,500 scholarship from the Duchy of Lancaster includes a 12-month estate management position.

Sports facilities include a shooting ground as well as a gymnasium, heated outdoor swimming pool, rugby, cricket, football and hockey pitches, tennis courts and an all-weather sports pitch. A rowing club operates from nearby Shrewsbury. The campus has its own local, the Welly Inn, as well as the students' union Main Bar.

Accommodation, more than half of it catered, is guaranteed on campus to those from abroad, or who are disabled or have left care.

Tuition fees

» Fees for UK students	£9,250
» Fees for International students 2022–23	£11,250
Veterinary	£33,000
» For scholarship and bursary information see www.harper-adams.ac.uk/apply/finance/	
» Graduate salary	£23,500

Student numbers

Undergraduates	2,360	(1,760)
Postgraduates	95	(460)
Applications/places		2,625/510
Applications per place		5.1
Overall offer rate		70%
International students – EU		1.1%
Non-EU		3%

Accommodation

University provided places: 774
Catered costs: £134–£166 per week
Self-catered £122–£130
First years given priority for accommodation
www.harper-adams.ac.uk/university-life/accommodation

Where do the students come from?

State schools (non-grammar)	76.1%	Low participation areas	7.1%	
Grammar schools	9.4%	All ethnic minorities	2.8%	
Independent schools	14.5%	White working-class males	5.6%	
First generation students	36.2%	Black achievement gap	n/a	

Social inclusion ranking: 28

Disabled	18%
Mature (over 21)	11.3%

Hartpury University

Making its debut in our academic league table, Hartpury – which is four miles north of Gloucester – gained university status three years ago. Founded in 1948 as an agricultural institute, it was part of the University of the West of England from 1997 until it began awarding its own degrees in 2017 and became a fully-fledged university the year after. Reflecting its history and countryside setting, courses cover a broad land-based selection, while the curriculum has grown to encompass animal, equine, sport and veterinary nursing degrees.

University life centres around a commercial farming business. The main Home Farm on campus occupies 72 hectares while four others are nearby. Students learn how to farm cows, calves, sheep and arable land in the 400-hectare "classroom" and the business supplies Sainsbury's, Müller and Glencore among others.

Hartpury was awarded gold in the Teaching Excellence Framework three years ago, just before gaining university status. The panel praised course design and assessment practices that provided a high level of stretch and challenge. It also highlighted the "inquiry-based" approach to teaching and learning and its "optimum contact hours, which secure high levels of engagement and commitment to learning and study from students".

Most degrees include a placement and an integrated placement year is compulsory on some courses.

A new £1.25million Digital Innovation Farm is being added on campus, giving students and agri-businesses the equipment to research and create products that boost productivity and profitability. The development is phase two in Hartpury's ten-year vision to lead the future of digital farming, which began with the 2019 launch of the Agri-Tech Centre. Featuring smart technology, precision tools and robotics, it helps students to gain insights into the productivity, profitability and sustainability of livestock production, and other global food challenges.

Hartpury has spent £50million on facilities in recent years. The university also has a dairy bull-beef rearing unit, a sheep handler and a 296-cubicle dairy unit. An advanced dairy parlour, designed to benefit cows and students reduces milking times and improves hygiene and welfare for the university's 250-strong award-winning herd.

Bovine studies also benefit from a new herd of 50 pedigree Guernsey cattle. Agriculture students will be able to carry out research into the breed within an applied, commercial setting.

Building on Hartpury's aim to set the standards in the world of horses, the university has invested £700,000 into an Equine and Animal Assisted Arena (EAAA) and round

Hartpury House
Gloucester GL19 3BE
01452 702 244
admissions@hartpury.ac.uk
www.hartpury.ac.uk
studentsunion@hartpury.ac.uk
Open days: see website

The Times and The Sunday Times Rankings

Overall Ranking: =112 (last year: n/a)

Teaching Quality	78.3%	=18
Student Experience	73.4%	=29
Research quality	n/a	
Entry standards	117	=85
Graduate prospects	61.6%	114
Good honours	62.9%	131
Expected completion rate	n/a	
Student/staff ratio	22.2	127
Services and facilities	£3,012	27

pen. It will support students on equine and canine degrees with their practical learning, as well as equine research and development projects. Hartpury is to host the 2022 FEI (Fédération Equestre Internationale) Dressage and Eventing European Championships for Young Riders and Juniors there.

Equine provision also includes a rider performance centre, therapy centre, international competition arenas and stabling for 230 horses – used by students and by equestrian athletes in training. Students can even bring their own horse to university (not many places can say that) with stabling and livery options available.

A degree in equine behaviour and welfare welcomed its first students in September 2021, as did top-up degrees in animal training and performance, and in canine training and performance.

Hartpury achieved such glowing scores from its students in the 2020 National Student Survey (NSS) that it would have finished joint top for satisfaction with teaching quality in our *Guide's* previous edition, had it been included in our tables then. It has suffered a hefty drop in levels of satisfaction in 2021, however, in the wake of the Covid pandemic, but still manages a UK top 20 placing. The sharp decline in scores is perhaps unsurprising given the applied nature of Hartpury's courses, which would have posed more of a challenge to translate into digital format than classroom-based degrees. The majority of teaching was back on campus for the 2021–22 academic year.

Sport commands a high profile. A sports academy costing £8.8million opened in 2019, which includes biomechanics and human performance laboratories, an anti-gravity treadmill, an altitude chamber, and high-speed cameras and digital mirrors to map body movement. There are also medical and physiotherapy rooms, a rehabilitation suite and a large multi-sports hall. There is a golf driving range and Hartpury University RFC recruits many students.

Hartpury is also the training centre for the British Rowing World Class and Pentathlon GB Pathway programmes. Its link with Gloucester Rugby provides work experience opportunities for sports students.

Hartpury endeavours to allocate student accommodation for first-years, but does not offer a guarantee. Most student bedrooms are on campus where social life is lively and Gloucester and Cheltenham are five and ten miles away for a bigger night out.

Tuition fees

» Fees for UK students	£9,250
» Fees for International students 2022–23	£13,000
» For scholarship and bursary information see www.hartpury.ac.uk/university/facilities/ life-at-hartpury/finance/	
» Graduate salary	£20,000

Student numbers

Undergraduates	1,725	(45)
Postgraduates	40	(185)
Applications/places		2,890/705
Applications per place		4.1
Overall offer rate		n/a
International students – EU		3.6%
Non-EU		4.5%

Accommodation
Catered costs: £136–£153 per week
Self-catered: £136–£155
First years given priority for accommodation
www.hartpury.ac.uk/university/facilities/life-at-hartpury/accommodation

Where do the students come from?

State schools (non-grammar)	90.1%	Low participation areas	11.5%		Disabled	9.2%
Grammar schools	2.7%	All ethnic minorities	5.6%		Mature (over 21)	16.7%
Independent schools	7.2%	White working-class males	5.9%			
First generation students	48.1%	Black achievement gap	n/a			

Social inclusion ranking: 82

Heriot-Watt University

Two hundred years after its foundation as the world's first mechanics institute, Heriot-Watt is maintaining its reputation for innovation and excellence in engineering education through the establishment of the National Robotarium on its Riccarton campus in Edinburgh. Working in collaboration with the University of Edinburgh, the new centre will open in 2022. One of its first research projects will bring together academics from Heriot-Watt, Imperial College London and the University of Manchester to research trust in autonomous systems, pooling expertise in robotics, cognitive science and psychology.

The robotarium is said to be the largest and most advanced facility of its type in the UK and a centre of excellence for research into robotics and artificial intelligence. It augments existing laboratories for human robotic interaction and assisted living and will explore interaction between humans, robots and their environments.

The new development follows the opening in 2019 of the Grid (Global Research, Innovation and Discovery) building, a technology hub with open learning spaces to encourage collaboration between global industry partners and students and academics on Heriot-Watt's campuses around the world.

These take in Malaysia and Dubai, in addition to the home bases in Edinburgh and Galashiels. The university's Go Global programme offers students the opportunity – pandemic permitting – to move between campuses for a semester, a year, or longer with courses following the same programme and academic criteria on each campus. Heriot-Watt won our 2018 International University of the Year award. The new Dubai campus has capacity for up to 4,000 students.

Heriot-Watt's outward-looking approach to higher education makes for graduates who are capable of making an immediate impact in the workplace. Eighty-one per cent of Heriot-Watt graduates were in high-skilled jobs or postgraduate study, the latest Graduate Outcomes survey found, ranking the university in the UK top 40.

Many degree programmes include industry placements and projects and carry professional accreditation; the university teams up with an average of 200 big companies every year for a variety of projects. Its portfolio of 37 spin-out companies ranks the university 4th in Scotland and 21st in the UK.

In a further nod towards employers, Heriot-Watt has one of the largest graduate apprenticeship (GA) programmes of any Scottish university, with 500 GA students at last count. It plans to recruit over 200 more across the nine existing programmes including engineering, design and manufacturing; IT management for business; IT software development; civil engineering; built environment (quantity

Edinburgh EH14 4AS
0131 451 3376
studywithus@hw.ac.uk
www.hw.ac.uk
www.hwunion.com
Open days: see website

EDINBURGH
Belfast
London
Cardiff

The Times and The Sunday Times Rankings
Overall Ranking: =30 (last year: 35)

Teaching quality	73%	88
Student experience	73.1%	=33
Research quality	36.7%	28
Entry standards	170	13
Graduate prospects	74.3%	46
Good honours	82.6%	39
Expected completion rate	84.6%	=63
Student/staff ratio	17.3	=91
Services and facilities	£3,723	9

surveying); business management; data science; and instrumentation measurement and control.

New degrees that launched in September 2021 include accelerated (three-year) programmes in international business management, economics, accountancy and finance, and marketing, as well as BAs in communication design, and fashion branding and promotion. The last is based at the Scottish Borders campus, 35 miles south of Edinburgh in Galashiels, which specialises in textiles, fashion and design.

Heriot-Watt's blended learning approach to the pandemic was adjudged more successful by its students than has been the case among many of its peer institutions. It was just outside the top 30 in the UK for the smallest decline in year-on-year scores, leading to significant gains this year in our rankings for teaching quality and student experience.

The panel awarding Heriot-Watt silver in the Teaching Excellence Framework praised its course design "directly informed by research activity", more than 80% of which was rated world-leading or internationally excellent in the most recent Research Excellence Framework, published in 2014. Heriot-Watt was among the leaders in the UK in mathematics, general engineering and architecture, planning and the built environment, where it made joint submissions with the University of Edinburgh. It features in the top 30 of our research ranking.

The university drops three places this year in our Scottish social inclusion ranking but secures a UK top 20 ranking for its performance in recruiting white working-class males, one of the key groups underrepresented on Britain's campuses. There is a generous bursary system, with awards of up to £3,100 per year towards living costs for students recruited from homes with income of less than £25,000 in England, Wales and Northern Ireland. Minimum entry offers are made where possible to students from the 20% of areas considered most deprived in Scotland.

The main Riccarton campus hosts Oriam, Scotland's national centre for performance in many sports, where world-class facilities are available to Heriot-Watt students. The £33million complex features a Hampden Park replica pitch, outdoor synthetic and grass pitches, a 12-court sports hall, a 3G indoor pitch and a fitness suite, plus medical facilities.

The Edinburgh halls of residence are conveniently placed and house more than 1,800 students. Regular bus services link the campus to the city centre and its wide range of nightlife and cultural events.

Tuition fees
- » Fees for Scottish students £0–£1,820
  RUK fees (capped at £27,750 for 4-year courses) £9,250
- » Fees for International students 2022–23 £16,000–£20,584
- » For scholarship and bursary information see www.hw.ac.uk/study/fees-funding.htm
- » Graduate salary £25,000

Student numbers

Undergraduates	7,605	(545)
Postgraduates	1,945	(1,060)
Applications/places	9,025/1,240	
Applications per place	7.3	
Overall offer rate	79.4%	
International students – EU	5.6%	
Non-EU	17.4%	

Accommodation
University provided places: 1,823
Self-catered: £147–£215 per week
First years guaranteed accommodation
www.hw.ac.uk/uk/edinburgh/accommodation.htm

Where do the students come from?

State schools (non-grammar)	83.9%	Deprived areas	11%	
Grammar schools	4.2%	All ethnic minorities	15%	
Independent schools	11.9%	White working-class males	7.7%	
First generation students	32.7%	Black achievement gap	-16%	

Social inclusion ranking (Scotland): 8

Disabled	5.2%	
Mature (over 21)	23%	

University of Hertfordshire

Students at the University of Hertfordshire have gained new social facilities. The redevelopment of the Forum nightclub on the College Lane campus has created two areas – an informal bar and a second-floor nightclub, each with 530-person capacities. The redesign has also repurposed the Forum's auditorium as teaching space, featuring a 250-seat lecture theatre and breakout areas for collaborative learning, as part of an increasingly flexible approach to teaching and learning.

Blended learning was well-established at Hertfordshire before the pandemic, making the rapid move to remote learning less complex than at some institutions. Teaching rooms have lecture-capture facilities, allowing students to listen back remotely, and live online lectures are also recorded to be watched afterwards.

Hertfordshire welcomed the shift from examinations to assessments that remote learning necessitated. The university feels these are a more authentic measure and wants to develop how it approaches assessments in future.

When upgrading Hertfordshire to a gold award in 2018, the Teaching Excellence Framework (TEF) judging panel commended the strong emphasis on work-based learning, entrepreneurship and enterprise, with employability and transferable skills embedded in the curriculum. There had been high levels of investment in physical and digital resources and courses benefited from "vocationally informed pedagogy supported by the university's educational research network".

The De Havilland campus, housing Hatfield's £12million Enterprise Hub, has spaces for students, staff and the business community along with an incubator for start-ups and graduate entrepreneurs. The new Institute of Sport at De Havilland brings modern facilities for students in the School of Life and Medical Sciences.

Professional accreditations or approvals are often built into courses, and students leave with CV extras such as Microsoft qualifications or City & Guilds awards. Most courses offer work placements and the careers team supports students for four years after graduation, helping them to find opportunities, prepare for interviews or start-up their own enterprise. The Flare Ignite ideas challenge gives entrepreneurial Herts students and alumni up to £3,500 prize money plus training to bring their winning ideas to life.

The opportunity to study at one of more than 170 universities around the world is promoted to students – for a term, a summer or a whole year. The Go Herts award gives students formal recognition for extracurricular activities.

More than 700 higher and degree apprentices are enrolled on Hertfordshire's 15 apprenticeship programmes. Fields include

College Lane
Hatfield AL10 9AB
01707 284 800
ask@herts.ac.uk
www.herts.ac.uk
www.hertfordshire.su
Open days:
see website

The Times and The Sunday Times Rankings
Overall Ranking: =96 (last year: 99)

Teaching quality	74.6%	=72
Student experience	70.2%	=56
Research quality	5.6%	=86
Entry standards	103	=126
Graduate prospects	69.4%	=69
Good honours	70.3%	115
Expected completion rate	82%	=84
Student/staff ratio	15.6	=61
Services and facilities	£2,793	=42

digital and technology solutions, engineering, nursing and sports management.

Applications to Hertfordshire have fallen by more than a third over the past decade, but the number of students starting courses has decreased less sharply, by just under a fifth, over the same period.

College Lane, Hertfordshire's original campus, is a 20-minute walk from the purpose-built £120million De Havilland base and the two are linked by a free shuttle bus, footpaths and cycle lanes. The Hutton Hub is home to student services on the College Lane site, which also has a £50million science building and an art gallery. The Automotive Centre on College Lane delivers up-to-date engineering teaching and many Formula One teams have Hertfordshire graduates on their staff.

The university has its own teaching observatory for hands-on learning in astronomy and astrophysics six miles from Hatfield. Bayfordbury Observatory features some of the latest technology in the field, including seven large optical telescopes, four radio telescopes and a high-definition planetarium.

In the 2014 Research Excellence Framework, more than half the work submitted by Hertfordshire was placed in one of the top two categories. The best results were in history.

Few universities have more students drawn from ethnic minorities than the near six in ten taking courses here, which is unusual for a non-urban location in southern England. Few can beat its recruitment from non-selective state schools, at 95%.

There are widening participation links with schools across Hertfordshire and the university runs outreach events such as GCSE booster workshops, student shadowing and summer schools.

The £15million Hertfordshire Sports Village was selected as one of 17 training camps for athletes competing in the 2012 London Olympics. It features a 110-station health and fitness centre, 25m pool, physiotherapy and sports injury clinic and a large multipurpose sports hall.

There are 4,600 study bedrooms across both campuses, enough to guarantee one for all first-years. The three Ask Herts Hubs are a fresh initiative on campus designed to give students a consistent place to go to have their questions answered.

Trains to King's Cross take 25 minutes, though there is also plenty to do in the network of local Hertfordshire towns, including St Albans, Watford and Broxbourne.

Tuition fees

» Fees for UK students	£9,250
Foundation courses	£6,165
» Fees for International students 2022–23	£14,000
» For scholarship and bursary information see www.herts.ac.uk/study/fees-and-funding	
» Graduate salary	£24,900

Student numbers

Undergraduates	15,370 (2,435)
Postgraduates	4,200 (3,520)
Applications/places	19,845/3,270
Applications per place	6.1
Overall offer rate	70.6%
International students – EU	3.9%
Non-EU	12.3%

Accommodation
University provided places: 4,600
Self-catered: £100–£210 per week
www.herts.ac.uk/life/student-accommodation

Where do the students come from?

State schools (non-grammar)	95.3%	Low participation areas	7%	Disabled	5.4%
Grammar schools	2.5%	All ethnic minorities	57.1%	Mature (over 21)	23.9%
Independent schools	2.2%	White working-class males	3.6%		
First generation students	50.9%	Black achievement gap	-23.7%		

Social inclusion ranking: 53

University of the Highlands and Islands

Spread over 13 campuses and more than 70 local learning centres across some of the remotest parts of northern Scotland, the University of the Highlands and Islands (UHI) is unlike any other institution in this guide. Blended learning – such a cultural revolution to other institutions – has been the norm since its inception more than 20 years ago. How else could it reach its far-flung students?

UHI's blended learning approach combines online and face-to-face tuition with small class sizes and extensive use of video conferencing, although some courses are already available entirely online.

The online elements of courses have expanded even here during the pandemic and some will continue alongside academic, support and social activities delivered on-campus to enhance the wider student experience. The university also recognises that some students will need access to in-person teaching because of home, health or digital issues.

More than half the students are aged over 21 when they enrol, and more than 3,000 undergraduates study part-time. That leaves some 5,500 studying full-time, attached to one of the campuses or learning centres.

The university does not publish two offers – standard and minimum – for its courses, preferring to set its standard offer at the minimum level required to successfully complete a course. This supports its wider remit to widen access to higher education.

UHI rises two places in our Scottish social inclusion ranking this year, partly because of its success in recruiting white working-class males, one of the most underrepresented groups in higher education. About one in nine students at UHI come from this demographic, a rate bettered by just five universities.

The course portfolio reflects the needs of each campus' locality. UHI works with organisations as diverse as the Crown Estate, Scottish Land and Estates, the Cairngorms National Park Authority, the Dounreay Partnership and SSE, the Perth-based energy company. A partnership with software giant IBM has spawned the innovative BSc in applied software development, giving students access to the latest technologies replicating modern software development practices, guest speakers, industry mentors from around the world, and enhanced IBM Cloud access to complement students' learning.

Boeing, Lockheed Martin and Liberty have been partners in developing STEM (science, technology, engineering and mathematics) subjects, including aerospace and advanced technology. And the optometry sector, including Specsavers, have collaborated in developing UHI's optometry degree, designed to support employment demand in rural areas. There

---

Executive Office
12b Ness Walk, Inverness IV3 5SQ
01463 279 190
info@uhi.ac.uk
www.uhi.ac.uk
www.uhi.ac.uk/en/students/
get-involved/
students-association/
Open days: see website

The Times and The Sunday Times **Rankings**
Overall Ranking: n/a
No data available

are two graduate apprenticeships supporting the civil engineering and childcare sectors in Scotland via a BEng (Hons) in civil engineering, and a BA (Hons) in early learning and childcare.

Newly-launched degrees include moral and philosophical studies with religious education, geography (as a single subject or as a joint degree with a number of humanities subjects), and sustainable development (also as a single subject or jointly with humanities subjects).

All students and graduates have access to FutureMe, UHI's online careers platform. This incorporates the JobShop, where local, national and international employers advertise job and placement opportunities.

The same features of part-time and distance learning that are virtues in helping UHI serve its region and country make comparison with other universities nigh on impossible. UHI was withdrawn from our rankings in 2017 on account of its dissipated nature and the large numbers of part-time staff and further education students within its various colleges.

These stretch from Shetland in the far northeast to Campbeltown in the southwest; from Lews Castle College, set in 600 acres of parkland, on the Isle of Lewis in the northwest to Perth College in the east. Students live mostly locally to the colleges, but the university offers just over 600 places in student accommodation, about half of them at UHI Inverness College.

Some colleges are relatively large and located in the urban centres such as Perth, Elgin and Inverness, while others are smaller institutions, including some where the primary focus is research. There are a dozen specialist research facilities in all, as well as an enterprise and research centre on the Inverness campus. They helped to produce some extremely good results in the 2014 Research Excellence Framework, in which 70% of the submission was classified as world-leading or internationally excellent.

UHI Sabhal Mòr Ostaig is the only Gaelic-medium college in the world, set in stunning scenery on the Isle of Skye. Across the university, many courses can be studied in the language. UHI was the first in Scotland to produce a Gaelic Language Plan, which includes proposals to enhance the curriculum, produce more bilingual resources for students and hold more Gaelic events. Donnie Munro, the former Runrig frontman, has been director of development, fundraising and the arts here since stepping back from the band in 1997.

Tuition fees

» Fees for Scottish students	£0–£1,820
RUK fees (capped at £27,000 for 4-year courses)	£9,000
» Fees for International students 2022–23	£12,360–£13,62
» For scholarship and bursary information see www.uhi.ac.uk/en/studying-at-uhi/first-steps/ how-much-will-it-cost/	
» Graduate salary	£22,500

Student numbers

Undergraduates	5,510	(3,160)
Postgraduates	405	(830)
Applications/places	4,505/1,095	
Applications per place	4.1	
Overall offer rate	59.5%	
International students – EU	2.6%	
Non-EU	0.4%	

Accommodation

University provided places: 612
Catered: £125 per week
Self-catered: £107–£150 per week
www.uhi.ac.uk/en/studying-at-uhi/first-steps/accommodation/

Where do the students come from?

State schools (non-grammar)	97.4%	Deprived areas	10.5%
Grammar schools	0%	All ethnic minorities	3.9%
Independent schools	2.6%	White working-class males	11.1%
First generation students	43.9%	Black achievement gap	n/a

Social inclusion ranking (Scotland): 7

Disabled	1.7%		
Mature (over 21)	51.1%		

University of Huddersfield

The merger of the University of Huddersfield's School of Art, Design and Architecture with the School of Music, Humanities and Media has created a new School of Arts and Humanities, one of the largest faculties of its kind.

It offers students courses in an environment that should foster interdisciplinary working – in particular around the university's new Yorkshire Film and Television School, which has a 300 sq m film studio along with live broadcast television studios, virtual reality and motion-tracking sensors and music and sound production facilities. New degrees launched in 2021 include film-making; television studies and production; performance for screen; and screenwriting.

The School of Arts and Humanities is another step in Huddersfield's continuing commitment to maintaining the same level of teaching and learning experience for students that earned it gold in the Teaching Excellence Framework (TEF). The TEF panel commended the university's effective use of learning analytics to target timely interventions that boost students' results. It also praised an institution-wide strategy for assessment and feedback, which ensures that all students are challenged to achieve their full potential.

To date this has not translated into stellar scores in the National Student Survey, even before the pandemic knocked the scores for six. In a comparison of 2021 outcomes with those of 2020, just 33 institutions saw bigger falls in student satisfaction, with students marking Huddersfield down heavily in the learning resources and learning community sections of the survey.

Huddersfield's single-site campus is two minutes' walk from the town centre. Investment in teaching and research facilities has brought plenty of modern, purpose-built resources. The £30million Barbara Hepworth Building opened in 2019 for the study of art, design and architecture. Featuring creative studios and technology facilities that combine digital and physical innovation, it overlooks the Huddersfield Narrow Canal, which runs through the campus. The £31million Joseph Priestley Building has teaching spaces, workshops and laboratories for science subjects, as well as its own student hub and social area.

The curriculum has been reshuffled, a process that was already underway in our last edition. Apart from the new media courses, additions include natural sciences; environmental and analytical science; mathematics MMath; chemistry with environmental science; and education with psychology. Part-time degrees in education with various specialisms have also launched. The Huddersfield Business School has withdrawn, added and changed the titles of a significant tranche of its courses across the fields of law, marketing, economics, business and accounting.

Queensgate
Huddersfield HD1 3DH
01484 472 625
study@hud.ac.uk
www.hud.ac.uk
www.huddersfield.su
Open days: see website

Overall Ranking: 75 (last year: =73)

Teaching quality	72%	=105
Student experience	64.7%	=112
Research quality	9.4%	61
Entry standards	121	=74
Graduate prospects	65.3%	95
Good honours	78.9%	56
Expected completion rate	83.5%	=75
Student/staff ratio	13.7	=23
Services and facilities	£2,567	63

Huddersfield's portfolio of degree apprenticeships is growing. New for January 2022 are programmes in pre-registration nursing, with four specialism options: adult, child, learning disability and mental health. The university introduced blended learning nursing degree apprenticeships in 2021, with the same range of specialisms. Its suite of health-related programmes also gained physiotherapy, occupational therapy and midwifery degree apprenticeships.

Employability initiatives include internships via a link with Santander, work-ready content delivered by employers within courses and an alliance with the Chartered Management Institute (CMI) that provides all students with a CMI leadership qualification. Companies at which students undertook work placements in 2020–21 include PwC, Oxfam, Sony, Walt Disney and HMRC.

Some of the most successful subject areas for Huddersfield in the 2014 Research Excellence Framework were in the arts and social sciences. The university did well overall, entering almost a third of its academics for assessment. Nearly 60% of their work was rated world-leading or internationally excellent. There were particularly good results in music, drama and performing arts, as well as in English, social work and social policy.

The year-long Progression Module builds on Huddersfield's proud record for widening participation in higher education. The skills-boosting programme is worth 12 UCAS tariff points to those who complete it, which they can use towards entry requirements at Huddersfield, Leeds Beckett and Leeds Trinity universities.

Aspire to Uni is a ten-year outreach programme for pupils from target primary schools, designed to improve their results and progression from Sats up to post-16 courses. Almost 57% of 2020's new students were the first in their family to go to university, a proportion that puts Huddersfield in the top 20 institutions nationally.

Digs is Huddersfield's preferred accommodation provider. It has more than 1,600 rooms – most of them in the Storthes Hall Park student village. There are 280 spaces at Ashenhurst, just over a mile from the campus.

The £22.5million Student Central building has sports facilities that include an 80-station gym, two dance studios, a physiotherapy treatment room and a sports hall. The town's leisure centre is within ten minutes' walk of campus. Huddersfield's 20,000-strong student population ensures a lively social life, while Leeds and Manchester are accessible by train.

Tuition fees

» Fees for UK students	£9,250
» Fees for International students 2022–23	£15,000–£18,000
» For scholarship and bursary information see www.hud.ac.uk/undergraduate/fees-and-finance	
» Graduate salary	£22,000

Student numbers

Undergraduates	12,315 (1,280)
Postgraduates	2,030 (1,675)
Applications/places	17,245/2,930
Applications per place	5.9
Overall offer rate	76.2%
International students – EU	2.6%
Non-EU	13.7%

Accommodation

University provided places: 1,660
Self-catered: £70–£115 per week
www.hud.ac.uk/uni-life/accommodation

Where do the students come from?

State schools (non-grammar)	95.4%	Low participation areas	15.3%	Disabled	8.3%
Grammar schools	3.4%	All ethnic minorities	44.2%	Mature (over 21)	21.2%
Independent schools	1.2%	White working-class males	6%		
First generation students	56.7%	Black achievement gap	-14.2%		

Social inclusion ranking: 20

University of Hull

The University of Hull is an official partner of Team GB – the first and only university to have this close link. The special relationship resulted in a variety of CV-boosting opportunities for students in the run-up to the Tokyo 2020 Olympics. Internships, live briefs for marketing undergraduates and a virtual reality project that enabled athletes to familiarise themselves with Tokyo ahead of the games were among the activities. A research project is exploring the heritage of the Olympic Games and there are three new PhD research projects with Team GB.

Now in the third year of this exclusive six-year partnership, Hull has also secured triple Olympic champion gymnast Max Whitlock MBE as an ambassador for the university, in a relationship designed to inspire success in students.

Teaching and learning facilities at Hull's single-site redbrick campus have been upgraded. The media centre has been brought together on one site and gained the augmented/virtual reality equipment required for games-design degrees. A crime scene investigation house – which simulates the inside of a domestic home – has been added, to enhance the experience of students.

For those on law courses, a second court has been built, with judge's chambers, in addition to the established moot court. Hull has also re-launched its legal mediation centre, which provides final-year students with real-world experience of civil law disputes. Elsewhere, at the Nidd building a newly installed professional business lounge is facilitating business networking among students and external partners.

Hull also has industry-standard recording and performance facilities in Middleton Hall and an art gallery in the upgraded £28million Brynmor Jones library.

When awarding Hull silver in the Teaching Excellence Framework the judging panel praised the university for its course design and assessment practices that stretch and challenge students. Assessors were also impressed by Hull's investment in physical and digital infrastructure.

The university has stated that it is providing digitally enhanced education, anchored to the campus, so that teaching can be delivered on campus and/or online, depending on the circumstances of the pandemic. Across all faculties, seminars, tutorials, workshops and labs on campus will be enhanced by digital quizzes, presentations, podcasts and videos with a view to ensuring a mix of real-time and "anytime" delivery. Lectures and seminars are recorded and made available for students to access afterwards, whether they have attended in person or not.

This approach led to one of the stronger

Cottingham Road
Hull HU6 7RX
01482 466 100
admissions@hull.ac.uk
www.hull.ac.uk
www.hullstudent.com
Open days: see website

The Times and The Sunday Times Rankings		
Overall Ranking: =52 (last year: =60)		
Teaching quality	76.6%	=38
Student experience	71.9%	41
Research quality	16.7%	54
Entry standards	124	=65
Graduate prospects	73.9%	49
Good honours	77.2%	71
Expected completion rate	80.9%	=94
Student/staff ratio	15.5	=56
Services and facilities	£2,561	64

pandemic performances in this year's National Student Survey (NSS). Hull ranked in the top 50 when 2021 NSS outcomes were compared with the pre-pandemic results from 2020.

The university launched a five-year education strategy in 2020, committing to inclusivity as well as investigating the challenges of the fourth industrial revolution and equipping graduates with skills needed for a fairer, brighter and carbon-neutral future. Under a new international strategy Hull is providing overseas opportunities for all students who want them – via work placements, studying abroad, summer schools or international study tours.

Hull achieves one of the highest rankings among pre-1992 universities in our social inclusion index – putting it among the top 20 this year.

The university's wide-ranging environmental research projects place it at the heart of the Humber region's push towards a low-carbon economy. More than 60% of the work entered for the 2014 Research Excellence Framework was rated as world-leading or internationally excellent, although Hull made a relatively small submission for a pre-1992 university. The best results were in the allied health category, while geography and computer science also did well.

The university won a Queen's Anniversary Prize for its research into slavery and played a key role in shaping the UK's Modern Slavery Act. Hull's strength in politics is reflected in a steady flow of graduates into the House of Commons. The Westminster-Hull internship programme offers a year-long placement for British politics and legislative studies students.

Hull's curriculum introduced new degrees in graphic design; media production; professional policing; and creative industries (subject to validation) in 2021.

The medical school Hull shares with the University of York has expanded after being awarded another 90 places. In the £25million Allam medical building, opened by the Queen and partly paid for by the local philanthropist Assem Allam, medical students can work alongside nursing, midwifery and allied health undergraduates, as well as PhD students, advanced nurse practitioners and physician associates.

First-years are guaranteed a place in halls of residence, and if they want to stay for their second and third years that is usually possible too. The city itself is kind on the student wallet and there is plenty of local nightlife.

Tuition fees

» Fees for UK students	£9,250
Foundation courses	£7,500
» Fees for International students 2022–23	£15,400–£18,300
Medicine	£38,500
» For scholarship and bursary information see www.hull.ac.uk/choose-hull/study-at-hull/money	
» Graduate salary	£23,000

Student numbers

Undergraduates	11,045	(890)
Postgraduates	1,430	(890)
Applications/places		11,165/2,460
Applications per place		4.5
Overall offer rate		75.7%
International students – EU		2.6%
Non-EU		9.6%

Accommodation

University provided places: 2,312
Self-catered: £125–£210 per week
First years guaranteed accommodation
www.hull.ac.uk/choose-hull/student-life/accommodation

Where do the students come from?

State schools (non-grammar)	91.9%	Low participation areas	27.6%		
Grammar schools	3.7%	All ethnic minorities	11.5%		
Independent schools	4.4%	White working-class males	8.4%		
First generation students	50.3%	Black achievement gap	-10.8%		

Social inclusion ranking: 19

Disabled	7.4%
Mature (over 21)	31.9%

Imperial College London

Our University of the Year 2022 is the only UK university to focus exclusively on science, medicine, engineering and business. The institution has been at the heart of the country's coronavirus response, its academics now familiar faces as they have dissected the latest Covid data. Its own problem-solving approach to learning during the pandemic got the thumbs up from students, anointing Imperial our University of the Year for Student Experience also. It was one of only two institutions where student satisfaction improved in our analysis of National Student Survey (NSS) scores between 2020 and 2021.

The coronavirus has dominated the work of the university's School of Public Health, which will move to new premises by 2023 at a cost of £100million. The school has been responsible for more than 40 reports on the spread and control of Covid, the most influential authored by epidemiologist Professor Neil Ferguson, director of the Jameel Institute for Disease and Emergency Analytics.

The university was also well-prepared to roll out the rapid shift to remote learning that the pandemic necessitated, thanks to its experienced network of educational technologists and digital learning pioneers who have developed and shared best practices. Among its advances in online learning, Imperial sent miniaturised lab experiments around the world and recreated field trips in virtual settings.

The result has been a turnaround in a hitherto lacklustre performance in the annual survey seeking students' views on the university experience. Imperial achieved the biggest jump in student satisfaction this year of any university, a remarkable achievement at the height of the pandemic, when students elsewhere used the NSS to express a vote of no confidence in their university experience in 2020–21.

Undergraduates in most subjects are based at the original South Kensington campus, which is home to the business school and the Dyson School of Design Engineering.

There are nine sites in the capital, with teaching bases attached to a number of hospitals in central and west London. The Faculty of Medicine is one of Europe's largest in terms of staff and student numbers. The UK's first Academic Health Science Centre (AHSC), run in partnership with Imperial College Healthcare NHS Trust, aims to translate research advances into patient care. Imperial is also a partner in a medical school in Singapore, run jointly with Nanyang Technological University.

The latest chapter in Imperial's history, the ambitious 23-acre White City campus, brings together academia, business, the third sector and

---

South Kensington Campus
Exhibition Road
London SW7 2BU
Engineering.admissions
@Imperial.ac.uk
Medicine.ug.admissions
@Imperial.ac.uk
Ns.admissions@Imperial.ac.uk
www.imperial.ac.uk
www.imperialcollegeunion.org
Open days: see website

The Times and The Sunday Times **Rankings**
Overall Ranking: 4 (last year: 5)

Teaching quality	77.7%	=28
Student experience	79.3%	3
Research quality	56.2%	2
Entry standards	197	6
Graduate prospects	92%	=2
Good honours	92.4%	6
Expected completion rate	97.5%	3
Student/staff ratio	11.1	3
Services and facilities	£4,047	2

the community. Its overarching mission is to turn cutting-edge research into real-world benefits for society. The 13-storey Sir Michael Uren building opened in 2020, dedicated to biomedical engineering research, followed by Scale Space – a building designed to support life sciences and tech firms to grow their businesses.

Ranked seventh in the 2022 QS World University rankings, Imperial's reputation as a global academic elite institution is well earned. It counts 14 Nobel Prize winners among its alumni – including Sir Alexander Fleming who discovered penicillin. It received stellar plaudits in the 2014 Research Excellence Framework, when its research was found to have the greatest impact on the economy and society of any university. Of its submission, 90% was rated world-leading or internationally excellent, an outcome bettered only by Cambridge.

Its gold-rated performance in the government's Teaching Excellence Framework was similarly impressive, with assessors praising Imperial for providing an "exceptionally stimulating and stretching academic, vocational and professional education that successfully challenges students to achieve their full potential".

The university topped the new graduate prospects measure in our previous edition, and won our University of the Year for Graduate Employment award. Its graduates continue to be heavily in demand, with 92% in high-skilled or graduate-level employment or further study within 15 months.

Imperial's record on social inclusion is improving in some areas; notably it has the third lowest black achievement gap of any UK institution, and the 19th-highest proportion of UK students recruited from ethnic minorities. However, it continues to attract among the largest contingents from private schools, and in the 2020 admissions cycle only just over four in ten students arrived from non-selective state comprehensive schools – placing Imperial bottom on this measure. It remains four places off the bottom of our social inclusion ranking.

A five-year plan to widen access is underway. New admissions schemes guarantee interviews or lower offers for applicants from underrepresented groups; outreach programmes are targeting black students; a free digital platform has been rolled out to support students taking further maths A-level; and a maths sixth form school will target underrepresented groups.

There were 2,865 residential spaces for 2021 entry. All first-years are guaranteed a space.

Tuition fees

» Fees for UK students		£9,250
» Fees for International students 2022–23	£34,000–£36,200	
Medicine		£46,650
» For scholarship and bursary information see www.imperial.ac.uk/study/ug/fees-and-funding/		
» Graduate salary		£33,500

Student numbers

Undergraduates	10,475	(0)
Postgraduates	7,300	(1,630)
Applications/places	25,650/3,045	
Applications per place	8.4	
Overall offer rate	42.9%	
International students – EU	15.3%	
Non-EU	34.1%	

Accommodation

University provided places: 2,865
Self-catered: £91–£316 per week
First years guaranteed accommodation
www.imperial.ac.uk/study/campus-life/accommodation/

Where do the students come from?

					Social inclusion ranking: 112	
State schools (non-grammar)	42.4%	Low participation areas	4.1%	Disabled		2.3%
Grammar schools	23.4%	All ethnic minorities	60.6%	Mature (over 21)		9.7%
Independent schools	34.1%	White working-class males	2.2%			
First generation students	24.3%	Black achievement gap	-3.8%			

Keele University

The friendly, safe community that students enjoy on the University of Keele's 600-acre parkland campus is known affectionately as the "Keele bubble". Located in the heart of England, near Stoke-on-Trent, the self-contained campus has all the amenities of a small town – giving students access to shops, a bank, a health centre and a pharmacy along with bars and restaurants. The newly opened 150-room Courtyard by Marriott hotel is the latest addition, nestled in the university's Science and Innovation Park.

The university developed its Flexible Digital Education model during the pandemic – a framework of online materials and live online engagement designed to complement in-person teaching and learning.

Keele is a former winner of our University of the Year for Student Experience, and a strong endorsement from students this year for its handling of the pandemic has seen the university rise nearly 20 places in our rankings for this measure, placing it back in the UK top 30.

The Teaching Excellence Framework (TEF) awarded Keele gold. The panel commended an institutional culture that "demonstrably values teaching as highly as research", with outstanding levels of student engagement and excellent teaching and assessment practices resulting in a commitment to learning.

The Keele Curriculum, introduced in 2012, came in for particular praise in the TEF assessment. It covers voluntary and sporting activities, as well as the academic core, contributing to the Keele University Skills Portfolio, which is accredited by the Institute of Leadership and Management.

One of the first UK universities to declare a climate emergency, Keele has reduced its carbon emissions by 39% – exceeding its 2020 target and en route to its goal of being carbon neutral by 2030. Two wind turbines and 12,500 solar panels are being installed on campus in a partnership between the university and a low-carbon energy company. When completed they will generate up to half of Keele's electricity. Meanwhile, with HyDeploy – a UK-first trial – Keele has successfully blended hydrogen into the campus's closed gas network to reduce carbon emissions.

Research at Keele's recently launched Institute for Sustainable Futures is focused on issues such as food security, climate change and clean energy. The university was awarded Sustainability Institution of the Year at the 2021 Green Gown awards, which celebrate such efforts within higher education institutions.

In the 2014 Research Excellence Framework more than 70% of the work submitted by Keele was placed in the top two categories of world leading or internationally excellent. Research in primary care and health sciences, pharmacy, chemistry, science

---

Keele ST5 5BG
01782 734 010
admissions@keele.ac.uk
www.keele.ac.uk
www.keelesu.com
Open days: see website

The Times and The Sunday Times **Rankings**

Overall Ranking: 48 (last year: =51)

Teaching quality	75.9%	=51
Student experience	73.4%	=29
Research quality	22.1%	53
Entry standards	121	=74
Graduate prospects	77.5%	27
Good honours	77.1%	68
Expected completion rate	88%	51
Student/staff ratio	14.8	=43
Services and facilities	£2,225	88

and technology, the life sciences, and history scored particularly well.

From 2011 to 2020 the number of students starting courses swelled by more than a quarter, while applications decreased by about the same proportion – against a rising offer rate. Applications were 18% higher at the end of March 2021 than at the same point the year before – an uplift the university credits to its popular health programmes, particularly in medicine, nursing, physiotherapy and radiography along with a growing curriculum. It has launched an integrated Master's paramedic science degree and greatly expanded its offer within the areas of business, computing and geology. New courses in conservation and data science have also been introduced.

Keele doubled its portfolio of degree apprenticeships from two to four with the introduction of new programmes in district nursing and research science, joining courses in registered nursing and advanced clinical practice.

The second cohort of trainee vets enrolled in 2021 at Keele's new Vet School, a collaboration with Harper Adams University. One of only ten vet schools in the UK, it offers 72 places each year, delivered at both campuses. A veterinary hospital and a clinical skill centre on campus is due to be completed in 2022.

Sir David Attenborough opened the life sciences laboratories in recent years and, elsewhere, the Keele Business School has a big-data laboratory and a business incubator. The £34million Central Science Laboratory brings together practical teaching across a range of disciplines.

Keele is more successful than many pre-1992 universities in our social inclusion index, where it ranks 40th this year. Contextual information relating to applicants' backgrounds and experiences is considered for most applications, and those eligible for a contextual offer receive up to a two-grade reduction. The medical school runs a widening participation scheme to support underrepresented groups.

The university has about 2,800 residential spaces. International students who apply by the deadline are guaranteed accommodation, with first-years the next in line. The students' union organises events on campus every day and night of the week during term, and nearby Newcastle-under-Lyme has options for off-campus nights out. Sports facilities include a full-size 3G football pitch suitable for all-weather play in a variety of sports to supplement the indoor facilities.

Tuition fees

» Fees for UK students £9,250
» Fees for International students 2022–23 £14,700–£24,000
  Foundation courses £14,800; Medicine £39,000
» For scholarship and bursary information see
  www.keele.ac.uk/study/undergraduate/tuitionfeesandfunding/
» Graduate salary £24,000

Student numbers

Undergraduates	7,965	(525)
Postgraduates	655	(1,740)
Applications/places	14,475/2,020	
Applications per place	7.2	
Overall offer rate	77.9%	
International students – EU	2.1%	
Non-EU	4.9%	

Accommodation

University provided places: 2,800
Self-catered: £90–£171 per week
First years guaranteed accommodation
www.keele.ac.uk/discover/accommodation/

Where do the students come from?

				Social inclusion ranking: 40	
State schools (non-grammar)	84.4%	Low participation areas	19.8%	Disabled	7.8%
Grammar schools	8.9%	All ethnic minorities	34.1%	Mature (over 21)	15%
Independent schools	6.7%	White working-class males	5.9%		
First generation students	43.7%	Black achievement gap	-15.2%		

University of Kent

The curriculum at the University of Kent has gained a swathe of new degrees fit for the fourth industrial revolution. In 2021, Kent undergraduates began degrees in the fields of artificial intelligence; data science; computer science (cybersecurity); digital design; and electronic and computer engineering. The options of a year in industry or abroad are offered with most.

The review of the university's portfolio of programmes aligns with the Kent 2025 strategy, which targets growth in science, engineering, medicine, and creative, cultural and digital programmes.

The second intake of trainee doctors have begun courses at the Kent and Medway Medical School, a collaboration with Canterbury Christ Church University, which opened in September 2020. The school's Pears building on Kent's 300-acre Canterbury campus provides undergraduates with a GP simulation suite along with a 150-seat lecture theatre, seminar rooms and social spaces.

Only a handful of UK universities have a college system – Kent among them. Every student is attached to a college, the epicentre of social life, especially in the first year, with academic as well as residential facilities. There are six colleges at the Canterbury campus and one at the Medway site on the old Chatham naval base, which is shared with Greenwich and Canterbury Christ Church universities. The £50 million School of Pharmacy and the purpose-built Centre for Music and Audio Technology are at Medway too, with the refurbished business school.

Awarding Kent gold, the Teaching Excellence Framework panel praised the college system as a vital element underpinning a "flexible and personalised" approach to academic support. Assessors also praised Kent's "outstanding" Student Success Project, which identifies trends in results and completion rates, and acts to help those likely to fall behind.

Most Kent lectures were already being recorded pre-pandemic – whether they were delivered in person or online. This is continuing for the 2021–22 academic year and will be developed further in response to staff and student feedback. Students make particular use of the recorded sessions when preparing for exams, the university has found.

Results from the 2021 National Student Survey (NSS) suggest that Kent got the balance for course delivery during the pandemic about right. NSS scores for 2021 were down overall in all bar two universities, but only 40 institutions experienced a smaller decline than Kent. This has resulted in a sharp improvement this year in the university's ranking for teaching quality and student experience.

Kent has more than 630 degree apprentices on 12 programmes across sectors including bio

The Registry
Canterbury CT2 7NZ
01227 768 896
www.kent.ac.uk/contact-us
www.kent.ac.uk
www.kentunion.co.uk
Open days: see website

The Times and The Sunday Times **Rankings**
Overall Ranking: 46 (last year: 48)

Teaching quality	74.5%	=74
Student experience	70.4%	55
Research quality	35.2%	33
Entry standards	125	=63
Graduate prospects	68.2%	=77
Good honours	81.4%	42
Expected completion rate	88.2%	=46
Student/staff ratio	16.7	=80
Services and facilities	£1,985	110

science, clinical trials, social work and chartered management. A foundation year is being added to law from September 2022, and a suite of modern languages is also launching.

Almost three-quarters of the work submitted for the 2014 Research Excellence Framework was judged world-leading or internationally excellent. Led by successes in social work and social policy, music and drama, and modern languages, Kent achieves its highest ranking across our nine performance measures for the quality and quantity of its research.

There were 164 nationalities represented at Kent at the last count and there are postgraduate sites in Brussels and Paris. Under its #AllInternational banner, students are offered opportunities such as international study placements; global engagement modules as part of some courses; and worldwide online hangout events. The Kent Global Passport is an online app designed to assess students' cultural intelligence.

The university offers more generous financial help to undergraduates than most. Its Kent Financial Support Package (KFSP) is worth £1,500 per academic year (up to £4,500 maximum) to state-educated students from England whose household income is below £42,875 and who also meet other criteria, such as living in social housing. For 2021's intake up to 746 KFSPs were available.

Merit-based awards include the Kent Scholarship for Academic Excellence – a single £2,000 payment that is not means-tested but may be paid on top of the KFSP, awarded to students with AAA at A-level, or equivalent qualifications, or AAB if one of the subjects is either maths or a foreign language.

With 5,384 residential spaces at the Canterbury campus and a further 725 at Medway, Kent guarantees a place to all first-years who apply by the deadline.

A modern £3 million hub in the Park Wood student village on the Canterbury campus includes a shop, café/bar and dance studios. The Pavilion playing fields complex opposite is also the site of the cycle hub. The Sports Centre has a fitness suite, strength and conditioning training area and three multipurpose sports halls.

There are plenty of student-centric venues among Canterbury's cobbled streets and the seaside charms of Whitstable and Margate are easily reached by public transport. During term time a free shuttle bus connects the campuses at Canterbury and Medway.

Tuition fees

» Fees for UK students	£9,250
» Fees for International students 2022–23	£17,400–£21,200
EU fees	£13,000–£15,900
Medicine	£48,200
» For scholarship and bursary information see	
www.kent.ac.uk/finance-student/fees/index.htm	
» Graduate salary	£24,000

Student numbers

Undergraduates	14,070	(950)
Postgraduates	2,430	(1,255)
Applications/places	22,245/3,685	
Applications per place	6	
Overall offer rate	88.6%	
International students – EU	6.4%	
Non-EU	10.7%	

Accommodation

University provided places: 6,109
Catered costs: £144–£270 per week
Self-catered: £128–£210 per week
First years guaranteed accommodation
www.kent.ac.uk/accommodation/

Where do the students come from?

State schools (non-grammar)	90.3%	Low participation areas	10.2%	Disabled	5.6%
Grammar schools	3.3%	All ethnic minorities	42.7%	Mature (over 21)	8.5%
Independent schools	6.4%	White working-class males	5.4%		
First generation students	46.4%	Black achievement gap	-21.3%		

Social inclusion ranking: 80

King's College London

Applications to King's College London (KCL) hit a record high in 2020, when almost 57,500 students applied to study there – 10% more than the year before and a 51% uplift since 2011. A record number of places were awarded, with 7,875 enrolments in 2020 – a 17% increase. Since 2011 they have more than doubled.

KCL's popularity is showing no sign of slowing down – applications were 19% higher at the end of March 2021 than at the same point the year before. New courses have joined the curriculum, among them a master's in nursing (dual-award) with registration for adult and mental health nursing. The university has noticed a broader interest across all courses, especially those aligned to medicine and nursing, triggered by the pandemic's spotlight.

Dentistry undergraduates have 70 new phantom heads on which to practice their skills, after a £3million upgrade of facilities at Guy's Hospital Tower Wing. The investment has also afforded 12 haptics technology units and the latest in online platforms, including true-colour fast and accurate intra-oral scanners.

Dentistry regularly features among the top five degrees for career prospects, as almost all graduates go straight into work. Across all subjects King's graduates are among the most sought after, and the university ranks just outside the top ten in this year's Graduate Outcomes Survey, which records the proportion of graduates in high-skilled graduate-level jobs or further study 15 months after leaving.

Opportunities for students to engage with employers contributed to a silver award in the Teaching Excellence Framework. The panel highlighted the "excellent" extent to which students were stretched academically and the "strong research-led culture" that requires all research staff to teach.

Twelve Nobel Prize winners have studied or worked at KCL, which is in our top ten for research after 85% of the work submitted to the 2014 Research Excellence Framework was judged to be world-leading or internationally excellent. Law, education, clinical medicine and philosophy all ranked in the top three.

Some of the biggest advances in modern life have had input from KCL, including the discovery of DNA and the development of radar. The university continues to team up with hundreds of businesses – not least by co-ordinating the Covid-19 Research Registry. A new Department of Engineering opened in 2019, building on strengths in robotics, telecommunications and biomedical engineering.

Students rated King's' response to the pandemic higher than that of all but 17

Strand
London WC2R 2LS
020 7848 5454
Admissions@kcl.ac.uk
www.kcl.ac.uk
www.kclsu.org
Open days: see website

The Times and The Sunday Times **Rankings**
Overall Ranking: 18 (last year: 30)

Teaching quality	71.5%	112
Student experience	65.6%	=105
Research quality	44.0%	9
Entry standards	164	=18
Graduate prospects	82.8%	12
Good honours	88.1%	15
Expected completion rate	91.3%	=30
Student/staff ratio	11.7	=6
Services and facilities	£3,242	21

universities across the UK, according to our comparison of results in the 2021 National Student Survey (NSS) with those from 2020. This helped the university to move out of the bottom ten in our rankings for teaching quality and student experience to sit 13 and 21 places higher respectively.

The upturn in student satisfaction has contributed to King's rising to 18th in our overall academic ranking; a 12-place gain, bigger than any other among top 30 universities this year. Its QS World Universities Ranking for 2022 (which doesn't consider student satisfaction) is 35th.

KCL is one of the oldest and largest colleges of the University of London, with more than 30,000 students – a third of them from outside the UK. Four of KCL's campuses are within a square mile of each other near the banks of the Thames. A fifth campus in Denmark Hill, south London, hosts the Institute of Psychiatry, Psychology and Neuroscience and some dentistry facilities.

Most non-medical departments are located at the Strand, including KCL's Dickson Poon School of Law which has expanded into the east wing of the iconic Somerset House. Bush House, former headquarters of the BBC World Service, now houses KCL's business school, the faculty of science and some student services.

Nursing and midwifery and some biomedical subjects are based at Waterloo, while medicine and dentistry are mainly at Guy's Hospital, near London Bridge, and the St Thomas' Hospital campus, across the river from the Houses of Parliament.

KCL ranks third for social inclusion among the Russell Group universities, behind only Queen Mary, University of London and Sheffield. More than six in ten students are from ethnic minorities and the narrow black achievement gap is bettered by just 12 other universities.

About 40% of the student intake qualifies for financial help. The King's Living bursary of up to £1,600 is awarded to those from households with incomes up to £42,875.

Accommodation is guaranteed to all first-years who apply by the deadline. More than 1,000 places are at the lowest end of the rent scale and just 11 cost the top whack of £465 a week. Students can self-assign their rooms.

Sports grounds, south of the city centre, have facilities for all the main sports, plus rifle ranges, two gyms and a swimming pool.

Tuition fees

- » Fees for UK students £9,250
- » Fees for International students 2022–23 £21,840–£29,460
  Medicine £42,840; Dentistry £47,880
- » For scholarship and bursary information see
  www.kcl.ac.uk/study/undergraduate/
- » Graduate salary £29,000

Student numbers

Undergraduates	18,500	(870)
Postgraduates	9,140	(4,605)
Applications/places		57,470/6,655
Applications per place		8.6
Overall offer rate		59.4%
International students – EU		15.8%
Non-EU		23.5%

Accommodation
University provided places: 5,212
Catered costs: £302–£313
Self-catered: £155–£465 per week
First years guaranteed accommodation
www.kcl.ac.uk/accommodation

Where do the students come from?

State schools (non-grammar)	64.6%	Low participation areas	3.7%		
Grammar schools	12.2%	All ethnic minorities	63%		
Independent schools	23.4%	White working-class males	2%		
First generation students	37.2%	Black achievement gap	-9.7%		

Social inclusion ranking: 85

Disabled	6.4%
Mature (over 21)	21.3%

Kingston University

Kingston University is digging deep to invest in the student experience. A £100million project to upgrade halls of residence at its Seething Wells and Kingston Hill sites should be completed in 2022. Students will benefit from modern, energy-efficient bedrooms – 1,216 of them refurbished and 117 new rooms. Listed buildings at Seething Wells are being transformed into a café and events space, while at Kingston Hill kitchens are being expanded and shared social spaces are having a facelift.

This overhaul follows Town House, the university's £50million six-storey building at Penrhyn Road which opened in 2020. The development has fast become the focal point of the campus while also attracting plaudits for its striking architecture. It has given students access to facilities that include dance studios, an auditorium, informal learning spaces and a studio theatre, plus a library and archive.

At nearby Knights Park, where the Kingston School of Art is based, the Mill Street Building has been the focus of a £29million renovation. Students here now have more than 9,000 square-metres of creative teaching, workshop and studio space.

Our analysis of the 2021 National Student Survey (NSS) results puts Kingston just inside the top half for its Covid response – a respectable performance, although the shiny new facilities had to be at arm's length because of social distancing.

Most teaching has returned to in-person delivery. Some elements of blended learning are continuing, however, such as the recording of lectures for students to listen back to remotely. Bookable online support sessions with academic tutors – introduced during the pandemic – extended the hours that staff were available, a boon for students who have external commitments.

Penrhyn Road and Knight's Park campuses are close to Kingston town centre; the Kingston Hill site is a couple of miles away, near Richmond Park. The fourth campus is in Roehampton Vale, where a former aerospace factory now contains a technology block. Kingston is the UK's largest provider of undergraduate aerospace education, with its own Learjet and flight simulator.

The health, social care and education faculty is run jointly with St George's and there is a link with the Royal Marsden School of Cancer Nursing and Rehabilitation, enabling some to spend half of their course on clinical placements.

Applications to Kingston were up 22% by the end of March 2021 compared with the same point the year before, boosted by a 46% uplift in applications in the fields of health, social work and education. However, since a high point a decade ago applications have more than halved, although the number

Holmwood House
Penrhyn Road
Kingston upon Thames
KT1 2EE
020 3308 9932
admissionsops@kingston.ac.uk
www.kingston.ac.uk
www.kingstonstudents.net
Open days: see website

KINGSTON UPON THAMES

Edinburgh
Belfast
Cardiff
London

The Times and The Sunday Times **Rankings**
Overall Ranking: =101 (last year: 104)

Teaching quality	75.1%	=62
Student experience	69.2%	73
Research quality	5.1%	=91
Entry standards	116	=91
Graduate prospects	62.2%	110
Good honours	73.7%	100
Expected completion rate	82.4%	83
Student/staff ratio	17.6	=98
Services and facilities	£2,589	61

starting courses has remained steadier. Of 2020's intake, 29% came via Clearing.

Kingston's creative courses are among its most successful. In the 2014 Research Excellence Framework, art subjects achieved some of the best results alongside history and English. It entered relatively few academics – just 16% of eligible staff – but 60% of the submission reached the top two categories and there was some world-leading research in each of the nine areas assessed.

The university fared less well in the government's Teaching Excellence Framework (TEF), holding bronze – the lowest rating. The TEF assessors did compliment the university's award-winning focus on black and other ethnic minority students, and a completion rate in line with the average for Kingston's courses and student profile. Completion figures have improved even more since the TEF assessment.

Building on this strength and reflecting one of the country's more diverse student populations (63% from ethnic minorities), Kingston's Elevate accelerator programme is tailored to black UK-domiciled students. Designed to empower and equip them with commercial awareness and skills, Elevate provides access to industry events along with inspiring stories of successful black professionals. The programme ends with practical support for job applications and advice on professional opportunities – including starting a business.

Degree apprenticeships are a relatively small but growing area; programmes in social work and adult nursing have joined three options around construction and programmes to train nursing associates and environmental scientists. Kingston expects to have more than 600 student apprentices by September 2022. Undergraduate provision also gains a degree in business and accounting next year.

The university will award 400 entry bursaries of £2,000 to new undergraduates who meet certain criteria for widening participation. Those who have been in care, or who are adult carers, qualify for separate bursary provision.

The Tolworth Court outdoor sports facilities are three miles from the main campus and there is a gym on the Penrhyn Road site that offers student rates. Kingston has spent more than £20million extending and upgrading its student accommodation and all new entrants are guaranteed one of 2,340 residential places. Its riverside location and its relative proximity to London's bright lights are a big selling point.

Tuition fees
- » Fees for UK students £9,250
  Foundation courses (Early years £6,000) £7,800
- » Fees for International students 2022–23 £13900–£16,200
- » For scholarship and bursary information see www.kingston.ac.uk/undergraduate/fees-and-funding/
- » Graduate salary £24,500

Student numbers

Undergraduates	11,865	(905)
Postgraduates	3,915	(1,385)
Applications/places	21,455/3,215	
Applications per place	6.7	
Overall offer rate	71.9%	
International students – EU	4%	
Non-EU	9.5%	

Accommodation
University provided places: 2,340
Self-catered: £112–£360 per week
First years guaranteed accommodation
www.kingston.ac.uk/accommodation/

Where do the students come from?

State schools (non-grammar)	95.2%	Low participation areas	6.1%	Disabled	6.9%
Grammar schools	1.9%	All ethnic minorities	62.6%	Mature (over 21)	24.4%
Independent schools	2.9%	White working-class males	3.3%		
First generation students	52.7%	Black achievement gap	-19.3%		

Social inclusion ranking: 59

Lancaster University

After a glut of applications in 2020 – up more than 14% – and record admissions, Lancaster University's applications dipped slightly in the 2021 recruitment cycle, but overall the university has never been more in demand. An outstanding teaching record and its green, self-contained campus attracts students from all around the world.

Lancaster has featured consistently in our top ten in recent years: in 2018 it was our University of the Year and in 2019 it was our International University of the Year, with global outposts including a joint institute near Weihai, Shandong province, China, a branch campus in Ghana and another in Leipzig, Germany.

Its rankings for teaching quality and the wider student experience, derived from the 2021 National Student Survey (NSS), have risen sharply, despite falls in outright positivity for both due to the pandemic. However, Lancaster's declines were more modest than most, with just 15 universities doing better in our comparison with the previous year. Scores for course organisation and management were virtually unchanged, testament to this university's strong structures.

With leadership from chancellor Alan Milburn, the former chairman of the Social Mobility Commission, Lancaster has continued to widen participation. It recently launched an access programme to school students from year 9 and above. This includes information and skills-based workshops and, for those who complete the course, a typical offer two grades below the advertised requirements. The university also makes contextual offers to UK students one grade below the published entry grade and expects eligible applications to increase for 2022 entry.

Accordingly, its social inclusion rank has improved slightly in the past year. Although it is still in the bottom 30 in our table for England and Wales, it outperforms 17 of the 21 English or Welsh Russell Group universities. Almost eight in ten students come from non-selective state schools, and more than one third are from homes where neither parent or carer went to university.

About a third of the 2021 and 2022 intakes are expected to qualify for some form of financial assistance, and this includes a £1,000 annual bursary for UK students with a household income of less than £30,000. A £1,000 Lancaster scholarship is awarded to all UK entrants with at least AAA at A-level (or the equivalent) and five GCSEs at grade A/7 or above.

Lancaster's impressive physical facilities continue to grow. The management school has completed a significant modernisation, while the university has been working on a Health Innovation Campus to unite academics with

Bailrigg
Lancaster LA1 4YW
01524 592 028
ugadmissions@lancaster.ac.uk
www.lancaster.ac.uk
www.lancastersu.co.uk
Open days: see website

The Times and The Sunday Times **Rankings**

Overall Ranking: 11 (last year: =10)

Teaching quality	77.3%	34
Student experience	74.3%	23
Research quality	39.1%	15
Entry standards	144	=38
Graduate prospects	79.9%	19
Good honours	83.1%	34
Expected completion rate	93.3%	=17
Student/staff ratio	13	=12
Services and facilities	£3,509	14

local government, businesses, citizens and healthcare providers.

After a second phase of development, the sports centre now has a second hall, strength and conditioning room and a "human performance lab", while the library's three-floor extension has created 400 new study spaces and 120 for silent work. In 2020 Lancaster opened a high-tech architecture studio providing specialist facilities for up to 48 students, joined to the Lancaster Institute for the Contemporary Arts.

Lancaster's eco-friendly student residences on the 560-acre parkland campus have won the best halls award in the National Student Housing Survey eight times since 2010. In recent years, between 96% and 100% of undergraduate students who wanted a room on campus were offered one, and everyone who lists it as their first choice is guaranteed a place as long as they apply before the deadline.

Academically, the university has a strong offer, winning gold in the Teaching Excellence Framework (TEF), for making students feel valued, supported and challenged academically. The TEF panel said its "culture of research-stimulated learning" provided the knowledge, skills and understanding that is most highly valued by employers.

In the 2014 Research Excellence Framework, 83% of Lancaster's work was considered world-leading or internationally excellent, with particular success in business and management, sociology, English, and maths and statistics. The next nationwide research assessment is due to be published in April 2022.

One distinctive feature at the university is a college system. Everyone is allocated to one of nine colleges, which has its own advisory team dedicated to student support and can signpost help from the wellbeing, counselling and mental health services. These clinics, groups and one-on-one support are offered in person (pandemic allowing) as well as online.

The university's strong business links include its special business development and knowledge exchange team's use of European funds to support local businesses, which by extension help students to leverage their studies in the world of work. Four in five graduates are in high-skilled work or postgraduate study within 15 months of leaving, an excellent record that places Lancaster inside the UK top 20 on this measure.

Tuition fees

» Fees for UK students £9,250
» Fees for International students 2022–23 £20,930–£25,270
  Medicine £38,500
» For scholarship and bursary information see https://www.lancaster.ac.uk/study/undergraduate/fees-and-funding/
» Graduate salary £24,500

Student numbers

Undergraduates	11,385	(20)
Postgraduates	2,850	(1,415)
Applications/places	23,085/3,565	
Applications per place	6.5	
Overall offer rate	85.4%	
International students – EU	10%	
Non-EU	19.3%	

Accommodation
University provided places: 10,634
Catered costs: £146–£203 per week
Self-catered: £94–£171 per week
First years guaranteed accommodation
www.lancaster.ac.uk/accommodation/

Where do the students come from?

State schools (non-grammar)	78.6%	Low participation areas	8.2%	**Social inclusion ranking: 89**	
Grammar schools	10.7%	All ethnic minorities	18.9%	Disabled	7.2%
Independent schools	10.6%	White working-class males	5.3%	Mature (over 21)	4.4%
First generation students	35.2%	Black achievement gap	-17.2%		

University of Leeds

Leeds was well-positioned for the pivot to remote learning at Covid-19's outbreak, having had a digital education service in place since 2013. Its lecture-capture technology and multimedia management systems record lectures and virtual classroom sessions, supplementing the face-to-face experience. Students are able to refer back to the recorded content through an online learning environment, which includes subtitles along with the audio recording.

A new role of deputy vice-chancellor for digital transformation has been created, to oversee a strategy that builds on the positives of recent experience and embeds the effective use of digital technologies, data and digital approaches into all education.

Leeds ranks in the upper half of universities for its Covid response in our analysis of National Student Survey (NSS) results – having suffered a less severe drop in student satisfaction scores than many other institutions. This has translated into modest gains in our rankings for teaching quality and student experience, which are both derived from the pandemic-hit 2021 NSS.

Professor Simone Buitendijk, the new vice-chancellor, took up her role mid-pandemic after four years as vice-provost (education) and professor of maternal and child health at Imperial College London. Dutch scholar Buitendijk, the university's 13th vice-chancellor, has taken over from Sir Alan Langlands, who led the university for seven years. She has hit the ground running with a ten-year strategy governed by the elements of community, culture and impact. It sets out a blueprint which aims to tackle inequalities, achieve societal impact and drive change.

Investment in the bricks and mortar campus continues. The Bragg Building provides a new engineering and physical sciences hub for undergraduates and postgraduates, with facilities to engineer materials at atomic and molecular scales. Other modern developments include the Laidlaw Library and the refurbished Edward Boyle Library. A £17million upgrade to the students' union building, once famed for having the longest bar in the country, has improved social spaces and performance venues, and boosted facilities for clubs and societies.

Leeds secured gold in the Teaching Excellence Framework, impressing with a strong emphasis on education inspired by "discovery, global and cultural insight, ethics and responsibility, and employability". Assessors found that students take charge of their experiences with academic and co-curricular opportunities that can enhance their learning while preparing them for the world beyond university.

There are more than 500 undergraduate programmes, with students encouraged to take courses outside their main subject. The Leeds

---

Woodhouse Lane
Leeds LS2 9JT
0113 343 2336
study@leeds.ac.uk
www.leeds.ac.uk
www.luu.org.uk
Open days: see website

The Times and The Sunday Times **Rankings**

Overall Ranking: 15 (last year: =15)

Teaching quality	73.6%	82
Student experience	69.6%	67
Research quality	36.8%	27
Entry standards	159	22
Graduate prospects	79.7%	=20
Good honours	88.5%	13
Expected completion rate	93.4%	=15
Student/staff ratio	13.7	=30
Services and facilities	£3,211	23

Curriculum promotes the broadening of intellectual horizons and requires undergraduates to produce a research project in their final year.

More than 80% of the research assessed in the 2014 Research Excellence Framework was considered world-leading or internationally excellent, placing Leeds in the top ten for 30% of its subject areas. It is in the top 100 in the QS World University Rankings.

The Leeds Cancer Research Centre has opened with state-of-the-art infrastructure in discovery biology, physical sciences, engineering, artificial intelligence and clinical research, designed to accelerate the translation of new treatments and technologies to improve the prevention, diagnosis and treatment of cancer.

The new National Pig Centre aims to enable Leeds academics to help lower the environmental footprint of pig farming, while ensuring high welfare standards.

Our 2017 University of the Year remains one of the most popular in the country, attracting more than 62,000 applicants last year – only Manchester and Edinburgh had more. Applications were up a further 6% by the end of March 2021 compared with the same point 12 months earlier.

Two-thirds of Leeds students come from families with a history of university education and three in ten are drawn from independent or selective state secondary schools. This means that Leeds has one of the lower proportions of students from non-selective state schools in the UK.

Among its widening participation schemes are contextual offers for applicants from deprived neighbourhoods, and an access scheme that rewards those who complete it with a lower-than-published offer. The Alternative Entry Scheme takes account of mature students' work and life experiences if they lack formal entry qualifications. Leeds's financial support package benefits 30% of admissions.

The university's 98-acre site is walking distance from the city centre, although much of the accommodation is further out. There are 9,175 student bedrooms, enough to guarantee accommodation to first-years. Those living in halls get free access to the Edge sports centre (discounted rates are offered university-wide), which has one of the largest fitness suites of any UK university. The facility is complemented by the Brownlee Centre, the UK's first purpose-built triathlon training base, housed at Sports Park Weetwood, three miles from the main campus.

Tuition fees

»	Fees for UK students	£9,250
»	Fees for International students 2022–23	£20,750–£25,250
	Medicine	£36,500
»	For scholarship and bursary information see www.leeds.ac.uk/undergraduatefees	
»	Graduate salary	£25,000

Student numbers

Undergraduates	25,570	(390)
Postgraduates	8,835	(1,535)
Applications/places	62,250/7,155	
Applications per place	8.7	
Overall offer rate	65.7%	
International students – EU	4.2%	
Non-EU	12.1%	

Accommodation

University provided places: 9,175
Catered costs: £162–£207 per week
Self-catered: £91–£191 per week
First years guaranteed accommodation
www.accommodation.leeds.ac.uk/

Where do the students come from?

				Social inclusion ranking: 102	
State schools (non-grammar)	70%	Low participation areas	8.1%	Disabled	6.9%
Grammar schools	11.6%	All ethnic minorities	22.1%	Mature (over 21)	7.5%
Independent schools	18.3%	White working-class males	3.8%		
First generation students	32.9%	Black achievement gap	-18.8%		

Leeds Arts University

For the first time, Leeds Arts University has submitted work for assessment in the Research Excellence Framework. It is a bold step by the former Leeds College of Arts, which only became a university in 2017. It chose to showcase its work with local and global communities, including research into "drawing as a collaborative tool in community visualisation". Results are due to be published in April 2022.

The university's new chancellor, Skin – the lead singer of Skunk Anansie, DJ, fashion icon, actress and activist – began her ambassadorial role in January 2021. The artist, who took part in the university's Creative Networks events programme and masterclass in 2019, said: "I am really impressed with the students and staff, and look forward to being able to support everybody in their creative talents."

The north of England's only specialist arts university, Leeds Arts was our 2019 University of the Year for Student Retention. Its dropout rate continues to be low at 2.8% – about one third of the level expected (8.3%), putting it on a par with the likes of Warwick and Bath even though it has a considerably more diverse intake.

During the pandemic, remote delivery of practical arts courses proved to be a challenge. Leeds Arts committed to giving students access to on-campus facilities and teaching whenever guidance allowed and introduced a blended learning model using video conferencing for some teaching and one-to-one contact. Submissions for assessment were adapted to be digital, using photography or recordings.

However, after years of excellent scores in the National Student Survey, the pandemic hit Leeds Arts hard. Students passed a harsh judgment on its efforts, with scores for overall satisfaction falling 19 percentage points. Only one university (Bournemouth) lost more ground in our comparison of student satisfaction scores.

The small student community of about 2,000 undergraduates is based on the Blenheim Walk campus, ten minutes from Leeds city centre. Opened in 2019, it has studios for film, music and photography as well as a 230-seat auditorium, enhanced fashion design studios and a large specialist arts library.

Professional-standard equipment includes large-format digital printers, 3D scanners and industrial-grade machinery for working with wood, metal and plastics. Acoustically insulated sound booths, which record the quietest and loudest sounds, can be used to create radio or television advertisements. At Vernon Street, the original base in the city centre, further education courses are taught.

The opening exhibition at the Blenheim

Blenheim Walk
Leeds LS2 9AQ
0113 202 8039
admissions@leeds-art.ac.uk
www.leeds-art.ac.uk
www.leedsartsunion.org.uk
Open days: see website

The Times and The Sunday Times **Rankings**

Overall Ranking: =103 (last year: 55)

Teaching quality	72.3%	=98
Student experience	64.9%	111
Research quality	n/a	
Entry standards	149	=29
Graduate prospects	51.7%	131
Good honours	76.7%	=76
Expected completion rate	93.5%	14
Student/staff ratio	15.1	=49
Services and facilities	£1,287	131

Walk Gallery featured the work of Yoko Ono. In 1966 she performed her *Bag Piece* at the Vernon Street building with her then husband, Anthony Cox.

Leeds Arts is no stranger to famous names and counts Henry Moore and Barbara Hepworth, who were contemporaries, among its alumni. More recently Damien Hirst and Marcus Harvey emerged from Leeds Arts to lead the way in the YBA (Young British Artists) scene. The comedian and actor Leigh Francis, better known as Keith Lemon, began his career there with a diploma in art and design.

When it was still Leeds College of Art, the institution was awarded silver in the Teaching Excellence Framework. The panel was impressed that a significant number of teaching staff were practising artists or designers, enhancing the students' exposure to the creative industries, and praised the level of support for mature students and those with disabilities.

Easter and summer schools are among activities to widen participation. There is also a free after-school art club, specialist workshops and taster sessions for learners of all ages. The university has the eighth-highest proportion of disabled students of any in our guide and 93.1% of the intake is state-educated, a slightly higher proportion than expected given its courses and entry standards.

All students receive two £55 payments in their first year to help with the cost of materials, and an extra £75 in the third year. Bursaries add up to £1,100 over three years to undergraduates whose family income is below £25,000 a year.

Students build their portfolios through paid external projects, forging industry links through live briefs and opportunities to show their work at trade fairs, studios and in galleries. A careers portal lists jobs and other creative opportunities for students and recent graduates.

As well as Skin, guest speakers at the university's Creative Networks events have included the artist Jake Chapman, the historian and broadcaster Andrew Graham-Dixon, and Frances Morris, director of Tate Modern.

Leeds Arts is one of the city's four universities and the social scene is energetic. University accommodation is owned and managed privately: there are places for about 70% of students who want to live in. If accommodation is full, the students' union provides links to private rental companies.

Tuition fees

» Fees for UK students	£9,250
» Fees for International students 2021–22	£15,800–£16,900
» For scholarship and bursary information see www.leeds-art.ac.uk/apply/finance/	
» Graduate salary	£20,000

Student numbers

Undergraduates	2,075	(0)
Postgraduates	30	(40)
Applications/places		4,805/760
Applications per place		6.3
Overall offer rate		43.5%
International students – EU		2.6%
Non-EU		6.8%

Accommodation

University provided places: 673
Self-catered: £120–149 per week
First years given priority
www.leeds-art.ac.uk/life-in-leeds/accommodation

Where do the students come from?

State schools (non-grammar)	93.1%	Low participation areas	13.1%		
Grammar schools	1.4%	All ethnic minorities	9.8%		
Independent schools	5.5%	White working-class males	4.1%		
First generation students	42.4%	Black achievement gap	n/a		

Social inclusion ranking: 64

Disabled	12.5%
Mature (over 21)	9.6%

Leeds Beckett University

Two Leeds Beckett students have brought home medals from the Tokyo Olympic Games as part of a university sporting contingent that performed better than many countries. Alex Yee, 23, who is studying for a BSc in sport and exercise science, won gold in the triathlon mixed relay and silver in the men's triathlon. With 19-year-old criminology student Keely Hodgkinson's silver in the 800m, Leeds Beckett's medals haul equalled South Africa's at the Games.

Their triumphs capped an astonishing performance by an Olympic team featuring no less than 18 athletes who had graduated from the university or trained at its world-class Carnegie School of Sport through the elite programme run in partnership with British Athletics: the Leeds Talent Hub. The environmental chambers at the school's new £45million facility were vital to help the competitors prepare for the hot and humid conditions in Tokyo.

A 60m covered rooftop sprint track for performance training and analysis is among the facilities at the school, which opened in 2020 on the Headingley campus. As well as research laboratories and a teaching kitchen, the building has enhanced strength and conditioning spaces. The university's other partnerships include Leeds Rhinos rugby league and Yorkshire County Cricket.

A £300million development programme is continuing to upgrade the Headingley and City campuses. The £80million School of Arts building has 11 floors of specialist facilities for 3,000 students taking 40 courses in creative technologies, fashion marketing, film, music and sound, and the performing arts. Students have access to a 180-seat theatre, a 220-seat cinema, industry-standard film and green screen studios, a black box theatre, sound recording studios, acoustic labs and post-production suites. The school's history stretches back at least 170 years and the university hopes the new base will become a cultural hub for the city's arts scene.

The focus on boosting the quality of student life seemed to be paying off for Leeds Beckett in 2020 when it reached the top 25 in the National Student Survey (NSS) for student satisfaction with the broad experience, and the top 40 for satisfaction with teaching quality. But the students' verdict on their pandemic experience was negative, placing Leeds Beckett was only 31 places off the bottom, leading to heavy falls in our rankings for teaching quality and student experience.

One-to-one interview rooms for confidential guidance and support have been installed as part of a drive to improve wellbeing services. A multi-disciplinary wellbeing team works directly with students and with academic schools to identify problems early. Students can also self-refer for consultations.

City Campus
Leeds LS1 3HE
0113 812 3113
admissionenquiries@
leedsbeckett.ac.uk
www.leedsbeckett.ac.uk
www.leedsbeckettsu.co.uk
Open days: see website

The Times and The Sunday Times Rankings		
Overall Ranking: =112 (last year: 107)		
Teaching quality	74.9%	=64
Student experience	69.4%	=68
Research quality	4.1%	=101
Entry standards	104	=124
Graduate prospects	66.2%	=91
Good honours	75.7%	89
Expected completion rate	77.6%	112
Student/staff ratio	20	=118
Services and facilities	£2,384	80

The Law School has loaded many textbooks on a database for easier access and the School of Social Sciences opened a cold case unit in September 2020, where students gain experience by working on real missing persons cases. The School of Health and Community Studies has a new speech and language therapy suite.

Fourteen new courses include visual effects, geography, sports journalism, digital marketing, cybersecurity and a distance learning option in primary education – accelerated route (Montessori). From 2022, the options will include degrees in English and creative writing, and history and politics.

A silver award from the Teaching Excellence Framework came with praise for Leeds Beckett's employability strategies for students, who can learn real-world skills through live project briefs, case studies, practice-related assessments, and placements.

The university has launched a graduate internship scheme to support the region's small to medium-sized businesses as they recover from pandemic. The scheme offers businesses a bursary to recruit a Leeds Beckett graduate.

From its beginnings in its predecessor institutions – the Leeds Mechanics Institute, founded in 1824, and the City of Leeds Training College (1913) – Leeds Beckett has been known for widening access to higher education. Although it remains in the bottom half of our social inclusion rankings for England and Wales, it has climbed 14 places to rank 70th this year.

In research, Leeds Beckett has built a reputation in applied fields with three interdisciplinary research institutes for health, sport and sustainability, and there are ten centres with a more specialist focus. Six research centres under the Carnegie School of Sport explore rugby, sport coaching, human performance, social justice in sport and society, active lifestyles, and obesity.

All students can take part in sport – even if they don't aspire to be an Olympian. A dedicated fitness app allows students to manage bookings at an extensive range of indoor and outdoor facilities while also tracking their fitness and adding personal goals. The Athletic Union has 38 sports clubs with more than 80 teams. Recreational and outdoor activities include tchoukball, sub-aqua and snow sports.

Leeds Beckett guarantees accommodation to all first-years who make the university their firm choice and apply by the deadline. Lively and relatively affordable, Leeds nightlife is a big draw for students.

Tuition fees

»	Fees for UK students	£9,250
»	Fees for International students 2022–23	£14,000
	Foundation courses	£12,500
»	For scholarship and bursary information see www.leedsbeckett.ac.uk/undergraduate/financing-your-studies/	
»	Graduate salary	£21,000

Student numbers

Undergraduates	15,895 (1,810)
Postgraduates	2,185 (3,400)
Applications/places	25,550/4,685
Applications per place	5.5
Overall offer rate	78.1%
International students – EU	1.4%
Non-EU	3.2%

Accommodation
University provided places: 2,633
Self-catered: £106–£256 per week
www.leedsbeckett.ac.uk/student-experience/accommodation/

Where do the students come from?

State schools (non-grammar)	91.9%	Low participation areas	17.2%	Disabled	6.5%
Grammar schools	3%	All ethnic minorities	21.7%	Mature (over 21)	13.5%
Independent schools	5%	White working-class males	7.8%		
First generation students	39.1%	Black achievement gap	-19.4%		

Social inclusion ranking: =70

Leeds Trinity University

Leeds Trinity's commitment to supporting access to higher education for communities that are hard to reach, without a university tradition or lacking aspirational role models is borne out by its success. Of the four Leeds universities, Trinity is the most socially inclusive, this year ranking just outside the top 20 in England and Wales. Six in ten students are the first in their family to go to university, almost one in five comes from an area of low participation and 62% are aged over 21 – all among the highest proportions in the UK.

Initiatives to widen participation include contextualised admissions, foundation years, pre-16 support, and, for local year 12 students, taster days and a summer school – after which most enrol at Leeds Trinity the next year. The university's personalised approach to study and support is galvanised in its strapline: "At Leeds Trinity you are a name not a number", a supportive ethos that has helped to attract students who previously lacked confidence. The university was the first in Yorkshire to receive the Race Equality Charter bronze award in recognition of its work to improve representation, progression and success of black, Asian and minority ethic students (who make up just under half the student body and staff).

Based at a single site in Horsforth, six miles northwest of Leeds city centre, the university experienced a surge in scores for student satisfaction with both teaching quality and the wider experience in the previous edition of our *Guide*. However, the gains were lost in the National Student Survey (NSS), undertaken at the height of the pandemic, with just five universities experiencing a bigger decline in scores.

From ranking just outside the top 50 for teaching quality and student experience last year, Leeds Trinity now finds itself well outside the top 100 on both measures. Scores for learning resources were down 25.1 percentage points (the third biggest fall on this measure), learning community scores were down 17.2 percentage points and overall satisfaction down 15.6 percentage points.

The lecture-capture technology installed during the pandemic will continue to be a learning tool, but the university is aware that students place a higher value on in-person learning. Recent upgrades to facilities should help to boost satisfaction now that the campus has re-opened. Trinity launched a new fitness suite in early 2020 and has since created another for sports therapy. A new motion-capture analysis lab is for use by students on sport and media courses. Photography students have access to two new studios and a modern darkroom.

Accommodation is also being upgraded, doing away with Kirkstall Hall's part-catered provision and creating bigger kitchens to suit self-catering. Older residences have been

Brownberrie Lane
Horsforth
Leeds LS18 5HD
0113 283 7123
admissions@leedstrinity.ac.uk
www.leedstrinity.ac.uk
www.ltsu.co.uk
Open days: see website

The Times and The Sunday Times Rankings
Overall Ranking: 124 (last year: 110)

Teaching quality	71.1%	113
Student experience	63.9%	=118
Research quality	2.0%	121
Entry standards	103	=126
Graduate prospects	61.8%	=111
Good honours	81.8%	41
Expected completion rate	81.3%	91
Student/staff ratio	22.9	131
Services and facilities	£2,031	105

refurbished and have also gained kitchen space.

Teacher training remains the strongest suit at Leeds Trinity, which has its roots in two Catholic teacher-training colleges established in the 1960s, while today welcoming students of all faiths or none. New courses – in psychology with criminology or sociology; physical education and school sport; and strength and conditioning science – welcomed their first intakes in 2021.

All Leeds Trinity degrees include professional work placements without students needing to take a sandwich year. Volunteering is also credited as a placement, which students have opportunities to do abroad. All graduates leave with at least three months' work experience on their CV, with references from employers. A network of partnerships places students at local, national and global organisations.

The placement scheme contributed to a silver award in the Teaching Excellence Framework. The panel highlighted high-quality support mechanisms for employability, including professional placements, as well as excellent use of technology and innovative assessment and feedback.

The Centre for Apprenticeships, Work-based Learning and Skills co-ordinates Leeds Trinity's degree apprenticeship programmes and has specialist tutors and support staff. Digital marketer degree apprentices began training in February 2021, as did those on courses in children, young people and family practice. A police constable programme is run in partnership with the West Yorkshire force. Other options lead to qualifications as a chartered manager, supply-chain leadership professional and business-to-business sales professional.

Only 20 academics were entered for the 2014 Research Excellence Framework, but there were good results in communication, cultural and media studies, and library and information management. The flagship research group, the Leeds Centre for Victorian Studies, has a national and international reputation.

A spin studio and two floors of gym equipment feature in the campus fitness suite, with free weights and a training rig. Other facilities include 3G and grass pitches, an athletics track and outdoor hard courts for netball and tennis.

While the university is not able to guarantee accommodation, everyone who applied for a room in the current academic year was allocated one. A small number are still catered.

Tuition fees

»	Fees for UK students	£9,250
	Foundation degrees	£5,000
»	Fees for International students 2022–23	£12,000
»	For scholarship and bursary information see www.leedstrinity.ac.uk/study/fees-and-finance/	
»	Graduate salary	£20,000

Student numbers

Undergraduates	4,175	(45)
Postgraduates	495	(265)
Applications/places	6,355/990	
Applications per place	6.4	
Overall offer rate	86.4%	
International students – EU	1.6%	
Non-EU	0.2%	

Accommodation

University provided places: 683
Catered costs: £135 per week
Self-catered: £98–£133 per week
www.leedstrinity.ac.uk/accommodation/

Where do the students come from?

State schools (non-grammar)	96.1%	Low participation areas	19.8%	Social inclusion ranking: =22	
Grammar schools	2.2%	All ethnic minorities	45.8%	Disabled	4.9%
Independent schools	1.7%	White working-class males	4.1%	Mature (over 21)	62.1%
First generation students	59.8%	Black achievement gap	-17.6%		

University of Leicester

From autumn 2022 students at the University of Leicester will benefit from its £150million Freemen's campus. Featuring buildings within landscaped gardens and tree-lined pathways, the flagship development combines a new teaching and learning centre with 1,200 bed spaces, the first of which have already opened.

In addition to the centre's modern lecture theatres, teaching rooms and study areas the site will house a high-tech games area and cinema suite among its resources.

The new base is next to the main campus in a leafy suburb a mile from the city centre. A £21million extension to the Percy Gee students' union building doubled social learning spaces there and added a large food court at the heart of the campus. Elsewhere, there has been redevelopment at the historic Brookfield site, a few minutes from the main campus. Home to the School of Business, it has teaching rooms, lecture theatres, a trading room and breakout areas.

Further afield, the Leicester International Institute/Dalian University of Technology in Panjin, China, offers degrees taught in English in chemistry, mechanical engineering and mathematics.

Leicester fared well in the 2021 National Student Survey (NSS), experiencing one of the smaller falls in student satisfaction through the pandemic-affected academic year. It ranked in the top 30 of our analysis that compared NSS scores from both years, ranking universities on the scale of their year-on-year decline.

Remote learning continues to play an important role in undergraduate course delivery as part of a blended approach, which typically combines multiple on-campus and online delivery modes. These include in-person seminars, webinars, workshops and Q&A sessions and recorded lectures, presentations and scenario simulations. Lecture-capture technology is available to all students.

Leicester's effective remote learning pivot was in part down to already having a suitable infrastructure – as highlighted by Teaching Excellence Framework (TEF) assessors when awarding a silver rating. The panel praised Leicester's system for filming lectures, introduced in response to student feedback. The TEF panel also congratulated the university on engaging students with the latest research.

Leicester offers undergraduates the flexibility to choose single, joint or major/minor programmes. Those taking the latter route are able to combine a range of subjects, spending three-quarters of their time on the major element.

Although applications have dipped a little, Leicester has retained healthy enrolments across the past decade, with nearly 20% more first-years joining in 2020 than in 2011. The 2020 admissions round experienced a 13%

University Road
Leicester LE1 7RH
0116 252 5281
study@le.ac.uk
www.le.ac.uk
www.leicesterunion.com
Open days: see website

The Times and The Sunday Times Rankings
Overall Ranking: 37 (last year: 37)

Teaching quality	74.5%	=74
Student experience	71.3%	=45
Research quality	31.8%	=37
Entry standards	129	=55
Graduate prospects	73.5%	=51
Good honours	82.9%	=35
Expected completion rate	90.5%	35
Student/staff ratio	13.8	26
Services and facilities	£2,871	36

increase and made successful use of the clearing process, recruiting 29% of the intake this way.

Building on its longstanding commitment to space research, the university has opened its Space Park. Dedicated to companies developing space technology or using space-enabled data, it aims to be a world-leading centre for research, enterprise and education in space and Earth observation. Students will be part of its collaborative community of academics and industry partners.

Three quarters of the work submitted to the Research Excellence Framework was rated as world-leading or internationally excellent, with the School of Museum Studies producing the best work. Results were also good in clinical medicine, biology, earth science and general engineering.

Leicester is celebrating its centenary in 2021. "Citizens of Change 100" scholarships are worth £2,500 per year of study (up to £7,500 maximum) to ten UK students, or half-price tuition fees for the first year for 20 international students. Successful applicants have to create a video of up to 60 seconds – with TikTok and Instagram Reels as the suggested format – that answers the question: "What do you want to change?" Applications are welcomed from those who have applied late or through clearing, as well as those who already hold an offer and who have made Leicester their firm choice.

Further scholarships available include awards worth £1,000 per year of study

to students who have completed access programmes, or who come from households with incomes of less than £25,000. About a third of the intake are expected to receive some form of scholarship or bursary.

Leicester may make reduced offers of up to two grades across most undergraduate courses based on contextual data, even without applicants asking for a grade reduction. Outreach activities include workshops, campus visits, residential programmes, mentoring and academic taster days. Those who complete Leicester's post-16 progression programmes qualify for reduced offers and financial support.

Both of the university's sports centres have a gym, swimming pool, spa, sauna and steam room, and studios. The campus centre also has a sports hall and there are floodlit tennis courts, all-weather courts and rugby pitches at the Stoughton Road playing fields in Oadby.

Students enjoy the city of Leicester's manageable size, decent nightlife and reasonably priced restaurants. There is guaranteed space in student accommodation for those who apply before September 1.

Tuition fees

» Fees for UK students	£9,250
» Fees for International students 2022–23	£17,500–£21,750
Medicine (clinical years)	£40,140
» For scholarship and bursary information see	
www.le.ac.uk/study/undergraduate/fees-funding	
» Graduate salary	£25,000

Student numbers

Undergraduates	11,185	(215)
Postgraduates	3,565	(1,215)
Applications/places	19,475/2,590	
Applications per place	7.5	
Overall offer rate	74.2%	
International students – EU	4.2%	
Non-EU	12%	

Accommodation

University provided places: 3,482
Self-catered: £88–£96 per week
First years guaranteed accommodation
www.le.ac.uk/study/accommodation

Where do the students come from?

State schools (non-grammar)	81.1%	Low participation areas	10.1%	
Grammar schools	9.7%	All ethnic minorities	57.3%	
Independent schools	9.1%	White working-class males	3.4%	
First generation students	39.4%	Black achievement gap	-15.3%	

Social inclusion ranking: 73

Disabled	5.8%
Mature (over 21)	9.4%

University of Lincoln

Set in a modern campus overlooking Brayford Pool in a medieval cathedral city, the University of Lincoln has gone from strength to strength. A vastly broadened curriculum has almost doubled student numbers in the past dozen years or so, and largely buoyant student satisfaction rates indicate that an expanding academic scope is hitting the right notes with undergraduates.

The winner of our 2021 Modern University of the Year has invested more than £375million into the Brayford Pool campus over the past two decades.

The Lincoln Medical School – established in collaboration with the University of Nottingham, whose BMBS (Bachelor of Medicine, Bachelor of Surgery) degree the students take – has a new home in the heart of campus. Its £21million dedicated building houses lecture theatres, clinical skills and anatomy suites, laboratories and diagnostic tools among its specialised teaching and learning facilities. A biomedical and health sciences library and mock consultation rooms are on site, supported by the latest technologies.

The school launched in 2018 and its first cohort of students started their degrees in 2019. A foundation year widens access to the medical school, which was awarded an extra 20 places in its second year of operation. Grounded in the university's civic role within England's second-largest county, its graduates will be encouraged to complete their junior doctor training locally and apply for jobs in the region.

In common with almost all UK universities, Lincoln lost ground in this year's National Student Survey (NSS) as students voiced their dissatisfaction with their Covid experience – although Lincoln's scores were down more significantly than most, with just 50 universities experiencing a greater impact. However, such was the strength of the university's NSS outcomes in 2020, that it remains just outside and just inside the top 40 respectively for satisfaction with teaching quality and the student experience this year.

A variety of digital learning tools continue to be used at Lincoln, with the aim of maintaining the flexibility and inclusivity that a blended model allows. These may include online collaboration and video-based communication, professional digital tools to underpin student learning, and extra learning resources delivered online from experts – such as guest lectures. Lecture-recording technology is used in most face-to-face teaching sessions, enabling students to review content.

Lincoln achieved a gold rating in the government's Teaching Excellence Framework. Assessors complimented the university on a strong approach to personalised learning through highly engaged personal tutors, with access to analytics to monitor progress

---

Brayford Pool
Lincoln LN6 7TS
01522 886 644
enquiries@lincoln.ac.uk
www.lincoln.ac.uk
www.lincolnsu.com
Open days: see website

The Times and The Sunday Times Rankings
Overall Ranking: 49 (last year: 45)

Teaching quality	76.5%	=41
Student experience	72.2%	38
Research quality	10.3%	58
Entry standards	118	=79
Graduate prospects	68.4%	=75
Good honours	78%	65
Expected completion rate	88.1%	=48
Student/staff ratio	15.7	=63
Services and facilities	£2,409	77

proactively. It found that students were involved in the design of courses, which enabled them to develop their independence, understanding and skills to reflect their full potential.

Degrees in business with English; health, exercise and nutrition; international accounting; international logistics and supply chain management; and mechatronics have been introduced. In 2022, biomedical engineering will join them.

Lincoln's stable of degree apprenticeships has gained a course in cultural heritage conservatorship – making 16 in total – with about 520 students on programmes. Roles range from social worker, nursing associate and laboratory scientist to chartered manager, academic professional and agricultural/horticultural adviser.

More than half of a large submission to the 2014 Research Excellence Framework was rated internationally excellent or world-leading. Lincoln was in the top ten in the health category for the quality of its output. Research in agriculture, veterinary and food science got the university's best results.

Home to the world's first Centre for Doctoral Training for agri-food robotics, the university has completed a building for Lincoln's Centre of Excellence in Agri-food Technology at Holbeach. It follows the success of its nearby National Centre for Food Manufacturing and will act as an innovation hub to promote robotics and automation across the food supply chain.

Efforts to widen participation focus on Lincolnshire's higher education "cold spots", as defined by the Office for Students, aiming to raise aspirations and offer opportunities. Outreach initiatives in low-participation neighbourhoods appear to be paying off, and Lincoln has among the ten highest proportions in the country of white working-class male students – an underrepresented group. It ranks in the UK top 20 for the proportion of students recruited from areas with low participation. During the pandemic the university livestreamed talks for students considering their post-18 options, with guest speakers including Dame Carol Ann Duffy (former poet laureate), Dr Alex George (UK youth mental health ambassador), and the naturalist and broadcaster Chris Packham.

There are 4,300 residential spaces and Lincoln guarantees all first-years a spot. A sports centre includes a hall and outdoor pitches. There is a £6million performing arts centre too, with a 450-seat theatre and three large studio spaces.

Tuition fees

- » Fees for UK students £9,250
- » Fees for International students 2022–23 £14,700–£15,900
  Medicine (clinical years) £43,500
- » For scholarship and bursary information see www.lincoln.ac.uk/home/studywithus/undergraduatestudy/feesandfunding/
- » Graduate salary £21,000

Student numbers

Undergraduates	12,545 (1,550)
Postgraduates	1,230 (1,100)
Applications/places	17,300/3,715
Applications per place	4.7
Overall offer rate	83%
International students – EU	1.1%
Non-EU	4.1%

Accommodation
University provided places: 4,300
Self-catered: £114–£206 per week
First years guaranteed accommodation
www.lincoln.ac.uk/home/studentlife/accommodation/

Where do the students come from?

State schools (non-grammar)	93.2%	Low participation areas	19.4%	
Grammar schools	3.8%	All ethnic minorities	10.1%	
Independent schools	3%	White working-class males	9%	
First generation students	52.1%	Black achievement gap	-29.5%	

Social inclusion ranking: 65

Disabled	6.7%
Mature (over 21)	10.5%

University of Liverpool

The University of Liverpool had a good pandemic from its students' perspective, ranking in the upper half of UK universities in our analysis of the year-on-year National Student Survey (NSS) results. Although scores are heavily down on those from 2020, Liverpool has actually risen in our rankings for teaching quality to the fringes of the top 50 because other institutions have fallen away more sharply. It is now one of the better-performing Russell Group universities in our two measures of student satisfaction that are based on the NSS.

The university took the challenges presented by Covid-19 as an opportunity to re-think its teaching and learning environment and accelerate the adaptation of delivery methods. Liverpool's plans for the current academic year were largely informed by feedback from students, who expressed their appreciation of being able to pause, rewind, review and learn at their own pace, but who also made clear how highly they value meeting with their peers and tutors on campus.

Advances set to continue at Liverpool include online study tools, workshops, skills development sessions, a virtual careers studio and enhanced library resources. The university is aiming for all lectures to be recorded. Extracurricular activities (virtual and on-campus) are listed on the My Liverpool app, which students can add to their personalised planner throughout their time at university.

Liverpool has also been investing heavily in its city-centre campus, where recent launches include a modern teaching hub and a new home for the School of Law and Social Justice. Next up is the Digital Innovation Factory, which brings together computer science, robotics and engineering research within a centre of excellence in simulation and virtual reality.

The Tung auditorium adding a 400-seat auditorium and accommodating a 70-piece orchestra is expected to open in 2022. Drawing on the city's arts heritage, it will host concerts, lectures and exhibitions for people of all ages and backgrounds.

The developments will help to make room for Liverpool's growing student population. Applications and enrolments in 2020's admissions round reached new records. The number of students starting courses was up 10% on the year before and 46% higher than a decade before. A suite of product design engineering degrees joins the curriculum from 2022.

Partnerships with a wide range of institutions in 26 countries, from Austria to the US, provide opportunities for students to study part of their degree abroad. Liverpool has pledged to expand this offer, so most of its programmes will include the chance to

Liverpool L69 7ZX
0151 794 5927
ug-recruitment@liverpool.ac.uk
www.liverpool.ac.uk
www.liverpoolguild.org
Open days: see website

The Times and *The Sunday Times* Rankings		
Overall Ranking: =30 (last year: 29)		
Teaching quality	75.9%	=51
Student experience	72.4%	37
Research quality	31.5%	40
Entry standards	140	=43
Graduate prospects	75.6%	38
Good honours	81.3%	=43
Expected completion rate	91.3%	=30
Student/staff ratio	13.9	27
Services and facilities	£3,387	16

spend a year studying at one of its partner universities. The university also has a campus in the Chinese city of Suzhou, run in partnership with Xi'an Jiaotong University, and offers joint courses with the Singapore Institute of Technology.

Liverpool holds silver in the Teaching Excellence Framework. In the 2014 Research Excellence Framework, the university entered a relatively low proportion of its eligible academics compared with other Russell Group institutions. This holds it back in our research ranking even though 70% of the work was judged to be world-leading or internationally excellent. More than half of its chemistry research was considered world-leading. Computer science and general engineering also scored particularly well.

Like most Russell Group universities, Liverpool struggles in our social inclusion ranking with just nine of the 21 Russell Group institutions in England and Wales ranking lower. Its strongest performance comes in recruitment of students from areas with low participation in higher education, who accounted for about one in 12 of the intake in the most recent figures. Long-term engagement with local disadvantaged schools and colleges underpins the university's widening participation agenda.

About a third of UK undergraduates receive Liverpool bursaries, worth £750 or £2,000 per year, depending on household incomes up to £35,000. An £800 housing discount for those who receive the Liverpool bursary or other bursaries is a rare scheme among UK universities. About a quarter of students living in halls of residence receive the saving, at a cost of about £920,000 to the university each year. Accommodation is guaranteed to first-years.

Industry partnerships include close links with AstraZeneca, HSBC, IBM, Network Rail and Unilever. The Career Studio delivers an employer-led programme of activity for students, designed to boost their networking skills and get hired.

The campus sport and fitness centre includes a swimming pool, two sports halls, a squash course, a bouldering wall and spin studios. Off campus at the Wyncote Sports Ground, the university has ten pitches for football and rugby, one for lacrosse, a floodlit all-weather pitch and 3G rugby facilities.

Student life in Liverpool combines nights out, affordability and a friendly atmosphere.

Tuition fees

» Fees for UK students	£9,250
Foundation courses	£5,140
» Fees for International students 2022–23	£20,000–£24,500
Dentistry £39,000; Medicine £37,350; Veterinary Science £37,350	
» For scholarship and bursary information see www.liverpool.ac.uk/study/undergraduate/finance	
» Graduate salary	£24,000

Student numbers

Undergraduates	22,150	(535)
Postgraduates	4,570	(2,340)
Applications/places		43,365/5,295
Applications per place		8.2
Overall offer rate		78.1%
International students – EU		2.4%
Non-EU		23.5%

Accommodation
University provided places: 4,800
Catered costs: £219–£220 per week
Self-catered: £143–£196 per week
First years guaranteed accommodation
www.liverpool.ac.uk/accommodation/

Where do the students come from?

State schools (non-grammar)	74.5%	Low participation areas	8.6%	
Grammar schools	13.1%	All ethnic minorities	16.8%	
Independent schools	12.3%	White working-class males	4.8%	
First generation students	40.6%	Black achievement gap	-24.2%	

Social inclusion ranking: 104

Disabled	6.3%
Mature (over 21)	7.4%

Liverpool Hope University

An academic restructuring has divided Liverpool Hope's faculties into nine schools and departments, each with a range of subject areas and their own teaching and research strengths. Courses fall within the Schools of Business; Creative and Performing Arts; Health Sciences; Geography and Environmental Science; Humanities; Psychology; Mathematics, Computer Science and Engineering; Social Science; and Education.

Formed by the 1980 merger of two Catholic and one Church of England teacher-training colleges, Liverpool Hope achieved university status in 2005. Teaching is based at the main campus, Hope Park, in the leafy suburb of Childwall four miles from the city centre, and at the Creative Campus, close to the heart of Liverpool.

At Hope Park the School of Social Sciences building features a simulation suite, where social work students can tackle common scenarios and assess their performance via video and audio recordings. The physiotherapy and sports rehabilitation clinic provides access to clinical teaching and training spaces. An £8.5million health sciences building has laboratories for nutrition, genomics, cell biology and psychology, along with a 25m biomechanics sprint track.

Resources at the Creative Campus include two theatres, an arts centre, studios for fine and applied art courses, a recording studio and dance studios. There is also a hub for student services. Study spaces and library facilities have been updated.

Liverpool Hope was the only higher education institution in the city to achieve gold in the Teaching Excellence Framework (TEF). Assessors commented on "outstanding levels of stretch provided through judicious partnerships, good curriculum design and extracurricular activities". The panel also acknowledged a strategic approach to ensuring outstanding outcomes, and recognition of the value of an inclusive community of diverse learners.

The university is an accredited Duke of Edinburgh Gold Award provider and bases the expedition part of the CV-boosting programme at its outdoor education centre, Plas Caerdeon, in Snowdonia National Park. Hope's own Service and Leadership Award (SALA) scheme credits hours spent volunteering by students, who also receive training in health, safety, leadership and diversity and inclusion.

In common with many other universities that offer lots of practical-based degrees, Liverpool Hope fared poorly in the eyes of its students for its pandemic response and ranks in the bottom 20 nationally. The result compares starkly with the high levels of student satisfaction reported by undergraduates in the

Hope Park
Taggart Avenue
Liverpool L16 9JD
0151 291 3899
admission@hope.ac.uk
www.hope.ac.uk
www.hopesu.com
Open days: see website

The Times and The Sunday Times Rankings
Overall Ranking: 81 (last year: =80)

Teaching quality	75.4%	=58
Student experience	67.3%	=90
Research quality	9.2%	=62
Entry standards	113	=102
Graduate prospects	61.3%	=116
Good honours	74.4%	=96
Expected completion rate	82.6%	81
Student/staff ratio	14.8	=43
Services and facilities	£2,170	93

previous NSS, which put Liverpool Hope in the top 20 UK institutions for teaching quality.

Face-to-face teaching resumed on practical programmes from March 2021, and for those on all undergraduate degrees from May – which should bring satisfaction levels back towards their previous heights. Some online teaching material is still available for students including lecture-capture where possible.

New degrees include film, TV, radio and media production; physical activity, nutrition and health; applied biomedical health; data science; and software engineering. Combined honours options in interactive and immersive performance; musical theatre; and conservation biology have also launched.

Student numbers are buoyant at this relatively small institution. A second consecutive rise in applications in 2020 brought the demand for places to a record level. Enrolments saw a bigger hike of 24%, bringing them to their highest to date.

Liverpool Hope has fallen 30 places to sit outside the top 50 of our social inclusion ranking this year, due notably to a wide black achievement gap. It does well on other measures of social inclusion, however, with a quarter of the intake coming from the UK's most deprived areas, a greater proportion of white working-class male students than most universities, and a population of disabled students that is among the 25 highest nationally.

More than half the university's eligible staff were entered for the 2014 Research Excellence Framework (far more than at most post-1992 universities) and there were good results in theology and education. There are research-led seminars in the final year of degree courses to introduce undergraduates to a research culture, and all students produce a dissertation or advanced research project.

A flagship collaborative research project with Everton Football Club examines brand loyalty and the socio-economic impact of the club in the local community. In another collaboration, Liverpool Hope's augmented-reality team is developing its strategic relationship with Oculus, a Facebook Technologies company.

The university's sports psychologists exchange knowledge with British Universities and Colleges Sport (BUCS) and have helped to shape policy. The £5.5million Sports Complex includes a sports hall, squash courts, fitness suite, dance studio and artificial pitches.

Most residential places are at the Aigburth Park residential campus, three miles from the Hope Park site, and accommodation is guaranteed for first-years.

Tuition fees

» Fees for UK students	£9,250
» Fees for International students 2022–23	£11,400
» For scholarship and bursary information see www.hope.ac.uk/undergraduate/feesandfunding/	
» Graduate salary	£21,000

Student numbers

Undergraduates	3,815	(80)
Postgraduates	705	(380)
Applications/places		9,955/1,490
Applications per place		6.7
Overall offer rate		88.1%
International students – EU		2.5%
Non-EU		1%

Accommodation

University provided places: 1,142
Self-catered: £88–£126 per week
First years guaranteed accommodation
www.hope.ac.uk/halls

Where do the students come from?

State schools (non-grammar)	89.7%	Low participation areas	24.9%	
Grammar schools	8.8%	All ethnic minorities	12.8%	
Independent schools	1.5%	White working-class males	8.9%	
First generation students	50.2%	Black achievement gap	-27.2%	

Social inclusion ranking: 62

Disabled	10.5%
Mature (over 21)	19.2%

Liverpool John Moores University

Liverpool John Moores' (LJMU) new Student Life Building and Sport Building are now welcoming students. Occupying three-and-a-half acres of Liverpool's city centre on Copperas Hill, connecting the university's Mount Pleasant and City campuses, the £64.5million development is further evidence of LJMU's continued investment in the student experience and in advancing its research capabilities. The project has also regenerated the area near Lime Street station, thus chiming with its commitment to benefit the wider community.

The students' union has moved into the five-storey Student Life Building, which gives LJMU the student hub that it previously lacked. It is the focal point for careers advice, information on international exchanges and wellbeing support. There is also a chaplaincy, a café and a study area as well as teaching spaces.

Next to it, the sports building provides access to a modern gym and two multipurpose halls; its eight-court hall has a viewing gallery. Nursing and allied health students have benefited from a new extension at the Tithebarn Building. The four-storey development has added six technology-enhanced simulation suites, two flexible-use 75-seat lecture theatres and three IT suites.

Now that teaching and learning can largely take place on campus again, these improved facilities should help to lift student satisfaction scores. In our analysis of the National Student Survey (NSS) results, LJMU ranks in the bottom 25 nationally for its Covid response, measured by the size of the fall in its pandemic-influenced NSS outcomes in 2021 compared with those from 2020.

It performed much better in the Teaching Excellence Framework, holding a silver award. Assessors complimented its "highly effective institutional strategic drive to improve satisfaction with assessment and feedback", strong recognition of teaching excellence and a consistent commitment to student engagement.

The Liverpool Screen School is housed at the £37.6million Redmonds Building (along with the schools of business and of law) and has links with the northwest's creative industries such as the BBC in Salford and ITV Northern Lights. Students use industry-standard television and radio studios and undertake placements.

Through the business faculty's Liverpool Business Clinic, students work in a consultancy team tackling real challenges presented by the region's businesses. Similarly, law undergraduates can gain real-world, *pro bono* experience from the first year of study at the university's Legal Advice Centre, which has provided legal counsel worth more than £500,000 since 2014.

LJMU attracts consistently buoyant application and enrolment figures. In 2020 it received the highest number of undergraduate

Exchange Station
Tithebarn Street
Liverpool L2 2QP
0151 231 5090
courses@ljmu.ac.uk
www.ljmu.ac.uk
www.jmsu.co.uk
Open days: see website

The Times and The Sunday Times Rankings
Overall Ranking: 93 (last year: 85)

Teaching quality	72.4%	=96
Student experience	67.8%	=83
Research quality	8.9%	=67
Entry standards	143	42
Graduate prospects	67%	=86
Good honours	76.6%	78
Expected completion rate	82.7%	=79
Student/staff ratio	17.3	=91
Services and facilities	£1,826	117

applications since 2015, and a record number of students started courses. New degrees from 2021 include computing, human evolution and behaviour, and sport nutrition. All are offered with or without a foundation year.

The university was among the pioneers of degree apprenticeships and offers 17 programmes with more than 1,300 learners at the last count. Courses include healthcare, civil engineering, construction management, risk and safety management, quantity surveying, professional policing practice, and digital and technology solutions.

LJMU enjoys a burgeoning research reputation and more than 60% of the work submitted for the 2014 Research Excellence Framework was rated world-leading or internationally excellent. The proportion topped 80% in physics, where the results covered astronomy. Researchers and students use the university's robotic telescope in the Canary Islands. LJMU was ranked second in the UK for sports science and fourth among post-1992 universities for law and education.

The Football Exchange (FEX) at the School of Sport and Exercise Sciences has engaged in research for several Premier League clubs and governing bodies such as UEFA.

LJMU's roots go back to the Industrial Revolution. University status came in 1992 and with it the John Moores moniker, in honour of the Liverpool entrepreneur and philanthropist who helped to fund its forerunner institutions. Almost nine in ten students arrive from state schools and LJMU does well at attracting white working-class male students. Its outreach work has helped it recruit more students from Northern Ireland than any university outside the province itself.

Close to 40% of entrants have qualified for some form of financial help in recent years. The £500 LJMU bursary is paid automatically to eligible students for each year of study. Thanks to the support of Yoko Ono, the John Lennon Imagine awards pay a £1,000 cash bursary to low-income students who have been in care or are estranged from their families.

The university endorses 4,000 residential spaces in privately operated halls of residence. All first-years are guaranteed a room in the heart of the city.

Liverpool makes a strong case as a student city with its thriving nightlife, relative affordability and cultural wealth. There are opportunities to get involved in sport at elite or just-for-fun level in activities including men's and women's Gaelic football, tennis, basketball and athletics.

Tuition fees

» Fees for UK students	£9,250
» Fees for International students 2022–23	£16,100–£16,600
Foundation years	£11,000
» For scholarship and bursary information see www.ljmu.ac.uk/discover/fees-and-funding/	
» Graduate salary	£22,000

Student numbers

Undergraduates	18,605 (1,500)
Postgraduates	2,235 (2,710)
Applications/places	32,955/6,830
Applications per place	4.8
Overall offer rate	80.6%
International students – EU	1.3%
Non-EU	4.9%

Accommodation

University provided places: 4,000
Self-catered: £80–£171 per week
First years guaranteed accommodation
www.ljmu.ac.uk/discover/your-student-experience/accommodation

Where do the students come from?

State schools (non-grammar)	88.8%	Low participation areas	17.3%	Social inclusion ranking: =57	
Grammar schools	8.5%	All ethnic minorities	13.1%	Disabled	4.7%
Independent schools	2.7%	White working-class males	11.1%	Mature (over 21)	17.3%
First generation students	52.2%	Black achievement gap	-22.1%		

London Metropolitan University

London Metropolitan University outdid all but four universities in its Covid response as seen through students' eyes, according to our analysis comparing National Student Survey scores in 2020 and 2021. Satisfaction with teaching quality improved year-on-year, a rare feat on disgruntled British campuses in a difficult period.

These positive outcomes have lifted London Met 25 places to reach its highest-ever position in our overall academic rankings. The university's achievement is all the more remarkable given the high proportion of practical-based subjects it offers. Institutions with similar subject mixes have largely experienced the most acute tumbles in student satisfaction compared with those that have a greater focus on classroom-based subjects.

Within a week of the first lockdown, teaching had moved online and London Met noted that student engagement was extremely positive throughout the enforced period of remote learning. The university worked with its students' union to evaluate how people felt about course delivery. London Met is now bringing as much teaching and learning back to campus as possible, while livestreaming and recording lectures for those who cannot attend.

Most of London Met life takes place at the extensive Holloway Road campus with its angular, steel-clad graduate centre designed by Daniel Libeskind. The School of Art, Architecture and Design is nearly four miles away in Aldgate. Created by the merger of London Guildhall University and the University of North London in 2002, London Met's origins date from the mid-19th century.

The university has one of the UK's most socially diverse intakes, with almost seven in ten undergraduates aged over 21 when they start their studies, 62% drawn from ethnic minority backgrounds and more than half the first in their family to go to university. It retains its place this year among the 30 most socially inclusive universities in England and Wales in our unique ranking.

London Met has developed fresh student-facing resources over the past year, including new offices for each school combining administrative, course and pastoral support in one place. The Careers Education Framework is being extended across the university, enabling students to find the ideal work placement to mesh with their past experience.

Another new development, London Met Lab, gives students the opportunity to work with university staff to tackle real-world challenges in the vibrant – and complex – capital city. A module called Empowering London sets the scene for students to work closely with a grassroots community project to

166–220 Holloway Road
London N7 8DB
020 7133 4200
courseenquiries@londonmet.ac.uk
www.londonmet.ac.uk
www.londonmetsu.org.uk
Open days: see website

The Times and The Sunday Times Rankings
Overall Ranking: 100 (last year: 125)

Teaching quality	81%	6
Student experience	74.9%	=17
Research quality	3.5%	111
Entry standards	100	=129
Graduate prospects	57.1%	127
Good honours	66.7%	125
Expected completion rate	68%	129
Student/staff ratio	18.5	=106
Services and facilities	£3,817	8

identify and potentially solve a local problem.

London Met dropped the name of "Sir John Cass" from its School of Art, Architecture and Design in 2020 because of the 18th-century politician and philanthropist's early links to the slave trade. It also established an Education for Social Justice Framework, fully in operation from 2022, which aims to reflect the diversity of London Met students and create a truly inclusive education.

The Science Centre's Superlab on Holloway Road is among the largest teaching laboratories in Europe, with audiovisual systems that can transmit 12 practical lectures simultaneously for different groups of students – a handy tool in the switch to remote learning during the pandemic. A social learning hub at the centre has high-spec classrooms and a café.

London Met is one of only 22 universities around the world to be a member of the UN Language Careers Network. Another strong subject is cybersecurity, backed up by a research centre that is the first of its kind in the UK, bringing together students and businesses.

In the Teaching Excellence Framework, London Met was awarded bronze in the light of student achievement "notably below benchmark across a range of indicators". Assessors noted a range of positive strategies to improve student satisfaction but expressed concern that comparatively few carried on to postgraduate study.

The university entered just 15% of eligible academics in the 2014 Research Excellence Framework – far fewer than in the previous round in 2008 – although half of its submission was rated world-leading or internationally excellent. English and health subjects scored well.

Continuing its outreach work to support underrepresented and disadvantaged students, London Met runs national Saturday Clubs, which offer 30 weeks of workshops for 12 to 16-year-olds covering topics such as art and design, writing and talking, and developing confidence. The Upward Bound programme on alternate Saturdays targets key stage 3 to 4 pupils and aims to raise their GCSE attainment.

London Met does not own any halls of residence but works with private accommodation providers to find new entrants somewhere to live. Holloway Road has reasonably priced pubs and a burgeoning independent foodie scene, while buzzing Islington is among London's most popular haunts and Aldgate is in the thick of hipster territory. Membership of the university's modern gym and sports hall is free for all students.

Tuition fees

- » Fees for UK students   £9,250
- » Fees for International students 2022–23   £15,576–£17,110
- » For scholarship and bursary information see www.londonmet.ac.uk/applying/funding-your-studies/undergraduate-tuition-fees/
- » Graduate salary   £23,000

Student numbers

Undergraduates	7,520	(735)
Postgraduates	1,150	(985)
Applications/places		12,845/1,425
Applications per place		9
Overall offer rate		87.5%
International students – EU		6.4%
Non-EU		3.4%

Accommodation

University provided places: 0
Self-catered: £150–£411 per week (private providers)
www.londonmet.ac.uk/services-and-facilities/accommodation/

Where do the students come from?

State schools (non-grammar)	96.9%	Low participation areas	6.9%	
Grammar schools	1.2%	All ethnic minorities	62.4%	
Independent schools	2%	White working-class males	2.3%	
First generation students	54.2%	Black achievement gap	-24.9%	

Social inclusion ranking: 29

Disabled	5.3%
Mature (over 21)	69%

London School of Economics and Political Science

Students at the London School of Economics and Political Science (LSE) were more satisfied with how their university handled the pandemic than those at most other UK institutions. Our analysis of National Student Survey (NSS) results ranks the LSE's Covid response among the top 20 in the country by comparing scores in the 2021 pandemic edition of the NSS with those recorded in 2020.

The LSE notes that paying care and attention to planning the broader student experience (including community-building and wellbeing) along with teaching, learning and assessment were central to its effective shift to remote learning.

The university's notable performance for its Covid response is more remarkable given the improvement in student satisfaction it represents; LSE finished in bottom place (130th) for teaching quality and the broader student experience in 2018's NSS, but as the result of this year's strong performance now ranks 61st and 65th respectively on these measures.

The heavy investment in campus developments and efforts to improve the student experience appear to be paying off. A significant makeover in recent years has provided the Centre Buildings on Houghton Street with a new hub on the central London campus, off Aldwych. Open spaces have also been added and student facilities improved.

In 2022 the Marshall Building will open on the corner of picturesque Lincoln's Inn Fields. It will house a new sports centre, café, arts rehearsal facilities, music practice rooms and a teaching and learning hub. It will also be a base for the departments of management, finance and accounting as well as the Marshall Institute for Philanthropy and Social Entrepreneurship, funded by a £30million donation from hedge fund founder Sir Paul Marshall.

Demand for places at LSE remains high, undimmed by the bronze rating awarded in the last Teaching Excellence Framework reflecting poor student satisfaction. The promising graduate prospects are a big attraction. Applications in the 2020 admissions round reached record levels and have risen by a quarter in the decade since 2011. The LSE is among the UK's most selective universities, one of the UK's few institutions that does not participate in clearing.

To enhance students' future job prospects LSE embeds "real world" perspectives into their time via work experience, internships, volunteering and support for entrepreneurship. Placement years have been introduced on some programmes.

Active relationships with more than 15,000 organisations in the UK and worldwide facilitate the career-building opportunities.

Houghton street
London WC2A 2AE
020 7955 6613
www.lse.ac.uk/ask-LSE
www.lse.ac.uk
www.lsesu.com
Open days: see website

Edinburgh
Belfast
Cardiff
LONDON

The Times and The Sunday Times Rankings
Overall Ranking: 5 (last year: 4)

Teaching quality	75.3%	61
Student experience	69.8%	65
Research quality	52.8%	4
Entry standards	175	12
Graduate prospects	92%	2
Good honours	94.1%	3
Expected completion rate	96.5%	5
Student/staff ratio	12.4	8
Services and facilities	£2,983	30

A volunteer centre runs a brokerage service with 300 to 400 partner organisations per year, helping more than half of undergraduates to volunteer during their time at LSE. An entrepreneurship programme supports students' and graduates' start-ups.

The 2021 QS World Rankings ranked LSE top in Europe and second in the world in social sciences and management subjects. Only Harvard beat it.

Economics and politics may lead the way, but the university offers courses in more subjects than its name suggests, including maths, law and environmental policy. A degree in data science has joined the curriculum and one in politics and data science starts in 2022. More than 30 past or present heads of state have studied or taught at the LSE, as have 16 winners of the Nobel Prize in economics, literature and peace.

The school has been no stranger to political involvement, since its foundation by Beatrice and Sidney Webb, pioneers of the left-leaning Fabian movement. More recently a group of students launched a campaign called LSE Class War with a radical manifesto calling for a "private school free" LSE. This would require a momentous turnaround; with just 47% recruited from non-selective state schools the LSE ranks in the bottom three institutions for this measure. It is far more successful in reducing the black achievement gap, for which it ranks fifth best among UK universities.

Efforts to widen access include year 11 and 12 pupils shadowing undergraduates and travel bursaries to attend open days and other campus events. There are long-term widening participation programmes for pupils in years 12 and 13, such as Pathways to Law, and Pathways to Banking and Finance.

The LSE had more world-leading research than any other university in the 2014 Research Excellence Framework. It was the leader in the social sciences, with particularly good results in social work and social policy, and communication and media studies. A £10million donation from alumnus Firoz Lalji has since created an academic centre focused on Africa.

Around four in ten residential spaces are in catered halls of residence. Accommodation is guaranteed for first-years as long as they book online by the end of May.

The new sports centre in the Marshall Building due to open in early 2022, will add a sports hall, two squash courts and a heavy weights room to provision. The university's 23-acre sportsground is a train ride away in New Malden, Surrey.

Tuition fees

»	Fees for UK students	£9,250
»	Fees for International students 2022–23	£23,330
	For scholarship and bursary information see www.lse.ac.uk/study-at-lse/undergraduate/fees-and-funding	
»	Graduate salary	£32,000

Student numbers

Undergraduates	5,130	(30)
Postgraduates	6,535	(360)
Applications/places	22,115/2,180	
Applications per place	10.1	
Overall offer rate	36.5%	
International students – EU	12.7%	
Non-EU	40.2%	

Accommodation

University provided places: 3,594
Catered costs: £117–£315 per week
Self-catered: £168–£431 per week
First years guaranteed accommodation
www.lse.ac.uk/accommodation

Where do the students come from?

State schools (non-grammar)	47%	Low participation areas	4.8%	
Grammar schools	20.1%	All ethnic minorities	61.4%	
Independent schools	32.9%	White working-class males	2.4%	
First generation students	31.3%	Black achievement gap	-5.4%	

Social inclusion ranking: 105

Disabled	4.2%
Mature (over 21)	1.8%

London South Bank University

London South Bank University (LSBU) has been improving and expanding its facilities, with a new hub containing flexible study space, a gym and sports centre, catering options and library on the main Southwark campus. The biggest development is the new Croydon campus, the university's second largest.

Based in the town centre, the campus opened in 2021 and has a health focus, addressing a severe shortage of nurses across south London and the Gatwick triangle. It also offers business courses and includes student support and learning resources, and informal study spaces.

The university already has health students based in hospitals in Romford, Leytonstone and Havering, in east London. With the addition of the Croydon campus, LSBU has launched the Institute of Health and Social Care to underpin its mission to become the university of choice for the NHS and healthcare workforce in London. The move to an institute model will also see the opening of the LSBU Health Skills Centre in partnership with Guy's and St Thomas' NHS Foundation Trust, to encourage more local people into health and social care.

Three-quarters of LSBU's students are from London and 70% are drawn from ethnic minorities, helping to keep the university in the top 20 for social inclusion, although it has dropped out of the top ten this year. Widening participation has always been a priority at LSBU, which makes lower offers to disadvantaged applicants and has partnerships with colleges and academies in south London to encourage progression to higher education.

LSBU has been paying particular attention to the gap in performance in degree classifications between black, Asian and ethnic minority students and the rest, which had widened to more than 22% in the latest statistics. It has been trying to boost completion rates for those with financial problems by providing grants of up to £500 a year to about 400 students from its Student Retention Fund.

Applications were up by 5.5% at the end of March 2021, reflecting continued growth in the demand for nursing and other health courses, as well as the attractions of the new Croydon campus. Ten new degrees have been launched, mainly in economics and business, but also in dental hygiene and therapy. Five more have been approved for 2022, in politics and international relations, design, digital media production, film and television, and surveying.

LSBU is also expanding its already extensive portfolio of apprenticeships, which range from level 4 (the equivalent of a foundation degree) to level 7, a Masters

103 Borough Road
London SE1 0AA
0800 923 8888
course.enquiry@lsbu.ac.uk
www.lsbu.ac.uk
www.lsbsu.org
Open days: see website

Edinburgh

Belfast

Cardiff

LONDON

The Times and The Sunday Times Rankings
Overall Ranking: 127 (last year: 123)

Teaching quality	71.8%	=108
Student experience	63.1%	121
Research quality	9.0%	=64
Entry standards	106	=118
Graduate prospects	65.4%	94
Good honours	71.2%	112
Expected completion rate	75.2%	123
Student/staff ratio	16.8	=83
Services and facilities	£2,391	79

equivalent. It already has 2,000 apprentices and is aiming for 3,400 by September 2022, with new offerings in healthcare science, chartered surveying, radiography and the academic profession.

The university operates its own employment agency to help students find part-time work while they study and also provides strong support for start-up companies. However, it was one of the institutions to lose out heavily from last year's change in the way graduate prospects are measured in our rankings. LSBU was our University of the Year for Graduate Employment in 2018 and 2019, but slipped down the rankings under the new system, which bases scores on the numbers in high-skilled work 15 (rather than six) months after leaving. And it remains there in the latest figures published in 2021, which showed just 65.4% of graduates in high-skilled jobs, a decline on the previous year.

Before a reverse last year, LSBU's ranking had been improving, but it has slipped further in this edition after a big drop in student satisfaction. Ratings for teaching quality and the broader student experience have declined by substantially more than the national average during the pandemic, pushing the university into the bottom ten for the latter.

However, the university has a silver rating in the Teaching Excellence Framework, and LSBU entered more academics for the 2014 Research Excellence Framework than it had for previous assessments and scored well on the external impact of its research, with almost three-quarters of the submission placed in the top two categories as world-leading or internationally excellent. The university boasts the UK's first inner-city green technology research facility, the Centre for Efficient and Renewable Energy in Buildings.

The students' union and many support services have been brought together to make them more accessible. Sports facilities include a multipurpose hall, therapy services and a fitness suite, dance studio and injury clinic.

All 1,423 rooms in halls of residence are less than ten minutes' walk away. First-year full-time students are only guaranteed accommodation if they have accepted an unconditional offer by mid-June, but the university expects to have enough rooms to satisfy the remainder. As a so-called commuter university, only 23% of first-years applied for accommodation last year, and 85% received an offer.

Tuition fees

» Fees for UK students	£9,250
» Fees for International students 2022–23	£14,900
» For scholarship and bursary information see www.lsbu.ac.uk/study/undergraduate/fees-and-funding	
» Graduate salary	£27,000

Student numbers

Undergraduates	9,090 (3,635)
Postgraduates	1,725 (2,385)
Applications/places	22,185/3,340
Applications per place	6.6
Overall offer rate	69.5%
International students – EU	3.4%
Non-EU	5.8%

Accommodation

University provided places: 1,423
Self-catered: £135–£222 per week
www.lsbu.ac.uk/student-life/accommodation

Where do the students come from?

State schools (non-grammar)	95.7%	Low participation areas	6%	
Grammar schools	2%	All ethnic minorities	70.4%	
Independent schools	2.3%	White working-class males	3.1%	
First generation students	52.2%	Black achievement gap	-22.5%	

Social inclusion ranking: 18

Disabled	8.8%
Mature (over 21)	47%

Loughborough University

Loughborough is our Sports University of the Year for a third time after a total haul of 14 medals at the Tokyo Olympics. Athletes with a connection to the university – those who used its training facilities, current students or alumni – brought home three gold, six silver and five bronze medals.

If Loughborough was a country, it would have ranked 23rd in the final medals table, ahead of Sweden, Switzerland and Belgium. At the Rio Olympics in 2016 it was 17th, with five gold medals in its total of 12.

If you're serious about sport, Loughborough must be in your sights as a destination, with the best university sports facilities this side of the Atlantic; it boldly claims to have "the best facilities in one square mile anywhere in the world".

Investment of £60million over the past 15 years means that the unprepossessing campus on the edge of a small Leicestershire market town has the resources to allow anyone already of national and international standard to flourish, while also uncovering raw talent and developing it.

Adam Peaty, the Tokyo double-gold medallist, is one to make a splash in the 50m, eight-lane training pool, one of two British Swimming National Centres. The triathlete Alex Yee, who won gold and silver in Tokyo, trained at the British Triathlon Performance Centre. The indoor Seb Coe High Performance Athletics Centre and the Paula Radcliffe Athletics Track pay tribute to two world-class alumni. The university also hosts the National Performance Centre for the England and Wales Cricket Board, and England Netball. Loughborough has been selected as the high-performance partner for British Wheelchair Basketball and achieved Paralympics success in a range of sports in Tokyo, winning six golds.

The university's human performance laboratories, technical analysis suites, nutritional analysis and sports medicine services are second to none.

Loughborough regularly tops our rankings for sports science and leads the QS World University rankings for sport-related subjects again in 2021. All-round academic excellence, coupled with sustained high levels of student satisfaction, has twice won Loughborough our University of the Year title. No university has been shortlisted for our main award more times in its 23-year history.

Applications and admissions hit record levels in 2020. In the past decade applications have soared 59% and enrolments have climbed 38%.

Student satisfaction held up during the pandemic. Just 25 universities experienced a

Epinal Way
Loughborough LE11 3TU
01509 274 403
admissions@lboro.ac.uk
www.lboro.ac.uk
www.lsu.co.uk
Open days: see website

The Times and The Sunday Times Rankings

Overall Ranking: 10 (last year: 7)

Teaching quality	78.3%	=18
Student experience	80.6%	2
Research quality	36.3%	=30
Entry standards	150	=27
Graduate prospects	80.6%	15
Good honours	86%	22
Expected completion rate	93.4%	=15
Student/staff ratio	13.5	=20
Services and facilities	£3,425	15

smaller decline in National Student Survey scores between 2020 and 2021.

A contextual offer scheme lowers the high asking rate on many courses for those whose social and educational background fits the criteria. There are plans to extend the scheme for 2022 admissions. About one in seven students benefit from some form of bursary or scholarship.

As yet, the impact of such measures has not filtered through to Loughborough's social inclusion ranking, which sits just outside the bottom 20 in England and Wales. However, the university does finish ahead of 17 of the 21 English or Welsh Russell Group universities, which are Loughborough's principal competitors.

It mixes in the same company for graduate employment, a consistent strong point. Loughborough ranks 15th in the UK – behind ten Russell Group universities. More than four in five students are in high-skilled work or graduate-level study 15 months after graduating. All undergraduates are offered a year-long industrial placement. A Year in Enterprise placement for students wanting to start their own business has supported 69 students to set up their own company since 2012.

Loughborough was awarded gold in the Teaching Excellence Framework. Students from all backgrounds achieve consistently outstanding outcomes, assessors found, thanks to a culture of personalised learning and a comprehensive pastoral and academic tutorial programme.

New courses include a BA in design as well as physics or chemistry with computing, psychology in education, international relations or humanities with a foundation year at Loughborough or abroad. A new BA in liberal arts will be introduced in 2022.

Only eight universities entered such a high proportion of their eligible staff, 88%, in the Research Excellence Framework in 2014. Almost three-quarters of their research was judged to be world-leading or internationally excellent, with sport and exercise sciences producing the best results in the UK and six other subject areas featuring in the top ten.

The 440-acre campus is the hub around which most student life revolves. A further 95 acres has been purchased recently for future expansion. The addition of 600 new en-suite rooms in the Claudia Parsons Hall brings the total to about 6,200. The university can usually house all first-years who apply by September 1.

The prizewinning students' union, among the most popular in the country with its members, is undergoing an extensive refurbishment.

Tuition fees

» Fees for UK students £9,250
» Fees for International students 2022–23 £19,750–£25,700
» For scholarship and bursary information see www.lboro.ac.uk/study/undergraduate/fees-funding/
» Graduate salary £27,000

Student numbers

Undergraduates	13,680	(205)
Postgraduates	3,435	(975)
Applications/places		34,390/4,055
Applications per place		8.5
Overall offer rate		74.9%
International students – EU		4.5%
Non-EU		8.5%

Accommodation

University provided places: 6,155
Catered costs: £143–£200 per week
Self-catered: £100–£182 per week
First years guaranteed accommodation
www.lboro.ac.uk/services/accommodation/

Where do the students come from?

State schools (non-grammar)	68.5%	Low participation areas	7.9%	Disabled	8.4%
Grammar schools	15.2%	All ethnic minorities	24.9%	Mature (over 21)	1.9%
Independent schools	16.3%	White working-class males	5.3%		
First generation students	32.9%	Black achievement gap	-12%		

Social inclusion ranking: =95

University of Manchester

Among the lasting images of the pandemic on British campuses were pictures of students tearing down fences around University of Manchester halls of residence. Although the university management swiftly changed its approach, the response to Covid-19 precipitated one of the biggest falls in student satisfaction of any UK institution, according to our year-on-year analysis. Never Manchester's strong point, scores in the National Student Survey have dropped well outside the top 100 for satisfaction with teaching quality and the wider student experience.

This has not deterred prospective students, however. Applications, already the highest in the country, climbed a further 12% by the end of March 2021 compared with the same point in the cycle in 2020. Manchester has promised to distil the best aspects of online learning to a blended approach for the future. The balance between the two will vary across different subjects and will be adapted to circumstances in the university's four global centres in Dubai, Hong Kong, Shanghai and Singapore. Manchester's flipped model of teaching has moved explanatory material online, allowing students to learn at their own pace to prepare for workshops and seminars.

Manchester is the biggest university in our table, with more than 40,000 students.

The broad course offering had 27 additions for September 2021, more than half adding entrepreneurship to an existing degree programme. A BSc in mathematics with an integrated placement year will be another option from September 2022.

Students arriving then will be the first to benefit from the largest construction project undertaken by any UK university. Four engineering schools and two research institutes will share the £400million Manchester Engineering Campus, connecting facilities along Oxford Road as part of a £1billion redevelopment to create a unified "world-class" campus.

Social responsibility is a core aim at Manchester and all undergraduates are set three "ethical grand challenges": sustainability, social justice and workplace ethics. Manchester was named as the world's top university for action to support the United Nations Sustainable Development Goals in the *Times Higher Education* Impact Rankings 2021.

The Stellify Award recognises extracurricular activities alongside degree studies and is designed to make Manchester students highly employable. *The Times* Top 100 Graduate Employers 2021 ranks Manchester second for graduates targeted by top employers.

While Manchester's performance in UK rankings, which take account of student satisfaction, has been variable, the university places greater store in its success in research-

Oxford Road
Manchester M13 9PL
0161 275 2077
study@manchester.ac.uk
www.manchester.ac.uk
www.manchesterstudentsunion.com
Open days: see website

The Times and The Sunday Times **Rankings**
Overall Ranking: 23 (last year: 18)

Teaching quality	69.8%	119
Student experience	65.1%	=109
Research quality	39.8%	13
Entry standards	161	20
Graduate prospects	79.4%	22
Good honours	84.8%	29
Expected completion rate	93%	=21
Student/staff ratio	13.1	=14
Services and facilities	£3,222	18

focused international comparisons. It is in the top 30 in the QS World University Rankings 2021 and 35th in the Academic Ranking of World Universities, compiled in Shanghai.

Demonstrating its strength in research, Manchester won the biggest slice of funding in British higher education in 2020–21. It won 119 research and innovation grants worth £98million. It also topped the table for knowledge transfer partnerships, published by Innovate UK in August 2021.

World-leading or internationally excellent research was found in more than 80% of the work entered for the 2014 Research Excellence Framework. Manchester has had 25 Nobel laureates, most recently Sir Andre Geim and Sir Konstantin Novoselov, who shared the prize in physics in 2010 for discovering graphene, the strongest material ever measured. The university hosts the National Graphene Institute, set up to explore its industrial potential.

Jodrell Bank, the university's famed radio observatory, was made a UNESCO World Heritage Site in 2019 and is used for teaching and a focus for public engagement with research. Manchester also hosts the recently renovated Whitworth art gallery and the expanded Alliance Manchester Business School.

Efforts to broaden the intake focus on increasing recruitment from the city and its surrounding area. It admits more low-income students than any other Russell Group

institution and surpasses its national benchmarks for widening participation. It is the fourth-highest ranked Russell Group university in our social inclusion table for England and Wales, and more than a third of students are the first in their family to go to university.

In 2020, nearly 3,000 applicants were made contextual offers requiring grades lower than the standard offer to allow for disadvantage in their previous education. One-third of UK undergraduates receive financial support and scholarships are available in languages, science and engineering and at the business school.

The city's youth culture, plentiful accommodation and huge student population remain great attractions for applicants. Manchester owns or endorses 7,350 residential places, enough to guarantee rooms for all new entrants who apply, and usually accommodating 70% of first-years. There are first-rate sports facilities and the university's teams frequently rank near the top of the British Universities and Colleges Sport league.

Tuition fees

» Fees for UK students	£9,250
» Fees for International students 2022–23	£20,000–£24,500
Medicine, Dentistry (clinical years)	£47,000
» For scholarship and bursary information see	
www.studentsupport.manchester.ac.uk/finances/	
» Graduate salary	£25,000

Student numbers

Undergraduates	26,490	(140)
Postgraduates	10,250	(3,610)
Applications/places	79,925/9,065	
Applications per place	8.5	
Overall offer rate	59.7%	
International students – EU	8.3%	
Non-EU	23.1%	

Accommodation

University provided places: 7,350
Catered costs: £147–£203 per week
Self-catered: £109–£164 per week
First years guaranteed accommodation
www.accommodation.manchester.ac.uk/ouraccommodation/

Where do the students come from?

State schools (non-grammar)	71.9%	Low participation areas	8.9%	
Grammar schools	12.3%	All ethnic minorities	32.8%	
Independent schools	15.7%	White working-class males	3.2%	
First generation students	33%	Black achievement gap	-13.7%	

Social inclusion ranking: 90

Disabled	7.1%
Mature (over 21)	8.2%

Manchester Metropolitan University

Landmark developments are set to boost key strengths at Manchester Metropolitan University (MMU). The £35million School of Digital Arts (SODA) welcomed its first 1,000 students in September 2021 to study film, animation, UX (user experience) design, photography, games design and artificial intelligence, providing a collaborative space to work on live projects with industry partners. The Institute of Sport and Exercise Sciences is due to open in 2022, bringing together the Department of Sport and Exercise with researchers in musculoskeletal science, sports business experts and specialists in health, psychology and social care.

After a £400million development programme, the university aims to create a world-class learning environment where students and elite athletes will want to enrol – but first MMU must address one of the biggest slumps in student satisfaction during the pandemic. Its scores in the National Student Survey sank almost 60 places for satisfaction with the student experience this year, with highly publicised lockdowns of accommodation prompting a feisty reaction.

The university has planned a "full, on-campus university experience" for the 2021–22 academic year, continuing its block teaching approach, in which small groups of students learn together in four blocks of seven weeks, including an assessment week at the end of each block. The MMU website also outlines how social distancing measures or lockdowns would impact teaching if they had to be imposed later in the year.

Despite the cool reception from students to the university's response to Covid-19, MMU performs well in our rankings. Named our University of the Year for Student Retention 2021, MMU has continued to keep the dropout rate well below the national average for its subject and social mix. Its "whole student life cycle" programme, the First Generation Scheme, begins working with year 12–13 pupils in local sixth-form colleges, providing a summer school and twilight sessions – then continues to offer support for those who take up a place, even after they graduate.

Only three British universities recruit more undergraduates than MMU and none can match the size and scope of its degree apprenticeship portfolio. The first degree apprentices arrived in 2015 and more than 2,000 are now signed up with 400 employers in 15 fields from architecture, management and leadership to technology, digital marketing, digital user experience, health and social care, retail and science.

The northwest region's first public poetry library on the MMU campus is designed to cultivate a wider following for the art form and support the creation and performance

All Saints Building
All Saints
Manchester M15 6BH
0161 247 6969
www2.mmu.ac.uk/contact/
course-enquiry/
www2.mmu.ac.uk
www.theunionmmu.org
Open days: see website

Belfast
Edinburgh
MANCHESTER
London
Cardiff

The Times and The Sunday Times **Rankings**
Overall Ranking: 71 (last year: 65)

Teaching quality	72.3%	=98
Student experience	64.1%	117
Research quality	7.5%	75
Entry standards	127	=58
Graduate prospects	63.6%	105
Good honours	77.9%	66
Expected completion rate	85.5%	=57
Student/staff ratio	16	=70
Services and facilities	£3,152	24

of new writing. It shares a new arts and humanities building alongside the Manchester Writing School, where Carol Ann Duffy, the former poet laureate, is creative director.

Among the university's other star attractions are the Manchester School of Architecture, run in collaboration with the University of Manchester, which placed 11th in the QS 2021 rankings. Fashion is a particularly successful subject area at MMU, with the multidisciplinary Manchester Fashion Institute providing undergraduate and postgraduate training in design, business, promotion, fashion buying and technology.

Recent investment has provided new student hubs, mental health support, and online services. The Togetherall platform provides round-the-clock online wellbeing support for students. The university has been granted approval to pedestrianise some of the roads surrounding its main campus, creating a performance area and more green space.

Under MMU's employability strategy, undergraduates are offered work placements of up to a year. Tuition fees are waived during a placement year for up to 250 students with an annual family income of less than £25,000. The university has introduced a new placement with a Formula One team to encourage young people from underrepresented backgrounds to pursue a career in engineering and motorsport. Full funding, including living expenses, is available for a mechanical

engineering student who is female, black, Asian, or from an ethnic minority.

The university has a longstanding commitment to widening access to higher education. About 40% of undergraduates qualify for financial support and more than half of new entrants are the first in their family to go to university.

Almost two-thirds of MMU graduates stay and work in the northwest. The Talent Match service, run in partnership with the Greater Manchester Chamber of Commerce, helps to identify skilled graduates to meet the needs of local employers.

All first-years are guaranteed a room if they apply in time. The university owns or endorses more than 3,500 residential places in Manchester and is planning to increase capacity.

There are good sports facilities and the city's attractions help to boost recruitment levels. The Sugden Sports Centre, across the road from the All Saints campus, was redeveloped in 2018, and Manchester Aquatics Centre, with three gyms and a 50m pool, is also on the doorstep.

Tuition fees

» Fees for UK students	£9,250
» Fees for International students 2022–23	£15,500–£18,000
Architecture	£25,000
» For scholarship and bursary information see www2.finance.mmu.ac.uk/students/	
» Graduate salary	£21,000

Student numbers

Undergraduates	24,815	(1,620)
Postgraduates	3,725	(3,260)
Applications/places		48,270/7,790
Applications per place		6.2
Overall offer rate		69.1%
International students – EU		2.2%
Non-EU		4.3%

Accommodation

University provided places: 3,548
Self-catered: £112–£138 per week
First years guaranteed accommodation
www.mmu.ac.uk/study/accommodation/

Where do the students come from?

State schools (non-grammar)	93.5%	Low participation areas	14%	Disabled	5%
Grammar schools	3.4%	All ethnic minorities	38.6%	Mature (over 21)	14%
Independent schools	3.1%	White working-class males	5.4%		
First generation students	50.6%	Black achievement gap	-20.5%		

Social inclusion ranking: =70

Middlesex University

Middlesex invited students and staff to co-design courses to make sure that teaching from September 2021 would be an improvement on pandemic-hit 2020. Students are back on campus, but some online sessions have been retained where they have been shown to add value. The university has set itself the challenge of ensuring that no student will do worse than they would have done without a pandemic.

Change will be welcome: although student satisfaction scores edged up in the latest National Student Survey, indicating a more favourable judgment on provision in Covid times than that passed on most institutions in 2020–21, Middlesex remains outside the top 100 for teaching quality and only just inside the top 100 for the wider experience. The university hopes that its "learning through doing" approach, delivering practical courses with personalised support, will win hearts and minds.

Applicants may need more convincing. While university applications were climbing across the UK at the end of March 2021, they declined 6% at Middlesex compared with the same point in the cycle in 2020. The university said reduced demand from the European Union – a longstanding recruiting ground – helped to explain the dip. Middlesex has also dropped its aviation courses and expected a short-term fall in applications after bringing

in a new strategy to attract "better prepared" students who are more likely to accept an offer.

Investment in technology has transformed the scope for students to gain practical experience. Student nurses use virtual reality headsets to replicate real-life care settings and Middlesex led a project to develop an electronic practice assessment document (ePAD), now introduced in nursing courses across London. Simulated hospital wards will open in September 2022.

Middlesex will also open a purpose-built facility for its London Sport Institute within the new West Stand at the Saracens rugby ground in September 2022, where students will learn using the latest technology for motion capture, force sensing plates and full body scanning.

Students can complete part of their degree abroad. Although the campus in Malta will close in 2022, the two outposts in Dubai and one in Mauritius are thriving.

For the majority of students based in northwest London, further improvements are on the way at the main Hendon campus, where £200million has been spent to bring together library services and add two academic buildings at the business school.

Middlesex offers a flexible course system, allowing students to start on some courses in January.

The university hopes to double the numbers of degree apprentices to 2,600 by 2022. There

The Burroughs
Hendon
London NW4 4BT
020 8411 5555
enquiries@mdx.ac.uk
www.mdx.ac.uk
www.mdxsu.com
Open days: see website

The Times and The Sunday Times **Rankings**
Overall Ranking: 123 (last year: 121)

Teaching quality	71.6%	=110
Student experience	66.8%	97
Research quality	9.7%	60
Entry standards	105	=121
Graduate prospects	59.3%	121
Good honours	72.2%	109
Expected completion rate	76.2%	=118
Student/staff ratio	17.5	97
Services and facilities	£2,645	57

is a choice of 11 programmes aimed at careers as a police constable, social worker, teacher, nurse, and healthcare science or environmental health practitioner. At the Centre for Apprenticeships and Skills, academics and businesses work together to ensure courses meet the needs of trainees and employers.

In a study of graduates from 121 UK universities since 2000, Middlesex came tenth for the proportion who had gone on to become chief executive officers, managing directors, or started their own business. The on-campus branch of the recruitment service Unitemps won a national award in June 2021 for helping thousands to find paid work during their studies. However, our graduate outcome statistics put Middlessex in the bottom 20 in the UK for the proportion of graduates in high-skilled jobs or further study 15 months after completing their course.

Almost all the British students are state-educated, and Middlesex ranks in the top 30 in our social inclusion table. Three quarters are from black, Asian or ethnic minority backgrounds and more than half have parents who did not attend university. A new contextual admissions policy results in offers on average one grade lower than standard requirements for candidates facing the greatest barriers.

A Summer Support Fund helps disadvantaged students who need money urgently to cover living costs, and technology costs for online learning over the long vacation. Subject-specific initiatives include issuing iPads and Apple pencils to all maths undergraduates to ensure they have the same technology regardless of personal circumstances.

A new integrated postgraduate research hub is planned for the Hendon campus, in line with the university's ethos of practice-oriented, interdisciplinary research. More than a third of the eligible staff were entered for the 2014 Research Excellence Framework and 58% of their work reached one of the top two categories. Art and design produced the best results, with three-quarters of the research assessed as world-leading or internationally excellent.

Middlesex has more than 1,100 residential places on or close to campus, including 630 in a privately run development near Wembley Stadium. New entrants are guaranteed accommodation if they apply by the end of June.

Sports facilities are extensive, they include a bouldering wall and fitness pod and a real tennis court. London's many attractions are a Tube journey away.

Tuition fees

» Fees for UK students	£9,250
» Fees for International students 2022–23	,700
» For scholarship and bursary information see www.mdx.ac.uk/study-with-us/fees-and-funding/undergraduate-finance	
» Graduate salary	£23,733

Student numbers

Undergraduates	14,000	(880)
Postgraduates	2,435	(2,855)
Applications/places		21,275/2,730
Applications per place		7.8
Overall offer rate		68.3%
International students – EU		10.2%
Non-EU		13.4%

Accommodation

University provided places: 1,139
Self-catered: £151–£185 per week
First years guaranteed accommodation
www.mdx.ac.uk/student-life/accommodation

Where do the students come from?

State schools (non-grammar)	98.2%	Low participation areas	4%	**Social inclusion ranking: 27**	
Grammar schools	0.7%	All ethnic minorities	76.4%	Disabled	5.7%
Independent schools	1.1%	White working-class males	2.8%	Mature (over 21)	34.3%
First generation students	57.5%	Black achievement gap	-15.5%		

Newcastle University

For a high-level, party university, some of the lights went out at Newcastle during the pandemic. The city centre-based institution, a Russell Group university that performs outstandingly well in terms of teaching and research, has also traditionally been a place to enjoy the legendary northeastern nightlife.

A year of pandemic teaching and a severely curtailed nightlife have dealt a serious blow to Newcastle's scores in the National Student Survey (NSS), dropping more than any other Russell Group university in our analysis. Coming on top of several years of decline, Newcastle now stands 121st and 120th in our NSS-derived rankings for teaching quality and the wider student experience. Students were critical of learning resources and the learning community during the past year, while positive scores for overall satisfaction dropped from 82% to 69.5%.

The net effect of this pandemic slump has been to make Newcastle the lowest ranked of the Russell Group universities in our institutional table for the first time.

However, there are clearly hopes that the all-round student experience will improve now that in-campus teaching has restarted with online learning alongside, as applications have gone up by 8% in 2021. One of the big pulls for students is a wide range of excellent facilities, spread across four campuses and supporting Newcastle's strengths in research areas ranging from greener energy and future cities to dementia and video gaming.

A new round of investment has been completed at the impressive £350million urban regeneration project at Newcastle Helix (formerly Science Central), with the city council and Legal & General Capital. In 2019, the university completed the £34million Frederick Douglass Centre, named after the renowned American author and abolitionist, and equipped with a 750-seat auditorium and 200-seat lecture theatre. The centre was opened by a descendant of the activist and celebrated with a week of events themed around global social justice, and now it is a key part of teaching for the university's school of computing and business school.

Opened in 2020, the Catalyst building on Newcastle Helix houses the UK's National Innovation Centre for Ageing, National Innovation Centre for Data and the National Institute for Health Research Innovation Observatory, providing students and science-based companies top-notch facilities.

Other leading-edge facilities include the Emerson Cavitation Tunnel research centre, used to test propellers and turbine blades; the Hatton art gallery; and sports facilities that have recently had a £30million cash injection. Fresh sporting assets such as a gait track, environmental chamber and nutrition kitchen

Newcastle upon Tyne
NE1 7RU
0191 208 3333
apps.ncl.ac.uk/contact-us/
general-enquiry
www.ncl.ac.uk
www.nusu.co.uk
Open days: see website

The Times and The Sunday Times Rankings
Overall Ranking: 42 (last year: =31)

Teaching quality	69.4%	121
Student experience	63.5%	120
Research quality	37.7%	=21
Entry standards	144	=38
Graduate prospects	76.4%	33
Good honours	85.2%	=27
Expected completion rate	94%	13
Student/staff ratio	14.9	=47
Services and facilities	£2,675	55

are good news for the new BSc in sports and exercise.

Although student satisfaction scores are at a low ebb, Newcastle is still an academic centre of excellence. It won a gold award in the Teaching Excellence Framework, is one of only 12 universities in the world (and four in the UK) to achieve a five-plus Star rating from international assessors QS Quacquarelli Symonds and has been ranked 11th in the world for its impact on society and leadership in sustainable development.

However, as with many Russell Group universities, it doesn't do so well in terms of social inclusion. Although its rank improves by one place this year, only ten universities sit beneath it in our table. About a quarter of Newcastle applicants come from independent schools, and only about one in eight are drawn from areas with the lowest participation rates in higher education, despite its location in the English region with the lowest take-up of higher education overall.

Things might be changing, though. The university has started a partnership with Newcastle United Foundation to work on outreach, education and research programmes across the region, focusing on work placement and volunteering opportunities, and improving employability for a wider range of students.

About a third of entrants are the first generation of their family to go to university.

The university offers support for low-income students and those with dependent children, and 27.5% of admissions qualified for some financial assistance last year.

All first years are usually able to live in. However, students in later years of study live out in the city, with Jesmond, Fenham and Heaton among popular areas.

As a launchpad for careers, Newcastle does well at cultivating links with business. It works with Siemens on tackling all kinds of technological, health and manufacturing challenges, and has three National Innovation Centres working with industry on issues from data insight to the potential for rural economies.

A Europe-funded Arrow scheme has matched more than 50 local firms with academics to carry out innovation projects. And on the prestigious Helix site, all kinds of innovative companies are flourishing – and on the lookout for studious recruits.

Tuition fees

» Fees for UK students £9,250
» Fees for International students 2022–23 £20,400–£25,200
  Dentistry £39,300; Medicine £36,000
» For scholarship and bursary information see
  www.ncl.ac.uk/undergraduate/fees-funding
» Graduate salary £24,818

Student numbers

Undergraduates	21,255	(45)
Postgraduates	5,420	(1,350)
Applications/places		34,550/5,550
Applications per place		6.2
Overall offer rate		80.2%
International students – EU		4.6%
Non-EU		14.7%

Accommodation

University provided places: 4,159
Catered costs: £137–£197 per week
Self-catered: £97–£173 per week
First years guaranteed accommodation
www.ncl.ac.uk/accommodation/

Where do the students come from?

State schools (non-grammar)	64.8%	Low participation areas	8.3%
Grammar schools	10.7%	All ethnic minorities	14%
Independent schools	24.5%	White working-class males	4.8%
First generation students	33%	Black achievement gap	-12.3%

Social inclusion ranking: 106

Disabled	4%
Mature (over 21)	5.5%

Newman University Birmingham

More places are likely to be available at this small Catholic university in 2022. Growth is the aim in Newman's five-year strategy for 2020–25 – by recruiting more students and improving the retention rate for those already enrolled. It hopes to increase awareness of the distinct student experience it offers.

Almost one third (29%) of undergraduates entered through clearing in the 2020 intake. Applications edged up 4% by March 2021 compared with the same point in the cycle in 2020. This is, perhaps, partly explained by the introduction of degrees in applied writing, counselling, policing and sport management, and the introduction of foundation years in several subjects. Degree courses in sociology and social work will accept their first students in 2022.

Every full-time degree has a work placement module and the university stresses the development of transferable skills useful for further study or employment after graduation. The approach helped to secure a silver award in the Teaching Excellence Framework.

Student satisfaction declined further at Newman than at most universities during the pandemic, our analysis of National Student Survey scores in 2020–21 shows. For satisfaction with teaching quality, Newman has dropped from a top ten position in 2020 to a place in the top 30. For satisfaction with the wider student experience, it has fallen from the top ten to just outside the top 30, with an inevitable impact on the university's overall position in our table.

With fewer than 2,000 undergraduates, the former teacher-training college is one of the smallest universities in our guide. Despite its size, however, the student population is sufficiently diverse to place Newman just outside the top ten in our social exclusion index. Nearly all the undergraduates are state-educated and three-quarters are the first in their family to go to university, the highest proportion in the UK. More than four out of ten come from black, Asian or ethnic minority backgrounds, but the achievement gap between black students and others is also among the highest.

The campus is in a quiet residential area eight miles southwest of Birmingham city centre, with views over the Bartley reservoir and the Worcestershire countryside. Named after John Henry Newman, a 19th-century cardinal who wrote *The Idea of the University*, the institution is still guided by his vision of a community of scholars. It offers students the personal touch and claims to be a "different kind of university" with small class sizes and an interactive learning style. Its Catholic ethos has been retained, but students are recruited

Genners Lane
Bartley Green
Birmingham B32 3NT
0121 476 1181
admissions@newman.ac.uk
www.newman.ac.uk
www.newmansu.org
Open days: see website

The Times and The Sunday Times **Rankings**
Overall Ranking: 122 (last year: =112)

Teaching quality	78%	=25
Student experience	73.1%	=33
Research quality	2.8%	115
Entry standards	103	=126
Graduate prospects	63.8%	102
Good honours	68.4%	121
Expected completion rate	75.3%	122
Student/staff ratio	17.7	=100
Services and facilities	£1,899	112

from all faiths and none. Rebranding in 2018 added Birmingham to the university's title to emphasise to applicants its proximity to the city.

More than £20million has been invested in upgrading teaching facilities and building new halls of residence for 200 students. A mock law court, a new computer science laboratory and a careers and employability hub all opened in 2020 and work is continuing to make the campus more environmentally sustainable. It already has the top rating under the Eco Campus grading system.

Students returned to campus for the 2021–22 academic year but Newman expects to increase online learning in most subjects, especially for lectures. There will be variations for practical subjects or those accredited by professional, statutory and regulatory bodies, but the university says the pandemic has shown that while students value on-campus interaction and learning, they also welcome flexibility in the way they learn.

While comparatively low at 23, the number of academics entered for the Research Excellence Framework doubled between 2008 and 2014. Education and history produced the best results, but less than a third of the university's submission reached the top two categories. Newman does not employ staff for research alone, to ensure that students have regular contact with active researchers.

Newman is part of the Aimhigher West Midlands consortium, with the four other Birmingham universities and Worcester, which offers a range of activities, information, advice and guidance for young people aged 13–19. It runs its own outreach programmes and has partnerships with schools and further education colleges in the region, offering intensive support and opportunities to students.

No bursaries are available for students in the 2021–22 academic year except two Sanctuary Scholarships for asylum seekers and their families. However, student support payments of up to £1,750 are available and Newman issues supermarket and travel vouchers to those in hardship.

First-year students are guaranteed a place in university-owned accommodation. The halls of residence are close to the teaching areas and library and sports facilities are all on campus. There is a well-equipped fitness suite and performance room, as well as a 3G sports pitch, sports hall, gymnasium and squash courts. Birmingham city centre, with its cultural attractions and student-oriented nightlife, is within easy reach.

Tuition fees

» Fees for UK students	£9,250
» For scholarship and bursary information see www.newman.ac.uk/study/student-finance/	
» Graduate salary	£22,000

Student numbers

Undergraduates	1,855	(315)
Postgraduates	290	(335)
Applications/places		3,075/460
Applications per place		6.7
Overall offer rate		87%
International students – EU		0.5%
Non-EU		0%

Accommodation
University provided places: 291
Self-catered: £105–£195 per week
www.newman.ac.uk/study/why-newman/accommodation

Where do the students come from?

					Social inclusion ranking: =12	
State schools (non-grammar)	98.3%	Low participation areas	18.4%	Disabled	11.4%
Grammar schools	1.2%	All ethnic minorities	44.1%	Mature (over 21)	43%
Independent schools	0.5%	White working-class males	4.6%		
First generation students	75.2%	Black achievement gap	-30.9%		

University of Northampton

Northampton's impressive new campus seems yet to strike a chord with aspiring students. Applications were down for the fourth year in a row in 2020, almost 33% below the level recorded a decade ago. The university has not disclosed figures for the current admissions round.

Enrolments have remained more stable and Northampton was awarded gold in the government's Teaching Excellence Framework before the new campus opened. But the university is now outside the top 100 for teaching quality and the other areas of student experience covered by the National Student Survey (NSS) after a poor showing in the pandemic-influenced edition of the NSS. Overall, it has been dropping down our league table consistently, falling into the bottom ten this year.

The university had already adopted a system of "active blended learning" before the pandemic struck, combining face-to-face and online provision, and making use of the new configuration of the campus, which was designed for a "flipped learning" model where students prepare in advance for their teaching sessions and interact more with their peers and staff. Big lecture theatres have been replaced by classrooms for up to 40 people and smaller lecture spaces.

The 58-acre Waterside Campus is a few minutes' walk from the town centre, with a four-storey Learning Hub, where most teaching takes place, as its focal point. The whole development cost £330million and, uniquely in UK higher education, was funded by a bond backed by Treasury guarantee.

Northampton has combined two of its best-known features in a new subject area: The fusion of fashion and leather is expected to provide fresh opportunities for teaching and research in areas such as luxury design, high tech materials and environmental sustainability. The new alignment is a response to students' desire for a suite of fashion courses that recognise leather's significance in footwear and clothing design. (Northampton is a key centre for the shoe industry in the UK.)

The university has also joined the University of Leicester and hospitals in Northampton and Kettering to create the University Hospitals of Northamptonshire (UHN) NHS Group. The alliance will provide more placements for students in the Faculty of Arts, Science and Technology and the Faculty of Health, Education and Society, as well as new research opportunities.

Northampton was the first university in the UK to be named a Changemaker Campus by the Ashoka global network of social entrepreneurs and has since been ranked top in the country for social enterprise. Every student has the opportunity to work in a social enterprise, developing entrepreneurial

---

Waterside Campus
University Drive
Northampton NN1 5PH
0300 303 2772
study@northampton.ac.uk
www.northampton.ac.uk
www.northamptonunion.com
Open days: see website

***The Times and The Sunday Times* Rankings**
Overall Ranking: =108 (last year: 111)

Teaching quality	72.2%	101
Student experience	64.4%	115
Research quality	3.2%	113
Entry standards	104	=124
Graduate prospects	69.3%	=71
Good honours	68.1%	122
Expected completion rate	79.2%	104
Student/staff ratio	16.8	=83
Services and facilities	£3,363	17

skills to make them more employable.

The Northampton Employment Promise guarantees an internship of at least three months or a postgraduate course to any graduates who have not found full-time work within a year of leaving with at least a 2:2 degree or Higher National Diploma. The university also works closely with the Northamptonshire Growth Hub, assisting local businesses as well as highlighting opportunities for student placements and part-time jobs. Graduate prospects are among the university's strongest suits in our academic ranking.

There are nine degree apprenticeship programmes in areas ranging from manufacturing engineering to nursing, occupational therapy and policing. The university also co-sponsors a Technical College at Silverstone motor-racing circuit.

Northampton remains in the top 40 in our social inclusion table. Almost all undergraduates are from non-selective state schools and more than half have parents who did not go to university. A third are over 21 on entry.

Among the measures designed to broaden the intake further is the gift of a laptop to every new undergraduate. A wide variety of outreach activities includes STEAM Northants, which promotes science, technology, engineering, arts and maths courses and careers through interactive events.

In the 2014 Research Excellence Framework only 30% of its research was placed in the top two categories, but the university entered just a quarter of its eligible staff. Results were outstanding in history, where two-thirds of the work was considered world-leading or internationally excellent.

Five research centres focus on subjects from contemporary fiction to exploring psychic and paranormal claims. The China and Emerging Economies Centre studies changes to global business networks.

Northampton is one of few universities in the UK to offer all students free access to sports facilities. The students' union provides any necessary kit. The sports dome is used for teaching as well as recreation, and there is a pavilion, outdoor games areas and an artificial pitch.

This year, for the first time, all new full-time students who applied by May 21 and paid a £300 deposit were guaranteed a room in the halls of residence, either on or off campus.

The town centre has a number of popular bars including the Platform, a students' union venue housing a nightclub, bar and café.

Tuition fees

»	Fees for UK students	£9,250
	Foundation years	£6,780
»	Fees for International students 2022–23	£14,000
»	For scholarship and bursary information see	
	www.northampton.ac.uk/student-life/fees-and-funding/	
»	Graduate salary	£24,000

Student numbers

Undergraduates	8,135	(1,015)
Postgraduates	1,545	(1,370)
Applications/places		12,890/2,405
Applications per place		5.4
Overall offer rate		79.5%
International students – EU		3.5%
Non-EU		8.1%

Accommodation

University provided places: 2,500
Self-catered: £77–£171 per week
First years guaranteed accommodation
www.northampton.ac.uk/student-life/accommodation

Where do the students come from?

State schools (non-grammar)	97.2%	Low participation areas	16.8%	Disabled	5.7%
Grammar schools	1.3%	All ethnic minorities	42.3%	Mature (over 21)	34.2%
Independent schools	1.5%	White working-class males	4.5%		
First generation students	52.2%	Black achievement gap	-23.6%		

Social inclusion ranking: 35

Northumbria University

Academics at Northumbria pitched their skills into the effort to analyse and respond to the pandemic. As a partner in the Covid-19 Genomics UK Consortium, the Newcastle upon Tyne university made available its DNA sequencing research facility for the rapid sequencing of thousands of SARS-CoV-2 genomes. Such involvement epitomises one of Northumbria's overarching missions: to be a research-intensive modern university.

The second prong of its goal, responding to the needs of business and industry, is also exemplified by recent activities. It launched its first medtech spinout company for a new diagnostic tool developed by Northumbria researchers that can detect diseases, including Covid-19, via breath samples instead of swabs or blood tests.

Professor Andrew Wathey, the vice-chancellor, steps down in May 2022. He will leave a university transformed under his leadership since 2008, having become a research-rich, business-focused institution. Formerly Newcastle Polytechnic, university status came in 1992 and Northumbria's excellent reputation includes consistently being a top-performing modern university in this guide.

The university has partnerships with global organisations such as Santander, Unilever, IBM and Nissan and more than 560 employers and 60 professional bodies sponsor or accredit Northumbria's programmes. Through these links students benefit from teaching that is allied to the work-ready skills needed by employers, as well as research projects, work placements and job opportunities. The university ranks in the top 50 for the number of students in high-skilled jobs or further study within 15 months of leaving.

However, students were unimpressed by university life over the past year, leading to significant falls in our two rankings for teaching quality and student experience derived from the 2021 National Student Survey. Core teaching has returned to campus – including seminars, workshops, specialist lab sessions and tutorials – supported by online content including recorded lectures, which should prompt a recovery in both ratings.

Among a clutch of achievements Northumbria was ranked 50th in the world for sustainability in this year's *Times Higher Education* Impact Rankings and it ranked second in the UK for graduate start-ups in the Higher Education Business and Community Interactive Survey (Hebcis) of 2018/19.

Awarding Northumbria a silver rating in the Teaching Excellence Framework, assessors praised it for high attainment through a range of academic and personal support services, plus graduate start-up and careers assistance. High-quality physical and digital resources are used effectively in teaching and by students.

Sutherland Building
Newcastle upon Tyne
NE1 8ST
0191 227 4646
ask4help@northumbria.ac.uk
www.northumbria.ac.uk
www.mynsu.co.uk
Open days: see website

The Times and The Sunday Times **Rankings**
Overall Ranking: =62 (last year: 57)

Teaching quality	71.8%	=108
Student experience	64.2%	116
Research quality	9%	=64
Entry standards	139	45
Graduate prospects	73.8%	50
Good honours	80.8%	49
Expected completion rate	82.5%	82
Student/staff ratio	15.5	=56
Services and facilities	£2,482	69

More than £250million has been invested in excellent facilities over the past decade at the two campuses, one in the city centre and the other three miles away at Coach Lane (home to students from the Faculty of Health and Life Sciences). The university also has a base in London and more recently has started to offer courses taught in Amsterdam.

Among 13 new and revised degrees are courses in international business management (with or without French or Spanish); automotive engineering; accounting; and tourism events management.

Three new degree apprenticeships are available in occupational therapy; specialist community public health nursing; and district nursing. This brings the number of earn-while-you-learn options to 26. Solicitor, architect, chartered surveyor and police constable are among the longer-established programmes.

Unusually, Northumbria holds similar rankings in our tables for both academic measures and social inclusion, placing =62nd and 61st. Just under one in five students is recruited from areas with low progression rates to higher education, well above its benchmark level and reflective of successful recruitment within the northeast, the area with England's lowest participation rate.

The university has built on a strong showing in the Research Excellence Framework, in which 60% of the submitted work was adjudged to be world-leading or internationally excellent. Recent work includes a collaboration with the UK Space Agency to develop the world's first commercially available laser-based satellite communication system.

Northumbria is partnering with the University of Newcastle on the launch of a £9million Centre for Digital Citizens. In another study with Newcastle, construction has begun on the OME, the world's first living building – which generates its own energy and processes its own waste. Northumbria offers alumni a 20% discount on postgraduate fees.

There is a strong sporting tradition. The £30million Sport Central development at the City site was refurbished in 2019 and has a pool, sports science laboratories, sports halls and a 3,000-seat arena. Big-hitting alumni include England rugby players Owen Farrell, Anthony Watson and Mako Vunipola.

En-suite accommodation is guaranteed to all first-years. Newcastle's legendary nightlife is back firing on all cylinders, while the region's varied galleries, theatres and cinemas offer more peaceful activities – as do the Northumberland coast's stunning beaches.

Tuition fees

» Fees for UK students	£9,250
» Fees for International students 2022–23	£16,500
» For scholarship and bursary information see www.northumbria.ac.uk/study-at-northumbria/ fees-funding/	
» Graduate salary	£24,000

Student numbers

Undergraduates	18,865 (1,590)
Postgraduates	5,220 (2,650)
Applications/places	24,080/5,360
Applications per place	4.5
Overall offer rate	85.7%
International students – EU	4.7%
Non-EU	7%

Accommodation

University provided places: 2,875
Catered costs: £121–£122 per week
Self-catered: £80–£176 per week
First years guaranteed accommodation
www.northumbria.ac.uk/study-at-northumbria/accommodation/

Where do the students come from?

State schools (non-grammar)	89.7%	Low participation areas	17.5%		
Grammar schools	3.9%	All ethnic minorities	11.2%		
Independent schools	6.4%	White working-class males	8.4%		
First generation students	51.3%	Black achievement gap	-25.2%		

Social inclusion ranking: 61

Disabled	6.3%
Mature (over 21)	19.7%

Norwich University of the Arts

It may have been forged in a pandemic, but Norwich University of the Arts (NUA) believes that it has found a method of teaching and learning that reflects the way the creative industries operate and will help to prepare graduates for their careers. The approach involves a blend of on-campus practical sessions, live-streamed digital sessions and pre-recorded digital materials that are available on demand.

Students are expected to attend all the taught sessions included on their timetable. There are group teaching sessions and students can book time on campus to access a workshop, computer or studio space via NUA's virtual learning environment.

Assessment will be carried out in a variety of ways, including group reviews in which students present their work for discussion. Self-evaluation and peer evaluation are used to help them engage with learning and understand their progress.

Degrees include the option of a foundation year, giving students the chance to develop the skills to study at that level. All applicants are interviewed, with places awarded on the quality of their portfolio rather than predicted grades.

Students obviously approved of the arrangements at the height of the pandemic. The satisfaction rate in the National Student Survey (NSS) for the quality of teaching fell by less than a single percentage point; NUA is now in the top ten on this measure, up more than 40 places on pre-pandemic levels. Scores in the sections of the NSS covering the broader student experience fell by rather more, but the university still rose in the rankings on account of heavier falls elsewhere.

Professor Simon Ofield-Kerr has moved from University of the Arts London to head NUA after the retirement of Professor John Last, whose 12 years in charge brought the granting of university status and the development of multiple facilities. The latest is NUA's largest building project. The seven-storey building, beside the River Wensum in the heart of Norwich, adjoins the library and will create more teaching space and 100 bedrooms for first-year students.

Other recent developments have provided a new base for the students' union, a café and lounge, as well as laboratories and other teaching facilities for courses including film and moving image production, photography, and fashion communication and promotion. The Sir John Hurt Film Studio, named after the late actor and NUA chancellor, is in a grade II listed building that also houses the School of Architecture and won an award for its renovation.

Francis House
3–7 Redwell Street
Norwich NR2 4SN
01603 610 561
admissions@nua.ac.uk
www.nua.ac.uk
www.nuasu.co.uk
Open days: see website

The Times and The Sunday Times Rankings
Overall Ranking: 56 (last year: 77)

Teaching quality	79.8%	10
Student experience	69.7%	66
Research quality	5.6%	=86
Entry standards	129	=55
Graduate prospects	58%	124
Good honours	71.1%	113
Expected completion rate	83.7%	=73
Student/staff ratio	15.6	=61
Services and facilities	£2,931	34

The university makes a virtue of focusing entirely on the arts, design and media without branching out into business or the humanities and social sciences, as other former art schools have done. However, it has paid the price in our measure of graduate prospects, finishing in the bottom ten this year and last, with four in ten graduates not in high-skilled jobs or postgraduate study 15 months after leaving. Art and design subjects have been among the lowest scoring nationally in the new measure of graduate outcomes adopted last year.

However, NUA does better on other indicators. It was our 2020 University of the Year for Student Retention and has a gold rating in the Teaching Excellence Framework (TEF). The panel found that course design and assessment practices encouraged experimentation, creative risk-taking and team-working, providing "outstanding levels of stretch for students".

Its origins can be traced to 1845, when the Norwich School of Design was established by followers of the Norwich school of painters, known for their landscapes. Former tutors include the artists Lucian Freud, Lesley Davenport and Michael Andrews. NUA graduates and other experienced professionals give workshops for today's students.

Almost all the undergraduates are state-educated and more than one in six is from an area of low participation in higher education.

Up to half the entrants are expected to qualify for financial support in 2022, which includes a contribution towards the cost of materials, equipment and other expenses where household income is below £25,000. NUA has its own shop offering art supplies at discounted prices.

More than half of the work submitted to the 2014 Research Excellence Framework was judged to be world-leading or internationally excellent, with 90% in the top two categories for its impact on the broader cultural and economic landscape.

NUA does not have its own sports facilities but its students have access to the University of East Anglia's Sportspark, which includes an Olympic-sized swimming pool. The city of Norwich is popular with students and is one of the safest and greenest in the UK.

The new residential spaces will allow NUA to guarantee accommodation to all first-year students, as well as those from overseas in all years. In addition to its own stock, the university keeps a register of 1,000 private residential places.

Tuition fees
»	Fees for UK students	£9,250
»	Fees for International students 2022–23	£15,900
»	For scholarship and bursary information see www.nua.ac.uk/study-at-nua/fees-funding/	
»	Graduate salary	£19,400

Student numbers
Undergraduates	2,265	(0)
Postgraduates	50	(45)
Applications/places	3,465/1,020	
Applications per place	3.4	
Overall offer rate	69.3%	
International students – EU	3.6%	
Non-EU	3.9%	

Accommodation
University provided places: 900
Self-catered: £102–£155 per week
www.nua.ac.uk/university-life/accommodation/

Where do the students come from?
State schools (non-grammar)	93.8%	Low participation areas	18.2%	
Grammar schools	3.5%	All ethnic minorities	11.5%	
Independent schools	2.7%	White working-class males	8.8%	
First generation students	45.8%	Black achievement gap	-20.5%	

Social inclusion ranking: 39
Disabled	13.1%
Mature (over 21)	13.4%

University of Nottingham

The motto at Nottingham University is "normal never changed the world", and in an abnormal year it has stepped up to help its students.

It invested another £200,000 in student mental health and welfare support during the pandemic, on top of its normal £1million budget, and offers 300 short-style "virtual appointments" each week so that students can get advice and be referred on to specialised professionals if necessary.

Meanwhile, our 2019 Sports University of the Year also has a new "empower" sports programme to motivate less active female students and boost their mental health, and a parallel "men's health active" initiative to open doors through exercise and to stress that "there's no strength in silence". Students benefit from excellent facilities at the £40million David Ross Sports Village, where resources include an indoor sprint track, hydrotherapy pool and 200-station fitness suite.

This type of student support helped the institution perform better than most during the pandemic year, according to our analysis of the latest National Student Survey (NSS) results. Like all but two UK universities, Nottingham's scores dropped in our two NSS-derived ranking measures for teaching quality and student experience, but due to failings of universities elsewhere, Nottingham rose about 20 places in our rankings for both measures.

One of Nottingham's great strengths is its links with the working world and it was recently ranked in the top 10% of universities for "working with business" and in the top 20% for research partnerships in Research England's Knowledge Exchange Framework. It has strong links with graduate recruiters such as PwC, Unilever, Rolls-Royce, IBM and GlaxoSmithKline (GSK).

Nottingham is in the top five universities targeted by Britain's leading graduate employers, according to the High Fliers survey. More than four in five students land high-skilled jobs or go into graduate-level study within 15 months of leaving, among the strongest performances of any university.

The university has embraced degree apprenticeships and counts 191 apprentices enrolled on eight programmes in subjects including architecture, chemical lab science, bioinformatics, senior leadership and data science. It expects to have 600 student apprentices on courses by September 2022.

Nottingham was awarded gold in the Teaching Excellence Framework (TEF), outperforming many other Russell Group universities. It drew praise for high levels of contact time, which is prescribed and monitored; a culture of personalised learning that ensures all students are challenged to achieve their full potential; and exceptionally high student engagement with technology-

University Park
Nottingham NG7 2RD
0115 951 5559
www.nottingham.ac.uk/studywithus/enquiry.aspx
www.nottingham.ac.uk
www.su.nottingham.ac.uk
Open days: see website

The Times and The Sunday Times **Rankings**
Overall Ranking: 28 (last year: 26)

Teaching quality	73.5%	83
Student experience	68.4%	=78
Research quality	37.8%	20
Entry standards	146	=34
Graduate prospects	81%	14
Good honours	84.7%	30
Expected completion rate	93%	=21
Student/staff ratio	14.8	=43
Services and facilities	£3,009	29

enhanced learning.

The 330-acre University Park campus is one of the most attractive in the UK, winning several environmental awards in recent years. The performing arts studio has recently had a full refurbishment.

Much of the latest development has been on the Jubilee campus in the city, where the Advanced Manufacturing Building, opened in 2019, hosts collaborations with companies such as Rolls-Royce and Siemens. It has a Centre for Sustainable Chemistry, part-funded by GSK, featuring the UK's first carbon-neutral laboratories and has recently been working on a £17million Power Electronics and Machines Centre. There's a rolling £21million programme to refurbish and redevelop student accommodation here, while at University Park, 200 bedrooms in the oldest hall of residence, Florence Boot Hall, are being refurbished.

A third campus, 12 miles south of the city, at Sutton Bonington, focuses on the biosciences and veterinary medicine. Here, the North Lab has recently had an £8million renovation and extension while an expansion of facilities for the School of Veterinary Science continues and will include a new mock vet practice building.

Nottingham was among the pioneers of overseas campuses, exporting a well-known and trusted educational brand to China and Malaysia, where its sites are centres of research as well as teaching; it was our 2019 International University of the Year. Undergraduates are encouraged to transfer between campuses and, with thousands of international students coming to Nottingham, the university markets itself as a global institution.

However, social inclusiveness within the UK is more of a challenge. Although almost 30% of entrants are from a minority ethnic background, the university has one of the lowest recruitment rates of white working-class males (3.2% of entrants) and only about one in fourteen students come from postcodes with low participation rates in higher education. It is in the bottom ten of our social inclusion ranking for England and Wales.

Attempts to broaden the intake include university-organised activities with local schools and colleges, and roughly a third of UK applicants in 2020 qualified for a contextual offer, one A-level grade lower than Nottingham's official requirements.

The 2020 access and participation plan awarded financial assistance in the form of bursaries to around 30% of the intake.

Tuition fees

» Fees for UK students	£9,250
» Fees for International students 2022–223	£19,000–£25,000
Medicine (clinical years)	£43,500
Veterinary surgery	£33,250
» For scholarship and bursary information see www.nottingham.ac.uk/fees/tuition-fees-student-services.aspx	
» Graduate salary	£26,000

Student numbers			Accommodation
Undergraduates	25,655	(325)	University provided places: 9,208
Postgraduates	7,060	(1,800)	Catered costs: £176–£250 per week
Applications/places		54,170/7,005	Self-catered: £108–£221 per week
Applications per place		7.1	First years guaranteed accommodation
Overall offer rate		75.2%	www.nottingham.ac.uk/accommodation
International students – EU		3.2%	
Non-EU		13.3%	

Where do the students come from?

					Social inclusion ranking: 108	
State schools (non-grammar)	63.4%	Low participation areas	7.1%		Disabled	5.5%
Grammar schools	15.4%	All ethnic minorities	29.6%		Mature (over 21)	7.4%
Independent schools	21.2%	White working-class males	3.2%			
First generation students	30.1%	Black achievement gap	-18.7%			

Nottingham Trent University

Nottingham Trent University (NTU) has been enjoying its most successful period in terms of demand for places and accolades from guides such as this one. It was our 2018 Modern University of the Year and has continued to grow after recruiting more than 9,000 students in each of the past three years.

With another 2.7% increase in applications to March 2021 and clearing continuing into September, NTU's popularity shows no signs of abating. New facilities are being added in Nottingham and elsewhere in the region to support the influx of students while boosting research and a commitment to the local economy.

The £23million Medical Technologies Innovation Facility (MTIF) and the Dryden Enterprise Centre, providing facilities and support to entrepreneurs, start-ups and more established companies, opened in 2021. The university has pledged £1million towards an automated distribution and manufacturing centre in nearby Ashfield, which will be a training centre for construction and civil engineering students.

There are plans for a new building for the School of Art and Design to open in the city centre in 2023. It will include specialist teaching spaces, quiet study areas, an innovation lab and a collaborative hub for social learning.

However, like many universities, NTU struggled to satisfy its students during the pandemic. Scores for the student experience in the latest edition of the National Student Survey have plunged more than 14 percentage points, taking NTU from a position on the verge of the top ten to one where it is only just inside the top 100. It was a similar story in the sections covering the quality of teaching, although the decline was less steep.

The university has introduced new student support initiatives, including the appointment of a dedicated project officer to help with money management and budgeting. There will also be mandatory consent awareness training and extra support for care leavers and estranged students.

One new degree is planned for 2022: a BA in youth work. Further expansion is in the pipeline for degree apprenticeship programmes with the addition of data science and hygiene specialisms. There should be 1,500 places available in September 2022.

The main City campus is close to the centre of Nottingham and is the academic base for about half of NTU's students. The Clifton campus, just outside the city, houses the arts and humanities, and science and technology, as well as the Nottingham Institute of Education. At the Brackenhurst campus on a countryside estate 14 miles away, ARES (animal, rural and environmental sciences) courses are based. Recent

50 Shakespeare Street
Nottingham NG1 4FQ
0115 848 4200
ntu.ac.uk/askntu
www.ntu.ac.uk
www.trentstudents.org
Open days: see website

***The Times and The Sunday Times* Rankings**
Overall Ranking: 70 (last year: 53)

Teaching quality	74%	=80
Student experience	67.1%	=92
Research quality	6.5%	80
Entry standards	120	=77
Graduate prospects	65.8%	93
Good honours	73.4%	102
Expected completion rate	88.4%	=44
Student/staff ratio	15.3	=54
Services and facilities	£2,430	73

developments there have included a new teaching and reception building, dining area, lecture theatre and exhibition space.

The university has been branching out across the East Midlands, with NTU in Mansfield now offering foundation degrees in partnership with Vision West Nottinghamshire College. Subjects include business, computing, education and sport and exercise science, and training for ambulance technicians. There is an option to transfer to the Nottingham campus to upgrade to a bachelor's degree. The university also has plans to open a health campus in Worksop, run with Bassetlaw Hospital and the University of Derby.

NTU, which has a gold rating in the Teaching Excellence Framework, is among the leading universities for the number of students on year-long work placements. Most courses include placements of at least four weeks and a dedicated employment team can help students to find international opportunities.

A recently introduced system of contextual offers, reducing A-level requirements for eligible applicants by up to two grades, is expected to raise the numbers of socially disadvantaged students on campus. Almost a third of undergraduates benefit from a range of bursaries and scholarships. NTU co-leads the National Social Mobility Research Centre, although it does not set the world alight in our unique social inclusion

table, ranking in the bottom 30 in England and Wales.

Nottingham Trent has a more developed research function than most of its peer group. More than half of the work submitted to the 2014 Research Excellence Framework was considered world-leading or internationally excellent. The best results were in health subjects and general engineering, where more than 80% of the work was placed in the top two categories.

There is accommodation on every campus, and new entrants may book one of the 6,250 rooms owned or endorsed by NTU as soon as they have a firm offer of a place. They are guaranteed accommodation if they apply by mid-June. The university has a strong sporting reputation, frequently reaching the top 20 in the BUCS (British Universities and Colleges Sport) league.

Social life varies between campuses, but all have access to the city's lively cultural and clubbing scene.

Tuition fees

- » Fees for UK students £9,250
- » Fees for International students 2022–23 £15,600–£16,200
- » For scholarship and bursary information see www.ntu.ac.uk/study-and-courses/undergraduate/fees-and-funding
- » Graduate salary £22,000

Student numbers

Undergraduates	27,520	(1,390)
Postgraduates	3,665	(3,205)
Applications/places		46,670/9,430
Applications per place		4.9
Overall offer rate		88.6%
International students – EU		3.2%
Non-EU		6.2%

Accommodation

University provided places: 5,994
Self-catered: £106–£188 per week
First years guaranteed accommodation
www.ntu.ac.uk/life-at-ntu/accommodation

Where do the students come from?

State schools (non-grammar)	87.2%	Low participation areas	13.4%
Grammar schools	4.5%	All ethnic minorities	28%
Independent schools	8.3%	White working-class males	5.5%
First generation students	42.8%	Black achievement gap	-27.4%

Social inclusion ranking: 87

Disabled	7%
Mature (over 21)	9.7%

The Open University

Teaching has been largely unaffected by Covid-19 at the Open University (OU), the global pioneer of distance learning that the rest of the higher-education sector has had to try to catch up with during the pandemic.

Some face-to-face tutorials are expected to have returned by October 2022 at the OU's base in Milton Keynes, Buckinghamshire. All students are classified as part-timers, regardless of whether they study at full-time intensity or not, which allows them to complete their studies without any benefits being affected.

The OU has long championed widening participation in higher education, welcoming students for whom further study was once out of reach. Set up by Harold Wilson's 1960s Labour government, the university continues to accept students without traditional qualifications.

An OU degree is also considerably cheaper than one gained from a conventional university – a fact not lost on OU students, who pay £6,336 a year compared with £9,250 plus living costs elsewhere.

For those who have not studied for some time or who want to build their confidence or study skills, there are 30-credit access courses, available at half the cost (£792) of other 30-credit programmes, or free of charge to those (in England, Wales and Northern Ireland) from households with an income below £25,000 a year. In Scotland, a full-fee waiver is available for students with an individual income of up to £25,000. About 3,700 access students are expected to gain a free OU place in the 2021–22 academic year.

The university has a Disabled Veterans' Scholarship Fund that aims to provide 50 full-fee waivers to veterans of military service. The waiver can cover everything from an introductory access module up to an entire undergraduate or postgraduate qualification. There are up to ten full-fee waivers available under the Carers' Scholarship Fund, three of which are for young carers aged 18–25. These are open to those from households with income under £25,000 a year, who can show they care for someone for an average of 15 hours per week, or that they have been a carer within the past two years until a bereavement.

These two funds demonstrate the lengths to which the university will go to ensure that no one who might benefit from one misses out on an OU education. There is also means-tested help available to cover the cost of wifi, travel, childcare and study materials. The age profile of OU students is steadily coming down and now stands at 27, with 70% of students continuing to work while they study.

The university offers a full range of undergraduate courses and modules, including a remodelled Bachelor of Laws degree

---

Walton Hall
Milton Keynes
MK7 6AA
0300 303 5303
general-enquiries@open.ac.uk
www.open.ac.uk
www.oustudents.com

The Times and The Sunday Times **Rankings**
n/a
No data available

introduced in October 2021 and a new BSc in geology from 2022. The OU also offers seven degree apprenticeships in England, with more than 3,150 trainees for roles such as chartered manager, senior leader, digital and technology solutions, social worker, police constable, registered nurse and advanced clinical practitioner, and one higher nursing associate apprenticeship. In Scotland, there are three graduate apprenticeships (covering BScs in cybersecurity, software development and an MSc in cybersecurity) while in Wales the OU offers an applied software engineering degree apprenticeship.

Our rankings have never included the OU because the absence of campus-based undergraduates would place it at a disadvantage in comparison with traditional universities. There are no entrance requirements, for example, and no need for physical facilities for students.

Where comparisons are possible, the OU generally performs well. Just under three-quarters of its submission for the Research Excellence Framework in 2014 was considered world-leading or internationally excellent. Music was outstanding, with 94% of work submitted reaching the top two categories. Art and design, and electronic engineering also did well.

More than two million students in 157 countries have benefited from an OU education since its inception in 1969 and an enduring partnership with the BBC has allowed programming to reach an estimated 264 million people.

The university employs thousands of part-time tutors around the country to guide students through their degrees. Its "supported open learning" system allows students to work where they choose: at home, in the workplace or at a library or study centre. Tutorials, day schools or online forums and social networks provide contact with fellow students (subject to Covid restrictions) and work is monitored by continual assessment, examination or assignment.

Efforts to expand the university's reach continue. From its beginnings as a pilot scheme with a single Job Centre Plus office, the OU's Open Doors to Success programme of courses offers free training to jobseekers to increase their employability from more than 750 centres. Participants can earn digital badges to add to their CV.

Tuition fees

» Fees for England, Scotland, Northern Ireland (current) £3,168
   Wales £1,284
   All per 60-credit module. Full-time study represents
   Two modules per year. Honours degree = 360 credits.
» Fees for International students £3,168
» For scholarship and bursary information see
   www.open.ac.uk/courses/fees-and-funding
» Graduate salary n/a

Students		**Accommodation**
Undergraduates	265 (120,175)	Not applicable
Postgraduates	260 (8,720)	

Where do the students come from?
Not applicable

University of Oxford

Oxford did what universities aim to do in times of national crisis. Apply brilliant minds and come up with a solution.

The work of Professor Dame Sarah Gilbert, Dr Catherine Green and the Oxford Vaccine Group is already the subject of a book. Their work to create and successfully trial a vaccine in record time, in partnership with AstraZeneca, helped enable Britain to protect its people against Covid-19. The vaccine is expected eventually to be administered to about one fifth of the world's population.

The global significance of this vaccine work was key in Oxford winning our University of the Year award last year. An important secondary factor, and one that has a more direct impact on undergraduate opportunities and the student experience, is the university's determination to be more socially inclusive.

Professor Louise Richardson, Oxford's vice-chancellor, has committed to change, with a target of 25% of admissions coming from hitherto underrepresented groups by 2023. The intake in 2020 reflected the new dynamic with 68.4% of an expanded number of admissions coming from state schools, non-selective and selective, compared with 62.3% the year before.

"We know some groups are still underrepresented among our students, but we are determined to increase the pace of change," the university told us.

Our social inclusion ranking confirms this. We look at admissions from non-selective state schools only, which now stand at 45.6%, up from 39.4% in our first ranking published in 2018. The proportion of students from ethnic minorities (23.8%) is good enough to rank Oxford 63rd out of 131 universities and is up from 17.6%. The university's black achievement gap is bettered by just three British universities.

The fact that Oxford slips a place in our social inclusion ranking this year, to sit next to bottom with only Cambridge beneath it, is simply an indication of accelerating change elsewhere in its Russell Group peer group, which dominates the foot of our table.

Oxford's UNIQ outreach programme offers sustained mentoring to high-performing state school students. Further work targets areas such as Wales and northeast England where young people are less likely to go into higher education.

About a quarter of all students receive some non-repayable bursary support, with those from families with income of less than £27,500 per year receiving Crankstart awards of £5,000 a year.

Selection is in the hands of the 30 undergraduate colleges, which vary considerably

---

University Offices
Wellington Square
Oxford OX1 2JD
01865 288 000
www.ox.ac.uk/ask
www.ox.ac.uk/admissions/
undergraduate
www.oxfordsu.org
Open days: see website

The Times and The Sunday Times **Rankings**

Overall Ranking: 2 (last year: 2)

Teaching quality	n/a	
Student experience	n/a	
Research quality	53.1%	3
Entry standards	198	5
Graduate prospects	89.2%	4
Good honours	95.1%	=1
Expected completion rate	99.1%	1
Student/staff ratio	10.1	=1
Services and facilities	£3,610	11

in their atmosphere and student mix. For example, at Mansfield College last year 94.4% of its intake was educated in state schools, while at Hertford College 54% were. At St Peter's, 30.1% came from ethnic minorities, compared with 17% at Lincoln and Somerville.

Sound advice on the colleges' academic strengths and social vibe is essential for applicants to give themselves the best chance of winning a place and finding an environment where they can thrive. Chapter 14 of this book, *Applying to Oxbridge*, provides details for each college.

Applicants are allowed to make an open application without specifying a college, but most do make a choice. This is especially important for arts and social science students, where tuition is based in college. Science and technology subjects are mainly taught in central facilities. There are written admission tests for certain subjects and interviews for all.

Facilities are constantly being upgraded. The Biochemistry Completion opened in January 2021, adding laboratory space and facilities to encourage interdisciplinary collaboration. A Life and Mind Building for psychological and life sciences and an Institute of Development and Regenerative Medicine are under construction.

Oxford has a gold award in the Teaching Excellence Framework and had the best results in nine subject areas in the 2014 Research Excellence Framework, when 87% of its submission was rated as world-leading or internationally excellent. It has a slightly lower overall score than Cambridge in our research ratings because it entered a lower proportion of eligible staff.

Oxford continues to outdo Cambridge in international rankings, in contrast to ours where Cambridge has come out on top more often. In the tightest finish yet seen in our academic ranking, Oxford has overtaken Cambridge for the first time in nine years, only to find itself overtaken in turn by St Andrews.

Oxford is second in the QS World Universities ranking this year, one place ahead of Cambridge, while it has topped the *THE* World University Rankings for the past five years.

Terms are just eight weeks long, but students pack a lot in. Sports facilities at university and college level are high class. The Iffley Road sports complex has been upgraded with a new gym and sports hall.

The deadline for applications to Oxford is October 15 and it is not possible to apply to Oxford and Cambridge in the same year.

Tuition fees

»	Fees for UK students	£9,250
»	Fees for International students 2022–23	£27,840–£39,010
	Medicine (clinical years)	£48,600
»	For scholarship and bursary information see www.ox.ac.uk/admissions/undergraduate/ fees-and-funding	
»	Graduate salary	£30,000

Student numbers

Undergraduates	11,730 (3,540)
Postgraduates	7,755 (2,885)
Applications/places	23,735/3,480
Applications per place	6.8
Overall offer rate	21.5%
International students – EU	6.2%
Non-EU	10.7%

Accommodation

College websites provide accommodation details
See chapter 13 for individual colleges

Where do the students come from?

State schools (non-grammar)	45.6%	Low participation areas	4.2%
Grammar schools	16%	All ethnic minorities	23.8%
Independent schools	37.8%	White working-class males	2.1%
First generation students	14.8%	Black achievement gap	-4.1%

Social inclusion ranking: 115

Disabled	7.9%
Mature (over 21)	2.2%

Oxford Brookes University

Oxford Brookes is in the top five modern universities after rising three places in our academic ranking. However, a drop in average entry grades and falling student satisfaction during the pandemic has slowed its march up our table to reclaim the top spot in the modern sector which it held a decade ago. Satisfaction with teaching quality remains in the bottom 20 in the country.

The university has streamlined its degree system, introducing more interdisciplinary courses favoured by employers – such as information technology for business, which accepted its first students in September 2021. Liberal Arts is one of three new courses on the way for September 2022. Applications in 2020 experienced an upturn but have fallen by about a third since 2015.

The main curriculum expansion planned for 2022 is for degree apprenticeships. Programmes for specialist community public health nurses, district nurses, digital and technology solutions specialists, town planners, chartered surveyors and social workers are being added to the five existing higher or degree apprenticeships.

The university's latest strategy sets out its goals for 2035, which include a 25% increase in the number of "employer-led" students. The business school has already been awarded the Small Business Charter Award for outstanding support for small businesses, student and social entrepreneurship, as well as its overall commitment to the local economy.

The strategy promises "personalisation of the student learning experience" at the institution, awarded silver in the Teaching Excellence Framework. Learning analytics are used to track students' progress and will be developed further in anticipation of more online learning continuing beyond the pandemic.

Oxford Brookes has four campuses. Change is afoot at the engineering base at Wheatley, seven miles from Oxford, which is to be redeveloped for housing. Courses are due to be transferred to the main city campus in Headington in 2022. Harcourt Hill, three miles from the city centre, houses education, English, communication, philosophy and sport students, while nursing is based in a business park in Swindon.

The university is part of an innovative collaboration sharing education, clinical practice and research in nursing, midwifery and allied health professions with two NHS trusts, Oxford University Hospitals NHS Foundation Trust and Oxford Health NHS Foundation Trust.

A £220million investment programme, continuing until 2025, has already provided specialist computing equipment for the Faculty of Health and Life Sciences at Headington.

There has been a growing emphasis on the university's international profile, with new

Headington Campus
Oxford OX3 0BP
01865 741 111
admissions@brookes.ac.uk
www.brookes.ac.uk
www.brookesunion.org.uk
Open days: see website

The Times and The Sunday Times **Rankings**		
Overall Ranking: 54 (last year: 56)		
Teaching quality	70.9%	=115
Student experience	67%	=94
Research quality	11.4%	57
Entry standards	114	=99
Graduate prospects	74.7%	44
Good honours	81.3%	=43
Expected completion rate	90.7%	34
Student/staff ratio	14.2	=30
Services and facilities	£2,246	86

partnerships with the Metropolitan College in Greece, and Chengdu University of Technology in central China. Through a global partnership with the Association of Chartered Certified Accountants, Brookes has more than 200,000 students taking its qualifications in other countries, far more students than any other UK university.

International mobility is encouraged for the university's own students. It has been awarded funding for up to 90 to work or study in Japan under the government's new Turing Scheme. More than 30% of the students will be from disadvantaged backgrounds.

Slipping into the bottom 20 this year in our social inclusion ranking for England and Wales, the university has been stepping up efforts to broaden its intake, with an outreach programme covering more than 120 schools, summer schools and taster sessions. Nearly 30% of the undergraduates are privately educated, the most in a modern university – easily the highest among non-specialist post-1992 universities and three times the national average for its subjects and entry grades.

A contextual admissions policy allows for lower offers to recognise educational disadvantage, and support for students from low-income households includes subsidised bus passes. The university offers one of the most valuable bursaries at any UK university: the Tessa Jane Evans bursary for nursing, worth £30,000 over three years to three mature students who have no other forms of funding.

Oxford Brookes excelled in the 2014 Research Excellence Framework, entering more academics than most of its peers and still having almost 60% of its work rated as world-leading or internationally excellent. Results were especially good in architecture, English and history.

Applicants who make Oxford Brookes their firm choice are guaranteed one of the 5,600 rooms owned or endorsed by the university. Those who hold the university as their insurance choice are still guaranteed accommodation, but not necessarily one of their preferred choices. The institution is hoping to add another 600 places to the 1,300 already available in its student village by 2023.

Impressive sports facilities include a 25m swimming pool and nine-hole golf course. Oxford Brookes is especially strong in rowing, while the cricketers join those from the "other" university in town to take on county teams.

The students' union runs one of the biggest entertainment venues in Oxford.

Tuition fees

»	Fees for UK students	£9,250
	Foundation courses	£7,570
»	Fees for International students 2022–23	£14,600–£15,500
	Foundation courses	£9,270
»	For scholarship and bursary information see www.brookes.ac.uk/studying-at-brookes/finance/	
»	Graduate salary	£24,200

Student numbers

Undergraduates	12,065	(650)
Postgraduates	1,885	(2,300)
Applications/places	18,940/3,625	
Applications per place	5.2	
Overall offer rate	78.8%	
International students – EU	4.3%	
Non-EU	9%	

Accommodation

University provided places: 5,603
Self-catered: £92–£203 per week
First years guaranteed accommodation
www.brookes.ac.uk/studying-at-brookes/accommodation/

Where do the students come from?

State schools (non-grammar)	64.8%	Low participation areas	6.9%	Social inclusion ranking: 98	
Grammar schools	5.1%	All ethnic minorities	19.6%	Disabled	9.3%
Independent schools	30.1%	White working-class males	3.5%	Mature (over 21)	15.9%
First generation students	37.5%	Black achievement gap	-22.3%		

Plymouth University

With a £100million campus development and 30 new courses planned, Plymouth is hoping to regain the ground lost in the past 10 years, which have seen enrolments decline by 30% and applications fall by 26%. Ten new degrees started in September 2021 with 20 more to follow in 2022 in subjects as diverse as musical theatre, international relations, criminology and dietetics.

Work has begun on developing a landmark building for engineering and design that will repurpose some old facilities and incorporate a new-build addition, using world-leading sustainability practices. It should be ready by the start of the 2023–24 academic year.

A new brain research and imaging centre has opened on Plymouth Science Park and a new centre for nursing and health education is on the way at the 11-storey Intercity House, located at the city's rail station. It is being converted and refurbished as a teaching and clinical skills space for nurses, midwives, paramedics, physiotherapists and other allied health professionals.

The university had already opened a school of nursing in Exeter. It is the largest provider of nursing, midwifery and health professional education and training in the southwest of England, with other nursing courses in Plymouth and Truro.

Applications showed a 1,000 increase across the 2019 and 2020 cycles following five successive falls. Enrolments have yet to follow suit, but there was only a small decline in 2020, when the region was still experiencing a steep fall in the 18-year-old population.

Plymouth is proud of its record as an environmentally conscious university. *Times Higher Education* magazine ranked it among the top 25 in the world for its response to the United Nations Sustainable Goals, and top for the goal relating to "life below water". The university won a Queen's Anniversary Award in 2019 – its third – for its research on microplastics and marine litter.

Only two post-1992 universities produced better results than Plymouth in the 2014 Research Excellence Framework. Its submission involved a far bigger proportion of its academics than most of its peers yet nearly two-thirds was judged world-leading or internationally excellent.

Plymouth gained a silver award in the Teaching Excellence Framework. Although it has dropped out of our top 30 for student satisfaction with teaching quality after disappointing scores from the 2021 cohort in the National Student Survey, affected by the pandemic, it remains comfortably in the top third of universities on that measure.

Plymouth has developed support services to help students negotiate blended and distanced learning. One is the new Digital

Drake circus
Plymouth PL4 8AA
01752 585 858
admissions@plymouth.ac.uk
www.plymouth.ac.uk
www.upsu.com
Open days: see website

The Times and The Sunday Times **Rankings**
Overall Ranking: =58 (last year: 59)

Teaching quality	76.5%	=41
Student experience	70.7%	51
Research quality	15.9%	56
Entry standards	125	=63
Graduate prospects	73.1%	=53
Good honours	81%	=45
Expected completion rate	84%	71
Student/staff ratio	17.1	89
Services and facilities	£2,378	81

Writing Café, where trained mentors help fellow students adjust to writing across different disciplines. The facility was cited by the Office for Students as an example of how some universities had made positive changes as a result of the pandemic. A new student hub has brought support services together in the main library at the heart of campus.

The university draws 87% of its undergraduates from state schools and colleges, and 45% are the first in their family to go to university, helping Plymouth to achieve a mid-table ranking for social inclusion.

Twenty partner colleges are located mainly in the southwest and the Channel Islands, where students can follow Plymouth degree courses. There are also opportunities to study in Europe, America and Canada. Plymouth is a partner in the new South West Institute of Technology, established by the government to train students in technical subjects.

In 2020 the first 250 degree apprentices graduated from Plymouth and there were 700 students at the last count, on 15 programmes. Numbers are expected to rise to 1,100 by 2022 with the addition of programmes in leadership and management, nursing and allied health professions, digital and technology solutions, civil and mechanical engineering, town planning and clinical psychology.

Plymouth has the only partnership in Britain between a university and theatre to teach the performing arts. Undergraduates at its conservatoire divide their time between the university and the Theatre Royal Plymouth.

Plymouth also has one of the country's leading business incubation facilities, focusing on small and medium-size enterprises. About 12,000 students undertake work-based learning or placements, while the Plymouth Award recognises extracurricular achievements. Contributing to a strong outcome in our analysis of graduate prospects, the Cube business service works with more than 1,000 students a year.

There are 1,754 residential places in Plymouth, with 235 in Truro. Applicants holding Plymouth as their firm choice are guaranteed a place in one of the managed halls or an accredited private hall if they apply by mid-June.

On campus there is a sports hall, fitness centre, dance studio and squash courts. The university has upgraded its facilities for watersports and sessions are run exclusively for students at the city's international-standard swimming and diving centre. Plymouth city centre has plenty of student-oriented nightlife.

Tuition fees

»	Fees for UK students	£9,250
»	Fees for International students 2022–23	£14,200
	Dentistry & Medicine (clinical years)	£22,100–£41,100
»	For scholarship and bursary information see www.plymouth.ac.uk/fees	
»	Graduate salary	£24,000

Student numbers

Undergraduates	14,335	(1,330)
Postgraduates	1,255	(1,495)
Applications/places	18,675/3,430	
Applications per place	5.4	
Overall offer rate	72.2%	
International students – EU	2.4%	
Non-EU	7.1%	

Accommodation

University provided places: 1,989
Self-catered: £102–£183 per week
First years guaranteed accommodation
www.plymouth.ac.uk/student-life/services/accommodation

Where do the students come from?

State schools (non-grammar)	87.4%	Low participation areas	15.1%	
Grammar schools	7.1%	All ethnic minorities	13%	
Independent schools	5.5%	White working-class males	7.4%	
First generation students	45%	Black achievement gap	-24.1%	

Social inclusion ranking: 60

Disabled	10%
Mature (over 21)	29.3%

Plymouth Marjon University

Plymouth Marjon has leapt 18 places into the top four universities for student satisfaction with teaching quality. It is also back in the top ten for satisfaction with the wider student experience, helping to propel the small Church of England university up our overall league table.

Just four universities performed better than Marjon in our analysis of National Student Survey outcomes in 2021 compared with 2020. One reason that satisfaction rates barely dropped during the pandemic may be that commuting students – of which Marjon has many, some travelling long distances – embraced the online teaching that others yearning for the full campus experience found so frustrating. Where possible, the university is aiming to give students the choice of face-to-face or online learning in the 2021–22 academic year.

Marjon is first in England in the 2021 survey for its "learning community", a section assessing student involvement in their course. It was also top for satisfaction with the students' union and second in England for learning opportunities.

High satisfaction levels and a silver award in the Teaching Excellence Framework have helped to produce a generally upward trend in applications. They rose 17.6% by the end of March 2021 compared with the same point in the cycle a year before, one of the biggest rises in the country. Demand for places was up across the board, but was particularly strong in teaching, psychology, health and journalism.

Marjon was only 40 students off its target of attracting 1,000 students per cohort in 2020 and should easily surpass it in 2021–22. To cater for the new entrants, it has a ten-year development plan for its attractive campus on Plymouth's north side.

Social learning spaces and versatile new teaching accommodation have been added and the next phase will feature investment in the quad at the heart of campus and a new fitness trail with outdoor gym stations. The university is moving towards becoming a zero-carbon campus, having won significant funding for efficiency measures such as ground-source heat pumps and solar panels.

Four new degrees are planned for 2022 in the liberal arts, education and management, secondary education in STEM (science, technology, engineering and maths) subjects, and the esports industry.

Marjon was already investing in teaching and learning technology before the pandemic hit, introducing a Moodle virtual learning environment and installing interactive television screens in the main lecture rooms. All lectures are filmed for later viewing by students on mobiles or computers.

Almost all courses have some form of

Derriford Road
Plymouth PL6 8BH
01752 636 890
admissions@marjon.ac.uk
www.marjon.ac.uk
www.marjonsu.com
Open days: see website

The Times and The Sunday Times Rankings
Overall Ranking: =101 (last year: 115)

Teaching quality	81.6%	4
Student experience	77.2%	8
Research quality	0%	127
Entry standards	117	=85
Graduate prospects	61.8%	=111
Good honours	77.4%	70
Expected completion rate	78.3%	109
Student/staff ratio	16.4	=74
Services and facilities	£983	132

work placement for students, in organisations including NHS hospitals, local football clubs and media outlets. There is an increasing focus on health-related courses.

The university has been awarded £250,000 by the Office for Students and Research England to develop its student-led programmes in community clinics into a model for other institutions to follow. Researchers and students work with NHS patients to help them to manage disease through lifestyle and behavioural changes.

Marjon suffers in our academic rankings for a decision not to take part in the 2014 Research Excellence Framework, which leaves it in last place in our table for research quality. One of its key aims for 2025 is to develop a credible entry for future assessment.

Nearly all Marjon's undergraduates are state-educated and the proportion admitted from areas with low participation is nearly twice the national average. Widening participation is a priority for student recruitment, demonstrated by the university's highest-ever placing in our social inclusion table. Marjon has long-term progression agreements with 12 local schools or colleges and makes lower offers to promising applicants from disadvantaged backgrounds.

Once the College of St Mark and St John, which was established in London as a teacher-training institution in 1840 and moved to Plymouth in 1973, Marjon retains Church of England control and welcomes students of all faiths and none. Teacher education remains a strength.

Sport is another main area and the university's excellent sports facilities are all available to the public. They include a floodlit 3G pitch for rugby, lacrosse and football, two other floodlit all-weather pitches, a climbing wall, 25m indoor swimming pool and gym. There is also a rehabilitation clinic and sports science laboratory with a climate chamber and an anti-gravity treadmill.

There are student bedrooms on campus, a short bus ride from the lively city centre, for 459 students in seven halls of residence and 38 village houses. First-year students are given priority for accommodation. If there are none left they are found approved rooms off campus.

Tuition fees

» Fees for UK students	£9,250
Foundation courses	£6,000
» Fees for International students 2022–23	£12,500
» For scholarship and bursary information see www.marjon.ac.uk/courses/fees-and-funding/	
» Graduate salary	£23,000

Student numbers

Undergraduates	2,105	(110)
Postgraduates	300	(235)
Applications/places		2,860/805
Applications per place		3.6
Overall offer rate		84.4%
International students – EU		1%
Non-EU		0.6%

Accommodation

University provided places: 459
Self-catered: £95–£145 per week
First years guaranteed accommodation
www.marjon.ac.uk/student-life/accommodation/

Where do the students come from?

State schools (non-grammar)	97.2%	Low participation areas	19.3%	Social inclusion ranking: 3	
Grammar schools	0.4%	All ethnic minorities	6.4%	Disabled	15.6%
Independent schools	2.4%	White working-class males	13.4%	Mature (over 21)	37.8%
First generation students	58.2%	Black achievement gap	-29.6%		

University of Portsmouth

Portsmouth has made plans for 80% of its teaching to be face-to-face in the 2021–22 academic year. Its new "blended and connected" approach promises students every opportunity to be on campus for practical, studio and workshop work.

The university has adopted a core principle that all students should have access to learning from all formal teaching sessions, regardless of whether they are able to physically attend. Academic staff have been encouraged to generate a range of online support materials, such as enhanced notes in lecture slides, written summaries of sessions, audio summaries and narrated presentations. Field and lab-based activities will continue with safety measures in place.

The promises are more specific than at most other universities and should be welcomed by students who, in the National Student Survey, delivered a harsh verdict on Portsmouth's pandemic provision. Our analysis comparing outcomes in 2020 and 2021 showed that Portsmouth had one of the steepest falls, dropping 50 places overall for student satisfaction and almost 60 places for the wider student experience.

High levels of student engagement and commitment to learning were noted by assessors, who awarded Portsmouth gold in the Teaching Excellence Framework. Applications, however, have declined for six years in a row, falling by more than a quarter in that time. Enrolments have stayed steadier, but the university has dropped out of the top 100 for average entry grades.

Portsmouth has announced £400million of spending over ten years. The striking new £57million Ravelin Sports Centre at the heart of the campus opened at the end of 2021, built to be one of the most environmentally sustainable facilities of its type in the UK. Plans have been submitted for a new academic building in the city centre with large, flexible spaces for teaching, research and collaboration.

Other investment has been concentrated on teaching through real-life and simulated facilities to give students the hands-on experience favoured by employers. Students on healthcare courses learn to dispense medicines in a pharmacy and to treat NHS patients at a dental clinic. Portsmouth has also opened a forensic innovation centre where students work alongside police officers.

The £12million Future Technology Centre, opened in 2019, enables students on BEng (Hons) and MEng Innovation Engineering courses to confront real-world health, humanitarian and environmental problems using specialist technology. Additional teaching facilities are available on the city centre campus through Highbury College's City Learning Centre.

University House
Winston Churchill Avenue
Portsmouth PO1 2UP
023 9284 5566
admissions@port.ac.uk
www.port.ac.uk
www.upsu.net
Open days: see website

The Times and The Sunday Times Rankings		
Overall Ranking: 88 (last year: 72)		
Teaching quality	72.8%	=90
Student experience	66.5%	=98
Research quality	8.6%	70
Entry standards	111	=107
Graduate prospects	68.2%	=77
Good honours	76.3%	82
Expected completion rate	83.5%	=75
Student/staff ratio	16.3	73
Services and facilities	£2,405	78

Three new degrees were launched this year, in criminology and criminal justice; language; and counterterrorism, intelligence and cybercrime. Considerable growth is expected in Portsmouth's degree apprenticeship programme, introducing courses including architecture and manufacturing engineering, chartered surveying and risk management to boost numbers from 800 to 1,200 by 2022.

Health subjects produced the best results in the 2014 Research Excellence Framework. About 90% of the work submitted in dentistry, nursing and pharmacy was assessed as world-leading or internationally excellent. Health research links are expected to grow stronger after the local hospital trust was renamed the Portsmouth Hospitals University NHS Trust in 2020, marking a decade-long partnership.

The university has pioneered new approaches to student wellbeing. Academic staff, including personal tutors, are trained in mental health awareness and how best to support their students. Portsmouth was the first university to use WhatsUp? a mental health app that promotes better communication between students and pastoral services.

Portsmouth spends almost £1million a year funding student support, including scholarships to encourage progression to postgraduate courses where this will help career plans. There is a growing range of MRes programmes to develop research skills. Students are also encouraged to take up opportunities for UK and global work placements and can use the year to set up their own business.

More than a third of Portsmouth undergraduates qualify for financial support. The university is in the top 40 of this year's social inclusion ranking, with 30% of its undergraduates drawn from ethnic minorities. Nearly half are the first in their family to go to university.

Most of the accommodation is close to the central Guildhall campus, although many students live in neighbouring Southsea. The university has almost 4,000 residential places.

A £6.5million student centre includes alcohol-free areas. Sports facilities at the new Ravelin centre include an eight-lane 25m swimming pool, an eight-court sports hall, a 175-station fitness suite, squash courts and a ski simulator, while outdoor facilities are at the Langstone Sports Village, three miles away.

The seaside location provides an excellent base for watersports and other leisure activities, while the city's nightlife is lively.

Tuition fees

- » Fees for UK students — £9,250
- » Fees for International students 2022–23 — £16,200–£19,600
- » For scholarship and bursary information see www.port.ac.uk/study/undergraduate/undergraduate-fees-and-student-finance
- » Graduate salary — £24,000

Student numbers

Undergraduates	19,350 (2,660)
Postgraduates	2,800 (1,965)
Applications/places	23,920/4,450
Applications per place	5.4
Overall offer rate	85.9%
International students – EU	4.6%
Non-EU	12.8%

Accommodation

University provided places: 3,948
Catered costs: £134–£173 per week
Self-catered: £99–£163 per week
First years guaranteed accommodation
www.port.ac.uk/student-life/accommodation

Where do the students come from?

State schools (non-grammar)	91.5%	Low participation areas	15.6%	
Grammar schools	5.3%	All ethnic minorities	30.3%	
Independent schools	3.2%	White working-class males	7.7%	
First generation students	48.1%	Black achievement gap	-20.2%	

Social inclusion ranking: 38

Disabled	8.5%
Mature (over 21)	13.3%

Queen Margaret University Edinburgh

Queen Margaret (QMU) attracted a record intake in 2020 and with applications up by 11% in the current admissions round, it is making good progress on its plan for five years of growth. Most of last year's entrants were from Scotland but a fifth came from EU countries, which have since lost their entitlement to free tuition for new students.

Always a close-knit community, the university believes that the pandemic brought staff and students closer together in some ways. Students' union representatives continued to play a key part in the university's business continuity group, for example, and there was a joint student and staff Stories of Covid virtual exhibition, describing life in the pandemic.

Both internal surveys and the latest edition of the National Student Survey (NSS) suggest that such efforts have been appreciated. Although satisfaction levels have dipped slightly, QMU has moved up to the verge of the top 20 for teaching quality and is only four places lower for the broader student experience, compared with 95th in the previous edition. Just eight institutions performed better than QMU in our comparison of NSS outcomes from 2021 with those of the previous year.

In 2021–22 academic year, QMU planned for seminars, workshops, studio work, clinics and other small-group work to take place on campus, with lectures for more than 50 students online.

The university promises a "student-centred approach" with a culture of personalised support. Nearly a quarter of QMU's workforce has been trained in mental health first aid, offering a bigger network than any other in Scotland.

QMU's award-winning campus opened in 2007 and remains one of the most environmentally sustainable in the UK. Based in the seaside town of Musselburgh, it is ten minutes by train from the centre of Edinburgh.

The university's strategic plan promises to address sustainability in all courses, so graduates leave with a "rounded understanding of the sustainability challenges facing the world and the tools to contribute to solutions". QMU aims to reduce its own carbon footprint and to be one of the greenest institutions in the UK.

QMU has also set its sights on being Scotland's top modern university for graduate employment, partly by increasing the opportunities for students to take work experience. The Business Innovation Zone encourages entrepreneurial and business skills and its first Entrepreneur in Residence has a brief to advance female entrepreneurship.

A highly successful employer mentoring scheme matches third and fourth-year students with professionals who have relevant

University Way
Musselburgh
Edinburgh EH21 6UU
0131 474 0000
admissions@qmu.ac.uk
www.qmu.ac.uk
www.qmusu.org.uk
Open days: see website

Overall Ranking: 66 (last year: 89)

Teaching quality	78.2%	=21
Student experience	74%	25
Research quality	6.6%	79
Entry standards	160	21
Graduate prospects	66.8%	88
Good honours	80.4%	=52
Expected completion rate	81.5%	89
Student/staff ratio	20.8	121
Services and facilities	£1,541	130

experience. QMU is also developing the £40million Edinburgh Innovation Park on land next to the campus. However, at present all bar one Scottish university ranks above it in our graduate prospects measure, with just 66.8% of students in high-skilled work or graduate-level study within 15 months of leaving.

Three-quarters of the 3,500 undergraduates are female, and more than half qualify for bursaries of up to £2,000 a year. QMU is fourth in Scotland in our social inclusion index and has committed to recruiting greater numbers from disadvantaged groups. About one in five of last year's entrants were asked for grades below the norm, or made an unconditional offer, because of their background and educational experience.

Originally a cookery school for women, the institution was established in 1875 and named after Saint Margaret, the 11th-century wife of King Malcolm III of Scotland. It remains strong in teaching and research on hospitality and food, and has Dame Prue Leith, the restaurateur and *Great British Bake Off* host, as chancellor.

QMU also has the broadest range of allied health courses in Scotland and is one of only three universities north of the border to offer paramedic science. Health and rehabilitation is regarded as one of the three "flagship areas", together with sustainable business and creativity and culture.

Only 22% of the eligible staff were entered in the 2014 Research Excellence Framework but almost 60% of their work was considered world-leading or internationally excellent. The submission in speech and language sciences was the most successful, with 92% of it rated in the top two categories, placing the university second in the UK and first in Scotland in this area.

QMU has 800 residential places on campus and a good range of sports facilities. It does not guarantee accommodation for new entrants, although all those who wanted one were offered a place in 2020. Priority goes to students from outside the Edinburgh area, as well as those who have disabilities or have been in care.

There are a variety of services to help new students settle in and assist with their mental health subsequently. They include two dogs belonging to the students' union, who are registered Therapets and are popular figures on campus. Students can spend time with them either on a drop-in or appointment basis.

Tuition fees

» Fees for Scottish students £0–£1,820
  RUK fees (capped at £27,750 for 4-year courses) £9,250
» Fees for International students 2022–23 £7,000–£15,500
» For scholarship and bursary information see www.qmu.ac.uk/study-here/fees-and-funding/
» Graduate salary £23,000

Student numbers

Undergraduates	3,105	(410)
Postgraduates	655	(960)
Applications/places		6,535/1,080
Applications per place		6.1
Overall offer rate		57.3%
International students – EU		17.7%
Non-EU		1.9%

Accommodation

University provided places: 800
Self-catered: £121–£146 per week
www.qmu.ac.uk/campus-life/accommodation/

Where do the students come from?

State schools (non-grammar)	97.6%	Deprived areas	13.8%	Disabled	12%
Grammar schools	1.2%	All ethnic minorities	7.6%	Mature (over 21)	38%
Independent schools	1.2%	White working-class males	6.3%		
First generation students	38.2%	Black achievement gap	n/a		

Social inclusion ranking (Scotland): 4

Queen Mary, University of London

Runner-up for University of the Year in our previous edition, Queen Mary, University of London's (QMUL) success in our academic and social inclusion leagues is enduring. This year it adds a top 15 ranking for its Covid response to its achievements, as shown by a *Good University Guide* analysis of National Student Survey (NSS) results.

Satisfaction levels with teaching quality and the wider student experience dropped at almost all UK universities during the past year, but students at QMUL recorded a much smaller decline overall than those at most other institutions, which speaks highly of how their university handled the challenges of teaching and learning in a pandemic.

Even pre-Covid-19, QMUL was moving towards a "flipped classroom" model of education, in which students come together in person to discuss material they have digested beforehand. That shift was accelerated by the rapid pivot to remote learning. The university's aim now is to combine the best of online and in-person delivery, while offering a full range of on-campus social activities, from clubs and sports to volunteering.

Most of QMUL's undergraduates are taught and housed on a self-contained campus in Mile End, east London. Its large medical school, Barts and the London School of Medicine and Dentistry, is based in nearby Whitechapel.

The School of Mathematical Sciences has been transformed by an £18million investment that has provided seminar and workshop teaching rooms and a new lecture theatre. Study spaces for private and group work are built-in, with a 42-computer IT lab and a social hub.

Elsewhere, the School of Engineering and Materials Science has benefited from a £30million makeover that has added a creative hub with specialist equipment.

The improvements follow the development of a graduate centre and a new dental school. The university's £100million investment in its estate over recent years has also added the Neuron Pod, an extension of QMUL's award-winning Centre of the Cell science education centre. The art deco People's Palace, built to bring culture, entertainment and education to Victorian-era Eastenders, has been restored to host events.

QMUL was awarded silver in the Teaching Excellence Framework (TEF), impressing assessors with the quality of its coaching programmes, mentoring schemes and employer engagement programmes, which help students to find jobs. The QMUL Model accounts for 10% of a degree, covering activities such as work experience, volunteering, overseas travel, project work with local businesses and

327 Mile End Road
London E1 4NS
020 7882 5511
admissions@qmul.ac.uk
www.qmul.ac.uk
www.qmsu.org/
Open days: see website

Edinburgh
Belfast
Cardiff
LONDON

The Times and The Sunday Times Rankings
Overall Ranking: 40 (last year: 41)

Teaching quality	72.1%	=102
Student experience	69.3%	=70
Research quality	37.9%	19
Entry standards	146	=34
Graduate prospects	74.6%	45
Good honours	87.5%	17
Expected completion rate	91.6%	28
Student/staff ratio	13	=12
Services and facilities	£2,146	=96

organisations, learning a language, or taking modules from other subjects.

QMUL's success in our social inclusion index, ranking 47th, sets it 32 places ahead of all other Russell Group institutions, which tend to fare poorly in this measure, but strongly in our academic ranking. More than three quarters of students are from black and minority ethnic backgrounds (only four UK universities have a higher proportion) and the black achievement gap at QMUL is among the narrowest in the country.

Many QMUL students grew up near its campuses in the east London borough of Tower Hamlets (one of the UK's most deprived areas) and rub shoulders with students from around the world, who make up about a quarter of undergraduates.

The number starting courses has mushroomed by 57% since the university joined the Russell Group in 2012, after a record year for applications and enrolments in 2020. Six new degrees launch in September 2022: in modern languages and international relations; liberal arts; human geography with business management; physical geography with business management; global development; and accounting and management.

The university is also adding new pathways to 15 established programmes across economics, finance, marketing and business – with January starts and foundation years, or years abroad or in industry.

Degree apprenticeships are offered, in digital and technology solutions; business management for social change; digital technology solutions; and clinical education. There is also a programme to train senior professional economists. There should be about 500 degree apprentices by September 2022.

Medicine and other health subjects did well in the 2014 Research Excellence Framework, but the best results came in the humanities. About 95% of the research in linguistics and in music, drama and the performing arts was rated as world-leading or internationally excellent. More than 85% of QMUL's entire submission reached the top two categories.

Last year more than a third of students received the Queen Mary University of London Bursary, worth up to £1,700 per year. With the wide range of other scholarships and bursaries offered around a half of undergraduates receive some sort of financial award.

QMUL students can use the sports facilities at the nearby Queen Elizabeth Olympic Park, including the Copper Box indoor arena and the Aquatic Centre's swimming pool.

Tuition fees

»	Fees for UK students	£9,250
»	Fees for International students 2022–23	£20,000–£25,150
	Dentistry, Medicine	£42,500
»	For scholarship and bursary information see	
	www.qmul.ac.uk/undergraduate/feesandfunding/	
»	Graduate salary	£28,000

Student numbers

Undergraduates	14,825	(5)
Postgraduates	5,260	(1,580)
Applications/places	34,340/3,750	
Applications per place	9.2	
Overall offer rate	64.6%	
International students – EU	8.2%	
Non-EU	14.5%	

Accommodation

University provided places: 3,122
Self-catered: £133–£183 per week
First years guaranteed accommodation
www.qmul.ac.uk/study/accommodation

Where do the students come from?

State schools (non-grammar)	81%	Low participation areas	3.6%		
Grammar schools	11.5%	All ethnic minorities	76.5%		
Independent schools	7.5%	White working-class males	2.5%		
First generation students	46%	Black achievement gap	-5.7%		

Social inclusion ranking: 47

Disabled	6.5%
Mature (over 21)	9%

Queen's University Belfast

Queen's is on the verge of the top 20 in our league table for the first time in many years, moving up seven places with some of the best graduate prospects in the UK and improved rankings for student satisfaction during the pandemic.

Satisfaction rates at Queen's have held up better than at most universities, despite some rocky moments, with more than 200 students suspended for breaching Covid-19 regulations. Although scores in the National Student Survey (NSS) have dipped slightly, Queen's has moved up 40 places in the sections devoted to teaching quality and by more than 50 places in the remaining areas covering the wider student experience, rankings derived from the 2021 pandemic-hit NSS results.

Northern Ireland's leading university has improved its position in our table consistently over recent years and is also just outside the top 200 in the QS World University Rankings. Hillary Clinton was installed as chancellor as part of an internationalisation drive, which is intended to double the number of students coming from overseas.

A member of the Russell Group, Queen's saw increased enrolments in 2020, especially from outside the UK, up by about 33%. Applications were up again in the latest admissions round.

Most undergraduates come from Northern Ireland, two thirds of them from grammar schools, which educate a much larger proportion of the population in the province than elsewhere in the UK. Because of this the university does not feature in our social inclusion ranking. Our index measures recruitment from non-selective state schools, a figure that is unduly depressed at Queen's, Belfast and Ulster.

Queen's has been increasing its efforts to broaden its intake and about 30% of undergraduates received some financial support in 2020/21. The Pathway Opportunity Programme guarantees Northern Irish students living in disadvantaged areas a conditional offer that may be two grades lower than the norm.

The university won a seventh Queen's Anniversary prize for higher education in 2020 for its pioneering work in shared education, which facilitates collaboration between schools serving different faiths. For more than 100 years the university's own charter has guaranteed non-denominational teaching as well as student representation and equal rights for women.

Queen's has invested £350million in facilities over the past ten years. Recent developments have included the £39million School of Biological Sciences, which is expanding the university's work in areas such as agriculture, food science and the

University Road
Belfast BT7 1NN
028 9097 3838
admissions@qub.ac.uk
www.qub.ac.uk
www.qubsu.org
Open days: see website

The Times and The Sunday Times **Rankings**
Overall Ranking: 24 (last year: =31)

Teaching quality	74.5%	=74
Student experience	72.8%	35
Research quality	39.7%	14
Entry standards	148	=32
Graduate prospects	83.1%	11
Good honours	86.1%	21
Expected completion rate	91%	33
Student/staff ratio	14.6	39
Services and facilities	£2,410	76

environment, and a Precision Medicine Centre of Excellence, which is developing artificial intelligence solutions to enable early, rapid and accurate diagnoses of cancers.

A £2.1million grant will pay for a high-performance computing facility and Queen's has a newly revamped echo-free chamber for work on developing higher frequencies for advanced wireless systems, such as 5G. The university is also collaborating with Rakuten, the Japanese mobile network operator, to set up an Edge computing hub in Belfast.

Queen's plays a leading role in the Belfast City Region deal, a 15-year programme to boost growth. It has been rated top in the UK in successive years in an assessment of entrepreneurial impact by Octopus Ventures, praised for its highly effective approach to developing spinouts. It is co-leader of a national programme to promote the commercialisation of university research.

Queen's is in our top 20 for research after entering 95% of its academics for the 2014 Research Excellence Framework, a proportion matched only by Cambridge. Fourteen subject areas were ranked in the UK's top 20 and 77% of the research was considered world-leading or internationally excellent.

The campus, on the south side of the city, has a cinema, an art gallery and theatre, all of which are open to the wider community. The city centre has plenty of nightlife, but the social scene is mainly concentrated on the students' union and the surrounding area.

Most of the 4,000 residential places are at the nearby Elms student village, while a recent development of 1,200 rooms with its own services, including pastoral care, security and social activities, has added the option of city centre living. A new agreement with a private provider will increase the options further, with rooms for the same rent as Queen's own halls. First-year students, including those taking foundation degrees, are guaranteed a place.

The university's sports facilities, which include a cottage for climbers in the Mourne Mountains, have benefited from a £20million programme of investment. An international standard hockey pitch with floodlights and a 100-seat stand was added in 2020. There is an arena pitch which can host football, rugby or Gaelic sport, another 14 pitches, a recreational trail and conference facilities. The Physical Education Centre includes two swimming pools, and there is a boathouse on the River Lagan.

Tuition fees

»	Fees for Northern Ireland students	£4,530
	Students from England, Scotland and Wales	£9,250
»	Fees for International students 2022–23	£17,900–£22.800
	Medicine (clinical years)	£42,800
»	For scholarship and bursary information see www.qub.ac.uk/Study/Undergraduate/Fees-and-scholarships/Tuition-fees/	
»	Graduate salary	£23,500

Student numbers

Undergraduates	15,310 (3,005)
Postgraduates	4,035 (2,570)
Applications/places	26,115/4,945
Applications per place	5.3
Overall offer rate	73.7%
International students – EU	2.9%
Non-EU	8.8%

Accommodation

University provided places: 4,024
Catered costs: £90–£189 per week
Self-catered: £85–£175 per week
First years guaranteed accommodation
www.qub.ac.uk/accommodation

Where do the students come from?

State schools (non-grammar)	32%	Low participation areas	7.2%
Grammar schools	66.4%	Ethnic minorities	4.6%
Independent schools	1.6%	Mature (over-21)	18.7%
First generation students	35.7%		

Social inclusion ranking: n/a

Ravensbourne University, London

Occupying an eye-catching building next to the O2 Arena on the Greenwich Peninsula, Ravensbourne is only three years into achieving university status. Originally formed in 1962 by the merging of Bromley, Beckenham and Sidcup art schools, its degrees were validated by the University of the Arts London until 2018. The specialist design and digital media institution moved to the burgeoning Greenwich design district in 2010, where its new Institute for Creativity and Technology opened last year.

Described by Ravensbourne as "a place where hi-tech collides with lo-tech and no-tech", the aluminium-clad building houses the university's postgraduate provision alongside its CreativeLab in-house creative agency, incubation and research activities. Facilities for 3D digital printing, creative coding, laser cutting and rapid prototyping are among new equipment.

The institute should boost Ravensbourne's already strong links with creative technology businesses and entrepreneurship. Recent industry collaborations have included fashion students creating a denim brand in ten weeks for the denim trade's Kingpins Show. Digital photography students gained experience with the new creative communication platform Lenslife, while those on computing, gaming and animation courses have had access to the Amazon Future Engineer Bursary, which offers financial support, mentoring and internship opportunities at Amazon.

The university's extensive collaboration with industry was praised by assessors in the Teaching Excellence Framework, when Ravensbourne was awarded silver.

Ravensbourne remains one place off the bottom of our table (now expanded to 132 institutions), anchored by its low rates of student satisfaction. Taking account of its scores in the 2021 National Student Survey, impacted by the pandemic, Ravensbourne drops two places to be third from bottom in our rankings for student satisfaction with teaching quality. For satisfaction with the wider experience, it falls two places to record the poorest score in the UK.

It continues to be hampered by the absence of a score for research quality because it did not enter the Research Excellence Framework (REF) in 2014. A submission was made to the 2021 REF round, however, which should improve its ranking in our next edition of this guide, after REF results are published in 2022.

Ravensbourne fares much better in our social inclusion ranking, rising 43 places to be just outside the top 20. It performs particularly well for the recruitment of students from ethnic minorities and has one of the UK's narrower black achievement gaps. Progression

6 Penrose Way
Greenwich Peninsula
London SE10 0EW
020 3040 3500
hello@rave.ac.uk
www.ravensbourne.ac.uk
www.ravesu.co.uk
Open days: see website

The Times and The Sunday Times **Rankings**
Overall Ranking: 131 (last year: 130)

Teaching quality	65.8%	128
Student experience	54.7%	130
Research quality	n/a	
Entry standards	113	=102
Graduate prospects	61.4%	115
Good honours	80.9%	=47
Expected completion rate	79.7%	103
Student/staff ratio	22.6	130
Services and facilities	£1,561	128

agreements are in place with schools and colleges that have high proportions of pupils on free school meals, and where there are low levels of progression to higher education. All new students receive a £100 voucher towards course materials, rising to £500 for those from low-income households.

Demand for places reached the highest level for four years in 2020, while the number of students starting courses surpassed 1,000 for the first time. The first digital content creation students began their courses in September 2021, as did the first games programming undergraduates. A top-up degree in digital photography was also introduced, allowing students to upgrade their existing qualification to a Bachelor of Arts. Degrees in computer science; fashion management; business and management; and digital production are due to begin in September 2022.

Ravensbourne has its sights on being recognised as a national and international leader in creative industries education and training. A partnership with Berghs School of Communication, in Stockholm, brings Swedish students to the university. The minimum entry requirements are two Cs at A-level, or equivalent. Candidates are also interviewed and their portfolio or showreel is assessed.

Ravensbourne's best-known alumni include the fashion designers Clare Waight Keller of Givenchy, who designed the dress that Meghan Markle wore for her wedding to Prince Harry, and Stella McCartney, who studied her foundation degree at Ravensbourne College of Design and Communication – as the university was formerly named. Jay Osgerby, the co-designer of the Olympic 2012 torch, and the stand-up comedian Andi Osho also studied there.

The university does not own or manage halls of residence, but it works with a number of private providers and host families to offer accommodation and secure discounts for those on low incomes. For sports, students have easy access to local facilities across Greenwich and into Charlton, in the absence of any facilities within the university itself.

Students can straddle two hemispheres at the same time at the nearby Royal Observatory Greenwich. The Cutty Sark and National Maritime Museum add to the rich cultural seam that helped to earn World Heritage Site status for the Maritime Greenwich area. A renowned market and plenty of pubs, bars and restaurants provide local entertainment.

Tuition fees

»	Fees for UK students	£9,250
	Foundation courses	£5,421
»	Fees for International students 2022–23	£16,500
	Foundation courses	£12,100
»	For scholarship and bursary information see www.ravensbourne.ac.uk/information/ prospective-students/fees-and-funding/	
»	Graduate salary	£22,300

Student numbers

Undergraduates	2,455	(0)
Postgraduates	40	(5)
Applications/places		3,455/835
Applications per place		4.1
Overall offer rate		92.9%
International students – EU		6.9%
Non-EU		7.6%

Accommodation

University provided places: 100
Self-catered: £143–£385 per week
www.ravensbourne.ac.uk/information/prospective-students/accommodation/

Where do the students come from?

State schools (non-grammar)	92.9%	Low participation areas	5.9%
Grammar schools	2.2%	All ethnic minorities	48.3%
Independent schools	4.8%	White working-class males	6.1%
First generation students	46.6%	Black achievement gap	-13.9%

Social inclusion ranking: 21

Disabled	8.6%
Mature (over 21)	17.4%

University of Reading

Reading launched more than 50 degree programmes in 2021 – more than any university in our survey, although a number involved the addition of a foundation or placement year to an existing degree. The expansion, including seven more programmes starting in 2022, is part of Reading's effort to be a "larger, vibrant and more sustainable institution" by the time of its centenary in 2026.

After successive gains in our previous two editions, Reading drops back slightly this year after less than stellar scores in the pandemic-influenced 2021 National Student Survey (NSS). The impact of the student vote means Reading's ranking in our NSS-derived measure of teaching quality falls out of the UK top 100.

The university is investing more than £200million on capital projects, many of which respond directly to student demands for more study space and better technical resources. A prime example being the £40million refurbishment of the main campus library, increasing study space and improving key facilities.

Among the latest additions are a new health and life sciences building, which includes one of the largest teaching labs in the UK and the Cole Museum of Zoology, which is open to the public. Lecture theatres have been refurbished under the 2026: Transform programme and new traffic-free walking, cycling and running routes added on the Green Flag Award-winning Whiteknights campus, which is set in 320 acres of parkland on the outskirts of Reading.

The university was on target to surpass its target of 45% carbon reduction by 2021 even before the Covid-19 lockdown began. Reading is one of the leading universities for research into climate change and has a long tradition of environmental awareness.

Ranked just outside the top 200 universities in the QS World University Rankings, Reading draws about a quarter of its undergraduates from outside the UK. Its global engagement strategy includes a target for one student in three to have some experience of studying abroad by 2026, beginning with summer schools at its branch campus in Malaysia, as well as at longstanding partner institutions in Moscow and Nanjing, China.

Closer to home, the university has a second campus in town and 2,000 acres of farmland at nearby Sonning and Shinfield for its highly regarded agricultural degrees. The other main site houses its business school, formerly Henley Management College, which has an attractive position on the banks of the Thames. It offers postgraduate and executive programmes, while business undergraduates are taught on the Whiteknights campus.

Whiteknights
PO Box 217
Reading RG6 6AH
0118 378 8372
www.reading.ac.uk/question
www.reading.ac.uk
www.rusu.co.uk
Open days: see website

***The Times* and *The Sunday Times* Rankings**

Overall Ranking: 34 (last year: =31)

Teaching quality	72%	=105
Student experience	68.3%	=80
Research quality	36.5%	29
Entry standards	122	=72
Graduate prospects	76.5%	32
Good honours	85.6%	23
Expected completion rate	91.4%	29
Student/staff ratio	16.4	=74
Services and facilities	£2,859	37

Reading has a silver rating in the Teaching Excellence Framework. All first-degree students can take work placements, as well as career management skills modules that contribute five credits towards their degree classification.

Second-year students have access to the prizewinning RDGgrad programme over the summer vacation and into the autumn of their final year to prepare for graduate job applications. The activities include a mock assessment centre for 150 students and personal contact with careers consultants and successful alumni.

The Reading Experience and Development (RED) Award certificates extracurricular activities that might be of interest to employers. Two new tiers (Plus and Xcel) were added in 2020 to give students the opportunity to progress further after the initial award. These initiatives bear fruit in a competitive graduate employment record, with more than 76% of students in high-skilled jobs or graduate-level study 15 months after leaving.

The student welfare team is integrated with an academic tutor system to address personal problems and enhance students' professional development. There is also a wide range of scholarships and bursaries, including 50 for international students that are worth £4,000 for each year of a course.

Reading entered more academics for assessment in the 2014 Research Excellence Framework than most of its peers, and almost 80% of its research was rated as world-leading or internationally excellent. Real estate, planning and construction management were among the top-performing areas.

Almost 5,000 residential places are either on or within easy walking distance of the Whiteknights campus, allowing the university to guarantee a hall place to all new entrants. The SportsPark, on the edge of the campus, has extensive indoor and outdoor facilities including dance and yoga studios, a soccer park, badminton, squash and indoor tennis courts. There are also boathouses on the Thames and a sailing and canoeing club nearby.

Reading may not be the most fashionable town, but it has plenty of nightlife and is within easy reach of London. There is an award-winning shopping centre, although the cost of living is high. Almost £3million has been spent on the student union's popular 3sixty nightclub. A £1million capital fund allows the union to select its own projects. So far, they have included free charging points in lecture theatres, more lockers and a "relaxation zone".

Tuition fees

» Fees for UK students	£9,250
» Fees for International students 2022–23	£19,500–£23,700
» For scholarship and bursary information see www.reading.ac.uk/ready-to-study/study/fees-and-funding	
» Graduate salary	£25,000

Student numbers

Undergraduates	12,195	(435)
Postgraduates	3,110	(2,995)
Applications/places	20,320/3,090	
Applications per place	6.6	
Overall offer rate	85.8%	
International students – EU	6.3%	
Non-EU	14.1%	

Accommodation

University provided places: 4,982
Catered costs: £130–£201 per week
Self-catered: £131–£268 per week
First years guaranteed accommodation
www.reading.ac.uk/ready-to-study/accommodation

Where do the students come from?

State schools (non-grammar)	73.6%	Low participation areas	7%	
Grammar schools	10.3%	All ethnic minorities	33.2%	
Independent schools	16%	White working-class males	3.4%	
First generation students	35.1%	Black achievement gap	-16.3%	

Social inclusion ranking: 92

Disabled	7.4%
Mature (over 21)	8.3%

Robert Gordon University

Teams of entrepreneurial students at Robert Gordon University (RGU) have the opportunity to solve global challenges via a five-month Innovation Accelerator programme. In response to evolving worldwide issues posed by the pandemic the modern Aberdeen university adapted its established start-up programme to include support for students' inspired solutions for specific problems.

Teams working on innovative projects, social enterprises and initiatives – as well as start-ups – receive mentoring, city centre office space and access to £2,000 seed funding as part of the programme, which is run in partnership with North East Scotland College and is also open to staff and alumni.

Stellar student satisfaction scores spurred RGU to win Scottish University of the Year in our previous edition. It has also been our leading post-1992 university for graduate prospects, remaining in the top 20 for this measure until 2016 during some of the peak years of the North Sea oil and gas industry based off Aberdeen. Performance more recently has tailed off, with the proportion of students in high-skilled jobs now close to the UK average.

Diversifying its drive to give students work-ready skills is one aim at RGU, which has also launched a creative entrepreneurship short course for graduates to transition their creative practice into a business. Since establishing a new eHub Jobs board facility, RGU has advertised vacancies for more than 1,000 companies. Students have access to employer partners from early in their studies and depending upon their degree will gain experiences including industry projects, placements and insight days.

The university gained gold in the Teaching Excellence Framework (TEF) and has developed a strategy to be an "innovative, disruptive force in higher education". The TEF panel was impressed by the range of opportunities for students to develop knowledge, understanding and skills that are most highly valued by employers, and to engage "consistently and frequently" with developments at the forefront of professional practice.

The Garthdee campus is the hub of all teaching, and overlooks the River Dee on the south side of Aberdeen. Named after an 18th-century philanthropist, RGU has more than 250 years' history in education. Its landmark green glass library tower symbolises its future ambitions after a £135million capital programme. The Clinical Skills Centre houses a wide range of simulations including a ward, home setting, radiography suite, physiotherapy suite and gym, and a community pharmacy.

Equipment within the engineering department includes a wind tunnel, offshore

Garthdee House
Garthdee Road
Aberdeen AB10 7AQ
01224 262 728
UGOffice@rgu.ac.uk
www.rgu.ac.uk
www.rguunion.co.uk
Open days: see website

The Times and The Sunday Times Rankings
Overall Ranking: =62 (last year: 66)

Teaching quality	79.7%	11
Student experience	75.4%	15
Research quality	4.0%	=104
Entry standards	154	24
Graduate prospects	71.9%	58
Good honours	73%	105
Expected completion rate	84.3%	69
Student/staff ratio	18.7	=110
Services and facilities	£2,001	108

platform models, a wave tank and a remotely operated vehicle pool for underwater robotics and subsea projects. RGU's drilling simulator, which is part of the DART (Dynamic Advanced Response Training) simulation suite, provides real-time training within a virtual drilling environment using 3D graphics to represent a rig floor and oil and gas industry equipment and drilling processes.

The university made a relatively small submission to the 2014 Research Excellence Framework, but more than 40% of the work was placed in the top two categories. Health subjects and communication and media studies provided the best results. RGU's present strategy promises investment in sustainable transportation, data and analytics, pharmacy, smart cities and biomedical toxins.

RGU is in the upper half of universities for its Covid response, according to our analysis of National Student Survey results from 2021 and 2020. The university provides virtual support for students covering areas such as writing, study skills, maths and statistics. Aimed at enabling students to become independent learners, the sessions include collaborations with the library, employability and counselling and wellbeing teams.

Full-time undergraduates who come from Scotland's most deprived postcodes can apply for free accommodation in standard single rooms at RGU's Woolmanhill flats.

There are also discounted options elsewhere. Students who have been in care qualify for a 20% accommodation discount in their first year. For everyone else, nearly half of the 912 residential places cost less than £100 a week to rent and there is usually space for all who want a room, although there is no formal guarantee.

Scotland's third largest city is home to two universities and Aberdeen offers a student-friendly atmosphere with excellent transport links. Three gyms, a swimming pool, badminton courts, bouldering and climbing facilities and a sports hall are available on campus. RGU also has a physiotherapy clinic and offers sports scholarships.

Tuition fees

» Fees for Scottish students	£0–£1,820
RUK fees	£5,000–£8,500
» Fees for International students 2021–22	£14,000–£17,700
» For scholarship and bursary information see www.rgu.ac.uk/study/courses	
» Graduate salary	£24,000

Student numbers

Undergraduates	8,080	(1,005)
Postgraduates	1,345	(2,235)
Applications/places		9,875/2,285
Applications per place		4.3
Overall offer rate		66.3%
International students – EU		10%
Non-EU		3.8%

Accommodation

University provided places: 912
Self-catered: £98–£160 per week
www.rgu.ac.uk/life-at-rgu/accommodation

Where do the students come from?

State schools (non-grammar)	94.3%	Deprived areas	5.2%	Disabled	6.1%
Grammar schools	0.3%	All ethnic minorities	10%	Mature (over 21)	34.6%
Independent schools	5.3%	White working-class males	6.9%		
First generation students	34.4%	Black achievement gap	-32.5%		

Social inclusion ranking (Scotland): 12

University of Roehampton

Occupying a 54-acre campus near Putney and Hammersmith in southwest London, Roehampton's fine setting blends historic buildings, woodland walks and ponds with modern facilities. The university has invested in esport provision and has a dedicated room for multiplayer video game competitions, whose already-growing popularity boomed amid the pandemic's shuttered stadiums and stay-at-home mandates.

Roehampton also offers the UK's first esports scholarships, worth £1,500 per year for talented students, as well as Europe's first Women in esports scholarships, offered with the aim of increasing diversity in the field. The subject's popularity is not limited to those studying related degrees; of the university's many student societies, esports was the largest last year.

Under a new partnership with Croydon College, Roehampton will begin validating its degrees this year and has installed a study centre in Croydon. It is also delivering an adult nursing degree at the college's university centre, with further joint degree offerings in the pipeline.

The university ranks in the country's top 100 for its Covid response, according to our analysis of the National Student Survey (NSS). In common with other institutions,

Roehampton is continuing to embrace the flexibility offered by recording live lectures for its students, who can access the content from home at a time that suits them and refer back to it when revising for exams.

Small group teaching is the focus of activities on campus in the 2021–22 academic year, while students have the choice between online or in-person tutorials. A Proactive Student System has been developed with the aim of enabling timely and regular contact between students and tutors – often a bone of contention among undergraduates.

Student wellbeing officers provide help on wide-ranging topics such as managing finances and personal safety. A free, confidential short-term counselling service is offered to all students, in tandem with therapeutic groups and workshops. Bus services between the campus and local stations at Barnes and Wimbledon, e-bikes and "college kitchens" support commuting students.

The recently opened £13million Sir David Bell Building houses Roehampton's digital media hub. Students have access to industry-standard film studios, editing suites and newsrooms, and can use resources for media, photography and sound production. A cinema and computing facilities are included too, with study spaces and a gallery area for student displays and creative industry events.

Roehampton was upgraded to silver in the Teaching Excellence Framework in 2019.

Grove House
Roehampton Lane
London SW15 5PJ
020 8392 3232
ug.information@roehampton.ac.uk
www.roehampton.ac.uk
www.roehamptonstudent.com
Open days: see website

The Times and The Sunday Times Rankings
Overall Ranking: 65 (last year: 78)

Teaching quality	73.1%	=86
Student experience	68.3%	=80
Research quality	24.5%	50
Entry standards	100	=129
Graduate prospects	60.2%	=119
Good honours	71.4%	111
Expected completion rate	77.5%	=113
Student/staff ratio	15.2	53
Services and facilities	£3,596	12

The panel complimented the university on the reduction in the attainment gap for black, Asian and minority ethnic students, and for support to find work experience.

One of the country's most socially inclusive universities, ranked in the top 30 overall in our table, Roehampton counts more than six in ten students from ethnic minorities, more than four in ten aged over-21 and 96% are recruited from non-selective state schools.

After an 8% rise in applications in the 2020 admissions cycle there had been a further 15% uplift by the end of March 2021, compared with the same point the year before. The increase is due in part to expanding computer science provision. Of 2020's UK intake, 44% entered via clearing. From September 2022 Roehampton will offer degrees in education practice; liberal arts; and sports therapy. Top-up degrees in dance and drama are also launching.

Having been founded in 1841, Whitelands – one of the university's four historic constituent colleges, along with Digby Stuart, Froebel and Southlands – pioneered the training of women as teachers. Education courses remain a significant area for Roehampton, and account for about a quarter of students.

The university has additional study locations in Holborn in central London, Birmingham and Manchester, where business and computing degrees are taught by staff from QA Higher Education, a private company.

Two-thirds of Roehampton's eligible academics submitted work in the 2014 Research Excellence Framework and 66% of it was rated world-leading or internationally excellent. The university outperformed all post-1992 universities and had the most highly rated dance department in the UK, with 94% of research placed in the top two categories. The results in education and English were among the best in London. These successes produced a 40% increase in funding for research.

Roehampton's dance programmes are renowned, buoyed by four dance studios on campus. Gym Roehampton, also on site, is run by Nuffield Health. Close to central London but offering a campus community environment, Roehampton gives students a best-of-both-worlds experience, while college balls and formal dinners provide an extra dimension to undergraduate social life. All first-years are guaranteed a room in on-campus halls of residence.

Tuition fees

» Fees for UK students	£9,250
» Fees for International students 2022–23	£13,474–£14,732
» For scholarship and bursary information see www.roehampton.ac.uk/undergraduate-courses/tuition-fees/	
» Graduate salary	£23,300

Student numbers

Undergraduates	9,890	(475)
Postgraduates	1,215	(915)
Applications/places		7,245/1,410
Applications per place		5.1
Overall offer rate		89.3%
International students – EU		3.1%
Non-EU		4.8%

Accommodation

University provided places: 1,849
Self-catered: £98–£194 per week
First years guaranteed accommodation
www.roehampton.ac.uk/accommodation

Where do the students come from?

State schools (non-grammar)	96.3%	Low participation areas	4.2%
Grammar schools	1.4%	All ethnic minorities	63.9%
Independent schools	2.3%	White working-class males	5.3%
First generation students	49.2%	Black achievement gap	-24.3%

Social inclusion ranking: 30

Disabled	5.9%
Mature (over 21)	43.6%

Royal Agricultural University

Countless townies dreamt of escaping to the country when faced with urban life under Covid-19 restrictions. Some of them were budding students, this year's 20% uplift in applications to the Royal Agricultural University (RAU) suggests.

Based in 25 bucolic Cotswolds campus acres just outside Cirencester and with 491 hectares of nearby farmland, the university's small student numbers, collegiate feel and sporty social life are an appealing prospect.

It has added foundation years on all BSc courses, a widening participation effort that it believes is reflected in the increased demand for places.

Hands-on learning takes place at Coates Manor Farm next to the campus, at Kemble Farms dairy complex and at Leaze Farm. A new partnership with Gloucestershire's Bathurst Estate gives students access to 15,000 acres of farmland, forestry, environmentally managed land, real estate and heritage properties, along with a range of rural enterprises for teaching, research and knowledge exchange.

Students may spend a sandwich year in industry as part of their degree, a 2020-launched innovation. Entrepreneurial activity is encouraged too, supported by schemes such as an enterprise programme for student start-ups, which offers access to local business mentors. RAU's Cotswold Hills wine business is a student-run social enterprise, as is its 2007-founded Muddy Wellies beer operation.

An environment, food and society degree and a rural entrepreneurship and enterprise degree, both with foundation year options, began in September 2020. Informed by industry needs, the courses are part of a wider £2.5million initiative in partnership with the Countryside and Community Research Institute and University College of Estate Management. The aim is to create leadership in the agri-food and land management industries, post-Brexit. Their content has been shaped by experts from the food supply chain, farming, land management, banking and NGOs (Non-Governmental organisations), including Waitrose and Barclays.

Agri-food recruitment company De Lacy, real estate consultants Knight Frank and the conservation organisation Slimbridge Wetland Centre were among employers to engage with RAU students at events recently, while work placements at companies including Bayer, Miele UK, St James's Place and Intel have provided valuable experience.

Once the initiatives bear fruit, they should help RAU gain ground on our measure of graduate prospects, where it has dropped into the bottom 30, with only 63.2% of graduates in high-skilled jobs or further study 15 months after finishing.

The university did better in the eyes of its students for its Covid response, taking less of a

Stroud Road
Cirencester GL7 6JS
01285 889 912
admissions@rau.ac.uk
www.rau.ac.uk
rausu.unioncloud.org
Open days: see website

The Times and The Sunday Times Rankings

Overall Ranking: 116 (last year: =73)

Teaching quality	72.4%	=96
Student experience	68.5%	77
Research quality	1.1%	125
Entry standards	111	=107
Graduate prospects	63.2%	107
Good honours	67.9%	123
Expected completion rate	89.5%	=37
Student/staff ratio	21.7	124
Services and facilities	£3,214	22

hit to its National Student Survey (NSS) scores in pandemic-affected 2021 than many others. Even so, undergraduates' recent satisfaction with teaching quality and the wider experience at RAU has suffered declines that have contributed to its fall down our main league table this year, to well outside the top 100.

The RAU was awarded silver in the government's Teaching Excellence Framework, winning praise for its specialist facilities. Assessors were impressed by the employer-informed course design, work placements and extracurricular opportunities for students to develop skills and attributes valued by employers.

RAU's Cultural Heritage Institute in Swindon, opened in 2021, is the base for postgraduate courses including an MBA and research opportunities.

This development may help improve future research rankings, the RAU having achieved one of the lowest scores in the 2014 Research Excellence Framework, when only 12 staff were entered and just 7% of their work was placed in the top two categories.

Every monarch since Queen Victoria has visited RAU since its 1845 foundation. Its nickname "Oxbridge of the countryside" reflects the high proportion of privately educated students who enrol, four in every 10, at last count. Just 55% are recruited from comprehensives.

The university's graduate diploma in agriculture has become a source of second career training for those leaving professions such as the armed forces. Relevant experience as well as formal qualifications count in the RAU's assessment of applicants and contextual offers lower than the published tariffs are made to those from disadvantaged and underrepresented backgrounds. As education partner of the Royal Three Counties Show the RAU supports efforts to raise awareness of education and careers in the land-based sector within Gloucestershire, Herefordshire and Worcestershire. RAU also supports Agrespect, the rural LGBT organisation.

University polo is played at a club about 12 miles from campus, rowing is at Gloucester Rowing Club and shooting is held at Hollow Fosse. Sports facilities range from lacrosse, hockey and rugby to tennis, croquet and netball. Kennels for the university's beagle pack are run by student masters alongside a kennel huntsman. The beagles meet twice a week during term time.

Three-quarters of the 334 rooms in eight halls of residence on campus are catered. There is space for about 80% of first-years.

Tuition fees

»	Fees for UK students	£9,250
»	Fees for International students 2022–23	£13,500
»	For scholarship and bursary information see www.rau.ac.uk/study/undergraduate/ funding-your-time-at-university	
»	Graduate salary	£24,000

Student numbers

Undergraduates	980	(35)
Postgraduates	95	(20)
Applications/places		1,115/305
Applications per place		3.7
Overall offer rate		n/a
International students – EU		2.6%
Non-EU		7.9%

Accommodation

University provided places: 334
Catered costs: £156 per week
Self-catered: £161–£231 per week
www.rau.ac.uk/university-life/accommodation

Where do the students come from?

State schools (non-grammar)	54.7%	Low participation areas	2.3%
Grammar schools	5.1%	All ethnic minorities	4.4%
Independent schools	40.2%	White working-class males	3%
First generation students	38.4%	Black achievement gap	n/a

Social inclusion ranking: 113

Disabled	9.5%
Mature (over 21)	22.1%

Royal Holloway, University of London

Royal Holloway is endeavouring to broaden the horizons of its students. The Surrey-based member of the University of London is expanding partnerships with overseas institutions, so that students may access more global opportunities, pandemic permitting. Undergraduates on all courses already have the flexibility to take an additional year to complete their degree. Through the Optional Placement Year scheme, they can spend their third year gaining work experience related to their course or in an area that interests them. Alternatively, they can opt to spend it volunteering, studying abroad – or a combination of all three.

Students can apply for the scheme from the autumn term of their second year and successfully taking part contributes to their overall result, formally recognised on degree certificates. In another move towards internationalisation and in partnership with the University of London, Royal Holloway is increasing its distance-learning courses to enable study from anywhere in the world.

When awarding silver in the Teaching Excellence Framework assessors praised the level of investment in e-learning facilities, and said students were engaged with developments from the forefront of research, scholarship and professional practice.

The university finished in the middle reaches of our analysis of the 2021 scores in the National Student Survey (NSS). Its scores for satisfaction with teaching quality and student experience fell less sharply than many.

Based on a 135-acre woodland campus in green-belt Egham, not far from Windsor and Heathrow, Royal Holloway's success across our league table's measures (including research, student satisfaction and graduate prospects) earned it shortlisting for our University of the Year award two years ago.

The campus is distinguished by its palatial red-brick Founder's Building, modelled on a French château and opened by Queen Victoria. Its more recent developments include the SuperFab world-class "cleanroom" in the physics department, which has advanced electronic nanofabrication equipment for research and development of the technology needed for medical imaging and quantum computers.

The Beatrice Shilling Building, named after the pioneering British aeronautical engineer and amateur racing driver, houses the Department of Electronic Engineering, opened in 2017. One of its aims is to attract more female engineering students – fittingly for an institution formed from the merger of two colleges (Royal Holloway and Bedford) that were among the first British institutions to educate women. Bedford's early students included Sarah Parker Remond, the first black

Egham Hill
Egham TW20 0EX
01784 414 944
study@royalholloway.ac.uk
www.royalholloway.ac.uk
www.su.rhul.ac.uk
Open days: see website

The Times and The Sunday Times **Rankings**
Overall Ranking: 26 (last year: 22)

Teaching quality	74.5%	=74
Student experience	70.5%	=52
Research quality	36.3%	=30
Entry standards	130	54
Graduate prospects	72.5%	=55
Good honours	86.5%	20
Expected completion rate	91.2%	32
Student/staff ratio	15.1	=49
Services and facilities	£2,820	39

woman to carry out a lecture tour around Britain about slavery, the artist Barbara Bodichon and the novelist George Eliot.

A record intake of new students in 2020's admissions round, represents a 50% increase in the numbers starting courses in a decade. Applications were also at their highest yet in 2020 and have swelled by nearly 30% in ten years.

Twenty-two new undergraduate degrees launch in September 2022, among them drama with acting; English with world literatures; philosophy with politics, law with modern languages (French, German, Italian or Spanish); and integrated master's options in corporate finance; economics and econometrics; finance; economics; and law and economics.

More than 80% of the work assessed in the 2014 Research Excellence Framework was judged to be world-leading or internationally excellent, placing Royal Holloway in the top 30 institutions on this measure.

Geography achieved the best results in England, while earth sciences, psychology, mathematics, music, media arts, and drama and theatre all reached the top ten in their subject areas. Royal Holloway was named by the government as one of eight academic centres of excellence in cybersecurity research.

Building on this pedigree, Royal Holloway is focusing on challenge-led research such as immersive and digital technologies, climate change, cybersecurity and quantum science that contribute to addressing key contemporary issues.

More than a third of 2020's intake qualified for some sort of financial award out of a £3.3million spend on scholarships and bursaries. These include bursaries for students from low participation areas, low-income households or those who have attended a local partner school. Scholarships are awarded competitively to recognise various academic, sport and music achievements.

The Reed Innovation scholarship, worth £15,000 over three years, is awarded to undergraduates studying any degree, who have proven innovative and creative problem-solving skills and who are expected to achieve AAA at A-level or equivalent.

Royal Holloway is one of the University of London's top sporting colleges, with more than 80 teams and good facilities. There is a fitness studio and multi-use sports hall and outdoor facilities such as a 3G pitch.

A quarter of the 3,158 residential spaces on campus are catered and new entrants are guaranteed a room if they apply in time. It is a 40-minute hop to London's bright lights.

Tuition fees

» Fees for UK students £9,250
» Fees for International students 2022–23 £19,300–£23,200
» For scholarship and bursary information see www.royalholloway.ac.uk/studying-here/fees-and-funding
» Graduate salary £23,000

Student numbers

Undergraduates	8,325	(205)
Postgraduates	2,210	(790)
Applications/places	17,885/2,775	
Applications per place	6.4	
Overall offer rate	86%	
International students – EU	8%	
Non-EU	13.7%	

Accommodation

University provided places: 3,158
Catered costs: £120–£182 per week
Self-catered: £145–£191 per week
First years guaranteed accommodation
www.royalholloway.ac.uk/student-life/accommodation/

Where do the students come from?

State schools (non-grammar)	76.1%	Low participation areas	5.5%
Grammar schools	10.9%	All ethnic minorities	52.1%
Independent schools	13.1%	White working-class males	3.3%
First generation students	39%	Black achievement gap	-16.8%

Social inclusion ranking: 83

Disabled	7.6%
Mature (over 21)	5.7%

University of St Andrews

In topping our institutional table this year, St Andrews has done something no university has achieved in the near 30-year history of our (or any other UK) ranking. Displacing Cambridge and Oxford from the top of our academic tree is no mean feat.

And no fluke, either. For several years, St Andrews has been closing in on the top spot with levels of student satisfaction that other elite universities would envy. It flipped its small-class teaching model to online delivery during the pandemic, registering only a tiny decline in satisfaction rates across nine areas of the annual National Student Survey (NSS), when scores elsewhere fell off a cliff. It tops our NSS-derived rankings for teaching quality and student experience. In both instances, the lead is statistically huge – at about four percentage points.

Remarkably, St Andrews students registered increased satisfaction levels for teaching on their courses, learning opportunities and overall satisfaction, the latter coming in with a positive score of 93.3%. "In a time when most of us were being told what we couldn't do, the University of St Andrews took the bold step of taking on a new "can do" mantra during the Covid-19 outbreak," the university told us. "The joint initiative between the university and the Students' Association was established to help students reimagine, experiment with, and contribute to the world-renowned St Andrews student experience."

A taskforce worked on extracurricular events, encouraged people to set up online study groups and offered advice such as using the local beach for social contact. Spaces were bookable via union and library websites, and a marquee on the lawn hosted gatherings of up to 30 people. For some groups, such as certain students with a disability, remote learning has had significant advantages, which the university is determined to maintain.

Student satisfaction is well founded. The university also has the highest entry standards, the third best student-to-staff ratio, the fifth highest level of expenditure per student, and outstanding graduate employment rates and research outcomes. It may be the third oldest university in the English-speaking world, but St Andrews is a thoroughly modern, globalised institution.

In September 2021, its degrees in Chinese studies began with 14 joint honours combinations including six languages, economics and international relations, looking at China's popular and dissident cultures.

Having the Duke and Duchess of Cambridge as students at the start of the century gave St Andrews a global PR boost.

College Gate
North Street
St Andrews KY16 9AJ
01334 462 150
admissions@st-andrews.ac.uk
www.st-andrews.ac.uk
www.yourunion.net
Open days: see website

The Times and The Sunday Times **Rankings**
Overall Ranking: 1 (last year: 3)

Teaching quality	86.5%	1
Student experience	84.2%	1
Research quality	40.4%	11
Entry standards	207	1
Graduate prospects	80.4%	=16
Good honours	91.8%	7
Expected completion rate	95.7%	7
Student/staff ratio	11.1	=3
Services and facilities	£3,943	5

In 2020–2021, it had students from 130 countries, and 40% came from outside Britain, with 16% recruited from Scotland (a number capped by the government) and the rest from the UK.

In normal times, they all benefit from exchange and study opportunities in Australia, New Zealand, Hong Kong, Singapore, Canada and the US. St Andrews scored highly in the most recent Research Excellence Framework, especially for work with Edinburgh University on chemistry and physics. It is also renowned for its marine research, pioneering medical work at the Sir James Mackenzie Institute for Early Diagnosis, and the Handa Centre for the Study of Terrorism and Political Violence.

A fundraising appeal for the university's 600th anniversary in 2013, led by the Duke of Cambridge, raised £100million to improve facilities. A £14million redevelopment of the sports centre at Hepburn Gardens offers a 120-station gym, technical climbing wall, strength and conditioning suite for performance athletes, indoor sports arena with space for 400 spectators and 13 grass pitches.

There are six halls of residence encircling University Park, where all first-years are guaranteed a place if they apply in time. Students live out in the small coastal town in later years, blurring the lines between town and gown. St Andrews, perhaps more than any other location, is dominated by its university.

Unlike many Scottish institutions, St Andrews does not align its fees with English universities, so students from the rest of the UK pay £9,250 for each year of their four-year courses. However, more than £1million is awarded in scholarships and bursaries each year, supporting almost 1,000 students in 2020–21.

Professor Sally Mapstone, principal and vice-chancellor of St Andrews, led Scotland's work on contextual admissions. The scheme has been embraced by St Andrews, allowing offers up to two A-level grades lower than standard.

In 2020, 14% of Scottish applicants and 32% from elsewhere in the UK received a contextual offer. Recent efforts in this area see the university move off the foot of our Scottish social inclusion ranking for the first time this year.

The university is one of a very small minority to require all students to undertake compulsory training in sexual consent, equality, diversity and inclusion. This comes after a spate of sexual misconduct allegations last year, many of them made against members of an American-style fraternity.

Tuition fees

»	Fees for Scottish students	£0–£1,820
	RUK fees	£9,250
»	Fees for International students 2022–23	£26,350
	Medicine	£33,570
»	For scholarship and bursary information see	
	www.st-andrews.ac.uk/study/fees-and-funding/	
»	Graduate salary	£26,000

Student numbers

Undergraduates	7,790	(680)
Postgraduates	1,770	(295)
Applications/places	20,580/2,215	
Applications per place		9.3
Overall offer rate		41%
International students – EU		6.1%
Non-EU		33.4%

Accommodation

University provided places: 3,597
Catered costs: £168–£255 per week
Self-catered: £142–£232 per week
First years guaranteed accommodation
www.st-andrews.ac.uk/study/accommodation/

Where do the students come from?

State schools (non-grammar)	57.5%	Deprived areas	11%
Grammar schools	6.4%	All ethnic minorities	15.3%
Independent schools	36.2%	White working-class males	3.4%
First generation students	18%	Black achievement gap	n/a

Social inclusion ranking (Scotland): 14

Disabled	5.7%
Mature (over 21)	8.9%

St George's, University of London

Long after the doorstep clapping drew to a close, the pandemic's spotlight on the health professions has continued to drive up applications to health-related degrees. It is a trend acutely evident at St George's, the University of London's specialist health university, where applications at the end of March 2021 had risen by nearly half compared with the same point in the cycle a year before. Founded more than 250 years ago, the Tooting-based institution was the second in the country to award medical degrees.

Students are immersed in a professional environment from the start, as the university has the unique advantage of sharing a campus with a teaching hospital as part of St George's University Hospitals NHS Foundation Trust. Options extend beyond medicine to include biomedical science and healthcare science degrees covering respiratory and cardiac physiology and sleep physiology. Paramedic science and radiography degrees are also taught on site in a partnership with Kingston University.

The shift to remote learning was a struggle for practical-based institutions, particularly those with a medical focus. The university duly suffered in National Student Survey scores in 2021 as final-year students gave their verdict on its pandemic teaching response. St George's is just outside the bottom ten in our analysis comparing student satisfaction scores in 2020 and 2021.

The Online Education Framework brought in to get around Covid restrictions is now evolving into a blended model of teaching and learning. St George's aim is to take the best of online delivery and combine it with interactive and skills-based sessions on campus. Students can listen back to most lectures, which are recorded.

The black achievement gap at St George's is the narrowest (and therefore best) in the country and the university has one of the highest proportions of students from ethnic minority backgrounds. However, its overall performance on social inclusion is affected by a large contingent of recruits from fee-paying or selective state schools, about one-third. St George's makes contextual offers up to two A-level grades lower than the standard to students who meet criteria for widening participation: those who are in care, the first in their family to go to university, from low-participation areas or who qualify for free school meals or Pupil Premium. In 2020 it accepted 43% of its students through clearing, considering this to be the fairest way to find high-quality candidates, and has not seen its entry tariff scores decline unduly as a result.

Applicants are interviewed for entry to all undergraduate courses except biomedical science and clinical pharmacology. A shadowing

---

Cranmer Terrace
Tooting
London SW17 0RE
020 3897 2032
study@sgul.ac.uk
www.sgul.ac.uk
www.sgsu.org.uk
Open days: see website

The Times and The Sunday Times **Rankings**
Overall Ranking: 78 (last year: 49)

Teaching quality	64.5%	129
Student experience	59.2%	=126
Research quality	22.2%	52
Entry standards	144	=38
Graduate prospects	94.4%	1
Good honours	80.5%	=50
Expected completion rate	93%	=21
Student/staff ratio	13.3	18
Services and facilities	£2,637	58

scheme offers sixth-formers from state schools in Wandsworth and Merton the opportunity to spend time with a consultant at St George's Hospital or a local GP.

St George's was the first UK institution to launch the MBBS graduate entry programme 21 years ago. The four-year fast-track degree in medicine is open to graduates in any discipline and has become an increasingly popular route into the medical profession. St George's also offers a four-year graduate-entry Bachelor of Surgery degree at the University of Nicosia in Cyprus. A preparatory centre for international students is based on the south London campus.

While the world was on an emergency footing during the pandemic, St George's released staff with clinical roles so they could treat patients. Its research scientists contributed to the lab-based diagnostic effort and research laboratories were repurposed to support expanding NHS pathology services. Its online course, Managing Covid-19 in General Practice, has been undertaken by nearly 20,000 people from more than 150 countries.

St George's is one of 11 universities in our rankings awarded bronze (the lowest grade) in the government's Teaching Excellence Framework. Although the panel gave it credit for an "embedded institutional culture that rewards excellent teaching, and promotes inclusivity among staff and students", it was held back by low levels of student satisfaction with assessment and feedback.

The university did much better in the Research Excellence Framework in 2014, where it was second only to Imperial College London for the impact of its work. Overall, 70% of its submission was considered world-leading or internationally excellent.

Historic developments in cardiac pacemakers and IVF are among St George's research achievements. Recently, the institution's expanding range of Covid-19 research projects has included work on a rapid antibody test. Its scientists are researching the biology of the disease and trialling potential treatments.

An active students' union offers 120 clubs, societies and community projects. The sports centre is five minutes' walk from campus and there are many competitive teams. Students have the use of a rowing club on the River Thames.

Applicants who have accepted St George's as their firm offer before the end of June are guaranteed one of Horton Hall's 486 rooms.

Tuition fees

» Fees for UK students	£9,250
» Fees for International students 2022–23	£19,250
Medicine	£38,500
» For scholarship and bursary information see www.sgul.ac.uk/study/undergraduate-study/fees-and-financial-support/	
» Graduate salary	£29,000

Student numbers

Undergraduates	3,075	(440)
Postgraduates	280	(530)
Applications/places		6,020/530
Applications per place		11.4
Overall offer rate		38.7%
International students – EU		1.6%
Non-EU		6.8%

Accommodation

University provided places: 486
Self-catered: £172–£182 per week
First-years guaranteed accommodation
www.sgul.ac.uk/study/life-at-st-georges/accommodation

Where do the students come from?

					Social inclusion ranking: 69	
State schools (non-grammar)	67.9%	Low participation areas	5.1%	Disabled	7.4%
Grammar schools	20.1%	All ethnic minorities	63.4%	Mature (over 21)	31.8%
Independent schools	12%	White working-class males	1.8%		
First generation students	35.3%	Black achievement gap	-1.1%		

St Mary's University, Twickenham

Listening to students was key to how St Mary's University, Twickenham navigated the rapid switch to remote learning last year. In our analysis of the latest National Student Survey (NSS) scores compared with last year's, the university had one of the ten smallest declines in student satisfaction in a difficult year when many universities sustained big falls in this key area.

The crash in student ratings elsewhere helped St Mary's rise into the top 10 of our rankings for both satisfaction with teaching quality and the wider student experience, fuelling a 19-place rise in our institutional ranking overall.

St Mary's also ensured that its academics were properly trained to integrate the new educational technologies involved, chose user-friendly virtual platforms and reconfigured all types of central support for the remote environment to minimise the impact on the student experience.

Lecture-capture technology can be supported in all of the teaching spaces at St Mary's and is being used wherever possible, with content uploaded to a virtual learning environment. Tutorials and seminars are being delivered predominantly face-to-face in 2021–22.

Founded in 1850 to train teachers for the growing number of poor Catholic children,

St Mary's is the largest of the UK's three Catholic universities yet admits students of all faiths or none. About one-third of the 5,000-strong undergraduate community are enrolled on teacher-training programmes.

All undergraduate provision is based in Twickenham, where St Mary's occupies an attractive 35-acre campus featuring gardens, parkland and the shimmering white gothic fantasy Strawberry Hill House near the River Thames – 30 minutes from central London. It also has a community building in the centre of Twickenham, with theatre space, studio rooms and a large conservatory area with a café. The Exchange offers training courses for local residents and companies, as well as providing more teaching space for students.

St Mary's was awarded silver in the Teaching Excellence Framework and assessors commended its high-quality resources and good staffing levels, which allowed personalised and small-group learning. Every student has an academic tutor tasked with answering their queries and helping to resolve any issues during their time at university. A team of learning and development lecturers provide further support, embedding skills workshops into courses covering topics such as referencing and exam revision.

In September 2021 new degree courses were introduced in sport and social change and in sports performance analysis and talent identification. The University is planning

Waldegrave Road
Strawberry Hill
Twickenham TW1 4SX
020 8240 2394
apply@stmarys.ac.uk
www.stmarys.ac.uk
www.stmaryssu.co.uk
Open days: see website

Overall Ranking: 67 (last year: 86)

Teaching quality	80.4%	8
Student experience	78.1%	5
Research quality	4%	=104
Entry standards	105	=121
Graduate prospects	66.6%	89
Good honours	78.6%	=60
Expected completion rate	81.1%	=92
Student/staff ratio	18	=103
Services and facilities	£1,879	116

to grow its allied health offer with new programmes in the coming years.

The university was granted research degree awarding powers in April 2021 and plans to expand postdoctoral programmes across a number of specialisms, starting with two options in strength and conditioning this year. St Mary's has also launched a postgraduate centre in Edinburgh, at the Gillis Centre, where master's programmes in theology and education are being delivered.

With 66% of graduates in high-skilled jobs or further study 15 months after finishing their degrees, St Mary's has improved its position in our graduate prospects measure this year. Industry collaborations include two courses run with the Chelsea Football Club Foundation and a partnership with the Royal Ballet in London's Covent Garden, where St Mary's faculty of sport, allied health and performance science provides strength and conditioning support to ballet dancers.

Sport is a well-established strength: alumnus Sir Mo Farah won a scholarship to the university's renowned Endurance Performance and Coaching Centre and trained at St Mary's for ten years in the run-up to his gold medal-winning performance in the 5,000m and 10,000m events at the London 2012 Olympics.

Sport scholarships are made in gold, silver and bronze ratings, depending on the level of competition student athletes are engaged in: senior international, junior national or county/regional. Alongside packages with free gym membership, access to the strength and conditioning suite and massage suite for all sport scholars, silver and gold recipients receive up to £3,000 in financial help.

There are generous academic scholarships too, worth £3,000 per year of study and awarded to students arriving with at least ABB at A-level, or equivalent, and who come from households with incomes under £25,000.

Indoor sports facilities include a performance hall, studio, tennis centre, and fitness and conditioning suite at the main campus, where outdoors the Sir Mo Farah Athletics Track and rugby pitches are located. The Teddington Lock campus is home to floodlit all-weather pitches.

All of St Mary's 600-plus self-managed halls of residence are catered – a highly unusual feature among UK universities – and on campus. These factors are likely to contribute to the university's buoyant rates of student satisfaction.

Tuition fees

- » Fees for UK students — £9,250
  Foundation courses — £5,140–£8,660
- » Fees for International students 2022–23 — £13,650
  Foundation years from £6,620; Two-year degrees £13,950
- » For scholarship and bursary information see www.stmarys.ac.uk/student-finance/undergraduate/tuition-fees.aspx
- » Graduate salary — £23,000

Student numbers

Undergraduates	3,445	(220)
Postgraduates	965	(885)
Applications/places		5,235/985
Applications per place		5.3
Overall offer rate		84.7%
International students – EU		4.7%
Non-EU		3.5%

Accommodation

University provided places: 650
Catered costs: £195–£248 per week
First years guaranteed accommodation
www.stmarys.ac.uk/student-life/accommodation/overview.aspx

Where do the students come from?

State schools (non-grammar)	91.8%	Low participation areas	6.8%	Disabled	7%
Grammar schools	2.3%	All ethnic minorities	31.9%	Mature (over 21)	23.3%
Independent schools	5.8%	White working-class males	6.5%		
First generation students	44.7%	Black achievement gap	-14.2%		

Social inclusion ranking: 68

University of Salford

The new £65million Science, Engineering and Environment Building, due to open on Salford's main Peel Park campus in summer 2022, supports an educational focus on robotics, digital and smart living at the university. Featuring a wind tunnel, robotics facility and the Morson Maker Space manufacturing and digital fabrication hub, the project has been designed to enable students, academics and industry partners to work together. It will also have high-spec laser laboratories.

The building fits in with an £800million plan in conjunction with the local authority to create a new 240-acre district linking the centre of Manchester with MediaCityUK, where Salford has another campus in the same development as the BBC and ITV. Courses in nursing, midwifery, psychology, social sciences, sports and health are based at the Frederick Road campus, ten minutes from Peel Park.

By the autumn term of 2022 another development, the North of England Robotics Centre, is due to open. Building on the university's 30-year history in the field, the £13million centre will house specialist facilities and teaching space tailored to robotics for intelligent infrastructure; digital automation and supply chain improvement;

and health, wellbeing, and integrated care technologies. The centre is intended to be a hub for Salford's robotics and automation specialists to collaborate with small and medium-size businesses to pilot the latest technologies.

At Peel Park the £55million New Adelphi teaching centre houses the latest facilities for art, performance, and design and technology students, including a 350-seat theatre, screen acting studios, six recording studios and a range of dedicated art and design workshops.

Founded in 1896 as the Royal Technical Institute to provide for the workforce that powered the Industrial Revolution, the University of Salford continues to foster industry links that benefit its students. For instance, an agreement with the BBC Philharmonic has allowed students first access to new technology that turns classical concerts into immersive musical experiences, while free virtual events run with the BBC Academy over the past year have covered topics from scriptwriting to location management.

A BSc in applied football studies is a collaboration with Leeds United Football Club. Delivered online, it teaches leadership, digital and business skills alongside coaching techniques to academy footballers. In another industry tie-in, the university offers an engineering degree in partnership with Siemens.

Salford prioritises real-world experience for students, building work experience

Maxwell Building
43 The Crescent
Salford
Greater Manchester
M5 4WT
0161 295 4545
enquiries@salford.ac.uk
www.salford.ac.uk
www.salfordstudents.com
Open days: see website

The Times and The Sunday Times **Rankings**
Overall Ranking: 98 (last year: 100)

Teaching quality	72%	=105
Student experience	65.6%	=105
Research quality	8.3%	71
Entry standards	126	=60
Graduate prospects	70.1%	68
Good honours	75.5%	=91
Expected completion rate	80.1%	100
Student/staff ratio	16.8	=83
Services and facilities	£2,416	75

placements and live briefs from industry experts into degree courses to boost employability. More than 70% of graduates were in high-skilled jobs or postgraduate study 15 months on from their degrees, the latest Graduate Outcomes survey showed – a strong showing that moves Salford up our graduate prospects measure this year.

However, the university was awarded bronze in the Teaching Excellence Framework (TEF) and an appeal to upgrade the assessment was rejected in 2018. Despite its good links with employers and a commitment to learning by students, the TEF panel found that progression to employment or further study remained "exceptionally low" – a position that the recent statistics suggest is well on the way to being countered.

Salford's portfolio of degree apprenticeships is growing, covering healthcare and a range of other roles. A nursing degree apprenticeship begins in 2022, joining established programmes such as social work, biomedical science and physiotherapy.

In our social inclusion ranking, the university is in the top half overall and reaches the top 20 for its proportion of students from comprehensive schools, which is almost 97%. Scholarship support for UK students targets those from low-income backgrounds, while Salford's international scholarships award high-achievers from around the world.

Salford entered only a third of its eligible academics for the 2014 Research Excellence Framework, but more than half of their work was assessed as world-leading or internationally excellent. The School of Health Sciences has an international reputation for the treatment of sports injuries.

Energy House 2.0, a £16million high-tech energy and buildings research facility, is under construction. When complete it will be used to investigate the future of housing, looking at issues such as off-site construction, smart homes, and energy use – complementing the university's initial Salford Energy House project.

A swimming pool, five fitness suites and a multiuse sports hall are among Salford's sports facilities. First-years are not guaranteed a room, but they are allocated most of the 2,111 available, and about 80% are able to live in. Less than two miles away, students have access to Manchester's legendary cultural and social scenes.

Tuition fees

»	Fees for UK students	£9,250
	Foundation courses	£8,250
»	Fees for International students 2022–23	£14,700–£17,100
»	For scholarship and bursary information see www.salford.ac.uk/undergraduate/fees	
»	Graduate salary	£24,000

Student numbers

Undergraduates	16,665	(660)
Postgraduates	2,005	(2,170)
Applications/places	25,235/5,095	
Applications per place	5	
Overall offer rate	75.7%	
International students – EU	2.3%	
Non-EU	4.5%	

Accommodation

University provided places: 2,111
Self-catered: £103–£159 per week
www.campuslivingvillages.co.uk/salford/

Where do the students come from?

State schools (non-grammar)	96.7%	Low participation areas	15.6%	Disabled	6.3%
Grammar schools	1.7%	All ethnic minorities	34.8%	Mature (over 21)	26.9%
Independent schools	1.7%	White working-class males	6.4%		
First generation students	46.1%	Black achievement gap	-26.2%		

Social inclusion ranking: =54

University of Sheffield

One of the 24 Russell Group universities and a global top-100 institution in the latest QS World University Rankings, Sheffield is burnishing its credentials by opening more research facilities. Its renowned Advanced Manufacturing Research Centre (AMRC), which provides work experience opportunities for students with industry giants such as McLaren, BAE Systems, Boeing and Rolls-Royce, is extending its footprint across the north.

The £20million AMRC North West on the Samlesbury Aerospace Enterprise Zone in Lancashire, houses a high-performing technical research and development team to enhance the county's manufacturing base.

The university has also installed one of only eight PET-MRI scanners in the UK to improve diagnosis of some of the most devastating diseases, including cancer, multiple sclerosis and cardiovascular disease. Researchers hope it will lead to the development of new treatments, giving patients in the region access to clinical trials. Sheffield's Translational Energy Research Centre began operations working on the latest carbon capture technologies.

Sheffield's main precinct stretches for a mile, ending near the city centre. Recent developments include Engineering Heartspace – home to its renowned Faculty of Engineering. The £23million Information Commons operates 24-hours throughout the year. In-person teaching remains central to the undergraduate experience and the university commendably kept going with face-to-face seminars and tutorials during the pandemic for much longer than many other institutions. Correspondingly, student satisfaction scores declined less than elsewhere, according to our analysis of National Student Survey scores. Seminars, tutorials and practical work returned to campus in September 2021, with lecture-capture continuing in tandem.

Rated silver in the Teaching Excellence Framework, assessors commended "high levels of stretch and challenge" which help students develop skills valued highly by employers.

On our measure of graduate prospects the university is among the top 30, with the latest figures showing that nearly eight in ten graduates were in high-skilled jobs or postgraduate study within 15 months of finishing. The university is one of Siemens's leading UK suppliers of graduates, who are targeted through unique hackathons, curriculum engagement and internships.

A 6% increase in applications in 2020 brought them to a new high, while enrolments experienced an even bigger 26% uplift. Of 2020's intake, 17% were placed through clearing. Sheffield is launching a politics, philosophy and economics (PPE) degree from September 2022. Degree apprenticeships for manufacturing engineers, social workers and

---

Western Bank
Sheffield S10 2TN
0114 222 8030
study@sheffield.ac.uk
www.sheffield.ac.uk
http://su.sheffield.ac.uk
Open days: see website

The Times and The Sunday Times **Rankings**
Overall Ranking: 22 (last year: =23)

Teaching quality	76.1%	=48
Student experience	73.7%	27
Research quality	37.6%	23
Entry standards	150	=27
Graduate prospects	77.4%	=28
Good honours	85.3%	26
Expected completion rate	92.8%	24
Student/staff ratio	14	28
Services and facilities	£2,497	68

nursing associates are among a portfolio of programmes, accounting for nearly 500 of Sheffield's undergraduates.

About 40% of 2021's intake received some form of financial help. Awards included more than 150 Experience Sheffield scholarships worth £3,600 for home and EU entrants from households with incomes of up to £50,000, who also met other widening participation criteria. Global Summer Experience scholarships for incoming first-years with A*AA (or higher) A-levels, covered their air fares to overseas summer schools, as well as tuition and accommodation fees while away. The Sheffield Bursary is worth between £250 and £1,000 per year to students from households with incomes up to £40,000.

Sheffield has moved up our social inclusion ranking this year, to 79th – outdoing all but Queen Mary, University of London among its English and Welsh Russell Group peers. A longstanding commitment to encouraging participation in higher education encompasses outreach initiatives with more than 500 local and regional schools and colleges.

Successful completion of access programmes earns entry grade reductions for applicants. Sheffield also takes contextual information into account, making alternative offers either one or two grades below the standard A-level requirements to those who qualify.

In the 2014 Research Excellence Framework, about 85% of the university's submission was considered world-leading or internationally excellent. Biomedical sciences, control and systems engineering, history and politics were all in the top three in the UK.

There are excellent sports facilities near the main precinct including five floodlit synthetic pitches, a large fitness centre, a swimming pool with sauna and steam rooms, sports hall, fitness studio, multipurpose activity room, four squash courts and a bouldering wall.

Outdoor pitches for rugby, football and cricket are a bus ride away. Sheffield has one of the biggest programmes of internal leagues at any university and scholarships for elite athletes contribute to its thriving high-performance sports.

Known for its green spaces and friendly atmosphere, Sheffield has a big student population, so its shops and bars cater to a student vibe. Regularly voted the best in the country, Sheffield's students' union (SU) is central to daily life. As well as housing the Foundry live music venue, the SU hosts events for the 350-plus student societies and is a focal point for the sports scene.

Tuition fees

» Fees for UK students £9,250
» Fees for International students 2022–23 £20,000–£25,670
   Dentistry £40,730; Medicine £38,050 (clinical years)
» For scholarship and bursary information see
   www.sheffield.ac.uk/undergraduate/fees-funding/
» Graduate salary £25,000

Student numbers

Undergraduates	18,575	(525)
Postgraduates	8,920	(2,035)
Applications/places	38,460/4,960	
Applications per place	7.8	
Overall offer rate	76.2%	
International students – EU	5.2%	
Non-EU	17.4%	

Accommodation

University provided places: 6,005
Self-catered: £80–£235 per week
First years guaranteed accommodation
www.sheffield.ac.uk/accommodation

Where do the students come from?

State schools (non-grammar)	76.3%	Low participation areas	10.4%	**Social inclusion ranking: 79**	
				Disabled	9.9%
Grammar schools	11.9%	All ethnic minorities	22.1%	Mature (over 21)	12%
Independent schools	11.8%	White working-class males	4.9%		
First generation students	32.7%	Black achievement gap	-8.7%		

Sheffield Hallam University

Work has begun on Sheffield Hallam's £110million upgrade to teaching and learning facilities at its city centre campus. New carbon-efficient buildings for the business school and the social sciences and humanities departments, green spaces and a revamped students' union will be finished over the next four years.

The development follows the £27million Heart of the Campus teaching and learning building on Hallam's Collegiate campus. The £30million Charles Street Building houses education courses. Hands-on learning resources include the largest PlayStation teaching lab in the world, in partnership with Sony, and a 3D virtual radiography room for healthcare students to practice cancer treatment.

The return to life on campus in the 2021–22 academic year should help student satisfaction to recover after poor reviews of the university's pandemic provision. Our analysis of the National Student Survey, comparing scores from 2020 and 2021, showed Sheffield Hallam to be one of the 30 institutions with the biggest declines in student satisfaction overall, prompting large falls in our rankings for satisfaction with teaching quality and the wider experience.

Face-to-face elements of the current blended approach include tutorials, practical work and employability-focused activities, alongside recorded lectures available on demand online, and digital community collaborations among students.

All new entrants are placed with three advisers – specialising in the academic side, employability and student support – who work together with a view to providing the best possible student experience. Unfortunately, this did not stop Hallam falling outside the top 100 for student satisfaction with the wider experience in this year's NSS.

Conversely, the university has accelerated 20 places up our social inclusion ranking to place 24th nationally – an achievement in line with its mission to transform students' lives and give everyone the chance to reach their full potential. Only two universities managed a narrower attainment gap between the proportions of black and white students gaining firsts and upper seconds. Hallam also succeeds in recruiting nearly a quarter of students from deprived areas – just ten universities attract more. More than half of Hallam undergraduates are the first in their family to enter higher education and almost all went to non-selective state schools.

Hallam leads the South Yorkshire Futures programme, the country's biggest university social mobility programme. The aim is to improve GCSE attainment and raise aspirations for young people, especially those from disadvantaged backgrounds.

City Campus
Howard Street
Sheffield S1 1WB
0114 225 5533
admissions@shu.ac.uk
www.shu.ac.uk
www.hallamstudentsunion.com
Open days: see website

The Times and The Sunday Times Rankings		
Overall Ranking: 72 (last year: 67)		
Teaching quality	73.1%	=86
Student experience	66%	104
Research quality	5.4%	=89
Entry standards	115	=96
Graduate prospects	73.5%	=51
Good honours	78.6%	=60
Expected completion rate	84.2%	70
Student/staff ratio	17.2	90
Services and facilities	£2,893	35

Its SHU Progress scheme recruits students from underrepresented groups and teams applicants with a named contact who guides them through the application process.

Undergraduates are promised work experience in every year of their degree. The university teams up with more than 1,000 organisations that offer opportunities such as workshops, consultancies, short placements and real-world projects. Many courses are accredited by professional bodies and Hallam works with employers on its course design.

Hallam's employability initiatives helped earn a silver award in the government's Teaching Excellence Framework (TEF), of which the university's vice-chancellor was chairman. He was not involved in the decision. The TEF panel complimented the institution on an exemplary commitment to the region and support for students to be retained in the area. Almost half of undergraduates come from Yorkshire and Humber and even more stay and work there after graduation.

One of the country's largest universities, Sheffield Hallam has 30,000 undergraduates, more than 1,700 of whom are enrolled on degree apprenticeship courses. It is a leading provider of the earn-as-you-learn higher education route, offering 30 programmes in nine study areas including policing, digital and technology, food and drink, management, and architecture and chartered planning, linked with 496 employers.

Eight new options are being introduced in 2021 and 2022, including teaching, paramedicine, social work, and therapeutic radiography, which will bring the number of degree apprentices to about 2,300.

Applications nudged up slightly in 2021, though they were still 40% lower than in 2011. The number of students starting courses has remained much steadier, however, helped by an increased offer rate, which equated to just under three quarters of applicants in 2020 being offered a place.

Only 16% of eligible academics entered the 2014 Research Excellence Framework and 65% of their work was considered world-leading or internationally excellent.

There are fitness suites and sports halls at both campuses. Hallam manages Sheffield's only athletics stadium, where the BUCS (British Universities and Colleges Sport) Championships have been hosted. Most outdoor pitches – grass, 3G and sand-dressed – are five miles from the city campus at Bawtry Road Sports Park, where there is also a cricket hall. All first-years who apply in time are guaranteed a space in one of the 15 halls of residence.

Tuition fees

» Fees for UK students   £9,250
» Fees for International students 2022–23   £14,415–£16,415
» For scholarship and bursary information see www.shu.ac.uk/study-here/fees-and-funding
» Graduate salary   £24,000

Student numbers

Undergraduates	21,660 (2,555)
Postgraduates	3,385 (3,365)
Applications/places	29,865/5,875
Applications per place	5.1
Overall offer rate	74.7%
International students – EU	1.4%
Non-EU	2.6%

Accommodation

University provided places: 4,457
Self-catered: £85–£169 per week
First years guaranteed accommodation
www.shu.ac.uk/study-here/accommodation

Where do the students come from?

State schools (non-grammar)	94.5%	Low participation areas	23.6%
Grammar schools	2.8%	All ethnic minorities	22.4%
Independent schools	2.6%	White working-class males	11.7%
First generation students	51.7%	Black achievement gap	-25.9%

Social inclusion ranking: 24

Disabled	8.5%
Mature (over 21)	20.1%

SOAS, University of London

SOAS (the School of Oriental and African Studies) was better placed than many institutions when the rapid pivot to remote learning had to be made last year. The university, which has a global reputation for its focus on Asia, Africa and the Near and Middle East, has been delivering distance learning and online degrees for more than 20 years.

Its experience shows in our analysis of National Student Survey (NSS) results, where SOAS ranks in the top 25 nationally for its Covid response, based on its performance in 2021 compared to outcomes from the previous year. Scores for learning opportunities went up year-on-year, a remarkable achievement in mid-pandemic and overall satisfaction was down a relatively low 3.1 percentage points.

In the 2021–22 academic year, face-to-face teaching, such as seminars and tutorials, and academic activities are being prioritised on campus. Larger group teaching, meanwhile, such as lectures, is being delivered mainly online through a mix of live and recorded content that allows students to work at their own pace.

The university offers more than 350 degree combinations across the social sciences, humanities and languages, all with its specialist focus. SOAS edged further up the QS world rankings by subject for arts and humanities this year, placing 44th globally. There were strong performances across other disciplines too, including development studies which was placed fifth in the world.

The school is based in the north block of Senate House, the imposing Bloomsbury headquarters of the University of London, which adjoins the SOAS precinct. The 2016 move to the five-storey site in its centenary year brought the school together at a single base for the first time in many years. It includes a student hub, hosting services such as accommodation, counselling, student finance and careers, and a plaza under a glass canopy.

A record number of new entrants joined SOAS in 2020, a welcome upturn after fluctuating student numbers. Applications decreased a little however, against a rising offer rate. Just under a fifth of first-years gained their places via clearing in the same admissions round.

A Race, Accountability and Listening Action Group launched in 2021, as part of SOAS's social justice mandate, committed to advocacy and accountability for the black community inside and outside the university. Drawing more than three-quarters of students from ethnic minority backgrounds, SOAS has one of the most ethnically diverse undergraduate populations in the country, ranking joint third and behind only City

10 Thornhaugh Street
Russell Square
London WC1H 0XG
020 3510 6974
study@soas.ac.uk
www.soas.ac.uk
http://soasunion.org
Open days: see website

The Times and The Sunday Times **Rankings**

Overall Ranking: 33 (last year: 50)

Teaching quality	72.1%	=102
Student experience	66.4%	=101
Research quality	27.9%	46
Entry standards	148	=32
Graduate prospects	67.8%	81
Good honours	85.2%	=27
Expected completion rate	83.5%	=75
Student/staff ratio	12.8	=9
Services and facilities	£3,304	19

among its University of London peers in this regard.

SOAS pioneered moves to "decolonise" the curriculum. It has also committed itself to challenging Eurocentrism and developed a toolkit for making teaching more inclusive and redressing disadvantage through racism and colonialism. There has been a student working group on the subject since 2016, prompted partly by SOAS's own colonial origins.

SOAS has also started a year-long consultancy with national trans-led charity, Gendered Intelligence, to create a trans, non-binary and intersex inclusion policy for its staff and students.

The university gained a silver award in the Teaching Excellence Framework, upgraded from bronze at the third attempt. The panel praised a strong institutional emphasis on personalised learning and small-group teaching, as well as a comprehensive student engagement system and outreach initiatives to widen participation.

The university offers a free week-long bridging course to prepare applicants who are the first in their family to go to university, are over 21, or are from a low-participation neighbourhood. Those with household incomes below £25,000 receive a bursary worth at least £1,500 a year.

In the Research Excellence Framework, music, drama and the performing arts produced the best results, when two-thirds of the submission was rated as world-leading or internationally excellent.

Students have their own bar, social space and catering facilities. The former University of London Union, now a student centre, is close at hand, with a swimming pool, gym and more bars.

There are 952 residential places available, enough to guarantee a space for all first-years, as additional spaces are sourced if needed. The students' union hosts sports clubs and teams such as basketball, baseball, aikido and table tennis – and students are welcome to set up their own. While the university does not own its own sports facilities it is well placed for plenty of public amenities.

Tuition fees

» Fees for UK students	£9,250
» Fees for International students 2022–23	£19,560
» For scholarship and bursary information see www.soas.ac.uk/registry/funding	
» Graduate salary	£24,000

Student numbers

Undergraduates	2,710	(30)
Postgraduates	1,880	(1,170)
Applications/places		5,790/880
Applications per place		6.6
Overall offer rate		78%
International students – EU		14.6%
Non-EU		20.3%

Accommodation

University provided places: 952
Catered costs: £249–£302 per week
Self-catered: £147–£261 per week
First-years guaranteed accommodation
www.soas.ac.uk/accommodation

Where do the students come from?

State schools (non-grammar)	79.9%	Low participation areas	2.8%	Disabled	8.1%
Grammar schools	5.4%	All ethnic minorities	73.3%	Mature (over 21)	15.2%
Independent schools	14.7%	White working-class males	1.8%		
First generation students	43.4%	Black achievement gap	-13.6%		

Social inclusion ranking: =76

Solent University

Based at sites across the centre of Southampton, Solent University was formed in 2005 through mergers between Southampton College of Art, the College of Technology and the College of Nautical Studies at Warsash. Maritime education remains a strength, and tuition for Merchant Navy senior officers, yacht certification, maritime safety management, leadership and security courses moved to the main campus after a £43million investment in simulation technology.

Students benefit from an immersive learning experience with specialist facilities that include Europe's largest maritime simulation centre. The university is unique in having its own fleet of 11 manned model ships, based at a training centre on Timsbury Lake. Solent offers the UK's only three-year officer cadetship training leading to a full honours degree approved by the UK Maritime and Coastguard Agency. Most cadets are sponsored by shipping companies such as Maersk, Carnival, Princess and Aramco.

The university's superyacht academy is also renowned within the industry. On the water, Team Solent Sailing teams compete successfully in national competitions. Elsewhere, courses are arranged under faculties of creative industries, architecture and engineering; sport, health and social sciences; and business, law and digital technologies. The university's £33million Spark building featured technology including lecture-capture facilities before the pandemic hit.

This ambition to increase the use of technology to support learning has been accelerated by the rapid shift to remote learning. The blend of online and in-person teaching in the 2021–22 academic year has been curated by course teams, to tailor a mix of in-person and virtual delivery. However, Solent's Covid response did not attract the high levels of student satisfaction it formerly enjoyed in the National Student Survey (NSS). Scores for teaching quality saw it fall 28 places to 50th, and for the wider undergraduate experience it has dropped to joint 75th, from 33rd in 2020. The declines have contributed to Solent falling outside our overall top 100.

The return to campus facilities and in-person interaction should improve things. A refurbishment programme is upgrading key buildings including the library. The improvements will make it easier for students to access the Student Hub. Administrative offices are being converted into extra teaching space for the new Faculty of Creative Industries, Architecture and Engineering.

Student support facilities are in one place, to promote easy access to advice on finance, accommodation and assessment. A "Sowlent" food garden is tended by students and has growing space for fruit and vegetables.

East Park Terrace
Southampton SO14 0YN
023 8201 5066
admissions@solent.ac.uk
www.solent.ac.uk
www.solentsu.co.uk
Open days: see website

The Times and The Sunday Times **Rankings**
Overall Ranking: =112 (last year: 93)

Teaching quality	76%	50
Student experience	68.8%	=75
Research quality	0.5%	126
Entry standards	110	=109
Graduate prospects	59.1%	122
Good honours	75.5%	=91
Expected completion rate	76.2%	=118
Student/staff ratio	16.1	72
Services and facilities	£2,146	=96

Furthering the university's diversity and inclusion initiatives, the Student Hub acts as a third-party hate crime reporting centre. All Student Hub and mental health advisers are being trained in gender awareness, and a specific point of contact is available for any student with concerns.

Solent was upgraded to silver in the Teaching Excellence Framework. Assessors were impressed by students' high levels of engagement and commitment to learning, and by the substantial investment in learning resources and successful integration of research and professional practice into the curriculum.

A guarantee to put real-world learning into undergraduate courses from September 2020 may help to boost employability in the future. Just under six in ten graduates were in high-skilled work or postgraduate study 15 months after their degrees, the latest figures show – a bottom 20 result. Students now have placement opportunities and paid assignments and will be assessed on tasks for employers or community organisations.

The university plans to keep expanding its portfolio of higher and degree apprenticeships. At present it offers 22, having gained new programmes in advanced clinical practice, health play, maritime, social work, healthcare science, artificial intelligence data and port maritime operations this year.

The university finished bottom in the 2014 Research Excellence Framework. It entered the lowest proportion of eligible academics

(7%) and none of its research was placed in the top two categories.

Solent has climbed up our social inclusion ranking. It has shown particular success in recruiting white working class men and students from deprived areas. It has introduced contextual offers, and bursaries of £500 to £1,500 are available to students from households with incomes under £25,000 – the larger sums reserved for those who are also care leavers, estranged from their families, or young carers.

A new sports complex features equipment for performance athletes and for general use. Sports scholars receive accommodation discounts and other valuable benefits. At Test Park there are pitches for football, American football and rugby union. Students have access to the Coalporters Rowing Club near campus and Spinnaker Sailing Club 18 miles away. All new students are guaranteed one of 1,249 rooms if they apply by June. Along with student-friendly pubs and clubs in the East Park area, Southampton's sea air and the nearby New Forest are big draws. Beaches dot the coast nearby, and the Isle of Wight is a ferry hop away.

Tuition fees

» Fees for UK students		£9,250
» Fees for International students 2022–23		£14,250
Foundation		£11,500
» For scholarship and bursary information see www.solent.ac.uk/finance/tuition-fees/		
» Graduate salary		£20,500

Student numbers

Undergraduates	8,865	(900)
Postgraduates	485	(260)
Applications/places		10,050/1,920
Applications per place		5.2
Overall offer rate		83.2%
International students – EU		14%
Non-EU		5.3%

Accommodation
University provided places: 1,249
Self-catered: £109–£154 per week
First years guaranteed accommodation
www.solent.ac.uk/studying-at-solent/accommodation

Where do the students come from?

					Social inclusion ranking: 32	
State schools (non-grammar)	96.2%	Low participation areas	18.3%	Disabled	5.5%
Grammar schools	0.8%	All ethnic minorities	18.4%	Mature (over 21)	35%
Independent schools	3%	White working-class males	11.4%		
First generation students	48.5%	Black achievement gap	-30.6%		

University of South Wales

At the University of South Wales's (USW) Pontypridd campus in Treforest a new chiropractic teaching centre and clinic is being developed. In line with the university's commitment to providing learning environments that simulate the demands of the workplace, the multimillion-pound development will include digital x-ray suites, treatment rooms and rehabilitation suites.

Situated in the heart of the lush green South Wales Valleys, the Pontypridd campus, ten miles from Cardiff, is USW's largest of three. Acute care simulation suites have been added at the university's clinical simulation centre, to improve teaching and learning for nursing and midwifery students, and USW has also begun refurbishing its halls of residence. Other recent developments at the Pontypridd base include a modern Law School and upgraded laboratories, as well as a £6million Learning Resource Centre.

Formed by a merger between Glamorgan and Newport universities, USW also has a Cardiff campus in the city centre, which is home to its creative industries courses, which benefit from industry-standard equipment for advertising, television and film set design, and fashion, as well as dance studios, rehearsal spaces and photographic studios. Cardiff is also the base for Startup Stiwdio, an incubation space.

The university moved to its Newport site in 2011 after the sale of the attractive Caerleon campus outside Newport – which subsequently found fame as the filming location for Netflix series *Sex Education*. Students were happy with the relocation to the £35million Newport City Campus, registering a big uplift in National Student Survey (NSS) satisfaction scores. Among courses based in Newport are cybersecurity, education and psychology, the latter of which gained new specialist facilities this term.

Students felt there was room for improvement in USW's handling of the pandemic, our analysis of year-on-year NSS results shows. The university ranks just inside the top 100 nationally. Satisfaction scores for teaching quality and the wider undergraduate experience have declined sharply from previously buoyant rates, in common with many other universities that focus significantly on practice-based courses. The return to the practical experiences, problem solving and active learning that USW employs on campus should bring satisfaction rates back up to their former standards. For the 2021–22 academic year the university is prioritising immersive activities for in-person learning, to get the best out of its specialist facilities and stimulate interaction, while providing lectures recorded virtually that can be re-visited later.

A Personal Academic Coaching scheme provides students with a series of conversations

1 Iantwit Road
Pontypridd
CF37 1DL
03455 76 77 78
admissions@southwales.ac.uk
www.southwales.ac.uk
www.uswsu.com
Open days: see website

Edinburgh

Belfast

PONTYPRIDD NEWPORT
CARDIFF London

The Times and The Sunday Times **Rankings**
Overall Ranking: 99 (last year: =90)

Teaching quality	75.5%	=56
Student experience	68.4%	=78
Research quality	4.0%	=104
Entry standards	116	=91
Graduate prospects	63.7%	=103
Good honours	73.1%	=103
Expected completion rate	81.8%	86
Student/staff ratio	15.5	=56
Services and facilities	£2,281	83

with a dedicated coach regarding their overall academic and professional progress.

Like many universities in Wales, USW has not entered the Teaching Excellence Framework. Of its relatively small submission in the 2014 Research Excellence Framework, half of the work was considered world-leading or internationally excellent. The best results came in a joint submission with Cardiff Metropolitan and Trinity St David universities in art and design. Results were also good for sport and exercise science, and social work and social policy.

The university offers eight degree apprenticeship programmes in Wales – including cybersecurity; data science; and mechanical, manufacturing, electrical and electronic engineering. A police constable degree apprenticeship operates with English forces.

The proportion of mature students aged over-21 is approaching four in ten and 96% of USW undergraduates went to non-selective state secondary schools, evidence of effective outreach activities. It ranks just outside the top 40 overall for social inclusion.

Degrees in music producing, applied engineering, biomedical science and sport and exercise science welcomed their first students in September 2021. Applications declined for the seventh consecutive year in 2020, as has the number of students starting courses – though less sharply. Maintaining entry standards, South Wales still turns down about three in ten applications.

Partnerships with the Welsh Rugby Union (WRU), Football Association of Wales Trust, police forces across England and Wales and Health Education Improvement Wales are among tie-ins that boost experience and opportunities for USW students.

However, the university ranks outside the top 100 in our graduate prospects measure, with the latest figures showing 64% were in high-skilled jobs or postgraduate study within 15 months of finishing their degree.

USW Sport Park has a 3G pitch and 270-seat stand used by student teams as well as Pontypridd FC. The Sport Park includes specialist equipment for sports degree studies and a centre for strength and conditioning with 12 lifting platforms and a full-size 3G indoor football pitch, the only one in Wales and one of five in the UK.

First-years are guaranteed a room in halls of residence, which are located at each of the university's campuses. Surrounded by coast and countryside all USW sites are near, or in, the buzzing student city of Cardiff, one of the UK's best places for undergraduate life.

Tuition fees

» Fees for UK students	£9,000
» Fees for International students 2022–23	£13,500–£13,800
» For scholarship and bursary information see www.southwales.ac.uk/study/fees-and-funding/	
» Graduate salary	£22,000

Student numbers

Undergraduates	14,290 (3,475)
Postgraduates	2,265 (3,060)
Applications/places	11,005/2,250
Applications per place	4.9
Overall offer rate	74.4%
International students – EU	4.5%
Non-EU	6.3%

Accommodation

University provided places: 1,656
Self-catered: £96–£135 per week
First years guaranteed accommodation
www.southwales.ac.uk/student-life/accommodation

Where do the students come from?

				Social inclusion ranking: 42	
State schools (non-grammar)	95.5%	Low participation areas	23.8%	Disabled	8.4%
Grammar schools	1.3%	All ethnic minorities	10.9%	Mature (over 21)	36.9%
Independent schools	3.1%	White working-class males	7%		
First generation students	44.5%	Black achievement gap	-33.1%		

University of Southampton

The University of Southampton has made consent training mandatory for all students. Many other institutions offer advice to undergraduates on issues including sexual consent but few have made such guidance a formal requirement. Southampton's students' union also provides compulsory Wide (welfare, inclusivity, diversity and equality) training for club and society committees.

Such decisive steps around student welfare and wellbeing add to the strong offer at Southampton, which is a founding member of the research-led Russell Group of universities. Established in 1862, it has climbed 13 places up the QS World University rankings this year, to 77th place globally, while retaining its place among our elite top 20 in the UK.

At the main Highfield campus, two miles from Southampton city centre, chemical engineering students will benefit from £5.3million of new teaching facilities in 2022, with specialist and design laboratories and an immersive virtual control room that simulates industrial facilities among the resources. Research within chemistry has also benefited from a £1.1million upgrade to crystallography equipment, bringing a new goniometer (to measure angles) and high-powered focusing optics.

Highfield's Centenary Building features teaching and learning facilities designed to enhance the student experience. Independent study spaces come with views across the campus and the city, seminar rooms are bookable and private study pods are plentiful.

EcoCampus Platinum status and a Bronze Hedgehog Friendly Campus award recognise some of Southampton's environmental initiatives. The university placed comfortably within the upper half of universities in our analysis of the 2021 National Student Survey results, effectively a measure on how well students thought the university handled the pandemic. It was in the top ten among its Russell Group peers.

After the experience of the pandemic the university has said it will increase the use of "pulse" surveys to keep up with student feedback and make necessary adjustments to the curriculum, resource delivery and accessibility. The university has also improved its NSS rankings for teaching quality (joint 53rd) and the wider undergraduate experience (42nd) this year – strong results especially in comparison with other research-intensive universities.

The Avenue campus houses most humanities departments and clinical medicine is based at Southampton General Hospital. Winchester School of Art and the National Oceanography Centre are among the university's other sites. Overseas, the university has a campus in Malaysia – originally dedicated to engineering, it began offering business courses too in 2020.

University Road
Highfield
Southampton SO17 1BJ
023 8059 9699
enquiry@southampton.ac.uk
www.southampton.ac.uk
www.susu.org
Open days: see website

The Times and The Sunday Times **Rankings**
Overall Ranking: 16 (last year: =15)

Teaching quality	75.8%	=53
Student experience	71.8%	42
Research quality	44.9%	7
Entry standards	151	26
Graduate prospects	76%	35
Good honours	87.3%	18
Expected completion rate	93.2%	20
Student/staff ratio	13.2	=16
Services and facilities	£2,772	49

Most Southampton degrees offer a year in employment and undergraduates are also encouraged to spend time studying abroad. The university does well in our measure of graduate prospects, with more than three-quarters of graduates in high-skilled jobs or postgraduate study within 15 months of finishing their degrees.

Southampton performed well in the 2014 Research Excellence Framework. It is in the top seven for research quality after entering nine out of ten eligible academics for assessment. More than 80% of their work was rated world-leading or internationally excellent. Research projects include work to calculate Southampton Football Club's carbon footprint over a three-year period.

The National Infrastructure Laboratory houses the latest teaching and research facilities for geomechanics, heavy structures, solid mechanics and infrastructure engineering. The laboratory is located at the £140million Boldrewood Innovation Campus, developed jointly with Lloyd's Register, and dedicated to marine engineering and engineering sciences.

Southampton is only just inside the top 100 in our social inclusion ranking, although this represents a more diverse intake than at most other Russell Group universities. More than two-thirds of students are from ethnic minority backgrounds and the university is making ground on narrowing the black attainment gap (which looks at the proportions of black and white students achieving firsts and upper seconds) – featuring among the top half of UK institutions for this measure.

About a quarter of admissions will receive some form of financial assistance in 2021, as was the case in 2020. Bursaries of £1,000 or £2,000 are awarded to students where household incomes are up to £30,000 or £16,000 respectively. International students awarded the university's merit scholarship qualify for a £3,000 tuition fee discount.

An indoor sports complex next to the students' union and a 25m pool add to Southampton's excellent facilities. There are numerous gyms at halls of residence, while the outdoor sports complex has multiple grass and synthetic pitches. Flying Formula is the university's Sigma 38 yacht, available for taster sessions or bareboat charter.

Southampton nightlife has a lively reputation, and students have the added bonuses of sandy beaches and the New Forest nearby. The university has more than 7,000 residential places, enough for all new entrants who apply by the deadline – and most others.

Tuition fees
- » Fees for UK students £9,250
- » Fees for International students 2022–23 £19,300–£23,720
  Medicine (clinical years) £25,000–£49,000
- » For scholarship and bursary information see www.southampton.ac.uk/courses/fees/undergraduate.page
- » Graduate salary £25,300

Student numbers

Undergraduates	14,665	(40)
Postgraduates	6,630	(1,330)
Applications/places	35,800/3,805	
Applications per place	9.4	
Overall offer rate	67.8%	
International students – EU	8.4%	
Non-EU	10.2%	

Accommodation
University provided places: 7,000
Catered costs: £154–£207 per week
Self-catered: £119–£340 per week
First years guaranteed accommodation
www.southampton.ac.uk/student-life/accommodation

Where do the students come from?

State schools (non-grammar)	72.3%	Low participation areas	7.4%	Disabled	6.1%
Grammar schools	14.8%	All ethnic minorities	23.2%	Mature (over 21)	8.9%
Independent schools	12.8%	White working-class males	4.8%		
First generation students	34.4%	Black achievement gap	-18.8%		

Social inclusion ranking: 97

Staffordshire University

There is dedicated space for higher and degree apprenticeships within Staffordshire's new £40million Catalyst building on the main Stoke-on-Trent campus, in step with the university's aim of having more than 6,300 student apprentices by 2030.

Staffordshire's portfolio of ten degree apprenticeship programmes covers business and administration, digital, health and science, manufacturing and engineering and law and policing. The university offers further options at higher apprenticeship level.

Beyond the Potteries, Staffordshire's Digital Institute campus in east London is expanding facilities for its games and esports degrees. A Megalab digital hive for cyber and computer science degrees is also being added. The new facilities will pave the way for courses in subjects including artificial intelligence and professional technologies.

Student satisfaction hit new heights at Staffordshire in 2020, when the university ranked 15th in the country for teaching quality in the National Student Survey (NSS). Results in 2021's NSS did not quite hit those levels, leading to a fall to just outside the top 20 in the ranking on this measure, as it was impacted by the pandemic-related challenges faced by many universities where the focus is on practical-based courses.

Supporting university families, Staffordshire has opened a £4.4million nursery and forest school close to the nature reserve on its Stoke-on-Trent campus. As well as providing 100 extra childcare spaces, the building has a classroom and observational facilities designated for use by student teachers, social workers and early years practitioners. A £5.5million investment in the Stafford campus incorporates clinical simulation and immersion suites.

Staffordshire holds a gold rating in the government's Teaching Excellence Framework (TEF), after an upgrade in 2019. The TEF panel said students from all backgrounds achieve outstanding outcomes and complimented the university on high rates of progression to high-skilled employment or further study as well as its strong commitment to supporting students' personal and professional development. The TEF panel noted the effectiveness of initiatives such as the Student Journey scheme – which was co-created by students and staff to address any areas of disadvantage. The Quiet Induction offers a calm, personalised registration and welcome experience for those on the autistic spectrum.

The university's goal to promote social mobility is evidenced by a seven-place rise to rank 6th in our social inclusion table. It recruited the second-highest proportion (12.4%) of white working-class male students in the country –

College Road
University Quarter
Stoke-on-Trent ST4 2DE
01782 294 000
enquiries@staffs.ac.uk
www.staffs.ac.uk
www.staffsunion.com
Open days: see website

Edinburgh
Belfast
STOKE-ON-TRENT
London
Cardiff

The Times and The Sunday Times Rankings
Overall Ranking: 76 (last year: 76)

Teaching quality	78.1%	=23
Student experience	70.5%	=52
Research quality	16.5%	55
Entry standards	117	=85
Graduate prospects	68%	80
Good honours	74.4%	=96
Expected completion rate	77.8%	111
Student/staff ratio	17.7	=100
Services and facilities	£2,063	102

the group least likely to go to university according to the Department for Education. Nearly three in ten students come from deprived postcodes – only two universities recruit more – and almost 60% are the first in their families to progress to higher education.

Students can apply for financial support to fund work or study placements, internships or international study. Addressing digital poverty, Staffordshire is increasing its stock of laptops available to students through a long loan scheme. Bursaries of £1,000 per year of study are offered to students who have left care or who are estranged from their families.

Externally funded support is being offered by the Denise Coates Foundation, which accepts applications from current and new Staffordshire students for bursaries of £1,500 for the first year of study and £1,000, in the second and third years. The bursary is not a hardship fund, it is intended to help towards trips and equipment or other items that will help students to progress their studies.

Primary teacher training programmes are based at Lichfield, where there is an integrated further and higher education centre, developed in partnership with South Staffordshire College. Nursing and midwifery students are based at the Royal Shrewsbury Hospital.

Applications increased by 5% in 2020 and a new partnership with Wilkes Academy of Performing Arts in Swindon contributed to a 12% rise by the end of March in the 2021

admissions cycle. Eight new degrees in 2021 included architecture, digital and social media marketing and climate change and society. Applications are open for Staffordshire's new degree in working with children, young people and families – which launches in September 2022.

Staffordshire increased the size and scope of its submission to the 2014 Research Excellence Framework, but still entered just 91 academics. The best results were in sport and exercise sciences, although all the university's work in psychology was placed in the top two categories for its external impact.

The Sir Stanley Matthews sports centre on the Stoke campus is close to university accommodation and includes a gym, grass and synthetic pitches, a sports hall and a strength and conditioning suite. There are 1,269 residential places and those who make Staffordshire their firm choice are guaranteed one.

The Hanley area is known for clubbing and nearby Newcastle-under-Lyme for its pubs. Students' union venues offer drinks, club nights and eating options. The Stoke campus is close to the city and transport links.

Tuition fees

» Fees for UK students £9,250
» Fees for International students 2022–23 £14,500–£19,000
» For scholarship and bursary information see www.staffs.ac.uk/courses/undergraduate/fees-and-funding
» Graduate salary £22,000

Student numbers

Undergraduates	8,745 (4,550)
Postgraduates	790 (1,590)
Applications/places	12,035/2,975
Applications per place	4
Overall offer rate	81.1%
International students – EU	1.2%
Non-EU	2%

Accommodation

University provided places: 1,269
Self-catered: £95–£125 per week
First years guaranteed accommodation
www.staffs.ac.uk/student-life/accommodation

Where do the students come from?

State schools (non-grammar)	97.2%	Low participation areas	28.4%		
Grammar schools	1.7%	All ethnic minorities	19.1%		
Independent schools	1.1%	White working-class males	12.4%		
First generation students	59.7%	Black achievement gap	-32.2%		

Social inclusion ranking: 6

Disabled	11.2%
Mature (over 21)	35.1%

University of Stirling

Stirling is emerging from the pandemic with rising applications and hopes to continue to attract more talent to its campus – one of the most beautiful in the UK – through its focus on widening access to higher education. Applications were up 9% at the end of March 2021 compared with the same point in the previous application cycle.

The first institution in the UK to pioneer an academic year of two 15-week semesters, the university rises five places to sixth in our Scottish social inclusion ranking. It works with local schools in low-participation areas and has a joint degree programme with Forth Valley College, whose students can enter Stirling's second or third year in programmes such as adult or mental health nursing.

Graduate apprenticeships are offered in data science and Stirling hopes to triple the number of trainees to 60 by next year. It is in talks with the Scottish Funding Council over plans to introduce more variety.

In 2020 about 6% of entrants received a contextual offer with lower target grades for those in deprived areas or those who have participated in Stirling's access programmes. A widening-participation officer is on hand to offer support during the admissions process and for those who gain a place, the university has a facility where students can borrow a laptop in the short term, free of charge.

An inspiring environment greets students of all backgrounds and nationalities: the 330-acre campus, centred on a loch beneath the Ochil hills, is perhaps the UK's most picturesque and the original 1960s design features the Pathfoot Building, an architectural masterpiece by John Richards. The university has promised that the £21.7million Campus Central project that is nearing completion will create facilities to match the stunning backdrop. The atrium at the heart of the campus was refurbished in 2020 and a new three-storey building will feature study and social spaces to enhance the student experience.

Like almost all UK universities Stirling has suffered a drop in student satisfaction over the pandemic period, yet it improved its position in our rankings as other institutions were impacted more severely by the student verdict on their pandemic learning experience. The university is in the top 40 in our analysis comparing National Student Survey outcomes from 2020 and 2021.

One explanation for its better performance on student satisfaction with teaching quality and the wider experience is Stirling's significant investment to innovate on teaching practice and learning infrastructure for courses delivered partly or fully online. Stirling has new software, a library of digital books and resources and has developed

---

Stirling
FK9 4LA
01786 467 044
admissions@stir.ac.uk
www.stir.ac.uk
www.stirlingstudentsunion.com
Open days: see website

The Times and The Sunday Times Rankings
Overall Ranking: 41 (last year: 38)

Teaching quality	77.9%	27
Student experience	73.3%	32
Research quality	30.5%	42
Entry standards	167	=15
Graduate prospects	71.5%	62
Good honours	75.1%	94
Expected completion rate	83.9%	72
Student/staff ratio	15.8	=65
Services and facilities	£2,191	92

platforms so students can interact with tutors and their student peers to complete coursework. The approach bodes well for blended learning in future.

Stirling has a proud research record. Almost three-quarters of the work submitted to the 2014 Research Excellence Framework was judged to be world-leading or internationally excellent. The best results were in agriculture, veterinary and food science, for which Stirling was ranked fourth in the UK. The university was top in Scotland for health sciences and third for psychology.

Its Institute of Aquaculture was awarded the Queen's Anniversary Prize in 2019 for its pioneering work in the world's fastest-growing food production sector in a bid to tackle global hunger. The university is now targeting its research on the government's "grand challenges" such as Scotland's aim to reach net zero greenhouse gas emissions by 2045.

Building on its solid research platform, Stirling has a global network for students, staff and alumni to share advice and seek mentorship, while the University of Stirling Innovation Park is a key hub for start-ups and established businesses, research collaboration and potential jobs.

Scotland's designated university for sporting excellence – and our UK Sports University of the Year 2020 – has an array of top-class facilities including fitness studios, a gym, three-court sports hall, indoor cycling studio, strength and conditioning areas and a high-performance suite, which opened in 2020.

There are also artificial pitches for hockey, football, rugby, Gaelic football, lacrosse and American football and an all-weather athletics track. The campus also hosts the National Swimming Academy and National Tennis Centre, which includes six indoor, two outdoor clay and two synthetic courts – where Sir Andy Murray and his brother Jamie began to build their careers. Sir Andy was awarded an honorary degree by Stirling in 2014.

Tuition fees

- » Fees for Scottish students   £0–£1,820
  RUK fees (capped at £27,750 for 4-year courses)   £9,250
- » Fees for International students 2022–23   £15,900–£18,800
- » For scholarship and bursary information see
  www.stir.ac.uk/study/fees-funding/
- » Graduate salary   £23,000

Student numbers

Undergraduates	8,100	(440)
Postgraduates	2,405	(1,596)
Applications/places		15,745/2,320
Applications per place		6.8
Overall offer rate		67.2%
International students – EU		10.4%
Non-EU		6.9%

Accommodation

University provided places: 2,894
Self-catered: £84–£179 per week
First years guaranteed accommodation
www.stir.ac.uk/student-life/accommodation

Where do the students come from?

State schools (non-grammar)	89.1%	Deprived areas	13.1%	Disabled	10.4%
Grammar schools	5.2%	All ethnic minorities	6.7%	Mature (over 21)	24.3%
Independent schools	5.7%	White working-class males	6.3%		
First generation students	38.1%	Black achievement gap	-5.7%		

Social inclusion ranking (Scotland): 6

University of Strathclyde

Strathclyde is elevated into our elite top 20 for student satisfaction after excellent results in the pandemic-influenced National Student Survey (NSS) of 2021. The university rose more than 50 places for satisfaction with teaching quality and 31 places for satisfaction with the wider experience to stand seventh in the UK.

Only three universities achieved better ratings for student satisfaction in our analysis comparing NSS outcomes in 2020 and 2021. The rapid move to remote learning when Covid loomed on campus was helped by this leading technological university's established infrastructure for delivering virtual degree courses.

Winner of our 2020 Scottish University of the Year award – and shortlisted for the UK University of the Year prize, too – Strathclyde expects future course delivery to be through a combination of on-campus, in-person and online learning, varying by subject area.

Strathclyde has ploughed £1billion into campus developments over the past decade and it's not finished yet. The flagship £60million Learning and Teaching building, at the heart of the John Anderson campus in Glasgow city centre, houses a raft of student-facing services in one location and adds extra study spaces. It should boost student satisfaction ratings further still. Elsewhere, facilities for biomedical engineering have had a £15.5million upgrade at the Wolfson Building.

There is more in the pipeline for Scotland's third-largest university, which was established in 1796 and continues to live by its founding mission to be a "place of useful learning". The university is transforming the site of the former Rottenrow maternity hospital and surrounding streets into a contemporary learning and teaching environment kitted out with smart features such as electric bike charging points and solar panels.

Bat and bird nesting boxes have also been included in designs, in tune with Strathclyde's commitment to cut carbon emissions by 70% over the next five years and to aim for net zero by 2040, or even sooner. The Centre for Sustainable Development, launched in 2020, has united all its work in this field – education, research and knowledge exchange – into the same strategic approach.

With more than 80% of graduates in high-skilled jobs or postgraduate study within 15 months of finishing their degrees, the university once again features in the top 20 on our measure for graduate prospects. Students benefit from well-established links that encompass partnerships with organisations such as Rolls-Royce, GlaxoSmithKline, Airbus, Boeing and ScottishPower/Iberdrola.

The Hunter Centre for Entrepreneurship, a unit endowed by the Scottish businessman

McCance Building
16 Richmond Street
Glasgow G1 1XQ
0141 548 4400
study-here@strath.ac.uk
www.strath.ac.uk
www.strathunion.com
Open days: see website

GLASGOW
Edinburgh
Belfast
London
Cardiff

The Times and The Sunday Times Rankings
Overall Ranking: 17 (last year: =23)

Teaching quality	77.5%	=31
Student experience	77.3%	7
Research quality	37.7%	=21
Entry standards	199	4
Graduate prospects	80.3%	18
Good honours	85.5%	=24
Expected completion rate	89.5%	=37
Student/staff ratio	18.9	=114
Services and facilities	£2,278	84

and philanthropist Sir Tom Hunter, is one of Europe's leading centres for the study of entrepreneurship, innovation and strategy and offers degrees in business enterprise.

The university delivers both Scotland's graduate apprenticeships and degree apprenticeships validated in England. Its growing portfolio already includes seven options such as senior leadership; civil engineering; and information technology.

Like most Scottish universities, Strathclyde did not enter the Teaching Excellence Framework, but it excelled in the 2014 Research Excellence Framework, taking it near the top 20 in our rankings. Almost 80% of an exceptionally large submission was rated world-leading or internationally excellent. The university was top in the UK for physics and top in Scotland for business.

Less than half of applications to Strathyclyde result in the offer of a place. Given its high entry standards and the calibre of its courses, it does well to recruit nine out of ten students from state schools. More than one-third of students have parents who did not go to university and Strathclyde ranks tenth in Scotland in our social inclusion index once again – proof that there is substance to its socially progressive outlook. The university became the first in Scotland to sign a commitment to support access to higher education for the Gypsy, Traveller, Roma, Showman and Boater communities.

Strathclyde offers a range of merit-based scholarships including financial awards for sport and engineering students. Scottish students benefit from the devolved government paying their tuition fees and to sweeten the deal for new entrants from the rest of the UK, the Strathclyde Accommodation Bursary helps with £1,000 towards rent in halls of residence. It also offers a cash bursary of £1,000, £2,000 or £3,000 per year of study to those from households with incomes less than £42,641.

The recently opened £31million sport centre has a six-lane, 25m swimming pool; two sports halls; squash courts; a café and specialist health facilities. Outdoor pitches are at the Stepps playing fields, five miles from the university's headquarters.

Accommodation is guaranteed in one of the university's 1,330 rooms as long as applications are received before the closing date. One of the UK's leading student cities, famously friendly Glasgow offers legendary nightlife, a student-centric vibe and plenty of culture.

Tuition fees

» Fees for Scottish students   £0–£1,820
    RUK fees (capped at £27,750 for 4-year courses)   £9,250
» Fees for International students 2022–23   £15,150–£22,400
» For scholarship and bursary information see www.strath.ac.uk/studywithus/feesfunding/
» Graduate salary   £27,000

Student numbers

Undergraduates	13,960	(2,155)
Postgraduates	5,745	(2,470)
Applications/places	27,700/4,055	
Applications per place	6.8	
Overall offer rate	48%	
International students – EU	3.5%	
Non-EU	6.7%	

Accommodation

University provided places: 1,300
Self-catered: £104–£141 per week
www.strath.ac.uk/studywithus/accommodation/

Where do the students come from?

State schools (non-grammar)	88.9%	Deprived areas	19.6%
Grammar schools	2.9%	All ethnic minorities	12.5%
Independent schools	8.1%	White working-class males	6.7%
First generation students	36.5%	Black achievement gap	-23.5%

Social inclusion ranking (Scotland): 10

Disabled	3.1%
Mature (over 21)	17%

University of Suffolk

Better student satisfaction has helped to lift Suffolk 18 places in our academic rankings. Satisfaction with teaching quality and the wider experience have both improved, a remarkable achievement given the challenging conditions of the pandemic.

Founded in 2007 as University Campus Suffolk, the institution was a satellite of the University of East Anglia (UEA) and Essex University and did not begin awarding its own degrees until 2015. It turns its modernity to its advantage, as its successful switch to remote learning attests. Suffolk ranks in the top 40 in the country in our analysis comparing scores in the National Student Survey in 2020 and 2021, indicating that the response to Covid restrictions was better received here than in many more renowned and historic institutions.

Suffolk adopted a "block" approach in its remote delivery, which streamlined course content and assessment and enabled students to better manage their time and academic focus. A lump sum was offered towards students' IT equipment. Face-to-face teaching has returned for the 2021–22 academic year and lectures are being livestreamed and recorded.

The curriculum is continuing to expand, as are Suffolk's student numbers which have now reached 8,320 undergraduates – exceeding the university's 2020 goal of growing to between 6,000 and 7,000. Computing, data science and artificial intelligence, and exercise prescription and public health were among new degrees to welcome their first students for the 2021–22 academic year.

A new Health and Wellbeing building features clinical simulation facilities, a working radiography imaging suite and counselling and physiotherapy rooms designed for use by students, practice partners and the community. The Hold, Suffolk's new £20million heritage research centre near Ipswich waterfront, opened in 2020 to house the region's historic treasures alongside learning spaces. Suffolk's new DigiTech Centre at Adastral park opened early in 2021 in a collaboration with BT, with £6.5million funding from the New Anglia Local Enterprise Partnership. Its specialist laboratories support information and communication technology (ICT) and digital creative courses.

The latest Graduate Outcomes survey showed that more than three-quarters of Suffolk graduates were in high-skilled jobs or postgraduate study 15 months after finishing their degrees – taking 41st place in our measure of graduate prospects, up 13 places since 2020.

The improvement is one example of the positive steps taken by Suffolk since

---

Waterfront Building
Neptune Quay
Ipswich IP4 1QJ
01473 338 348
admissions@uos.ac.uk
www.uos.ac.uk
www.uosunion.org
Open days: see website

The Times and The Sunday Times **Rankings**
Overall Ranking: 105 (last year: 122)

Teaching quality	76.1%	=48
Student experience	67.8%	=83
Research quality	n/a	
Entry standards	112	106
Graduate prospects	75.2%	41
Good honours	70.8%	114
Expected completion rate	65%	130
Student/staff ratio	16.5	=77
Services and facilities	£2,788	45

it was awarded bronze in the Teaching Excellence Framework. Assessors said it was "substantially" below its benchmarks for student satisfaction and graduate employment, although they acknowledged the contribution of employers to course design and found a "developing approach to the creation of research and practice-based communities of staff enabling students to benefit by exposure to scholarship, research and professional practice".

The absence of a research rating hampers Suffolk's league table position, because the 2014 Research Excellence Framework predated its establishment as an independent institution.

However, the university's upward trajectory continues in our social inclusion index, where it has entered the top ten. It has filled a higher education gap in the region and works actively to widen participation, engaging with schools and colleges to encourage progression to higher education. The proportion of students from disadvantaged areas is approaching a quarter (only nine universities have more) and Suffolk has achieved the lowest dropout rate in the country among this cohort. More than 77% of Suffolk students are aged over 21 when they enrol and almost six in ten are the first in their family to go to university.

Students from the European Union were offered a bargain deal on degrees for the 2021–22 academic year. Suffolk's EU Scholarship, paying up to £4,590 per year of academic study, is available for new undergraduate and postgraduate students, reducing their costs to pre-Brexit levels. There are also financial awards available to UK and international students.

There are plenty of sports facilities near the campus, though Suffolk does not have its own. The students' union co-ordinates activities for fun and competition. Lots of students live at home and Suffolk's 764 student rooms are usually enough to go round, although there is no formal accommodation guarantee.

Some of England's most beautiful spots, such as Dedham and Flatford in Constable country, are within easy reach of Ipswich for days out. Aldeburgh on the coast boasts award-winning fish and chips – best eaten on the shingle beach with views of the North Sea. The modern Waterfront development around Ipswich's marina is a popular hub of bars and restaurants.

Tuition fees

» Fees for UK students	£9,250
Foundation courses	£8,220
» Fees for International students 2022–23	£12,996–£14,598
» For scholarship and bursary information see www.uos.ac.uk/feesandscholarships	
» Graduate salary	£24,000

Student numbers

Undergraduates	8,320	(590)
Postgraduates	120	(530)
Applications/places		3.975/950
Applications per place		4.2
Overall offer rate		69.1%
International students – EU		9.1%
Non-EU		0.8%

Accommodation
Available places: 590
Self-catered: £90–£180 per week
www.uos.ac.uk/accommodation

Where do the students come from?

State schools (non-grammar)	97.3%	Low participation areas	23.7%	Disabled	5.3%
Grammar schools	1.2%	All ethnic minorities	32.8%	Mature (over 21)	77.1%
Independent schools	1.5%	White working-class males	2.6%		
First generation students	59.2%	Black achievement gap	-30%		

Social inclusion ranking: 7

University of Sunderland

Record numbers of students were admitted to Sunderland in 2020, the first-year undergraduate intake soaring above 4,000, virtually double the number of just three years before. This expansion has happened even as applications have fallen by 48% over the past decade.

The opening of a campus in London, offering business, healthcare, tourism and hospitality courses at undergraduate level, has changed the student demographic considerably, while triggering that sharp expansion in numbers. Just under half the students admitted come from the northeast – the region of England with the lowest participation rates in higher education. But just over a third now come from London, most of whom are not making the trek to the northeast but to Canary Wharf instead.

Sunderland, the University of the Year for Social Inclusion in our previous edition, is one of the leaders in offering university opportunities to those that might not be given them elsewhere. Ranked in the top ten overall in our social inclusion ranking, it sits second for the proportion of students admitted from postcodes with the lowest take-up of higher education, ninth for both the proportion of mature and first-generation students and 17th for the proportion of white working-class males among last year's intake.

The London outpost has helped make Sunderland the most ethnically diverse of the northeast's five universities, with 27.5% of students drawn from ethnic minorities. It works with more than 40 schools in the northeast, targeting middle-achieving children who have the capability but not the motivation to consider higher education. The First Choice Progression Scheme offers sessions to children on access to university, balancing finances, writing a CV, study skills and subject tasters. Successful completion is worth 16 UCAS tariff points.

This commitment to breaking the mould extends to the new School of Medicine which has just admitted its third intake, where one in five of all entrants meet criteria for widening participation. Attracting a socially diverse intake to medicine is a tough nut to crack. Sunderland delivers medical summer schools for year 12 pupils and targets schools in postcodes among the 40% with the lowest participation rates in higher education for outreach work.

One of five new medical schools around the country helping to address regional shortages of doctors and an imbalance of provision, Sunderland has teamed up with Keele University medical school to deliver the curriculum. A new cadaveric anatomy centre helps to train the next generation of medics. And a £1.4million midwifery suite has a full ward and a postnatal and immersive/

Edinburgh Building
City Campus
Chester Road
Sunderland SR1 3SD
0191 515 3000
student.helpline@sunderland.ac.uk
www.sunderland.ac.uk
www.sunderlandsu.co.uk
Open days: see website

The Times and The Sunday Times Rankings
Overall Ranking: 77 (last year: 103)

Teaching quality	79.6%	12
Student experience	74.9%	=17
Research quality	5.8%	=83
Entry standards	116	=91
Graduate prospects	61.8%	=111
Good honours	66.1%	128
Expected completion rate	77.4%	115
Student/staff ratio	15.5	=56
Services and facilities	£3,010	28

wellbeing suite, alongside areas to simulate home-birthing and birthing pool facilities.

All medicine undergraduates are offered free accommodation in their first year and a 50% discount for year two of their five-year course. Further support helps those recruited from homes where income is less than £42,875 per year. Academic scholarships were offered this year to the 130 students across all academic programmes who showed the largest increase in grades between GCSEs and A-level or equivalent qualifications.

The university rises in our academic ranking through excellent results in the pandemic-impacted 2021 National Student Survey (NSS). Where most universities haemorrhaged student satisfaction, just ten saw smaller declines in satisfaction than Sunderland between 2020 and 2021, an outstanding result that has boosted its ranking for teaching quality and student experience into the UK top 20.

Sunderland has a silver rating in the Teaching Excellence Framework. The panel said academic experiences were tailored to the individual, with personalised support available. It also praised the exposure of students to professional practice through engagement with industrial and community partners, and employers' involvement in course development. Partners regionally and nationally include Caterpillar, Sage, Accenture, Northumbria police, Santander, the BBC and South Tyneside and Sunderland NHS Foundation Trust.

There are plans to expand the portfolio of 16 degree apprenticeships with new offerings in occupational health and public health and to launch a postgraduate engineer apprenticeship. New BSc degrees with Qualified Teacher Status cover biology, chemistry, design technology, engineering and computing. Others include professional policing, sport and rehabilitation therapy and modern music industries.

There are two campuses in Sunderland, one in the city centre and the other, the Sir Tom Cowie campus, on the banks of the River Wear, built around a 7th-century abbey described as one of Britain's first universities and incorporating the National Glass Centre.

The city of Sunderland is fiercely proud of its identity and has the advantage of a riverside and coastal location. The city boasts the northeast's only 50m swimming pool and dry ski slope, as well as Europe's biggest climbing wall and a theatre that shows West End productions. A short Metro or bus journey brings the culture and legendary nightlife of Newcastle within reach.

Tuition fees

»	Fees for UK students	£9,250
	Foundation courses	£8,200
»	Fees for International students 2022–23	£13,000
»	For scholarship and bursary information see www.sunderland.ac.uk/about/your-finances/	
»	Graduate salary	£23,000

Student numbers

Undergraduates	11,200	(1,385)
Postgraduates	2,205	(960)
Applications/places	8,460/1,690	
Applications per place	5	
Overall offer rate	70.8%	
International students – EU	7.3%	
Non-EU	11.1%	

Accommodation
University provided places: 1,378
Self-catered: £78–£98 per week
www.sunderland.ac.uk/about/accommodation/

Where do the students come from?

State schools (non-grammar)	95.8%	Low participation areas	28.6%	**Social inclusion ranking: 9**	
Grammar schools	0.7%	All ethnic minorities	27.5%	Disabled	6.3%
Independent schools	3.5%	White working-class males	7.9%	Mature (over 21)	65.3%
First generation students	59.5%	Black achievement gap	-27.1%		

University of Surrey

Professional training placements of up to 12 months are offered on most degree programmes at Surrey, our University of the Year for Graduate Employment. Taken in between the second and third years in the UK or overseas, the placements mean that most Surrey students spend four years at university. New entrants apply for the placements via UCAS as sandwich courses when making their main application to Surrey.

The university has built a network of more than 2,300 national and international businesses where students can learn on the job, including Microsoft, KPMG, the civil service and GlaxoSmithKline. The connections are paying off for Surrey graduates: 81.5% were in high-skilled jobs or postgraduate study 15 months after leaving, the Graduate Outcomes survey found.

Surrey was one of only two UK universities that avoided a decline in student satisfaction levels throughout the pandemic. In our analysis comparing scores in the National Student Survey in 2020 and 2021, it ranks second only to Imperial College London. Surrey drew on the online-learning expertise of its academic staff across different faculties for a hybrid approach to the challenge of Covid-19.

A branded blend of face-to-face and remote online learning – SurreyLearn – was underpinned by the goal of achieving equity of learning opportunities. It aimed to reduce for students the cognitive load involved in navigating teaching delivery methods to free up their focus for learning activities.

Bite-size recorded lectures and entirely online assessment from briefs to submission to feedback, characterised Surrey's successful switch to lockdown-friendly higher education. From the start of the 2021–22 academic year, face-to-face learning and on-campus activities have taken precedence again over online delivery. The positive feedback from students took Surrey up 85 places in our teaching quality ranking and up 73 places for the wider student experience, putting it in the top ten for student satisfaction, where poor scores had dragged down its overall ranking in our league table in previous years.

The university was awarded gold in the Teaching Excellence Framework. A glowing reference from the panel described "innovative and personalised provision", "high levels of teaching excellence" and an effective approach to the development of professional skills and employability".

Beginning life in London in 1891 as Battersea Polytechnic Institute, the university was founded in its current form in Guildford in 1966. The two campuses, Stag Hill and Manor Park, just over a mile apart, are ten minutes' walk from the centre of Guildford.

Senate House
Guildford GU2 7XH
01483 682 222
admissions@surrey.ac.uk
www.surrey.ac.uk
www.ussu.co.uk
Open days: see website

Edinburgh
Belfast
Cardiff London
GUILDFORD

The Times and The Sunday Times Rankings
Overall Ranking: 32 (last year: 39)

Teaching quality	77.1%	35
Student experience	76.3%	=9
Research quality	29.7%	44
Entry standards	136	=46
Graduate prospects	81.5%	13
Good honours	81%	=45
Expected completion rate	89.3%	40
Student/staff ratio	16.7	=80
Services and facilities	£2,809	40

The separate Surrey Research Park is one of the largest in the UK still to be owned, funded and managed by its host university.

About £400million of ongoing investment has brought modern resources. Surrey's £45million School of Veterinary Medicine is expanding its partnership with CVS, one of the UK's largest integrated veterinary service providers, to provide a three-year residency in small animal internal medicine.

The university's £70million 5G Innovation Centre is one of the world's first research centres dedicated to mobile communications and future internet technologies. The £14million Kate Granger building, opened in 2020 at the Research Park, houses the School of Health Sciences and clinical simulation suites to train nurses, midwives, physicians' associates and paramedics.

The upward curve in enrolments in recent years came to a halt in 2020's admissions round, and applications also dipped. Entry standards remain demanding however, and Surrey turns down about four in ten applications.

Surrey, which ranks 11th in the world for hospitality and leisure management in the QS World Rankings 2021, is launching a new degree in professional international hotel management in September 2022. The first applied contemporary theatre students began courses in 2021 and two new law pathways were introduced: law and technology; and philosophy, politics and law.

Almost 80% of the work submitted to the 2014 Research Excellence Framework was assessed as world-leading or internationally excellent. The best results were in nursing and other health subjects. Surrey's research is organised around "grand challenges" such as global wellbeing, sustainable cities and connecting societies and cultures.

More than one-fifth of Surrey's students come from independent or selective grammar schools, so it has one of the lowest intakes from non-selective state schools. It is among the country's more ethnically diverse institutions, with more than a third of students from black, Asian or minority ethnic backgrounds.

The £36million Surrey Sports Park is on the Manor Park campus. Students can earn rewards for keeping active through the SurreyMoves+ app. Extensive facilities – both indoors and outdoors – are up to standard for elite athletes and used by teams including Harlequins rugby union, Surrey Storm netball and Guildford City swimming club.

First-years are guaranteed a place in halls of residence.

Tuition fees

» Fees for UK students	£9,250
» Fees for International students 2022–23	£17,900–£23,100
Veterinary Medicine	£35,500
» For scholarship and bursary information see www.surrey.ac.uk/fees-and-funding	
» Graduate salary	£25,714

Student numbers

Undergraduates	12,990	(495)
Postgraduates	2,725	(780)
Applications/places		29,805/2,595
Applications per place		11.5
Overall offer rate		63.8%
International students – EU		10.5%
Non-EU		13.1%

Accommodation

University provided places: 4,178
Self-catered: £72–£162 per week
First years guaranteed accommodation
www.surrey.ac.uk/accommodation

Where do the students come from?

State schools (non-grammar)	77.5%	Low participation areas	6.8%	Disabled	4.9%
Grammar schools	13.6%	All ethnic minorities	34.6%	Mature (over 21)	11.4%
Independent schools	8.9%	White working-class males	4.3%		
First generation students	41.5%	Black achievement gap	-17.5%		

Social inclusion ranking: 91

University of Sussex

A tactical approach to supporting students from application through to graduation and beyond has contributed to an exemplary record on student retention at Sussex. Based on the social and academic background of the intake, the university's benchmark dropout rate is 10.1%, yet in reality just 5% are projected to do so.

Such success at keeping students is usually the preserve of small institutions, but with more than 14,000 undergraduates Sussex is one of the larger universities – and a worthy winner of our University of the Year for Student Retention award.

Students are more likely to achieve above-average success and progression if they are engaged with university beyond their course, Sussex has found. To that end, its Learn to Transform strategy encourages them to become partners in the big decisions faced by the university.

The idea is to build undergraduates' confidence by boosting their investigative, technical, navigational and employability skills – offering paid summer research opportunities, mentoring and internships. The new Student Connectors initiative creates paid employment for students who work directly with staff to devise improvements to campus life.

At the university's Falmer campus just outside Brighton, which benefits from acres of rolling parkland on the edge of the South Downs National Park and listed Sixties architecture by Sir Basil Spence, a new £28million Student Centre is set to become a focal point, offering easier access to expert services, both digital and in-person.

A four-year project to transform the East Slope student village has tripled bed spaces to almost 2,200. Outdated 1970s digs have been replaced with en-suite bedrooms in terraced townhouses and flats arranged in clusters. There are common rooms and communal laundry rooms, bookable study spaces and secure cycle parking.

These facilities should improve student satisfaction levels, which have held Sussex back in our league table in recent years since its peak in our overall top 20 five years ago. For satisfaction with teaching quality, the university remains outside the top 100, but scores for satisfaction with the wider experience have risen 32 places.

Sussex has been recording lectures for several years and is continuing to do so as on-campus activities resume. In our analysis of National Student Survey satisfaction scores from 2020 and 2021, which indicated how final-year students felt about their university's Covid response, Sussex achieved a top-50 ranking.

The university continues to be driven by

Sussex House
Falmer
Brighton BN1 9RH
01273 876 787
ug.enquiries@sussex.ac.uk
www.sussex.ac.uk
www.sussexstudent.com
Open days: see website

The Times and The Sunday Times **Rankings**
Overall Ranking: 47 (last year: 44)

Teaching quality	71.6%	=110
Student experience	67.7%	85
Research quality	31.8%	=37
Entry standards	136	=46
Graduate prospects	68.2%	=77
Good honours	78.4%	=63
Expected completion rate	92.2%	25
Student/staff ratio	17.4	=94
Services and facilities	£2,450	72

its core values of collaboration, courage, kindness, inclusion and integrity. To address inequality, it has created a new role of pro-vice-chancellor for diversity, culture and inclusion. In the 2021 QS World University Rankings by subject, Sussex topped development studies for the fifth consecutive year.

One of the first organisations to declare a climate emergency in 2019, Sussex's work to help build sustainable cities and communities is reflected in its ninth place in the UK and 41st globally in the 2021 *Times Higher Education* World Impact Rankings, which assess universities against the United Nations Sustainable Development Goals (SDGs).

Sussex gained silver in the Teaching Excellence Framework, winning praise for its "outstanding" employment strategy. Undergraduates are encouraged to take work placements, study abroad and learn a language. They are also able to structure their course with a 75/25% split between major and minor subjects.

There is support for student start-ups, freelance careers and social enterprises via the Sussex Entrepreneurship programme. However, with less than 70% of graduates in high-skilled jobs or postgraduate study 15 months after finishing their degrees, Sussex has suffered a 25-place fall in our graduate prospects measure.

A new degree in banking and digital finance starts in 2022. The business school has an on-site Bloomberg financial markets lab simulating real-time trading.

A successful joint medical school is shared with the neighbouring University of Brighton, and students split their time between the Royal Sussex County Hospital and the two universities' Falmer campuses.

Three-quarters of the work submitted for the 2014 Research Excellence Framework was assessed as world-leading or internationally excellent and Sussex was among the leaders in history, English, psychology and geography.

About 30% of 2021's intake qualified for the Sussex bursary, worth £1,000 in the first year and £500 in subsequent years to those with household income below £25,000.

There are two sports halls, glass-backed squash courts, a well-equipped gym, a dance and martial arts studio and outdoor pitches. Brighton seafront offers volleyball and sand sports and Hove Lagoon hosts watersports.

Sussex has 5,055 residential spaces, almost all on campus – enough to guarantee a room to all first-years. A few minutes away by public transport, Brighton's nightlife, diversity and seafront are hard to beat.

Tuition fees

» Fees for UK students	£9,250
» Fees for International students 2022–23	£18,500–£22,500
Medicine (clinical years)	£37,293
» For scholarship and bursary information see www.sussex.ac.uk/study/fees-funding	
» Graduate salary	£24,000

Student numbers

Undergraduates	14,775	(5)
Postgraduates	3,525	(1,090)
Applications/places	17,780/3,160	
Applications per place	5.6	
Overall offer rate	89.3%	
International students – EU	8.4%	
Non-EU	18%	

Accommodation

University provided places: 5,055
Self-catered: £119–£173 per week
First years guaranteed accommodation
www.sussex.ac.uk/study/accommodation

Where do the students come from?

State schools (non-grammar)	80%	Low participation areas	7.9%	
Grammar schools	9%	All ethnic minorities	26.5%	
Independent schools	11%	White working-class males	4.7%	
First generation students	39.8%	Black achievement gap	-18.7%	

Social inclusion ranking: 86

Disabled	10%
Mature (over 21)	10.7%

Swansea University

Swansea is broadening its curriculum with a range of new courses such as a pharmacy degree, introduced in September 2021. A BSc in environmental science and the climate emergency is also new and, like many of Swansea's degrees, can be taken as a four-year course with a year spent in industry or abroad.

The university is building on its strong record for student satisfaction by developing its assessment and feedback processes – often a bone of contention among undergraduates. It moves into the top 30 this year for satisfaction with teaching quality after a decent performance in this year's National Student Survey, when other institutions found their scores hard hit by fallout from the pandemic.

A five-mile sweeping curve of sandy beach separates the university's original Singleton Park campus from the £450million, 65-acre Bay Campus, which opened in 2015 – doubling the size of the institution. The campus has direct access to the beach, and houses about 1,000 students in its on-site halls of residence.

Swansea celebrated its centenary in 2020. The foundation stone was laid by King George V at Singleton Park and the Prince's Foundation for Building Community, set up by his great-grandson, Prince Charles, helped to develop the Bay Campus. Along the way, developments at the original parkland campus include the Hillary Rodham Clinton School of Law, named after the former US secretary of state who received an honorary doctorate from Swansea in 2017. It has its own courtroom and law clinic.

Swansea was awarded gold in the Teaching Excellence Framework, thanks to its clear employability strategy and strong staff-student partnerships. With three-quarters of graduates in high-skilled jobs within 15 months of finishing their degrees, the university ranks just outside the UK top 40 on our graduate prospects measure. The Swansea Employability Academy provides paid internships and co-ordinates programmes for career development. More than 600 organisations – such as Tata Steel, Pfizer, Fujitsu and Rolls-Royce – advertise roles directly to alumni and provide networking opportunities. Many business partners have research bases at the Bay Campus.

Swansea's guaranteed offer policy promises all UK applicants a conditional offer for its programmes – excluding professional courses. Those who accept, benefit from flexibility with their grades. The university also offers a foundation year to candidates whose predicted grades or educational history indicate they are not ready for the undergraduate course for which they have applied. Other applicants may be offered an alternative course to which they would be better suited.

Applications rose about 3% in 2020 and another 13% by March 2021 compared with

Singleton Park
Swansea SA2 8PP
01792 295 111
admissions@swansea.ac.uk
www.swansea.ac.uk
www.swansea-union.co.uk
Open days: see website

***The Times* and *The Sunday Times* Rankings**

Overall Ranking: 39 (last year: 36)

Teaching quality	77.7%	=28
Student experience	73.5%	28
Research quality	33.7%	35
Entry standards	131	=52
Graduate prospects	82.6%	22
Good honours	80.4%	=52
Expected completion rate	89.4%	39
Student/staff ratio	14.8	=43
Services and facilities	£2,143	98

the same point in the cycle a year before, driven by a nationwide increase in interest in subjects allied to health and medicine. A record number of new students enrolled in 2020, more than one fifth having entered via Clearing. Students who achieve AAA at A-level or equivalent qualify for an excellence scholarship of £1,000 a year for three years. AAB or equivalent grades at A-level merit total scholarship payments of £2,000.

Swansea is continuing to expand its research facilities and is opening a Centre for Integrative Semiconductor Materials in 2022. The £35million Institute for Innovative Materials, Processing and Numerical Technologies (known as Impact) opened in 2019, where industry and academics are collaborating in advanced engineering and materials.

Four-fifths of the work submitted for the 2014 Research Excellence Framework was assessed as world-leading or internationally excellent, with health subjects, English and general engineering getting Swansea's best results.

The £20million Sports Village beside the Singleton campus has an athletics track, grass and all-weather pitches, squash and tennis courts, plus an indoor athletics training centre and 80-station gym. There are 50-metre and 25-metre pools at the Wales National Pool next door. The Bay campus, which has a sports hall, gym and two outdoor multi-use areas, is to gain a new covered multicourt development. At Singleton Park, Hockey Pitch 1 has been resurfaced with the same international-standard material that was used at the Tokyo Olympics.

The university's grass and 3G pitches at Fairfield, five miles away, were built in partnership with Swansea City Football Club. The university also has links with the Ospreys and Scarlets rugby clubs.

Respect, Swansea's educational module developed with the students' union, covers topics such as sexual misconduct and consent, drugs and alcohol. It is mandatory for all students from the 2021–22 academic year.

The students' union hosts more than 150 societies. Swansea offers a lively social scene at wallet-friendly prices. Mumbles seaside resort nearby is also popular for nights out. Further west, the Gower Peninsula has some of the UK's finest beaches including Rhossili and Three Cliffs Bay.

The university has 2,632 residential spaces – enough to guarantee accommodation to all first-years who apply by June 30.

Tuition fees

»	Fees for UK students	£9,000
	Foundation courses	£7,500
»	Fees for International students 2022–23	£15,850–£20,200
	Medicine (clinical years)	£39,750
»	For scholarship and bursary information see	
	www.swansea.ac.uk/undergraduate/fees-and-funding	
»	Graduate salary	£24,000

Student numbers

Undergraduates	15,505	(810)
Postgraduates	2,995	(1,070)
Applications/places	17,870/3,590	
Applications per place	5	
Overall offer rate	80.2%	
International students – EU	4.3%	
Non-EU	9.1%	

Accommodation

University provided places: 2,632
Catered costs: £143–£159 per week
Self-catered: £95–£162 per week
First years guaranteed accommodation
www.swansea.ac.uk/accommodation/

Where do the students come from?

State schools (non-grammar)	90.7%	Low participation areas	11.6%	
Grammar schools	1%	All ethnic minorities	18%	
Independent schools	8.3%	White working-class males	6.9%	
First generation students	36.9%	Black achievement gap	-13.5%	

Social inclusion ranking: =76

Disabled	4.8%
Mature (over 21)	19.7%

University of Teesside

Teesside is our University of the Year for Social Inclusion for the outstanding role it plays in making higher education an option for teenagers in a region with the lowest participation rate in England. More than three-quarters of Teesside's students are recruited from within northeast England, many from its hometown, Middlesbrough.

Ranked fourth in our social inclusion rankings overall, it is one of few institutions to have risen each year of publication since 2018. Behind the overall ranking lies considerable success in individual indicators that target some of the key areas of under-recruitment in most universities. It ranks first in England and Wales for recruitment of students from postcodes with the lowest participation rates in higher education, second for the proportion of admissions drawn from non-selective state schools, has the eighth-highest proportion of white working-class male students, and ranks 15th for the proportion of students whose parents or carers did not attend university.

A high dropout rate is often the price to pay for such diversity in the student body, but Teesside's students are strongly supported in their studies from the outset so that the dropout rate of about one in six students is marginally lower than the expected level.

The university makes wide use of foundation years as a route for students who have grades significantly below the minimum tariff for courses and engages in outreach work in schools and colleges with children from years six to 13 to raise aspirations and dispel myths about higher education. If they ask: "Will there be students like me?" the answer, at Teesside, is usually "yes".

Levelling up is assisted by the Teesside University Advance scheme, which provides all students beginning a full-time undergraduate degree with a new iPad and separate keyboard, and up to £300 of credits to purchase learning resources.

This makes a slump in student satisfaction more surprising. In our comparison of National Student Survey scores in 2020 and 2021 only four universities fell further as students reacted to their institution's response to the pandemic. Teesside fell 70 places for satisfaction with teaching quality and 66 places for satisfaction with the wider student experience, which largely explains its 26-place slump in our academic ranking this year.

Poor satisfaction scores are partly attributed to the high proportion of healthcare students among the responding cohort of final-year undergraduates. The loss of placements at hospitals and medical practices during the pandemic will have impacted their experience far more than those taking classroom-based subjects.

Middlesbrough
TS1 3BX
01642 218 121
enquiries@tees.ac.uk
www.tees.ac.uk
www.tees-su.org.uk
Open days: see website

The Times and *The Sunday Times* Rankings		
Overall Ranking: 118 (last year: 92)		
Teaching quality	72.1%	=102
Student experience	63.9%	=118
Research quality	3.6%	110
Entry standards	115	=96
Graduate prospects	74.1%	48
Good honours	74.2%	99
Expected completion rate	75.6%	121
Student/staff ratio	17.9	102
Services and facilities	£2,781	=46

A strong culture of partnership with students was acclaimed by the Teaching Excellence Framework, which awarded Teesside silver. Assessors were also impressed by innovative and well-resourced support for developing employability. Our analysis of the latest Graduate Outcomes figures places Teesside in the top 50 in the UK for the second successive year for its proportion of students in high-skilled jobs or further study 15 months after completing their course.

Teesside has a programme of more than 200 internships each year and industry mentor schemes are a feature of initiatives such as Advantage Tees Valley, supporting students from disadvantaged backgrounds to get graduate-level jobs locally. Digital technology continues to be central to the jobs strategy. The start-up centre Teesside Launchpad, which has fledged 25 fast-growing tech companies, has been refurbished and includes games studios, business units and hot-desk space.

Job-specific and vocational degree programmes also help to keep graduate employment rates on track. New courses available from September 2021 cover games development, software engineering, automation and digital engineering, business and data analytics, events management and supply chain management. There are also several new nursing studies degrees with specialisms.

There are plans to increase the number of higher and degree apprenticeship students from 1,250 to 2,000 by September 2022. Course options include business, computing, engineering, forensic science, life and physical sciences, nursing, midwifery and the health professions.

A £275million investment programme has brought improvements to the campus. The most recent addition, the Student Life building, amalgamates support services alongside social spaces and a digital learning hub.

The £21million Cornell Quarter for student residences has been completed and will house 300 students, increasing the accommodation stock by nearly a third to about 1,300 places – an important step towards broadening Teesside's appeal beyond the local region it serves so well.

Sports facilities are available on and off campus. The Olympia sports complex on campus incorporates a sports hall with capacity for 500 spectators, a climbing wall and gym. The Saltersgill Pavilion, two miles away, has four rugby union pitches, and the university is a stakeholder in the River Tees Watersports Centre offering waterskiing, rowing, kayaking, white water rafting and canoeing around the Tees barrage, four miles from campus.

Tuition fees

»	Fees for UK students	£9,250
	Foundation courses	£6,150
»	Fees for International students 2022–23	£13,000
»	For scholarship and bursary information see www.tees.ac.uk/sections/fulltime/fees.cfm	
»	Graduate salary	£24,000

Student numbers

Undergraduates	10,225 (5,250)
Postgraduates	2,390 (1,425)
Applications/places	11,800/2,850
Applications per place	4.1
Overall offer rate	74.3%
International students – EU	1.1%
Non-EU	5.1%

Accommodation
University provided places: 1,300
Self-catered: £65–£125 per week
www.tees.ac.uk/sections/accommodation

Where do the students come from?

State schools (non-grammar)	98.6%	Low participation areas	31%	Disabled	10.2%
Grammar schools	0.5%	All ethnic minorities	12.5%	Mature (over 21)	44.8%
Independent schools	0.9%	White working-class males	10.5%		
First generation students	57.2%	Black achievement gap	-20.3%		

Social inclusion ranking: 4

University of Wales, Trinity St David

Prioritising the opening of its key facilities as soon as safely possible post-lockdown, the University of Wales Trinity St David (UWTSD) ensured that students had access to resources such as art studios and the Advanced Manufacturing academy, based at its SA1 waterfront campus in Swansea. On-track testing facilities for UWTSD's motorsport engineering students were also among the first to reopen.

UWTSD enjoys a strong record on student satisfaction in the National Student Survey (NSS) and has done well to rank 13th nationally for teaching quality this year under the challenging conditions of the pandemic. Alongside personalised on-campus experiences, remote learning is continuing to be a key component of undergraduate course delivery. Access to remote learning provides a level of flexibility and inclusivity that is valued by UWTSD's students, says the university, hence digital provision – as part of a blended model – is here to stay.

Created in its present form by the 2010 merger of Trinity University College Carmarthen with University of Wales Lampeter, the multicampus university is based in Carmarthen, Lampeter, Swansea and Cardiff after a subsequent absorption of Swansea Metropolitan University in 2013. A campus in London opened in 2012, where courses in computing, business management, accounting, and health and social care are offered. There are about 10,000 students spread across its bases.

The original Lampeter institution is the third-oldest university in England and Wales after Cambridge and Oxford – with an original royal charter, as St David's College, dating from 1822. Occupying an ancient castle and modelled on an Oxbridge college, the Lampeter campus offers subjects including anthropology, archaeology and medieval studies.

UWTSD's success in our social inclusion survey enables it to break into the top ten in England and Wales for the first time. Almost all, 98%, of students attended non-selective state schools. The university has the sixth-highest proportion of disabled students, 14%, and two-thirds of undergraduates are aged over-21 – only seven universities have more mature students.

The Carmarthen site, established in 1848 to train teachers, offers programmes in the creative and performing arts, as well as a growing portfolio within the school of sport, health and outdoor education. A mile from the campus, is the refurbished centre for outdoor education on the Wales Coast Path at Cynefin, which offers direct access to the River Towy, its own bushcraft, campsite and bike track.

The original Swansea campus began as a college of art, but its automotive engineering courses – especially those focused on motorsport – have become its best-known. Automotive

Carmarthen Campus
College Road
Carmarthen SA31 3EP
0300 500 5054
admissions@uwtsd.ac.uk
www.uwtsd.ac.uk
www.tsdsu.co.uk
Open days: see website

***The Times and The Sunday Times* Rankings**
Overall Ranking: =83 (last year: =101)

Teaching quality	79.5%	13
Student experience	70%	=60
Research quality	2.6%	116
Entry standards	136	=46
Graduate prospects	60.7%	118
Good honours	74.4%	=96
Expected completion rate	78.8%	107
Student/staff ratio	18.8	=112
Services and facilities	£2,153	95

engineering students work as part of a race team involved in UK events, using an on-campus simulator for big data analysis that feeds into the vehicle design for on-track testing. The university has good links with Aston Martin, Jaguar Land Rover and McLaren Automotive.

The Construction Wales Innovation Centre is another feature of the Swansea campus. It provides laser measurement and surveying equipment for hands-on learning, offering students the use of cutting-edge technologies, including virtual reality construction applications and drones.

UWTSD was one of six Welsh universities to enter the Teaching Excellence Framework (TEF) in 2017. An initial bronze rating was upgraded to silver in 2019, with the panel praising "optimal" contact time, leading to outstanding personalised provision.

The TEF panel also drew attention to UWTSD's lower-than-expected performance on graduate prospects. The latest Graduate Outcomes data shows an improvement on last year's figures – with just under 61% of graduates in high-skilled employment or postgraduate study 15 months after the end of their course, lifting the university just above the bottom ten.

The university's new Graduate Attributes Framework may help further improve professional outcomes for students. Modules are designed to develop career-focused skills such as digital competency, research and project management. The framework also teaches personal competencies including communication, creativity, self-reflection, resilience and problem-solving.

An upturn in the numbers choosing postgraduate courses should also start to trickle through in the near future, thanks to the £3,000 scholarships that UWTSD began offering as master's tuition fee discounts last year.

UWTSD had 825 degree apprentices on 14 programmes, at last count, across fields that include engineering, policing, computing, archaeological practice, and materials science. Growth is planned for the earn-while-you-learn stable of courses, and the university expects 1,000 degree apprentices by September 2022.

First-years are guaranteed accommodation. Sports facilities are available at the Carmarthen, Lampeter and Swansea campuses, offering plenty of indoor and outdoor facilities. A 40ft climbing wall at Carmarthen is a good place to practice before students scale the nearby crags of Pembrokeshire.

Swansea offers the big-city university experience; Lampeter and Carmarthen something more intimate and niche.

Tuition fees

» Fees for UK students	£9,000
» Fees for International students 2022–23	£13,500
Foundation courses	£10,250
» For scholarship and bursary information see www.uwtsd.ac.uk/student-finance/	
» Graduate salary	£20,000

Student numbers

Undergraduates	9,145	(1,535)
Postgraduates	1,100	(920)
Applications/places		3,040/845
Applications per place		3.6
Overall offer rate		87.4%
International students – EU		2.7%
Non-EU		1.2%

Accommodation

University provided places: 641
Self-catered: £75–£140 per week
www.uwtsd.ac.uk/accommodation

Where do the students come from?

State schools (non-grammar)	98%	Low participation areas	13.6%	Social inclusion ranking: 8	
Grammar schools	0.4%	All ethnic minorities	6.5%	Disabled	14.2%
Independent schools	1.6%	White working-class males	5.9%	Mature (over 21)	66.6%
First generation students	45.9%	Black achievement gap	-12.2%		

Ulster University

Ulster has notched up its best performance yet in our league table and was shortlisted for our University of the Year 2022 award. Its expanded campus in Belfast's Cathedral Quarter marks a new chapter for the university, as well as for the city's regeneration, as one of the largest single-site higher education developments in Europe. Such ambition has come at a cost – reportedly almost £364million, more than 40% over budget.

The campus has 75,000 square metres of digitally smart and socially connected academic and leisure space – enough to accommodate more than 15,500 students and staff, whose relocation from the Jordanstown campus seven miles north of Belfast is due to be completed in 2022.

Ulster had one of the 20 strongest performances in this year's pandemic-affected National Student Survey, boosting its rankings for teaching quality and student experience into the UK top 30 in both instances. Elements of remote learning have long been part of Ulster's teaching and learning, but the highly anticipated new campus will precipitate the return to increased face-to-face learning.

At Ulster's Magee campus in Derry, refurbishments are underway to provide specialist facilities for the new medical school. The launch of a graduate-entry medicine degree has boosted applications to Ulster this year. Run in partnership with St George's, University of London, the four-year MBBS programme is open to graduates from science and non-science backgrounds and is intended to fulfil a shortfall of doctors in Northern Ireland.

Adding to provision for health-related courses at Magee, a nursing and paramedic skills suite has been developed, catering for the increase in nursing students and for students on the new paramedic science degree which launched in 2021. By September 2022 the School of Health Science will have entirely relocated its undergraduate programmes to Magee – bringing 800 students – after the closure of most provision at the Jordanstown site.

Degrees in marine science, education with digital learning, and international business also join the roster from 2022. Fourteen degree apprenticeship programmes are offered within areas such as design and innovation, accountancy and finance, built environment, business studies, civil engineering, computing, health science and management.

Ulster's degree programmes often feature a work-based learning component. More than 2,000 students annually undertake a professional practice placement or a placement year, and employers are engaged in the design and delivery of many courses. The Go Global scheme offers the chance to study, work or

Cromore Road
Coleraine BT52 18A
028 9036 6565
study@ulster.ac.uk
www.ulster.ac.uk
http://uusu.org
Open days: see website

COLERAINE   Edinburgh

Belfast

London

Cardiff

The Times and The Sunday Times Rankings
Overall Ranking: 44 (last year: =51)

Teaching quality	77.7%	=28
Student experience	74.6%	19
Research quality	31.8%	=37
Entry standards	126	=60
Graduate prospects	72.1%	57
Good honours	80.9%	=47
Expected completion rate	87.1%	53
Student/staff ratio	18.9	=114
Services and facilities	£2,792	44

volunteer abroad. A Global Mobility team and Study Abroad Tutor network can help match students to vacancies and academic opportunities.

Such efforts are reflected in Ulster ranking in the top half of our graduate prospects measure, with more than 72% of graduates in high-skilled jobs or postgraduate study 15 months after finishing their degrees.

Northern Ireland's emergence as a leading film and television centre has inspired many students, who gain insight into the industry at a £6.5million media centre opened four years ago at Coleraine on the Atlantic coast. It has a BBC television studio at its heart, with a multimedia newsroom and editing suites. Screen production facilities are being boosted at the Belfast campus, too, where a cinema screening room, virtual production studio, green room and editing suite are being added.

The Centre for Molecular Biosciences, at Coleraine, produced the university's most highly rated work in the 2014 Research Excellence Framework. More than 70% of Ulster's submission was considered world-leading or internationally excellent, notably in law, nursing and health science.

Almost all undergraduates are from state schools, but the university does not feature in our social inclusion ranking because the education system in Northern Ireland is radically different from the rest of the UK, with selective grammar schools making up a significant proportion of state secondary schools. Our ranking measures recruitment from non-selective state schools, a figure that is unduly depressed at Ulster and Queen's, Belfast.

Outreach programmes encompass summer schools, lectures, laboratory experiments, workshops and school visits. The university's Tutoring in Schools initiative places hundreds of student volunteers annually in primary, post-primary and special needs schools in disadvantaged areas.

The High Performance Sports Centre, which houses the Sports Institute of Northern Ireland, will stay in Jordanstown. It is next in line for a multimillion-pound extension to accommodate sports clubs and academic activities. Cameras have been installed in the sports hall and three outdoor pitches, enabling performance analysis and live-streamed matches. Jordanstown's outdoor and indoor sprint tracks, sports science and sports medicine facilities remain available to students.

A place in one of the university's 2,125 rooms is guaranteed for all first-year students who apply by the deadline.

Tuition fees

» Fees for Northern Irish students	£4,530
RUK fees	£9,250
» Fees for International students 2022–23	£15,360–£17,200
» For scholarship and bursary information see www.ulster.ac.uk/student/fees-and-funding	
» Graduate salary	£22,000

Student numbers

Undergraduates	14,865 (6,000)
Postgraduates	2,540 (4,275)
Applications/places	28,475/5,435
Applications per place	5.2
Overall offer rate	82.3%
International students – EU	3.5%
Non-EU	14.6%

Accommodation

University provided places: 2,125
Self-catered: £83–£133 per week
First years guaranteed accommodation
www.ulster.ac.uk/accommodation

Where do the students come from?

State schools (non-grammar)	59.1%	Low participation areas	9.5%	Social inclusion ranking: n/a	
Grammar schools	40.7%	All ethnic minorities	2.9%	Disabled	n/a
Independent schools	0.2%	White working-class males	n/a	Mature (over 21)	23.9%
First generation students	45.2%	Black achievement gap	n/a		

University College London

Students joining University College London (UCL) for the 2022–23 academic year will be among the first to populate its ambitious UCL East campus in Stratford. The phased opening of the 50,000 square-metre site, based at Queen Elizabeth Olympic Park, begins in spring 2022.

The design is guided by the principle of collaboration, with spaces where academics, students, local communities and industry can put their heads together in an open culture. UCL East will house up to 4,000 students who will live and study in one location.

UCL is determined that the new campus will break down the barriers that have limited the traditional university model, by making faculties distinct and keeping apart its teaching and learning operations from its research side. About 260 staff will be based at UCL East specialising in engineering, architecture, arts, humanities, social sciences, life sciences and population health studies, and there will be opportunities for those from different disciplines to work together. From London St Pancras station, close to UCL's main Bloomsbury campus, trains to nearby Stratford International take an average of just seven minutes.

The university is developing 60 new degree programmes with an accent on "learning by doing" as part of its drive to give students the right skills for the "fourth industrial revolution" by building on overlapping physical, digital and biological advances. New degrees in media, global humanitarian studies and experimental linguistics have been introduced for 2021–22.

This new chapter in the history of UCL, founded in 1826, comes after a strong year for the university. It has climbed two places in the 2022 QS World University Rankings to =8th. With 30 Nobel laureates among its staff and graduates, immense strength in research stimulates undergraduate life. Every student gets the opportunity to engage in research as part of the connected curriculum framework.

In the 2014 Research Excellence Framework UCL had the most world-leading research in medicine and the biological sciences, the largest volume of research in science, technology, engineering and maths, and the biggest share of top grades in the social sciences.

UCL has tended to have by far the largest contingent of European students in the UK (more than 5,000 in 2018–19) but, in spite of Brexit, applications rose almost 7% in 2020 to nearly 59,000. They rose another 16% by the end of March 2021, compared with the same point in the cycle a year earlier. There is stiff competition for places and UCL requires a foreign language (or British sign language) at grade C or above at GCSE. However,

Gower Street
London WC1E 6BT
020 8059 0939
undergraduate-admissions
@ucl.ac.uk
www.ucl.ac.uk
http://studentsunionucl.org
Open days: see website

The Times and The Sunday Times **Rankings**
Overall Ranking: 7 (last year: 8)

Teaching quality	72.8%	=90
Student experience	69.9%	=62
Research quality	51.0%	5
Entry standards	177	=10
Graduate prospects	85.3%	9
Good honours	92.6%	5
Expected completion rate	94.3%	12
Student/staff ratio	10.1	=1
Services and facilities	£2,961	32

students who did not take a language at school are allowed to reach this standard during their degree instead.

The medical school, with several associated teaching hospitals, is among the largest in Europe. UCL was a founding partner in the Francis Crick Institute (named after one of its Nobel laureates), which undertakes research in health and disease and became one of London's leading Covid-19 vaccine centres.

Early in the pandemic, engineers and clinicians from UCL, University College Hospital and Mercedes AMG HPP came together to rapidly develop and manufacture the CPap Ventura breathing aid for seriously ill Covid-19 patients. The device is now being used in more than 115 hospitals in the UK and the design and manufacturing instructions have been distributed to more than 100 countries.

Comfortably the biggest of the University of London's colleges, UCL opened a new student centre in 2019 with 1,000 extra study places, as well as areas for group collaboration. UCL's Institute of Education has also been refurbished.

UCL ranks a respectable 29th (and eighth among Russell Group universities) in our analysis of student satisfaction over its Covid response, based on a comparison of scores in the National Student Survey in 2020 and 2021. It is delivering a blended model of online and in-person teaching for 2021–22.

With a student population that is one of the most ethnically diverse in the country, UCL also has the eighth lowest black achievement gap of any UK university. On our other measures of social inclusion, however, it fares less well. Just over half of its students are from selective state secondaries or independent schools – the latter accounting for more than one-third, one of the highest proportions. Only a quarter of entrants are the first in their family to go to university. UCL runs summer schools, outreach activities and campus programmes to try to make its intake more diverse.

Close to the West End and with its own theatre and recreational facilities, UCL offers plenty of things to do during down time. More than 7,000 residential places are owned or endorsed, enough to guarantee accommodation for first-years. Indoor sports and fitness facilities are close at hand, but the main outdoor pitches are a (free) coach ride away in Hertfordshire.

Tuition fees

» Fees for UK students	£9,250
» Fees for International students 2022–23	£24,000–£35,100
Medicine (clinical years)	£43,733
» For scholarship and bursary information see	
www.ucl.ac.uk/students/fees-and-funding	
» Graduate salary	£30,000

Student numbers

Undergraduates	19,140	(575)
Postgraduates	15,805	(5,575)
Applications/places		58,690/7,550
Applications per place		7.8
Overall offer rate		56.6%
International students – EU		15.2%
Non-EU		36.2%

Accommodation

University provided places: 7,251
Catered costs: £193–£284 per week
Self-catered: £131–£397 per week
First years guaranteed accommodation
www.ucl.ac.uk/accommodation

Where do the students come from?

State schools (non-grammar)	50.6%	Low participation areas	3.8%	Disabled	4.5%
Grammar schools	16.7%	All ethnic minorities	55.5%	Mature (over 21)	8%
Independent schools	32.7%	White working-class males	1.7%		
First generation students	26.7%	Black achievement gap	-5.9%		

Social inclusion ranking: 100

University of Warwick

Winner of our University of the Year for Teaching Quality award, Warwick has never been outside the top ten in our academic ranking and moves up two places this year. It landed our teaching prize, along with being runner-up for University of the Year, thanks to strong student endorsement of its Covid response, expressed through this year's National Student Survey (NSS). Among Russell Group institutions, only Imperial College London did better in a comparison of this year's NSS outcomes with last.

Actively engaging students in co-creating new ways of learning was key to its successful rollout of blended and online learning, the university has said, alongside clear and consistent communication, an area that hampers many universities.

Developments continued through the pandemic, most notably the eight-storey Faculty of Arts, which makes a statement at the heart of Warwick's 750-acre site. This £57.5million landmark offers spaces for study, collaborative work, teaching and socialising.

Specialist facilities cater for the different arts and humanities departments housed here. Among them is an antiquities room for classics and ancient history, creative writing and film screening rooms, theatre studios, a media lab and an edit suite.

Another arts-focused project – the expansion of Warwick Arts Centre – was completed in 2021. The space now includes a concert hall, theatre and café. Its opening coincided with nearby Coventry's investiture as European City of Culture. (The market town of Warwick is a longer seven-mile journey from the university's campus, despite its name.)

Research-led since its foundation in 1965, Warwick places 61st in the 2022 QS World Rankings. Space to bring together 300 biomedical researchers has been added on campus at the £50million Interdisciplinary Biomedical Research Building. Here, academics from the School of Life Sciences and Medical School are helping to research and advance human health and fight disease.

Almost 90% of the work submitted for the 2014 Research Excellence Framework was rated as world-leading or internationally excellent, confirming Warwick's place among the top eight universities for research. English and computer science produced the best results, and Warwick ranked in the top ten in 14 subject areas.

The university's large business school has a London base in the Shard, which delivers part-time programmes. Further afield, Warwick partners with universities across Europe, North America, South America, Australasia and east Asia to offer study abroad opportunities for

Admissions Office
University House
Coventry CV4 8UW
024 7652 3723
ugadmissions@warwick.ac.uk
www.warwick.ac.uk
www.warwicksu.com
Open days: see website

The Times and The Sunday Times **Rankings**
Overall Ranking: 8 (last year: =10)

Teaching quality	78.5%	16
Student experience	74.5%	=20
Research quality	44.6%	8
Entry standards	169	14
Graduate prospects	85.4%	8
Good honours	87.8%	16
Expected completion rate	95.1%	9
Student/staff ratio	12.8	=9
Services and facilities	£2,649	56

undergraduates depending on discipline.

Global sustainable development students spend part of their second year at Monash University – either in Melbourne, Australia, or Kuala Lumpur, in Malaysia. The history department takes students to Venice in a partnership with the University of Venice Ca'Foscari, that gives access to its libraries and other facilities. Students' immersion in Venetian life is encouraged by a buddy scheme with University of Venice students.

Warwick's portfolio of degree apprenticeships is growing, with a new programme for electro-mechanical engineers in place and four more from September 2022 for environmental practitioners, research scientists, coaching professionals and career development professionals.

More than 85% of Warwick's graduates were in high-skilled jobs or postgraduate study within 15 months of completing their degrees, the latest figures showed, ranking it eighth in our graduate prospects measure. It is also among the top six recruiting grounds in the *Times* Top 100 Graduate Employers survey.

In the government's 2017 Teaching Excellence Framework (TEF), though, Warwick was restricted to silver, in spite of consistent high achievement by its students and staff, excellent completion and employment rates and exceptional employer feedback – criteria usually suitable for a gold award.

The TEF panel was impressed by the culture of research-stimulated learning, but said Warwick had missed its benchmarks for student satisfaction and continuation rates among some groups. It is in our top ten for completion rates, however, with just 3% of students dropping out.

Warwick has edged inside the top 100 of our social inclusion ranking this year, its position boosted by a narrowing black achievement gap and an ethnically diverse intake of students. Its proportion of students recruited from independent or selective state grammar schools is one of the highest in the country, however.

A £49million sports and wellness hub includes a 230-station gym, a 25m swimming pool, fitness studios, bouldering and climbing walls, a sports hall, and 4G outdoor pitches.

First-years are guaranteed accommodation. The university aims to house them on campus where it has more than 7,000 spaces. It also manages 1,883 rooms off site. The new Cryfield Village campus residences round off a £62million investment in student accommodation that has added 830 rooms.

Tuition fees

»	Fees for UK students	£9,250
	Foundation courses	£6,750
»	Fees for International students 2022–23	£22,280–£28,410
	Medicine (clinical years)	£25,997–£45,326
»	For scholarship and bursary information see	
	www.warwick.ac.uk/services/wss/studentfunding/funding	
»	Graduate salary	£29,000

Student numbers

Undergraduates	16,315 (1,320)
Postgraduates	6,340 (2,850)
Applications/places	42,840/5,955
Applications per place	7.2
Overall offer rate	68.7%
International students – EU	12.1%
Non-EU	17.3%

Accommodation

University provided places: 7,076
Self-catered: £77–£198 per week
First years guaranteed accommodation
www.warwick.ac.uk/services/accommodation/

Where do the students come from?

State schools (non-grammar)	62.4%	Low participation areas	6.6%	**Social inclusion ranking: 99**	
Grammar schools	17.9%	All ethnic minorities	42.5%	Disabled	5.7%
Independent schools	19.7%	White working-class males	3.2%	Mature (over 21)	9%
First generation students	31.2%	Black achievement gap	-11.2%		

University of West London

Continuing to go all-out to enhance the student experience, the University of West London (UWL) has developed a new leisure centre in partnership with two local councils. Located in Gunnersbury Park, near UWL's Ealing campus, its gym has more than 100 machines and outdoor facilities span eight tennis courts, two all-weather floodlit pitches and ten grass pitches for football, rugby and cricket. Students began using the new centre in April 2021.

UWL's successful focus on supporting students earned it top five scores for teaching quality and the wider experience in last year's National Student Survey (NSS) – and our University of the Year for Student Experience award. The Street on campus houses student-facing services including careers support, counselling and wellbeing advice, which can now be accessed via an online booking system.

The university rolled out its UWLFlex blended on-campus and online learning approach in 2020, with bespoke content and tools designed to ensure a seamless interface between in-person and virtual learning environments. It also brought in one-to-one online sessions for careers support, counselling and wellbeing advice.

Even after the pandemic dip in student satisfaction, as experienced by most institutions, UWL still retains a top ten ranking in our measure for satisfaction with teaching quality and is in the top 20 for student experience.

Students have returned to UWL's specialist learning facilities, which are designed to prepare graduates for the world of work. Among them are a Boeing 737 flight simulator, a mock courtroom and replica hospital wards.

The new School of Biomedical Sciences opened last year – in line with UWL's research strategy: "today's problems, tomorrow's solutions". It has benefited from £1.5million of investment in specialist laboratories to aid teaching in areas such as genetics, immunology, pharmacology, bioinformatics and molecular biology.

At UWL's Brentford campus, the Paragon Building is the headquarters of one of the largest healthcare faculties in Britain. The university also has a Reading outpost, the Berkshire Institute of Health, for nursing and midwifery students.

UWL achieved silver in the government's Teaching Excellence Framework (TEF). The panel complimented the university on its investment in high-quality physical and digital resources, with students fully involved in the design of the new facilities.

Applications increased by 11% in the 2020 admissions round and had increased by a further 17% by the end of March in the

St Mary's Road
Ealing
London W5 5RF
0208 231 2220
admissions@uwl.ac.uk
www.uwl.ac.uk
www.uwlsu.com
Open days: see website

Edinburgh
Belfast
Cardiff
LONDON

The Times and The Sunday Times Rankings
Overall Ranking: 74 (last year: =60)

Teaching quality	80.3%	9
Student experience	75.5%	14
Research quality	1.6%	122
Entry standards	117	=85
Graduate prospects	62.4%	109
Good honours	78.8%	=57
Expected completion rate	77.5%	=113
Student/staff ratio	15.9	=68
Services and facilities	£2,526	66

2021 cycle. UWL's first quantity surveying students began courses in September 2021, as did those on the new biological sciences degree. Applications are open for degrees in data science, biomedical engineering, and biochemistry – which launch in September 2022.

The latest figures showed that more than 62% of UWL graduates were in high-skilled work or postgraduate study 15 months after finishing their degree – placing it outside the top 100 of our graduate prospects measure. Helping to lift these figures, graduates are given lifelong access to UWL's careers service, which offers placement opportunities, industry workshops and careers counselling.

UWL works with local schools to raise aspirations and attainment, offering activities such as Saturday clubs in art and design, while its UWL in the Community scheme delivers key skills to mature learners. The success of such efforts is evidenced by the university's top ten ranking in our social inclusion table. More than two-thirds of undergraduates are from ethnic minority backgrounds and just under six in ten are aged over 21 when they enrol. More than a third of the university's academic staff are also from black and ethnic minority backgrounds.

Around half of full-time students qualify for some form of financial assistance. Provision includes 400 undergraduate bursaries of £500 per year of study to students from low-income households. Path to Success

scholarships help those taking a four-year degree with a foundation year. Aspire cards provide £200 funds for use in the online student shop (£100 for part-time students), and core textbooks.

Working to develop its research profile UWL has opened three new research centres. The Geller Institute of Ageing and Memory focuses on improving the quality of life for older adults and those affected by dementia. The Centre for Levelling Up addresses diversity and equality in education – building on UWL's partnership with the Social Mobility Pledge. A new Institute for Policing Studies is bringing together UWL's extensive activity in professional police training with research into shaping policing across the world.

As well as the new sporting development at Gunnersbury Park, UWL has an on-campus sports centre with two gyms, two large fitness studios and plenty of changing-room space.

As most students live out the 456 university endorsed or managed rooms provide enough space for all first-years to be guaranteed a spot.

Tuition fees

» Fees for UK students	£9,250
» Fees for International students 2022–23	£13,250
» For scholarship and bursary information see www.uwl.ac.uk/study/undergraduate-study/ fees-and-funding-undergraduates	
» Graduate salary	£24,500

Student numbers

Undergraduates	8,910	(905)
Postgraduates	1,220	(955)
Applications/places	14,070/1,780	
Applications per place	7.9	
Overall offer rate	59.9%	
International students – EU	12.1%	
Non-EU	8.1%	

Accommodation

University provided places: 456
Self-catered: £161–£290 per week
www.uwl.ac.uk/student-life/accommodation

Where do the students come from?

State schools (non-grammar)	94.9%	Low participation areas	7.2%	**Social inclusion ranking: =10**		
Grammar schools	0.6%	All ethnic minorities	66.7%	Disabled	8.5%
Independent schools	4.4%	White working-class males	3.1%	Mature (over 21)	57.6%
First generation students	53.2%	Black achievement gap	-21.5%		

University of the West of England Bristol

Specialist teaching and learning spaces populate UWE Bristol's Frenchay, City and Glenside campuses – complementing the university's practice-based curriculum. A recent addition, the Engineering Building brings the different engineering disciplines to life for students in its workshops, laboratories and digital facilities and enables them to tackle real-world problems via live industry briefs.

Boosting work-ready skills for its graduates is central to activities at UWE Bristol, which has one of the largest internship programmes at any university. In a recent snapshot of activity the scheme had almost 11,000 contacts registered across 5,800 organisations and was advertising 370 vacancies.

Student consultancy projects are a growing arm of the internship programme. Reimagined for 2020's pandemic landscape, the scheme partnered with Santander Universities to offer undergraduates and graduates fully-funded eight-week opportunities with local employers – who could not have employed an intern at the time without the university's support. Such efforts translate into a better than average showing in our graduate prospects ranking with three-quarters of students in high-skilled work or graduate-level study within 15 months of leaving.

After stellar results in the National Student Survey (NSS) in our *Guide's* previous edition (when UWE Bristol finished sixth for students' satisfaction with the wider undergraduate experience and 13th for their assessment of teaching quality), there was one of the sharpest downturns during the pandemic year – although scores for both NSS-derived rankings in our table still remain within the UK top 50. The university created more outdoor covered spaces so that students could connect socially and safely during the pandemic and added outside catering outlets. The return to hands-on learning should help to restore satisfaction levels.

The university received a gold rating in the government's Teaching Excellence Framework (TEF). The panel noted the above-benchmark levels of student satisfaction with academic support and rates of progression to high-skilled employment. TEF assessors also commended UWE Bristol's outstanding learning resources at institutional and subject-specific levels, the systematic embedding of enterprise and entrepreneurship throughout curricula, and successful approaches to personalised learning. Student representation at all levels of the institution was found to be comprehensive.

The City campus in Bower Ashton benefits from modern design studios added as part of a £37million investment in facilities for creative industries. Featuring flexible workshops and collaborative learning areas, they also house the Fabrication Centre and the Centre for Fine Print Research.

Frenchay Campus
Coldharbour Lane
Bristol BS16 1QY
0117 328 3333
admissions@uwe.ac.uk
www.uwe.ac.uk
www.thestudentsunion.co.uk
Open days: see website

The Times and The Sunday Times Rankings
Overall Ranking: 73 (last year: 58)

Teaching quality	76.4%	=43
Student experience	70.9%	50
Research quality	8.8%	69
Entry standards	123	=67
Graduate prospects	74.2%	47
Good honours	75.6%	90
Expected completion rate	82%	=84
Student/staff ratio	15.8	=65
Services and facilities	£1,888	113

The £5million optometry and clinical skills centre on the Glenside campus is housed in a grade II listed former NHS laundry. It is now the base for trainee paramedics, occupational therapy students and nurses as well as undergraduates on the optometry programme.

A newly refurbished learning space featuring a simulated crime scene was in place for the second cohort of police constable degree apprentices at the Frenchay campus in 2021. The university offers a further 19 degree apprenticeships with more than 1,640 learners on programmes in fields including healthcare science, town planning, architecture, advanced clinical practice. Nursing (adult) launched as a degree apprenticeship in 2021.

More than 60% of the work submitted for assessment in the 2014 Research Excellence Framework was rated as world-leading or internationally excellent. Health subjects and communication and media studies produced the best results.

Funding from Research England has boosted facilities at the Centre for Fine Print Research, allowing the university to increase its work in transformative technologies for practice-led design; innovative print techniques (reconstructing historic reprographic methods); novel print processes and materials for physical and tactile surfaces.

UWE Bristol ranks in the lower half of our social inclusion table, but only just. More than 91% of students come from non-selective state schools and the university succeeds in recruiting one of the higher proportions of working-class white male students.

About a third of a year's intake usually qualifies for some form of financial assistance from the university. The UWE Bursary of £500 per year benefits low-income students, boosted to £1,500 per year for care leavers, those with caring responsibilities or those estranged from their families.

The Frenchay campus has fitness suites next to student residences as well as a sports hall, indoor climbing wall, squash courts and an all-weather pitch. Sports teams including soccer, American football and rugby are based at the £4.5million Hillside Gardens facility a few miles away, which has artificial and grass pitches and undercover spectator seating.

Frenchay is gaining an extra 2,250 student bedrooms, the first phase of which will be ready for occupation in September 2023. For now, the university owns 3,364 rooms and allocates a further 1,909 in privately-owned halls of residence. Those who apply for a space by the early June deadline are guaranteed one.

Tuition fees

» Fees for UK students	£9,250
» Fees for International students 2022–23	£14,250
» For scholarship and bursary information see www.uwe.ac.uk/courses/fees	
» Graduate salary	£24,000

Student numbers

Undergraduates	21,405 (1,705)
Postgraduates	2,930 (4,640)
Applications/places	32,010/6,230
Applications per place	5.1
Overall offer rate	71%
International students – EU	3.9%
Non-EU	9.9%

Accommodation

University provided places: 5,273
Self-catered: £96–£226 per week
www.uwe.ac.uk/life/accommodation

Where do the students come from?

State schools (non-grammar)	91.3%	Low participation areas	15.6%
Grammar schools	3.1%	All ethnic minorities	19.4%
Independent schools	5.7%	White working-class males	6.9%
First generation students	42.5%	Black achievement gap	-31.1%

Social inclusion ranking: 66

Disabled	9.3%
Mature (over 21)	24.9%

University of the West of Scotland

One of Scotland's largest modern institutions, the University of the West of Scotland (UWS) is also one of its most socially inclusive. Founded from the 2007 merger of Paisley University and Bell College in Hamilton (both of which served areas of low participation in higher education), UWS is now based at four Scottish campuses and one in London.

The university's commitment to opening the doors to higher education is evidenced by the broad social and economic spectrum of its student community. About three in ten students, the highest proportion, are from areas deemed the poorest by the Scottish Index of Multiple Deprivation – proof that UWS's adjusted entry thresholds for those from disadvantaged backgrounds are bearing fruit.

The university considers applicants based not only on their qualifications but also their life and work experiences, and personal circumstances. More than half of students are 21 or older when they enrol and a similar proportion have parents who did not go to university.

Its success at reducing inequalities helped UWS to earn first place in Scotland and 14th in the UK for the measure in *Times Higher Education's* Global Impact rankings, which rate institutions according to the United Nations Sustainable Development Goals.

The £110million Lanarkshire site in Hamilton International Technology Park is powered by 100% renewable energy sources and houses courses in health, computing and some business and social science subjects.

The UWS headquarters are at the Paisley campus, while at the Ayr site £81million of investment has added facilities including a prizewinning library shared with Scotland's Rural College. The smallest campus, Dumfries, shares an 85-acre parkland site with the University of Glasgow and Dumfries and Galloway College.

The London campus, launched in 2017, offers professionally-focused programmes in areas including business, health, project management and accounting. It moved to the Docklands area in 2020 where it benefits from technology-rich teaching and learning spaces.

Eco measures across UWS campuses have resulted in a 42% reduction in carbon emissions – more than double its 2020 goal. By 2040 the university has committed to net zero emissions. Most undergraduate degrees combine academic learning with work placements and work-related practical assessments. The professional links translated to almost seven in ten UWS graduates being in high-skilled jobs or further study 15 months after finishing their degrees, placing the university joint 71st in our graduate prospects measure.

However, in common with many other

Paisley Campus
Paisley PA1 2BE
0800 027 1000; +44 141 849 4101 (international)
ask@uws.ac.uk
www.uws.ac.uk
www.sauws.org.uk
Open days: see website

The Times and The Sunday Times **Rankings**

Overall Ranking: =110 (last year: 116)

Teaching quality	72.8%	=90
Student experience	65.5%	107
Research quality	4.3%	=98
Entry standards	136	=46
Graduate prospects	69.3%	=71
Good honours	77%	=72
Expected completion rate	78.1%	110
Student/staff ratio	20.9	=122
Services and facilities	£2,559	65

institutions with similar practical-based subject mixes, UWS took a hit in student satisfaction during the pandemic and experienced one of the ten biggest falls in scores when teaching quality and student experience was compared in the 2021 National Student Survey.

In-person lectures will play a decreasingly important role within UWS's teaching and learning, with online delivery the preferred method for this kind of content. On campus the focus is on interactive learning such as workshops, seminars and laboratory work.

Financial assistance supports the university's widening participation agenda, such as the £1.11million funds it uses to help eligible student parents meet childcare costs. There are also discretionary funds set aside to help eligible students meet their basic costs of living while studying.

Applications were up by around 4% in March 2021, compared with the same point the year before. The first mathematics students began their courses in September 2021, as did those on the new criminal justice and forensic science degree.

The School of Health, Nursing and Midwifery, the largest in Scotland, produced the university's best results in the 2014 Research Excellence Framework, in which 44% of the submission reached one of the top two categories.

Recent research projects at UWS include working with Alzheimer Scotland to investigate the benefits of walking football for men aged over 70 with dementia. In another football-related project, UWS became Celtic Football Club's first Youth Academy sports science partner in 2020, a relationship that provided students with the chance to support elite youth football development.

Professor Sheila Rowan, chief scientific adviser for Scotland, opened the thin films laboratory on the Paisley campus in early 2020, after its £12million refurbishment. The lab is part of the UWS Institute of Thin Films, Sensors and Imaging – whose pioneering work helped produce film-based chips used in non-contact thermometers, the type frequently seen during the Covid-19 pandemic.

Most students live at home, which means the university's 196 student bedrooms at the Ayr campus and 491 at the Paisley site are enough for all first-years who want to live in.

Students have free membership to gym and fitness facilities, and Wednesday afternoons are kept free from classes to encourage students to take part in sport and social activities.

Tuition fees

- » Fees for Scottish students £0–£1,820
  RUK fees (capped at £27,750 for 4-year courses) £9,250
- » Fees for International students 2022–23 £14,500–£17,250
- » For scholarship and bursary information see www.uws.ac.uk/money-fees-funding/
- » Graduate salary £24,500

Student numbers

Undergraduates	11,900	(1,565)
Postgraduates	1,570	(1,070)
Applications/places		19,675/3,895
Applications per place		5.1
Overall offer rate		57%
International students – EU		4.2%
Non-EU		1.5%

Accommodation
University provided places: 687
Self-catered: £95–£160 per week
www.uws.ac.uk/university-life/accommodation

Where do the students come from?

State schools (non-grammar)	98.4%	Deprived areas	29.6%		
Grammar schools	0.2%	All ethnic minorities	9.3%		
Independent schools	1.3%	White working-class males	7.5%		
First generation students	47%	Black achievement gap	-22.4%		

Social inclusion ranking (Scotland): 2

Disabled	1.5%
Mature (over 21)	54.2%

University of Westminster

With its headquarters on Regent Street in the West End of London, the University of Westminster occupies some of the capital's most central locations. Law courses are based around the corner on Titchfield Street, while the nearby Cavendish campus is the focus of programmes including engineering, psychology and biological and biomedical sciences.

Westminster's Marylebone campus near Regent's Park houses teaching and learning in a wide range of subject areas including architecture, data science, tourism and accounting – and is also the site of central student support services. The media, arts and design faculty, its best-known feature, enjoys a more suburban setting in Harrow, northwest London, where specialist facilities include studios for music, film and television, plus extensive, well-equipped creative arts spaces.

An international perspective at Westminster goes two ways; the university recruits a high proportion of overseas students (although it experienced a small decline in applications from EU students in the 2021 cycle) and its courses are taught in nine overseas countries, from Sri Lanka to Uzbekistan. UK students have opportunities to gain international experience via exchange partnerships with more than 100 institutions across 26 countries. The Polylang programme offers a wide range of free language tuition, including Arabic, French and Chinese.

Founded as the UK's first polytechnic in 1838, the university remains a practice-focused institution. Building on experiences during the pandemic, Westminster is expanding its blended and technology-enhanced teaching and learning approaches, coupled with an on-campus focus on practical and active learning methods. This means a reducing emphasis on traditional exam assessments and an increase in "authentic" means of evaluation – based on the competencies, knowledge, skills and attitudes professional and civic life require.

Despite a significant fall this year, Westminster has generally performed well in our social inclusion table, a reflection of its success at widening participation in higher education. Seven in ten undergraduates come from ethnic minorities, ranking the university in the top 10 for ethnic diversity, and more than half are the first in their family to go to university.

Westminster was given a bronze rating in the Teaching Excellence Framework, which takes account of the backgrounds of students. An unusually brief commentary by the awarding panel praised the consistent support for students at risk of dropping out and acknowledged a strategic approach and commitment to improving employment and entrepreneurship.

However, Westminster has sunk to the bottom ten of our graduate prospects measure, with just over 57% of graduates in high-skilled jobs or postgraduate study within

309 Regent Street
London W1B 2HW
020 7915 5511
admissions@westminster.ac.uk
www.westminster.ac.uk
www.uwsu.com
Open days: see website

The Times and The Sunday Times **Rankings**
Overall Ranking: 129 (last year: 126)

Teaching quality	70.7%	=117
Student experience	66.5%	=98
Research quality	9.8%	59
Entry standards	118	=79
Graduate prospects	57.3%	126
Good honours	70.2%	=116
Expected completion rate	80.2%	=98
Student/staff ratio	20.9	=122
Services and facilities	£1,992	109

15 months of finishing their degrees. Along with the falls in student satisfaction this has contributed to Westminster dropping three places down our main league table to sit just three places off the bottom.

The university is in our top 60 for research, however, comfortably its best position among the nine measures in our academic table and one of the best performances for research among post-1992 universities. It held its position among the leading institutions for communication and media studies in the 2014 Research Excellence Framework, when almost two-thirds of the work submitted was judged to be world-leading or excellent. There were even better results in art and design, and a good performance in English, although less than 30% of eligible staff entered.

The first sports management students began courses in September 2021, as did those on digital marketing and digital media degrees. Applications for 2020 entry were higher than they have been for five years, and the largest number of new students started courses yet in an admissions round that drew around 20% via clearing.

Westminster has launched a new, much bigger suite of degree apprenticeships. Eleven undergraduate programmes began in September 2021 in building surveying, quantity surveying and commercial management, real estate, applied biomedical science, building control surveying, project management, and construction management. The university expects to have around 370 degree apprentices on courses by September 2022.

There are 481 residential places in Wembley and 447 in Harrow not enough to meet demand. Students are advised to apply early and can be helped to find alternative accommodation if they have missed the boat with halls.

Sports facilities include gyms with qualified exercise trainers at the Regent Street and Harrow campuses. The Quintin Hogg sports ground, 45 acres overlooking the River Thames in Chiswick, can accommodate football, rugby, hockey, lacrosse, cricket, tennis and netball, and has its own pavilion. Across the road is the boathouse. The rowing club is one of more than 100 sports clubs and societies fielded by the students' union.

London has earned the top spot in the 2021 "World's Best Cities" index for the fifth year running according to Resonance Consultancy, a leading advisor in tourism, real-estate and economic development. With campuses re-opened this year, Westminster students have the capital's culture and nightlife at their fingertips.

Tuition fees

» Fees for UK students	£9,250
» Fees for International students 2022–23	£14,400
» For scholarship and bursary information see www.westminster.ac.uk/study/fees-and-funding/	
» Graduate salary	£24,000

Student numbers

Undergraduates	13,425 (1,960)
Postgraduates	2,330 (1,755)
Applications/places	26,980/4,310
Applications per place	6.3
Overall offer rate	80.7%
International students – EU	11.8%
Non-EU	17.5%

Accommodation

University provided places: 928
Self-catered: £181–£211 per week
www.westminster.ac.uk/study/accommodation

Where do the students come from?

State schools (non-grammar)	94.7%	Low participation areas	4.3%		
Grammar schools	1.9%	All ethnic minorities	70.2%		
Independent schools	3.5%	White working-class males	3.3%		
First generation students	55.3%	Black achievement gap	-23.2%		

Social inclusion ranking: 63

Disabled	5.2%
Mature (over 21)	15.7%

University of Winchester

Winchester's broadening curriculum has added more than 50 new degrees in recent years. Maths provision was boosted in September 2021 with three options: mathematics and science; mathematics with data science; and an integrated masters maths degree. The first nutrition and dietetics students also began courses, as did those on degrees in physical education and sport; and sports therapy.

A Bachelor of Science in social and criminal justice launches in September 2022, by which time Winchester's incoming vice-chancellor, Professor Sarah Greer, will have taken the helm.

Overlooking the cathedral city, a 10-minute walk away, Winchester's King Alfred campus quarter occupies a wooded hillside. Most of student life happens here, within faculty buildings, performing arts studios and a multimedia centre.

At the West Downs quarter, the £50million learning and teaching building opened in 2021, featuring a drum-shaped auditorium and housing the university's computer and digital-related degrees and business and management programmes.

A life-size statue of the Swedish environmentalist Greta Thunberg was unveiled at the West Downs building, and met with criticism from the students' union which felt the money could have been better spent during a difficult year. "We know that many find her a controversial figure. As a university we welcome debate and critical conversations," wrote Professor Joy Carter, the outgoing vice-chancellor, in an email to students.

The West Downs development was built to exacting eco-standards, in line with Winchester's remit to be "the university for sustainability and social justice." In the 2021 *Times Higher Education* Global Impact Rankings, which rate universities worldwide for their success in delivering the United Nations' 17 Sustainable Delivery Goals (SDGs), it is placed second in the UK for quality education, in recognition of its focus on sustainability and social responsibility.

Demonstrating these values further, Winchester has signed the Race Equality Charter. It is focusing on decolonising the curriculum at the university, which was first established as a Church of England foundation for teacher training and known as King Alfred College until 2004.

Winchester has a silver rating in the Teaching Excellence Framework. The panel was impressed by its "appropriate" contact hours, tutorials and buddy schemes that produce personalised learning and high levels of commitment from students. Most are stretched sufficiently to make progress, and acquire the knowledge, skills and understanding valued by employers, assessors added.

Winchester has improved its ranking in

Sparkford Road
Winchester SO22 4NR
01962 827 234
admissions@winchester.ac.uk
www.winchester.ac.uk
www.winchesterstudents.co.uk
Open days: see website

The Times and The Sunday Times **Rankings**

Overall Ranking: =106 (last year: 96)

Teaching quality	72.5%	95
Student experience	65.3%	108
Research quality	5.8%	=83
Entry standards	108	=113
Graduate prospects	63.7%	=103
Good honours	76.5%	=79
Expected completion rate	84.4%	68
Student/staff ratio	17.4	=94
Services and facilities	£1,754	122

our graduate prospects measure this year, though with just under 64% of graduates in high-skilled jobs or postgraduate study 15 months after finishing their degrees it has yet to break into the top 100.

Applications edged upwards to reach record levels in 2020's admissions round, in step with the university's expanding course options. Winchester also offers six degree apprenticeships, covering a range of digital and technology specialisms; senior leadership; and social work. Programmes for nurse associate, and for registered nursing (adult, child or mental health) are being introduced from 2022. A network engineering specialism of digital and technology solutions is also joining the stable.

Winchester held its own in the 2014 Research Excellence Framework. Almost 45% of its work was considered world-leading or internationally excellent and its best results were recorded for communications and history.

The university rises 13 places in our social inclusion ranking this year to sit comfortably in the top half. Its widening participation objectives focus on increasing low progression rates to higher education among local communities and increasing the diversity of the student body.

There are also residential activities for children-in-care, young carers, forced migrants and service children. Targeted support packages are provided in tandem – offering contextualised admissions, designated support staff, access to year-round housing, and financial help.

The two-floor university gym is at the heart of the £12million Burma Road student village and offers daily classes at no extra charge to members. On campus there is also a fitness studio, a sports hall and a multi-use games area. The Winchester Sports Stadium nearby has an athletics track and a floodlit all-weather pitch.

With 1,949 residential spaces, the university guarantees accommodation to all first-years. A popular relocation destination for those seeking tranquillity and low crime rates, Winchester is also home to Europe's longest medieval cathedral. Students benefit from being able to get to know each other relatively quickly and nightlife is both student-centric and of manageable proportions.

Support for students' mental health and wellbeing begins with a pre-arrival orientation and welcome for first-years. The wellbeing team works with colleagues on disability, academic skills and student money teams – among others – to dovetail help. Mental wellbeing workshops through the year cover topics such as managing anxiety and stress; presentation skills; and "look after your mate".

Tuition fees

»	Fees for UK students	£9,250
»	Fees for International students 2022–23	£13,800
»	For scholarship and bursary information see www.winchester.ac.uk/accommodation-and-winchester-life/students-and-money/	
»	Graduate salary	£22,000

Student numbers

Undergraduates	6,300	(395)
Postgraduates	610	(695)
Applications/places	10,095/2,265	
Applications per place	4.5	
Overall offer rate	86.7%	
International students – EU	1.7%	
Non-EU	4.2%	

Accommodation

University provided places: 1,949
Catered costs: £173 per week
Self-catered: £12–£165 per week
First years guaranteed accommodation
www.winchester.ac.uk/accommodation-and-winchester-life/accommodation

Where do the students come from?

					Social inclusion ranking: 46	
State schools (non-grammar)	93.8%	Low participation areas	14.9%		Disabled	12.1%
Grammar schools	2.4%	All ethnic minorities	11.5%		Mature (over 21)	18.4%
Independent schools	3.9%	White working-class males	6.3%			
First generation students	49.6%	Black achievement gap	-26.8%			

University of Wolverhampton

A busy schedule of developments at Wolverhampton did not slacken during the pandemic. The university opened its £45million School of Architecture and Built Environment at the Springfield campus in 2020, part of a £120million regeneration of a 12-acre derelict brewery into a supercampus.

The university has headquarters in its home city and an expanding regional footprint. At the Telford campus, a £5million health and social care training centre opened in May 2021, providing hands-on learning facilities for key workers. The new facilities are well-timed given Wolverhampton's significant rise in applications to health-related courses in 2021–22.

In Hereford, work has completed on the Midlands Centre for Cybersecurity, a joint venture with Herefordshire council providing research and development resources out of three cyber-laboratories. The university also has a site in Walsall.

Wolverhampton was awarded silver in the Teaching Excellence Framework in 2018, upgraded from bronze. It still missed its benchmarks for student satisfaction and progression to high-skilled employment, but the panel praised the commitment to enhancing students' learning experience, as well as the involvement of employers in the development and review of courses. It was also impressed by mental health provision and support systems.

Student satisfaction with teaching quality and with the wider experience declined at Wolverhampton during the pandemic-hit year – as it did at almost every other university. In our previous edition the university featured in the top half of UK institutions for teaching quality and was not far outside the upper half for the wider experience too. That seems a long way off this year, but the university will hope that the return to campus should get satisfaction rates back to those levels.

Going forward, the university expects more sessions to contain a hybrid of student attendance in the classroom both physically and virtually. Tutorials and seminars are likely to be delivered in this mixed-mode, with some students accessing their tutors and support on-campus and others using the online learning environment.

The launch of nine new degrees has added depth to Wolverhampton's performing arts and creative provision. The first acting and theatre students began courses in September 2021, while degrees in dance and creative performance; music (with or without education); audio technology and production; and digital production arts for theatre degrees also launched. A management and leadership degree has also been added.

Wolverhampton has climbed out of the bottom 20 of our graduate prospects measure to feature just inside the top 100. The

Wulfruna Street
Wolverhampton WV1 1LY
01902 323 505
admissions@wlv.ac.uk
www.wlv.ac.uk
www.wolvesunion.org/
Open days: see website

The Times and The Sunday Times Rankings
Overall Ranking: 128 (last year: 128)

Teaching quality	74.4%	=78
Student experience	67.1%	=92
Research quality	5.9%	82
Entry standards	107	=116
Graduate prospects	64.6%	=99
Good honours	70.2%	=116
Expected completion rate	71.4%	128
Student/staff ratio	17	=87
Services and facilities	£2,161	94

Graduate Outcomes survey found just under 65% of Wolverhampton graduates in high-skilled employment or postgraduate study 15 months after leaving.

A partnership with Santander Universities provides funding for scholarships and awards to boost students' employability and entrepreneurship, and the careers department offers a programme of micro placements and work experience.

Through new links with the BBC, the university is promoting media internships and graduate opportunities to those on courses ranging from software engineering to journalism. This chimes with the BBC's drive to increase diversity among its workforce – as Wolverhampton recruits one of the most socially inclusive student populations in the country. Two-thirds are the first in their family to go to university, the third highest proportion at any university; more than one-fifth come from the country's most deprived postcodes and nearly half are aged over 21.

At last count, the university had more than 1,000 students on its suite of 16 higher and degree apprenticeships. Options include nursing, occupational therapy, teaching and social work.

By far the best results in the Research Excellence Framework were in information science, where almost 90% of the work submitted was considered world-leading or internationally excellent. The new cyber hub in Hereford will provide significant resources for the Wolverhampton Cyber Research Institute.

The new National Brownfield Research Institute focuses on the practical application of regeneration and has a dedicated building under construction on the Springfield campus.

The high-quality sports facilities at Walsall campus are the base for the university's research centre for sport, exercise and performance. They include grass and 3G pitches, outdoor courts for tennis and netball, a gym and strength facility and a 200m running track. Sports scholarships of up to £4,500 over three years come with access to physiotherapy, strength and conditioning training and mentoring.

All first-years qualify for a £300 travel fund – for use towards public transport costs. They can still apply for further bursary or scholarship awards. Access bursaries for care leavers include £250 for graduation costs as well as £2,000 payments in years one and two of a degree.

With 1,251 university-owned residential rooms, 80% of first-years who apply for one can be accommodated.

Tuition fees

» Fees for UK students £9,250
   Foundation courses £8,400
» Fees for International students 2022–23 £12,950–£13,450
» For scholarship and bursary information see www.wlv.ac.uk/apply/funding-costs-fees-and-support/
» Graduate salary £24,000

Student numbers

Undergraduates	12,430 (2,770)
Postgraduates	1,450 (2,215)
Applications/places	16,915/3,206
Applications per place	5.3
Overall offer rate	83.9%
International students – EU	0.8%
Non-EU	6.1%

Accommodation

University provided places: 1,251
Self-catered: £90–£108 per week
www.wlv.ac.uk/university-life/accommodation

Where do the students come from?

State schools (non-grammar)	97%	Low participation areas	21.7%	Disabled	8.6%
Grammar schools	1.2%	All ethnic minorities	51.2%	Mature (over 21)	46.5%
Independent schools	1.8%	White working-class males	4.6%		
First generation students	66.4%	Black achievement gap	-22.8%		

Social inclusion ranking: 15

University of Worcester

The first medical students at Worcester start their courses in September 2022, following a four-year push for the creation of the Three Counties Medical School. Serving Gloucestershire, Herefordshire and Worcestershire, the new school will focus on primary care.

Extra facilities are due to open by the end of 2022 through the transformation of the former *Worcester News* building and print factory into a new Centre for Health and Medical Education – where an anatomy suite and simulation rooms to teach consultation skills will be among the specialist facilities.

Worcester already has a strong reputation for health-related courses and was shortlisted as Nurse Education provider of the Year (pre-registration) for a record seventh time in the *Student Nursing Times* Awards in August 2021. The new building will house its wide range of health disciplines.

In common with many universities, Worcester's student satisfaction scores dipped in the National Student Survey (NSS) in 2021 as final-year students gave their verdict on pandemic provision. It has a strong record in the NSS and remains in the top 25, however, for satisfaction with teaching quality and the wider experience.

Worcester pledged to make in-person teaching the priority for 2021–22, backed up by recorded lectures.

"Excellent" levels of contact time and teaching that encourage high levels of student engagement and commitment were among the attributes praised by assessors from the Teaching Excellence Framework when awarding Worcester a silver rating.

Located in the historic cathedral city on the banks of the River Severn, Worcester's ranking in our league table overall has risen by 15 places – a significant improvement that brings it comfortably inside the top 100. An improvement in graduate prospects has contributed, with an above average proportion of graduates (73%) in high-skilled employment or postgraduate study 15 months after finishing.

Work placements of up to 12 months are offered within degree courses. Students in the School of Sport and Exercise Science have secured placements with local teams such as the Worcester Warriors rugby club and Worcestershire County Cricket Club, and also with elite Spanish basketball club Valencia Basket.

Industry initiatives at the School of Arts include monthly masterclasses and guest lectures, plus links with organisations that include the Writers' Guild, Channel 4 and ITV Central.

The university's three teaching campuses are less than a mile apart in the city centre. The attractive City campus incorporates the former

Henwick Grove
Worcester WR2 6AJ
01905 855 111
admissions@worc.ac.uk
www.worcester.ac.uk
www.worcsu.com
Open days: see website

The Times and The Sunday Times Rankings
Overall Ranking: 86 (last year: =101)

Teaching quality	78.1%	=23
Student experience	74.5%	=20
Research quality	4.3%	=98
Entry standards	114	=99
Graduate prospects	73.1%	=53
Good honours	66.6%	126
Expected completion rate	85.3%	59
Student/staff ratio	16.9	86
Services and facilities	£1,885	114

Worcester Royal Infirmary and the Hive library along with the business school, health and wellbeing centre and Jenny Lind law building.

Just opposite is the Art House, opened in 2019, which has modern facilities for art and illustration courses in a grade II listed art deco building. St John's campus, the headquarters, houses science facilities, the National Pollen and Aerobiology Research Unit, the digital arts centre and drama studio.

The curriculum gained new degrees in medical sciences in 2021–22, and in creative writing and media and culture. The foundation year of a new environmental management and sustainability degree has also launched, which the main three-year programme follows in 2022. Among the course's residential field trips is the opportunity to visit India and stay in a tiger reserve.

Worcester was one of the most improved universities in the 2014 Research Excellence Framework: it went up 20 places, partly because it entered five times as many academics as it had in 2008. A third of the work submitted was considered world-leading or internationally excellent, with history and art and design achieving the best scores.

Sports facilities include a rubber crumb pitch at St John's and a sport therapy suite at City. The Lakeside campus has 50 acres of open grass and woodland for bushcraft. University rowing benefits from amenities at Worcester Rowing Club.

Worcester's commitment to – and facilities for – disability sport are exceptional. Its 2,000-seat indoor sporting arena on the Riverside campus is designed for wheelchair athletes as well as the able-bodied. At the Lakeside campus, a 10-acre lake has been adapted for inclusive watersports.

The university is in the top half of our social inclusion ranking, recruiting more than 95% from non-selective state schools. More than one in ten students is disabled, the 12th highest proportion in any university. Contextual offers have joined Worcester's widening participation initiatives.

Reach card credits of £50 or £100 are given to full-time undergraduates to help with essentials such as e-text books. Scholarships of £1,000 are awarded to students with the best academic profiles.

Accommodation is guaranteed to first-years in 1,200 spaces. One in ten of Worcester's residents are students, making for a student-centric local vibe. Tudor buildings, riverside scenery and the nearby Malvern Hills create a charming backdrop, while clubs and societies play an active role in the social scene.

Tuition fees

» Fees for UK students	£9,250
» Fees for International students 2022–23	£13,400
» For scholarship and bursary information see www.worcester.ac.uk/study/fees-and-finance/	
» Graduate salary	£24,000

Student numbers

Undergraduates	7,685	(715)
Postgraduates	845	(936)
Applications/places	10,010/2,165	
Applications per place	4.6	
Overall offer rate	83.3%	
International students – EU	4.8%	
Non-EU	5.8%	

Accommodation

University provided places: 1,200
Self-catered: £108–£184 per week
First years guaranteed accommodation
www.worcester.ac.uk/life/accommodation

Where do the students come from?

State schools (non-grammar)	95.2%	Low participation areas	14.7%	Disabled	11.6%
Grammar schools	1.9%	All ethnic minorities	12.6%	Mature (over 21)	35.6%
Independent schools	2.9%	White working-class males	6%		
First generation students	51.2%	Black achievement gap	-24.1%		

Social inclusion ranking: 49

Wrexham Glyndŵr University

Wrexham Glyndŵr has begun a £1million upgrade to teaching facilities at its main Plas Coch campus and Regent Street art school. The updates are part of a £60million Campus 2025 programme to improve facilities at all sites. One of them, Glyndŵr University Racecourse Stadium, is shared with Wrexham Football Club, which has secured headline-grabbing investment from the Hollywood stars Ryan Reynolds and Rob McElhenney.

For the fourth consecutive year Wrexham Glyndŵr is the most socially inclusive university in England and Wales – befitting an institution named after Owain Glyndŵr, the 15th-century Welsh prince who championed the establishment of universities throughout Wales. One in five students has a registered disability (the highest proportion of any UK university) and only two beat Wrexham Glyndŵr for the high proportion (76%) of students aged over 21 when they enrol. The proportion who come from postcodes with the lowest participation in higher education is approaching three in ten.

The university provides advice, guidance and support to students in the communities it serves, with the aim of breaking down barriers specific to underrepresented groups. Taster sessions on campus and in local schools are among outreach activities, and entry grade requirements are adjusted for students who meet widening participation criteria.

Making higher education accessible and flexible for students is among Wrexham Glyndŵr's core values, and it has found that blended learning offers an inclusive approach. The development of its on-campus and digital Active Learning Framework was accelerated by the pandemic and some aspects of remote delivery are remaining as students return to hands-on learning.

The university has succeeded where many others with a similar focus on practice-based courses fell down in the past year. Students endorsed its efforts through the pandemic with some stellar scores in the National Student Survey, lifting Wrexham Glyndŵr to second place behind St Andrews in our ranking based on students' assessment of teaching quality.

The university gained silver in the Teaching Excellence Framework (TEF), scoring well for its part-time courses. Part-timers who live in Wales are eligible for a scholarship waiving 40% of the tuition fee. The TEF panel was impressed by the high levels of interaction with industry, business and the public sector and commented favourably on the quality of work-based learning that matches the region's priorities.

The Centre for the Creative Industries on the Wrexham campus features high-quality studios used by television production students

---

Mold Road
Wrexham LL11 2AW
01978 293 439
enquiries@glyndwr.ac.uk
www.wgu.ac.uk
www.wrexhamglyndwrsu.org.uk
Open days: see website

The Times and The Sunday Times **Rankings**

Overall Ranking: =110 (last year: 124)

Teaching quality	82%	2
Student experience	73.8%	26
Research quality	2.3%	119
Entry standards	113	=102
Graduate prospects	64%	101
Good honours	76.2%	=83
Expected completion rate	73.2%	125
Student/staff ratio	21.9	=125
Services and facilities	£1,773	121

and is the regional home of BBC Cymru Wales. Other specialist facilities include a complementary medicine clinic, laboratories for computer game development and for the study of crime scenes – as well as a flight simulator and supersonic wind tunnel.

The rural Northop campus in Flintshire specialises in animal studies and biodiversity courses and has a small animal unit and an equine centre. The St Asaph campus in Denbighshire is a research centre for the opto-electronics industry, focusing on the technology to make high-resolution telescopes. The campus incubator offers a programme for space industry start-ups.

A 5% increase in applications in 2020 went some way to reversing four years of decline, although fewer students started courses in 2020, with enrolments experiencing a 23% dip. Applications for 2021 looked encouraging by the end of March, when they were 15% higher than at the same point the year before.

A new law degree launched in 2021 to provide a foundation for those wanting to pursue a career in law in England and Wales. The curriculum also gained options in product design; law and criminal justice; biochemistry; biomedical science; and media production.

In partnership with Airbus, which has a large plant nearby, Wrexham Glyndŵr's Advanced Composite Training and Development Centre in Broughton carries out research to help improve the efficiency of aircraft, and feeds into the university's engineering courses.

The university entered only 34 academics for the 2014 Research Excellence Framework, but a third of their work was judged to be internationally excellent, with some world-leading, notably in media subjects.

The university owns the Racecourse stadium, which is leased by Wrexham AFC. It is the world's oldest international football ground currently in use and hosted the first Welsh home international match in 1877. Students across the university from journalism, business and history to sports make use of it within their studies.

The campus also has a modern sports centre with two floodlit artificial pitches, a human performance laboratory and indoor facilities. Many students live at home, which allows Wrexham Glyndŵr to guarantee accommodation to first-years who apply by the deadline within 321 rooms at Wrexham Village. The Lazy Lion students' union bar offers pizza and doubles as a venue, while local pubs and clubs run dedicated student nights.

Tuition fees

» Fees for UK students	£9,000
» Fees for International students 2022–23	£11,750
» For scholarship and bursary information see www.glyndwr.ac.uk/fees-and-funding/	
» Graduate salary	£22,500

Student numbers

Undergraduates	2,555	(2,330)
Postgraduates	195	(965)
Applications/places	1,735/385	
Applications per place	4.5	
Overall offer rate	68%	
International students – EU	9.2%	
Non-EU	1.5%	

Accommodation

University provided places: 321
Self-catered: £115–£168 per week
www.glyndwr.ac.uk/accommodation

Where do the students come from?

					Social inclusion ranking: 1	
State schools (non-grammar)	97.9%	Low participation areas	27.1%	Disabled	20%
Grammar schools	0.5%	All ethnic minorities	5%	Mature (over 21)	76.2%
Independent schools	1.6%	White working-class males	6.2%		
First generation students	60.6%	Black achievement gap	-23.3%		

University of York

Shortlisted for our University of the Year award, social justice is a prevailing theme at 1963-founded York, which became a University of Sanctuary in 2020 to demonstrate its commitment to refugees, asylum seekers and other forced migrants. York has cemented its place in our top 20 institutions, having weathered a challenging year, which included being thrown in the pandemic deep end when a Chinese student became one of the first official Covid-positive patients in the UK.

York, which now ranks above all but four of its fellow Russell Group members in our social inclusion ranking, was the first of its research-led peers to sign the Social Mobility Pledge – a coalition of businesses and universities that have vowed to put levelling up at the heart of their operations. There was no pandemic pause to its efforts to widen participation either. Undergraduates worked with academic staff and local business mentors to support secondary school pupils engaged in York's outreach and access programmes.

Set on a 200-acre parkland campus within walking distance of the historic cathedral city, the university is one of a handful to operate a collegiate system. Their student communities cross year groups and academic disciplines,

and are the bases for accommodation, social activities, inter-college sports and support networks. Anne Lister (York's tenth college) opened in 2021 with 348 student bedrooms, to be joined by a further 1,000 rooms in summer 2022.

York did well to gain ground on its rankings for student satisfaction with both teaching quality and the wider experience this year – placing in the top 40 for each measure. It ranks respectably in the upper half of universities for its Covid response too, our year-on-year analysis of National Student Survey results show.

The positives gleaned from the rapid shift to remote learning, dubbed "Covid-keeps" by York, include podcast-style recorded lectures and a move away from invigilated exams to open assessments.

More than 78% of York graduates were in high-skilled employment or postgraduate study in the latest Graduate Outcomes survey, placing it in the top 25.

Career-planning begins early for undergraduates via initiatives such as York Futures, which helps students develop CV-enhancing skills and experiences, set up their own enterprise or prepare for further study. The York Strengths programme runs in tandem, providing opportunities for students to work out what careers suit them and to build confidence around communicating their strengths.

York's employability efforts were among the factors behind its upgrade to gold in the Teaching Excellence Framework in 2018. The panel found

Heslington
York YO10 5DD
01904 324 000
ug-admissions@york.ac.uk
www.york.ac.uk
www.yusu.org
Open days: see website

The Times and The Sunday Times **Rankings**
Overall Ranking: 19 (last year: 20)

Teaching quality	76.7%	37
Student experience	72.1%	=39
Research quality	38.3%	17
Entry standards	149	=29
Graduate prospects	78.1%	25
Good honours	82.9%	=35
Expected completion rate	93.3%	=17
Student/staff ratio	13.6	22
Services and facilities	£2,273	85

excellent academic support and a research-strong environment that engages students and provides outstanding levels of stretch.

Recent developments include the Church Lane building – the management school's new facility – complete with a modern, flexible working environment and outdoor social spaces. The Hull York medical school has benefited from a recent redesign and gained clinical skills spaces nearby.

Dedicated to research into innovations such as driverless cars the York Institute for Safe Autonomy opened in 2021, housing specialist laboratories and testing facilities for robotics and the new Eleanor and Guy Dodson building provides cutting-edge research facilities for determining protein structure.

In the 2014 Research Excellence Framework, York submitted a lower proportion of its academics for assessment than most leading universities. Nevertheless, more than 80% of the research was considered world-leading or internationally excellent. York was in the top ten for the impact of its research and remains in the top 20 for research quality overall.

Applications have been consistently healthy, and an 11% increase brought enrolments to a new record in the 2020 admissions round. The first law and criminology students began courses in 2021.

York's outreach initiatives are showing evidence of success – it now ranks inside the top 100 of our social inclusion table. Its black achievement gap is among the 25 narrowest in the country. However, the proportion of students recruited from independent or selective state schools is among the 25 highest nationally.

Around a quarter of UK undergraduates benefit from York bursaries and scholarships. It offers care leaver students free year-round accommodation for the duration of their studies, both on and off-campus.

The York Sports Village features a 25m pool, trainer pool, 120-station gym, 3G pitch and five-a-side pitches. The university has the only outdoor velodrome in Yorkshire, a 1km cycling track, an athletics track and a boathouse on the River Ouse.

First-years who apply by the deadline are guaranteed accommodation. According to urban legend, York has a pub for every day of the year. The cobbled-street city bursts with culture and the college system makes for a sociable campus. Student wellbeing officers are embedded in academic departments and the Open Door mental health team has gained extra practitioners.

Tuition fees

» Fees for UK students	£9,250
» Fees for International students 2022–23	£19,600–£24,000
Medicine (Hull-York Medical School)	£38,500
» For scholarship and bursary information see www.york.ac.uk/study/undergraduate/fees-funding/	
» Graduate salary	£25,000

Student numbers

Undergraduates	13,740	(335)
Postgraduates	4,040	(1,675)
Applications/places		24,785/4,085
Applications per place		6.1
Overall offer rate		81.4%
International students – EU		4%
Non-EU		11%

Accommodation

University provided places: 6,054
Catered costs: £136–£201 per week
Self-catered: £99–£179 per week
First years guaranteed accommodation
www.york.ac.uk/study/accommodation/

Where do the students come from?

					Social inclusion ranking: =95	
State schools (non-grammar)	70.9%	Low participation areas	9.5%	Disabled	6.9%
Grammar schools	11.2%	All ethnic minorities	14.3%	Mature (over 21)	6.1%
Independent schools	17.9%	White working-class males	5.1%		
First generation students	31.9%	Black achievement gap	-12.9%		

York St John University

The curriculum continues to evolve at York St John (YSJ), founded in 1841 as a teacher training college. The first nursing students began their degrees in adult and mental health specialisms in 2021 and programmes in cybersecurity and forensic psychology are on the way in 2022.

A new creative centre on the main 11-acre Lord Mayor's Walk campus near York city centre provides extra space for a growing student population. The three-storey building, with views over York Minster from its atrium, features a 210-seat theatre and specialist teaching facilities for music, drama, dance and acting as well as computer science programmes.

A strong record in the National Student Survey (NSS) has ranked YSJ in the top 10 for student satisfaction with teaching quality for the past two years, alongside buoyant levels of contentment with the wider undergraduate experience. Students were less pleased with their university's response to the pandemic however, and YSJ registered one of the larger year-on-year declines in NSS scores.

Even with such a dip, it still places in the upper third nationally for both measures of student satisfaction. A 7.2% dropout rate, considerably below the expected level, shows evidence of the positive experiences students have at YSJ – a university that is proud to foster a strong sense of community on its campuses. Graduation ceremonies take place in the inspiring splendour of York Minster.

While some lecture-capture facilities remain available in the 2021–22 academic year, the main focus is in-person teaching and learning activities on campus, where more than £100million has been ploughed into developments. The modern Fountains Learning Centre houses the library, IT facilities and a lecture theatre and the striking De Gray Court building provides a contemporary reception area.

The Haxby Road sports campus, a mile away, has modern sports science laboratories and teaching rooms, set within 57 acres of outdoor space and facilities such as 3G pitches, outdoor courts and a sprint track. An indoor tennis centre and sports barn are also on-site. Further afield, YSJ opened a postgraduate London campus in 2018.

Low rates of graduate employment in high-skilled jobs contributed to a bronze rating in the Teaching Excellence Framework but the panel was impressed by a scheme that involves undergraduates in research and by the innovative measures to support vulnerable students, including those with mental health difficulties.

Progression to high-skilled jobs continues to hold York St John back in our league table also. With almost 65% of graduates in high-skilled work or postgraduate study, it is only

Lord Mayor's Walk
York YO31 7EX
01904 876 598
admissions@yorksj.ac.uk
www.yorksj.ac.uk
http://ysjsu.com
Open days: see website

The Times and The Sunday Times **Rankings**
Overall Ranking: =83 (last year: =83)

Teaching quality	77.5%	=31
Student experience	71.3%	=45
Research quality	4.1%	=101
Entry standards	108	=113
Graduate prospects	64.7%	98
Good honours	76.1%	=85
Expected completion rate	84.5%	=65
Student/staff ratio	18.1	=105
Services and facilities	£2,203	90

just inside the top 100 of our measure for graduate prospects, a small improvement on last year.

Psychology produced the best results in the 2014 research ratings, when the 30% of research regarded as world-leading or internationally excellent represented a big improvement on the 2008 assessments. The strategy promotes interdisciplinary research, targeting further improvement in the 2021 exercise.

YSJ expects to have around 700 learners on its seven degree apprenticeships by 2022, an ambitious projection given there were fewer than 250 apprentices at last count, but one that is in line with the strategic goal to have at least 10,000 students across all courses by 2026. The current programmes include senior leadership, data science, project management, healthcare science and policing.

York St John recruits about a fifth of its students from the lowest-participation postcodes, although it has fallen significantly in our wider social inclusion ranking. It expects 40% of students to qualify for new financial awards tailored to support disadvantaged students and those in hardship post-Covid.

Other financial awards are based on merit and/or widening participation criteria, such as scholarships of £800 a year for students from black, Asian and ethnic minority backgrounds with a household income below £42,000, and for care leavers and students estranged from their families. Students from households with an income below £25,000 are eligible for £250 a year.

The university makes discounted entry grade offers on a wide range – but not all – of its courses, taking into account students' age, whether they have a disability, have spent time in care, where they live and the performance of their school. Around 30% of applicants qualify for such offers, which typically amount to a 24-UCAS tariff point reduction (equivalent to three A-level grades) from the standard offer.

The Lord Mayor's Walk campus has a sports hall, climbing wall, basketball, netball, indoor football and cricket nets, while a 15-minute walk brings students to the sports park's extensive facilities.

The students' union hosts more than 50 clubs and societies, but if there's nothing that suits, students are invited to start their own. Quiz nights, karaoke, live sport and live music are among the entertainments hosted at the campus venue.

Tuition fees

» Fees for UK students	£9,250
Foundation degrees	from £4,200
» Fees for International students 2022–23	£12,750
» For scholarship and bursary information see www.yorksj.ac.uk/students/your-finances/	
» Graduate salary	£21,000

Student numbers

Undergraduates	5,590	(115)
Postgraduates	880	(420)
Applications/places		8,720/1,625
Applications per place		5.4
Overall offer rate		88.5%
International students – EU		1.4%
Non-EU		3%

Accommodation
University provided places: 1,465
Self-catered: £102–£187 per week
First years guaranteed accommodation
www.yorksj.ac.uk/study/accommodation

Where do the students come from?

State schools (non-grammar)	94.8%	Low participation areas	19.8%	Disabled	8.1%
Grammar schools	1.9%	All ethnic minorities	6.6%	Mature (over 21)	19.3%
Independent schools	3.3%	White working-class males	6.3%		
First generation students	47.5%	Black achievement gap	-40.1%		

Social inclusion ranking: 88

Specialist and Private Institutions

1 Specialist colleges of the University of London

This listing gives contact details for specialist degree-awarding colleges within the University of London not listed elsewhere within the book. Those marked * are members of GuildHE (**www.guildhe.ac.uk**). Fees are for a single year of study.

Courtauld Institute of Art
Somerset House Strand
London WC2R 0RN
020 3947 7711
www.courtauld.ac.uk
Fees: £9,250 (Overseas £23,500)

London Business School
Regent's Park
London NW1 4SA
020 7000 7000
www.london.edu
Postgraduate only

London School of Hygiene and Tropical Medicine
Keppel Street
London WC1E 7HT
020 7636 8636
www.lshtm.ac.uk
Postgraduate medical courses

Royal Academy of Music
Marylebone Road
London NW1 5HT
020 7873 7373
www.ram.ac.uk
Fees: £9,250 (Overseas £25,300)

Royal Central School of Speech and Drama*
Eton Avenue
London NW3 3HY
020 7722 8183
www.cssd.ac.uk
Fees: £9,250 (Overseas £20,083–£23,383)

Royal Veterinary College
Royal College Street
London NW1 0TU
020 7468 5000
www.rvc.ac.uk
Fees: £9,250 (Overseas £15,190–£38,600)

University of London Institute in Paris
9–11 rue de Constantine
75340 Paris Cedex 07, France
(+33) 1 44 11 73 83
https://ulip.london.ac.uk
Degrees offered in conjunction with Queen Mary and Royal Holloway colleges
Fees: £9,250 (Overseas £12,000)

2 Specialist colleges and private institutions

This listing gives contact details for other degree-awarding higher education institutions not mentioned elsewhere within the book. All the institutions listed below offer degree courses, some providing a wide range of courses while others are specialist colleges with a small intake. Those marked * are members of GuildHE (**www.guildhe.ac.uk**). Fees are the latest available for a single year of study.

Arden University
Business, finance, health and others
Arden House,
Middlemarch Park,
Coventry CV3 4FJ
  Campuses in London, Birmingham,
  Manchester & Berlin
0800 268 7737
www.arden.ac.uk
Fees vary – blended learning

BPP University
Mainly law, business & health
Aldine Place, 142–144 Uxbridge Road,
London W12 8AW
  Campuses in Abingdon, Birmingham,
  Bristol, Cambridge, Doncaster, Leeds,
  Liverpool, London, Manchester,
  Maidstone, Milton Keynes, Newcastle,
  Nottingham, Reading, Southampton
03300 603 100
www.bpp.com
Fees vary by subject and course

Conservatoire for Dance and Drama
Comprised of:
  Bristol Old Vic Theatre School, Central
  School of Ballet, London Academy of
  Music and Dramatic Art (LAMDA),
  London Contemporary Dance School,
  National Centre for Circus Arts,
  Northern School of Contemporary
  Dance, Rambert School of Ballet and
  Contemporary Dance, Royal Academy of
  Dramatic Art (RADA)*
14–16 Great Chapel Street,
London W1F 8FL

020 7387 5101
www.cdd.ac.uk
Fees: £9,250 (Overseas: contact school)

Dyson Institute of Engineering and Technology
Tetbury Hill Malmesbury
Wiltshire SN16 0RP
01285 705228
dysoninstitute@dyson.com
www.dysoninstitute.com
Paid degree courses – no fees

Glasgow School of Art
167 Renfrew Street, Glasgow G3 6RQ
0141 353 4500
www.gsa.ac.uk
Fees: Scotland, no fee,
RUK £9,250 (Overseas £18,960)

Guildhall School of Music and Drama
Silk Street, Barbican,
London EC2Y 8DT
020 7628 2571
www.gsmd.ac.uk
Fees: £9,250 (Overseas £21,800 - £23,120)

The University of Law*
Birmingham, Bristol, Guildford, Leeds,
London (Bloomsbury and Moorgate),
Manchester, Nottingham
0800 289 997
www.law.ac.uk
Fees: £11,100 – two-year course
(Overseas £16,875)
£9,250 – three-year course
(Overseas £14,150)

Liverpool Institute for Performing Arts*
Mount Street,
Liverpool L1 9HF
0151 330 3084
www.lipa.ac.uk
Fees: £9,250 (Overseas £17,200)

The London Institute of Banking and Finance*
4–9 Burgate Lane
Canterbury, Kent CT1 2XJ
01227 818609
   Student campus:
   25 Lovat Lane, London EC3R 8EB
   020 7337 6293
www.libf.ac.uk
Fees: £9,250 (Overseas £13,000)

New College of the Humanities*
Devon House,
St Katharine Docks,
London E1W 1LP
020 7637 4550
www.nchlondon.ac.uk
Fees: £9,250 (Overseas £14,000)

Pearson College*
Business, law & video games
190 High Holborn,
London WC1V 7BH
020 3944 8529
www.pearsoncollegelondon.ac.uk
Fees: £9,250 (Overseas £15,500)

Plymouth College of Art*
Tavistock Place,
Plymouth PL4 8AT
01752 203402
www.plymouthart.ac.uk
Fees: £9,250 (Overseas £15,500)

Regent's University London*
Business, design, media & psychology
Inner Circle,
Regent's Park, London NW1 4NS
020 7487 7700
www.regents.ac.uk
Fees: £18,500-£21,500

Rose Bruford College of Theatre and Performance*
Lamorbey Park,
Burnt Oak Lane,
Sidcup, Kent DA15 9DF
020 8308 2600
www.bruford.ac.uk
Fees: £9,250 (Overseas £18,000)

Royal College of Music
Prince Consort Road,
London SW7 2BS
020 7591 4300
www.rcm.ac.uk
Fees: £9,250 (Overseas £25,990)

Royal Conservatoire of Scotland
100 Renfrew Street,
Glasgow G2 3DB
0141 332 4101
www.rcs.ac.uk
Fees: Scotland, no fee;
RUK £9,250 (Overseas £18,393)

Royal Northern College of Music
124 Oxford Road,
Manchester M13 9RD
0161 907 5200
www.rncm.ac.uk
Fees: £9,250 (Overseas £24,000)

Royal Welsh College of Music and Drama
Castle Grounds, Cathays Park,
Cardiff CF10 3ER
029 2034 2854
www.rwcmd.ac.uk
Fees: £9,000 (Overseas £22,505)

St Mary's University College*
Teaching & liberal arts
191 Falls Road, Belfast BT12 6FE
028 9032 7678
www.stmarys-belfast.ac.uk
Fees: £4,530; RUK £9,250
(Overseas contact college)

Scotland's Rural College
Agriculture, environment & land
management
Peter Wilson Building,
The King's Buildings,
West Mains Road,
Edinburgh EH9 3JG
 Campuses at Aberdeen, Ayr, Cupar,
 Dumfries, Oatridge, West Lothian and
 Edinburgh
0131 535 4000
www.sruc.ac.uk
Fees: Scotland, no fee;
RUK £7,500 (Overseas £15,000)

Stranmillis University College
Teaching courses
Stranmillis Road, Belfast BT9 5DY
028 9038 1271
www.stran.ac.uk
Fees: £4,530; RUK £9,250 (Overseas £17,400)

Trinity Laban Conservatoire of Music and Dance
King Charles Court
Old Royal Naval College,
Greenwich, London SE10 9JF
020 8305 4444
www.trinitylaban.ac.uk
Fees: £9,250 (Overseas £14,060–£22,710)

University Academy 92
Business, media & sport
UA92 Campus,
Brian Statham Way, Old Trafford,
Manchester M16 0PU
0161 507 1992
www.ua92.ac.uk
Fees: £9,250 (Overseas £14,466)

University College, Birmingham (UCB)
Further and Higher Education courses
Mainly hospitality, tourism, business, sport
and education
Summer Row,
Birmingham B3 1JB
0121 604 1000
www.ucb.ac.uk
Fees: £9,250 (Overseas £13,500)

UCFB (University Campus of Football Business)*
Wembley Stadium
London HA9 0WS
Etihad Campus, Manchester M11 3FF
0333 241 7333
www.ucfb.ac.uk
Fees: £9,250 (Overseas £14,950)

Writtle University College*
Land management
Lordship Road,
Chelmsford, Essex CM1 3RR
01245 424200
www.writtle.ac.uk
Fees: £9,250 (Overseas £12,700)

Index

A-levels
  choosing 30
  UCAS tariff 32
Aberdeen, University of 14, 316–7
Abertay, University of 318–9
Aberystwyth University 320–1
Academic World Ranking of Universities 134
Access agreements 315
accommodation 100
  home, living at 103
  security 108
  sharing 108
  tenancy agreements 109
accounting and finance 148
Adjustment, UCAS 86
admissions tests 34
Adult Dependants' Grant 72
Advanced Highers, and UCAS tariff 32
aeronautical engineering 151
African studies 243
agriculture 152
America, studying in 125
American studies 153
anatomy 154
Anglia Ruskin University 322–3
animal science 156
anthropology 157
application process 77
application timetable 5–6, 82
Apply, UCAS 78
apprenticeships 10, 39
archaeology 158
architecture 160
Arden University 587
art, history of 220
art and design 162
Arts University Bournemouth 324–5
Arts, University of London 326–7
Aston University 328–9
astronomy 253
audiology 275
Augar review 10, 11, 49, 60

Bangor University 330–1
Bath, University of 14, 332–3
Bath Spa University 334–5
Bedfordshire, University of 95, 336–7
bio and biomedical engineering 165
biological sciences 167
Biometric Residence Permit 143
Birkbeck, University of London 12, 37, 338–9
Birmingham, University of 57, 113, 340–1
Birmingham City University 342–3
Birmingham, University College 589

Bishop Grosseteste University 344–5
Bolton, University of 14, 346–7
Black achievement gap 84
Blair, Tony 60
Blended learning 9, 314
Bournemouth University 348–9
BPP University 39, 45, 62, 587
Bradford, University of 350–1
Brexit 10, 55, 64, 128, 136
Brighton, University of 352–3
Bristol, University of 354–5
British Council 141
British Universities and Colleges Sport (BUCS) 113
Brunel University London 356–7
Buckingham, University of 39, 62, 358–9
Buckinghamshire New University 360–1
budget, student 69
building 170
bursaries 61–69, NHS 66
business studies 171
buzzword 78

Cambridge, University of 9, 14, 362–3
  application process 32, 34, 79, 288
  College profiles 302–313
  Tompkins Table 283
Canterbury Christ Church University 364–5
Cardiff Metropolitan University 368–9
Cardiff University 13, 366–7
Cathedrals Group 44
Celtic studies 175
Central Lancashire, University of 370–1
chemical engineering 176
chemistry 177
Chester, University of 372–3
Chichester, University of 374–5
Childcare Grant 67, 72
China, studying in 130
cinematics 194
City, University of London 376–7
civil engineering 179
classics and ancient history 181
Clearing 87
colleges, private 45, 586–9
Combined Honours 37
communications 182
complementary therapies 275
completion measure 21
computer science 185
conditional offer 74
Confirmation of Acceptance for Studies 142
Conservatoire for Dance & Drama 587

Council tax, and students 111
counselling 275
course, choosing 28
courses, online 38
Courtauld Institute 586
Covid-19, effects 9, 112, 282
Coventry University 378–9
Creative Arts, University of 380–1
creative writing 188
criminology 190
cross border studying, finance of 64
Cumbria, University of 382–3

dance 194
De Montfort University 384–5
deferred place 79, 89
degree apprenticeships 10, 39, 63
degree results, and league table 21
dentistry 193
Derby, University of 386–7
diplomas 33
Disabled Students' Allowance 71
Discover Uni 47, 55
distance learning 38
drama 194
Dropout rates 90
Dundee, University of 388–9
Durham University 390–1
Dyson, Institute of Eng & Tech 46, 587
Dyson School of Design Eng 432

East Anglia, University 392–3
East Asian studies 197
East European languages 265
East London, University of 394–5
economics 198
Edge Hill University 13, 396–7
Edinburgh, University of 66, 398–9
Edinburgh Napier University 400–1
education 201
Education and Library Board 97
electrical & electronic engineering 204
England, fees in 60–65
English 206
English tests 141
entry standard measure 20, 144
environmental sciences 213
Erasmus 12, 129
Essex, University of 402–3
Ethnic minorities 90
EU students, fees 10, 12, 134
Europe, studying in 128
exchange programmes 129
Exeter, University of 404–5

Falmouth, University of 406–7
fees, tuition 60–64

Ferguson, Sir Alex 410
Ferguson, Prof Neil 432
First generation students 85
food science 209
Football college (UCFB) 589
forensic science 158
forestry 152
Foundation degree 38
French 211
Fulbright Commission 125
Further Education Colleges 45, 62

gap year 88
general engineering 212
geography 213
geology 216
German 217
Glasgow, University of 13, 408–9
Glasgow Caledonian University 410–11
Glasgow School of Art 587
Gloucestershire, University of 412–3
Goldsmiths, University of London 14, 414–5
good honours measure 20
graduate earnings and employment 48–50
graduate prospects measure 20, 50, 145
Graphene Institute 471
Greenwich, University of 416–7
Guildhall School of Music & Drama 587
GuildHE 44

hardship fund, university 72
Harper Adams University 418–9
Hartpury University 420–1
health sciences 275
helicopter parents 124
Heriot-Watt University 422–3
Hertfordshire, University of 424–5
HESA 18, 21
Higher Education, Colleges 45
Highers, and UCAS tariff 32
High Fliers report 57
Highlands and Islands, University of 426–7
history 218
history of art 221
home, living at 103
hospitality 222
Huddersfield, University of 428–9
Hull, University of 430–1

Iberian languages 224
Imperial College 13, 61, 432–3
information systems and management 226
insurance for property at university 111
insurance choice 43, 74
International Baccalaureate 31, 32

international students 136
    application process 142
    employment and entry regulations 142
    English language requirements 141
    subjects studied 140
    universities favoured 139
interviews 84
Interest on loans 67
Islamic Finance 342, 347
Italian 227

Joint Honours 37

Keele, University of 434–5
Kent, University of 436–7
King's College London 14, 438–9
Kingston University 62, 440–1

Lancaster University 442–3
land management 228
Landscape 279
Languages – decline 12
Law, University of 46, 63, 587
law 229
league tables, value of 17–18
Leeds, University of 444–5
Leeds Arts University 14, 446–7
Leeds Beckett University 448–9
Leeds Trinity University 450–51
Leicester, University of 452–3
liberal arts 233
librarianship 226
Lincoln, University of 16, 454–5
linguistics 234
Liverpool, University of 456–7
Liverpool Hope University 458–9
Liverpool Inst for Performing Arts 588
Liverpool John Moores University 30, 460–61
living costs 100
Llewellyn, Dr David 418
loans, entitlement and repayment 66–67
London Business School 586
London, University of 314, 586
London Institute of Banking and Finance 588
London Metropolitan University 462–3
London School of Economics 33, 61, 464–5
London Sch of Hygiene & Trop Med 586
London South Bank University 466–7
Loughborough University 11, 468–9

Maintenance loans 65, 66
Manchester University 470–71
Manchester Metropolitan University 13, 472–3
manufacturing engineering 149

materials technology 235
mathematics 236
measures, league table 18–21
measures, subject tables 145
mechanical engineering 238
media studies 182
medicine 241
    subjects allied to 275
Mental health 123
Middle Eastern studies 243
Middlesex University 474–5
Million Plus 44
MOOC 38
music 244

National Student Survey 19, 144
natural sciences 246
New College of the Humanities 46, 62, 588
Newcastle University 476–7
Newman University 478–9
New Model In Technology & Engineering 46
NHS bursaries 66
Non-selective schools 92
Norrington Table, Oxford 284
Northampton, University of 480–81
Northern Ireland, fees & loans 75
Northumbria University 482–3
Norwich University of the Arts 484–5
Nottingham, University of 13, 486–7
Nottingham Trent University 488–9
nursing 247
nutrition 275

occupational therapy 275
offers 84
offer rates, high & low 40
Office for Fair Access (OFFA) 62
Office for Students 62, 90, 141
Ofsted 201
Online learning 38
open days 42, 315
Open University 38, 490–91
ophthalmology 275
optometry 275
osteopathy 275
overseas degrees, recognition of 134
Oxford Brookes University 494–5
Oxford, University of 9, 13, 80, 492–3
    application process 32, 34, 79, 288
    College profiles 288–301
    Norrington Table 284

parental role 122
Parents' Learning Allowance 99
part-time course 37, 59
part-time work 72

Pearson College 588
Perry, Grayson 326
personal statement, UCAS 80
pharmacology & pharmacy 250
philosophy 251
physics 253
physiology 154
physiotherapy 255
planning 278
Plymouth College of Art 588
Plymouth, University of 496–7
Plymouth Marjon University 498–9
podiatry 275
politics 256
Portsmouth, University of 500–501
private universities 587–9
professional qualifications 35
property management 227
psychology 260
Purnell, James 326

QS World University Ranking 133
Queen Margaret University 502–3
Queen Mary, University of London 14, 504–5
Queen's University Belfast 14, 506–7

radiography 263
Ravensbourne University, London 508–9
Reading, University of 510–11
recreation 222
reference, UCAS 81
Regent's University 46, 62, 588
rejection by university 88
Religious Studies 278
Remote learning 38
Research Excellence Framework (REF) 19, 144
research quality measure 19, 145
results day 86
Robert Gordon University 13, 62, 66, 512–3
Roehampton University 514–5
Rose Bruford College 588
Royal Academy of Music 586
Royal Agricultural University 14, 516–7
Royal Central Sch of Speech & Drama 586
Royal College of Music 588
Royal Conservatoire of Scotland 588
Royal Holloway, University of London 518–9
Royal Northern College of Music 588
Royal Veterinary College 586
Royal Welsh College of Music & Drama 588
Russell Group 30, 43, 93
Russian 264

St Andrews, University of 9, 66, 520–21
St George's, University of London 522–3
St Mary's College, Belfast 589
St Mary's University, Twickenham 524–5
Salford, University of 526–7
sandwich course 35, 58
scholarships 71
Scotland, fees in 73–74
Scotland, financial support 74
Scotland's Rural College 589
Scottish Highers 32, 76
security, student 111
services and facility spend measure 21
Sexual assault 118
Sheffield, University of 528–9
Sheffield Hallam University 530–31
SOAS, University of London 532–3
Social Inclusion 90
social policy 265
social work 267
sociology 269
soft subjects 31
Solent University 534–5
South Asian studies 197
South Wales, University of 536–7
Southampton, University of 538–9
Spanish 224
Specialist & private institutions 586–589
speech therapy 275
sports science 272
Staffordshire University 540–41
standard offers 41
Stirling, University of 542–3
Stormzy scholarships 362
Stranmillis College 589
Strathclyde, University of 544–5
student cities, global 128
student experience measure 19, 146
student finance, and parents 68
student–staff ratio measure 21
students, most satisfied 44
study abroad destinations 128
subject choice 30–35, 56
subjects – most popular 35
Suffolk, University of 546–7
Sunderland, University of 548–9
Surrey, University of 13, 550–1
Sussex, University of 13, 552–3
Swansea, University of 554–5

Teaching Excellence Framework 13
teaching quality measure 19, 145
Teesside, University of 13, 556–7
THE world ranking 134
theology 278
Tier 4, visa system 142

Tompkins Table, Cambridge 283
tourism 222
town planning 279
Track, UCAS 73
Trinity Laban Conservatoire 589
Trinity St David, University of Wales 558–9
tuition fees & loans 60–65
Turing scheme 12, 40, 129

UCAS application process 77
  Apply 78
  Extra 85
  Progress 88
  tariff 32
  Track 83
UCFB 589
UK, coming to study in 136
Ulster, University of 13, 560–61
unconditional offer 85
Unialliance 44
United States, studying in 125
University Academy 92, 589
University Alliance 44
University of the Arts London 326–7
University College Birmingham 589
University College London 562–3
university profiles, definitions 314–5

veterinary medicine 280
visa regulations 142
vocational subjects 33, 35–6

Wales, fees and grants in 75
Warwick, University of 13, 564–5
West London, University of 16, 61, 230, 566–7
West of England, University of 568–9
West of Scotland, University of 570–71
Westminster, University of 572–3
Whitty, Chris 10, 52
Winchester, University of 574–5
Wolverhampton, University of 12, 576–7
Worcester, University of 578–9
work experience 58, 80
work placement fee 62
World university table 131
Wrexham Glyndŵr University 96, 580–81
Writtle College 589

York, University of 13, 582–3
York St John University 584–5
Young Students' Bursary, Scotland 74